D1569851

CONCEPTUAL FOUNDATIONS OF BEHAVIORAL ASSESSMENT

THE GUILFORD
BEHAVIORAL ASSESSMENT SERIES
John D. Cone and Rosemery O. Nelson, Editors

Conceptual Foundations of Behavioral Assessment
Rosemery O. Nelson and Steven C. Hayes, Editors

Behavioral Assessment of Adult Disorders
David H. Barlow, Editor

Behavioral Assessment of Childhood Disorders
Eric J. Mash and Leif G. Terdal, Editors

CONCEPTUAL FOUNDATIONS OF BEHAVIORAL ASSESSMENT

Edited by

Rosemery O. Nelson
University of North Carolina at Greensboro

Steven C. Hayes
University of Nevada-Reno

THE GUILFORD PRESS

New York   London

© 1986 The Guilford Press
A Division of Guilford Publications, Inc.
200 Park Avenue South, New York, N.Y. 10003

Printed in the United States of America

Library of Congress Cataloging-in-Publication Data

Conceptual foundations of behavioral assessment.

   (Guilford behavioral assessment series)
   Includes bibliographies and index.
   1. Behavioral assessment.   I. Nelson, Rosemery O.
II. Hayes, Steven C.   III. Series.   [DNLM:
1. Behavior.   2. Personality.   3. Psychological Tests.
4. Psychological Theory.   BF 176 C744]
BF176.5.C66   1986   194.19'43   85-27363
ISBN 0-89862-142-9

To my parents, David, and Stony Brook (R.O.N.)

To Irving Kessler
Who started me down the behavioral path (S.C.H.)

CONTRIBUTORS

BEATRICE H. BARRETT, PhD, Behavior Prosthesis Laboratory, W. E. Fernald State School, Belmont, Massachusetts

BILLY BARRIOS, PhD, Department of Psychology, University of Mississippi, University, Mississippi

JOHN D. CONE, PhD, Department of Psychology, West Virginia University, Morgantown, West Virginia

IAN M. EVANS, PhD, Department of Psychology, University Center at Binghamton, State University of New York, Binghamton, New York

DONALD P. HARTMANN, PhD, Department of Psychology, University of Utah, Salt Lake City, Utah

MIKE F. HAWKINS, PhD, Department of Psychology, Louisiana State University, Baton Rouge, Louisiana

ROBERT P. HAWKINS, PhD, Department of Psychology, West Virginia University, Morgantown, West Virginia

STEPHEN N. HAYNES, PhD, Department of Psychology, Illinois Institute of Technology, Chicago, Illinois

STEVEN C. HAYES, PhD, Department of Psychology, University of Nevada-Reno, Reno, Nevada

ROBIN B. JARRETT, PhD, Department of Psychiatry, University of Texas Health Science Center at Dallas, Dallas, Texas

JAMES M. JOHNSTON, PhD, Department of Psychology, Auburn University, Auburn, Alabama

ELIZABETH C. McDONEL, MA, Department of Psychology, Indiana University—Bloomington, Bloomington, Indiana

RICHARD M. McFALL, PhD, Department of Psychology, Indiana University—Bloomington, Bloomington, Indiana

PAUL McREYNOLDS, PhD, Department of Psychology, University of Nevada-Reno, Reno, Nevada

ROSEMERY O. NELSON, PhD, Department of Psychology, University of North Carolina at Greensboro, Greensboro, North Carolina

H. S. PENNYPACKER, PhD, Department of Psychology, University of Florida, Gainesville, Florida

ARTHUR W. STAATS, PhD, Department of Psychology, University of Hawaii, Honolulu, Hawaii

WILLIAM F. WATERS, PhD, Department of Psychology, Louisiana State University, Baton Rouge, Louisiana

DONALD A. WILLIAMSON, PhD, Department of Psychology, Louisiana State University, Baton Rouge, Louisiana

PREFACE

From the time of Witmer, the assessment of psychological functioning has been the cornerstone of clinical psychology. Each of the major eras of clinical psychology has been marked by corresponding eras in assessment, from the days of the child guidance clinics with their emphasis on intellectual and achievement testing to the heyday of psychoanalysis with its emphasis on projective testing. It should not be surprising, then, that behavioral assessment has emerged as a strong force as the behavioral movement has gained ascendance within the clinical disciplines more generally.

Behavioral assessment, as this book shows, is the result of several distinctive historical and intellectual forces. It has been influenced by researchers who take a "natural science" approach, by empiricists, and by functional analysts. It replies to assessment questions from behavior therapy, applied behavior analysis, ethology, school psychology, behavioral medicine, cognitive therapy, and other fields. It admits to no population or psychological problem outside of its reach. In short, behavioral assessment is now ready to present itself as a comprehensive assessment approach.

The present volume is the first text to focus exclusively on the conceptual basis of behavioral assessment. It perhaps is a mark of the maturity of the field that we are now ready to "take stock" in this manner. The volume is meant for students, clinicians, and researchers interested in assessment.

The perspective taken in this book is that behavioral assessment is an *approach* to assessment of persons and their activities, and therefore has its own identity. Its identity does not lie with a particular set of techniques. The same assessment techniques can be used from different theoretical approaches. Similarly, its identity does not lie with a particular subject matter to be assessed. The uniqueness of behavioral assessment is not that it assesses behavior, whereas neuropsychological assessment assesses brain-behavior relationships, personality assessment assesses personality, and so on. The distinctive approach of behavioral assessment is a behavioral perspective that rests on behavior theory. A major purpose of this book is to explicate the ways in which behavior theory impacts on assessment issues, concerns, procedures, and questions. By so doing, the book provides a response to a concern, expressed by Kendall (1985), "that the lack of a conceptual framework has hindered the advance of behavioral assessment.

This lack has had several effects. For instance, due to the lack of a theoretically rich network of interrelationships, the thoughtful and theoretical talents of many researchers and clinicians were not being challenged." A hope of the editors is that the placement of behavioral assessment within its proper theoretical framework by means of this book will heuristically guide future research in and conceptual development of behavioral assessment.

The book is organized into four major sections. The first examines from *where* behavioral assessment comes—the conceptual underpinnings of behavioral assessment. It analyzes its history, nature, level of analysis, and distinctive features. The second section examines the *what* of behavioral assessment. It analyzes the question "What are the important and critical features of a person behaving in context?" The third section examines the *why* of behavioral assessment: selecting targets and treatments and assessing outcome. Finally, the last chapter examines the *whether* of behavior assessment—how do we know whether the assessment task has been adequately accomplished?

An effort of this kind takes the cooperation and forebearance of many. We would like to acknowledge our patient publisher, Seymour Weingarten; all of our excellent authors; Cindy Harrill and David Gray (for reasons they know all too well); and the enzymatic qualities of our students.

> Rosemery O. Nelson
> Steven C. Hayes
> Greensboro, NC—June 1986

REFERENCE

Kendall, P. C. (1985). Behavioral assessment and methodology. In C. M. Franks, G. T. Wilson, P. C. Kendall, & K. D. Brownell (Eds.), *Annual review of behavior therapy: Volume 10*. New York: Guilford.

CONTENTS

I
THE CONCEPTUAL FRAMEWORK
OF BEHAVIORAL ASSESSMENT

1

THE NATURE OF BEHAVIORAL ASSESSMENT

ROSEMERY O. NELSON
University of North Carolina at Greensboro
STEVEN C. HAYES
University of Nevada-Reno

Our intention in this chapter is to provide an introduction to the topic of this volume: the conceptual foundations of behavioral assessment. First, the philosophical roots of behavioral assessment are presented. These philosophical roots in behavior theory provide the main distinction between behavioral and traditional assessment. Second, the specific assumptions of behavioral assessment (extensions of these philosophical roots) are described, along with the implications of these assumptions for the assessment process. Finally, the goals of behavioral assessment are summarized. The other chapters in this volume serve to elaborate these conceptual foundations of behavioral assessment.

PHILOSOPHICAL ROOTS OF BEHAVIORAL ASSESSMENT

The philosophical roots of behavioral assessment lie in behavior theory. Behaviorism, in turn, has many historical antecedents.

MIND–BODY PROBLEM

The distinction between the mind and the body has a long history, but in modern terms it is typically traced to René Descartes (1596–1650). According to Cartesian dualism, human voluntary behavior was governed by the mind, while human involuntary behavior was purely physical and mechanical (Rachlin, 1970). "Mind" did not mean brain, but was a nonphysical realm that interacted with the brain. Thoughts and motor behaviors were given different ontological status: thoughts were causal and mental (again, in the sense of nonphysical), whereas motor behaviors were effects and physical. The literal dualism inherent in the word "mind" remains to this day. The Oxford English Dictionary defines "mind" as "the mental or psychical being or

3

faculty." An elaborating definition explains that "mind" is "the seat of a person's consciousness, thoughts, volitions, and feelings; the incorporeal subject of the psychical faculties, the spiritual side of a human being; the soul as distinguished from the body. . . . Mental being; opposed to matter."

In contrast with Cartesian dualism, behaviorism embraces the philosophical position of monism: "[the] behavioristic hypothesis [is] that what one observes and talks about is always the 'real' and 'physical' world (or at least the 'one' world)" (Skinner, 1945, p. 276). Typically, behaviorists are described as physical monists, but as the last part of the quotation above shows, this is not due to a kind of naive realism. The dictionary defines physical as "matter," and matter is said to be "the stuff of which things are made." In essence, anything that has a beginning or end (exists in time), or form, mass, appearance, and so on (exists in space) is "physical" in a scientific sense. Anything studied by science must be "physical" in the sense of existing in space or time. Thus, behaviorism holds a physically monistic position (see Hayes & Brownstein, in press, for a more detailed analysis of this issue). There is a physical substrate common to all phenomena (i.e., all knowable events occur in space and time). Behavior itself is a relational and not a static event, but that makes it no less physical. Behaviorism is not, however, reductionistic; it views behavior as a legitimate level of analysis in its own right that need not be reduced to its physiological substrate to achieve legitimacy.

A reflection of this physical monist position in behavioral assessment is the measurement of the triple response system (Lang, 1968; see also Chapter 5 by Evans in this volume). Thoughts, feelings, and actions are all considered to be behaviors and physical events. In some forms of behaviorism, behavior can only be an effect ultimately produced by environmental causes. In others (e.g., in the type embraced by most "cognitive–behavioral" assessors), thoughts may be given causal properties. All behavioral positions, however, acknowledge the physical substrate of behaviors such as thoughts (see Chapter 9 by Williamson, Waters, and Hawkins in this volume). A detailed discussion of views of causality held by different kinds of behaviorists is beyond the scope of this chapter (see Hayes & Brownstein, in press; Reese, 1984). We will, however, show why behaviorists themselves have differing views of causality in a later section.

NATIVISM–EMPIRICISM

The central difference between nativists and empiricists is the relative emphasis placed on the role of experience in forming ideas or patterns of behavior (Rachlin, 1970). Nativists emphasize innate ideas or patterns of behavior. Empiricists, like John Locke and other British Associationists, hold that all knowledge comes from the senses and from experience.

Behaviorists fall toward the empiricist end of this continuum. The principal way that humans are influenced by experience is through interactions with the environment that result in learning.

Behavioral assessors acknowledge their empiricist roots in at least three ways. Clients' current behavior patterns are viewed as the result of past learning history; thus, past experiences are an appropriate object of assessment. Moreover, current behavior is seen to be the product of current environmental influences. These influences must also be assessed, for example, through functional analysis. In addition, behavior within the assessment situation is acknowledged to be influenced by environmental variables. Relevant variables, that is, those designed to produce the behavior of interest, are deliberately introduced into the assessment situation. To illustrate, the phobic stimulus is included within the Behavioral Avoidance Test (Lazarus, 1961). Irrelevant variables, that is, those producing unwanted variability in behavior, are deliberately identified and controlled. For example, the effects of demand characteristics on clients' performance during the Behavioral Avoidance Test have been studied (Bernstein & Nietzel, 1973); these results are useful in controlling unwanted variability in performance.

FUNCTIONALISM–STRUCTURALISM

In biology, structuralism examined the structure of an organ or tissue, whereas functionalism asked what the function of the organ or tissue was in the life of the organism. As first used in psychology, structuralism examined structures of the mind, such as images or sensations, whereas functionalism examined functions of the mind, such as remembering, imagining, and attending (Murray, 1983). As currently used in psychology, structuralism focuses on *how* people behave, that is, what the form or topography of the behavior is, or upon supposed structures that underlie this behavior. Functionalism emphasizes *why* people behave as they do (Skinner, 1974). In a behavioral view, "why" questions are answered by specifying the contextual relationships into which behavior enters and showing how these in turn influence behavior. This is the question addressed by functional analysis (Ferster, 1965). Inspired by Darwin's evolutionary theory, functionalists concentrate on the functions that organismic activity served in its struggle to cope with a complex environment (Rachlin, 1970).

Radical behaviorism stems primarily from the functionalist tradition. Behavior is defined and understood in terms of its relationship to a given context—in given situations a given type of behavior produces given effects.

In a behavioral view, understanding is shown by the degree to which we can predict and control behavior in a variety of situations. In order to predict and control, the contextual events that produce behavior must be understood—its causes must be identified. This type of behaviorism focuses on the concrete "whys" of behavior.

Conversely, stimulus–response psychology and the neobehavioristic position that stemmed from it are largely structuralistic positions for reasons that are discussed in the next section. Because of this mix of traditions, behavioral assessment houses a considerable conflict, as this volume shows, between structuralistic and functionalistic positions.

Early questions within behavioral assessment tended to be dominated by structuralism. Examples include: Is behavior consistent or inconsistent across situations? Is behavior synchronous or asynchronous across the triple response system? Conversely, the actual use of behavioral assessment devices emerged in large part out of the functional analysis tradition (see Chapter 2 by McReynolds in this volume). More recently, functional questions within behavioral assessment per se have evolved. Examples include: *Why* is behavior consistent or inconsistent across situations? *Why* is behavior synchronous or asynchronous across the triple response system?

Similarly, psychometrics as a method of evaluating the quality of an assessment device stems from the structuralist tradition. In psychometrics, the relationship between scores on repeated administrations of the same device (test–retest reliability) or between scores on different devices (concurrent validity) is described. Some behaviorists, influenced by S–R psychology and its heirs, argue that psychometrics provides an adequate basis for the evaluation of behavioral assessment (for example, see Chapter 3 by Barrios & Hartmann in this volume).

For behaviorists in touch with functional–analytic roots, it seems more appropriate to evaluate the quality of behavioral assessment devices and procedures in terms of their accuracy and the *functions* that are served. The rationale is that, in psychometrics, one measure is evaluated against another measure, rather than a measure being evaluated against "reality." The former has been labeled "vaganotic" measurement; and the latter, "idemnotic."

> Vaganotic measurement refers to the creation of scales and units of measurement on the basis of variation in a set of underlying observations. . . . We have chosen the term *idemnotic* to denote the type of measurement that incorporates absolute and standard units whose existence is established independently of variability in the phenomena being measured. (Johnston & Pennypacker, 1980, pp. 64–71)

In a concrete illustration, the quality of observational data can be evaluated in two different ways. Using the psychometric tradition, quality is determined by interobserver agreement, or observer *reliability*, where the data obtained by one observer are compared with data obtained by a second observer. The alternative is observer *accuracy* where observational data are compared with a standard, such as mechanically obtained data (Foster & Cone, 1980).

Psychometrics is a structural means of evaluation that could be replaced by more functional alternatives: Do these devices and procedures enhance our understanding of behavior (conceptual utility) and contribute to treatment effectiveness (treatment utility)? To paraphrase a famous quotation from Titchener (1899) in order to apply it to assessment: "[Assessment], from a structural standpoint, is observation of an is: [assessment] from the functional standpoint, is observation of an is-for." This issue will be discussed in detail in Chapter 13 of this volume.

WORLD VIEW

Stephen Pepper, in his classic work on world views (1942), distilled the major defensable philosophical perspectives into four basic types: organicism, mechanism, formism, and contextualism. Pepper's idea is that the major world views are each built around a central metaphor that provides the coordinating model behind the specific theoretical positions in the system. Organicism takes as its "root metaphor" the growing, developing organic system. Mechanism adopts the metaphor of a machine. Formism relies on the metaphor of similarity, while in contextualism it is "the act in context." Modern behaviorism has two separate philosophical streams within it. Traditional S-R psychology and its direct descendents such as cognitive psychology and certain forms of social learning theory largely adopt mechanism while radical behaviorism, Kantorian interbehaviorism, and related positions are largely forms of contextualism.

The major disagreements and distinctions between various types of behaviorism and other psychological perspectives are often readily reducible to differences among these world views. For example, the dispute between radical behaviorism and developmentalism can usually be distilled into an argument between contextualism and organicism. Contextualists are dissatisfied with explaining changes in an organism's behavior by appealing to "stages of growth" or other organic metaphors. Contextualists want to know "in what evolutionary or ontogenic contexts" such "stages" appear.

The dispute between radical behaviorism and both S-R psychology and cognitive psychology can often in part be reduced to an argument between contextualism and mechanism. In mechanism, the structure of the machine is itself an explanation for the action of the machine. A car moves because it has spark plugs, pistons, and so on. Thus, the mechanist is inherently a structuralist and seeks to explain behavior by identifying the structural aspects of the machine that produce given effects. The computer metaphor of modern cognitive psychology, for example, readily leads a theorist to point to certain causal mechanisms, such as memory systems or processing capacity, that are thought to be in the machine itself. The contextualist objects that these mechanisms have emerged and can have their effects only within certain contexts. When these contextual sources of control are thoroughly explained, they believe that the concept of a mechanism is no longer needed. Thus, by recognizing that various forms of behaviorism exist and that they reflect various world views, we can examine several central philosophical conflicts with greater perspective.

Seeing radical behaviorism as a contextualistic world view also helps explain certain difficult issues in radical behaviorism. For example, radical behaviorists often insist that the word "cause" should be reserved for events that are at least theoretically manipulable. This, of course, has been roundly criticized by social-learning theorists (e.g., Bandura, 1981) and others (e.g., Schwartz & Lacey, 1984) who come from different parts of the behavioral tradition. It can be justified, based on the pragmatic need for manipulability so as to predict *and* control; but this does not do full justice to the issue. In a comprehensive form of contextualism, events in an analysis are fluid—each is defined and understood in terms of all the others. This can incapacitate one's ability to function intellectually, especially when it is realized that even one's own behavior of analyzing events is itself an event to be understood in context. Requiring that causes be manipulable provides a route out of the whirlpool a thoroughgoing contextualism creates. Thus, understanding that radical behaviorism is a form of contextualism dignifies certain key positions in radical behaviorism that would otherwise be viewed as relatively arbitrary or mere matters of convenience (Reese, 1984). Conversely, the mechanism inherent in social-learning theory and other neobehavioristic positions explains why self-efficacy and other such phenomena such as self-reinforcement or self-evaluation can be viewed as causal within this position. Rather than more behavior to be explained, a mechanist can view structural characteristics of the behavioral system as behavioral mechanisms, and thus causal entities.

The contextualistic aspects of behavioral assessment are most readily revealed by the tendency of behavioral assessors to define behavioral units based on the relationship of behavior to context (e.g., "attention getting behavior"; see Chapter 6 by Barrett, Johnston, & Pennypacker and Chapter 7 by McFall & McDonel in this volume); by a concern with ecological validity or naturalistic assessment; by environmental assessment; by a selective view of causality; and by other such aspects. The mechanistic tradition within behavioral assessment is revealed by its tendency at times to treat response skills as traits (e.g., "social skills"), by the use of one behavior to explain another (e.g., "self-efficacy"), and similar aspects.

IDIOGRAPHIC-NOMOTHETIC POSITIONS

It has been a behavioral tradition to focus on the individual (see Chapter 4 by Cone in this volume). In behavioral science, general principles have been built inductively, from the level of the individual to the level of generalizations across individuals. In behavioral practice, the emphasis is on the individual client. For each client, target behaviors must be identified, treatment strategies selected, and outcome measures determined.

The traditional approach to assessment tends to be nomothetic, especially as shown in (1) diagnosis or classification; and (2) psychometrics. The basis of classification systems is the identification of commonalities within groups of individuals (within-group homogeneity), and the identification of differences between groups of individuals (between-group heterogeneity). The focus is nomothetic—on groupings of individuals.

Variability in scores produced by a group of individuals forms the foundation of psychometrics, as described by Johnston and Pennypacker (1980; see also Chapter 6 in this volume). Historically, central contributors were Legendre who, in 1806, developed a mathematical procedure to derive the one best value from a series of variable values; Adolphe Quetelet who, about 1835, concluded that human characteristics were normally distributed, and that variability could be analyzed to determine ideal values of these characteristics; Francis Galton who, in the early 1900s, assumed that among the human characteristics that were normally distributed and assessed through analyses of variability was intelligence or mental ability; and Karl Pearson who, in 1896, developed the product moment correlation to describe the relationship between two variable distributions.

In contrast with this interest in variability within a group of people, behaviorism is generally interested in understanding the variability in the behavior of an individual across situations and across time. Variability is not seen as normal variation or as error variance, but rather variability is considered to be the product of to-be-identified variables (Cone, 1981; Johnston & Pennypacker, 1980). It is from an understanding of this variability that general principles can inductively be derived.

While the relative emphasis in behavioral assessment is on the individual, nomothetic approaches have proven useful in behavioral assessment in three ways: (1) the use of normative data; (2) the use of general principles from the field of abnormal psychology; and (3) the use of diagnostic labels for communication purposes. First, the use of normative data, collected from a group of individuals thought to be similar to or distinctly different from the client, has been useful to behavioral assessors. From normative data, target behaviors that are deviant from the norm can be selected. An example is O'Connor's work (1969) with socially withdrawn nursery school children. The actual social interactions of children who were referred by their teachers for social isolation and of nonreferred children were observed. Only referred children who displayed a very low rate of social interaction (fewer than five of 32 observation intervals) compared with their peers (who averaged interacting in 9.1 of 32 observation intervals) were subsequently treated for social isolation. Norms are not only useful in the initial selection of target behaviors, but also in the final evaluation of treatment success. If, as the result of treatment, the client's behavior is now in the normal range compared with his or her peers, then the treatment program has produced clinically significant or socially valid changes (Kazdin, 1977; Nelson & Bowles, 1975). Following a treatment of symbolic modeling, O'Connor's socially withdrawn children increased their rate of interactions to an average of about 11.0, slightly higher than the normative rate (1969).

The general principles of abnormal psychology demonstrate another use of a nomothetic approach beneficial to behavioral assessors. These general principles include information about (1) response covariation, or target behaviors that frequently covary; (2) typical controlling variables for a particular behavior problem, both organismic and environmental controlling variables; and (3) treatments that have a history of success with this particular behavior problem. Of course, these general principles must be applied idiographically to the client in question.

Finally, diagnostic labels, especially widely accepted labels like those of the Diagnostic and Statistical Manual of Mental Disorders (DSM-III; American Psychiatric Association, 1980) are useful to behavioral assessors, despite their nomothetic basis. These labels are useful for professional communication (e.g., when making referrals or when seeking assistance from the research literature), for reimbursement by insurance companies for psychological treatment, and for statistical record keeping.

A COMPARISON OF BEHAVIORAL AND TRADITIONAL ASSESSMENT

Thorough comparisons of behavioral and traditional approaches to assessment have been provided by Barrios and Hartmann in Chapter 3 of this volume, and previously by Hartmann, Roper, and Bradford (1979) and by Goldfried and Kent (1972). We also discuss this issue in more detail in

Chapter 13 of this volume. Although any comparison undoubtedly simplifies both approaches, the comparison here is in terms of the differing philosophical bases of the two approaches. It is in the differing philosophical bases and theoretical assumptions that the central differences lie. The central differences are *not* in techniques, since in fact, the two approaches share several assessment devices (e.g., interviews, questionnaires, standardized tests).

Traditional assessment typically emphasizes personologism. Psychopathology is thought to result from relatively stable intraorganismic variables that lie within the person. While the environment may have been important in laying down personality traits or mental disorders initially (e.g., Freud's emphasis on the early child-rearing environment), for assessment of adults, more emphasis is placed on intraorganismic causes of behavior than on environmental causes. Moreover, these intraorganismic causes often have a mentalistic ring to them, as do, for example, Freudian fixations or Rogers's need for self-actualization. These mentalistic causes are viewed as determinants of overt behavior. Hence, during assessment, behavior or appearance is interpreted as a *sign* of these underlying variables (Goldfried & Kent, 1972; Goodenough, 1949). The focus of assessment is on what the person *has* (Mischel, 1968). Thus, traditional assessment requires a high level of inference (Goldfried & Kent, 1972).

In contrast with the emphasis on personologism, most behavioral assessors hold either a situational (e.g., Mischel, 1968) or an interactionist (e.g., Mischel, 1973) point of view, that behavior is a result of environmental factors or of environmental factors interacting with organismic variables. Thus, given this emphasis on the empiricist tradition, the current environment is stressed more in behavioral assessment than in traditional assessment. Behavior is viewed as a *sample* of responding in a particular assessment situation (Goldfried & Kent, 1972; Goodenough, 1949). The focus of assessment is on what the person *does* rather than on what he or she *has* (Mischel, 1968). Thus, a lower level of inference is required in behavioral assessment than in traditional assessment. Moreover, in at least the operant tradition in behaviorism, the ultimate causes of behavior are typically thought to lie in the environment, not within the organism. It is recognized, however, that the behavioral effects of past interactions with the environment (both in a phylogenic and ontogenic sense) can alter the current effects of the environment in profound ways. In this limited sense, current behavior or behavioral repertoires can be thought of as "causal" (See Chapter 8 by Staats in this volume). Not only overt behavior, but also thoughts and feelings, have the same status as effects or products of these environmental variables. Thus, in behavioral assessment, motor behavior, thoughts, and feelings are assessed as separate but equal behaviors, within the heuristic of the triple response system.

Among the main goals of traditional assessment are the description of personalities and the diagnosis or classification of abnormalities (Hartmann et al., 1979). These largely tend to be nomothetic enterprises in that they focus on commonalities within groups of people and on differences between groups of people. Recently, however, there have been attempts within traditional assessment circles to describe personality using an idiographic approach (Harris, 1980; Lamiell, 1981).

The relative focus in behavioral assessment is idiographic in that, for each client, target behaviors must be identified (see Chapter 10 by Hawkins in this volume), treatment strategies selected (see Chapter 11 by Haynes in this volume), and outcome measures determined (see Chapter 12 in this volume). While nomothetic findings and principles may be useful in reaching these goals, caution must be exercised in applying these at the level of the individual.

Finally, another way that traditional assessment demonstrates its roots in nomothetic approaches is its emphasis on psychometrics as the proper way to evaluate the quality of assessment techniques. Psychometrics is a nomothetic approach in that psychometric data (i.e., reliability or validity coefficients) require scores from a group or groups of individuals. In contrast, some behavioral assessors (Cone, 1981; Nelson, 1983; Nelson & Hayes, 1979) believe that more idiographic and more functional approaches should replace psychometrics as the appropriate way to evaluate the quality of behavioral assessment devices and procedures. Among the idiographic approaches to behavioral assessment that have been suggested, in addition to the functional analysis, are (1) Shapiro's hypothesis-testing model (1966, 1970), elaborated by Turkat and his colleagues (Carey, Flasher, Maisto, & Turkat, 1984; Turkat & Maisto, 1985), in which hypotheses about individual clients are formulated and tested; and (2) Cone's (1980) template-matching approach in which target behaviors for an individual client are identified by matching the client's current behavior to a template of individually determined ideal behaviors. Other idiographic and functional approaches to evaluating behavioral assessment are described by Hayes, Nelson, and Jarrett in Chapter 13 of the present volume.

ASSUMPTIONS OF BEHAVIORAL ASSESSMENT

The assumptions of behavioral assessment can be neatly summarized by the convenient acronym, SORC, or Stimulus–Organism–Response–Consequences (Goldfried & Sprafkin, 1976). The *response* is the problematic behavior that is identified for modification. Behavioral difficulties are the focus of treatment. The other SORC components represent the controlling variables of

which this response is a function. In the context of interactionism, both immediate environmental and organismic controlling variables are considered
to be important. The immediate environmental variables are represented as
S, the *stimuli* that precede the target behavior, and C, the *consequences* that
follow the target behavior. The *organismic* variables are represented by O and
include both physiological states and past learning history. The assumptions
of behavioral assessment have implications for the assessment process. Each
of the SORC components, along with its implications for the assessment
process, is described subsequently.

STIMULI: THE IMPORTANCE OF SITUATION SPECIFICITY

Background

The emphasis that behavioral assessors place on the environmental stimuli
that control behavior can be viewed within the context of a historical debate.
The focus of this debate is whether the causes of behavior lie primarily
within the person (personologism), or primarily within the environment
(situationism), or whether causality lies in an interaction between person
and environment (interactionism). This debate is hotly contested, especially
within the arena of personality theory, but it also has clinical ramifications,
as later noted. The major protagonists in this debate and the various positions that they espouse are described in detail elsewhere in this volume in
Chapter 8 by Staats and Chapter 7 by McFall and McDonel.

A research question intended to resolve this theoretical debate is
whether behavior is consistent or inconsistent across different environmental situations. If the causes of behavior lie primarily within the person, the
personologist prediction is that behavior should be consistent, despite varying environmental situations. As McFall and McDonel (Chapter 7, this volume) stress, it is not absolute consistency that is predicted, but rather
relative consistency. In other words, a person's rank order on a certain
dimension compared with other individuals should remain consistent across
situations. Conversely, if the causes of behavior lie primarily within the
environment, the situationist prediction is that the behavior of the same
individuals should be inconsistent across different environmental situations.
Finally, the interactionist prediction falls in the middle, that behavior of the
same individuals should be moderately consistent across situations, since
both personal and environmental variables contribute to behavior.

Two types of research methodologies have been widely used to examine
the consistency of behavior across situations. In one type, the same subjects'
responses are correlated across different situations. For example, a classic

study by Hartshorne and May (1928) correlated children's "honesty responses" in the home, party games, athletic contests, and classroom tests. There is general agreement that the resultant correlations in studies of this type are low to moderate, which support the interactionist position (McFall & McDonel, this volume). In a second type of methodology, researchers calculated the proportion of the variance that can be accounted for by subjects, situations, and their interaction, typically by using an analysis of variance statistical procedure. To illustrate, with aggressive boys in six different situations (e.g., breakfast, structured games, arts and crafts), Rausch, Dittman, and Taylor (1959) found that more variance was accounted for by the individual by situation interaction than by either main effect of individual or of situation. This result is common in studies of this type and is taken as further support of the interactionist position. Summaries of relevant studies may be found in two very influential books by Mischel (1968) and by Peterson (1968).

Reactions to Interactionist Data

The data described earlier are generally interpreted as supporting an interactionist position. These data have generated several different reactions.

One reaction is that nomothetic or group questions and conclusions should be abandoned in favor of idiographic or individual questions and conclusions. The supposition is that there may be varying degrees of behavioral consistency across situations in different individuals. To illustrate, Bem and his colleagues (Bem, 1972; Bem & Allen, 1974; Bem & Funder, 1978) have proposed that there are individual differences in trait stability. For some individuals, certain traits may be stable in certain types of situations. Predictions are made that some types of behavior of some individuals will be consistent across some situations, but that this is not invariant across individuals. While Bem emphasizes different trait structures across individuals, idiographic approaches to the study of behavioral consistency have also been advocated by behaviorists. For example, after examining the baseline data of several subjects across several days, Jones (1972) concluded: "such *behavioral variability* over time may be the salient clinical characteristic for some subjects" (p. 8). Also examining individual differences, both Jones, Reid, and Patterson (1975) and Mash and Mercer (1979) concluded that there was more consistency across different situations in deviant children than in nondeviant children.

Another reaction to the interactionist data is a critique of the methodology used to generate these data. Epstein (1979, 1980) has argued that the consistency in behavior would be more apparent if larger numbers of behavioral samples were obtained. Indeed, Epstein's data support this contention.

Critiques of this approach have been provided by McFall and McDonel (this volume) and by Mischel and Peake (1982) and include the following: (1) situations were not varied systematically in these studies, so the same situations may have recurred; (2) the longitudinal consistency of behavior is not by itself support for cross-situational consistency, a point to be elaborated later, or for the existence of traits; (3) averaging or aggregating clumps of behavior across time does not allow precise predictions for individual behaviors at specific times in specific situations.

A third reaction to the interactionist data is that it is more advantageous in the long run to seek *reasons* for the consistency or inconsistency in behavior across situations than to continue to collect data demonstrating consistency or inconsistency. This reaction is elaborated by Staats in Chapter 8 of this volume. It typifies a functional (causative) rather than a structural (descriptive) approach to the question of consistency–inconsistency. Staats presents his reasons for consistency or inconsistency within the context of social behaviorism. If two situations both require the same elements from the person's basic behavioral repertoire and if the same reinforcement system is operative, then behavior will be consistent across the two situations. The reasons given by Mischel (1968) for consistency–inconsistency in behavior were stimulus generalization or discrimination, which were dependent on the individual's past reinforcement history: stimulus generalization produced consistent responding, and stimulus discrimination produced inconsistent responding. Mischel (1973) later presented more cognitive or mediational reasons for consistency–inconsistency: If the person perceived two situations to be similar, consistent behavior resulted. These perceptions varied across individuals, depending on such organism variables as "construction competencies" or "encoding strategies and person constructs" (Mischel, 1973).

Implications for Behavioral Assessment

The fact that behavior is at least somewhat situation specific has several implications for behavioral assessment. First is that a problematic response cannot be assessed in isolation from its situational controlling variables. To illustrate, if a client's target behavior is deviant sexual responding, then the stimuli that produce this deviant responding must be included within the assessment situation in order to measure the target behavior (Barlow, 1977).

A second implication is that progress must be made on the assessment of situational variables. The criterion situation in which the client's problem behaviors are occurring and in which therapeutic change must be demonstrated is the client's natural environment (Kazdin, 1979). To observe the problem behaviors and subsequent improvements in the treatment setting, the stimulus elements that control these behaviors in the natural environment must be reproduced in the treatment setting. The problem is in determining whether the "same" stimuli are being used in different settings. This determination, which involves the measurement of the environment, is both difficult (Frederiksen, 1972; McReynolds, P., 1979; Moos, 1973) and critical to behavioral assessment. To date, generally qualitative topographic distinctions are made in determining whether situations are the same or different; e.g., a classroom setting is different from a home setting, but presentation of fear-provoking stimuli are similar whether in the clinic or in the natural environment. Occasionally, more precise quantitative measurement of environmental stimuli occurs, for example, the number of feet between the subject and the snake during a behavioral avoidance test for a snake phobic. Much work is needed to provide measurements of the environment, in structural units and especially in functional units. Only then can there be any certainty that the "same" stimuli or situations are being utilized during assessment in the treatment setting as occur ordinarily in the natural environment.

A third implication of the relative situation specificity of behavior is that situational differences influence the data produced by behavioral assessment devices. Generic questions about the quality of behavioral assessment cannot be meaningfully addressed. For example, the generic question, "Can human observers collect accurate data?" cannot be answered without information about a host of situational variables that have been shown to influence observational data, like the type of training the observers receive, the complexity of the observation code the observers use, and the feedback given to observers about data that they collect (e.g., Kent & Foster, 1977). Similarly, the generic question, "Are self-recorders accurate?" cannot meaningfully be addressed. Generally, self-recorders are accurate only if they are well trained, if they record specific ongoing behaviors with appropriate units of measurement, if they are aware that their accuracy can be determined, and if they are rewarded for accuracy (McFall, 1977; Nelson, 1977).

A fourth and final implication of situational influences on behavior is that an overly strict interpretation of situation specificity obviates the assessment enterprise. Kazdin (1979) has labeled the dilemma produced by situation specificity "the two-edged sword of behavioral assessment (p. 27)." The problem is that it seems as if the assessment situation in the clinic is never exactly like the criterion situation in the natural environment. Even assessment in the natural environment has its problems, for the mere collection of data can alter the naturalistic situation. Reactivity, or alterations in behavior due to data collection, has been demonstrated, either when outside observers enter the environment (e.g., Kent & Foster, 1977) or when participant observers begin data collection in the environment (e.g., Hay, Nelson, & Hay,

1980). This problem makes it more apparent that we must be able to identify stimuli of situational variables that have *functional* similarity, if the assessment enterprise is to continue with any success.

CONSEQUENT VARIABLES

The environmental variables that contribute to the problematic behavior include both antecedent stimuli that precede the response, and consequent stimuli that follow the response. For problematic behavior, there are generally two types of consequences: short-term positive consequences that are maintaining the problem, and long-term negative consequences that make the response a problem. In terms of Mowrer's neurotic paradox (1950), abnormal behavior may be both "self-perpetuating" (i.e., have positive consequences) and "self-defeating" (i.e., have negative consequences). Given the gradient of reinforcement, the short-term positive consequences may often be more powerful than long-term negative consequences.

In remediating behavioral deficits and in replacing present maladaptive behavior, it is important to identify consequences surrounding possible alternative behaviors. For example, what would happen if a presently nonassertive woman became more assertive? Or how can a child, who currently receives adult attention for inappropriate behavior, receive attention in more appropriate ways?

The purpose of identifying or assessing the consequences of behavior is to understand and treat the client's problems. If the consequences surrounding a problem behavior are identified, understanding of the behavior's *maintaining* factors is increased. The distinction between etiological and maintaining factors should be noted. For example, the fact that a parent's solicitous attention is maintaining a child's phobia has no necessary implication for the etiology of that phobia. Similarly, the belief that the negative reinforcement of anxiety reduction is maintaining a person's compulsive behavior has no necessary implication for the etiology of that compulsion.

The identification of antecedent and consequent variables has treatment implications through the functional analysis. The variables of which a certain behavior is a function are identified. The variables identified in assessment are altered in intervention, thereby changing the target response. As an illustration, take three disruptive children in a classroom. If assessment reveals that the disruptive behavior of the first child is maintained by teacher attention, then a "praise and ignore" treatment strategy might be implemented in which the teacher is taught to praise appropriate behavior and to ignore inappropriate behavior (Madsen, Becker, & Thomas, 1968). If assessment reveals that the disruptive behavior of the second child is maintained by peer attention, then the Good Behavior Game might be selected as the treatment strategy (Barrish, Saunders, & Wolf, 1969). In this game, the class is divided into two teams; points are awarded to the team for appropriate behavior, and/or points are taken away from the team for inappropriate behavior. If assessment reveals that the disruptive behavior of the third child is related to his or her inability to perform the assigned academic work, the recommended treatment might be the provision of curriculum materials that are appropriate to the child's skills level. In summary, the functional analysis has direct treatment implications. Considerations surrounding this statement are elaborated in a subsequent section of this chapter.

ORGANISM VARIABLES

In addition to environmental variables, the other main class of variables that contribute to problematic responses are organism variables. There are two types of organism variables: physiological variables, and past learning history. Each of these contribute to the uniqueness of the individual. Because of these variables, different individuals make different responses to the same environmental situations.

Physiological Variables

A variety of physiological variables affect behavior. Genetic variables make long-term contributions to both abnormal behavior (e.g., schizophrenia) and normal behavior (e.g., Eysenck's neuroticism and intraversion, Eysenck, 1963). Environmental events, for example, a car accident, produce changes in physiology, such as a back injury, that in turn produce changes in behavior. Behavior can also produce changes in physiology during the lifetime of an individual, for example, through overeating, smoking, or drug abuse. Ontogenetic development produces changes in physiology that have an impact on behavior, for example, physical size increases, or visual acuity dissipates. Ephemeral physiological states such as hunger or fatigue also contribute to behavior. A biobehavioral model, along with its implications for behavioral assessment, is presented in Chapter 9 by Williamson, Waters, and Hawkins, in this volume.

There are two main reasons for identifying critical physiological variables during behavioral assessment: to increase our understanding of behavior and to treat it more effectively. As an example of the former contribution, our understanding of a person's current strange behavior may be better understood in light of a family history of schizophrenia or a recently diagnosed brain tumor. Identification of some physiological variables also can have treatment implications. For example, in one of our cases, a child was referred for stealing at school. Interviews and observations revealed that the stolen goods were always food or money, and that her foster home provided little to eat. Her behavior problem of stealing was treated by moving her to a more provident foster home, thereby removing the hunger cues. Furthermore, some cases of sexual dysfunction are related to physiological variables, including disease states, drug use, and poor hygiene. As a final example, a deficit in social interactions might be related to obesity or to some culturally devaluated aspect of appearance. Treatment might include a weight control program and a visit to a beauty parlor.

Past Learning History

Longitudinal Consistency of Behavior

Behavior tends to be both temporally consistent and situation specific. To elaborate, when a cross-section is taken of an individual's behavior, it most likely contains many different situations and, therefore, many different behaviors. In contrast, when a longitudinal section is taken, different situations may repeat, and therefore the set of different behaviors recurs. In Mischel's (1979) words: "No one seriously questions that lives have continuity and that we perceive ourselves and others as relatively stable individuals who have substantial identity and stability over time, even when our specific actions change across situations" (p. 742). The notable temporal stability of behavior has prompted Mischel (1968) to conclude: "Unless the environmental maintaining conditions change markedly, past behavior tends to be the best predictor of future behavior in similar situations" (p. 292).

Various explanations have been offered for the temporal consistency of behavior. These explanations occur at different levels of analysis, including behavioral, cognitive, and physiological, and include the following: (1) Behavior is temporally consistent because the same environmental situations repeat. These situations call forth the same behavior in the individual due to learning, both classical and operant conditioning, (Mischel, 1968) or due to perceived similarities in the situations (Mischel, 1973). By the "same environment" it is meant that the environment is functionally the same, not necessarily that it appears the same to an observer. In many situations, environments are clearly *functionally* the same, despite their formal differences. (2) Because a person receives intermittent reinforcement for the same behaviors that occur in the same situations, the behaviors are highly resistant to extinction (Mischel, 1968). (3) Trait labels (e.g., aggressive, alcoholic) or role labels (e.g., mother, student, ex-convict) may contribute to behavioral stabilities. According to Mischel (1968), "trait and role labels are likely to have particularly strong stabilizing effects on behavior when they lead the labeled person into special consistent environments in which he regularly encounters people who model the labeled behavior or who reinforce behaviors congruent with the label" (p. 287). (4) A person's "cognitive and behavioral construction competencies" (Mischel, 1973, p. 266), that is, his or her cognitive skills and capacity to generate behavior, contribute to behavioral stability, especially the stability in cognitive–intellectual performance (Mischel, 1968). (5) A person's physiological needs recur, for example, for sleep or for food, and the concomitant behaviors therefore recur, for example, sleeping or eating. (6) A person's physical appearance remains relatively the same, thus serving as a constant stimulus to those in the environment (e.g., according to cultural norms, a person is attractive or unattractive, or appears to be "athletic" or "intellectual"; Staats, 1975). (7) One's current behavioral repertoire sets limits on one's future behavioral repertoires (Staats, 1975). Many behaviors occur in complicated hierarchies, and there are limitations as to how many hierarchies an individual is capable of mastering. The repertoire that receives reinforcement is likely to be repeated and subjected to continued refinement. To illustrate, skiing is a temporally consistent behavior for an Olympic skier, and playing the piano is a temporally consistent behavior for a concert pianist, but probably not vice versa. (8) One's learned motivational system (Staats, 1975) or the perceived value of an expectancy for particular reinforcers (Mischel, 1973) enhances the temporal consistency of behavior. A person who likes to bowl may bowl over a long period of time, whereas someone who likes to read may read over a long period of time, but not necessarily the other way around. (9) A person's self-regulatory system or lack thereof may contribute to behavioral consistencies across time (Mischel, 1973). It is clear that these different explanations for the temporal stability of behavior within an individual include different levels of analysis: cognitive, physiological, and behavioral. Some of these explanations are elaborated in Staats's chapter on "personality" from a behavioral perspective (Chapter 8 in this volume).

Assessment Implications of Past Learning History.

Assessment of a person's past learning history contributes to our understanding and treatment of his or her problematic behaviors. The duration of a problem may predict the probability of treatment success. A therapist may teach an old dog new tricks, but it will be harder because the old tricks have been rewarded so many times. The history of a sexual deviant may implicate treatment prognosis. It is generally held that the probability of treatment success is greater for sexual deviants who have had some prior heterosexual experience than for those who have not (Feldman & MacCulloch, 1965), possibly because they need only to suppress deviant arousal, rather than simultaneously to increase appropriate arousal and social skills as well (Barlow & Abel, 1976).

Sometimes, current functional variables can be identified through assessment of the individual's history. One illustration is Wolpe's (1958) case of a man with pervasive anxiety. The man reported an incident in his past in which he had been both sexually attracted to and repulsed by a woman with whom he had intercourse at night in a hotel room. Only the dark outlines of objects were visible in the dimly lit room. The pervasive anxiety was assessed to worsen around sexual stimuli and dark heavy objects. This information about the client's past revealed clues about current functional stimuli. These stimuli could be included in a subsequent treatment program, for example, systematic desensitization or reinforced practice.

RESPONSES

What Should Be Assessed

As was previously noted, in behavioral assessment, behaviors or responses are assessed as *samples* of the person's usual responding in a particular stimulus situation. In contrast, traditional assessment is considered to be more inferential, with behavior interpreted as a *sign* of an underlying trait or disorder (Goldfried & Kent, 1972).

A large range of assessment techniques fall within the purview of behavioral assessment, including direct observations in naturalistic, role-played, or analogue situations; self-monitoring; participant observation; questionnaires; interviews; intelligence and achievement tests; and psychophysiological measures. The techniques of behavioral assessment and of traditional assessment may overlap. The critical distinction is the interpretation given to data obtained through the technique: whether the data are given a *sample* interpretation or a *sign* interpretation (Nelson & Hayes, 1979).

There is some current feeling that behavioral assessment has drifted from its behavioral roots, away from the measurement of *behavior* toward the measurement of *constructs* (Barrett, Johnston, & Pennypaker, Chapter 6 in this volume; Johnston & Pennypacker, 1980). Examples of this drift toward constructs are attempts to measure assertiveness, anxiety, social skills, or depression. A correlate of the call to return to the measurement of *behavior* is the eschewing of some of the behavioral assessment techniques noted above. Instead, a return to measuring *response frequency* is proposed, through automated counting or at least direct and continuous observation. In part, this conflict is due to the two strains of behaviorism reflected in the behavioral assessment movement.

The Issue of Response Covariation

A more detailed consideration of response covariation is provided in this volume by Evans (Chapter 5). An overview is presented here.

Triple Response System

The central way in which response covariation has been addressed in behavioral assessment is the triple response system. The triple response system refers to motoric, physiological, and cognitive aspects of behavior. This concept originated with Lang (1968) who noted asynchrony among the different response systems in the measurement of anxiety. This asynchrony has now been demonstrated numerous times, both when behavior is measured at some static moment of time (e.g., Hartshorne & May, 1928) and when behavior is measured repeatedly in the context of treatment (e.g., Leitenberg, Agras, Butz, & Wincze, 1971).

The implication of this asynchrony in the triple response system for behavioral assessment is that a thorough assessment will necessitate examination of each response system thought to be important before, during, and after treatment. In many cases, all three types of behavior must be assessed. This strategy is frequently used in the assessment of phobias, for example, where motoric avoidance, verbal ratings of fear, and physiological measures are simultaneously taken in the context of the behavioral avoidance test (Borkovec, Weerts, & Bernstein, 1977).

This notion of the triple response system has provoked at least four types of reactions. First, some attempts have been made to speculate about causes of asynchrony or synchrony among the three response systems. For example, Hodgson and Rachman (1974) propose that synchrony may increase as intensity of emotion increases. Merely demonstrating synchrony or asynchrony is a structural approach; identifying the controlling variables of which synchrony or asynchrony is a function is a functional approach.

Second, conceptual concerns have been raised about the idea of the triple response system (Kozak & Miller, 1982). The concern is that the surprise over asynchrony reflects an assumption that there is a hypothetical construct (e.g., fear) that should produce synchrony. This concern is related to the stance, earlier presented, that behavioral assessors should focus on data and responses, as opposed to constructs.

Third, methodological concerns have been raised. Cone (1979) has proposed that asynchrony may be a methodological artifact, due to a method by content confound. Two basic methods of assessment are self-report and direct observation. Content of assessment is motoric, physiological, or cognitive responses. As an example of this method by content confound, direct observations of motor content are usually compared with self-report of cognitive content, with a typically low correlation resulting. Cone (1979) advocates a reexamination of the triple response system, without this confound. Some data, collected prior to Cone's proposal, substantiate his view. Higher agreement (95%) was reached when motoric content was assessed by both direct observation (Behavioral Avoidance Test) and by self-report (statements predicting performance on the BAT) than when motoric content was assessed by direct observation (BAT) and when cognitive content was assessed by self-report (ratings of fear on the Fear Survey Schedule) (61%) (McReynolds & Stegman, 1976).

A fourth concern about the triple response system is that the data supporting asynchrony are nomothetic. Typically, correlations are obtained among motoric, physiological, and verbal measures from a *group* of subjects. The concern is that the group data may camouflage synchrony in the behavior of individuals. A dissertation in our laboratories conducted by Arlinza Turner in fact did show synchrony in the behavior of several subjects among motoric, physiological, and verbal measures of sexual arousal, even though the group-based correlations evidenced asynchrony (Turner & Hayes, 1984). Other concerns about the nomothetic–idiographic distinction are elaborated in a chapter in this volume by Cone.

Classification or Diagnosis

The idea that individual behaviors can and do covary in a regularly occurring, systematic manner across persons is the basis for diagnostic systems. In Kazdin's terminology, the individual behaviors are "symptoms," whereas the constellation of symptoms that occur together and covary over time is a "syndrome" (Kazdin, 1983). The former are the traditional target behaviors of behavioral assessment. Systematic covariations in behavior have only recently received attention in behavioral circles (Voeltz & Evans, 1982; Wahler, 1975).

While the symptom and syndrome levels of conceptualization in psychiatric diagnosis are compatible with contemporary behavioral thought, the next two levels delineated by Kazdin (1983) are less so. The third level of conceptualization is the "disorder": a syndrome becomes a disorder when

> evidence exists that the constellation of symptoms is useful to view as independent of other, more general, conditions. The evidence may consist of information about the natural course of the disorder, family history, possible biological correlates, and response to treatment. (Kazdin, 1983, p. 85)

The fourth level of conceptualization is the "disease": "The notion of disease is invoked for a disorder when there is a specific known etiology and an identifiable underlying (pathophysiological) process" (Kazdin, 1983, p. 86).

The current diagnostic or classification system in wide use is DSM-III (Diagnostic and Statistical Manual of Mental Disorders, 3rd edition, American Psychiatric Association, 1980). DSM-III has received its share of criticism (e.g., Harris, 1979; McReynolds, W. T., 1979; Schact & Nathan, 1977). To these could be added its basis in structuralism (a static or structural view of response covariation) as opposed to functionalism (response covariation based on common controlling variables), and its nomothetic quality (emphasis on differences among groups of clients) as opposed to an idiographic quality (emphasis on individual). Nonetheless, it is our view that it has utility for behavioral assessors (see also Nelson & Barlow, 1981).

One advantage of DSM-III is that it allows communication with other professionals. Such communication is important for describing our clients in journal articles or in professional referrals, for classifying clients for insurance or accountability purposes, and for grant proposals.

A second advantage is that DSM-III brings behavioral assessors in contact with research in abnormal psychology. Although the particular response covariations (syndromes) of DSM-III were identified by authority rather than empirically, such covariations cannot be ignored. When a client evidences some of the behaviors (symptoms) characteristic of a particular syndrome, a behavioral assessor would be wise to assess the presence or absence of other behaviors in the syndrome. Diagnoses may also be useful in suggesting controlling variables to assess. Certain syndromes seem more or less influenced by immediate environmental versus organismic variables. For example, for a client exhibiting depressive behaviors, controlling variables to assess include: familial history of depression (bipolar or unipolar), sudden environmental changes, and loss of reinforcers. Diagnoses may also be useful in suggesting treatments that have been found to be effective for clients with similar problems—phobics generally respond to exposure treatments, for example. Selecting a treatment based on diagnosis is further discussed in a subsequent portion of this chapter.

THE GOALS OF BEHAVIORAL ASSESSMENT

The assumptions of behavioral assessment have been summarized through use of the acronym SORC (stimulus–organism–response–consequence, Goldfried & Sprafkin, 1976). Behaviors or responses are a function of both environmental variables (stimuli and consequences) and organism variables (physiology and past learning history). In agreement with these assumptions, the goals of behavioral assessment are (1) to identify the target behaviors; (2) to select a treatment strategy; and (3) to evaluate the effectiveness of the treatment strategy. Each of these goals is elaborated here, and in other chapters of this volume.

IDENTIFICATION OF TARGET BEHAVIORS

Specification of Target Behavior

The first step in behavioral assessment is to specify the target behavior(s). This no easy task because clients are typically trait theorists who talk the language of traits rather than of behaviors (Mischel, 1968). Various strategies are available to help specify more global complaints. Clients can be asked to give examples of their problems, or to explain what evidence would be required of problem amelioration. Lazarus has suggested the strategy of the "three wishes" in which clients are asked to describe three ways in which their lives could be improved (Lazarus, 1971). One general purpose of behavioral assessment devices is to help in the process of identifying specific target behaviors.

The notion of selecting specific and singular target behaviors has recently provoked thoughtful new consideration. Evans's concern (Evans, 1985; Voeltz & Evans, 1982; see also Chapter 5 in this volume) is that the complexity of behavior may be missed if the focus is on singular responses. Responses interrelate, covary, and form complex response systems. In addition to reiterating this concern, Kazdin (1985) raises the issue of the relationship between the target behavior identified by the assessor and the clinical problem as experienced by the client. He asks: "To what extent does this behavior as defined and assessed correspond with the behavior as defined and evaluated by the client or significant others?" (p. 36). These lines of thought may modify target selection of the future.

Who Decides What the Target Behavior Should Be?

Generally, the therapist and client together select the goals: "the practice of behavior therapy is typically guided by a contractual agreement between both client and therapist specifying the goals and methods of intervention" (Davison & Stuart, 1975, p. 755). Obviously, the goals of the client cannot be ignored, but neither can the values of the therapist: Would the therapist agree to desensitize an anxious bank robber (a silly example) or to change the sexual orientation of a homosexual (a serious example)?

Sometimes the client is not in a position to contribute fully to decision making, for example, a child, a retarded person, a schizophrenic, a prison inmate. The views of significant others of the client may then be sought. According to Davison and Stuart (1975):

> There are times when there may be differences between the values of the client, significant others (e.g., parents, teachers, spouses), and the therapist. When this happens, treatment efforts are held in abeyance until consensus is achieved. (p. 755)

To help make the process of target behavior selection concrete, various nonempirical and empirical guidelines have been proposed. These are described briefly below, and are augmented and elaborated by Hawkins in Chapter 10 of this volume.

Nonempirical Guidelines For Selecting Target Behaviors

Various guidelines have been proposed that seem to reflect a philosophical stance more than an empirical base; a number of these will be reviewed here. (1) Behavior should be changed that is physically dangerous to the client or to others. (2) Behavior is abnormal if it is aversive to others, especially those in power, by virtue of its deviance from norms or its unpredictability (Ullmann & Krasner, 1969). (3) Behavior should be changed so that it maximizes the flexibility of the client's repertoire and the long-term individual and social good; one aspect of this view is maximizing the client's long-term reinforcers (Krasner, 1969; Myerson & Hayes, 1978). (4) Behavior to be changed should be stated in positive or constructionist terms, as opposed to negative or eliminative terms (Goldiamond, 1974; Hawkins, this volume; McFall, 1976; Winett & Winkler, 1972). The rationale is that undesirable behavior may fall by the wayside without extinction, punishment, or other eliminative processes when desirable behavior is established, and that constructive procedures produce long-term behavior change whereas eliminative procedures sometimes lead to quick relapse. (5) Optimal, not merely average, levels of performance (e.g., as determined by normative data) should be sought (Foster & Ritchey, 1979; Van Houten, 1979). (6) Select for modification only those behaviors that the environment will continue to maintain, that is, teach only those behaviors that will continue to be reinforced after training (Ayllon & Azrin, 1968). (7) Target behaviors should be selected that fall within the aegis of the clinician's treatment repertoire: "when intervention strategies are not available, the behavioral analysis becomes an academic exercise of no consequence" (Kanfer & Grimm, 1977, p. 9).

Empirical Guidelines to Select Target Behaviors

In addition to the philosophically driven guidelines summarized above, various empirically based guidelines have been proposed by which to select target behaviors. First, the use of normative data has been suggested for two purposes (Kazdin, 1977; Nelson & Bowles, 1975): (1) before treatment, the client's behavior can be compared with norms to determine if it is statistically abnormal, and (2) following treatment, the client's behavior can again be compared with the norms to determine whether treatment has brought the behavior into the normal range. Normative data may be especially useful in the selection of children's target behaviors because children's behavior changes rapidly through physical maturation and learning experiences. Normative data are provided for children's academic behavior though intelligence and achievement tests (Nelson, 1980). Norms can also be collected for children's social behavior. An illustration of this is O'Connor's work (1969) in which socially withdrawn preschoolers were identified on the basis of norms prior to treatment; these norms were also used posttreatment to judge the clinical significance of the treatment changes.

A second empirical strategy has been the use of regression equations to identify meaningful target behaviors. Potential target behaviors are entered as predictor variables in a regression equation; the targets that relate highly to the criterion variable become the focus of intervention. To illustrate, the four behaviors of attending to the assigned task, talking to another student about academic material, compliance with teacher requests, and low rates of pupil self-stimulation were found to relate highly to arithmetic achievement in fourth grade children, even when cross-validated in another school (Cobb, 1972). As another illustration, the conversational behavior by college males of personal attention (operationally defined as using "you" in a question or statement) was related to the criterion variable of female attraction, whereas other conversational behaviors (encouraging statements, and self-talk) were not related (Kupke, Hobbs, & Cheney, 1979).

A third empirically based strategy to select target behaviors is the known groups method (McFall, 1976). Known groups are identified, consisting of persons considered to be normal and persons displaying a particular problem (e.g., depression, schizophrenia). Then the two groups are compared in an attempt to identify the specific behaviors that differentiate them. As an illustration, groups of high frequency daters and low frequency daters were compared on behavioral, self-report, and partner rating measures of social competence and attractiveness (Glasgow & Arkowitz, 1975). Physical attractiveness differentiated the groups, but specific behavioral measures did not.

A fourth empirically based strategy is to solicit ratings from community consumers of behavior change, a concept that falls under the rubric of social validation (Kazdin, 1977; Wolf, 1978). In an example, community judges rated from videotapes the conversational abilities of nondelinquent junior high and college students (Minkin, Braukmann, Minkin, Timbers, Timbers, Fixsen, Phillips, & Wolf, 1976). The behaviors that were correlated with high ratings were asking questions, providing feedback or responding to the other individual, and duration of talking. These behaviors were subsequently taught to predelinquent girls.

A fifth strategy is the use of Goldfried and D'Zurilla's (1969) behavior analytic model, which is elaborated in Hawkins's chapter in this volume. An excellent example of this strategy is the identification of behavior important for employment success by Mathews, Whang, and Fawcett (1980). First, a list of 13 commonly identified job-related situations was generated (e.g., telephoning to request an interview); this stage was called situational analysis. Second, appropriate responses for each situation were delineated, a stage called response enumeration. Third, employers were asked to rate the importance of these responses in a stage called response evaluation. Finally, an assessment instrument was created and tested that included the situations and the important responses. The important responses could become target behaviors, as needed, in subsequent treatment programs.

A sixth and last empirically based strategy is the use of treatment validity (Nelson & Hayes, 1979; Hayes, Nelson, & Jarrett, Chapter 13 of this volume). A question asked in treatment validity research is: Does the selection of one target behavior lead to better treatment outcome than the selection of another target behavior? In one example of the strategy, the depression of women who had irrational cognitions improved more when they received cognitive therapy than when they received social skills training; conversely, the depression of women who had social skills deficits improved more when they received social skills training than when they received cognitive therapy (McKnight, Nelson, Hayes, & Jarrett, 1984). Choice of a target behavior was critical to treatment outcome. In another example, male college students were rated as more attractive to females when they were trained in the target behavior of personal attention (operationally defined as using "you" statements or questions) than when they were trained in the target behavior of using encouraging phrases (Kupke, Calhoun, & Hobbs, 1979).

Choosing Efficient Target Behaviors

Often, a client has several problems. The question, then, is where to begin treatment. In other words, which target behavior should be the first focus of treatment? One alternative is to change first the behavior that is most irritating to the significant others of the client (Tharp & Wetzel, 1969). The rationale is that the significant others, or mediators, are likely to continue cooperation with treatment if they benefit from the intervention.

Second, the behavior that is easiest to change could become the first target of intervention (O'Leary, 1972). The rationale is that treatment success will encourage further treatment efforts.

Third, behaviors that produce therapeutic response generalization should be altered first. For example, the reinforcement of academic accuracy has been shown to alter both academic correctness and on-task behavior, but the reinforcement of on-task behavior had no effect on academic accuracy (Hay, Hay, & Nelson, 1977). Similarly, children's oppositional behavior decreased more when they were rewarded for solitary play than when they were rewarded for cooperative parent–child activities (Wahler & Fox, 1980).

Fourth, and related to the third alternative, if different behaviors comprise a response chain, it is wise to begin intervention at the beginning of the response chain. By way of example, the multiple problems of clients referred to a drug treatment program were displayed in a diagram depicting the behavioral interrelationships (Angle, Hay, Hay, & Ellinwood, 1977). Treatment could then begin with the "keystone" or "pivotal" behavior that then affected other behaviors. The importance of assessing response systems in the selection of target behaviors has also been stressed by Evans (1985). An elaboration of the assessment of response hierarchies and response clusters is provided by Hawkins in Chapter 10 of this volume.

CURRENT RESEARCH ON TARGET BEHAVIOR SELECTION

Reliability of Target Behavior Selection

One focus of research has been on the reliability of target behavior selection. In other words, when different assessors are presented with the same information, will they agree on choice of target behaviors? The answer seems to be negative. When four assessors interviewed the same four adult clients, they generally agreed on the *number* of problem areas of each client, but not on the *specific* problem areas (Hay, Hay, Angle, & Nelson, 1979). Similarly, when 118 behavioral assessors were asked to identify target behaviors from written child case descriptions, their agreement across different experimental conditions (type of disorder and number of problems included in the case descriptions) varied considerably (Wilson & Evans, 1983).

Treatment Validity of Target Behavior Selection

While descriptive data about reliability (or lack thereof) of target behavior selection may be interesting, it is also important to know if choice of target behaviors is *relevant*. Reliability or agreement on choice of target behaviors is relevant only if that choice has some bearing on treatment outcome. Treatment validity research, as described earlier, answers the question, Are better treatment results obtained if one target is selected rather than another target? Treatment validity research progresses in two stages. First, likely target behaviors are hypothesized, through the known groups method, for example, or by normative data, or by regression equations. Second, two or more of these behaviors are treated in an experimental design that permits a comparison of the relative effectiveness in treating one behavior rather than another. The work described earlier by McKnight and colleagues (1984) and by Kupke, Calhoun, and Hobbs (1979) helped to establish the treatment validity of target behavior selection for some disorders.

SELECTION OF INTERVENTION STRATEGY

Elaboration of the multiple considerations required in selecting an intervention strategy is provided by Haynes's chapter in this volume. Three main strategies are presented here: the functional analysis, the keystone behavior strategy, and the diagnostic strategy (Nelson, 1984).

The Functional Analysis

The functional analysis is the classic strategy that links behavioral assessment and treatment. The environmental variables controlling the target behavior are identified in assessment and are subsequently modified in treatment (Goldfried & Pomeranz, 1968). In Ferster's (1965) words: "Such a functional analysis of behavior has the advantage that it specifies the causes of behavior in the form of explicit environmental events that can be objectively identified and that are potentially manipulable" (p. 11). For example, depression is sometimes attributed to a loss of reinforcement (e.g., Ferster, 1965). According to this view, reinforcement contingencies shift so that the depressed person is no longer reinforced for normal behavior, but instead receives attention and other rewards contingent on depressed behavior. Using this functional analysis of depression, Liberman and Raskin (1971) trained the family of a depressed client in contingency management. Reinforcing task completion and ignoring depressive behavior produced a correspondent decrease in depression, as shown by a single-subject reversal design.

While the functional analysis often appears to lead to successful treatment, one should bear in mind that generally the functional analysis performed in assessment is not truly a *functional* analysis. The controlling variables are usually hypothetical; no independent test is made to ascertain whether these indeed are the variables controlling the problem behavior. As evidence of this point, Haynes (Chapter 11 of this volume) reviewed 41 single case studies published in behavioral journals in 1981 to determine whether hypothesized causal factors (including but not limited to functional analyses) were independently verified prior to their manipulation in treatment. Of the 41 cases, in only 35% was there an independent verification of hypothesized causal factors before treatment.

In some sense, one purpose of behavioral assessment is to identify controlling variables. For example, the purpose of the Fear Survey Schedule (Geer, 1965) is to identify specific stimuli that provoke reports of fear in the client; as another illustration, role-playing might be used to identify specific situations in which the client manifests poor social skills; as a final example, in a search for consequences using an interview format, a mother might be asked how she responds when her son refuses to go to bed at the prescribed time. Using the words of O'Leary and Wilson (1975)

> behavioral assessment can be described as a series of mini-experiments in which the assessor tries to systematically expose the client to those relevant environmental and self-imposed stimuli which appear to be affecting the client's functioning so as to ascertain whether and how they control behavior. (p. 27)

Behavioral assessment is composed of mini-experiments only in a rudimentary sense, since the population of possible controlling variables is seldom systematically sampled and since controls are seldom used to identify which aspect of the situation produced the observed response.

The suggestion to *test* hypotheses about the patient prior to intervention was first made by Shapiro (1966). This suggestion has been revitalized by Turkat and his colleagues (Carey et al., 1984; Turkat & Maisto, 1985). Turkat advocates the construction of clinical experiments that can serve to validate a priori case formulations. As an example, in the case of a woman who ate excessively and who drank alcohol excessively, a deficit in impulse control was hypothesized (that is, responding to short-term contingencies). To test this proposed case formulation, the woman was asked to carry out a task of crossing out certain letters on a typewritten sheet, while choosing between two types of consequences: a small, immediate conseqence of one cigarette for each line completed versus a delayed, larger consequence of three cigarettes one month later for each line completed. Her choice of the small, immediate consequence over the larger delayed consequence was viewed as verification of the hypothesis.

The use of operant methodology to validate functional analyses has been suggested by Weiss (1968)—for example, a Taffel-task could be used to establish the effectiveness of a social reinforcer. In a Taffel-task, the subject constructs sentences; certain categories of words or phrases are preselected for verbal conditioning. In a study by Brannon and Nelson (in press), a Taffel-task was used to assess in a priori fashion the social reinforcement value of the significant other who had agreed to implement a contingency management procedure with depressed clients.

While the proposition of independently validating a functional analysis prior to implementing treatment based on that functional analysis is intuitively appealing, this proposition raises two issues. One issue is the situation specificity of behavior (e.g., Mischel, 1968). Even if the hypothesized controlling variables are validated in a clinical test of a case formulation, there is no guarantee that these are indeed the controlling variables for the actual clinical problem behavior. Second, research is needed to ascertain if treatment based on *tested* functional analyses is consistently more effective than treatment based on *hypothesized* functional analyses.

The validity of a hypothesized functional analysis is usually determined by treatment outcome. If the treatment based on the hypothesized functional analysis is successful, then the functional analysis might be assumed to be correct. Examples of this logic are provided by the implementation of contingency management procedures. For example, if teacher attention is altered and child behavior changes, then teacher attention probably contributed to prior child behavior (e.g., Harris, Wolf, & Baer, 1964). This is indirect validation at best, since the effectiveness of treatment based on a different functional analysis is seldom determined (Haynes, Chapter 11 of this volume).

In an important exception, Carr and Durand (1985) compared treatment outcomes when treatments were based on different functional analyses. Their assumption was that children's behavior problems (e.g., self-injury, tantrums, aggression) might serve a communicative function. For individual children, it was hypothesized (by observing children's behavior under easy or difficult task conditions) that behavior problems served either an escape function or (by observing children's behavior under conditions involving frequent versus infrequent adult attention) attention-getting function. Behavior problems assessed as serving an escape function were reduced when the children were taught an alternative form of communication, such as asking for help. Behavior problems did not improve when they were taught to ask: "Am I doing good work?" Conversely, behavior problems assessed as serving an attention-getting function were reduced when the children were taught to ask "Am I doing good work?" but not when they were taught to say, "Help me."

Keystone Behavior Strategy

An alternative link between assessment and treatment is the keystone behavior strategy. In this strategy, first, different response classes are identified that are believed to contribute nomothetically to a particular disorder. Second, for a specific client, a particular response class is identified that is thought to be the keystone behavior in ameliorating the disorder for that person. Unlike the functional analysis, which relies on stimulus–response

relationships, the keystone behavior strategy rests on response–response
relationships (Evans, 1985; Kazdin, 1983).

Using the example of depression, various response classes are thought
to contribute: ratio of pleasant and unpleasant events experienced by the
depressed person, the depressed person's level of social skills, and irrational
cognitions held by the depressed person (Beck, Rush, Shaw, & Emery, 1979;
Coyne, 1976; Lewinsohn & Arconad, 1981). In the keystone behavior strategy, one of these response classes would be idiographically selected for
treatment in each depressed person.

Some evidence for the effectiveness of the keystone behavior strategy in
the assessment and treatment of depression was provided by McKnight and
colleagues (1984). Depressed women with assessed problems in social skills
improved significantly more in both social skills and depression after receiving the related treatment of social skills training as compared with the
unrelated treatment of cognitive therapy. Conversely, depressed women
with assessed problems in irrational cognitions improved significantly more
in both cognitions and depression after receiving the related treatment of
cognitive therapy as compared with the unrelated treatment of social skills
training. These results showed that identification and treatment of the
correct keystone behavior was critical in ameliorating each woman's depression.

Diagnostic Strategy

A third and last strategy that links assessment and treatment is the diagnostic strategy. Diagnosis is based on the form, topography, or structural
properties of behavior, as opposed to its functional properties. If a person
displays certain behaviors, such as those specified in DSM-III (American
Psychiatric Association, 1980), he or she qualifies for a particular diagnosis,
regardless of the reasons for or causes of those behaviors. Diagnosis is based
on a "static" analysis, as opposed to a "functional" analysis (Ferster, 1965).

In the diagnostic strategy, after the person is diagnosed, he or she is
administered the treatment that has been found nomothetically to be most
effective in treating that disorder. For example, a phobic might receive exposure treatment (Barlow & Wolfe, 1981), a depressive might receive cognitive therapy (Beck et al., 1979), and an exhibitionist might receive covert
sensitization (Maletzky, 1980).

It is interesting to note that there is greater agreement among behavioral assessors on treatment choices than on hypothesized controlling variables (Felton & Nelson, 1984). Six clinicians assessed the same three clients,
with problem areas already identified for the clinicians. Agreement was
greatest on treatment proposals, followed by consequence, stimulus, and

organism variables, in that order. Perhaps the clinicians were using the diagnostic strategy in devising treatment proposals rather than the strategy of the functional analysis.

Comparison of the Three Strategies

The relative merits of the three strategies for selecting effective treatments has yet to be evaluated. Consistent with behavioral assumptions, it is generally believed that idiographic and functionally based assessment leads to more effective treatment than nomothetic and statistically based assessment; but there is no available evidence for this belief (Haynes, 1979).

In Chapter 11 of this volume, Haynes argues that a diagnostic strategy may be just as effective as an idiographic strategy: if (1) clients within a particular diagnostic category are relatively homogeneous; (2) a powerful treatment is available for the disorder; and (3) the cost of an idiographic assessment outweighs its additive benefits.

Nathan (1981) proposed that different assessment strategies might be suitable for different disorders. For disorders with a relatively biological etiology, the diagnostic strategy might be most useful in selecting treatment (e.g., phenothiazines for schizophrenics). Conversely, for disorders in which environmental variables appear to be relatively more influential, a functional analysis might be required for effective treatment (e.g., anxiety disorders).

Empirical comparisons using the three strategies for different disorders are needed. For example, different groups of depressives could receive treatments selected by different assessment strategies. For one group, treatment would be idiographically designed for each subject using the functional analysis. For a second group, treatment would be idiographically selected for each subject using the keystone behavior strategy. For the third group, treatment would be nomothetically selected for the whole group, perhaps a package treatment that contained all the components received idiographically by the subjects in the second group. Pre-post measures of depression would be compared to determine if one strategy that linked assessment and treatment was superior to other strategies in producing greater amelioration of depression.

EVALUATION OF TREATMENT OUTCOME

In addition to identifying a target behavior and to selecting an intervention, the third goal of behavioral assessment is to evaluate treatment outcome. The two tools needed to evaluate treatment outcome are single subject experimental design, and repeated and quantified dependent measures.

There are three reasons for systematically evaluating treatment outcome, as elaborated by Hayes and Nelson (Chapter 12 of this volume). First, the quality of client service is frequently improved. Repeated measurement provides feedback to the therapist in a timely fashion. Successful treatment can be pursued with renewed vigor, while unsuccessful treatment can be altered. Second, the collection of repeated and quantified measures provides an accountability system for evaluating client outcome. Convincing evidence can be presented to document requests for government and third-party payment for professional services. Third, systematic treatment evaluation advances clinical science. Demonstrations with internal validity of replicable and effective treatments are helpful in expanding our treatment armamentarium and in enhancing our understanding of specific disorders.

The two components needed for treatment evaluation are single-subject experimental designs and quantified, repeated measurement (Barlow, Hayes, & Nelson, 1984). Regarding the former, a minimum of a case study, or an A (baseline)–B (treatment) design, is needed to measure client progress and to be accountable. Case studies, however, lack internal validity (since other nontreatment events may have caused the observed improvements), and hence are not suitable for contributing to clinical science. An important exception is a series of replicated case studies, which may be also considered as a multiple baseline across subjects (Hayes, 1985). Other single-subject designs with internal validity include the reversal design, the changing criterion design, various multiple baseline designs, and the alternating treatments design (Barlow & Hayes, 1979; Barlow & Hersen, 1984; Hayes, 1981).

Regarding quantified and repeated measurement, several alternative types of measurement are possible. These include various observational measures, including self-monitoring, observation by the therapist, and observation by significant others; role-playing and observational measures in other analogue situations; questionnaires, interviews, and other forms of self-report; and physiological measures (Barlow et al., 1984; Nelson, 1981). These measures may be collected either in the natural environment or in the treatment setting. Guidelines in the use of these measures are described in the chapter by Hayes and Nelson (Chapter 12 of this volume).

SUMMARY

The main assumptions of behavioral assessment are conveniently summarized in the acronym SORC (stimuli–organism–response–consequences, Goldfried & Sprafkin, 1976). Responses or behaviors are a function of both immediate environmental variables (stimuli and consequences) and organismic variables (physiology and past learning history). The first goal of behavioral assessment is to identify the problematic responses. Sometimes this identification leads immediately to the second goal of behavioral assessment, selection of treatment, since interventions can often be chosen on the basis of responses (diagnoses or keystone response classes). At other times, the environmental controlling variables are identified in assessment and modified as the basis of treatment. The third goal of behavioral assessment is to evaluate treatment outcome to increase the probability of client improvements, to assure accountability, and to enhance clinical science.

REFERENCES

American Psychiatric Association (1980). *Diagnostic and statistical manual of mental disorders* (3rd ed.). Washington, D.C.: Author.

Angle, H. V., Hay, L. R., Hay, W. M., & Ellinwood, E. H. (1977). Computer assisted behavioral assessment. In J. D. Cone & R. P. Hawkins (Eds.), *Behavioral assessment: New directions in clinical psychology* (pp. 369–380). New York: Brunner/Mazel.

Ayllon, T., & Azrin, N. (1968). *The token economy.* New York: Appleton-Century-Crofts.

Bandura, A. (1981). In search of pure unidirectional determinants. *Behavior Therapy, 12,* 30–40.

Barlow, D. H. (1977). Behavioral assessment in clinical settings: Developing issues. In J. D. Cone & R. P. Hawkins (Eds.), *Behavioral assessment: New directions in clinical psychology* (pp. 283–307). New York: Brunner/Mazel.

Barlow, D. H., & Abel, G. G. (1976). Sexual deviation. In W. E. Craighead, A. E. Kazdin, & M. J. Mahoney (Eds.), *Behavior modification: Principles, issues, and applications* (pp. 341–360). Boston: Houghton Mifflin.

Barlow, D. H., & Hayes, S. C. (1979). Alternating treatments design: One strategy for comparing the effects of two treatments in a single subject. *Journal of Applied Behavior Analysis, 12,* 199–210.

Barlow, D. H., Hayes, S. C., & Nelson, R. O. (1984). *The scientist–practitioner: Research and accountability in clinical and educational settings.* New York: Pergamon.

Barlow, D. H., & Hersen, M. (1984). *Single-case experimental designs: Strategies for studying behavior change* (2nd ed.). New York: Pergamon.

Barlow, D. H., & Wolfe, B. E. (1981). Behavioral approaches to anxiety disorders: A report of the NIMH-SUNY, Albany, research conference. *Journal of Consulting and Clinical Psychology, 49,* 448–454.

Barrish, H. H., Saunders, M., & Wolf, M. M. (1969). Good behavior game: Effects of individual contingencies for group consequences on disruptive behavior in a classroom. *Journal of Applied Behavior Analysis, 2,* 119–124.

Beck, A. T., Rush, A. J., Shaw, B. F., & Emery, G. (1979). *Cognitive therapy of depression.* New York: Guilford.

Bem, D. J. (1972). Constructing cross-situational consistencies in behavior: Some thoughts on Alker's critique of Mischel. *Journal of Personality, 40,* 17–26.

Bem, D. J., & Allen, A. (1974). On predicting some of the people some of the time: The search for cross-situational consistencies in behavior. *Psychological Review, 81,* 506–520.

Bem, D. J., & Funder, D. C. (1978). Predicting more of the people more of the time: Assessing the personality of situations. *Psychological Review, 85,* 485–501.

Bernstein, D. A., & Nietzel, M. T. (1973). Procedural variation in behavioral avoidance tests. *Journal of Consulting and Clinical Psychology, 41,* 165–174.

Borkovec, T. D., Weerts, T. C., & Bernstein, D. A. (1977). Assessment of anxiety. In A. R. Ciminero, K. S. Calhoun, & H. E. Adams (Eds.), *Handbook of behavioral assessment* (pp. 367–428). New York: Wiley.

Brannon, S., & Nelson, R. O. (in press). Contingency management treatment of outpatient unipolar depression: A comparison of reinforcement versus extinction, and the nature of response covariation. *Journal of Consulting and Clinical Psychology.*

Carey, M. P., Flasher, L. V., Maisto, S. A., & Turkat, I. D. (1984). The a priori approach to psychological assessment. *Professional Psychology, 15,* 515–527.

Carr, E. G., & Durand, V. M. (1985). The social–communicative basis of severe behavior problems in children. In S. Reiss & R. Bootzin (Eds.), *Theoretical issues in behavior therapy* (pp. 220–254). New York: Academic.

Cobb, J. A. (1972). Relationship of discrete classroom behaviors to fourth grade academic achievement. *Journal of Educational Psychology, 63,* 74–80.

Cone, J. D. (1979). Confounded comparisons in triple response mode assessment research. *Behavioral Assessment, 1,* 85–95.

Cone, J. D. (1980, November). *Template matching procedures for idiographic behavioral assessment.* Paper presented at the meeting of the Association for Advancement of Behavior Therapy, New York.

Cone, J. D. (1981). Psychometric considerations. In M. Hersen & A. S. Bellack (Eds.), *Behavioral assessment* (pp. 38–68). New York: Pergamon.

Coyne, J. C. (1976). Depression and the response of others. *Journal of Abnormal Psychology, 85,* 186–193.

Davison, G. C., & Stuart, R. B. (1975). Behavior therapy and civil liberties. *American Psychologist, 30,* 755–763.

Epstein, S. (1979). The stability of behavior: I. On predicting most of the people much of the time. *Journal of Personality and Social Psychology, 37,* 1097–1126.

Epstein, S. (1980). The stability of behavior: II. Implications for psychological research. *American Psychologist, 35,* 790–806.

Evans, I. M. (1985). Building systems models as a strategy for target behavior selection in clinical assessment. *Behavioral Assessment, 7,* 21–32.

Eysenck, H. J. (1963). Biological basis of personality. *Nature, 199,* 1031–1034.

Feldman, M. P., & MacCulloch, M. J. (1965). The application of anticipatory avoidance learning to the treatment of homosexuality: I. Theory, technique, and preliminary results. *Behaviour Research and Therapy, 3,* 165–183.

Felton, J. L., & Nelson, R. O. (1984). Inter-assessor agreement on hypothesized controlling variables and treatment proposals. *Behavioral Assessment, 6,* 199–208.

Ferster, C. B. (1965). Classification of behavioral pathology. In L. Krasner & L. P. Ullmann (Eds.), *Research in behavior modification* (pp. 6–26). New York: Holt, Rinehart, & Winston.

Foster, S. L., & Cone, J. D. (1980). Current issues in direct observation. *Behavioral Assessment, 2,* 313–338.

Foster, S. L., & Ritchey, W. L. (1979). Issues in the assessment of social competence in children. *Journal of Applied Behavior Analysis, 12,* 625–638.

Frederiksen, N. (1972). Toward a taxonomy of situations. *American Psychologist, 27,* 114–123.

Geer, J. H. (1965). The development of a scale to measure fear. *Behaviour Research and Therapy, 3,* 45–53.

Glasgow, R. E., & Arkowitz, H. (1975). The behavioral assessment of male and female social competence in dyadic heterosexual interactions. *Behavior Therapy, 6,* 488–498.

Goldfried, M. R., & D'Zurilla, T. J. (1969). A behavioral-analytic model for assessing competence. In C. D. Spielberger (Ed.), *Current topics in clinical and community psychology: Vol. 1.* (pp. 151–196). New York: Academic.

Goldfried, M. R., & Kent, R. N. (1972). Traditional versus behavioral assessment: A comparison of methodological and theoretical assumptions. *Psychological Bulletin, 77,* 409–420.

Goldfried, M. R., & Pomeranz, D. M. (1968). Role of assessment in behavior modification. *Psychological Reports, 23,* 75–87.

Goldfried, M. R., & Sprafkin, J. N. (1976). Behavioral personality assessment. In J. T. Spence, R. C. Carson, & J. W. Thibaut (Eds.), *Behavioral approaches to therapy* (pp. 295–321). Morristown, NJ: General Learning Press.

Goldiamond, I. (1974). Toward a constructional approach to social problems: Ethical and constitutional issues raised by applied behavior analysis. *Behaviorism, 2,* 1–85.

Goodenough, F. L. (1949). *Mental testing.* New York: Rinehart.

Harris, F. R., Wolf, M. M., & Baer, D. M. (1964). Effects of adult social reinforcement on child behavior. *Young Children, 20,* 8–17.

Harris, J. G., Jr. (1980). Nomovalidation and idiovalidation: A quest for the true personality profile. *American Psychologist, 35,* 729–744.

Harris, S. L. (1979). DSM-III—Its implications for children. *Child Behavior Therapy, 1,* 37–46.

Hartmann, D. P., Roper, B. L., & Bradford, D. C. (1979). Some relationships between behavioral and traditional assessment. *Journal of Behavioral Assessment, 1,* 3–21.

Hartshorne, H., & May, M. A. (1928). *Studies in the nature of character: Vol. 1. Studies in deceit.* New York: Macmillan.

Hay, L. R., Nelson, R. O., & Hay, W. M. (1980). Methodological problems in the use of participant observers. *Journal of Applied Behavior Analysis, 13,* 501–504.

Hay, W. M., Hay, L. R., Angle, H. V., & Nelson, R. O. (1979). The reliability of problem identification in the behavioral interview. *Behavioral Assessment, 1,* 107–118.

Hay, W. M., Hay, L. R., & Nelson, R. O. (1977). Direct and collateral changes in on-task and academic behavior resulting from on-task versus academic contingencies. *Behavior Therapy, 8,* 431–441.

Hayes, S. C. (1981). Single case experimental design and empirical clinical practice. *Journal of Consulting and Clinical Psychology, 49,* 193–211.

Hayes, S. C. (1985). Natural multiple baselines across persons: A reply to Harris and Jenson. *Behavioral Assessment, 7,* 129–132.

Hayes, S. C., & Brownstein, A. J. (in press). Mentalism, private events, and scientific explanation: A defense of B. F. Skinner's view. In S. Modgil & C. Modgil (Eds.), *B. E. Skinner: Consensus and controversy.* Sussex, England: Falmer Press.

Haynes, S. N. (1979). Behavioral variance, individual differences, and trait theory in a behavioral construct system: A reappraisal. *Behavioral Asssessment, 1,* 41–49.

Hodgson, R., & Rachman, S. (1974). II. Desynchrony in measures of fear. *Behaviour Research and Therapy, 12,* 319–326.

Johnston, J. M., & Pennypacker, H. S. (1980). *Strategies and tactics of human behavioral research.* Hillsdale, NJ: Erlbaum.

Jones, R. R. (1972, April). *Intraindividual stability of behavioral observations: Implications for evaluating behavior modification treatment programs.* Paper presented at the meeting of the Western Psychological Association, Portland, OR.

Jones, R. R., Reid, J. B., & Patterson, G. R. (1975). Naturalistic observation in clinical assessment. In P. McReynolds (Ed.), *Advances in psychological assessment: Vol. 3* (pp. 42–95). San Francisco: Jossey-Bass.

Kanfer, F. H., & Grimm, L. G. (1977). Behavioral analysis: Selecting target behaviors in the interview. *Behavior Modification, 1,* 7–28.

Kazdin, A. E. (1977). Assessing the clinical or applied importance of behavior change through social validation. *Behavior Modification, 1,* 427–452.

Kazdin, A. E. (1979). Situational specificity: The two-edged sword of behavioral assessment. *Behavioral Assessment, 1,* 57–75.

Kazdin, A. E. (1983). Psychiatric diagnosis, dimension of dysfunction, and child behavior therapy. *Behavior Therapy, 14,* 73–99.

Kazdin, A. E. (1985). Selection of target behaviors: The relationship of the treatment focus to clinical dysfunction. *Behavioral Assessment, 7,* 33–47.

Kent, R. N., & Foster, S. L. (1977). Direct observation procedures: Methodological issues in naturalistic settings. In A. R. Ciminero, K. S. Calhoun, & H. E. Adams (Eds.), *Handbook of behavioral assessment* (pp. 279–328). New York: Wiley.

Kozak, M. J., & Miller, G. A. (1982). Hypothetical constructs versus intervening variables: A re-appraisal of the three-systems model of anxiety assessment. *Behavioral Assessment, 4,* 347–358.

Krasner, L. (1969). Behavior modification—values and training: The perspective of a psychologist. In C. M. Franks (Ed.), *Behavior therapy: Appraisal and status* (pp. 537–566). New York: McGraw-Hill.

Kupke, T. E., Calhoun, K. S., & Hobbs, S. A. (1979). Selection of neterosocial skills: II. Experimental validity. *Behavior Therapy, 10,* 336–346.

Kupke, T. E., Hobbs, S. A., & Cheney, T. H. (1979). Selection of heterosocial skills. I. Criterion-related validity. *Behavior Therapy, 10,* 327–335.

Lamiell, J. T. (1981). Toward an idiothetic psychology of personality. *American Psychologist, 36,* 276–289.

Lang, P. J. (1968). Fear reduction and fear behavior: Problems in treating a construct. In J. M. Schlien (Ed.), *Research in psychotherapy: Vol. 3* (pp. 90–102). Washington, DC: American Psychological Association.

Lazarus, A. A. (1961). Group therapy of phobic disorders by systematic desensitization. *Journal of Abnormal and Social Psychology, 63,* 504–510.

Lazarus, A. A. (1971). *Behavior therapy and beyond.* New York: McGraw-Hill.

Leitenberg, H., Agras, W. S., Butz, R., & Wincze, J. (1971). Relationship between heart rate and behavioral change during the treatment of phobias. *Journal of Abnormal Psychology, 78,* 59–68.

Lewinsohn, P. M., & Arconad, M. (1981). Behavioral treatment of depression: A social learning approach. In J. F. Clarkin & H. I. Glazer (Eds.), *Depression: Behavioral and directive intervention strategies* (pp. 33–67). New York: Garland.

Liberman, R. P., & Raskin, D. E. (1971). Depression: A behavioral formulation. *Archives of General Psychiatry, 24,* 515–523.

Madsen, C., Jr., Becker, W., & Thomas, D. (1968). Rules, praise, and ignoring: Elements of elementary classroom control. *Journal of Applied Behavior Analysis, 1,* 139–150.

Maletzky, B. M. (1980). Self-referred versus court-referred sexually deviant patients: Success with assisted covert sensitization. *Behavior Therapy, 11,* 306–314.

Mash, E. J., & Mercer, B. J. (1979). A comparison of the behavior of deviant and non-deviant boys while playing alone and interacting with a sibling. *Journal of Child Psychology and Psychiatry, 20,* 197–207.

Mathews, R. M., Whang, P. L., & Fawcett, S. B. (1980). Development and validation of an occupational skills assessment instrument. *Behavioral Assessment, 2,* 71–85.

McFall, R. M. (1976). Behavioral training: A skill-acquisition approach to clinical problems. In J. T. Spence, R. C. Carson, & J. W. Thibaut (Eds.), *Behavioral approaches to therapy* (pp. 227–259). Morristown, NJ: General Learning Press.

McFall, R. M. (1977). Parameters of self-monitoring. In R. B. Stuart (Ed.), *Behavioral self-management: Strategies, techniques, and outcomes* (pp. 196–214). New York: Brunner/Mazel.

McKnight, D. L., Nelson, R. O., Hayes, S. C., & Jarrett, R. B. (1984). Importance of treating individually-assessed response classes in the amelioration of depression. *Behavior Therapy, 15,* 315–335.

McReynolds, P. (1979). The case for interactional assessment. *Behavioral Assessment,, 1,* 237–247.

McReynolds, W. T. (1979). DSM-III and the future of applied social science. *Professional Psychology, 10,* 123–131.

McReynolds, W. T., & Stegman, R. (1976). Sayer versus sign. *Behavior Therapy, 7,* 704–705.

Minkin, N., Braukmann, C. J., Minkin, B. L., Timbers, G. D., Timbers, B. J., Fixsen, D. L., Phillips, E. L., & Wolf, M. M. (1976). The social validation and training of conversation skills. *Journal of Applied Behavior Analysis, 9,* 127–140.

Mischel, W. (1968). *Personality and assessment.* New York: Wiley.

Mischel, W. (1973). Toward a cognitive social learning reconceptualization of personality. *Psychological Review, 80,* 252–283.

Mischel, W. (1979). On the interface between cognition and personality: Beyond the person-situation debate. *American Psychologist, 34,* 740–754.

Mischel, W., & Peake, P. K. (1982). Beyond deja vu in the search for cross-situational consistency. *Psychological Review, 89,* 730–755.

Moos, R. H. (1973). Conceptualizations of human environments. *American Psychologist, 28,* 652–665.

Mowrer, O. H. (1950). *Learning theory and personality dynamics*. New York: Ronald Press.

Murray, D. J. (1983). *A history of western psychology*. Englewood Cliffs, NJ: Prentice-Hall.

Myerson, W. A., & Hayes, S. C. (1978). Controlling the clinician for the clients' benefit. In J. E. Krapfl & E. H. Vargas (Eds.), *Behaviorism and ethics*. Kalamazoo, MI: Behaviordelia.

Nathan, P. E. (1981). Symptomatic diagnosis and behavioral assessment. In D. H. Barlow (Ed.), *Behavioral assessment of adult disorders* (pp. 1-11). New York: Guilford.

Nelson, R. O. (1977). Assessment and therapeutic functions of self-monitoring. In M. Hersen, R. M. Eisler, & P. M. Miller (Eds.), *Progress in behavior modification: Vol. 5* (pp. 263-308). New York: Academic.

Nelson, R. O. (1980). The use of intelligence tests in behavioral assessment. *Behavioral Assessment, 2*, 417-423.

Nelson, R. O. (1981). Realistic dependent measures for clinical use. *Journal of Consulting and Clinical Psychology, 49*, 168-182.

Nelson, R. O. (1983). Behavioral assessment: Past, present, and future. *Behavioral Assessment, 5*, 195-206.

Nelson, R. O. (1984, November). *Is behavioral assessment the missing link between diagnosis and treatment?* Invited address presented at the Meeting of the Association for Advancement of Behavior Therapy, Philadelphia.

Nelson, R. O., & Barlow, D. H. (1981). An overview of behavioral assessment with adult clients: Basic strategies and initial procedures. In D. H. Barlow (Ed.), *Behavioral assessment of adult disorders* (pp. 13-43). New York: Guilford.

Nelson, R. O., & Bowles, P. E. (1975). The best of two worlds—observations with norms. *Journal of School Psychology, 13*, 3-9.

Nelson, R. O., & Hayes, S. C. (1979). Some current dimensions of behavioral assessment. *Behavioral Assessment, 1*, 1-16.

O'Connor, R. D. (1969). Modification of social withdrawal through symbolic modeling. *Journal of Applied Behavior Analysis, 2*, 15-22.

O'Leary, K. D. (1972). The assessment of psychopathology in children. In H. C. Quay & J. S. Werry (Eds.), *Psychopathological disorders of childhood* (pp. 234-272). New York: Wiley.

O'Leary, K. D., & Wilson, G. T. (1975). *Behavior therapy: Application and outcome*. Englewood Cliffs, NJ: Prentice-Hall.

Pepper, S. C. (1942). *World hypotheses*. Berkeley: University of California Press.

Peterson, D. R. (1968). *The clinical study of social behavior*. New York: Appleton-Century-Crofts.

Rachlin, H. (1970). *Introduction to modern behaviorism*. San Francisco: Freeman.

Rausch, H. L., Dittmann, A. T., & Taylor, T. J. (1959). Person, setting, and change in social interaction. *Human Relations, 12*, 361-378.

Reese, H. W. (1984, May). *Historical and philosophical analysis of causality*. Paper presented at the meeting of the Association for Behavior Analysis, Nashville.

Schact, T., & Nathan, P. E. (1977). But is it good for psychologists? Appraisal and status of DSM-III. *American Psychologist, 32*, 1017-1025.

Schwartz, B., & Lacey, M. (1984). What is behaviorism? *Contemporary Psychology, 29*, 675-676.

Shapiro, M. B. (1966). The single case in clinical–psychological research. *Journal of General Psychology, 74*, 3-23.

Shapiro, M. B. (1970). Intensive assessment of the single case: An inductive–deductive approach. In P. Mittler (Ed.), *The psychological assessment of mental and physical handicaps* (pp. 645-666). London: Methuen.

Skinner, B. F. (1945). The operational analysis of psychological terms. *Psychological Review, 52*, 270-276.

Skinner, B. F. (1974). *About behaviorism*. New York: Knopf.

Staats, A. W. (1975). *Social behaviorism*. Homewood, IL: Dorsey Press.

Tharp, R. G., & Wetzel, R. J. (1969). *Behavior modification in the natural environment*. New York: Academic.

Titchener, E. B. (1899). Structural and functional psychology. *Philosophical Review, 8*, 290-299.

Turkat, I. D., & Maisto, S. A. (1985). Application of the experimental method to the formulation and modification of personality disorders. In D. H. Barlow (Ed.), *Clinical handbook of psychological disorders* (pp. 502–570). New York: Guilford.

Turner, A. E., & Hayes, S. C. (1984). Nomothetic versus idiographic responses interrelationships: II. Sexual behavior. Paper presented at the meeting of the American Psychological Association, Toronto.

Ullmann, L. P., & Krasner, L. (1969). *A psychological approach to abnormal behavior.* Englewood Cliffs, NJ: Prentice-Hall.

Van Houten, R. (1979). Social validation: The evolution of standards of competency for target behaviors. *Journal of Applied Behavior Analysis, 12,* 581–591.

Voeltz, L. M., & Evans, I. M. (1982). The assessment of behavioral interrelationships in child behavior therapy. *Behavioral Assessment, 4,* 131–165.

Wahler, R. G. (1975). Some structural aspects of deviant child behavior. *Journal of Applied Behavior Analysis, 8,* 27–42.

Wahler, R. G., & Fox, J. J. (1980). Solitary toy play and time out: A family treatment package for children with aggressive and oppositional behavior. *Journal of Applied Behavior Analysis, 13,* 23–39.

Weiss, R. L. (1968). Operant conditioning techniques in psychological assessment. In P. McReynolds (Ed.), *Advances in psychological assessment: Vol. 1* (pp. 169–190). San Francisco: Jossey-Bass.

Wilson, F. E., & Evans, I. M. (1983). The reliability of target-behavior selection in behavioral assessment. *Behavioral Assessment, 5,* 15–32.

Winett, R. A., & Winkler, R. C. (1972). Current behavior modification in the classroom: Be still, be quiet, be docile. *Journal of Applied Behavior Analysis, 5,* 499–504.

Wolf, M. M. (1978). Social validity: The case for subjective measurement or how applied behavior analysis is finding its heart. *Journal of Applied Behavior Analysis, 11,* 203–214.

Wolpe, J. (1958). *Psychotherapy by reciprocal inhibition.* Stanford: Stanford University Press.

2

HISTORY OF ASSESSMENT IN CLINICAL AND EDUCATIONAL SETTINGS

PAUL McREYNOLDS

University of Nevada—Reno

Though many of the technical accoutrements that we associate with the assessment enterprise are quite new, the idea of assessment is very old. Indeed, it is probable that people always have been sufficiently curious about the behavior of their fellows to engage in some kind of naive, implicit assessment of each other.

The discipline of psychological assessment is, to be sure, something considerably more than the casual, untutored evaluations that ordinary individuals routinely make of one another. The discipline of assessment involves the systematic application to the objects of assessment—persons, situations, or persons-in-situations—of carefully developed procedures by individuals recognized by society as having special expertise. All this too, however, can be traced far back into the past. Thus, the notions of systematized assessment procedures and of specialists in employing these procedures were by no means unknown in antiquity, and were prominent in the medieval and Renaissance periods. Furthermore, the general theme of person assessment was widespread in the 19th-century even prior to the work of the well-known figures of Galton and Cattell.

Contemporary assessment is, of course, not only more advanced technically, but also differs in many other respects from earlier methods of psychological evaluation. It would be easy to overdraw the similarities between historical and present approaches to assessment. Nevertheless, it is undeniably true that the current premises and procedures in this field, as in any other area of technology and culture, grew out of their past. There are several reasons why an examination of this past may be useful to the contemporary assessment psychologist.

First, an awareness of the historical background of assessment offers one a deeper understanding of, and a better appreciation for the current scene in assessment. Second, the past is interesting and important in its own right, as part of the grand sweep of culture that comprises our human heritage. Third, it is always possible that specific approaches or directions employed by our predecessors, and then forgotten, may be discovered to have value for the present.

From the perspective of the present, many artifacts and episodes in the history of any area of human creativity have a way of looking quaint, and sometimes humorous. So it is in the history of cosmology, chemistry, medicine, and—yes, assessment too. Nevertheless we must realize that however preposterous earlier methods of assessment appear to us, they were taken quite seriously, and exercised great influence in their own day. In this context, the lessons of history permit us to wonder with what tolerance assessors of the future will view our own imperfect efforts.

This chapter traces the story of assessment from the earliest times to the present. Because of the breadth of coverage, the treatment is necessarily more in the nature of a systematic overview than an in-depth accounting. Thus, my aim is to provide an overall picture of the scope and background of assessment, rather than a detailed guide. Though the present chapter encompasses the entire field of assessment, special attention, in keeping with the general theme of this volume, is given to the historical bases of behavioral assessment.

ASSESSMENT IN ANTIQUITY

The major methods of psychological assessment in the ancient world were astrology and physiognomy (McReynolds, 1975). It is impossible to say which was the earlier of these, but both were in widespread use by the Hellenistic period. Furthermore, the notion of certain individuals having special expertise in these forms of assessment was already in vogue. By the end of Greek intellectual hegemony, both astrology and physiognomy had become intermixed with humoral concepts in a broad, fairly systematic conceptualization that purported to explain and permit the prediction of a wide range of behavior.

Let us briefly consider each of these approaches. First, take astrology. The idea that events, including human behaviors, might be influenced by the movements of the heavenly bodies appears to have begun in ancient Sumer, the earliest known civilization. It may, of course, have had an even earlier, unknown origin. In any event, it would seem that during the early part of the first millenium B.C., if not earlier, Mesopotamian diviners were employing two methods for predicting future events: first, the practice of hepatoscopy, based on examinations of the livers of sacrificial sheep; and second, astrology. Both of these approaches were at first devoted to the prediction of important political or natural events. Later—possibly as early as the 5th century B.C.—the idea of the personal horoscope, in which the positions of the planets are used to assess the characteristics of individuals, was born.

From Mesopotamia the astrological theme spread to the rest of the then civilized world. It is possible, however, that it had an independent origin in China. It was in Hellenistic Greece, in the hands of the inventive yet systematic Alexandrian Greeks, that the approach was transformed into the complex conceptual system that we know today. The general premises of personal astrology, sometimes called natal or genethlialogical astrology, are that individuals are particularly sensitive to the influence of the planets at the moment of their birth, and furthermore that the nature of these influences is a function of the relative positions of the planets. Hence, it is possible, by knowing the location of the heavenly bodies at the time of a person's birth, to infer the nature of the individual's psychological makeup.

Horoscopal astrology attained a tremendous popularity in the later Greek period, and even such outstanding astronomers as Hipparchus and Claudius Ptolemy were taken in by it. One may wonder how people as enlightened as the Hellenistic Greeks could believe in astrology (actually, not all did: the Epicureans, for example, rejected it vigorously). The explanation, no doubt, lies partly in the fact that this was only the early morning of science. I am inclined to believe that it also reflects the fact that people have a tremendous need—particularly in periods of high anxiety, as the Alexandrian era was—to find answers, to understand themselves and their fellows.

Whereas astrology was Mesopotamian in origin, physiognomy was created, so far as we can tell, by the ancient Greeks. The general theme of physiognomics is that the psychological characteristics of an individual are revealed in, or represented by, the individual's physical features and overt movements. This is a much more reasonable assumption than that underlying astrology. Indeed it is involved, in one way or another, in such contemporary areas as somatotypy and nonverbal communication. Physiognomy represents an obvious advance over astrology in that the assessor focuses his or her attention on the person being assessed, rather than on something completely removed—the positions of the planets.

An early—perhaps the earliest—practitioner of physiognomics was Pythagoras, according to later accounts. Pythagoras is said to have had a school, or center of some kind, in southern Italy (at Crotone) in the 6th century B.C., and to have employed physiognomical techniques in examining applicants to his group. A later contributor to this approach was Aristotle, whose physiognomical conceptions are represented in a number of his works. There is an important—and entertaining—little book, titled *Physiognomics* (Hett, 1936) that has come down to us and which amounts to a kind of manual of physiognomical assessment. Though the traditional attribution of this work to Aristotle is not justified, it does appear to reflect his views on the subject. Here is a sentence from Aristotle's *Prior analytics* (Tredennick, 1967) which indicates the general physiognomic assumption: "It is possible to judge men's character from their physical appearance, if one grants that body and soul change together in all natural affections" (p. 527; 70b 7–9). Though this is a plausible enough premise, the cues actually employed by the early physiognomists were for the most part highly fanciful and esoteric. For example, a man's courage was evaluated in terms of the similarity of his facial features to those of a lion, conceived as the epitome of courage.

Astrological and physiognomic assessment, despite their obvious inadequacies, flourished for many centuries; indeed, they are still with us. It is instructive, from the historical perspective, to note the important contributions made by these early approaches. First, they pioneered the *idea* of assessment, the notion that the psychological makeups of individual persons can be accurately described. Second, they heralded the concept of individual differences—that persons differ significantly in behavioral profiles. Third, they stimulated the primitive development of a taxonomy of psychological variables, since any attempt to describe people necessarily involves the existence of a system of concepts in which to do so. And fourth, both horoscopal and physiognomic assessment highlighted the notion of a body of complex, even esoteric knowledge, and the accompanying recognition of specialists skilled in the application of this knowledge.

Another relevant Greek invention—the ancestor of later systematic personality theory—was humorology. This rather complex physiologic characterology dated back at least to Hippocrates in the 5th century B.C. and was systematically developed by Galen and others. Humorology posited the existence of four basic personality dimensions (sanguinity, irritability, melancholy, and placidity), each related to a specific bodily substance. This system, which proposed that individuals differ in terms of the degree of prominence of each of the dimensions, amounted, in an adumbral way, to a kind of psychological profile in terms of which persons could be described. It is interesting to note that humoral psychology emphasized—though in an indirect way—the influence of environmental factors. Thus, the relative amounts of given humors in a person's body were conceived to be influenced by weather and climate, and by one's diet.

Finally, I must call attention, albeit only briefly, to the Greek theory of the passions. This conceptualization, originally developed by the Stoics, included a listing of strong affects (most prominent: joy, sadness, fear, and hope). It thus contributed to the developing taxonomy of variables in terms of which individual differences could be categorized.

By the close of the Greco-Roman period the general idea of psychological assessment was well established. A considerable technology, albeit a largely invalid one, had been developed to implement it. Perhaps the main lesson to be learned from this early phase is the central, possibly inevitable role that assessment plays in complex societies.

ASSESSMENT THROUGH THE CENTURIES

In this section, I will carry the narrative forward to around the close of the 17th century. It is a striking fact that few innovations in assessment were made during this long period. Rather, the era can most succinctly be described, from our present perspective, as one in which the characterological themes of the Hellenistic Greeks—astrology, physiognomy, humorology, and the theory of the passions—were further elaborated, often in fantastic ways, and became intertwined with each other in pedantic and convoluted systems of thought. During the medieval period, as touch was lost with the Greco-Roman roots, the influence of astrological and physiognomic conceptions waned considerably. In the Renaissance, however, which reflected the rediscovery of the classical past, both of these approaches enjoyed a strong revival. In the Italian Renaissance, for example, it was commonplace for major decisions to be made on the basis of astrological advice; and all persons of importance had their horoscopes drawn as a matter of course. Physiognomical superstitions, too, abounded.

By the latter part of the period under review, however, we come to two works that clearly foreshadowed the future look of assessment, even though both of them were, in substance, still in the earlier tradition. The first and most important of these was *Examen de Ingenios para las Ciencas*, written by Juan Huarte and published in Spain in 1575, and translated into English as *The Tryal of Wits* (Huarte, 1575/1698). This fascinating work was a milestone in the history of assessment. For the first time, an author explicitly proposed a discipline of assessment, gave it a task to do, and offered some suggestions as to how it might proceed. Specifically, Huarte pointed out, first, that people differ from one another in particular talents; and second, that different vocations require different sets of talents in order for persons to succeed in them. Therefore, he argued, a system should be set up to determine the specific pattern of abilities of different persons in order that they might be guided into the appropriate kinds of education and occupation. This system, according to Huarte, would involve the appointment of a number of examiners ("Triers") who would carry out certain procedures ("Tryals") in order to determine a subject's specific capacities.

The other important work on assessment in this period was *Les Characteres des Passions* (1640–1662; 1650) by Marin Cureau de La Chambre, a French physician whose patients included Louis XIV (Diamond, 1968). La Chambre can be thought of as a transitional figure between the Renaissance and the impending Enlightenment. His approach to assessment was a curious blend of quaint astrological and physiognomic superstitions from the past and an emphasis on direct behavioral observations that heralded the future. La Chambre's writings on assessment were widely read, and were influential in further developing the theme of assessment in Western culture.

THE ROOTS OF MODERN ASSESSMENT

In the preceding sections, I surveyed some of the early forerunners of psychological assessment, and traced, in particular, the development of the *idea* of assessment. None of the techniques that I have discussed so far, however, had any appreciable validity as scientific ways of learning about human character or predicting human behavior. The beginnings of a valid, scientific approach to assessment occurred in the period that we turn to now, beginning in the latter part of the 17th and early 18th centuries.

The scene is the University of Halle, in the German state of Branden-burg. The year, 1691. On the last day of December, Christian Thomasius, professor of philosophy, completed a short article titled (as translated) "New discovery of a well-grounded and for the community most necessary science to know the secrets of the heart of other men from daily conversation, even against their will" (1692a). This was followed in 1692 by a more detailed account titled "Further elucidation by different examples of the recent pro-posal for a new science for obtaining a knowledge of other men's minds" (Thomasius, 1692b). These works, as is evident from their titles alone, are quite fascinating. Though little known to historians of psychology (McReyn-olds & Ludwig, 1984), they are of considerable significance in the history of assessment.

There are two main reasons for this importance. The first is that Thomasius developed a system of rating scales—the first in the entire history of psychology—for the assessment of what he considered the four basic characterological dimensions (sensuousness, acquisitiveness, social am-bition, and rational love). Rating scales are, of course, at the very heart of contemporary assessment methodology. Thomasius's system involved 60-point scales, set off in 5-point intervals. The importance of this development was not only in the invention of psychological rating scales as such, but also in the implication, momentous in its portent, that personality variables can be conceptualized in quantitative terms.

The second reason for assigning a high valuation to Thomasius's contri-butions is that, in gathering data on subjects in order to make his ratings, he rejected the centuries-old conceptions of humorology, physiognomy, and astrology. Instead, the ratings depended primarily on inferences drawn from the direct observation of the subject's behavior, including his or her conversation, interactions with others, and personal habits.

Despite—or perhaps because of—the novelty of Thomasius's conceptions, no one picked them up and carried them forward. From the perspective of history, his early quantitative approach appears as something of an anomaly in the chronicle of assessment. It is interesting to note that Christian von Wolff, who was an important early figure in the history of philosophical psychology, was a younger colleague of Thomasius at Halle. It was Wolff who first used the term "psychometry," a word now closely tied to the assessment enterprise. Wolff's usage, however, was more theoretical, and referred to mental processes (Ramul, 1960; Wolff, 1738), though no actual empirical data were involved. The differences between the two men were indicative of the future bifurcation in psychology: Thomasius—concerned with individual differences and the practical applications of psychological knowledge; and Wolff—interested in overall psychological theory and in the nature of mental processes of man-in-general.

The term "psychometry"—or variations of it in different languages—was employed throughout the 18th and 19th centuries mainly to apply to psychophysical measurements (e.g., Weber's law). Only in the present century has the usage shifted so that "psychometrics" now refers primarily to the assessment of individual differences. Another term that was sometimes utilized during this earlier period to refer to mental measurement, in both the generalized and the individual differences senses, was "anthropometry." Thus Galton, whom we will consider shortly, referred to his research facility, which was devoted primarily—though not exclusively—to psychological measurements, as an "anthropometric laboratory." In his empirical research reports, however, he preferred the term "psychometric." Because of his influence, this was the beginning of the switch of the meaning of the word "psychometric" from psychophysical to individual differences studies.

The 1700s constituted an impressive period in the progress of general psychology, with such key figures as Herbart, Berkeley, Hume, and Hartley; but advances in psychological assessment were hardly noteworthy. Around the end of the period, however, there was one development that contributed in an important, though indirect, way to later activity in assessment. This was the elaboration of faculty psychology by the Scottish philosopher-psychologist Thomas Reid and his follower Dugald Stewart. Their conceptualizations included the postulation of several dozen powers of the mind (e.g., self-esteem, gratitude, pity, judgment, memory). These powers constituted, in effect, a rather comprehensive taxonomy of dimensions on which individuals could vary, and thus provided a ready-made glossary of traits for later assessment psychologists.

The Reid–Stewart system—which itself was descended in part from the earlier taxonomies of the passion theorists—was first mined by the phrenologists, to whom we turn next. It was also influential on later taxonomists of the mind. It is also a rather direct line from the faculty psychologists to the later instinct theorists, such as James (1890) and McDougall (1933), and eventually to the motive classifications of Henry Murray (1938) and R. B. Cattell (1957), especially the latter.

Franz Gall, the founder of phrenology, was born in 1758, and was educated in anatomy at Strasbourg and Vienna. Gall and his younger collaborator, J. C. Spurzheim, were responsible for rather sophisticated research on the brain (Krech, 1962) for that period. It was Gall, for example, who developed the first modern conception of the functions of the cerebral cortex. Gall was particularly interested in the functions of different parts of the cortex. He formed the hypotheses that different cortical areas subserve different psychological capacities, that individuals differ in these capacities, and that the degree of these differences can be gauged by minute differences in the topography of the skull. The latter of these notions—that individual differences in psychological functions can be assessed through the shape of a person's skull—was never received into the mainstream of psychology, and eventually was demonstrated to be totally invalid. Nevertheless, the phrenological movement, though it is often properly held up as a prime example of a silly and obtuse practice, was indirectly of considerable importance in the history of assessment.

Phrenology was immensely popular in the United States during much of the 19th century. Merle Curti (1943), in his *The growth of American thought*, has delineated the widespread vogue for obtaining phrenological readings. The historian of psychology, David Bakan (1966), has observed that "In the 1830s phrenology swept the United States in a way that few other intellectual movements have" (p. 203). What was the reason for this great appeal? The answer is probably found in these words of E. G. Boring (1950): "The most important and greatest puzzle which every man faces is himself, and, secondarily, other persons. Here seemed a key to the mystery, a key fashioned in the scientific laboratory and easy to use" (p. 56).

Bakan (1966) has well summarized the overall influences of phrenology on psychology. I emphasize here the contributions of the phrenological movement to later assessment technology (McReynolds, 1975). These include: (1) *Mental taxonomy*. Like psychological assessors before and since, phrenologists found it necessary, in order to describe individual differences, to have a catalogue of mental or behavioral functions. As implied earlier,

Spurzheim (1834/1970) patterned his taxonomy in part after that of Reid and Stewart. (2) *Emphasis on individual differences.* Mainstream psychology during this period focused primarily on the generalized human being. Interest in psychological differences among persons, which is the primary interest of the common man and of assessment psychology, was carried and furthered by the phrenologists. (3) *Emphasis on practical applications of psychology.* The phrenologists—like Thomasius, Huarte, and others before them—were committed in principle to turning psychological knowledge to useful, practical ends. This orientation was reinforced by the prevailing ethos of the American culture, which has always highlighted practical achievement. (4) *Assessment paradigm.* The systematic notions of assessor and subject, the idea of a formal assessment session in which the professional person would gather data from the client, the development of standard, quantitative profiles of the characteristics of the subject, and the provision for structured written reports—all these and other accoutrements of later assessment practice were provided by the phrenologists. They thus left in the overall stream of thought an image of what assessment consists of. (5) *Rating scales.* Though Galton, whom we will consider shortly, is generally given credit for the invention of psychological rating scales, his usage was actually preceded by that of the phrenologists; and Thomasius, as already reported, was much earlier than either. It is unlikely that the phrenologists were aware of Thomasius's work, and in any event their usage was much more detailed. The forms provided by phrenological firms as early as 1845 (Bakan, 1966, p. 211) included systematic nine-point and seven-point scales, with detailed descriptions for each value. (6) *Attempts at objectivity.* While the standards of evidence of the phrenologists were incredibly loose, and while the movement included a number of deliberate charlatans, there were also a number of pioneering attempts to gather objective data on posited relations between behavioral variables and skull configurations. The statistical tool that the investigators lacked was the correlation coefficient, which had not yet been invented.

Up to this point in our account of the history of assessment, the approaches that we have reviewed were focused mainly on intrapersonal determinants of behavior. They essentially followed what today we would call a trait model of behavior. In other words, the influence of the environment, or stimulus situation, on behavior was as yet given little weight. This is not to say, however, that it was afforded no weight at all. The humorologists, as suggested earlier, considered that behavior was affected by such environmental factors as the weather, the seasons, and the food that one ate. It might be supposed that the phrenologists, with their emphasis on the topography of the skull, would have held to an exclusively intrapsychic view of the determinants of behavior. This, however, was not the case. Phrenological theory conceived that neural, and even skull changes could occur as the result of circumstances. Also, as Bakan (1966) has cogently observed, phrenology "manifested an inordinate optimism in connection with the possibilities of change through education and the modification of the environment, very similar to the optimism which was later displayed by John B. Watson" (p. 213).

GALTON, CATTELL, AND WITMER

What I have written so far is prelude to what is to follow. This is true in the sense that with Galton we come to the beginnings of scientific assessment. While history is all of a piece, and all intellectual breakthroughs have their essential antecedents, yet there are times when the pace of progress quickens. In this perspective, Galton occupies a key transitional place in the chronicle of psychological assessment. His historical role in the study of individual differences is analogous to the central role of Wundt in the history of experimental psychology (McReynolds, 1981).

Francis Galton, a cousin of Charles Darwin, was born in 1822 and died in 1911. A man of intense but varied interests, he was one of the scientific leaders of his time. After the publication of Darwin's (1859) *Origin of the species*, Galton became interested in questions concerning the inheritance of mental capacities and traits in humans, and devoted most of his career to this subject. Darwin's theory emphasized individual variations in psychological, as well as in physical dimensions. Galton, committed to this perspective, found it necessary to develop new ways of assessing individual differences. In the 1870s, in particular, he began to concentrate on the measurement of psychological variables, and in 1876 he began keeping a notebook on "Psychometric Inquiries."

In 1879 (the same year in which Wundt inaugurated his experimental laboratory at the University of Leipzig), Galton published two articles on psychometrics (1879a, 1879b), and in 1880 he reported work on individual differences in mental imagery. It was in this research that Galton utilized rating scales. In addition, he gathered data through the use of pencil-and-paper questionnaires—the ancestor of all contemporary inventories and data forms. In 1883 Galton's *Inquiries into human faculty and its development*—the first classic in assessment psychology—appeared; and, in 1884, he published an important paper on "Measurement of character." The term "personality" had not yet come into technical vogue, but "character" had essentially the same meaning. This article consisted of a plea, with some specific suggestions, for the development of ways to measure nonintellectual variables. It can be considered, in a programmatic sense, as the beginning of the subdiscipline later known as "personality evaluation." The article is particularly interesting in that it suggests, in a highly prescient way, certain behavioral, psychophysiologic, and expressive methods for measuring individual differences.

Galton largely created the bases for the quantitative assessment of individual differences. He pioneered the use of questionnaires, rating scales, word association techniques, test batteries, and other evaluative methods. His most important and lasting contribution, however, was in the development of statistical concepts. Though his formulation of the coefficient of "co-relation" (Galton, 1888) was completed by his follower Karl Pearson (1896), the core idea was Galton's. It is largely upon this basis that modern assessment technology has been constructed. Galton's interest in statistics derived from several sources. One was his personality: his maxim was "whatever you can, count" (Newman, 1954, p. 72). For example, on one occasion he counted the number of "fidgets" per minute among persons attending a lecture, in order to obtain a measure of boredom. Another source was his familiarity with the work of Quetelet (1835/1969), the Belgian mathematician who in 1835 had inaugurated the study of statistics in the social sciences. Finally, Galton discovered, as many would after him, that the systematic study of individual differences is impossible without adequate normative data of the quantitative kind.

Galton believed that intellectual capacities could be measured by various sensorimotor tasks, in particular by reaction time. Unfortunately, his own extensive but crude (by today's standards) empirical research in this area failed to support his hypothesis. Galton did, however, contribute in an interesting way to the development of a test that was to have a solid future—digit span. Joseph Jacobs (1887) had carried out some observations on immediate memory span, which he referred to as "prehension." These came to Galton's attention, and with the help of the psychologists Alexander Bain and James Sully, Galton (1887) carried out some tests at the Earlswood Asylum for Idiots. This was on June 18, 1886.

In 1886, the American psychologist James McKeen Cattell came under the influence of Galton. Cattell had been a student in Wundt's program at Leipzig from 1883 to 1886, when he received his doctorate. On his way home, he paused to visit with Galton and later returned to work with Galton in his laboratory at South Kensington. In 1888, Cattell took a position as professor of psychology—he was the first person in the world with this title—at the University of Pennsylvania. In 1890, he published an epochal paper titled "Mental tests and measurements." In this publication, which in a programmatic way marked the beginning of the mental test movement in the United States, Cattell argued that rigorous scientific procedures should be applied to the assessment of individual differences. He maintained that such measures, if carried out in a systematic, large-scale manner, would be both interesting and useful. The specific tests proposed by Cattell were adapted from the sensory–motor devices of Galton.

In 1891, Cattell moved to Columbia University, and shortly thereafter began a project in which approximately 50 freshmen were given a battery of tests each year. The idea was to demonstrate the meaningfulness of the tests by showing their relation to class grades. In 1901, Clark Wissler, a student of Cattell's, presented a detailed analysis of the findings, using the newly available correlation coefficient. The results were quite disappointing. Primarily because of these negative findings the attempt to assess intelligence from reaction time was discarded for the next three-quarters of a century, and has only recently been reopened (Jensen, 1982)—this time with better technology and more promising results.

When Cattell left Pennsylvania, his place there was taken by Lightner Witmer, who had been a junior member of the department. Witmer, like Cattell, was interested in individual differences. He also had an additional concern, however; this was the practical application of psychological knowledge to the resolution of real-life problems. Even as an undergraduate, Witmer had had the vision of going into a helping profession. The fact that he went into the brand new field of psychology was due probably to the influence of Cattell.

In 1896, Witmer brought his two interests together with the establishment of a "psychological clinic"—a new idea, and the first in the world—for the diagnosis and treatment of the academic and behavioral problems of children (though some adults were seen also). Now, diagnosis and treatment require assessment, and so here was the beginning of a new current in the overall system of assessment psychology. It should be noted that though Witmer was the first to organize a psychological clinic, he was not the first person in the newer psychology to be concerned with clinical issues (Bondy, 1974). Emil Kraepelin (1887), who studied under Wundt but took his degree in medicine, had begun his systematizing work in psychiatry. And Edouard Seguin (1842), who had been a pupil of Jean-Marc-Gaspard Itard and had emigrated to the United States in 1848, had stimulated a wide interest in the care and training of the mentally retarded. Witmer was, however, the first to develop a clinic for the diagnosis and treatment of a variety of clinical psychological problems, and to bring the resources of scientific psychology— meager as they were at this time—to the aid of clinical work.

When Witmer began his work, there were no useful tests available, and no background of proven treatment methods. In the beginning years of his practice, therefore, he depended very heavily on impressions gained by interviews, and on uncertain notions concerning the significance of speech patterns, gait, attentiveness, and other behaviors. Later, as psychological tests became available, Witmer adopted some of them, and devised two tests himself—the Witmer Formboard and the Witmer Cylinders. Both of these were employed in his clinic for many years. Several years ago I interviewed a woman who, many years before, had been a clinician on Witmer's staff, and she gave very eloquent testimony to the utility of Witmer's tests (McReynolds, 1979a). Eventually the Binet scales and their derivatives became the major tests used in the clinic; but Witmer never adopted tests in a wholesale way, and always maintained a skeptical attitude toward them. His methods of assessment, though they included tests, depended more on observational procedures, as the following quotations (Witmer, 1915) make clear:

> I am often asked for a list of the tests which we employ at the Psychological Clinic. I do not furnish such lists, because I am in doubt whether there is a single test which I can recommend to be employed with every case which comes to the Clinic for examination. . . . My very early experience with cases at the Psychological Clinic revealed the necessity for keeping the examination in a fluid state. I acquired a fear of the formalism of a blank, especially a blank filled in by some more or less adequately trained assistant. Experience also led me to believe in the inefficacy of the quantified results of a test, as for example the Binet test. . . . I believe that the clinical psychologist in conducting his examination must proceed directly to the work in hand. I want to know who brings or sends the child to the Clinic. Why is he brought? What do his parents or teachers complain of? (pp. 1–3)

Witmer's approach reminds us that psychological assessment is not limited to the administration and interpretation of formal tests, but includes a variety of clinical techniques. Witmer's methods, both in assessment and treatment, focused directly on the specific behaviors involved. While he did not employ the systematic techniques that workers in the behavioral assessment paradigm were to develop later, there is much in common between Witmer's orientation and theirs. In his own time, however, particularly during the 1920s and 1930s, Witmer's deemphasis of formal tests was largely obscured by the prevailing psychological ethos, which tended to exalt, and even to reify, test scores.

In 1906 Witmer founded *The Psychological Clinic* (Garfield, 1982). This served as the primary journal, until it ceased publication in 1935, for the reporting of clinical assessment through the medium of case studies. Witmer's clinic was the model for the many others earlier in this century, and his work was seminal in educational as well as in clinical psychological assessment. Many of his cases were referred directly by schools, and he was deeply interested in helping teachers to deal constructively with children's behavior problems.

ASSESSMENT COMES OF AGE: THE RISE OF PERSON TESTS

In 1896, in the same year in which Witmer in America established his Clinic, Alfred Binet and Victor Henri in France published an article titled "La Psychologie Individuelle," which presented the basis for a new approach to the assessment of intelligence. Binet, like Galton, was interested in the study of individual differences and in intellectual capacities, but he rejected Galton's view that mental capacity could be evaluated by sensorimotor measures. In their trailblazing article, Binet and Henri proposed instead that the proper approach would be to test the subject's performance on a variety of complex mental processes. Though this could hardly be done with the same precision that had become possible in the measurement of sensorimotor variables, it had the advantage of greater relevance to the behavior that one was trying to predict. In retrospect, we would say that the Binet approach amounted, in effect, to a sampling of the behaviors that it was designed to assay.

This was the beginning of the development of the first truly successful assessment device. As we will see later, it opened up a new direction for psychology and spawned a number of related instruments.

Binet was an indefatigable researcher. A clinical psychologist in the full sense of the term—though the term had not yet come into general useage—Binet was interested in individual differences, hypnosis, psychopathology, and psychological development. He founded the psychological laboratory at the Sorbonne in 1889, and the journal *L'Année Psychologique* in 1895. By 1900, he was ready to turn from theory to practice. He administered a series of tasks to the five children in a class considered by their teacher to be the brightest, and the five judged to be the least bright, in order to get a preliminary idea of what would work. In 1904, the Minister of Public Instruction set up a commission to study instructional procedures for mentally defective children. In 1905, Binet and Theodore Simon brought forth their first complete intelligence scale. This was further revised in 1908 and again in 1911.

Binet's approach included two key innovations: first, the sampling of complex processes; and second, the arrangement of tests in terms of the ages at which they could typically be passed. Both ideas, though new, were not without certain precedents. Ebbinghaus, as early as 1897, had developed a sentence completion method, in which the child provided a missing word or syllable, that appeared to differentiate good from poor students. And Jacobson and Galton, it will be recalled, had pioneered in the use of the digit span. Further, the idea of age-grading the behaviors of children was not new. In particular, as Goodenough (1949, p. 50) has noted, Stanford E. Chaille, medical professor at Tulane University, published in 1887 a description of characteristic developmental changes from 1 month to 3 years of age. Chaille's chronology, however, primarily concerned physical development and included relatively few systematic observations on cognitive development. A number of other attempts at mental assessment during the 1890s have been described by Reisman (1976, pp. 30–31). It was strictly a sign of the times, then, when the American Psychological Association (founded in 1892) set up a committee in 1895 to consider standardizing the tests developed in different laboratories. The committee included Witmer and Cattell, with the latter as chairman.

We have now come to the point in this narrative—that is, early in the 20th century—when new assessment techniques were being developed with great rapidity and frequency. These techniques were conceptualized in the main as "mental tests," but I will categorize them in this chapter as "person tests," since they deal with the assessment of individuals. The assessment enterprise began a period of growth and expansion, in both the technical and popular senses, that brought it into the center of important societal trends and issues, and which is still under way. However, it would be inappropriate to attempt in this chapter, which is designed to provide a broad historical background for the chapters to follow, to delineate in any detail the innumerable tests and test ventures that have characterized the period since Binet. Rather, I will now comment briefly on certain key trends and highlights in the test movement, and will then focus, in the succeeding two sections, on two relatively new areas—environmental assessment and, to a greater extent, behavioral assessment—that are particularly relevant to this volume.

One interesting trend, after the inaugural work of Galton, Cattell, and Binet, was the development of multitest manuals. It is fascinating, from today's perspective, to look back at some of these earlier handbooks. The first one, so far as I am aware, was that of Guy Montrose Whipple, of Cornell, which appeared in 1910. It was titled *Manual of mental and physical tests*,[1] and included instructions for obtaining a wide spectrum of measures of attention, perception, memory, imagination, vocabulary, and other areas. In 1911, Robert S. Woodworth and Frederic L. Wells—both had been students of Cattell—published a report, which amounted to a manual, on association tests. And in 1912, Shephard I. Franz, who was a professor at George Washington University and Scientific Director and Psychologist at the Government Hospital for the Insane, came out with his *Handbook of mental examina-*

---

1. This was preceded by the *Lehrbuch der psychologischen Untersuchungsmethoden* (1899), by Robert Sommer, a German psychiatrist. The *Lehrbuch* was primarily concerned with diagnostic evaluation, and is of limited significance in the history of psychological tests. S. I. Franz, who had an MD as well as a PhD, included a quotation from the *Lehrbuch* in his *Handbook* (1912, p. 2).

tion methods. This highly useful volume included a large variety of brief procedures that the clinician could employ in assaying a patient's different mental functions. In 1919, *The Psychological Clinic*—Witmer's journal—published a large special issue, "Reference book in clinical psychology and for diagnostic teaching" (Witmer, 1919). Many years later (1942) Wells, who is noted above, developed, with the psychiatrist Jurgen Ruesch, a pocket-size spiral-bound *Mental examiners' handbook*, which included a large number of short but relevant measurement techniques for the busy clinician. This was apparently the last of the brief multitest manuals, though the same tradition has been carried on, at a more detailed, technical level, by such later handbooks as those of Buros (1938–1978); Gambrill (1977, 1978); Hersen and Bellack (1976; 1981); Kent (1950); McReynolds (1968–1981); McReynolds and Chelune (1984); Rapaport, Gill, and Shafer (1945, 1946); Shafer (1948); and Woody (1980).

Following the successes of Binet and Simon in assaying the intellectual competences of school children, the zeitgeist of assessment focused for some time on intelligence tests. This is a complex but often-told story, from Binet to the present day, and I will mention only a few highlights here. Binet and Simon had thought in terms of levels of mental development, in which a child could be said to be, say, 1, 2, or 3 years retarded. This system, however, made it difficult to compare children of different ages. In 1911, the German psychologist William Stern (1911) suggested that this problem could be solved by dividing a child's mental age by his or her chronological age to yield a "mental quotient."

The two most important pioneers in the intelligence testing movement, after Binet, were Henry H. Goddard and Lewis M. Terman. Goddard, who had taken his PhD under G. Stanley Hall at Clark, in 1906 became head of research at the Vineland (New Jersey) Training School for Feebleminded Children. In 1910, he published an English translation of the Binet–Simon scale. Goddard was something of a crusader in the application of mental tests; and, under his inspiration, the Vineland School attained a national reputation. Terman, who also earned his PhD under Hall, was a more careful investigator than Goddard, but was equally imbued with the significance of intelligence assessment. Both Terman and Goddard had in common with Witmer the desire to make scientific psychology useful. Thus Terman's dissertation (1906), which was devoted to the systematic comparison of seven "bright" and seven "stupid" boys, begins with the sentence, "One of the most serious problems confronting psychology is that of connecting psychology with life" (p. 307).

In 1916, Terman, by then at Stanford, brought out a careful revision and improvement of the Binet–Simon scales. This Stanford Revision, as it was called, quickly became the standard for all other intellectual measures. It was in this test that the concept of the IQ, adapted from Stern's "mental quotient," first appeared. In 1937 Terman, in collaboration with Maude A. Merrill, published a further revision of the Stanford–Binet tests. The latest revision, completed in 1985 (Thorndike, Hagen & Sattler) is currently a widely used instrument for the assessment of children's intelligence.

The other major sequence of intelligence tests is that begun by David Wechsler in the 1930s, when Wechsler was chief psychologist at the Bellevue Psychiatric Hospital in New York. There was then a strong need for a suitable intelligence test for adults, and Wechsler produced this in the 1939 Wechsler–Bellevue Scale. The latest tests in the Wechsler series are the WPPSI (Wechsler Preschool and Primary Scale of Intelligence, 1967), the WISC-R (Wechsler Intelligence Scale for Children, Revised, 1974), and the WAIS-R (Wechsler Adult Intelligence Scale, Revised, 1981).

Interest in assessing personality characteristics, as contrasted with strictly cognitive functions, is, as we have seen, very old. In the modern era, this area of assessment can be said to have begun with Galton's (1884) article on the measurement of character. Binet and Henri, in their important 1896 article, which I have referred to earlier, had suggested that imagination might be evaluated by a subject's response to inkblots or by asking the subject to tell a story on a given topic. Association tests, invented by Galton, were discussed by Münsterberg in 1888, and systematically developed by Carl Jung in 1910. Personality assessment, in the modern mode, did not get actively under way, however, until Woodworth, referred to earlier as one of Cattell's first students at Columbia, developed the *Personal Data Sheet*, a 116-item inventory designed to help identify emotionally unstable soldiers in World War I (Ferguson, 1952; Franz, 1919; Woodworth, 1919). This was a highly innovative instrument, but it was not without important suggestive antecedents. We noted above that Galton had pioneered the use of the questionnaire method in psychology, and G. Stanley Hall—an early American genetic psychologist who, as I observed earlier, was the teacher of Goddard and Terman—had used questionnaires extensively in his studies of child psychology in the 1890s (e.g., Hall, 1897). Furthermore, as Goldberg (1971, p. 295) notes, several earlier attempts had been made to systematize signs of emotional disturbance in a manner that made them easily amenable to an interview-like inventory format. Woodworth's schedule was a clear step forward, however, and a harbinger of things to come in three key respects: (1) it was the first such questionnaire that could plausibly be conceptualized as a "test," (2) it was the first personality instrument to translate a series of responses into a single quantitative variable; and (3) it was the first inventory to be based on an empirical item selection procedure (House, 1926).

The descendants of the Woodworth inventory are too numerous to list here, and almost too numerous to count; but they include such later, widely used tests as the Bernreuter Personality Inventory (Bernreuter, 1933), the Minnesota Multiphasic Personality Inventory (Hathaway & McKinley, 1940), the California Psychological Inventory (Gough, 1957), and the Personality Research Form (Jackson, 1967). The development and proliferation of inventories has been interestingly recounted by Goldberg (1971). Attitude measures, a somewhat related genre, were pioneered by Thurstone (1931).

The idea of using blotches of paint as stimuli for imaginative responses goes back to Leonardo da Vinci. In 1857, the German poet–physician Justinus Kerner published a series of inkblots accompanied by verses stimulated by them (Alexander & Selesnick, 1966). Binet, as already noted, conceived that inkblot responses could be used to evaluate imaginativeness. Whipple's (1910) *Manual*, cited earlier, included an inkblot test of imagination. In 1917, Szymon Hens (Ellenberger, 1954) reported a study of the inkblot responses of 1200 subjects. It remained, however, for Herman Rorschach, a Swiss psychiatrist, to develop the first systematic personality test based on inkblot responses (Rorschach, 1921/1942). Rorschach's father was an art instructor, and Rorschach himself was something of an artist. It is fascinating to learn that Rorschach's boyhood nickname was "Kleck" (inkblot). Rorschach's main innovations were to posit specific personality meanings for form, movement, and color responses. His book does not refer to the interpretation of different shading in the blots, since such shadings were not part of the plates sent to the printer. Oddly enough, the shadings were created by the original poor job of printing (Ellenberger, 1954, p. 206). Rorschach's work was, of course, the stimulus for the later systems of Klopfer, Beck, and others, culminating in the current approach of Exner (1974), as well as of Holtzman's (Holtzman, Thorpe, Swartz, & Herron, 1961) Inkblot Test.

The other chief projective device (in addition to the Rorschach) in current use is the Thematic Apperception Test (TAT), which was introduced in 1935 by Christiana D. Morgan and Henry A. Murray (Morgan & Murray, 1935). The TAT consists of a series of pictures to which the subject tells stories. Though the idea that people may reveal their innermost selves through their fantasies was very old, the formal use of standard pictures to elicit stories appears to have been new. The TAT has, of course, led to numerous descendants. Other early approaches to personality assessment include the relative position rating method (Wells, 1917), Florence Goodenough's (1926) Draw-a-Man Test, and June Downey's (1923) procedures for assessing Will-Temperament. Two early books that describe numerous techniques not reviewed here are those by Hollingsworth (1922) and Symonds (1934).

I will now comment briefly on the history of the measurement of interests. Galton (1874), in a study of scientists, included several questions about their interests, but this was a rather casual effort. Next, Edward L. Thorndike, in 1912, presented some data on the consistency of interests over time; and Truman L. Kelley (1914) reported the use of a very brief interest questionnaire. The real beginning of interest inventories, according to David Campbell (1968), occurred shortly after World War I at Carnegie Tech, when there were several psychologists interested in this area. The first useful inventory was that of Bruce Moore (1921); this was concerned with the interests of engineers. However, the main figure in the development of interest inventories was Edward K. Strong, who had studied with Cattell and Thorndike at Columbia, and who went to Stanford—in part due to Terman's influence—in 1923. Strong published his first Vocational Interest Blank in 1927. This was the ancestor of all later interest assessment forms, including the current Strong-Campbell Interest Inventory (Strong & Campbell, 1981) and the Vocational Preference Inventory (Holland, 1978). For further details on the history of interest assessment, the reader is referred to Freyer (1931) and Campbell (1968).

The customers of psychological assessment fall mainly into four classes: typical, ordinary people, used in personality research and test norming; disturbed persons, for whom tests furnish diagnostic data; students, for whom tests provide academic achievement and diagnostic data; and workers, for whom tests offer information concerning placement and performance. Of these, the utilization of tests in education has always been the most extensive. The history of educational assessment is part and parcel of the overall story of psychological assessment, but the area also has a number of special roots. Some kind of evaluative process seems essential to the educational process, and no doubt is as old as systematic schooling. The earliest formal schools were those in Sumer (Kramer, 1963), but we have no knowledge of their evaluation procedures. Oral examinations for the doctoral degree dates back to about 1200, and written examinations were common in Europe by the early 19th century (Linden & Linden, 1968). In the 1860s George Fisher, an English schoolmaster, proposed a numerical scale for the evaluation of students' proficiencies in given subjects.

The actual beginning of systematic techniques for assessing children's progress in school dates from the 1890s. The person responsible was J. M. Rice, an American pediatrician–psychologist who became dissatisfied with the quality of schools and who conducted a series of studies on spelling, arithmetic, and other elementary school subjects. The most influential person in the rapid development of standardized educational testing earlier in this century, however, was Thorndike. A student of Cattel and a holder of the PhD degree who turned from his original interest in individual differ-

ences in animals to a concentration on children, Thorndike was largely responsible for the introduction into the psychological and educational professions
of the statistical concepts developed by Galton, Pearson, Spearman, and
others (Thorndike, 1904). In 1910, Thorndike published a carefully developed quantitative scale for assessing the quality of a pupil's handwriting.
One of Thorndike's students, C. W. Stone (1908), developed a series of
standard tests in arithmetic and reading. After World War I, group academic
testing, inspired in part by the Alpha examination that had been developed
during the war (Linden & Linden, 1968), spread rapidly, and led eventually to
the Stanford Achievement Tests (see Buros, 1978, pp. 96–107), the Metropolitan Achievement Tests (see Buros, 1978, pp. 63–71), and other similar
batteries.

   Meanwhile, a whole new field, with a reminiscent glance backward to
Huarte, was developing. This was the use of tests in identifying individual
aptitudes in occupational selection and assignment. Early work in this area
was brought together by Clark Hull in 1928—this was before he became
interested in learning theory—and by Donald G. Paterson and John G. Darley (1936). Walter Bingham's (1937) *Aptitudes and aptitude testing* amounted to a
kind of manual for the vocational assessor of that period. A later volume by
Ghiselli reviewed the area up to 1966.

   This section has summarized the period during which the major thrust
of assessment was the development of tests for the measurement of the
psychological characteristics of individuals. Concern with person tests was
the major theme—indeed, essentially the only theme—in psychological assessment during the first half of this century. Such an approach, though on
something of a plateau since about 1950, is still the largest thread in the
skein of assessment.

A NEW DIRECTION: ENVIRONMENTAL ASSESSMENT

In the last several decades, two new and somewhat related directions have
emerged in assessment. These are environmental assessment and behavioral
assessment. Of the two movements, behavioral assessment is the larger and
more pervasive, and I will give it more attention here. First, however, I will
briefly review the background of environmental assessment. The approach is
analogous to person assessment, but differs in that the focus is on the
behaviorally relevant characteristics of environments in which behaviors
occur, as contrasted with the more traditional emphasis upon person variables.

   Most directly, environmental assessment grew out of the broader area
of environmental psychology. Though it is only in the last decade or so that

this area has emerged as a recognized subdiscipline of psychology, its roots go much further back into the past. As I indicated earlier, adumbrations of an environmentalistic orientation can be traced back to the Greek period—as, for example, in Hippocrates' emphasis on climatic and geographic influences on behavior. However, the critical shift toward a fuller recognition of the importance of environmental, or situational factors in influencing behavior began in the Enlightenment period (Curti, 1943; Randall, 1976). The key figures in developing the position that Randall referred to as "the omnipotence of environment" (p. 315) were Locke, Hartley, Montesquieu, and Helvetius. The new view was most clearly and influentially presented by Locke (1690/1959), who maintained the absolute preeminence of sensory—that is, external—factors in the determination of behavior. Hartley (1749/1966) then transformed this premise into a full-fledged associationistic psychology. Helvetius (1758/1810) and Jeremy Bentham (1789/1948) emphasized the role of rewards and punishments in shaping behavior. Referring to the former's *Treatise on Man*, Robinson (1976) has noted that "hereditary differences are dismissed as negligible and . . . the effects of training, reward, punishment, and experience are accorded first place in determining the character and accomplishments of the individual" (p. 310).

The two modern psychologists most responsible for bringing environmental factors into a central systematic position were John Watson (1919) and Kurt Lewin (1951). Interestingly, they came from quite different theoretical stances, the former being a behaviorist and the latter a field theorist. The area that we now call environmental assessment owes more to the inspiration of Lewin, whereas behavioral assessment, which I will consider shortly, is descended mainly from Watson.

Closely related to the field of environmental psychology is ecological psychology; and, for our present purposes, environmental assessment and ecological assessment may be considered the same. The study of psychological ecology, under the aegis of Roger Barker and Herbert F. Wright, got under way in the 1950s and early 1960s (Barker, 1960, 1968; Barker & Wright, 1955) and environmental psychology gained its identity a little later (Craik, 1970; Proshansky, Ittelson, & Rivlin, 1970). In order to study the environment or the ecology, it is of course necessary to measure it. Our interest here is in the historical background of methods for assessing environmental variables.

In 1963, the book *Stimulus determinants of behavior*, edited by S. B. Sells, highlighted some of the environmental factors that influence behavior, and in 1964 Richard Wolf published a key article titled "The measurement of environments." Meanwhile, George Stern and his associates, beginning in the later 1950s, had been developing a series of "Environment Indexes," and these led in 1970 to the publication of Stern's *People in Context*. By 1971,

Kenneth Craik could begin his significant chapter on the assessment of places with the words, "At long last, the assessment of environments is beginning to gain its proper share of scientific investigation" (p. 40). The last development in environmental assessment that I will mention in this background chapter is the set of "social climate scales" developed by Rudolph Moos (1975). These scales focus on a variety of particular settings, including work environments, hospital ward atmospheres, correctional institution environments, and university residence environments.

Environmental assessment, when carried out by those in the ecological tradition of Barker and Wright, depends largely on systematic observations. An equally strong trend, however, has been the development of pencil-and-paper devices such as those of Stern and Moos, patterned more or less after the tradition of instruments designed for the assessment of persons. The history of environmental assessment to date is necessarily brief, but it promises to be a major theme in the future.

EMERGENCE AND DEVELOPMENT OF BEHAVIORAL ASSESSMENT

In the section "Assessment Comes of Age," I traced the development of tests designed to elicit systematic information about the psychological characteristics of individuals. This line of research and practice is, of course, a continuing one, with new tests constantly being developed and older ones being improved. There are, however, certain serious limitations in an exclusive dependence upon the person–test model of assessment. These include, first, a limitation in the test paradigm itself—that is, there are clearly important features about persons that cannot be captured in the space–time restrictions connoted by the term "test." A second limitation is the underlying premise of a simplistic person–test paradigm, namely, that a person's behavior is determined solely by the characteristics of the person. This premise is clearly untenable. These limitations in the prevailing assessment paradigm were among the factors—though they were not the only ones, as we will see shortly—that led to the rise of behavioral assessment, which emphasizes the direct observation of behavior and the influence of situational factors.

In order to put this movement, which constitutes the focus of this volume, in appropriate context, it will be necessary to back up a bit in our historical review. Behavioral assessment, we will see, is, though quite new, also very old.

The direct forbear of behavioral assessment is, of course, the behaviorist school in theoretical psychology, as founded by John B. Watson in the early part of this century. To quickly summarize a story already well known to psychologists, Watson, in 1913, published an article titled "Psychology as the behaviorist views it"; he followed this, over the next 15 years, by a series of books devoted to the development of the behaviorist position. The basic tenets of behaviorism were, first, an emphasis on the importance of observable behaviors, as opposed to inferences concerning mental processes; and, second, an insistence on the importance of environmental influences in the determination of behavior. Watson himself evidently found no conflict between behaviorism and person-oriented tests, since he dedicated his book *Psychology from the standpoint of a behaviorist* (1919) to Cattell and Adolf Meyer (a prominent psychiatrist at Johns Hopkins University, where Watson was also located), and included five pages on tests. And in a letter[2] dated May 22, 1917 to Henry Goddard at the Vineland Training School, Vineland, New Jersey, Watson, who was preparing to give a course to medical students specializing in psychiatry, requested a list of psychological tests that Goddard could recommend (Goddard did so, in a letter dated May 25). The closest Watson came to suggesting a special variety of behavioral tests appears to have been in his *Psychological care of infant and child* (1928, pp. 17–36), which describes a number of tests (e.g., for handedness) employed in experimental work.

Watson's behaviorism of course did not arise out of a vacuum. The intellectual climate that made it possible had a number of immediate antecedents, including the work of the biologist Jacques Loeb (1912) on a mechanistic interpretation of behavior, the conditional reflex model of Pavlov (1927), and the objective studies on animal behavior by Thorndike (1911). Another important theme leading up to behaviorism was the debate, in the latter part of last century, concerning the development of a positivistic psychology (Danziger, 1979). After Watson, behaviorism bifurcated into two main branches, of which the chief paradigms are the conditioning model of Hull and the operant model of Skinner. The former served as the basis of Wolpe's reciprocal inhibition therapy (Wolpe, 1958), and the latter led to the operant techniques grouped under the rubric of "behavior modification."

2. I came across this letter when doing research at the Archives of the History of American Psychology, at the University of Akron, in 1979. The letter, which is reprinted here with the kind permission of James B. Watson, reads as follows: "My dear Goddard: At Dr. Meyer's suggestion I am planning to give here in the Clinic next year a course on psychology in relation to medicine. Only students with medical degrees specializing in psychiatry will be admitted. I am planning during the first half of the year to present general psychological viewpoints and a discussion of methods in psychology. From this point I shall go on into the various psychological tests which may become medically useful. Psychiatrists are anxious to have a wider acquaintance with various psychological testing methods. Such information will assist them in dealing with the assets of individuals whose vocational future they must to a certain extent shape. I am writing to you in the hopes that it will not be too much trouble for you to give me a list of the tests which you think may or will prove useful in connection with psychiatric work. Please make a check mark on the tests which you actually employ in your work./With sincere apologies for the trouble this will cause you, I am/Sincerely yours, John B. Watson"(s).

There is currently a tendency (Krasner, 1971) to employ the term "behavior therapy" generically to encompass all treatments growing out of the behavioral perspective. We can thus say that it was the existence of behavior therapy—which grew rapidly during the 1960s and 1970s—and the needs of behavior therapists for ways to assess certain therapy-related variables that led directly to the development of behavioral assessment. As Goldfried put it in 1977, "The interest in behavioral assessment is an obvious by-product of the growing popularity of behavior therapy techniques" (p. 4).

While this tie is still very strong, it should also be noted that behavioral assessment techniques are increasingly being applied in nontherapeutic settings, such as schools, as well as in the study of important theoretical questions. It seems likely that as behavioral assessment becomes more and more technical, it will be increasingly independent of its therapeutic origins.

Later in this section, I want to review in more detail the historical connections between behavior therapy and behavioral assessment. First however, it will be instructive to briefly examine the antecedents of behavioral assessment in the broader past. One of the characteristic features of behavioral assessment is its emphasis on the direct observation of the behavior in which one is interested. Examples of this approach in earlier periods are not difficult to find. It is said that the physiognomic examinations conducted by Pythagoras (McReynolds, 1975) in the 6th century B.C. consisted largely of observations of the applicants' behavior in various contexts. A much later, but also clearer instance of the recognition of the importance of direct observation in assessment is furnished in Thomas Wright's (1604/1971) *Passions of the minde in generall*. Wright pointed out that:

> We cannot enter into a man's heart, and view the passions or inclinations which there reside and lay hidden; therefore, as Philosophers by effects find out causes, by proprieties essences, by rivers fountaines, by boughes and floures the kore and rootes; even so we must trace out passions and inclinations by some effects & externall operations. And there be no more than two, words and deeds, speech and action: of which two knowledge may be gathered of those affections we carie in our minds (p. 105).

This sentiment strikes a resonant chord in the emphasis among behaviorists on the priority of overt behavior and verb behavior in functional analysis.

Late in the same century, Christian Thomasius, as described earlier in this chapter, devised a system of characterological rating scales. The importance of this innovation, from our present perspective, is that Thomasius emphasized actual behavioral data, especially verbal data, as the basis for making the ratings. Then in the next century, in 1787, another German philosopher, Dietrich Tiedemann (Murchison & Langer, 1927), published the first systematic record of longitudinal observations on behavioral development in children. The scientific world was not yet ready for this objective approach; but, roughly a century later, Charles Darwin's (1877) observational record of the behavior of his young son received considerable attention. Shortly thereafter, Wilhelm Preyer (1882) published his influential *Die Seele des Kindes*. These works inaugurated a period of intense interest in diarylike reports on the observed behavior of children (see Goodenough, 1949, p. 31); this interest overlapped with, and was part of the growing child study movement in that era.

As these comments suggest, a major forerunner of the emphasis on the direct observation of behavior that characterizes contemporary behavioral assessment consisted of certain trends in the field that first was called genetic psychology, and later developmental psychology. It is not necessary to examine this historical record in detail here, but I do want to point up several particularly significant contributions. One of the first of these was the work of Arnold Gesell (e.g., Gesell, 1925), who, like Terman, had been a student of Stanley Hall, America's first important child psychologist. But whereas Hall developed questionnaire methodology, Gesell devised and utilized a variety of direct observational techniques, including the pioneering use of cameras, one-way screens, and coding systems, to chart the behaviors of infants. Witmer, then in the latter stage of his career, was very impressed with the work of Gesell. Another early contributor to the systematic observation of children's behavior was Florence Goodenough (1928). She developed the short-sample technique, in which the presence or absence of given behaviors during brief periods, for example, 10 minutes, are recorded. The method was particularly applicable to classrooms and playgrounds. The work of Dorothy Swaine Thomas (1929; Thomas, Loomis, & Arrington, 1933) was innovative in systematizing objective techniques for codifying and recording a variety of social interactions in nursery school children. W. C. Olson (1929), in a study of nervous habits, used two observers to record whether particular behaviors occurred in given time periods, and obtained satisfactory interobserver reliabilities. Theodore Newcomb (1929), in his investigation of "extrovert–introvert" tendencies in problem boys in camp situations, developed a standardized report form to indicate the presence or absence of specified behaviors.

Another early exponent of the application of observational techniques in the study of children was Charlotte Buhler (1930). In the same period, Esther Berne (1930) carried out an extensive study of the social behaviors of nursery school children, based on systematic behavioral ratings. Finally, we may note a nursery school study by Mildred Parten (1932) utilizing the short-sample approach of Goodenough.

These, then, are some of the important early studies on children that emphasized direct observation of behavior prior to the behavioral assessment movement. For an early review of the area see Murphy, Murphy, and Newcomb (1937, pp. 255–277), and for a recent, more comprehensive survey of the history of observational methods in child psychology see Wasik (1984).

In order to see what the analogous situation at the adult level was, we must turn to the social and personality area. Here too, we find considerable development of systematic observational methods in the first half of this century, though it is interesting to note that progress at the adult level was preceded by work with children. An important pioneer in the empirical study of personality was Henry Murray. His *Explorations in personality* (1938), written with his students, includes several experimental-observation approaches, including a section by R. N. Sanford (pp. 504–508) involving observation of interviews from behind a one-way screen. During World War II, Murray headed the personnel selection project for the U.S. Office of Strategic Services (OSS Assessment Staff, 1948). This project involved the development and application of a variety of simulated "real-life" behavioral situations.

Eliot Chapple (1940) was a pioneer in the empirical study of interpersonal relations. By the latter 1940s, investigators had begun the construction of systematic behavioral coding systems, and apparatuses for their application. Thus Robert Bales and Henry Gerbrands, in 1948, reported a device with a moving tape on which observed instances of behavioral interactions could be recorded. And in 1949, Chapple described his "interaction chronograph," an apparatus for systematically recording observations of the sequences of interactions among individuals. These apparatuses are the ancestors of counting and recording devices used by contemporary behavioral assessors. In 1951, Bales brought out his highly influential book, *Interaction process analysis*, which set forth a carefully developed method for categorizing interpersonal behaviors.

One of the more innovative techniques employed in Murray's OSS project was the improvisations procedure. This method, along with Jacob Moreno's earlier work in psychodrama, was the forerunner of today's strong interest in role playing assessment techniques (for a review of this area, including its historical background, see McReynolds & DeVoge, 1978).

A seminal figure in the development of the observational paradigm in the 1930s and 1940s was Kurt Lewin, who favored methods for quantifying overt behaviors in preference to the use of psychological tests in his wide-ranging research. An innovative study (Barker, Dembo, & Lewin, 1943) employed observational methods in the examination of frustration in young children. Later, Barker and Wright, who had been influenced by Lewin, inaugurated the field of ecological psychology, as I noted in the preceding section. In this enterprise (Barker & Wright, 1951; Wright, 1967), they developed reliable methods for categorizing and coding relevant "real-life" behaviors. Lewin's important role in the background of the direct observational approach now so favored by behavioral assessors is of special historical interest in that Lewin's own holistic orientation was at the opposite pole from the behaviorist perspective. This interchange illustrates the unpredictable and sometimes surprising way in which innovative ideas spread and have their influence.

In some respects, the ecological assessment and the behavioral assessment movements were to follow parallel paths. These paths converged in a Conference on Ecology and Behavior Analysis at the University of Kansas in 1976 (Rogers-Warren & Warren, 1977).

Another signal feature of behavioral assessment, as I have already indicated, is its emphasis on the environmental, or stimulus determinants of behavior. This view, as is well known, was strongly championed by Watson. From the historical perspective, however, Watson's doctrine is best appreciated as one outcropping of a long-developing historical current, as I observed in the section on environmental assessment. Watson and later behaviorists systematized and objectified the environmental perspective of the associationists, and in so doing shifted the emphasis from the global "environment" to particular situations and specific controlling stimuli.

In the above paragraphs, I pointed out some of the historical antecedents of contemporary behavioral assessment (for another treatment of this topic, see Nelson, 1983). Two qualifying points need to be added. First, it does not necessarily follow that those psychologists who actually developed the various modern behavioral assessment techniques were in fact influenced by the earlier work reviewed above, that is, precedence does not necessarily imply influence. A thorough examination of actual influences is beyond the scope of this chapter. It seems safe to assume, however, that the earlier work on behavioral observation and ecological assessment at the very least helped to create the kind of scientific climate in which behavioral assessment could grow and flourish. And second, it should not be thought that behavioral assessment is the only inheritor of the prior work on observational methods. On the contrary, observational approaches are now widely respected and practiced by exponents of all methodological orientations in psychology. It is true that applied behaviorists, to their credit, have been especially alert to the rich potential in observational assessment, but the approach has not been entirely overlooked by other therapeutic orientations. For example, observation of children's behaviors was a primary source of data in the late Anna Freud's (1965) clinic and school in London.

So far I have outlined some of the precursors of applied behaviorism. I want now to describe in more detail how this theoretical position eventually led to the field of behavioral assessment. The key link, as I noted earlier, was the development of behavior therapy. The historical background of this orientation to psychological treatment has been reviewed elsewhere (Hersen, 1976; Kazdin, 1978; Ullmann & Krasner, 1965), and need not be recited in detail here, though a few summary comments seem in order. The idea of desensitization (though not under that name) can be traced back at least as far as Francis Hutcheson (1726; cf. McReynolds, 1969, p. xiii). In the 1920s, Mary Cover Jones (1924) successfully treated a child's fear of rabbits by deconditioning; and, in the 1930s, Mowrer and Mowrer (1938) employed a behavioral approach in the treatment of enuresis. These are the milestones usually noted when the history of behavior therapy is recounted. However, there were also several other significant contributors to the origins of behavior therapy in the 1920s and 1930s. This story, which includes in particular some of the theoretical ideas of William Burnham (1925), E. R. Guthrie (1938), and John Dollard and Neal Miller (1950), and the innovative work of Edmund Jacobson (1938) on progressive relaxation—has been accurately reviewed by Ullman and Krasner (1965, pp. 50–59), and, more recently, and from a broader perspective, by Krasner (1982).

The first use in the literature of the term "behavior therapy," according to Krasner (1971, p. 484; see also Krasner, 1982) was a 1953 report, by Ogden Lindsley, B. F. Skinner, and H. C. Solomon, of their research on schizophrenia, carried out in an operant context. In 1958, Joseph Wolpe's highly influential book, *Psychotherapy by reciprocal inhibition*, appeared. Two years later, in 1960, H. J. Eysenck edited the first broad-range book on behavior therapy, *Behavior therapy and the neuroses*, and dedicated it "To the memory of J. B. Watson." Then, in 1963, the international journal, *Behaviour Research and Therapy*, was founded, under Eysenck's editorship; its first issue carried one article on assessment (Freund, 1963). With the publication of additional edited volumes by Eysenck (1964) on behavior therapy, and by Ullmann and Krasner (1965) and Krasner and Ullmann (1965) on behavior modification, the behavioral approach to treatment can be said to have emerged as a distinctive and recognized form of treatment.

How, then, did all this activity lead to behavioral assessment? At the beginning of the behavior therapy movement, the question of unique methods of assessment appears not to have been carefully considered. Wolpe's (1958) book, for example, recommends the use of personality inventories, in particular, the Willoughby Personality Schedule (pp. 107–111). However, as the behavior therapy movement gathered momentum and undertook to articulate its unique methodological bases, the characteristic attitude of behavior therapists toward assessment became largely one of disinterest, verging on antipathy, since the available instruments seemed to be incongruent with the behavioral rationale. In the long run, however, an attitude of disinterest proved not to be viable, since behavior therapists, no less than therapists of other orientations, do need a solid understanding of their clients' problems and circumstances in order to maximize the effectiveness of their treatments. What was needed, though this was not immediately apparent in all its ramifications, was an assortment of specific assessment procedures custom-made to provide the particular data required for behavioral treatments. This need has been the major force powering the development of behavioral assessment to the level and the diversity that it has reached today. Further, as the aims and rationale of behavior therapists have changed, so have assessment emphases (Mash & Terdal, 1981, pp. 6–8).

From the historical perspective, we are primarily interested in the early development of particular behavioral assessment techniques, and of the growth of the *idea* of behavioral assessment as a unique orientation. With respect to specific assessment instruments, the first assessment method to be accorded a standard place in the behavioral assessment repertoire was that of Fear Survey Schedules (FSS). An FSS is a pencil-paper instrument in which the patient or client indicates the degree of fear, or phobic anxiety he or she feels toward each of a number of listed stimuli. The answers are then used by the therapist in designing desensitization procedures. Though the early proliferation of FSS scales (Dickson, 1975) makes their course somewhat difficult to follow, the beginnings of the method seem clear (Wolpe & Lang, 1964). In 1954, Joseph Sandler, working in the psychoanalytic tradition, published a symptom inventory; and, in 1957, Dixon, DeMonchaux, and Sandler carried out an analysis of the 26 items of the inventory that referred to specific fears. Separately, Donald Akutagawa (1956), also in the psychoanalytic orientation, developed a schedule of specific fear stimuli for his dissertation. This inventory then served as the basis of the FSS's specifically developed for use in behavior therapy (Dickson, 1975; Lang & Lazovik, 1963; Wolpe & Lang, 1964). The first systematic assessment developed in the operant therapy context appears to have been the Reinforcement Survey Schedule (RSS), devised by Cautela and Kastenbaum (1967) to provide data on the different stimuli that a client finds reinforcing.

In the latter 1950s and early 1960s, the use of operant methods in psychiatric and educational settings, following Ogden Lindsley's (1956) utilization of operant conditioning technology in identifying behavior deficits in schizophrenics, developed rapidly. Among the diverse diagnostic areas encompassed (see Ullmann & Krasner, 1965) were chronic schizophrenia (Ayllon & Michael, 1959; King, Armitage, & Tilton, 1960), childhood autism (Ferster & DeMyer, 1962), phobias (Lang & Lazovik, 1963), and mental deficiency (Barrett & Lindsley, 1962). While these and similar studies did not emphasize behavioral assessment as such, they all involved some kind of behavioral measure of therapeutic effectiveness.

As noted earlier, contemporary behavioral assessment places particular emphasis on the direct observation of individual behaviors in natural settings, including the home and the school. Though all of the studies listed above involved this approach to some degree, the two most influential contributors to the development of systematic observational assessment were, in my view, the research programs of Sidney Bijou and colleagues, and of Gerald Patterson and colleagues. Both programs focused primarily on the assessment of children or young people. Bijou's systematic work, first reported in 1957 (see also Bijou and Orlando, 1961; for reviews see Bijou, 1965; Bijou and Peterson, 1971), emphasized analysis of the controlling stimuli for behaviors in an operant framework. The Patterson group, beginning in the mid-1960s (Patterson, 1965; Patterson, McNeal, Hawkins, & Phelps, 1967; reviewed by Jones, Reid, and Patterson, 1975) concentrated on the development of a sophisticated and reliable behavioral coding system.

I turn now to the historical development of the conception of behavioral assessment as an area in its own right, as a somewhat unique approach to assessment in the same sense that behavior therapy is a relatively unique approach to treatment. The first discussion of assessment in this context, to the best of my knowledge, was a section by Leonard Ullmann and Leonard Krasner in the Introduction to their 1965 book (see pp. 28–29). After rejecting the medical model, these authors wrote, "This does not mean, however, that there is no place for psychological assessment in behavior modification. It does mean that such assessment focuses on different variables and has different goals. Assessment in behavior modification is directly associated with treatment." Greenspoon and Gersten, in 1967, examined the nature of psychological testing from the behavioral perspective. Next, in 1968, three important articles—by Joseph Cautela; by Marvin Goldfried and David Pomeranz; and by Robert Weiss—appeared; all three articles carefully examined the place of assessment in the behavioral orientation. The first two of these articles were, I believe, the earliest anywhere to employ the term "behavioral assessment" in its present technical sense. In the same year, Walter Mischel, in his influential *Personality and assessment*, included a chapter on "Assessment for behavior change." A bit later, in 1971, Krasner devoted a brief section to assessment in his *Annual Review of Psychology* article on behavior therapy. Then, in 1972, the bases of behavioral assessment were explored in considerable detail in an important article by Goldfried and Ronald Kent.

These developments can be said to have marked the emergence of behavioral assessment as a distinctive applied and research area. This recognition was further established, during the following decade, by the publication of a number of important books (Ciminero, Calhoun, & Adams, 1977;

Cone & Hawkins, 1977; Gambrill, 1977; Hersen & Bellack, 1976; Kendall & Hollon, 1981; and Mash & Terdal, 1981) and the establishment of two journals, *Behavioral Assessment* and *The Journal of Behavioral Assessment*, in the area.

I have now brought the story of behavioral assessment essentially up to the point where it becomes part of the present scene, rather than history. Before closing this section, however, several general observations from the historical perspective seem in order. First, it is evident that the perspective termed behavioral assessment has certain unique and important features, and brings to the overall assessment enterprise a number of fruitful new directions, methods, and emphases, and serves both to extend and to correct certain aspects of earlier assessment practices. Second, behavioral assessment is, however, a part of the whole. When viewed in terms of its historical antecedents and its current functions and problems, it has much in common with other approaches to assessment. It is best conceptualized in terms of its place in the larger picture. And, third, though new in the sense of being a recently conceived and developed area, behavioral assessment can trace its forbears far back into the past.

SOME FINAL THOUGHTS

A chapter on history should end with a look at the future, since it is generally assumed that a study of the past can suggest certain insights into what is to come. Predicting the future is at best a hazardous task (McReynolds, 1982). If the past is a reasonably accurate guide, however, then certainly we may expect continued development of assessment technology, along with occasional quantum advances. One such advance, in my judgment, is the paradigm that brings together person variables and environmental or stimulus variables in the prediction of behavior. As our review has shown, both person factors and situational factors have received the concentrated attention of assessment psychologists. Development of the technology for systematically combining these data sources into a potentially more powerful interactional model (McReynolds, 1979b, 1985), however, is largely a task for the future.

Turning now to the broader perspective, we cannot fail to be impressed by the strides that various pioneers in assessment have made over the centuries. Our review has also suggested the ubiquity of assessment practices in different places and times. In this context, it is noteworthy that most civilized societies, reaching back to the ancient times, have included more or less formalized assessment procedures in their cultural matrices. This fact points out—in a way that is both challenging and humbling—the important role that assessment fills in our own society.

REFERENCES

Akutagawa, D. (1956). A study in construct validity of the psychoanalytic concept of latent anxiety and test of a projection distance hypothesis. (Doctoral dissertation, University of Pittsburgh; 1956) *Dissertation Abstracts, 16,* 2519.

Alexander, F. D., & Selesnick, S. T. (1966). *The history of psychiatry.* New York: Harper & Row.

Ayllon, T., & Michael, J. (1959). The psychiatric nurse as a behavioral engineer. *Journal of the Experimental Analysis of Behavior, 2,* 323–334.

Bakan, D. (1966). The influence of phrenology on American psychology. *Journal of the History of the Behavioral Sciences, 2,* 200–220.

Bales, R. F. (1951). *Interaction process analysis.* Cambridge, MA: Addison-Wesley.

Bales, R. F., & Gerbrands, H. (1948). The "interaction recorder": An apparatus and check list for sequential content analysis of social interaction. *Human Relations, 4,* 456–463.

Barker, R. G. (1960). Ecology and motivation. In M. R. Jones (Ed.), *Nebraska symposium on motivation* (pp. 1–49). Lincoln: University of Nebraska Press.

Barker, R. F. (1968). *Ecological psychology: Concepts and methods of studying the enviornment of human behavior.* Stanford, CA: Stanford University Press.

Barker, R. G., Dembo, T., & Lewin, K. (1943). Frustration and regression. In R. G. Barker, J. S. Kounin, & H. F. Wright (Eds.), *Child development and behavior* (pp. 441–458). New York: McGraw-Hill.

Barker, R. G., & Wright, H. F. (1951). *One boy's day.* New York: Harper & Row.

Barker, R. G., & Wright, H. F. (1955). *Midwest and its children: The psychological ecology of an American town.* New York: Harper & Row.

Barrett, B. H., & Lindsley, O. R. (1962). Deficits in acquisition of operant discrimination and differentiation shown by institutionalized retarded children. *American Journal of Psychology, 67,* 424–436.

Bentham, J. (1948). *The principles of morals and legislation.* New York: Hafner. (Original work published 1789.)

Berne, E. V. C. (1930). *An experimental investigation of social behavior patterns in young children* (University of Iowa Studies in Child Welfare, 4, no. 3). Iowa City: University of Iowa Press.

Bernreuter, R. G. (1933). The theory and construction of the personality inventory. *Journal of Social Psychology, 4,* 387–405.

Bijou, S. W. (1957). Patterns of reinforcement and resistance to extinction in young children. *Child Development, 28,* 47–54.

Bijou, S. W. (1965). Experimental studies of child behavior. In L. Krasner & L. Ullmann (Eds.), *Research in behavior modification* (pp. 56–81). New York: Holt, Rinehart & Winston.

Bijou, S. W., & Orlando, R. (1961). Rapid development of multiple-schedule performances with retarded children. *Journal of the Experimental Analysis of Behavior, 4,* 7–16.

Bijou, S., & Peterson, R. F. (1971). Functional analysis in the assessment of children. In P. McReynolds (Ed.), *Advances in psychological assessment* (Vol. 2) (pp. 63–78). Palo Alto, CA: Science and Behavior Books.

Binet, A., & Henri, V. (1895). La psychologie individuelle. *L'Année Psychologique, 2,* 411–465.

Binet, A., & Simon, T. (1905). Application des méthodes nouvellés au diagnostic du niveau intellectual chez des enfants normaux et anormaux d'hospice et d'école primare. *L'Année psychologique, 11,* 245–266.

Bingham, M. V. (1937). *Aptitudes and aptitude testing.* New York: Harper.

Bondy, M. (1974). Psychiatric antecedents of psychological testing (before Binet). *Journal of the History of the Behavioral Sciences, 10,* 180–194.

Boring, E. G. (1950). *A history of experimental psychology* (2nd ed.). New York: Appleton-Century-Crofts.

Buhler, C. (1930). *The first year of life* (P. Greenberg & R. Ripin, Trans.). New York: John Day. (Original published in German, 1927.)

Burnham, W. H. (1925). *The normal mind.* New York: D. Appleton.

Buros, O. K. (1938–1979). *Mental measurements yearbooks* (1st Yearbook, 1938; 2nd, 1940; 3rd,

1949; 4th, 1953; 5th, 1959; 6th, 1965; 7th, 1972; 8th, 1978). Highland Park, NJ: Gryphon Press.

Campbell, D. P. (1968). The Strong Vocational Interest Blank: 1927-1968. In P. McReynolds (Ed.), *Advances in psychological assessment* (Vol. 1) (pp. 105-130). Palo Alto, CA: Science and Behavior Books.

Cattell, J. M. (1890). Mental tests and measurements. *Mind, 15,* 373-381.

Cattell, R. B. (1957). *Personality and motivation structure and measurement.* New York: World Book Company.

Cautela, J. R. (1968). Behavior therapy and the need for behavioral assessment. *Psychotherapy: Theory, research and practice, 5,* 175-179.

Cautela, J. R., & Kastenbaum, R. (1967). A reinforcement survey schedule for use in therapy, training and research. *Psychological Reports, 20,* 1115-1130.

Chaille, S. E. (1887). Infants, their chronological process. *New Orleans Medical and Surgical Journal, 14,* 893-912.

Chapple, E. D. (1940). Measuring human relations: An introduction to the study of the interaction of individuals. *Genetic Psychology Monographs, 22,* 3-147.

Chapple, E. D. (1949). The interaction chronograph: Its evolution and present application. *Personnel, 25,* 295-307.

Ciminero, A. R., Calhoun, K. S., & Adams, H. E. (Eds.). (1977). *Handbook of behavioral assessment.* New York: Wiley-Interscience.

Cone, J. D., & Hawkins, F. P. (Eds.). (1977). *Behavioral assessment: New directions in clinical psychology.* New York: Brunner/Mazel.

Craik, K. H. (1970). Environmental psychology. In K. H. Craik, B. Kleinmuntz, R. L. Rosnow, R. Rosenthal, J. R. Cheyne, & R. H. Walters (Eds.), *New directions in psychology* (Vol. 4) (pp. 1-122). New York: Holt, Rinehart & Winston.

Craik, K. H. (1971). The assessment of places. In P. McReynolds (Ed.), *Advances in psychological assessment* (Vol. 2) (pp. 40-62). Palo Alto, CA: Science and Behavior Books.

Curti, M. (1943). *The growth of American thought.* New York: Harper & Bros.

Danziger, K. (1979). The positivist repudiation of Wundt. *Journal of the History of the Behavioral Sciences, 15,* 205-230.

Darwin, C. (1859). *The origin of species.* London: John Murray.

Darwin, C. (1877). A biographical sketch of an infant. *Mind, 2,* 285-294.

Diamond, S. (1968). Marin Cureau de La Chambre. *Journal of the History of the Behavioral Sciences, 4,* 40-54.

Dickson, C. (1975). Role of assessment in behavior therapy. In P. McReynolds (Ed.), *Advances in psychological assessment* (Vol. 3) (pp. 341-388). San Francisco: Jossey-Bass.

Dixon, J. T., DeMonchaux, C., & Sandler, J. (1957). Patterns of anxiety: The phobias. *British Journal of Medical Psychology, 30,* 34-40.

Dollard, J., & Miller, N. E. (1950). *Personality and psychotherapy.* New York: McGraw-Hill.

Downey, J. E. (1923). *The will-temperament and its testing.* Yonkers-on Hudson, NY: World Book Co.

Ebbinghaus, H. (1897). Ueber eine neue Methode zur Prüfung geistiger Fähigkeiten und ihre Anwendung bei Schulkindern. *Zeitschift für Psychologie, 13,* 401-459.

Ellenberger, H. (1954). The life and work of Hermann Rorschach. *Bulletin of the Menninger Clinic, 18,* 173-213.

Exner, J. E., Jr. (1974). *The Rorschach: A comprehensive system.* New York: John Wiley & Sons.

Eysenck, H. J. (Ed.). (1960). *Behaviour therapy and the neuroses.* Oxford: Pergamon Press.

Eysenck, H. J. (Ed.). (1964). *Experiments in behaviour therapy.* Oxford: Pergamon Press.

Ferguson, L. W. (1952). *Personality measurement.* New York: McGraw-Hill.

Ferster, C. B., & DeMyer, M. K. (1962). A method for the experimental analysis of the behavior of autistic children. *The American Journal of Orthopsychiatry, 32,* 89-98.

Franz, S. I. (1912). *Handbook of mental examination methods.* New York: Journal of Nervous and Mental Disease Publishing Co.

Franz, S. I. (1919). *Handbook of mental examination methods* (2nd ed.). New York: Macmillan.

Freud, A. (1965). *Normality and pathology in childhood.* New York: International Universities Press.

Freund, K. (1963). A laboratory method for diagnosing predominance of homo- or hetero-erotic interest in the male. *Behaviour Research and Therapy, 1,* 85–93.

Freyer, D. (1931). *The measurement of interests.* New York: Henry Holt.

Galton, F. (1874). *English men of science: Their nature and nurture.* London: Macmillan.

Galton, F. (1879a). Psychometric experiments. *Brain, 2,* 149–162.

Galton, F. (1879b). Psychometric facts. *Nineteenth Century, 6,* 425–433.

Galton, F. (1880). Statistics of mental imagery. *Mind, 5,* 301–318.

Galton, F. (1883). *Inquiries into human faculty and its development.* London: Macmillan.

Galton, F. (1884). Measurement of character. *Fortnightly Review, 36,* 179–185.

Galton, F. (1887). Supplementary notes on 'prehension' in idiots. *Mind, 12,* 79–82.

Galton, F. (1888). Co-relations and their measurement, chiefly from antropometric data. *Proceedings of the Royal Society, 45,* 135–145.

Gambrill, E. D. (1977). *Behavior modification: Handbook of assessment, intervention, and evaluation.* San Francisco: Jossey-Bass.

Garfield, S. L. (1982). Editorial: The 75th anniversary of the first issue of *The Psychological Clinic. Journal of Clinical and Consulting Psychology, 50,* 167–170.

Gesell, A. (1925). *The mental growth of the pre-school child.* New York: Macmillan.

Ghiselli, E. E. (1966). *The validity of occupational aptitude tests.* New York: John Wiley & Sons.

Goddard, H. H. (1910). A measuring scale for intelligence. *The Training School, 6,* 146–155.

Goldberg, L. R. (1971). A historical survey of personality scales and inventories. In P. McReynolds (Ed.), *Advances in psychological assessment* (Vol. 2) (pp. 293–336). Palo Alto, CA: Science and Behavior Books.

Goldfried, M. R. (1977). Behavioral assessment in perspective. In J. D. Cone & R. P. Hawkins (Eds.), *Behavioral assessment* (pp. 3–22). New York: Brunner/Mazel.

Goldfried, M. R., & Kent, R. N. (1972). Traditional versus behavioral personality assessment. *American Psychologist, 77,* 409–420.

Goldfried, M. R., & Pomeranz, D. M. (1968). Role of assessment in behavior modification. *Psychological Reports, 23,* 75–87.

Goodenough, F. L. (1926). *Measurement of intelligence by drawings.* Yonkers-on-Hudson, NY: World Book Co.

Goodenough, F. L. (1928). Measuring behavior traits by means of repeated short samples. *Journal of Juvenile Research, 12,* 230–235.

Goodenough, F. L. (1949). *Mental testing: Its history, principles, and applications.* New York: Holt, Rinehart & Winston.

Gough, H. G. (1957). *California Psychological Inventory Manual.* Palo Alto, CA: Consulting Psychologists Press.

Greenspoon, J., & Gersten, C. D. (1967). A new look at psychological testing: Psychological testing from the standpoint of a behaviorist. *American Psychologist, 22,* 848–853.

Guthrie, E. R. (1938). *The psychology of human conflict.* New York: Harper & Row.

Hall, G. S. (1897). A study of fears. *American Journal of Psychology, 8,* 147–249.

Hartley, D. (1966). *Observations on man, his frame, his duty, and his expectations.* Gainsville, FL. Scholars' Facsimiles and Reprints. (Original work published 1749.)

Hathaway, S. R., & McKinley, J. C. (1940). A multiphasic personality schedule (Minnesota): I. construction of the schedule. *Journal of Psychology, 10,* 249–254.

Helvetius, C. A. (1810). *Essays on the mind* (Anon. Trans.). London: Albion Press. (Original work published in French 1758.)

Hersen, M. (1976). Historical perspectives in behavioral assessment. In M. Hersen & A. S. Bellack (Eds.), *Behavioral assessment: A practical handbook* (pp. 3–22). New York: Pergamon Press.

Hersen, M., & Bellack, A. S. (Eds.). (1981). *Behavioral assessment: A practical handbook* (2nd ed.). New York: Pergamon Press.

Hett, W. S. (Ed. and Trans.) (1936). Physiognomics. In *Aristotle: Minor works* (pp. 81–137). Cambridge, MA: Harvard University Press.

Holland, J. L. (1978). *Vocational Preference Inventory.* Palo Alto, CA: Consulting Psychologist Press.

Hollingsworth, H. L. (1922). *Judging human character*. New York: D. Appleton.

Holtzman, W. H., Thorpe, J. S., Swartz, J. D., & Herron, E. W. (1961). *Inkblot perception and personality; Holtzman inkblot technique*. Austin: University of Texas Press.

House, S. D. (1926). A mental hygiene inventory. *Archives of Psychology, 14,* 1–112.

Huarte, J. (1698). *The tryal of wits* (E. Bellamy, Trans.). London: Richard Sare. (Original work published 1575 in Spanish.)

Hull, C. L. (1928). *Aptitude testing*. Yonkers-on-Hudson, NY: World Books.

Hutcheson, F. (1726). *An inquiry into the original of our ideas of beauty and virtue* (2nd ed.). London: Darby, Bettesworth, Fayram, Pemberton, Rivington, Hooke, Clay, Batley & Simon.

Jackson, D. N. (1967). *Personality Research Form Manual*. Goshen, NY: Research Psychologist Press.

Jacobs, J. (1887). Experiments on 'prehension'. *Mind, 12,* 75–79.

Jacobson, E. (1938). *Progressive relaxation*. Chicago: University of Chicago Press.

James, W. (1890). *Principles of psychology* (2 vols.). New York: Henry Holt.

Jensen, A. R. (1982). Reaction time and psychometric g. In H. J. Eysenck (Ed.), *A model for intelligence* (pp. 93–132). Berlin: Springer-Verlag.

Jones, M. C. (1924). A laboratory study of fear: The case of Peter. *Pedagogical Seminary and Journal of Genetic Psychology, 31,* 308–315.

Jones, R. R., Reid, J. B., & Patterson, G. R. (1975). Naturalistic observations in clinical assessment. In P. McReynolds (Ed.), *Advances in psychological assessment* (Vol. 3) (pp. 42–95). San Francisco: Jossey-Bass.

Jung, C. (1910). The association method. *American Journal of Psychology, 21,* 219–269.

Kazdin, A. E. (1978). *History of behavioral modification*. Baltimore: University Park Press.

Kelley, T. L. (1914). *Educational guidance. An experimental study in the analysis and prediction of ability of high school pupils*. New York: Columbia University Contributions to Education, No. 71.

Kendall, P. C., & Hollon, S. D. (Eds.). (1981). *Assessment strategies for cognitive-beahvioral interventions*. New York: Academic Press.

Kent, G. H. (1950). *Mental tests in clinics for children*. New York: D. Van Nostrand.

King, G. F., Armitage, S. G., & Tilton, J. R. (1960). A therapeutic approach to schizophrenics of extreme pathology. *Journal of Abnormal and Social Psychology, 61,* 276–286.

Kraepelin, E. (1887). *Psychiatrie. Ein kurzes Lehrbuch für Studierende und Aerzte* (2nd ed.). Leipzig: Abel.

Kramer, S. N. (1963). *The Sumerians: Their history, culture, and character*. Chicago: University of Chicago Press.

Krasner, L. (1971). Behavior therapy. *Annual Review of Psychology, 22,* 483–532.

Krasner, L. (1982). Behavior therapy: On roots, contexts, and growth. In G. T. Wilson & C. M. Franks (Eds.), *Contemporary behavior therapy* (pp. 11–62). New York: Guilford Press.

Krasner, L., & Ullmann, L. P. (Eds.). (1965). *Research in behavior modification*. New York: Holt, Rinehart & Winston.

Krech, D. (1962). Cortical localization of function. In L. Postman (Ed.), *Psychology in the making* (pp. 31–72). New York: Knopf.

Lang, P. J., & Lazovik, A. D. (1963). Experimental desensitization of a phobia. *Journal of Abnormal and Social Psychology, 66,* 519–525.

Lewin, K. (1951). *Field theory in social science*. New York: Harper & Row.

Linden, K. W., & Linden, J. D. (1968). *Modern mental measurement: A historical perspective*. Boston: Houghton Mifflin.

Lindsley, O. R. (1956). Operant conditioning methods applied to research in chronic schizophrenia. *Psychiatric Research Reports, 5,* 118–139.

Lindsley, O. R., Skinner, B. F., & Solomon, H. C. (1953). *Studies in behavior therapy. Status Report I*. Waltham, MA: Metropolitan State Hospital.

Locke, J. (1959). *An essay concerning human understanding* (2 vols.). New York: Dover. (Original work published 1690.)

Loeb, J. (1912). *The mechanistic conception of life*. Chicago: University of Chicago Press.

Mash, E. J., & Terdal, L. G. (Eds.). (1981). *Behavioral assessment of childhood disorders*. New York: Guilford Press.

McDougall, W. (1933). *The energies of men*. New York: Charles Scribner's Sons.

McReynolds, P. (Ed.). (1969). *Four early works on motivation*. Gainsville, FL: Scholars' Facsimiles & Reprints.

McReynolds, P. (1975). Historical antecedents of personality assessment. In P. McReynolds (Ed.), *Advances in psychological assessment* (Vol. 3) (pp. 477–532). San Francisco: Jossey-Bass.

McReynolds, P. (1979a). Unpublished interview with Genevieve Murphy, Bryn Mawr, PA, May 30, 1979.

McReynolds, P. (1979b). The case for interactional assessment. *Behaviorial assessment, 1,* 237–247.

McReynolds, P. (1968–1981). *Advances in psychological assessment* [Vol. 1 (1968), Vol. 2 (1971)]. Palo Alto, CA: Science & Behavior Books; [Vol. 3 (1975), Vol. 4 (1978), and Vol. 5 (1981)], San Francisco: Jossey-Bass.

McReynolds, P. (1981). Introduction. In P. McReynolds (Ed.), *Advances in psychological assessment* (Vol. 5) (pp. 1–21). San Francisco: Jossey-Bass.

McReynolds, P. (1982). The future of psychological assessment. *International Review of Applied Psychology, 31,* 117–139.

McReynolds, P. (1985). Psychological assessment and clinical practice: Problems and prospects. In C. D. Spielberger & James N. Butcher (Eds.), *Advances in personality assessment* (pp. 1–30). Hillsdale, NJ: Lawrence Erlbaum.

McReynolds, P., Chelune, G. J. (Eds.), (1984). *Advances in psychological assessment* (Vol. 6). San Francisco: Jossey-Bass.

McReynolds, P., & DeVoge, S. (1978). Use of improvisational techniques in assessment. In P. McReynolds (Ed.), *Advances in psychological assessment* (Vol. 4) (pp. 222–277). San Francisco: Jossey-Bass.

McReynolds, P., & Ludwig, K. (1984). Christian Thomasius and the origin of psychological rating scales. *Isis, 75,* 546–553.

Mischel, W. (1968). *Personality and assessment*. New York: Wiley.

Moore, B. (1921). Personnel selection of graduate engineers. *Psychological Monographs, 30,* No. 138.

Moos, R. (1975). Assessment and impact of social climate. In P. McReynolds (Ed.), *Advances in psychological assessment* (Vol. 3) (pp. 8–41). San Francisco: Jossey-Bass.

Morgan, C. D., & Murray, H. A. (1935). A method for investigating fantasies. *Archives of Neurology and Psychiatry, 34,* 289–306.

Mowrer, O. H., & Mowrer, W. M. (1938). Enuresis: A method for its study and treatment. *The American Journal of Orthopsychiatry, 8,* 436–459.

Münsterberg, H. (1888). *Die Willenshandlung. Ein Beitrag zur physiologischen Psychologie*. Freiburg: Mohr.

Murchison, D., & Langer, S. (1927). (Trans.). Tiedemann's observations on the development of the mental faculties of children. *Pedagogical Seminary and Journal of Genetic Psychology, 34,* 205–230. (Original work published 1787 by D. Tiedemann in German.)

Murphy, G., Murphy, L. B., & Newcomb, T. M. (1937). *Experimental social psychology* (rev. ed.). New York: Harper.

Murray, H. C. (1938). *Explorations in personality*. New York: Oxford University Press.

Nelson, R. (1983). Behavioral assessment: Past, present, and future. *Behavioral Assessment, 5,* 195–206.

Newcomb, T. M. (1929). The consistency of certain extrovert-introvert behavior patterns in 51 problem boys. New York: *Teachers College Contributions to Education,* No. 382.

Newman, J. R. (1954). Francis Galton. *Scientific American,* 190, 72–76.

Olson, W. C. (1929). *The measurement of nervous habits in normal children*. Minneapolis: University of Minnesota Press.

OSS Assessment Staff. (1948). *Assessment of men*. New York: Rinehart & Winston.

Parten, M. B. (1932). Social participation among preschool children. *Journal of Abnormal and Social Psychology, 27,* 243–269.

Paterson, D. G., & Darley, J. G. (1936). *Men, women, and jobs: A study in human engineering*. Minneapolis: University of Minnesota Press.

Patterson, G. R. (1965). Responsiveness to social stimuli. In L. Krasner & L. Ullmann (Eds.), *Research in assessment modification* (pp. 157–178). New York: Holt, Rinehart & Winston.

Patterson, G. R., McNeal, S., Hawkins, N., & Phelps, R. (1967). Reprogramming the social environment. *Journal of Child Psychology and Psychiatry, 8*, 181–195.

Pavlov, I. (1927). *Conditioned reflexes.* London: Oxford University Press.

Pearson, K. (1896). Mathematical contributions to the theory of evolution: regression, heredity and panmixia. *Philosophical Transactions, 187A*, 253–318.

Preyer, W. (1882). *Die Seele des Kindes.* Leipzig: Fernau. (Translation by H. W. Brown, *The mind of the child.* In two parts, 1888, 1889. New York: Appleton.)

Proshansky, H. M., Ittelson, W. H., & Rivlin, L. G. (1970). *Environmental psychology: Man and his physical setting.* New York: Holt, Rinehart & Winston.

Quetelet, L. A. J. (1969). *A treatise on man and the development of his faculties.* Gainsville, FL: Scholars' Facsimiles and Reprints. (Reprint of English edition of 1842; original work published 1835 in French.)

Ramul, K. (1960). The problem of measurement in the psychology of the eighteenth century. *American Psychologist, 15*, 256–265.

Randall, J. H. (1976). *The making of the modern mind* (5th ed.). New York: Columbia University Press.

Rapaport, D., Gill, M., & Schafer, R. (1945, 1946). *Diagnostic psychological testing* (2 vols.). Chicago: Year Book Medical Publishers.

Reisman, J. M. (1976). *A history of clinical psychology.* New York: Irvington.

Robinson, D. N. (1976). *An intellectual history of psychology.* New York: Macmillan.

Rogers-Warren, A., & Warren, S. F. (1977). *Ecological perspectives in behavior analysis.* Baltimore: University Park Press.

Rorschach, H. (1942). *Psychodiagnostics* (P. Lemkau & B. Kronenberg, Trans.). Berne: Hans Huber. (Original work published 1921 in German.)

Sandler, J. (1954). Studies in psychopathology using a self-assessment inventory, I. The development and construction of the inventory. *British Journal of Medical Psychology, 27*, 142–145.

Seguin, E. (1842). *Théorie et practique de l'education des enfans arriérés et idiots.* Paris: Bailliére.

Sells, S. B. (Ed.). (1963). *Stimulus determinants of behavior.* New York: Ronald Press.

Shafer, R. (1948). *The clinical applications of psychological tests.* New York: International Universities Press.

Sommer, R. (1899). *Lehrbuch der psycholgischen Utersuchungsmethoden.* Berlin and Vienna: Urban and Schwarzenberg.

Spurzheim, J. G. (1970). *Phrenology, or the doctrine of mental phenomena.* Gainsville, FL: Scholars, Facsimiles & Reprints, Ed. by A. A. Walsh (Original edition 1834).

Stern, G. (1970). *People in context.* New York: John Wiley & Sons.

Stern, W. (1911), *Die differentielle Psychologie in ihren methodischen Grundlagen.* Leipzig: Barth.

Stone, C. W. (1908). *Arithmetical abilities and some factors determining them.* New York: Teachers College, Columbia University.

Strong, E. K. (1927). Vocational interest test. *Educational Record, 8*, 107–121.

Strong, E. K., & Campbell, D. P. (1981). *Strong-Campbell Interest Inventory.* Palo Alto, CA: Consulting Psychologists Press.

Symonds, P. M. (1934). *Psychological diagnosis in social adjustment.* New York: American Book Co.

Terman, L. M. (1906). Genius and stupidity: A study of some of the intellectual processes of seven "bright" and seven "stupid" boys. *Pedagogical Seminary, 13*, 307–373.

Terman, L. M. (1916). *The measurement of intelligence.* Boston: Houghton Mifflin.

Terman, L. M., & Merrill, M. (1937). *Measuring intelligence: A guide to the administration of the new revised Stanford-Binet tests of intelligence.* Boston: Houghton Mifflin.

Thomas, D. S. (1929). *Some new techniques for studying social behavior.* New York: Teachers College, Columbia University.

Thomas, D., Loomis, A. M., & Arrington, R. C. (1933). *Observational studies of social behavior* (Vol. 1). Social behavior patterns. New Haven, CT: Yale University Press.

Thomasius, C. (1692a). *Das Verborgene des Herzens anderer Menschen auch wider ihren Willen laus der taglichen Conversation zuerkennen*. Halle, Germany: Christoph Salfeld.

Thomasius, C. (1692b). *Weitere Erleuterung durch untersciedene Exempel des Ohnelangst gethane Vorschlags wegen der neuen Wissenschaft Andere Menschen Gemuther erkennenaulernen*. Halle, Germany: Christoph Salfeld.

Thorndike, E. L. (1904). *An introduction to the theory of mental and social measurements*. New York: The Science Press.

Thorndike, E. L. (1910). Handwriting. *Teachers College Record, 11*, 83–175.

Thorndike, E. L. (1911). *Animal intelligence*. New York: Macmillan.

Thorndike, E. L. (1912). The permanence of interests and their relation to abilities. *Popular Science Monthly, 81*, 449–456.

Thorndike, R., Hagen, E., & Sattler, J. S. (1985). *Stanford Binet Intelligence Scale: Fourth Edition*. Chicago: Riverside Publishing Co.

Thurstone, L. L. (1931). The measurement of social attitudes. *Journal of Abnormal and Social Psychology, 26*, 249–269.

Tredennick, H. (Ed. & Trans.) (1967). *Aristotle's prior analytics*. Cambridge, MA: Harvard University Press.

Ullmann, L. P., & Krasner, L. (Eds.), (1965). *Case studies in behavior modification*. New York: Holt, Rinehart & Winston.

Wasik, B. H. (1984). Clinical applications of direct behavioral observation: A look at the past and the future. In B. B. Lahey & A. E. Kazdin (Eds.), *Advances in clinical child psychology* (Vol. 7). New York: Plenum Press.

Watson, J. B. (1913). Psychology as the behavorist views it. *Psychological Review, 20*, 158–177.

Watson, J. B. (1919). *Psychology, from the standpoint of a behaviorist*. Philadelphia: J. B. Lippincott.

Watson, J. B. (1928). *Psychological care of infant and child*. New York: W. W. Norton.

Wechsler, D. (1967). *Manual for the Wechsler Preschool and Primary Scale of Intelligence*. New York: Psychological Corporation.

Wechsler, D. (1974). *Wechsler Intelligence Scale for Children—Revised Manual*. New York: Psychological Corporation.

Wechsler, D. (1981). *WAIS-R Manual: Wechsler Adult Intelligence Scale-Revised*. New York: Psychological Corporation.

Weiss, R. L. (1968). Operant conditioning techniques in psychological assessment. In P. McReynolds (Ed.), *Advances in psychological assessment* (Vol. 1). Palo Alto, CA: Science and Behavior Books.

Wells, F. L. (1917). *Mental adjustments*. New York: D. Appleton.

Wells, F. L., & Ruesch, J. (1942). *Mental examiner's handbook*. New York: Psychological Corporation.

Whipple, G. W. (1910). *Manual of mental and physical tests*. Baltimore: Warwick & York.

Wissler, C. (1901). The correlation of mental and physical tests. *Psychological Monographs, 3*, No. 16.

Witmer, L. (1915). Clinical records. *Psychological Clinic, 9*, 1–17.

Witmer, L. (Ed.). (1919). Reference book in clinical psychology and in diagnostic teaching [Special issue]. *The Psychological Clinic, 12*, 145–288.

Wolf, R. (1966). The measurement of environments. In A. Anastasi (Ed.), *Testing problems in perspective* (pp. 491–503). Princeton, NJ: Educational Testing Service.

Wolff, C. (1738). *Psychologia Empirica* (2nd ed.). Frankfurt: A. Leipsig.

Wolpe, J. (1958). *Psychotherapy by reciprocal inhibition*. Stanford, CA: Stanford University Press.

Wolpe, J., & Lang, P. J. (1964). A fear survey schedule for use in behavior therapy. *Behaviour Research and Therapy, 2*, 27–30.

Woodworth, R. S. (1919). Examination of emotional fitness for warfare. *Psychological Bulletin, 16*, 59–60.

Woodworth, R. S., & Wells, F. L. (1911). Association tests. *Psychological Monographs, 13*, No. 5, Whole No. 57.

Woody, R. H. (Ed.). (1980). *Encyclopedia of clinical assessment* (2 vols.). San Francisco: Jossey-Bass.
Wright, H. F. (1967). *Recording and analyzing child behavior*. New York: Harper & Row.
Wright, T. (1971). *The passions of the minde in generall*. Urbana: University of Illinois Press. (Original work published 1604.)

3

THE CONTRIBUTIONS OF TRADITIONAL ASSESSMENT: CONCEPTS, ISSUES, AND METHODOLOGIES

BILLY BARRIOS

University of Mississippi

DONALD P. HARTMANN

University of Utah

Has there ever been a time when behavior therapists have not been embroiled in controversy, be it with the lay public or their fellow professionals? It does not seem so (e.g., Kihlstrom & Nasby, 1981; Klein, Dittmann, Parloff, & Gill, 1969; Nordheimer, 1974). Nor does it seem to be without good reason. Behavior therapists have brought upon themselves much of the negative attention and criticism that they have received. They have done so through their senseless baiting of advocates of other schools of psychotherapy and their expansive claim of therapeutic effectiveness—claims not quite as grandiose as Watson's (1913), but grandiose nevertheless.

Events of late have led behavior therapists to become less hostile in their view of other schools of psychotherapy and more humble in their claims of treatment success. Past presidents of the Association for Advancement of Behavior Therapy have alerted us to the fact that behavioral techniques are no panacea for psychological ailments (Barlow, 1980; Hersen, 1981; Kazdin, 1979a; Wilson, 1982). Summaries or meta-analyses of treatment outcome research have alerted us to the fact that diverse interventions produce similar levels of improvement (e.g., Landman & Dawes, 1982; but see Kazdin & Wilson, 1978, for a contrasting view). Acknowledging the limits of behavioral interventions and the benefits of nonbehavioral interventions has led behavior therapists to become more receptive to what other schools of psychotherapy have to offer.

This increased receptivity to what other schools of psychotherapy have to offer can be seen in the recent writings of behavior therapists. In these writings we find discussion of such topics as hypnosis (Spanos & Barber,

1976), client resistance (Jahn & Lichstein, 1980), and the therapist-client relationship (Mahoney, 1977). We also find a call for a rapprochement with traditional modes of psychotherapy (e.g., Goldfried & Padawer, 1982; Kendall, 1982). Calls for an integration with other schools of psychotherapy are nothing new; they have appeared throughout the history of behavior therapy (e.g., Beck, 1970; Birk, 1970; Brady, 1968; Landsman, 1974; Lazarus, 1967; Mahoney, 1974; Marks & Gelder, 1966; Watchel, 1975). What is new is that these calls are now being heeded.

Behavior therapists have toned down the rhetoric regarding their treatment of psychological disorders, but they have not toned down the rhetoric regarding their assessment of psychological disorders. In declaring that their approach to assessment is superior to all other approaches to assessment, behavior therapists appear to be headed down the same path they traveled vis-á-vis the treatment of psychological disorders. We find this disconcerting. The striking parallels between the development of behavioral assessment and the development of projective assessment is even more disconcerting. The two approaches have similar origins. Both arose out of a climate of discontent with orthodox methods of measurement. This discontent over the ability of available assessment instruments to provide information commensurate with current thinking about abnormal behavior was so great it resulted in the rejection of the orthodox instruments and the construction of alternative instruments that were more in line with current thinking.

Will behavioral assessment, similar in origin to projective assessment, suffer a similar demise (Hartmann, Roper, & Bradford, 1979)? We fear that behavioral assessment will show the same rapid rise and abrupt decline in stature and in use as projective assessment. But we believe that a sensitivity to the tenets of traditional testing may help behavioral assessment avoid an early death. What we are recommending here is not the wholesale adoption of traditional assessment devices nor the tailoring of traditional devices to suit the unique needs of behavior therapists (Greenspoon & Gersten, 1967; Landau & Goldfried, 1981). No, what we are arguing for is the recognition and acceptance of the conceptual issues, paradigms, and methodologies that transcend all approaches to assessment. These are conceptual issues, paradigms, and methodologies that must be attended to if any approach to assessment is to survive. To date, behavior therapists have paid little attention to these issues, paradigms, and methodologies, whereas students of traditional testing have been most mindful of them and, indeed, have attempted to design and evaluate their measurement practices in light of these preeminent concepts. The traditional approach to assessment is, therefore, quite germane to the behavioral approach to assessment, in that it illustrates for us how these preeminent concepts guide us in the development and evaluation of our measurement practices.

SIMILARITIES AND DIFFERENCES BETWEEN
TRADITIONAL AND BEHAVIORAL ASSESSMENT

Before describing the issues, paradigms, and concepts common to traditional models of assessment and of potential use to behavioral assessors, we will summarize the differences between traditional and behavioral assessment. The purpose of this digression is to identify clearly the two approaches for the discussion that follows. The comparison also indicates the extent to which our assumptions control—and in some cases fail to control—the nature of our assessment practices.

As previous chapters have indicated, neither traditional assessment nor behavioral assessment are monolithic, homogeneous edifices. Indeed, while differing "on average," both are highly fractionated and sometimes contradictory approaches. Traditional assessment, as used here, includes psychodynamic and trait-oriented approaches to assessment. Behavioral assessment has even more diverse constituents. It includes conceptual aspects of the applied behavioral, neobehavioristic mediational stimulus-response, cognitive-behavioral, and social learning models (see Kazdin & Wilson, 1978). Behavioral assessment also includes strategic aspects of behavioral-analytic, criterion-referenced, norm-based, as well as various idiographic approaches to assessment (see Chapter 4 in this volume; also see Kratochwill, 1982; Nelson & Hayes, 1981).

Table 3-1 summarizes the commonly mentioned general features distinguishing the traditional and behavioral orientations (Hartmann *et al.*, 1979). The most basic differences between the two general approaches to assessment lie in their assumptions about the nature of personality and the causes of behavior. Traditional approaches view personality as something the individual *has*, while the behavior approach is more interested in what the individual *does* (Mischel, 1968). Moreover, traditional assessors tend to invoke global personality constructs, presumably acquired in the past, as the underlying causes of current behaviors. Behavioral assessors, on the other hand, tend to employ more specific descriptive summaries of patterns of responses to particular situations and to search for the causes of such behavior in the interaction of characteristics of the individual with antecedent and consequent stimuli in the environment.

These very different conceptualizations have important implications for the role of behavior and of history, and the view of the stability of behavior in the two approaches. The traditional approach to assessment underplays the role of behavior and considers it important mainly as a sign of underlying traits or states. In the behavioral approach to assessment the test behavior itself is of interest as a representative sample of the person's behavior in the *assessment* situation. In the traditional approach to assessment, emphasis is

TABLE 3-1. Differences between Behavioral and Traditional Approaches to Assessment

	Behavioral	Traditional
Assumptions		
Conception of personality	Personality constructs mainly employed to summarize specific behavior patterns, if at all	Personality as a reflection of enduring underlying states or traits
Causes of behavior	Maintaining conditions sought in current environment or in environment–organism interactions	Intrapsychic or within the individual
Implications		
Role of behavior	Important as a sample of person's repertoire in specific situation	Assumes importance only insofar as it indexes or signifies underlying causes
Role of history	Relatively unimportant, except, for example, to provide a retrospective baseline	Crucial in that present conditions seen as a product of the past
Consistency of behavior	Behavior thought to be specific to the situation	Behavior expected to be consistent across time and settings
Uses of data	To describe target behaviors and maintaining conditions	To describe personality functioning and etiology
	To select the appropriate treatment	To diagnose or classify
	To evaluate and revise treatment	To make prognosis; to predict
Other characteristics		
Level of inferences	Low	Medium to high
Comparisons	Intraindividual or idiographic	Interindividual or nomothetic
Methods of assessment	Direct methods (e.g., observations of behavior in natural environment)	Indirect methods (e.g., interviews and self-report)
Timing of assessment	Ongoing	Pre- and perhaps posttreatment, or strictly to diagnose
Scope of assessment	Specific and extensive (i.e., multisetting, -time, and -response)	Global (e.g., of cure, or improvement) but only of the individual

Note. Table adapted from Hartmann, Roper, & Bradford, 1979.

placed on uncovering the historical roots of current intrapsychic problems. The behavioral approach is largely ahistorical, though Haynes (1978, p. 40) has enumerated a number of functional roles for historical information in behavioral assessment. Since the traditional approach considers behavior to be a function of stable and enduring underlying causes of traits, behavior is presumed to be consistent across time and different settings or situations. In the behavioral approach, however, behavior is considered to be a function of current and specific environmental conditions as well as of more or less enduring organismic variables; thus behavior would be expected to vary if the environment were changing.

The most significant practical difference between behavioral and traditional approaches to assessment is the uses to which the respective data are put. Traditional assessment data typically are used for description of the individual's personality structure, for diagnosis and classification, and for prediction. The major purpose of behavioral assessment data are to arrive at a description of the target behaviors and the variables controlling these behaviors such that an appropriate treatment can be implemented and evaluated.

The level of theoretical inference or abstraction distinguishes behavioral from traditional assessment. The level of inference is typically much higher in traditional assessment than in behavioral assessment, largely because of the former orientation's predilection for higher-level constructs (e.g., Goldfried & Kent, 1972). The types of comparisons made in the two approaches differ. Since the traditional approach is more concerned with classification and prediction, more emphasis is placed on differences between individuals, or nomothetic issues. The behavioral approach, on the other hand, is more concerned with comparing changes in behavior within an individual, or idiographic issues.

Finally, the methods, timing, and scope of assessment are different in the two approaches. Generally, behavior assessment employs more direct methods—methods in which the behavior of interest is actually observed in its natural context—than does traditional assessment. Behavioral assessment necessitates more continuous measurement in order to conduct an appropriate descriptive analysis of the conditions presumably affecting the individual's behavior, to select treatment in light of this descriptive analysis, and most importantly to evaluate treatment effectiveness.

Behavioral assessment is characterized by a focus on specific behaviors and conditions and the measurement of multiple variables. These variables include strengths and deficiencies, potentially controlling antecedent and consequent events, any relevant cognitive and physiologic variables, the target behaviors in other settings and across time, the potential effectiveness of change agents in the natural environment, and desirable and undesirable collateral effects of treatment (Haynes, 1978). Since traditional assessment focuses on stable underlying traits or states within the individual, more global and less numerous measures are required.

This summary clearly indicates that the conceptions, goals, and functions of behavioral and traditional assessment differ importantly over a broad range of dimensions. We must hasten to add, however, that summaries such as that given in Table 3-1 must be interpreted cautiously lest they misrepresent the wide variation in *assessment practices* reported by presumed behavioral assessors (Ford & Kendall, 1979; Swan & MacDonald, 1978; Wade, Baker, & Hartmann, 1979).

COMMON CONCEPTS, ISSUES, AND METHODOLOGIES

At first glance, the abyss separating the behavioral and the traditional assessment orientations would seem to prohibit traditional assessment from contributing anything of value to behavioral assessment. Lest our readers despair, we briefly describe here concepts and their associated issues and methodologies that are pertinent to assessment practices, irrespective of approach. These super-ordinate concepts emerged within the context of traditional assessment. As a result, we draw heavily upon the traditional assessment literature in our coverage of them.

All assessments ultimately are intended to facilitate decision making (e.g., Cronbach, 1970), and the objective of clinical assessment, whether behavioral or traditional, is to render clinical decisions (e.g., Evans & Wilson, 1983). The precision and accuracy, as well as the usefulness of these clinical decisions are a function of the veridicality of the data upon which they are based, and the extent to which these data are void of the contaminating presence of extraneous variables.

Gauging the extent to which assessment data are indicators of what they purport to be measuring is facilitated by sensitivity to the concepts of *standardization, reliability,* and *validity.* Once the data are collected, they must be interpreted or used in particular ways. Determining how best to use assessment data is relevant to the notions of *norms,* as well as the broader concepts of *decision-making models* and *utility.* We briefly review these concepts as well as the primary issues and methodologies involved in their application and investigation, and suggest their applicability to behavioral assessment (see also Cone, 1977, 1982; Goldfried, 1977; Hartmann, *et al.,* 1979; Nunnally, 1978).

STANDARDIZATION

Standardization refers to the extent to which an assessment device is applied uniformly across conditions of administration. The assessment protocol, including materials, time limits, instructions, scoring criteria, and the like all must be "held constant" if comparisons—whether they be across individuals, time, or occasions—are to reflect differences in the behavior of interest rather than variations in assessment procedures. It is clear that behavioral assessors have not always been sensitive to the importance of standardization. Even such popular devices as behavioral avoidance tests vary widely in their type and mode of instructions, as well as in their number of steps or tasks (Barrios, Hartmann, & Shigetomi, 1981). Because approach responses to feared objects have been shown to differ as a function of these procedural variations, the lack of standardization makes across-study comparisons with even this premier behavioral assessment technique "risky at best" (Barrios, *et al.*, 1981, p. 272).

RELIABILITY

The number of articles and chapters concerning reliability (see the review by Hartmann & Wood, 1982) that have appeared in behavioral journals in recent years is evidence that clinical behaviorists have not rejected the concept of reliability. It does seem to be the case, however, that certain aspects of reliability have been neglected, at least as reflected in published clinical behavioral research. This neglect may be due both to changes in underlying assumptions about behavior and to the inadequate development of computational and other operational procedures for assessing reliability in ways that are congruent with behavioral methodology (e.g., see Cone, 1977; Hartmann *et al.*, 1979; Nelson, Hay, & Hay, 1977). Whatever the reason for the neglect, its consequences are as clear for behavior assessors as for traditional assessors: inadequate evaluation of the reliability of an instrument limits attempts to improve or replace it, muddles the interpretation of weak or null stimulus-response (behavior) and response-response relations, and makes unclear the extent to which scores can be generalized.

The theory of generalizability proposed by Cronbach and associates (Cronbach, Gleser, Nanda, & Rajaratnam, 1972) makes explicit the relationship between reliability and generalizability. According to the theory, a score is determined by the specific conditions under which it is determined, such as test forms, items, observers (assessors), time, and contexts. When any of these dimensions—called facets in generalizability theory—produce substantial variability in performance, generalization from one condition or level of the facet to another (such as from one setting to another) can be associated with substantial inaccuracy. Three facets of generalizability deserve our particular attention: observers, settings or situations, and time.

Because of behavioral assessment's early emphasis on direct observations, its practitioners have been most sensitive to the observer facet of generalizability (Kelly, 1977). Despite this attention, assessment of the generalizability of results across observers has been plagued by a number of problems. For example, there is disagreement over the definitions of basic concepts such as accuracy, reliability, and agreement as well as disagreement over the relevance and applicability of these concepts to behavioral data (see Cone, 1977, 1982; Hartmann, 1982). There is also uncertainty over the level of data at which observer reliability should by assessed (e.g., Hartmann, 1977), and substantial concerns over the paucity of studies examining the reliability of clinical decisions including problem identification and treatment selection (e.g., Mash & Terdal, 1976). The methodology for investigating these latter reliability issues has been available for at least 35 years (e.g., Little & Shneidman, 1959), and deserves more frequent use by behavioral reseachers. [See Evans and Wilson (1983) for a review of the few studies investigating the reliability of clinical behavioral assessors' judgements.] Finally, investigators apparently cannot even agree on the appropriate method for summarizing reliability information (Kazdin, 1977a), or how this information should be used to aid in decision making (Morris & Rosen, 1982). Certainly these issues of interobserver reliability deserve the continuing attention of behavioral investigators.

Behavioral assessors' rejection of trait assumptions has been interpreted to imply that behaviors are temporally inconsistent and that the facet of time (test-retest reliability) is irrelevant to behavior assessment. The question of behavioral stability, however, must by answered *empirically*, and not by fiat or on the basis of theoretical partisanship. Because behaviors vary in their stability, an assessment instrument's test-retest reliability must be evaluated on the basis of what is known about the behavior it putatively measures.[1] (Of course, traditional assessors have long been aware of the necessity of variable test-retest reliability standards; e.g., consider the measurement of mood.) Consequently, low test-retest reliability does not necessarily threaten an instrument's integrity (e.g., Nelson *et al.*, 1977) unless a persuasive case can be made that the performance assessed was indeed stable. Nevertheless, information regarding behavioral stability or the lack thereof is a matter of substantial importance to behavioral assessors. For example, behaviors showing marked instability may be unsuitable targets for demonstration studies that require conformity to the demands of individual-subject designs (e.g., Kazdin, 1982b). Consequently, the assessment of temporal reliability would seem to be particularly important in experimental behavioral investigations, in order to determine whether and, if so, what kind of design adjustments may be required. When confronted with instability (e.g., trending or otherwise variable baselines), investigators are faced with the alternatives of grouping their data, extending their measurements by adding more samples of behavior, gaining additional control of measurement set-

---

1. Some responses, such as performance on general cognitive tasks, show very substantial stability (Mischel, 1968). Still other molar response classes such as friendliness and conscientiousness show moderate stability, while the component behaviors comprising these classes are only slightly stable (Mischel & Peake, 1982).

tings, or changing dependent variables in order to achieve specified purposes (Hartmann, 1982).

The third facet of generalizability, situations, concerns the degree to which performance measures display situational consistency. Again because of their dislike of traditional trait assumptions, behaviorists have emphasized situationally-induced discriminative responding rather than situationally consistent responding. While the evidence for discriminative responding across settings is strong (e.g., Mischel, 1968; Mischel & Peake, 1982), it is also apparent that the consistency issue is much more complex than first thought, and furthermore, that there are behaviors that display substantial cross-situational consistency (Bem, 1983; Epstein, 1983). As in the case of temporal stability, situationally inconsistent responding does not necessarily indict the instrument providing this performance pattern, unless there is incontrovertible, independent evidence of situational consistency. Eventually the accumulation of empirical facts will answer the consistency question for particular combinations of behaviors, individuals, and settings. Behavior assessors may find it burdensome to work with behaviors that are situationally inconsistent (Kazdin, 1979b). Behaviors failing to display situational consistency, whether serving as aids in treatment selection or as indices of treatment effectiveness, will be of limited utility—the measures of these behaviors may be meaningful only in the setting in which they were obtained. Thus while behavioral inconsistency may not have clear implications for evaluating assessment instruments, behavioral inconsistency may have critical implications for the conduct of assessments and for the design of treatments.

VALIDITY

The validity of a measurement device is in essence directly linked to its ability to accomplish specific objectives set forth by the assessor (Kaplan, 1964). Viewing the validity of an instrument in terms of the degree to which it serves as a means to an end meshes naturally with the goal-attainment orientation of behavior therapy (e.g., Rimm & Masters, 1979; Wilson & O'Leary, 1980). Appraising the validity of an assessment tool entails inspection of both its evidential and consequential data bases (Messick, 1980); that is, it necessitates judging the support for inferences and decisions made from the measurements and the impact of the actions initiated in light of those decisions. Validity thus denotes the tenability of inferences from assessment data. Since validity or adequacy itself is not a measurable entity, it too represents an inference (American Psychological Association, 1974).

Validity issues have not received much attention from behavioral investigators, particularly those using observational procedures (Hartmann & Wood, 1982). Indeed, observational data have been considered inherently valid, and thus serve as the criterion against which other sources of data were validated (e.g., Mash & Terdal, 1976). This assumption of inherent validity is clearly a serious error (Haynes, 1978). All forms of assessment data, including direct observations, include method-dependent sources of error and hence require validation (e.g., Baum, Forehand, & Zegiob, 1979; Haynes & Horn, 1982; Kazdin, 1982a).

At least three traditional forms of validity are relevant to behavioral assessors: content, criterion-related, and construct validity.[2] Content validity is especially important in the initial development of an assessment device. Content validity is determined by the adequacy with which an instrument samples the behavioral domain of interest (Cronbach, 1971). The requirements necessary to establish content validity—including definition of the relevant domain, representative sampling from this domain for inclusion in the instrument, and specification of scoring procedures—have been described by behavioral investigators (Linehan, 1980); with notable exceptions, these requirements have been applied to behavioral instruments (see Haynes & Kerns, 1979).

Criterion-related validity refers to the usefulness or accuracy of scores in predicting some performance criterion (predictive validity) or in substituting for some other established—and typically more costly—measurement procedure (concurrent validity). These two forms of criterion-related validity are clearly relevant to behavioral assessors (e.g., Haynes, 1978) and are central to two currently prominent issues in behavioral assessment (Hartmann & Wood, 1982): (1) the utility of behavioral assessment data for identifying problem behaviors and controlling stimuli, and for selecting effective treatments; and, (2) the substitutability of less expensive and less reactive data for naturalistic observational data. Investigations of both of these issues are susceptible to a variety of lethal flaws including restriction-in-range and criterion contamination. Fortunately, the generic problems associated with predictive and concurrent validity studies have been identified and catalogued, and effective solutions have been developed (Maher, 1978; Megargee, 1966; Wiggins, 1973).

Construct validity (Cronbach & Meehl, 1955) is indexed by the degree to which scores from an assessment device accurately measure some psycho-

---

2. Other forms of validity specifically designated by clinical behaviorists are also relevant to behavioral assessors: treatment validity (Nelson & Hayes, 1979), the extent to which an assessment device contributes to the development of effective treatments; and social validity (Kazdin, 1977b; Wolf, 1978), the degree to which decisions regarding the focus, the form, and the effectiveness of treatment are consistent with social criteria. Both of these forms of validity would seem to be subclasses of construct validity.

logical construct such as deviant behavior, assertiveness, or social skills. While some behavioral clinicians have argued that construct validation is "inappropriate to behavioral assessment" (Cone, 1981, pp. 46–47), other behavioral clinicians have conducted extensive series of studies to establish the construct validity of their assessment devices (e.g., Jones, Reid, & Patterson, 1975; Paul & Lentz, 1977). These studies attempt to answer such questions as which component responses belong to the construct? Which variables influence scores on the device? For example, are scores sensitive to dissimulation (fake-bad or fake-good) instructions? Does the device discriminate between members of known groups? While the methodologies employed in construct validation investigation vary substantially, a particularly important methodology is that of convergent and discriminant validation described by Campbell and Fiske (1959) and recently extended to triple response mode assessments by Cone (1979). According to this approach, two or more behaviors assessed with two or more methods are compared, in part, to determine the extent to which method artifacts confound measures of behaviors. In behavioral assessment, archival records, mechanical instrumentation, self-report, and nonparticipant observations applied to what is presumed to be the same behavior may yield very different results, and could lead to entirely different conclusions about behavior. In view of the ubiquity of measurement specific effects, construct validation is required if a behavior is to be considered independently of the specific procedures used to measure it (Hartmann et al., 1979).

Validity is the last of the concepts based in traditional assessment that concern the extent to which scores, from whichever device they are obtained, measure what they purport to be measuring. Validation procedures, because they also may indicate (e.g., by means of correlation coefficients) how well scores predict a criterion, also belong to the traditional concepts concerned with the interpretation or use of scores, a topic to which we now turn.

NORMS

The ambiguous meaning of test scores is a persistent problem in psychological measurement. Two popular methods of test construction are available for wresting meaning from scores. With the norm-referenced approach, an individual's performance is expressed (and given meaning) in relationship to the performance of other individuals on the same measuring device. In view of the interindividual emphasis implied in the use of norm-referenced assessment, it is not surprising that there are few behavioral assessment devices that include norms (Evans & Nelson, 1977).

With the alternative method, criterion-referenced testing, scores are directly interpretable in terms of some criterion, objective, or domain (Glaser & Nitko, 1971). In comparison to norm-referenced assessment, criterion-referenced assessment yields interpretations that are "direct, rather than comparative; emphasizes intra-individual change, rather than inter-individual differences; and gauges the level of attainment of relatively narrow, rather than broad, performance objectives" (Hartmann et al., 1979, p. 9). In view of these characteristics, it would seem that criterion-referenced testing is more in keeping with the treatment focus of behavior assessment. The potential value of norms should not be dismissed quickly by behavioral assessors, however, as norms may serve a variety of useful functions. Some of these include identifying problematic behaviors, classifying or grouping subjects, assessing the degree of convergence between measures, and evaluating the social validity of treatment effects (see Hartmann et al., 1979, for an extended discussion of the functions of norms).

The use of normative data for decision making requires careful standardization of materials as well as of administration and scoring procedures (see section on Standardization, above). Without adequate standardization, comparison of scores with norms is fraught with hazards. Other cautions should also be observed when using norms. For example, norms are not absolute, universal, or immutable (Anastasi, 1976), and they must be representative of the desired comparison group and relevant to the purpose they are to serve. If these warnings are heeded, norms can be of substantial use to behavior interventionists.

OTHER DECISION MODELS

Norms are but one method of making assessment decisions. Other methods are represented by more than a score of statistical and clinical prediction models described by Wiggins (1981). These models include regression approaches of varying complexity as well as automated, paramorphic, and unit-weighting clinical decision models. Based upon the current literature, neither these nor other decision models have attracted the attention of behavioral clinicians. Indeed, while an occasional voice has indicated that clinical decision making is a topic worthy of attention (e.g., Broadhurst, 1976; Lanyon & Lanyon, 1976), there appears to be a conspiracy of silence regarding the decision-making strategies used by behavioral clinicians. We know next to nothing about how behavioral assessors combine information, which sources of information are must useful for which decisions, and which errors in decision making require particular vigilance by assessors (e.g., Mash & Terdal, 1976). In fact, only recently have the important contributions of Tversky and Kahneman (1974) on judgmental heuristics and biases begun to appear in behaviorists' writings (e.g., Evans & Wilson, 1983; Kanfer & Busemeyer, 1982). As Evans and Wilson (1983) emphasize, the decision making of behavioral clinicians "must first be conceptualized . . . then research models can be brought to bear . . . [and finally novice behavior therapists can be trained] in the selection and use of information pertinent to their decision-making requirements" (p. 49). Almost certainly, accomplishment of the first two steps will be aided by attention to research on clinical decision making (e.g., Wiggins, 1981) as well as careful scrutiny of relevant work in cognitive psychology (e.g., Tversky & Kahneman, 1974).

UTILITY

The utility or value of behavioral assessment procedures must be based ultimately on their ability to enable investigators to make correct decisions regarding target behavior identification, selection of optimum treatment strategies, and the evaluation of outcomes (e.g., see Ciminero, 1977). The methods of determining the utility of assessment devices are generally well understood, and involve knowledge of the rates of correct and incorrect decisions using the technique, the values associated with these outcomes, and the cost of obtaining the assessment information (e.g., see Wiggins, 1973).[3]

When utility is conceptualized in this manner, it unfortunately is apparent that the value of behavior assessment procedures for making target identification and treatment selection decisions has hardly begun to be evaluated (e.g., Evans & Nelson, 1977; Felton & Nelson, 1984; Nelson, 1983; Nelson & Hayes, 1979). It is only in the evaluation of treatment effectiveness that a growing body of data supports the utility of behavioral assessment procedures (e.g., Kazdin & Wilson, 1978; Rachman & Wilson, 1980). Even in treatment evaluation, however, Karoly (1977, p. 227) suggests that "a sense of certainty about appropriate methods of assessment should be ruled premature at this stage of knowledge." From this cursory review, there is little doubt but that the methodology available for assessing utility (e.g., Wiggins, 1973) continues to be relevant to the field of behavioral assessment.

This brief description of the concepts of standardization, reliability, validity, norms, decision making, and utility does not sufficiently convey their relevance to behavioral assessment. Their importance is perhaps best

3. Not uncommonly, utility is expressed comparatively, as where one assessment–decision strategy is compared with another. The second assessment–decision strategy may be viewed as a control, as when using an optimizing strategy with baserate information.

illustrated through a detailed account of the phases of behavioral assessment, which is offered in the next section.

PHASES OF ASSESSMENT

A hallmark of the behavioral approach to clinical practice is a dynamic interplay between measurement and action (e.g., Hersen & Barlow, 1976). Assessment supplies information which the behavior therapist then draws upon to make various kinds of inferences. These inferences in turn dictate the design and conduct of therapeutic operations. The inferences vary in terms of the phenomena to be related, the width of the knowledge gap separating these phenomena, and the types of evidence required to support the bridge. It follows that different inferences require different types of information. When viewed in this light, the various functions of assessment are nothing more than changing requests on the part of the behavior therapist for information. How well an assessment satisfies a particular request rests upon an evaluation of the tenability of the inference, tenability being determined by an instrument's measurement properties (e.g., reliability, validity, and utility).

The phases and precise functions of behavioral assessment are summarized in Table 3-2. The phases resemble a funnel in that they begin with a broad scope and progessively narrow to a relatively circumscribed focus (Cone & Hawkins, 1977). As the level of inspection shifts from phase to phase so do the discrete functions that are assigned to each stage. Couched as questions, these functions are fulfilled when an assessment provides information that leads to an accurate reply. It is here in the rendering of an accurate reply, or to use the language heretofore employed, the positing of a tenable inference, that the traditional assessment concepts of reliability, validity, norms, decision making, and utility come into play. Exactly how they contribute is examined on a phase-by-phase, question-by-question basis in the sections that follow.

THE SCREENING PHASE

In the initial phase of screening and general disposition, the behavior therapist wishes to determine whether a case is suitable for the type of services offered, and if so, what additional data may be pertinent, and if not, to whom might the client be referred. For example, an agency specializing in the treatment of phobic disorders wishes to restrict their clientele to those whose principal disturbance is that of a marked fear to a specific object,

TABLE 3-2. Phases of Clinical Assessment

Phase	Questions addressed
Screening	Does this person have a problem? Where should this person be referred? Is further assessment required?
Problem definition and analyses	What is the extent and nature of the problem? What factors (e.g., environmental and organismic) maintain the problem? What is the precise rate or duration of the problem behavior?
Finalizing treatment objectives and intervention tactics	What are the behavioral objectives? What are the individual's assessments and liabilities (e.g., motivation and skills)? What additional resources can be brought to bear on the problem? What is the optimum intervention strategy?
Monitoring treatment progress	Are changes occurring in the target and collateral behaviors? Are the treatment changes adequate?

Note. Table based upon Cone & Hawkins (1977), Hawkins (1979), Haynes (1978), Kratochwill (1982), and Mash & Terdal (1976).

activity, or situation. Such an agency would like to weed out quickly those persons who have no circumscribed fear or for whom a phobia is merely an ancillary feature of a more debilitating condition, and then direct these individuals to an appropriate treatment facility. If all of this sounds vaguely familiar, it should, for it is nothing more than the practice of differential diagnosis. Clinical behaviorists may shy away from diagnostic labels, preferring the categories of performance deficits and excesses (e.g., Kanfer & Saslow, 1969); they cannot, however, avoid the task of classification.

To aid them in discriminating the appropriate from the inappropriate client, behavioral clinicians fashion from assessment data a rough sketch of the person's current life pattern. Because time is usually of the essence, assessors want to rule as swiftly as possible whether a prospective client should be taken on or referred to a more suitable agency. They also want their ruling to be correct; that is, they want to accept for care only those who are truly eligible for services and to exclude those who actually do not meet the imposed criteria. Of utmost importance, then, are the traditional assessment concepts of validity and utility.

As stated above, the function of assessments during this first phase is to assist the behavioral clinician in determining how well a prospective client matches with the selection or screening criteria. These criteria may be those of the diagnostic categories of the *Diagnostic and statistical manual of mental disorders* or criteria self-generated by the therapist or the parent agency.

Regardless of the source of the screening criteria, collectively they depict a performance pattern that the behavioral assessor is intent on identifying. It is from assessment data that the presence or absence of this performance pattern is inferred. Thus, in the initial phase of assessment, the primary concern or problem is that of criterion validation, a problem that is solved through the judicious use of measures that sensitively detect the criterion performance.

Although there might be many such measures, only those of greatest utility are employed. Our agency specializing in the treatment of phobic disorders may conduct a behavioral interview, administer a battery of self-report inventories, or solicit the observations of family members. All of these measures, let us say, have been found to correlate highly with more direct measures of the criterion performance. Nevertheless, they may be of little utility, as utility is a concept that is by no means mirrored by the magnitude of a correlation coefficient. Various factors enter into an evaluation of an instrument's utility, perhaps the most important of which is its predictive efficiency relative to base rates (e.g., Wiggins, 1973). Others are the time and expense associated with obtaining the assessment information (e.g., administering and scoring the instrument). Recall that the behavior therapist does not wish to spend an inordinate amount of time probing the person before settling on a disposition. All that is desired is sufficient information to formulate a prompt, yet accurate, diagnosis.

Thus, from the outset, the practice of behavioral assessment can profit from a fellowship with the more traditional measurement concepts, in this case, those of criterion validity and utility. For to answer efficiently the questions posed in the first phase of assessment, it is clear that not just any instrument will do, but only ones of proven diagnostic utility (Messick, 1980).

PROBLEM DEFINITION AND ANALYSIS

In the previous phase of screening and general disposition, the behavioral clinician was interested in merely skimming the surface, in capturing a simple outline of the client's functioning. This hasty sketch then serves as a springboard for a more fine-grain analysis from which specific problem areas are identified, and a general course of treatment mapped out. The designation of problem areas and their corresponding treatment programs are the products of inferences based on assessment data. These inferences are facilitated by attending to the traditional measurement concepts of content and construct validity, generalizability, norms, and decision making.

Identification of Problem Areas

The broad-band assessment of the screening phase provides the behavioral clinician with clues as to which aspects of the client's functioning might be problematic. The clinician then follows up on these leads by conducting an in-depth assessment of each problem area. Continuing with our example of the phobia clinic, assume that preliminary questioning of a client turns up apprehension over both driving and refusing unreasonable requests as areas of concern. Whether each problem necessitates treatment depends in part on information from content-valid assessment; that is, from measurement that adequately covers the performance pattern of interest.

Evidence for the adequacy of content coverage typically comes from two sources: an appraisal of the assessment's overlap with our conceptualization of the response pattern (Nunnally, 1978), and endorsements by those persons in the client's immediate environment for whom the performance has direct bearing (Goldfried & D'Zurilla, 1969). Take, for example, the assessment of fear and assertion. Among behaviorists, the prevailing view of fear is that of a tripartite phenomenon comprised of subjective, motoric, and physiologic response units (Lang, 1971). Consequently, an assessment that neglects to monitor all three response systems is automatically seen as insufficient (e.g., Borkovec, Weerts, & Bernstein, 1977; Lick & Katkin, 1976; Morris & Kratochwill, 1983). For assertion, the counterpart to the three-systems model might be McFall's (1982) formulation of social skill—a formulation that depicts an assertive act as composed of behavioral units mediated by cognitive-decoding, -decision, and -encoding processes. From such a framework, an assessment of an assertive act would be judged adequate only if it focused on both motoric and underlying cognitive features.

The upshot is that it is critical for an assessment instrument to measure what it is purposed to measure, that it satisfactorily address all aspects thought to constitute the response pattern. A mismatch between an instrument's coverage of a response pattern and our conceptualization of it opens the door to faulty deductions and misdirected treatment. For as noted earlier, it is from these assessment data that problem areas are inferred and corrective steps are generated. If the measures do not reflect performance as they are believed to, then miscalculations and treatment blunders are virtually inevitable.

Content valid assessment does not tell us whether or not a performance sequence is problematic, though it does set the occasion for such a determination. A ruling of the problem status of a pattern is generally reached by appraising the data against a background of normative or criterion performance. Norms, then, can be an invaluable aid to the behavioral clinician, particularly in these instances where there are no other definitive criteria as to what constitutes acceptable performance. Behavior therapists, however, have tended to shy away from norm-referenced measures, electing to use instead edumetric or criterion-referenced measures (e.g., Carver, 1974). On the surface, such a preference would appear to greatly simplify the process of pinpointing problem areas. Having a clear-cut demarcation that separates adequate from inadequate performance would eliminate much of the deliberating that takes place during this phase, or at least one would think so. Rarely, though, is the behavioral clinician interested in the assessed performance per se. Most assessments are conducted under contrived conditions that differ substantially from relevant aspects of the client's typical life circumstances. Yet it is from these assessments that typical responding is inferred. How safe is it for the behavioral clinician to generalize from the assessment context to important life-settings? How well does the measured performance mirror those displayed in pertinent life situations? Answers to these and related questions regarding the comparability of response measures can be obtained through generalizability analyses. They are certainly answers which the behavioral clinician must have if intelligent use is to be made of criterion-referenced assessment.

Norms and the methods of generalizability analysis are thus part and parcel to the process of problem identification. Data, even behavioral assessment data, have no intrinsic meaning. It is when assessment data are interpreted—set against the yardstick of normative and/or generalizability estimates—that they acquire significance (Kaplan, 1964; Mitroff & Sagasti, 1973).

Treatment Planning

At this juncture in the clinical sequence, the behavior therapist begins formulating a crude treatment plan, one that is built upon the insights gleaned from the assessment data. These insights are simply clues into the possible factors maintaining inadequate responding. It is in the provision of such clues that the love affair between the behavior therapist and a strict criterion-referenced approach to assessment turns sour. It is also here where the notion of constructs and construct-referenced assessment come into play.

First let us look at the inherent drawbacks of a purely criterion-referenced assessment. Our breakdown of the problem identification process showed criterion-referenced measures coupled with evidence of generalizability across relevant conditions to be a powerful intermediary. Beyond this step, though, such measures appear to have little value as they offer no hints as to the sources of inadequate performance. This is because a strict criterion-referenced approach to assessment shuns theorizing; it is concerned only with the accomplishment of the act itself. There is no causal blueprint to accompany criterion-referenced measures, therefore, there is no list of possible maintaining agents for one to explore.

Consider, for example, the criterion-referenced assessment of fear and assertion. When a client performs poorly on such tests, these areas may be tagged problematic and targeted for change. The concern is then to what to attribute this poor performance? Few behavior therapists would claim that failure to respond at criterion levels is irrefutable evidence of skill deficits, yet this is the implicit and sole interpretation put forth by an orthodox criterion-referenced analysis. Insufficient responding may be due to skill deficits, but it also may be a function of limited incentives, excessive arousal, physical impairments, insensitivity to stimulus cues, reactivity to testing per se, and a host of other possibilities.

The moment we begin generating and empirically eliminating these competing accounts of faulty responding, we enter the realm of construct validation (Guion, 1978; Messick, 1980). Through the evocation of constructs and the orderly process of their explication, assessment scores acquire an interpretive richness that easily eclipses that of criterion-referenced measures (Nunnally, 1978). Their superior richness lies in their body of established relationships with other measures, a body that is amassed from efforts at convergent and discriminant validation (Campbell & Fiske, 1959). And it is this body of relationships that supplies us with a list of factors most likely to be behind the disturbed performance. The list contains nomothetic variables, ones which have been found relevant for the group as a whole and which therefore may not be applicable for any isolated individual. Whether any or all of the variables are pertinent to the particular case at hand is determined in the next phase of assessment. Whatever the upshot of just such an inquiry might be, the fact remains that construct-referenced measures are perhaps the best starting point for treatment planning.

Decision making is obviously an integral part of both problem identification and treatment planning. Norms and criterion-referenced measures facilitate the interpretation of assessment scores; but they do not and can not issue a ruling on whether such scores indicate a problem area worthy of remedial action. Construct-referenced measures aid in designing an intervention, but they do not and can not dictate the program's exact nature. These are difficult decisions that the behavior therapist alone must make. How they are reached is at this time left solely up to the discretion of each individual therapist. For behavior therapy has yet to formulate a working model of decision making, as has already been noted.

It is difficult to imagine how this second phase of behavioral assessment could be carried out without an appeal to the concepts and methodologies of construct validation, generalizability theory, and decision making. Carried out efficiently, that is, for behavior therapists have and will doubtlessly continue to spot problem areas and draw up plans for their treatment. Even more difficult to imagine is how behavioral assessment can evolve from its present state to a well-articulated discipline without the aid of such concepts and methodologies, a point that we will pick up and discuss further in this chapter's concluding section.

FINALIZING TREATMENT OBJECTIVES AND INTERVENTION TACTICS

Having pinpointed problem areas, the behavior therapist must now locate their maintaining variables, establish treatment goals, and map out steps that will lead to goal attainment. It is assessment data that are looked to for guidance in carrying out each of these tasks, and it is the inclusion of constructs, norms, estimates of generalizability, and models of decision making which enhance their helpfulness. In the ensuing sections, we note the exact point(s) in this task sequence where each of these concepts and their accompanying methodologies cone into play. And in so doing, we also relate how they foster valid inferences, and thus expedite the treatment process.

Identifying Maintaining Variables

We work under the assumption that the variables responsible for a perfor- mance pattern are ones which systematically co-vary with it (e.g., see Maho- ney, 1978). And as was pointed out in the previous section, it is construct- and not criterion-referenced measures that furnish us with a pool of covar- iates. Of course, not all of the correlates are potential maintaining agents. Some are best seen as products rather than causes of the problem behavior, and some as simply irrelevant for the particular case at hand. Construct- referenced assessment, thus, does not provide us with a foolproof printout of the problem's maintaining agents, but rather provides us with a menu of interesting possibilities. It is this listing, though, which gives a focus and orderliness to what would otherwise be a hit-and-miss search for the prob- lem's maintaining variables.

   To illustrate, consider once again the client who expresses apprehension over driving an automobile. A criterion-based assessment would tell us whether the client's performance met some minimum level of acceptability, nothing more. A construct-referenced assessment, on the other hand, would tell us of variables that have been previously linked to the response pattern displayed by the client and also the strength of those relations. That is so because the tracing of such a network of relations is basic to the construct validation process (e.g., Nunnally, 1978). A host of situational and organismic variables, including the reactions of others, the client's mood state, and client's belief system may make up this network. The behavior therapist is free to pick and choose which among these variables might be sustaining the fear reaction of this specific client.

A construct-referenced assessment thus serves as a springboard for further assessment, for a closer look at these variables believed to be perpetuating the problem area. Before proceeding, though, the behavior therapist must decide first on the order in which these potential maintenance factors are addressed, then on the steps for determining whether or not they are indeed operative in this particular case. The sequence in which the variables are assessed may come from one or a combination of sources including theories, empirically derived hierarchies, previous experiences, and manpower constraints—to name but a few. Determining whether or not a variable is acting as a maintenance agent may come about in part through the use of norm- or criterion-referenced measures. Each offers a backdrop for interpreting the assessment data, but as in the indentification of problem areas neither can say what is and what is not a maintaining variable. Only the behavioral assessor can make such decisions.

Specifying Treatment Objectives

As the behavioral clinician moves on to the establishment of treatment goals, the need for a model of decision making becomes even more acute. Rare is the monosymptomatic client, who, having a single isolated problem, thus has a circumscribed treatment goal. More common is the client who expresses multiple complaints and displays a number of impairments, each of which is linked to a somewhat distinct goal state. With these individuals, the behavior therapist must arrange the order in which the various treatment objectives are tackled. Our hypothetical client serves as a case in point. In addition to being able to drive an automobile fearlessly and firmly refuse unreasonable requests, our client wishes to be orgasmic during coitus with her husband. The question then is: Which of these three treatment goals do we tackle first? Which second? And which third? When can they all be worked toward simultaneously? There are many factors on which we could base their relative standing such as the severity of the problem, the immediacy of therapeutic change, and the hypothesized and demonstrated interrelationships among the goals (e.g., Kazdin, 1982c, Mash & Terdal, 1981; Voeltz & Evans, 1982). The challenge is to arrive at the rank ordering that best promotes the attainment of rapid and lasting therapeutic change, a challenge that a model for decision making might help us meet.

Finalizing Intervention Tactics

Settling on the exact makeup of treatment is not as straightforward as a reading of clinical case studies and research reports would lead us to believe. Naturally, we would like our treatment efforts to neutralize those forces maintaining the problem performance and to create those conditions conducive to goal attainment. If there were only one change strategy that met these requirements, the matter would be cut-and-dry. But more often than not, there are several perfectly permissible techniques from which we can choose.

The goal of "fearlessly driving an automobile" is a good example of the type of situation in which more than one treatment technique is available. Which of the many fear reduction procedures do we select? Some may argue that it makes no difference which technique we select as the literature shows all of them to be effective. Even if we were to concede this point, it is highly doubtful that the various procedures are equivalent on all dimensions. They most likely would vary in terms of their complexity, their duration, their reliance on others, their social palatability, the responsibilities that they accord to the client, and the set of therapist's skills that they require for maximum efficiency. Obviously, then, there is much more to choosing the optimum intervention than comparing the published track records of the different procedures. Track records are unquestionably important, but so are the procedures' relative standing on these other dimensions. Selecting the treatment most likely to succeed for a particular client thus entails attending to an array of dimensions. The puzzle is how to arrange the information on these dimensions, such that it directs us to the most efficacious procedure. That is, of course, the function of a decision-making model.

To move through the clinical tasks of identifying maintenance variables, specifying treatment goals, and organizing intervention tactics is to render a succession of formidable decisions, or, if you will, inferences. With each decision serving as the foundation for the next, a single miscalculation could send us on an errant course, or worse, bring the entire inferential structure tumbling down. We believe, however, that the chances of this happening can be reduced, and as our review of these three tasks reveals, in part through the adoption of the traditional notions and methods of norms, construct validation, and decision-making models.

MONITORING TREATMENT PROGRESS

With the onset of treatment, the immediate purpose of assessment becomes that of tracking these responses which have been targeted for change.

Assessment offers insights into the intervention's impact, which in turn contribute to decisions regarding its continuation, alteration, or termination. Specifically, these are insights into response fluctuations and the adequacy of response changes. The precision of these insights, and thus the exactness with which performance changes are detected and their significance gauged, can be enhanced by a working knowledge of several orthodox measurement concepts. How they do so follows.

Detecting Changes in Target Responses.

The behavior therapist hopes both to observe the desired changes in performance and to attribute those changes to the influence of treatment. The realization of such hopes rests on a content-valid assessment, a rigorous functional analysis, and, of course, an active treatment. A sensitive content-valid assessment allows for the detection of fluctuations in responding; a rigorous functional analysis allows for the deduction of the therapy's influence. As noted earlier in the section on "Identification of Problem Areas," it is the overlap between our coverage of a response pattern and our conceptualization of it that makes for content-valid assessment. It is, however, reliable measurement that in part makes for a rigorous or internally valid functional analysis (e.g., Cook & Campbell, 1979; Kazdin, 1982b).

Reliability contributes to the analytic process by eliminating three sources apart from the intervention that might account for shifts in responding: inherent fluctuations in performance, variations in assessment administration, and variations in scoring. Their elimination opens the way for more confident attributions or inferences regarding the treatment's hold over responding. For, recall, the behavior therapist wishes to both detect performance changes and attribute those changes to the workings of the intervention. To do so, the behavior therapist must first reject those prima facie accounts of responding that have nothing whatsoever to do with treatment—three of which implicate some form of unreliability as responsible for the fluctuations in performance. Reliable assessment, that is, standardized assessment yielding measures of high temporal stability and inter-rater reliability, negates all three of these competing interpretations of the data. And in so doing, allows for more accurate deductions of treatment's role in the changes observed.

Judging the Adequacy of Therapeutic Changes

Once performance changes have been duly noted and attributed to treatment, they must then be judged for their acceptability. Typically this entails appraising the client's responses against a backdrop of behaviorally couched treatment goals, criterion levels of performance, normative estimates, and public opinion (Hartmann, Roper, & Gelfand, 1977; Kazdin, 1977b; Wolf, 1978). Each of these criteria holds certain strengths and weaknesses as a judgmental aid. Behaviorally defined treatment goals are, it would seem, the ideal reference point. They simplify the situation into a plain yes-or-no matter: either the client's performance matches the desired pattern or it does not. The twist is that such goals are rarely independent of the other back-drops, and in fact emanate from them. Thus the pluses and minuses of behaviorally couched treatment goals are the pluses and minuses of criter-ion-referenced assessment, norms, and social validation.

Earlier, in our discussion of the identification of problem areas, we underscored the value of criterion-referenced measures. Those same re-marks apply here. For when there is an incontrovertible standard for effec-tive responding, judging the acceptability of therapeutic change becomes a relatively straightforward matter. Unfortunately, there are few patterns that have clear demarcations between adequate and inadequate perfor-mance. At what point, for example, does one cross over from fearful to fearless responding, and from unassertive to assertive responding? In cases such as these, the behavior therapist must look elsewhere for help in evalu-ating the adequacy of therapeutic change. Two possibilities are the impres-sions of significant others and normative estimates.

Of the two, social validation data appear to be the favored frame of reference. Given behavior therapy's idiographic bent, this preference for the reactions of the client's immediate environment is not at all surprising. It would seem, then, that norms are of little use in judging the suitability of therapeutic changes. This, however, is not the case. Social validation data, though an important yardstick, on the one hand, may not necessarily denote the adaptiveness of the client's responses. The social milieu may be too harsh or too lenient a critic, either of which might be deterimental to the client's welfare. Norms, on the other hand, allow us to pinpoint how well the client performs relative to his or her peers. True, norms do not tell us whether performance is at an adaptive or competent level; they do, however, set limits on what we might realistically expect to see from our client. This moderating influence makes normative estimates the perfect companion to the more rigid judgmental aids of criterion-referenced and social validation measures.

Whatever form this backdrop takes—be it criterion-referenced assess-ment, social validation data, normative estimates, or some combination of the three—the behavior therapist must still translate the comparison into a verdict of either adequate or inadequate therapeutic change. And then, in light of that decision, map out a specific course of action. In the case of satisfactory performance, do we continue with treatment, revise it, or re-place it with a program designed to maintain or enhance adaptive functioning? In the face of unsatisfactory responding, do we extend the treatments trial period, alter its makeup, abandon it for another, or terminate it along with the entire therapist-client relationship? With so many alternatives from which to choose, it is clear that we need a framework that will prevent us from both becoming bogged down and acting impulsively; a framework that will enable us to weigh the relative merits of the different options and point us to the most promising one. Another name for such a framework is a decision-making model.

This casual overview of the phases of assessment has reacquainted us with the varied purposes of assessment, and has revealed to us the role that traditional measurement concepts and methodologies can play in the fulfillment of those functions. At each and every stage of assessment, there is some traditional notion or methodology that is relevant, if not necessary. And at each and every stage, the contribution is essentially the same, that of rendering more systematic and tenable the inferences that can be drawn from assessment data.

A CONCLUDING COMMENT

We began this chapter by recounting the parallels between projective techniques and behavioral assessment, and pointing out how both grew out of an atmosphere of discontent with conventional modes of measurement. We also expressed our fear that the two would suffer a similar fate, that of quickly falling into disrepute. For in the haste to come up with assessment practices that are more compatible with our premises, have we behavioral clinicians developed ones that are more scientific and less subjective than those of our predecessors? Is a behavioral assessment any less speculative than one based on a battery of projective tests? Our brief look into the nature and nuances of behavioral assessment suggests that it is an operation still steeped in subjectivism.

Elevating behavioral assessment from the status of an art form to that of a well-articulated, scientifically respectable discipline will require more than just hard work. There also will need to be a change in attitudes. One attitude requiring change is the misbegotten notion that makeshift, improvised, nonstandardized assessment is congruent with an idiographic approach to clinical practice. Another changeworthy attitude is that a "good old-fashioned functional analysis" is the answer to all our assessment needs. Such a viewpoint begs the question: It tells us nothing of how variables are selected for an analysis nor how the findings are to be interpreted. And finally, there is the need to utilize many of the traditional measurement concepts and methods that have heretofore been seen as largely antithetical to behavioral assessment. Their intelligent assimilation is, in our opinion, the key to a mature behavioral assessment. After all, only a mature behavioral assessment is assured of a long and venerable life.

REFERENCES

American Psychiatric Association. (1980). *Diagnostic and statistical manual of mental disorders* (3rd. ed.). Washington, DC: Author.

American Psychological Association, American Educational Research Association, and National Council on Measurement in Education. (1974). *Standards for educational and psychological tests.* Washington, DC: American Psychological Association.

Anastasi, A. (1976). *Psychological testing* (4th ed.). New York: Macmillan.

Barlow, D. H. (1980). Behavior therapy: The next decade. *Behavior Therapy, 11*, 315–328.

Barrios, B. A., Hartmann, D. P., & Shigetomi, C. (1981). Fears and anxieties in children. In E. J. Mash & L. G. Terdal (Eds.), *Behavioral assessment of childhood disorders* (pp. 259–304). New York: Guilford Press.

Baum, C. G., Forehand, R., & Zegiob, L. E. (1979). A review of observer reactivity in adult-child interactions. *Journal of Behavioral Assessment, 1*, 167–178.

Beck, A. T. (1970). Cognitive therapy: Nature and relation to behavior therapy. *Behavior Therapy, 1*, 184–200

Bem, D. J. (1983). Toward a response style theory of persons in situations. In M. M. Page (Ed.), *Personality—Current theory and research: Nebraska symposium on motivation 1982* (pp. 201–231). Lincoln: University of Nebraska Press.

Birk, L. (1970). Behavior therapy: Integration with dynamic psychiatry. *Behavior Therapy, 1*, 522–526.

Borkovec, T. D., Weerts, T. C., & Bernstein, D. A. (1977). Assessment of anxiety. In A. R. Ciminero, K. S. Calhoun, & H. E. Adams (Eds.), *Handbook of behavioral assessment* (pp. 367–428). New York: John Wiley & Sons.

Brady, J. P. (1968). Psychotherapy by a combined behavioral and dynamic approach. *Comprehensive Psychiatry, 9*, 536–543.

Broadhurst, A. (1976). Applications of the psychology of decisions. In M. P. Feldman & A. Broadhurst (Eds.), *Theoretical and experimental bases of the behaviour therapies* (pp. 269–287). London: John Wiley & Sons.

Campbell, D. T., & Fiske, D. W. (1959). Convergent and discriminant validation by the multitrait-multimethod matrix. *Psychological Bulletin, 56*, 81–105.

Carver, R. P. (1974). Two dimensions of tests: Psychometric and edumetric. *American Psychologist, 29*, 512–518.

Ciminero, A. R. (1977). Behavioral assessment: An overview. In A. R. Ciminero, K. S. Calhoun, & H. E. Adams (Eds.), *Handbook of behavioral assessment* (pp. 3–13). New York: John Wiley & Sons.

Cone, J. D. (1977). The relevance of reliability and validity for behavioral assessment. *Behavior Therapy, 8*, 411–426.

Cone, J. D. (1979). Confounded comparisons in triple response mode assessment research. *Behavioral Assessment, 1*, 85–95.

Cone, J. D. (1981). Psychometric considerations. In M. Hersen & A. S. Bellack (Eds.), *Behavioral assessment: A practical handbook* (2nd ed., pp. 38–68). New York: Pergamon Press.

Cone, J. D. (1982). Validity of direct observational assessment. In D. P. Hartmann (Ed.), *Using observers to study behaviors* (pp. 67–79). San Francisco: Jossey-Bass.

Cone, J. D., & Hawkins, R. P. (Eds.) (1977). *Behavioral assessment: New directions in clinical psychology.* New York: Brunner/Mazel.

Cook, T. D., & Campbell, D. T. (1979). *Quasi-experimentation: Design and analysis issues for field settings.* Chicago: Rand McNally.

Cronbach, L. J. (1970). *Essentials of psychological testing* (3rd ed.). New York: Harper & Row.

Cronbach, L. J. (1971). Test validation. In R. L. Thorndike (Ed.), *Educational measurement* (2nd ed., pp. 443–507). Washington, DC: American Council on Education.

Cronbach, L. J., Gleser, G., Nanda, H., & Rajaratnam, N. (1972). *The dependability of behavioral measurements: Theory of generalizability for scores and profiles.* New York: John Wiley & Sons.

Cronbach, L. J., & Meehl, P. E. (1955). Construct validity in psychological tests. *Psychological Bulletin, 52,* 281–302.

Epstein, S. (1983). A research paradigm for the study of personality and emotions. In M. M. Page (Ed.), *Personality—Current theory and research: Nebraska symposium on motivation 1982* (pp. 91–154). Lincoln: University of Nebraska Press.

Evans, I. M., & Nelson, R. O. (1977). Assessment of child behavior problems. In A. R. Ciminero, K. S. Calhoun, & H. E. Adams (Eds.), *Handbook of behavioral assessment* (pp. 603–681). New York: John Wiley & Sons.

Evans, I. M., & Wilson, F. E. (1983). Behavioral assessment as decision making: A theoretical analysis. In M. Rosenbaum, C. M. Franks, & Y. Jaffe (Eds.), *Perspectives on behavior therapy in the eighties* (pp. 35–53). New York: Springer.

Felton, J. L., & Nelson, R. O. (1984). Inter-assessor agreement on hypothesized controlling variables and treatment proposals. *Behavioral Assessment, 6,* 199–208.

Ford, J. D., & Kendall, P. C. (1979). Behavior therapists' professional behaviors: Converging evidence of a gap between theory and practice. *the Behavior Therapist, 2,* 37–38.

Glaser, R., & Nitko, A. J. (1971). Measurement in learning and instruction. In R. L. Thorndike (Ed.), *Educational measurement* (2nd ed., pp. 625–670). Washington, DC: American Council on Education.

Goldfried, M. R., (1977). Behavioral assessment in perspective. In J. D. Cone & R. P. Hawkins (Eds.), *Behavioral Assessment* (pp. 3–22). New York: Brunner/Mazel.

Goldfried, M. R., & D'Zurilla, T. J. (1969). A behavior-analytic model for assessing competence. In C. D. Spielberger (Ed.), *Current topics in clinical and community psychology* (Vol. 1, pp. 151–196). New York: Academic Press.

Goldfried, M. R., & Kent, R. N. (1972). Traditional versus behavioral assessment: A comparison of methodological and theoretical assumptions. *Psychological Bulletin, 77,* 409–420.

Goldfried, M. R., & Padawer, W. (1982). Current status and future directions in psychotherapy. In M. R. Goldfried (Ed.), *Converging themes in psychotherapy: Trends in psychodynamic, humanistic, and behavioral practice* (pp. 3–49). New York: Springer.

Greenspoon, J., & Gersten, C. D. (1967). A new look at psychological testing: Psychological testing from the standpoint of a behaviorist. *American Psychologist, 22,* 848–853.

Guion, R. M. (1978). Scoring of content domain samples: The problem of fairness. *Journal of Applied Psychology, 63,* 499–506.

Hartmann, D. P. (1977). Considerations in the choice of interobserver reliability estimates. *Journal of Applied Behavior Analysis, 10,* 103–116.

Hartmann, D. P. (1982). Assessing the dependability of observational data. In D. P. Hartmann (Ed.), *Using observers to study behavior* (pp. 51–65). San Francisco: Jossey-Bass.

Hartmann, D. P., Roper, B. L., & Bradford, D. C. (1979). Some relationships between behavioral and traditional assessment. *Journal of Behavioral Assessment, 1,* 3–21.

Hartmann, D. P., Roper, B. L., & Gelfand, D. M. (1977). An evaluation of alternative modes of child psychotherapy. In B. L. Lahey & A. E. Kazdin (Eds.), *Advances in clinical child psychology* (Vol. 1, pp. 1–46). New York: Plenum Press.

Hartmann, D. P., & Wood, D. D. (1982). Observational methods. In A. S. Bellack, M. Hersen, & A. E. Kazdin (Eds.), *International handbook of behavior modification and therapy* (pp. 109–138). New York: Plenum Press.

Hawkins, R. P. (1979). The functions of assessment: Implications for selection and development of devices for assessing repertoires in clinical, educational, and other settings. *Journal of Applied Behavior Analysis, 12,* 501–516.

Haynes, S. N. (1978). *Principles of behavioral assessment.* New York: Gardner Press.

Haynes, S. N., & Horn, W. F. (1982). Reactivity in behavioral observations: A methodological and conceptual critique. *Behavioral Assessment, 4,* 369–385.

Haynes, S. N., & Kerns, R. D. (1979). Validation of a behavioral observation system. *Journal of Consulting and Clinical Psychology, 47,* 397–400.

Hersen, M. (1981). Complex problems require complex solutions. *Behavior Therapy, 12,* 15–29.

Hersen, M., & Barlow, D. H. (1976). *Single case experimental designs: Strategies for studying behavior change.* New York: Pergamon Press.

Jahn, D. L., & Lichstein, K. L. (1980). The resistive client: A neglected phenomenon in behavior theory. *Behavior Modification, 4,* 303–320.

Jones, R. R., Reid, J. B., & Patterson, G. R. (1975). Naturalistic observation in clinical assessment. In P. McReynolds (Ed.), *Advances in psychological assessment* (Vol. 3, pp. 42–95). San Francisco: Jossey-Bass.

Kanfer, F. H., & Busemeyer, J. R. (1982). The use of problem solving and decision making in behavior therapy. *Clincial Psychology Review, 2,* 239–266.

Kanfer, F. H., & Saslow, G. (1969). Behavioral diagnosis. In C. M. Franks (Ed.), *Behavior therapy: Appraisal and status* (pp. 417–444). New York: McGraw-Hill.

Karoly, P. (1977). Behavioral self-management in children: Concepts, methods, issues, and directions. In M. Hersen, R. M. Eisler, & P. M. Miller (Eds.), *Progress in behavior modification* (Vol. 5, pp. 197–262). New York: Academic Press.

Kaplan, A. (1964). *The conduct of inquiry: Methodology for behavioral science.* San Francisco: Chandler.

Kazdin, A. E. (1977a). Artifact, bias, and complexity of assessment: The ABCs of reliability. *Journal of Applied Behavior Analysis, 10,* 141–150.

Kazdin, A. E. (1977b). Assessing the clinical or applied importance of behavior change through social validation. *Behavior Modification, 1,* 427–452.

Kazdin, A. E. (1979a). Fictions, factions, and functions of behavior therapy. *Behavior Therapy, 10,* 629–654.

Kazdin, A. E. (1979b). Situational specificity: The two-edged sword of behavioral assessment. *Behavioral Assessment, 1,* 57–75.

Kazdin, A. E. (1982a). Observer effects: Reactivity of direct observation. In D. P. Hartmann (Ed.), *Using observers to study behavior* (pp. 5–19). San Francisco: Jossey-Bass.

Kazdin, A. E. (1982b). *Single-case research designs: Methods for clinical and applied settings.* New York: Oxford University Press.

Kazdin, A. E. (1982c). Symptom substitution, generalization, and response covariation: Implications for psychotherapy outcome. *Psychological Bulletin, 91,* 349–365.

Kazdin, A. E., & Wilson, G. T. (1978). *Evaluation of behavior therapy: Issues, evidence, and research strategies.* Cambridge, MA: Ballinger.

Kelly, M. B. (1977). A review of the observational data-collection and reliability procedures reported in the Journal of Applied Behavior Analysis. *Journal of Applied Behavior Analysis, 10,* 97–101.

Kendall, P. C. (1982). Integration: Behavior therapy and other schools of thought. *Behavior Therapy, 13,* 559–571.

Kihlstrom, J., & Nasby, W. (1981). Cognitive tasks in clinical assessment: An exercise in applied psychology. In P. C. Kendall & S. Hollon (Eds.), *Assessment strategies for cognitive-behavioral interventions* (pp. 287–317). New York: Academic Press.

Klein, M. H., Dittmann, A. T., Parloff, M. B., & Gill, M. M. (1969). Behavior therapy: Observations and reflections. *Journal of Consulting and Clincial Psychology, 33,* 259–266.

Kratochwill, T. R. (1982). Advances in behavioral assessment. In C. R. Reynolds & T. B. Gutkin (Eds.), *The handbook of school psychology* (pp. 314–350). New York: John Wiley & Sons.

Landau, R. J., & Goldfried, M. R. (1981). The assessment of schemata: A unifying framework for cognitive, behavioral, and traditional assessment. In P. C. Kendall & S. B. Hollon (Eds.), *Assessment strategies for cognitive-behavioral interventions* (pp. 363–399). New York: Academic Press.

Landman, J. T., & Dawes, R. M. (1982). Psychotherapy outcome: Smith and Glass' conclusions stand up under scrutiny. *American Psychologist, 37,* 504–516.

Landsman, T. (1974, August). Not an adversity but a welcome diversity. Paper presented at the meeting of the American Psychological Association, New Orleans.

Lang, P. J. (1971). The application of psychophysiological methods in the study of psychotherapy and behavior modification. In A. E. Bergin & S. L. Garfield (Eds.), *Handbook of psychotherapy and behavior change: An empirical analysis* (pp. 75–125). New York: John Wiley & Sons.

Lanyon, R. I., & Lanyon, B. J. (1976). Behavioral assessment and decision-making: The design of strategies for therapeutic behavior change. In M. P. Feldman & A. Broadhurst (Eds.), *Theoretical and experimental bases of the behaviour therapies* (pp. 289–329). London: John Wiley & Sons.

Lazarus, A. A. (1967). In support of technical eclecticism. *Psychological Reports, 21*, 415–416.

Lick, J. R., & Katkin, E. S. (1976). Assessment of anxiety and fear. In M. Hersen & A. S. Bellack (Eds.) *Behavioral assessment: A practical handbook* (pp. 175–206). New York: Pergamon Press.

Linehan, N. M. (1980). Content validity: Its relevance to behavioral assessment. *Behavioral Assessment, 2*, 147–159.

Little, K. B., & Shneidman, E. S. (1959). Congruencies among interpretations of psychological test and anamnestic data. *Psychological Monographs, 73* (No. 6, Whole No. 476).

Maher, B. A. (Ed.) (1978). Clinical research methodology [Special issue]. *Journal of Consulting and Clinical Psychology, 46*(4).

Mahoney, M. J. (1974). *Cognition and behavior modification.* Cambridge, MA: Ballinger.

Mahoney, M. J. (1977). Reflections on the cognitive-learning trend in psychotherapy. *American Psychologist, 32*, 5–13.

Mahoney, M. J. (1978). Experimental methods and outcome evaluation. *Journal of Consulting and Clinical Psychology, 46*, 660–672.

Marks, I. M., & Gelder, M. G. (1966). Common ground between behavior therapy and psychodynamic methods. *British Journal of Medical Psychology, 39*, 11–23.

Mash, E. J., & Terdal, L. G. (1976). Behavior therapy assessment: Diagnosis, design and evaluation. In E. J. Mash & L. G. Terdal (Eds.), *Behavior therapy assessment* (pp. 15–31). New York: Springer.

Mash, E. J., & Terdal, L. G. (1981). Behavioral assessment of childhood disturbance. In E. J. Mash & L. G. Terdal (Eds.), *Behavioral assessment of childhood disorders* (pp. 3–76). New York: Guilford Press.

McFall, R. M. (1982). A review and reformulation of the concept of social skills. *Behavioral Assessment, 4*, 1–33.

Megargee, E. I. (1966). *Research in clinical assessment.* New York: Harper & Row.

Messick, S. (1980). Test validity and the ethics of assessment. *American Psychologist, 35*, 1012–1027.

Mischel, W. (1968). *Personality and assessment.* New York: John Wiley & Sons.

Mischel, W., & Peake, P. K. (1982). Beyond déjà vu in the search for cross-situational consistency. *Psychological Review, 89*, 730–755.

Mitroff, I. I., & Sagasti, F. (1973). Epistemology as general systems theory: An approach to the design of complex decision-making experiments. *Philosophy of Social Science, 3*, 117–134.

Morris, E. K., & Rosen, H. S. (1982). The role of interobserver reliability in the evaluation of graphed data. *Behavioral Assessment, 4*, 387–399.

Morris, R. J., & Kratochwill, T. R. (1983). *Treating children's fears and phobias: A behavioral approach.* New York: Pergamon Press.

Nelson, R. O. (1983). Behavioral assessment: Past, present, and future. *Behavioral Assessment, 5*, 195–206.

Nelson, R. O., Hay, L. R., & Hay, W. M. (1977). Comments on Cone's "The relevance of reliability and validity for behavioral assessment." *Behavior Therapy, 8*, 427–430.

Nelson, R. O., & Hayes, S. C. (1979). Some current dimensions of behavioral assessment. *Behavioral Assessment, 1*, 1–16.

Nelson, R. O., & Hayes, S. C. (1981). Nature of behavioral assessment. In M. Hersen & A. S. Bellack (Eds.), *Behavioral assessment: A practical handbook* (2nd ed., pp. 3–37). New York: Pergamon Press.

Nordheimer, J. (1974, May 28). Experts feel Miss Hearst may have undergone brainwashing. *New York Times*, p. 30.

Nunnally, J. (1978). *Psychometric theory* (2nd ed.). New York: McGraw-Hill.

Paul, G. L., & Lentz, R. J. (1977). *Psychological treatment of chronic mental patients: Milieu versus social-learning programs.* Cambridge, MA: Harvard University Press.

Rachman, S. J., & Wilson, G. T. (1980). *The effects of psychological therapy* (2nd ed.). New York: Pergamon Press.

Rimm, D. C., & Masters, J. C. (1979). *Behavior therapy: Techniques and empirical findings* (2nd ed.). New York: Academic Press.

Spanos, N. P., & Barber, T. X. (1976). Behavior modification and hypnosis. In M. Hersen, R. E. Eisler, & P. M. Miller (Eds.), *Progress in behavior modification* (Vol. 3, pp. 1-44). New York: Academic Press.

Swan, G. E., & MacDonald, M. L. (1978). Behavior therapy in practice: A national survey of behavior therapists. *Behavior Therapy, 9,* 799-807.

Tversky, A., & Kahneman, D. (1974). Judgement under uncertainty: Heuristics and biases. *Science, 185,* 1124-1131.

Voeltz, L. M., & Evans, I. M. (1982). The assessment of behavioral interrelationships in child behavior therapy. *Behavioral Assessment, 4,* 131-166.

Wade, T. C., Baker, T. B., & Hartmann, D. P. (1979). Behavior therapists' self-reported views and practices. *the Behavior Therapist, 2,* 3-6.

Watchel, P. L. (1975). Behavior therapy and the facilitation of psychoanalytic exploration. *Psychotherapy: Theory, Research, and Practice, 12,* 68-72.

Watson, J. B. (1913). Psychology as the behaviorist views it. *Psychological Review, 20,* 158-177.

Wiggins, J. S. (1973). *Personality and prediction: Principles of personality assessment.* Reading, MA: Addison-Wesley.

Wiggins, J. S. (1981). Clinical and statistical prediction: Where are we and where do we go from here? *Clinical Psychology Review, 1,* 3-18.

Wilson, G. T. (1982). Psychotherapy process and procedure: The behavioral mandate. *Behavior Therapy, 13,* 291-312.

Wilson, G. T., & O'Leary, K. D. (1980). *Principles of behavior therapy.* Englewood Cliffs, NJ: Prentice-Hall.

Wolf, M. M. (1978). Social validity: The case for subjective measurement or how applied behavior analysis is finding its heart. *Journal of Applied Behavior Analysis, 11,* 203-214.

4

IDIOGRAPHIC, NOMOTHETIC, AND RELATED PERSPECTIVES IN BEHAVIORAL ASSESSMENT

JOHN D. CONE

West Virginia University

Within psychology generally, and personality theory and assessment more particularly, there has been a long-standing argument over the relative importance of the universal and the unique. Articulating the differences between a psychology dealing with particulars on the one hand, and universals on the other, Allport (1937) referred to the former as "idiographic" and to the latter as "nomothetic." It is well known that Allport urged the pursuit of idiographic approaches to the study of personality, and, indeed, to psychology as a science. "As long as psychology deals only with universals and not with particulars, it won't deal with much" (Allport, 1960, p. 146).

Perhaps nowhere else in psychology is Allport's idiographic perspective more relevant than in the newly emerged subdiscipline of behavioral assessment. Mischel (1968) has observed that "behavioral assessment involves an exploration of the unique or idiosyncratic aspects of the single case, perhaps to a greater extent than any other approach" (p. 190), and Nelson and Hayes (1981) have recently argued that "behavioral assessment is always conducted at an idiographic or individualized level" (Nelson & Hayes, 1981, p. 29), but that certain nomothetic principles can be applied to its conduct. For example, nomothetic principles can be brought to bear on the primary goals of behavioral assessment, which include identifying target behaviors, determining controlling variables, selecting intervention strategies, and evaluating the impact of those strategies (Nelson & Hayes, 1981, p. 29).

NOMOTHETIC

The Greek word *nomos*, from which Windelband (1921) and later Allport (1962) developed the term "nomothetic," means "law." Over the years, nomothetic has been variously used to describe an approach to psychology that is concerned with (1) the discovery of *general laws* and (2) relating *universally applicable variables* in (3) research involving relatively large *numbers of subjects*. Such research may be said to be variable centered since it typically deals with a particular characteristic such as intelligence, depression, obesity, assertion, and so on. The concern is with learning more about the variable, that is, developing general laws relating it to other variables in research which commonly takes the form of correlating differences between persons on a measure of that variable with differences in their standing on some other variable. Persons rated high and low on the Beck Depression Inventory (BDI; Beck, 1972), for example, might be differentially exposed to various dosages of some medication (e.g., lithium carbonate) in order to learn more about the treatment of depression.

IDIOGRAPHIC

The Greek word *idios*, from which Windelband and later Allport (1962) developed the term idiographic, means "one's own, private." To take an idiographic approach to science is to be concerned with uniqueness. In psychology, it is to be concerned with the study of person A *qua* person A; to view person A as a "self-contained universe with its own laws" (Shontz, 1965, p. 244). Idiographic research is person-centered rather than variable-centered. Its concern is not so much with a particular variable or set of variables brought by the scientist, but instead with whatever characteristics are brought by the person (Bem & Allen, 1974). In other words, the psychologist starts at the level of the individual with all of that individual's uniqueness. Moreover, the psychologist does this, whenever possible, devoid of preconceptions developed and nurtured in a nomothetic history.

Unlike its nomothetic counterpart, the idiographic perspective emphasizes the discovery of relationships (laws) among variables uniquely patterned in each person. Moreover, it examines such relationships intensively in research conducted with the individual, obtaining the necessary variation within that person over time rather than between individuals at a single point in time.

PROBLEMS WITH A RIGID DISTINCTION

While these historical differences have been the basis for much of the dialectic in psychology concerning the two perspectives, a close look at the behavior of behavioral assessors, and, indeed, at that of clinicians generally, argues the difficulty of maintaining clear distinctions. It is hard to see, for example, how any one of us could approach a client totally devoid of nomothetically driven preconceptions. We are almost certain to assess the client in terms of a handful of pet characteristics, implicitly or explicity. Additionally, we are almost certain to formulate hypotheses about the client's functioning in terms of things we have learned from experience and "the literature" about relationships ("laws") among those characteristics. Indeed, we are likely to wonder how one could do otherwise and still be of help to the client. Such perplexity is the natural result of our thorough indoctrination in logical-positivist thought, or the "demonstrative" tradition as Rychlak (1977) termed it. Had we an alternative view of the world, such as the dialectical, it might be possible to appreciate how we could do otherwise.

Nonetheless, however useful it has proven historically, a simple nomothetic-idiographic dichotomy seems to offer only a half-opened window for viewing the activities of contemporary behavioral assessors. In addition to the customary characteristics summarized by these two perspectives, there are others that, when considered concurrently, lead to the differentiation of multiple approaches to behavioral assessment that seem to cut across traditional idiographic and nomothetic points of view.

These other dimensions are related to the idiographic-nomothetic distinction, but are not synonymous with it. For example, the distinction between inductive and deductive approaches to science is often associated with the idiographic-nomothetic distinction. It can be considered quite separately, however, as we shall see. To understand contemporary behavioral assessment, and the role of the idiographic-nomothetic distinction in it, a larger context must be established.

A CONTEMPORARY EXAMPLE OF "BEHAVIORAL ASSESSMENT"

To highlight some of the differences among behavioral assessors, let us consider a recent pair of studies conducted and reported by Kupke and colleagues (Kupke, Calhoun, & Hobbs, 1979; Kupke, Hobbs, & Cheney, 1979). The overall thrust of their research was to identify behavior of male college students that might be related to evaluations of their heterosocial competence by female peers. Verbal behaviors conceptualized by Kupke and colleagues as having social reinforcement value were examined. The rationale for their selection was that "interpersonal attraction has been related to the experiencing of reinforcing events" (Kupke, Hobbs, & Cheney, 1979, p. 328). Therefore, reinforcing verbalizations on the part of the males should lead to high ratings of heterosocial competence and attraction.

In the first study (Kupke, Hobbs, & Cheney, 1979), three conversational behaviors ("personal attention," "minimal encourages," and "self-talk") were related via stepwise-multiple regression to ratings of heterosocial competence by females. Only personal attention proved to be significantly related to the ratings. The usefulness of this conversational skill was then evaluated experimentally in the second study (Kupke, Calhoun, & Hobbs, 1979). Three groups of ten males each were trained to increase either personal attention, minimal encourages, or nothing (controls), and changes (pre–post) in their mean interpersonal attraction scores were examined. Only the men trained to increase their use of personal attention showed increases in rated interpersonal attractiveness. Kupke, Calhoun, and Hobbs (1979) concluded that the findings provided "considerable support for the experimental validity of personal attention" (p. 344).

ANALYZING THE EXAMPLES: FIVE QUESTIONS

Let us examine Kupke and colleagues' research in terms of the following five questions:

1. What was its overall purpose?
2. What was its subject matter?
3. What general scientific approach was taken?
4. Where were variations in the subject matter found/or how were they produced?
5. To what extent were currently operative environmental variables considered?

We can see the way idiographic and nomothetic dimensions relate to the general activities of behavioral assessors by examining these five questions. We will follow a specific example, but the implications are meant to apply to all of behavioral assessment.

OVERALL PURPOSE

The general or overall purpose of the research was to study interpersonal attraction. Kupke and colleagues hypothesized that this variable was related to heterosocial competence, such that persons (males in this case) judged more competent would similarly be viewed as more interpersonally attractive. In terms of purpose, then, the research was clearly concerned with a universal variable and not with the men serving as subjects. Moreover, the research was concerned with relationships (laws) among certain variables, and it looked for these in terms of correlations calculated across groups of subjects.

These attributes are sufficient to classify the studies of Kupke and co-workers squarely within the traditional nomothetic perspective. If we were to stop here, however, we would not have considered other important characteristics that might distinguish these studies from others and serve as a basis for pointing out the pluralistic nature of contemporary behavioral assessment.

SUBJECT MATTER

Consider the second question addressed above, that is, the subject matter of Kupke and colleagues' research. Specific, measurable verbal behavior of the male subjects was related to judgments of their interpersonal attractiveness. Thus, behavior was the subject matter of principal interest to these investigators. Within contemporary behavioral assessment, however, it is frequently the case that hypothesized traits or constructs presumed to underlie the behavior are the principal interest, either explicitly or implicitly. For example, much of the research relating cognitive, motor, and physiologic reactions to stressful circumstances is predicated on the assumption that a fear construct knits these reactions together (e.g., Odom, Nelson, & Wein, 1978). The notion that "all assessment systems, including behavioral observation, are based on inferences about some construct which they are assumed to measure" (Haynes, 1978, p. 177) further illustrates the point. (It should be noted that the mere grouping of behaviors on the basis of topographic or functional similarities does not imply an interest in traits or constructs. "Response classes" are nothing more than such groupings until their members are assumed to go together because they are reflective of something more basic, e.g., "fear.")

Whether behavior or traits are the subject matter of interest is of no small consequence. Indeed, there are crucial relationships among the subject matter of assessment, the methods chosen to assess it, and the procedures used to establish the adequacy of these methods (Cone, 1981, 1982; Johnston & Pennypacker, 1980). Thus, when traits and other hypothetical constructs are the subject matter, they are typically viewed as the relatively stable derivatives of early childhood experience which manifest themselves in various ways across a variety of settings. It is legitimate for the methods of the trait assessor to be less direct than those of the behavior assessor since they can be expected only to tap indicators, manifestations, or signs (Goodenough, 1949) of the trait and not the actual trait itself. Hence, the great reliance on verbal self-report measures, the adequacy of which is established via classical psychometric procedures concerned with reliability and validity.

The scientist interested in behavior, however, has a subject matter that is observable directly, and that is typically viewed as stable across time and situations only in proportion to the stability of contemporaneous environmental stimulation. Hence, great reliance is placed on direct observational assessment methods, the adequacy of which is established via attention to their accuracy, that is, their sensitivity to independently verifiable aspects of behavior. Of course, trait assessors sometimes use methods other than self-report, even direct observation, and behavior assessors sometimes use methods other than direct observation, even self-report.

In his discussion of the differences between nomothetic and idiographic approaches, Allport (1962) never distinguished the different subject matters that might be at issue. His own research and theorizing were thoroughly couched in the trait perspective. Other subject matters, however, can easily be considered within the traditional idiographic–nomothetic dialectic. Idiographic approaches can be taken with subject matters other than traits; indeed, much contemporary idiographic research has had behavior as its subject matter. As has already been seen, nomothetic research can also be behavior-oriented. Thus, it is important to examine contemporary behavioral assessment research both in terms of its purpose (i.e., the establishment of general laws among universal variables vs. the study of persons *qua* persons) and its subject matter. In doing this, the traditional idiographic–nomothetic distinction requires augmentation. When we look at the remaining questions posed earlier about Kupke's studies, it becomes even clearer that supplemental considerations can be useful.

SCIENTIFIC APPROACH

For example, given that Kupke studied relationships among specific behaviors for the purpose of formulating general laws, what can be said about the general scientific approach that was taken? Was it the general-to-specific, deductive emphasis characteristic of contemporary psychology or was it the movement-to-movement inductive emphasis characteristic of the experimental analysis of behavior? It seems fair to locate this research squarely within the hypothetico-deductive orientation. Verbal behavior conceptualized as having social reinforcement value was examined because "interpersonal attraction has been related to the experiencing of reinforcing events" (Kupke, Hobbs, & Cheney, 1979, p. 328). In familiar hypothetico–deductive terminology, if interpersonal attraction is related to experiencing reinforcing events, then increases in socially reinforcing verbal behavior should be related to increases in interpersonal attraction. Had Kupke, and colleagues taken an inductive approach, their selection of behavior to assess would not have been driven by such formal theoretical considerations. Instead, they might have taken a broader survey of behavior potentially related to interpersonal attraction. Successive analyses of an initially large pool of content would have produced smaller and smaller sets of behavior having progressively stronger relationships to attraction.

There may appear to be a natural affinity between an idiographic approach to assessment and inductive scientific strategy. Allport (1962) seemed to prefer inductive tactics, saying that "we should take the patient's own story as a starting point," avoiding the tendency to redact "this story into general categories, dismembering the complex pattern of the life into standard dimensions (abilities, needs, interest inventories, and the like)" (p. 413). Much earlier, another proponent of idiographic analyses warned against selecting target behaviors from universal lists, for example, inventories, because they can destroy "all possibility of discovering the unique characteristics of the single personality" (Baldwin, 1942, p. 170).

Nevertheless, classifying research such as that of Kupke and colleagues as nomothetic or idiographic would tell us little of its general scientific approach as it is being considered here. Certainly an idiographic analysis could be pursued deductively (e.g., Shapiro, 1961), just as a nomothetic one could be pursued inductively (e.g., Shontz, 1965). This is an extremely important distinction in the practice of clinical assessment, generally, and behavioral assessment, specifically.

There are dangers attending a deductive approach to behavioral assessment, especially when applied with individual clients. One is the tendency for the prior formulation of general categories to shut off or constrain further investigation. If the individual assessor always examines clients exclusively in terms of a set of favorite constructs or behaviors (e.g., as represented in a given inventory or battery of assessment devices), the discovery of important behavior not included in the set and of relationships between that behavior and relevant controlling stimuli can be discouraged.

It is probably not possible to take a wholly inductive approach to assessment because this would require that we release ourselves totally from our preconceptions. We could, however, achieve a much closer approximation given our present level of methodological sophistication and the technology available. In clinical work, an inductive perspective is important at many steps in the assessment process, from selecting items to include in initial screening, reducing these to intervention targets, monitoring change in the targets over time, and interpreting the outcome of our intervention strategy. Often we use deductive methods when inductive methods would be more desirable. Deductive groupings of items based on theoretical predilections rather than groupings based on empirically established covariations among the items over time are one example. Techniques to accomplish such empirical groupings have been available for some time. As early as 1942, Baldwin developed personal structure analysis as an informal, cluster-analytic-like way of grouping content on the basis of relative frequency and temporal contiguity. More recently, Wahler and colleagues have used correlational procedures to examine the structure of direct observations of multiple behaviors as they vary within and between persons over time and across settings (Kara & Wahler, 1977; Lichtstein & Wahler, 1976; Wahler, 1975; Wahler & Fox, 1980).

Most clinical assessment remains firmly wedded to deductive methods, however. For example, Shapiro (1961) used a deductive approach to grouping client-relevant content that he had initially developed using relatively inductive procedures. After using a standardized interview to develop a list of "symptoms" in the client's own words, Shapiro discussed these with the client's therapist and they interviewed the client jointly to clarify any questions about the nature of the symptoms. A rating scale for each symptom was then developed and used repeatedly over the course of intervention. In one example with a 28-year-old female, 20 items were monitored for 9 weeks. The items were grouped on a rational basis into six dimensions (e.g., hostility, depression, delusions of reference), and improvement was plotted in terms of the *average* score for each of these. Whether the individual items would have arranged themselves differently had groupings been allowed to emerge empirically cannot be determined. Other investigators (e.g., Block & Bennett, 1955; Nunnally, 1955; Pervin, 1977; Voeltz & Evans, 1979) have used factor analysis to produce such empirical groupings.

One major problem with the use of deduction at this stage of assessment is that our language will limit the available categories to be seen. There is overwhelming evidence that the structure of ratings by others is largely the result of the linguistic structures carried about in the heads of the rater (Mischel, 1968). That is to say, the grouping of various characteristics is more likely to reflect the semantics of the rater's language than any inherent arrangement in the person(s) being rated (cf. D'Andrade, 1965; Norman & Goldberg, 1966; Passini & Norman, 1966). This evidence, in combination with data showing that directly observed behaviors group themselves differently between persons and even within persons from one situation to another (Wahler, 1975), supports the conclusion that rational groupings are less desirable than empirical ones at this early stage in the development of behavioral assessment.[1] (For an extensive review of literature on the interrelationships among responses in behavioral assesssment interested readers should consult Voeltz & Evans, 1982). In fact, given evidence that early

---

1. It should be noted that other research has found some consistency in factors derived from direct observations of individual subjects, however (Evans & Voeltz, 1980; Harris, 1980; Kara & Wahler, 1977; Strain & Ezzell, 1978).

categorizations constrain our observations to events that fit these categories (e.g., Rubin & Shontz, 1960), and evidence that such organizations once established are relatively immutable (e.g., Meehl, 1960), it is likely that such deductively driven a priori formulations will be less sensitive to the changing behavior of individual clients than would inductively driven, empirical formulations.

It would seem, therefore, that an inductive approach to the initial *selection* of item content (which is fairly common clinically—e.g., in a clinical interview) could be followed most fruitfully by an empirical or inductive approach to *grouping* it into manageable categories. Selecting intervention targets from within these categories can also be achieved inductively on the basis of systematic relationships among category members (e.g., select the behavior having the highest correlations with others in the group). This approach is similar to the "keystone behavior" strategy suggested by Nelson (1984). Alternatively, items showing the strongest relationship to therapeutic procedures (as tried out in mini, pretherapy manipulations) could be targeted. Still another approach would be to select those behaviors shown to have the highest correlations with relevant extra therapy variables such as job performance, marital interactions, and so on. Interested readers should consult the series of articles on target behavior selection appearing in a recent issue of *Behavioral Assessment* (Evans, 1984; Kanfer, 1984; Kazdin, 1984; Kratochwill, 1984; Mash, 1984).

Once initial item content has been selected and categorized, and intervention targets have been selected, monitoring of those targets over time will be important. Change in these targets and perhaps in more general variables not specifically targeted will need to be examined to assess the outcome of the intervention effort. Again, as at the earlier stages, intervention can proceed in an inductive manner, with decisions controlled by changes in the targets, or it can proceed deductively, with decisions controlled by prior formulations of the therapist. These, in turn, are the product of more or less formalized theoretical predilections concerning relationships between client variables and various therapeutic maneuvers.

In summary, whether one's general approach to science is inductive or deductive can have a bearing on decisions made at various points in the assessment process. Together with purpose and subject matter, scientific approach can lead to important distinctions within behavioral assessment. With respect to Kupke and co-workers' research, it has been shown that its purpose was primarily nomothetic in that it was variable-focused and sought general laws relating that variable to others. Specific behavior was studied (as contrasted with traits or other hypothetical constructs), and the research was conducted within the hypothetico–deductive scientific tradition.

SOURCE OF VARIATION

Another important difference in the literature on behavioral assessment is the source of variation used in examining relationships among the variables of interest. Within psychology it is possible to differentiate two major approaches to obtaining the necessary variation: (1) differences *between* persons can be related to other variables of interest; and (2) differences *within* persons can be related to other variables. Chassan (1967) has referred to the study of between-person differences in the context of "extensive" designs; the study of within-person differences in the context of "intensive" designs. An interesting historical account of these perspectives is presented by Hersen and Barlow (1976).

The experimental tradition in psychology has consistently viewed differences between persons as error variance to be controlled and/or partialed out of research on the relationships between independent and dependent variables. The principal source of variation for investigators in this tradition has been between groups of individuals. Differences between persons have been viewed as meaningful and worthy of study in their own right by researchers more aligned with the correlational–descriptive, individual difference tradition (Cronbach, 1957).

Experimental psychologists have not sought the necessary variation exclusively between groups, however. A minority, largely under the rubric of the experimental analysis of behavior, has acknowledged the value of intensive study of individual or small numbers of subjects over time. In recent years, research designs have been refined so that increasingly stonger conclusions can be drawn about the relationships between independent and dependent variables (Barlow, Hayes, & Nelson, 1984; Hersen & Barlow, 1976; Kazdin, 1982; Kratochwill, 1978; Sidman, 1960). For such experimentalists, variation within subjects is seen as a window through which to examine lawful relationships between these variables. For them, behavioral variability is likely to be viewed as extrinsic and therefore largely controllable by the careful manipulation of environmental events.

Kupke, Hobbs, and Cheney (1979) chose to study differences among their male subjects in certain verbal behavior and related these in a stepwise multiple regression formula to differences between the subjects in terms of ratings given them by female confederates. Behavior shown to be correlated with the ratings was subsequently manipulated, and changes in the ratings were examined in terms of mean differences between groups of men. (Kupke, Calhoun, & Hobbs, 1979). Alternatively, Kupke and colleagues could have studied one or a small group of men intensively as their performance of the relevant behavior varied over time. Covariation between this behavior and ratings of interpersonal attraction also collected over time would establish the validity of the former.

This distinction has a bearing on the difference between idiographic and nomothetic perspectives. Idiographic research would probably most often examine changes within a person over time. Yet the two are not synonymous. Within-person variability could be examined nomothetically, for example (Harris, 1980).

ENVIRONMENTAL INFLUENCES

Finally, having considered overall purpose, subject matter, scientific approach, and whether between- or within-subject variability was studied, the extent to which environmental variables are given prominence in the research can be examined. It is probably safe to assert that most behavioral assessors consider their research to be interactionist. In that way, they are comparable to their counterparts in the personality assessment area (e.g., Bem & Funder, 1978; Bowers, 1973; Endler & Magnusson, 1976; Magnusson & Ekehammer, 1975). Behavioral assessment has consistently emphasized the need to assess environmental characteristics as well as behavior (Nelson & Hayes, 1979).

There is incomplete agreement on the extent and methods for considering environmental influences, however. At one extreme, behavioral assessors have sometimes merely described objective topographic features of behaviors without explicit reference to or actual assessment of environmental characteristics. At other times, simple description of behavior and antecedent and consequent stimuli has been considered sufficient. Finally, the establishment of functional relationships among behavioral and environmental variables has frequently been undertaken.

In addition to its active influence on behavior, the environment can be seen as a relatively passive source of information about the clients/subjects being assessed. An example is Nunnally's (1955) idiographic analysis of the self-concept of a single client as it changed over the course of therapy. The client Q-sorted a set of 60 descriptive statements specific to her. These statements had been distilled from the material of 12 clinical interviews, a variety of projective tests, and interviews with friends and relatives of the client. The environment (i.e., friends and relatives) contributed relevant information for the assessment. The outcome of therapy was evaluated in terms of the client's self-reports alone, however, and no systematic manipulation of environmental variables occurred.

In contrast, though the initial behavior in Kupke, Hobbs, and Cheney's

(1979) research was determined deductively from formal theoretical concepts, it was subsequently validated in correlations with environmental variables (e.g., judgments by female confederates). Further validation was established experimentally by manipulating the behavior of the subjects and examining its impact on the environment (i.e., confederates' judgments).

The systematic inclusion of environmental input is typical of research in applied behavior analysis (Baer, Wolf, & Risley, 1968). In one example, Madson, Becker, Thomas, Koser, and Plager (1968) examined the possibility that teachers might be contributing adversely to the very behavior of their students they wanted to change. In an ABABC time series design the frequency of teacher "sit down" commands given to first graders was systematically varied over the first four phases of the study. It was clearly demonstrated that when teachers increased their rate of commanding students to sit down (in the B phases) *more* students rather then fewer were found to be out of their seats. Eliminating "sit down" commands and instituting praise for sitting in the final (C) phase resulted in the fewest children out of their seats. Thus, a functional relationship was established between student behavior and the environmental variable comprised of the teachers' reactions to it.

Each of the examples above represents a different approach to the use of environmental input in the assessment process. Nunnally (1955) used it to establish initial assessment content, but then made no further reference to environmental input. Kupke and colleagues (1979) made no use of it in establishing initial assessment content, but they validated that content against subsequent changes in the social environment of their subjects. Madsen *et al.* (1968) used one type of environmental input (i.e., teacher complaints) to establish initial assessment content, and another (i.e., teacher commands) to bring about change in a behavior pinpointed from that content. Obviously the environment can be used in multiple ways and at different points in the assessment process.

At the same time, it is conceivable (if not desirable) that a behavioral assessor might not rely on environmental input at all. Thus, initial content might be restricted solely to client verbalizations and/or a set of descriptive statements routinely used by the assessor. Intervention targets might similarly derive from an analysis of the verbalizations or descriptive statements, and an intervention might be designed, implemented, and evaluated without any reference to extra therapy variables. Of course, a behavioral assessor pursuing such a course could argue that the relevant environmental variables are those within the assessment/therapeutic context, and that consideration of these thereby renders the perspective he or she uses an interactionist one. This may be a defensible point, but certainly most behavioral assessors look outside the assessment/therapy context for both the content to assess and the environmental variables against which to validate the content and the impact of subsequent interventions.

The point is that there are different ways in which environmental considerations can have an inpact on the work of behavioral assessors. It is not enough to say a behavioral assessor *considers* the influence of environmental events. *When* they are considered and *how* is likely to vary across and perhaps even within assessors, making the quality of their interactionist position an important difference between them.

SUMMARY

The purpose of considering answers to the five questions posed of the research of Kupke and colleagues was to illustrate that several dimensions are available for characterizing the activities of contemporary behavioral assessors. The customary idiographic–nomothetic dialectic is a starting point, but it cannot be adequately understood without describing several related but distinct dimensions. The issues of overall purpose, subject matter, scientific approach, source of variability, and type and timing of environmental input seem to take us further toward understanding what behavioral assessors do. Indeed, the simultaneous consideration of these five characteristics can even be used to produce a scheme for classifying different approaches to behavioral assessment, described briefly in the final section of this chapter.

TYPES OF BEHAVIORAL ASSESSMENT

The juxtaposition of each dimension with every other one is represented in Figure 4-1. In terms of the theme of this chapter, this scheme highlights the diversity within contemporary behavioral assessment. It is easy to see that the traditional emphasis on persons *qua* persons of the idiographic focus can be further differentiated into concern with behavior on the one hand, or traits on the other. (Incidentally, dichotomous dimensions have been used for ease of illustration. It is quite possible that more than two values could be distinguished rather meaningfully for some of these dimensions.) The former might be referred to as behavioral idiography and the latter as trait idiography. Similarly, behavioral and trait nomography could be identified.

It should also be apparent that behavioral or trait idiography (nomography) can be further differentiated in terms of the relative emphasis on deductive versus inductive approaches to science, and whether scientific knowledge is developed on the basis of variability within persons on the one

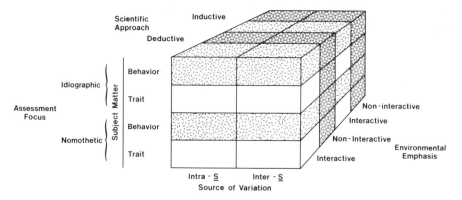

FIG. 4-1. Models of behavioral assessment research.

hand, or between them on the other. In other words, there is a logical constellation of related concepts that surrounds the idiographic/nomothetic distinction. These are not simply direct extensions of the traditional use of the distinction because it is possible to be idiographically oriented (in the traditional sense) and still be trait-oriented or deductive. Nevertheless, it is tempting to define preferred types of assessment within this framework and to suggest that behavioral assessment would be better off if everyone practiced it. The purest form of idiography might be one that studied behavior inductively as it varied over time within individuals. The purest form of nomography might be one that studied traits or other hypothetical constructs deductively as they varied between individuals at a given point in time. In this sense, behavioral assessment could probably benefit from a purer form of idiography than is usually practiced. Much of the current work in behavioral assessment is relatively pure nomography.

In case this all seems rather pedantic, abstract, theoretical, and irrelevant to behavioral assessment as currently practiced, it might be instructive to see how far we get with efforts to classify the research of Kupke and associates (1979) discussed above. We have already noted that the research was designed to study the variable of interpersonal attaction by examining specific behavior as it related to judgments of attractions. The approach was deductive, and general laws relating behavior to attraction were established in terms of variation between subjects. Environmental input was used to establish the validity of the specific behaviors studied. Thus, in terms of the model presented in Figure 4-1, Kupke and associates' research would be classified in the cross-hatched block on the right hand side, third row from the top on the front of the figure.

Now, suppose Kupke and colleagues had been clinicians in private practice concerned with thoroughly understanding the behavior of an individual client complaining of poor heterosocial relationships. Rather than deduce behaviors to assess based on theoretical speculations about interpersonal attraction being related to experiencing reinforcing events, Kupke and colleagues might have taken a broader-reaching, more inductive survey of the behaviors functionally related to heterosocial relationships of the client himself. The client might have been observed interacting with several different women of the type he found interesting. Narrative recordings of client and confederate behavior might have been analyzed for systematic, recurring sequences or patterns of interaction. These might then have been studied for functional relationships between client behavior and desirable confederate responses. Behaviors showing these relationships (and for which the client was deficient) would be targeted for intervention.

Having taken such an orientation, the research of Kupke and co-workers would be classified as "pure idiographic" or idiographic in a natural science perspective. In terms of the model, it would be located in the cross-hatched block just to the left of the previous one in Figure 4-1. It is possible that one may practice idiographic assessment with other than a natural science perspective, of course. In fact, most of the idiographic literature to date has had its theoretical foundation in alternative perspectives. It is also possible to practice idiographic *behavioral* assessment from other than a natural science point of view, but the very strong arguments for adopting the natural science viewpoint when behavior is the subject matter weigh heavily in its favor (cf., Bijou & Baer, 1961; Johnston & Pennypacker, 1980; Skinner, 1938, 1953). .

As with its traditional, trait-oriented forebearer, it could no doubt be argued that "pure" idiographic behavioral assessment is simple scientific "vagrancy" (Eysenck, 1954), has little value "in confirmatory aspects of scientific activity" (Kiesler, 1971, p. 66), and belongs more to history, art, or biography (Allport, 1961). Indeed, much of the application of the idiographic–nomothetic dialectic of psychology, generally, to behavioral assessment, specifically, will be viewed by some as nothing more than old wine in a new bottle. It is hoped, however, that the conceptual scheme represented in Figure 4-1 will take the discussion beyond the either/or arguments characteristic of much of the general discussion to date.

The example of the Kupke and colleagues studies should be illustrative of the inadequacies of classifying assessment practices into simple categories such as behavioral versus traditional, idiographic versus nomothetic, and so on. At this point in its development, there is not a unitary body of knowledge distinguishing the behavioral assessment literature from others. Most of us would probably classify the studies of Kupke and associates as examples of behavioral assessment despite the fact that, except for their concern with behavior, they are indistinguishable from traditional assessment practices. It seems of value to recognize more explicitly the pluralistic nature of the field and to call attention to meaningful differences in the diverse practices presently lodged therein. There is not one behavioral assessment; there are many. Perhaps a volume on conceptual foundations such as this will help sharpen the differences and lead to clearer definitions and ultimately to more rapid advancement of the field.

REFERENCES

Allport, G. W. (1937). *Personality: A psychological interpretation.* New York: Holt.

Allport, G. W. (1960). *Personality and social encounter.* Boston: Beacon Press.

Allport, G. W. (1961). *Pattern and growth in personality.* New York: Holt, Rinehart & Winston.

Allport, G. W. (1962). The general and the unique in psychological science. *Journal of Personality 34,* 405–422.

Baer, D. M., Wolf, M. M., & Risley, T. R. (1968). Some current dimensions of applied behavior analysis. *Journal of Applied Behavior Analysis, 1,* 91–97.

Baldwin, A. L. (1942). Personal structure analysis: A statistical method for investigation of the single personality. *Journal of Abnormal and Social Psychology, 37,* 163–183.

Barlow, D. H., Hayes, S. C., & Nelson, R. O. (1984). *The scientist practitioner: Research and accountability in clinical and educational settings.* New York: Pergamon Press.

Beck, A. T. (1972). *Depression: Causes and treatment.* Philadelphia: University of Pennsylvania Press.

Bem, D. J., & Allen, A. (1974). On predicting some of the people some of the time: The search for cross-situational consistencies in behavior. *Psychological Review, 81,* 506–520.

Bem, D. J., & Funder, D. C. (1978). Predicting more of the people more of the time: Assessing the personality of situations. *Psychological Review, 85,* 485–501.

Bijou, S. W., & Baer, D. M. (1961). *Child development (Vol. 1). A systematic and empirical theory.* New York: Appleton-Century-Crofts.

Block, J., & Bennett, L. (1955). The assessment of communications: III. Perception and transmission as a function of the social situation. *Human Relations, 8,* 317–325.

Bowers, K. S. (1973). Situationism in psychology: An analysis and a critique. *Psychological Review, 80,* 307–336.

Chassan, J. B. (1967). *Research design in clinical psychology and psychiatry.* New York: Appleton-Century-Crofts.

Cone, J. D. (1981). Psychometric considerations. In M. Hersen & A. S. Bellack (Eds.), *Behavioral assessment: A practical handbook* (2nd ed., pp. 38–68). New York: Pergamon Press.

Cone, J. D. (1982). Validity of direct observation assessment procedures. In D. P. Hartmann (Ed.), *New directions for methodology of behavioral science: Using observers to study behavior.* (pp. 67–79). San Francisco: Jossey-Bass.

Cronbach, L. J. (1957). The two disciplines of scientific psychology. *American Psychologist, 12,* 671–684.

D'Andrade, R. G. (1965). Trait psychology and componential analysis. *American Anthropologist, 67,* 215–228.

Endler, N. S., & Magnusson, D. (1976). Toward an interactional psychology of personality. *Psychological Bulletin, 83,* 956–974.

Evans, I. M. (1984). Building systems models as a strategy for target behavior selection in clinical assessment. *Behavioral Assessment, 7,* 21–32.

Evans, I. M., & Voeltz, L. M. (1980). "Developing empirical criteria for the selection of priority target behaviors in severely handicapped preschool children." Paper presented at the meeting of the American Association of Mental Deficiency, San Francisco, May.

Eysenck, H. J. (1954). The science of personality: Nomothetic! *Psychological Review, 61,* 339–342.

Goodenough, F. L. (1949). *Mental testing.* New York: Rinehart.

Harris, Jr., J. G. (1980). Nomovalidation and idiovalidation: quest for the true personality profile. *American Psychologist, 35,* 729–744.

Haynes, S. N. (1978). *Prinicples of behavioral assessment.* New York: Gardner Press.

Hersen, M., & Barlow, D. H. (1976). *Single case experimental designs.* New York: Pergamon Press.

Johnston, J. M., & Pennypacker, H. S. (1980). *Strategies and tactics of human behavioral research.* Hillsdale, NJ: Lawrence Erlbaum.

Kanfer, F. H. (1984). Target selection for clinical change programs. *Behavioral Assessment, 7,* 7–20.

Kara, A., & Wahler, R. G. (1977). Organizational features of a young child's behaviors. *Journal of Experimental Child Psychology, 24,* 24–39.

Kazdin, A. E. (1982). Single-case experimental designs. In P. C. Kendall & J. N. Butcher (Eds.), *Handbook of research methods in clinical psychology,* (pp. 461–490). New York: John Wiley & Sons.

Kazdin, A. E. (1984). Selection of target behaviors: The relationship of the treatment focus to clinical dysfunction. *Behavioral Assessment, 7,* 33–47.

Kiesler, D. J. (1971). Experimental designs in psychotherapy research. In A. E. Bergin & S. L. Garfield (Eds.), *Handbook of psychotherapy and behavior change* (pp. 36–74). New York: John Wiley & Sons.

Kratochwill, T. R. (Ed.) (1978). *Single subject research: Strategies for evaluating change.* New York: Academic Press.

Kratochwill, T. R. (1984). Selection of target behaviors in behavioral consultation. *Behavioral Assessment, 7,* 49–61.

Kupke, T. E., Calhoun, K. S., & Hobbs, S. A. (1979). Selection of heterosocial skills. II. Experimental validity. *Behavior Therapy, 10,* 336–346.

Kupke, T. E., Hobbs, S. A., & Cheney, T. H. (1979). Selection of heterosocial skills: I. Criterion-related validity. *Behavior Therapy, 10,* 327–335.

Lichstein, K. L., & Wahler, R. G. (1976). The ecological assessment of an autistic child. *Journal of Abnormal Child Psychology, 4,* 31–54.

Madsen, Jr., C. H., Becker, W. C., Thomas, D. R., Koser, L., & Plager, E. (1968). An analysis of the reinforcing function of "sit down" commands. In R. K. Parker (Ed.), *Readings in educational psychology* (pp. 265–278). Boston: Allyn & Bacon.

Magnusson, D., & Ekehammer, B. (1975). Perceptions of and reactions to stressful situations. *Journal of Personality and Social Psychology, 31,* 1147–1154.

Mash, E. J. (1984). Some comments on target selection in behavior therapy. *Behavioral Assessment, 7,* 63–78.

Meehl, P. E. (1960). The cognitive activity of the clinician. *American Psychologist 15,* 19–27.

Mischel, W. *Personality and assessment.* (1968). New York: John Wiley & Sons.

Nelson, R. O. (1984, November). *Is behavioral assessment the missing link between diagnosis and treatment?* Unpublished paper presented at the meeting of the Association for the Advancement of Behavior Therapy, Philadelphia.

Nelson, R. O., & Hayes, S. C. (1979). Some current dimensions of behavioral assessment. *Behavioral Assessment, 1,* 1–16.

Nelson, R. O., & Hayes, S. C. (1981). An overview of behavioral assessment. In M. Hersen & A. S. Bellack (Eds.), *Behavioral assessment: A practical handbook* (2nd ed., pp. 3–37). New York: Pergamon Press.

Norman, W. T., & Goldberg, L. R. (1966). Raters, ratees, and randomness in personality structure. *Journal of Personality and Social Psychology, 4,* 681–691.

Nunnally, J. C. (1955). An investigation of some propositions of self-conception: The case of Miss Sun. *Journal of Abnormal and Social Psychology, 50,* 87–92.

Odom, J. V., Nelson, R. O., & Wein, K. S. (1978). The differential effectiveness of five treatment procedures on three response systems in a snake phobia analog study. *Behavior Therapy, 9*, 936–942.

Passini, F. T., & Norman, W. T. (1966). A universal conception of personality structure? *Journal of Personality and Social Psychology, 4*, 44–49.

Pervin, L. (1977). The representative design of person-situation research. In D. Magnusson & N. S. Endler (Eds.), *Personality at the crossroads: Current issues in interactional psychology* (pp. 371–384). Hillsdale, NJ: Lawrence Erlbaum.

Rubin, M., & Shontz, F. C. (1960). Diagnostic prototypes and diagnostic processes of clinical psychologists. *Journal of Consulting Psychology, 24*, 234–239.

Rychlak, J. F. (1977). *The psychology of rigorous humanism*. New York: John Wiley & Sons.

Shapiro, M. B. (1961). A method of measuring psychological changes specific to the individual psychiatric patient. *British Journal of Medical Psychology, 34*, 151–155.

Shontz, F. C. (1965). *Research methods in personality*. New York: Appleton-Century-Crofts.

Sidman, M. (1960). *Tactics of scientific research: Evaluating experimental data in psychology*. New York: Basic Books.

Skinner, B. F. (1938). *The behavior of organisms*. New York: Appleton-Century-Crofts.

Skinner, B. F. (1953). *Science and human behavior*. New York: Macmillan.

Strain, P. S., & Ezzell, D. (1978). The sequence and distribution of behavioral disordered adolescents' disruptive inappropriate behaviors: An observational study in a residential setting. *Behavior Modification, 2*, 403–425.

Voeltz, L. M., & Evans, I. M. (1979, August). Covariation of behavior in a preschool handicapped child with multiple behavior problems. Unpublished paper presented at the Fifth International Congress of the International Association for the Scientific Study of Mental Deficiency, Jerusalem, Israel.

Voeltz, L. M., & Evans, I. M. (1982). The assessment of behavioral interrelationships in child behavior therapy. *Behavioral Assessment, 4*, 131–165.

Wahler, R. G. (1975). Some structural aspects of deviant child behavior. *Journal of Applied Behavior Analysis, 8*, 27–42.

Wahler, R. G., & Fox, III, J. J. (1980). Solitary toy play and time out: A family treatment package for aggressive and oppositional children. *Journal of Applied Behavior Analysis, 13*, 23–39.

Windelband, W. (1921). *An introduction to philosophy* (J. McCabe, Trans.). London: Unwin.

II

A BEHAVIORAL VIEW
OF PERSONALITY

5

RESPONSE STRUCTURE AND THE TRIPLE-RESPONSE-MODE CONCEPT

IAN M. EVANS

University Center at Binghamton, State University of New York

The relationship among responses within individual behavioral repertoires has been a relatively neglected topic in behavioral assessment research and theory. Using the word "neglect" implies a worth that is unappreciated—and in a systematic review of the child behavior modification literature, Voeltz and Evans (1982) documented that the issue is deserving of serious clinical attention. We showed just how frequently interventions supposedly directed toward single-target "problem" behaviors actually resulted in widespread consequences for the client, resulting in change in both positive behaviors (collateral benefits) and negative behaviors (side effects). Although behavior therapy research has predominantly represented both problems and outcomes in terms of levels of single, isolated responses, the implicit acceptance of response structures is abundantly evident. Recent examples might be Wahler's concept of the "keystone" behavior (see Wahler & Fox, 1982) and resurgent interest in the syndrome as a construct (Kazdin, 1982) that implies covariation of certain characteristic behaviors.

In fact, the topic of response relationships emerges in so many different forms and guises in behavior theory that the lack of appreciation is not so much for response covariation per se, but for its methodological underpinnings and theoretical implications. Theoretical models determine the basic nature of response organization hypothesized, and methodological conventions pose limits for the types of organization that can be observed. The purpose of this chapter is to elaborate on these two issues and examine their significance for one of the more popular response relationship concepts in behavioral assessment, the notion that there are three broad response systems, or "modes" discernible in human conduct. In the process, I will show that the underlying conceptual questions are rather fundamental ones, pertaining to the derivation of behavioral constructs and the endowment of our empirical observations with order and regularity through the assignment of discrete events to behavioral classes and to superordinate categories (fear, assertion, relaxation, aggression, and so on).

THE TRIPLE-RESPONSE MODE

The tripartite distinction among response systems began innocently enough
with a needed and heuristic reminder by Lang (1968) that as a construct *fear*
embraced response changes in three measurement modes—verbal, overt
motor, and somatic. Typically, correlations among measures obtained in
different modes were low. As there was no justification for considering one
mode primary, or more true than the others, the assessment of fear, it was
argued, should incorporate variables derived from each mode. Lang was at
pains to emphasize that the response systems are very much influenced by
each other, but that they can vary independently.

THE THREE RESPONSE MODES AS A TAXONOMY

From this beginning the model was quickly expanded in a number of directions. Most notable of these is the acceptance of Lang's categories as the
three fundamental categories for describing or classifying all behavioral
measures. Thus in their authoritative statement on the nature of behavioral
assessment, Nelson and Hayes (1979) comment: "Behavioral assessment also
includes [in addition to overt motor behavior] the measurement of physiological–emotional behavior and cognitive–verbal behavior" (p. 3). Most behavioral assessment texts (e.g., Nay, 1979) describe with approval the three
systems of cognitive, motoric, and psychophysiologic events. Mischel (1981)
writes: "We must consider what people do cognitively and affectively, not
just motorically" (p. 484).

    Descriptively, then, the three categories and the implicit divisions be-
tween them have been widely accepted in the field. As an organizational
model, however, it has certain drawbacks. For one thing, the boundaries
between the categories are arbitrary and (as can be seen from the terms
quoted above) often unclear; is speech, for example, a motor activity or a
cognitive one? Some modes are easily misinterpreted. For instance, the
cognitive mode cannot be equated with the subjective experience of an
emotion (Kozak & Miller, 1982). Furthermore, the three groups do not
coincide with physiologic realities—the anatomic distinctions made between
effector systems are usually the skeletal muscle system, the autonomic
nervous system, and the hormonal system. Also, other more comprehensive
categories have been proposed but given much less attention, such as
Staats' (1975) division of personality repertoires into the following general
systems: emotional–motivational, sensorimotor, and language–cognitive. As
Burns (1980) indicated, these three are conceptually quite different from the
conventional triple-response modes and they focus assessment on various

basic behavioral repertoires underlying each system. These repertoires typically involve skill interactions such as verbal–motor repertoires, or image–word repertoires (see Chapter 8, this volume).

A final, practical limitation as an organizational principle becomes obvious when one considers phenomena other than anxiety. Clinical concerns such as child behavior problems, drug addictions, or organic brain syndromes, for example, cannot be neatly divided into *equivalent* motor, cognitive, or physiologic components. Hence, assigning *equal* status or significance to the three categories seems inappropriate as a general rubric for clinical assessment.

THE TRIPLE-RESPONSE MODE AS AN EXPLANATORY CONCEPT

A second major direction in which the triple-response mode has been taken is to retain the specific focus on anxiety/fear measurement, but to elaborate on the explanatory rather than the taxonomic value of the concept. This approach is best exemplified by the work of Rachman and associates (Rachman, 1978). Rachman and Hodgson (1974; see also Hodgson & Rachman, 1974) have emphasized the lack of correspondence between overt avoidance behavior and other, typically autonomic, indices of fear. They made a distinction between discordance (low correlations between measures at a particular point in time) and desynchrony (low correlations between change scores), and went on to suggest circumstances under which separation would be most likely. For instance, they argued that discordance will be least evident during intense emotional arousal. Discordance will increase when there are unusual extraneous influences acting on a particular measure; a good illustration of these latter circumstances would be Bernstein's (1973) demonstration that subjects in direct avoidance tests could be persuaded through social pressure to approach a phobic object which they still reported fearing intensely. A third influence on discordance and desynchrony that Rachman and Hodgson proposed is the type of therapeutic intervention, so that synchrony itself could perhaps be seen as a desirable long-term dependent variable for treatment.

Whatever merits Rachman's (1978) argument has as a model of fear and emotional behavior, its implications for assessment are controversial. On the one hand, Eysenck (1979) asserted that the theory represents a "powerful guide in the selection of measuring instruments" (p. 83) for the evaluation of behavior therapy. Cone (1979) on the other hand, has seriously questioned the evidence for synchrony/desynchrony on the grounds that comparisons of measures representing different behavior "modes" are confounded with the different methods of measurement used in each case; that is, it is the method, not the mode, that may account for the existing evidence of low correlations. To determine the impact of method variance, Cone (1979) proposed an ingenious modification of the Campbell and Fiske (1959) multi-trait–multimethod matrix, with behaviors substituted for traits and an added dimension, "content," to represent the three modes.

To illustrate his argument, Cone (1979) provided a simplified matrix that has two modes or contents (motor and physiologic), two methods (self-report and direct observation), and four behaviors, two within each content, that can be measured either by self-report or direct observation. The example assumes that the response "perspire," for instance, falls within the physiologic *content* system and can be measured by self-report *methods* ("I often perspire") or direct observational *methods* ("He or she is perspiring"). It is certainly reasonable to consider perspiring a psychophysiologic response, yet content and method have been so confounded in previous work that self-reported perspiration would probably be classified by most investigators as a cognitive variable. Traditionally, the physiologic system would be represented only by direct electrophysiologic monitoring of a phenomenon such as perspiring. Thus while Cone's (1979) reformulation is an important conceptual advance, it does not closely match the conventional tripartite divisions.

Kaloupek and Levis (1983) have also presented a case for considering desynchrony to be largely an issue of measurement artifact and not a true phenomenon. One of the concerns is that of a scaling problem: if anxiety is considered a hypothetical construct, such theorizing would suggest that change in one "channel" would be accompanied by changes in the other, but not necessarily of an equivalent magnitude (in terms of scale scores). Therefore, different individuals' rank orders of magnitude for each measure would alter with any general change and so correlations across individuals will be low. Furthermore, there are often differences in procedures and stimulus conditions that produce uncontrolled variance. If a subject is asked to estimate, after a fear-arousing situation, the amount of increase in heartbeat rate, that self-report will reflect memory of the situation in addition to the actual heart rate that might have been recorded physiologically at the time.

If different measures of "anxiety"—or any other hypothetical construct—correlated perfectly, then the measures would be redundant. Kaloupek and Levis (1980) have also made this observation in their criticism of the desynchrony position; in other words we should not *expect* different measures of anxiety to correlate. Hugdahl (1981) elaborates on this as a logical problem. If three measurement components do not correlate (are not redundant or interchangeable) then they must be measuring at least somewhat different things. If any one measure can stand alone as representing the phenomenon of interest, then how do we know that we are not simply measuring three different emotions or three different phenomena, rather than the subcomponents of one unitary entity? This conceptual dilemma reflects certain implicit assumptions regarding personality constructs and their measurement, and so it is to this topic that we should now turn.

BEHAVIORAL CONSTRUCTS

In classic personality measurement theory, a construct represents a hypothesis that a variety of behaviors will correlate with one another in studies of individual differences and/or will be similarly affected by experimental treatments (i.e., the internal consistency of the construct). It is obvious that behavioral assessment uses constructs and that no science of behavior or model of behavioral measurement could exist without so doing. As Messick (1981) has argued, however, social behaviorists "do not so much eschew constructs as they do the attribution of [causality to] traits" (p. 582). As behaviorists we try to reduce our natural tendency to give reality status to a construct by suffixing as much as possible with the term "behavior"—much to the misery of the field's *litterati*. Thus, *assertive behavior* seems less likely to result in our explaining a particular response by reference to the hypothetical entity *assertiveness*, but it is equally a construct in which such diverse behaviors as "expressing a positive feeling" and "refusing an unreasonable request" are thought to be linked by some common conceptual feature.

TYPES OF CONSTRUCTS AND THEIR EXPLANATORY VALUE

The organizational principle that links different behaviors is closely related to the causal role or reality status given the construct. Thus some constructs are basically descriptive categories only, such as *play* which might encompass digging in the sand, splashing in a bathtub, or operating a video game. These behaviors would be recognized as exemplars by having certain criterial attributes, in this case including the source of reinforcement or the purpose of the activity. In a study of the effects of an intervention on play it might be possible to overgeneralize semantically and presume that more than one exemplar of the class of play behavior was influenced by the treatment, but usually the variants of play behavior are seen as independent.

If, however, different behaviors represent a construct because of a common underlying behavioral mechanism, then interest in the behavior itself is reduced relative to the underlying mechanism. For example, different social activities—such as meeting someone for the first time, being interviewed for a job, or going on a date—might share a common skill mechanism, such as the one postulated by McFall (1982). Various specific social behaviors would be studied to reveal the basic skills. For many of these types of constructs, the common feeling is often an emotional dynamic. A convenient example is parental overprotectiveness. Overprotectiveness may take many different forms, such as helping the child with difficult tasks and not allowing the child to be exposed to slightly dangerous situations. Each form, it could be argued, is causally related to a common element: anxiety regarding the safety of one's child.

Play, social skills, and overprotectiveness are illustrations of three levels of constructs in behavior theory with the common element becoming increasingly causal as one proceeds across levels. If parental anxiety explains overprotectiveness, then one would expect that different overprotectiveness behaviors would covary, such that any event which increased or decreased parental anxiety (including therapeutic interventions) would have impact on all behaviors covered by the construct. Personality traits are behavioral constructs at just that level. Since Mischel's influential monograph (1968), behavioral assessment has tended to view traits as being derived from assumptions regarding the cross-situational consistency of behavior, so that trait theory is challenged most by evidence that behavior is situationally specific. However, an equally important half of trait theory is the cross-behavioral consistency of the trait. That is, the trait is manifest in the correlations among physically different behaviors that are considered exemplars of the same general class or construct.

MEASUREMENT OF CONSTRUCTS

It is important to recognize the difference between the defining characteristics of a construct and the measurement of the degree to which an individual evinces that construct as a trait. Definitionally, constructs must remain constant, that is to say there must be criteria whereby a given instance of behavior can be judged as exemplifying the construct. Circularity, for instance, is a construct. The size of a circle can vary but its shape cannot. We can measure circumference to determine a property (size) of the circle, but it is determining a figure has radii that are all of equal length that identifies the figure as a circle. Similarly, for an act to be considered aggressive, it must have some invariant properties that define the construct—perhaps some element of force involved in gaining a personal advantage for the behaving individual. For an individual to be considered aggressive, he or she must emit responses fitting the construct definition in such a manner that others would judge such responses to be high frequency (relative to others), or a typical way of solving problems, or, so uniquely characteristic of the construct that its status as an aggressive response is indisputable (hitting another child to get a toy might be a less ambiguous incident than snatching the toy away).

Determining an individual's "disposition" from judgments regarding the frequency of behaviors exemplifying the construct has been called the "act frequency" approach to personality by Buss and Craik (1983). How individuals come to make such judgments, that is, what they report in ratings, will be considered later, but for now it might be worth returning to anxiety. There appears to be no invariant, defining properties of fear or anxiety as a construct. As an emotional construct, the subjective experience of anxiety might be considered the critical element. Avoidance behavior, therefore, is anxiety-motivated behavior, not an occasion of anxiety. A measure of avoidance behavior, by this reasoning, is not a measure of anxiety, although degree of anxiety can be *inferred* from degree of avoidance *when other sources of motivation* (e.g., social pressure not to avoid) *are controlled.*

If avoidance behavior is a manifestation of anxiety but not a measure of anxiety, the psychometric procedure of determining the construct validity by correlating one measure with another, is circular or futile, particularly if the correlations are across individuals. Subjective feelings of anxiety and avoidance behavior might well correlate, but that does not make them potentially equal measures of the construct. A construct cannot be validated simply by observing covariations across individuals. The validity of a construct should represent a judgment regarding its heuristic value in construction of a theory. One, but only one, method of determining the usefulness of a construct is the convergent/discriminant distinction popularized by Campbell and Fiske (1959). Behaviorally this type of validation is concerned with the discovery that various responses relate more closely to each other than to other responses considered to be outside the construct.

To illustrate this more closely, consider "Type A behavior." The validity of this construct emerges from demonstrating that individuals exhibiting job preoccupation are also likely to exhibit restlessness, impatient behavior and competitiveness. On the basis of this cluster of (lower-order) constructs, predictions can be made about behavior in new situations. To validate Type A behavior in young children, for instance, Corrigan and Moskowitz (1983) had preschool children rated for the above characteristics by their teachers. The children were then asked to perform a choice reaction time task under conditions predicted to elicit Type A behavior. Type A-rated children showed faster reaction times but not higher heart rates or observed impatient behaviors during the task. This study is a nice example of a common research strategy used by those holding a behavioral/trait interactionist position: A construct is identified through observation of a pattern of covariation among behaviors across individuals. The pattern or cluster is usually

first measured by means of self-ratings by others, either formally or informally. Once a verbally designated construct is identified, the specific defining
features are examined through more careful observation, and, if found
promising, the effects of the construct (as a mediating trait variable) on other
aspects of performance are examined. Thus, other aspects of behavior not
previously thought to be interrelated, are conceptually linked. This approach
is most forcefully argued by Eysenck (1967) in the first chapter of *The
biological basis of personality*.

RATINGS AND THE VALIDATION OF CONSTRUCTS

Widespread and accepted as this strategy has become, the assumption that a
construct first defined by ratings can then be validated by reference to other,
more directly observed, parameters of behavior, is of limited merit. Personality or behavioral constructs, as explained, represent hypotheses regarding
commonalities among physically different behavior. Ratings represent two
judgments: one, that different behaviors fall into the category of interest,
and two, that one individual exhibits such behaviors more frequently, to a
greater degree, or more precisely than another. The first of these processes
is clearly what persons engage in when initially deriving the implicit constructs of personality. Sometimes known as implicit personality theory, we
know from decision research that in general, perception of covariation
among events is subject to considerable error (Crocker, 1981). So, although
ratings may well represent convenient aggregations of many aspects of
behavior (see Cairns & Green, 1979), they can also be overly influenced by
specific, unique, or simply irrelevant characteristics of the phenomenon
being rated.

A useful illustration of this effect was provided by Stark in an unpublished master's thesis conducted in my research program. Stark (1981) relied
on a naturalistic, clinical situation to investigate implicit constructs developed
to explain the behavior of an autistic, severely handicapped adolescent girl.
The professional staff at the psychiatrically oriented treatment facility reported that this teenager had "off" days. Such a notion is not uncommon in
clinical settings, and in this case was used to justify why on certain days the
child was not being provided with systematic educational programming. By
measuring a wide variety of aspects of her behavior—including academic
performance—every day for a considerable time, Stark was able to demonstrate that the impression of global "bad" days, in which all aspects of her
performance deteriorated, was quite false. The staff's global ratings of
whether she was "on" or "off" did correlate with the frequency of echolalic

speech on any given day. The behavior, however, was not correlated negatively with any measure of competent, on-task performance.

In behavioral assessment theory, then, obtaining the correlation between a rating and observed behavior is a strategy for helping to discover the behavioral cues relied on by the raters in making their judgments. Another master's thesis from the University of Hawaii by Marlene Lindberg (1981) can be used to elaborate on this position. Digman (see Digman & Takemoto-Chock, 1981) has extensively investigated a "trait" in school-children, labeled Will to Achieve (also called Industriousness). Always derived from teacher ratings, scores on this construct are relatively independent of measured intelligence and ratings of Intellect or Friendly Compliance. Will to Achieve scores do, however, correlate strikingly with school and even occupational achievement many years later. Lindberg observed the classroom behavior of first- and second-grade children over 10 days. Behavior supposedly indicative of Will to Achieve (being on task, obtaining material's necessary for the task) correlated, implying a meaningful construct. Frequencies of those behaviors also correlated with teachers' ratings of Will to Achieve. In the trait tradition, this would be seen as validating the ratings scales; in behavioral theory the observed behaviors would be thought of as the referent behaviors from which the teachers made their judgments. In fact, however, the frequency of observed on-task behaviors correlated even more highly with teachers' ratings of Intellect (.71) and Friendly Compliance (.76). Although psychometrically these three scales are somewhat independent, it is clear that children with positive classroom behaviors, particularly compliance, will be rated high on characteristics generally considered positive.

A major thesis of this chapter is that behavioral constructs are best understood by examining the organization of behaviors, or their interrelationships. Correlations among behavioral indices across individuals, provide little information about response organization. Even when raters simply categorize individuals according to a personality construct, the pattern of behavior identified may be very different from that intuitively imagined. To emphasize and clarify this point, another study from my research program will be considered. Finkboner (1982) was interested in the construct "overprotectiveness" mentioned earlier, since as this term is used a great deal in clinical contexts when discussing the parents of handicapped children. The construct refers to a wide range of hypothesized characteristics, including maternal anxiety, restrictive rule-setting, and intrusiveness. We limited our analysis to maternal teaching style, being interested in enhancing the learning environments for mentally retarded children.

Mothers were first identified as overprotective (or effective) by preschool teachers and public health nurses, and the final comparison groups were selected from these groups of mothers on the basis of self-ratings of overprotectiveness or effectiveness. As expected, overprotective mothers were more likely to control their children and complete tasks for them during the direct observations of their interactions with the children. They were also significantly more likely to utilize scolding and negative physical contact. Their children, in turn, were more likely to be noncompliant, to cry and refuse tasks, to be unresponsive, and to engage in self-directed behaviors. Mothers considered effective actually initiated *more* instructional interactions; the overprotective mothers' attempts to do so were usually ignored or rebuffed by their children. The "response style" or cluster of maternal behaviors, therefore, was closely dependent upon the other responses in the mother–child dyad. As a result responses that may have internal organization would not necessarily simply correlate with each other, either across individuals or within individuals over time. Behaviorally referenced constructs are critical for understanding response interactions, as long as the responses are not seen merely as signs of the construct or trait.

As a final illustration of this position, one additional construct is worth considering, namely attachment in infants. Commonly relied on "measures" of attachment (looking, approaching, touching mother, and crying) do not correlate across infants, whether observations are separated by a few minutes or by days or months (Masters & Wellman, 1974). In an elegant and well-reasoned monograph on attachment behavior, Ainsworth, Blehar, Waters, and Wall (1978) discuss the implications of this fact and make certain excellent observations: "the data suggest that the behavioral items relevant to attachment are related in a complex but systematic way that suggests an underlying 'causal system.' They do not, however, suggest a unitary, generalized trait" (p. 297). Research indicates that the attachment system is related to certain general dimensions such as security versus anxiety or response to close body contact. Response relationships of this kind indicate that while it is not particularly helpful to think of attachment as a trait, it is still an organizational principle, not merely a collection of discrete behaviors. It is a propensity, an inner structure of behavior that is "responsible for the distinctive quality of the organization of the specific attachment behaviors through which a given individual promotes positively with a specific attachment figure" (Ainsworth, 1972, p. 123).

To summarize the discussion thus far, it should be reiterated that in behavioral assessment, constructs (including what are generally labeled "traits") represent hypothetical principles for organizing discrete behaviors. Many different organizational principles can be proposed by a theory, from simple concepts whereby different behavioral events can be classified together, to more elaborate suggestions regarding the behavioral mechanisms that regulate or control some coherent system of response interrelationships. Behavioral indices derived from different sources, therefore, are often measures of different things, or parts of the system, even though they may often have some commonalities. Ratings, for instance, reflect judgments based on repeated observations, implicit or intuitive theories of personality, and other decision making processes. Correlations between ratings and other indices, therefore, reveal most about the cues and the bases for judgment, not validation of the construct. To examine other relationships among different types of behavioral indices, let us consider the interface between self-report and external or "objective" measures.

SELF-REPORT AND OBJECTIVE MEASURES

It is crucial to separate self-report into different types or classes of information if we wish to make any sense of the connection between a self-report measure and an objectively derived measure. The categories suggested here are not totally comprehensive, but they do have implications for relationships between measures which seem important. The first category to consider is usually private but potentially verifiable events ("I had two cigarettes before breakfast"; "I went on three eating binges last week"). As these self-reports are typically much easier to obtain than direct observations, they can sometimes be substituted when frequencies or exact counts of behavioral events are required. Determining the accuracy of self-report has therefore received some attention in behavioral assessment; Nelson's (1977) and others' work on self-monitoring involves a special example of these investigations. The research she reviews reveals some of the circumstances under which self-reports might be least distorted, but one cannot establish a priori the veridicality of any self-report, given that they are so easily falsified. Nevertheless, within individual contexts the performance of "validity" checks by occasionally sampling the behavior objectively can be regarded as an agreement check between self-report and actuality. In an articulate example of this, Stephens, Norris-Baker, and Willems (1984) refer to such checks as establishing "data quality"—these investigators checked the accuracy of daily reports by patients in a rehabilitation setting on the amount of time they spent out of bed engaged in a variety of activities.

A second category is the verbal report of private, nonverifiable events in which the report is assumed not to be the psychological event itself—overtly expressed—but rather an account of it. Typically, these are reports of cognitive events ("I dreamed of you last night"; "I am seeing double"; "I told myself to take it easy"). As such they are essentially the reports of classical introspection, although the behavioral influence has tended to put a new slant on them as the making public of a covert behavioral event, such as how one went about solving a problem (a metacognition). In such cases, the lack of veridicality may come about because we do not always have access to information about such cognitive events (Nisbett & Wilson, 1977).

One reason that behavioral assessment has been willing to rely on self-reports is that, unlike psychoanalysis, there is no strong background theory claiming that unconscious processes distort the self-reported information. There are, however, recognized sources of error, so it is possible to analyze the situations under which the truest report might be obtained. However, due to the private nature of the experience, the report may be impossible to verify objectively. This is important to keep in mind because other, nonverbal measures are equally inferential and may be equally erroneous. For instance, an individual can solve a problem as though using a particular cognitive strategy, which would lend credence to the report of using that strategy, but no more so than the other way around, thus providing internal consistency but no criterion measure. If an individual reports having a headache, we assume a genuine "experience" and look for expected consistency in other equally indirect manifestations of the experience, for example, behavior such as taking aspirin, lying down, moaning, and so forth. Our belief in the reality of the experience of the subjective event also derives from other sources of consistency with our own private experience, such as knowledge of a likely causal event, for example, an injury or fatigue, to explain the headache.

A third general category of self-report is the verbal expression of an attitude, opinion, or belief, in which the expression is the content, that is, it is not a report of something, rather the report *is* the something. The verbal expression of an attitude ("I'm in favor of a nuclear freeze") is isomorphic to the attitude. The attitude may have counterparts in other behaviors (voting on a referendum, contributing to a political campaign, and so on) which allows one to judge the genuineness of the expression, but these are not thought of as equivalent manifestations of the attitudinal construct. Instead, the overt behaviors and the affective component of the expresssed attitude interact—various psychological theories tried to depict this interaction. Staats' (1975) behavior theory probably provides the best detailed model of the exact relationship between the verbal expression and its affective value. According to A-R-D theory, words have Attitudinal (emotional-eliciting) functions, Reinforcing functions, and Discriminative stimulus functions. This provides a theoretical model for why an avoidance behavior (from which we often infer an attitude) is related to the verbal expression of the feeling or opinion.

An interesting aspect of this type of self-report emerges when we consider belief statements about oneself. Generally we would *not* expect congruence with some other measure of reality. For example, a scale of perceived competence should reflect a person's self-image, not actual competence. Also, self-reports of traits are like ratings by others: they reflect aggregations of the individual's self-observation of behavior in a range of situations. Thus the rating reflects the variety of situations implicitly included in the judgment as well as the usual technical difficulty of scaling one person's attributes relative to another's. Thus a statement "I am a kind person" assumes an indeterminate number of situations in which kindly behavior may be exhibited and an unknown scale of how other people behave in comparable situations.

Of course, we have reason to believe that a person may adjust subsequent behavior in order to be consistent with this self-image. This presents another interesting issue for the investigator who hopes to measure strength of a fear by having an individual first provide belief/opinion type of self-rating and then carry out a specific action. Also, other persons learn about individuals partly through their self-expressions of individual characteristics; thus a person who described himself or herself frequently as "disorganized" might be perceived that way by others even though they have no direct evidence. There are many studies in the behavioral assessment literature in which intercorrelations are investigated between self-ratings of, for example, assertiveness, ratings by others, and observations of a single instance of social behavior in a simulted situation. Such correlations do not "validate" any of the measures. The three measures may or may not correlate depending upon whether the cues used by others to judge relative assertiveness are actual instances of behavior or the person's self descriptions. The simulted situations may not be one of the situations included in the aggregations of prior observations. And finally there are the various problems in scaling of such comparisons already mentioned.

SELF-REPORT OF POTENTIALLY ACCESSIBLE INTERNAL EVENTS

The fourth and final type of self-report is that in which an individual provides a self-report of a private event that is potentially measurable by objective psychophysiologic procedures ("My hands are sweating"; "My heart is beating faster"). This could merely be a special case of the first category, were it not for the fact that there seem to be considerable individual differences in the degree to which people are able to detect and report internal somatic events. Clearly, it is this type of report that is utilized in studies of the so-called "congruence" between cognitive and physiologic measures. Self-report of an internal state or somatic event could more accurately be described as the self-report of visceral perception, that is, the processing of information from the interoceptors. This is not the place to discuss the complex issue of whether interoception impinges directly on consciousness, as individuals can sense the action of visceral events in various ways. For instance, heart rate can be detected by mechanoreceptors in the muscles of the thorax, or by visual observation of an arterial pulse, or by its ballistic effect.

In my laboratory, we have observed that subjects asked to estimate the "degree of penile erection" relied on various cues, including peripheral cutaneous stimuli from the genital area as well as visual inspection. These estimates correlated very highly with circumference measures, at least over the range of tumescence for which circumference increase and degree of erection are actually related in a linear fashion (Farkas, Evans, Sine, Eifert, Wittlieb, & Vogelmann-Sine, 1979). Correlations between circumference (the objective physiologic measure) and continuously monitored self-report of "sexual arousal," however, were much more variable. They were high for some subjects, who presumably judged their sexual arousal by reference to their own tumescence, and negligible for others, who perhaps relied on other features of the general situation such as their appraisal of the erotic materials used to stimulate arousal. One could not argue that these latter individuals were showing desynchrony of their cognitive and physiologic system; they were reporting an experience, not monitoring an internal physiologic change. Of course, there does seem to be some clinical significance in certain individuals either not using visceral cues or being poor judges of visceral activity, or, as Schachter (1971) has argued, judging internal states on the basis of external cues. For instance, there has been some interest in whether alcoholics can estimate their blood alcohol levels (which can, of course, be measured objectively), and, if not, whether they can perhaps be taught to do so (Nathan, 1978).

Stunkard and Koch (1964) showed that obese people tended to report being hungry much of the time, whereas normal-weight individuals showed a distinct relationship between their reports of hunger and objective measures of gastric motility (stomach contractions). Again, we have to remember that part of the variability in these relationships is lexical, relating to the self-application of the term *hunger*, and not necessarily a question of visceral responsiveness per se. Assuming that there are striking individual differences in responsiveness to changes in the *milieu interieur*, Mandler, Mandler, and Uviller (1958) developed the Autonomic Perception Questionnaire. It appears, however, that this instrument measures the tendency of individuals to use certain terms in describing their experiences, rather than actually measuring the judgment of changes that can be objectively verified. As interoceptive sensations become labeled through strictly intrasubjective means—without the benefit of interindividual confirmation and feedback—the verbal reference system for reporting internal events is likely to be highly idiosyncratic. In addition, if we think of this category of self-report as report of sensations, then it would follow from signal-detection analyses that individuals will differ not just in their detection thresholds but in their reporting criteria. There is some similarity between this assumption and the long-standing interest in the notion of "repressors" and "sensitizors" in expression of emotion, except that reports of an emotion are circular compared to reports of visceral sensations. The thoughtful work of Borkovec (1976) provides a more extended discussion of this issue related to autonomic perception and its measurement.

In summary, correlations across individuals behavior self-report measures and other, public responses cannot be expected, nor typically interpreted. The usual psychometric position that one measure can be validated by such correlation, derives from an assumption that the measures of interest are substituted measures of some underlying construct. In fact, by cleverly twisting the English language, psychometricians have redefined *validity* as meaning the extent to which a measure can now be considered a measure of the construct. According to the analysis presented in this section, self-report measures vary, such that for some types of self-report accuracy (veridicality) is of importance because the self-report is an exact substitute for direct observation. For other types, where no measure of veridicality is possible (we can never "really know" whether the person truly has a headache or feels depressed or dislikes heights) interest shifts to the question of consistency among indices of the expression of the "state" or "feeling" or whatever affective construct is being used.

Correlations between measures of two or more responses *within* individuals can only be interpreted in the framework of some theory regarding response interrelationships. For instance, the correlation between self-report of an emotional feeling and some psychophysiologic parameter might indicate the autonomic afferent cues relied upon by the individual in making the self-report. Or, as many cognitive theorists would argue, the verbal expression of a feeling might alter an individual's autonomic reactions. Or the self-reported expression and the autonomic change may both be controlled independently be some third psychological event—perhaps some change in the state of the central nervous system such that a more primary emotional state can be inferred. One of the best ways to illustrate these issues is to consider the very extensive literature on the interactions among autonomic responses (the psychophysiologic "mode" of the three "response-systems").

RELATIONSHIPS AMONG AUTONOMIC RESPONSES

By this stage, one general theme of the chapter should be clear: The components of effector systems interact and influence one another. Psychophysiologic research has typically been oriented toward examining interrelationships among different components of theoretically derived constructs in order to understand the interactive mechanisms of control, or, sometimes, aimed at the identification of alternative physiologic indices of cognitive events. An example of this latter strategy is the use of pupillary dilation as an indicator of "processing load' in memory and reasoning tasks. The magnitude of brief, task-evoked, phasic decreases in pupil diameter relates rather precisely to the demands of various cognitive tasks (Beatty & Wagoner, 1978). Similarly, Lacey (e.g., 1967) has demonstrated that cardiac deceleration accompanies *intention*, or the anticipation of performing a voluntary motor act. Heart rate, therefore, is not a convenient measure of anxiety, nor is its relation to cognition simply a by-product—Lacey has argued that decreases in heart rate (and blood pressure) actually facilitate attention to external events and sensorimotor integration by decreasing baroreceptor-controlled inhibition of cortical activity.

Obrist and co-workers (Obrist, 1981) have meticulously studied the issue of inter-response control. Especially notable is the classic work on the relationship between heart rate and somatomotor activity. Since the cardiovascular system must adjust rapidly and precisely in accordance with the metabolic requirements of the muscles, one source of innervation is vagal (parasympathetic) and the integration (covariation) between somatic activity and heart rate is striking. What is particularly interesting in the present context is that the usual coupling between striate muscle and cardiac activity breaks down when sympathetic effects become predominant, such as when an organism is actively avoiding aversive stimuli. Hence, a clear relationship between autonomic and motor responses is seen only at certain tonic levels of autonomic activation. Obrist seriously questions the view that tonic heart rate is a useful index of emotional arousal: "to whatever extent cardiovascular adjustments are uniquely sensitive to behavioral events (independent of metabolic processes), these are but ripples in the wave and can at any time be inundated by the wave" (Obrist, 1981, p. 200).

Another major impetus for the study of dependence and independence among the components of autonomic behaviors was interest in the instrumental reinforcement of autonomic responses. Concern for the effect of specific contingencies on other autonomically mediated behaviors was partly methodological (concomitantly measured autonomic responses providing a possible within-subject control for artifactual and nonconditioning effects), and partly theoretical (concomitant effects may provide clues to the mediational mechanisms, if any, underlying the process of instrumental conditioning of the autonomic nervous system). Most of the early studies reported parallel, but not statistically significant changes in the other responses monitored. However, Kimmel (1967) showed that reinforcing digital vasoconstriction significantly increased—in comparison to yoked controls—both that response and the frequency of spontaneous skin resistance responses. However, when skin resistance responses were explicitly reinforced, there was no effect upon the frequency of concomitant vasoconstriction. Because spontaneous skin resistance responses are more frequent than vasoconstrictions, this result was attributed to the adventitious reinforcement of the more frequent response.

This interpretation, of course, is the familiar operant perspective on how a response "class" could be developed: Two previously independent responses come under a common source of external control, one adventitiously. This is the major mechanism for response structure proposed by Wahler and Fox (1982). However, as already explained with reference to Obrist's work, when dealing with autonomic processes our dominant biological model is that of a *system* in which change in one component is likely to be structurally and functionally related to change in others. An obvious concept, for instance, is general sympathetic arousal, involving heart beat acceleration, pupil dilation, and sweating—the arousal construct, in fact, arising from the observation that these sympathetic events often reveal concomitant change. We also seem ready to recognize subsystems of interdependent changes, such as the mutual and interactive influence of heart rate, arterial vasoconstriction and blood pressure.

In a subsystem like the cardiovascular system, autonomic changes regulate one another. Responses that serve a homeostatic or regulatory function will not correlate if we look at moment to moment fluctuations. They might well, however, show lead or lag correlations, particularly at resting levels. If the correlation is based on fluctuation of tonic level over a fairly long time period, it is possible that autonomic responses that actually are not related will be similarly and simultaneously aroused by fluctuating external levels. If longer total time spans and fairly lengthy intervals between data points are selected for investigation, psychophysiologic responses considered as concomitant time-series will appear to be related because they correlate. (A similar methodological issue arises when considering overt motor behaviors, as will be described in the next section, Inter-Response Structure).

Even though mutually regulatory functions characterize individual autonomic responses, specific interventions, such as biofeedback manipulations, may, in a sense, render the response independent of its usual system by overriding its customary regulatory sources. Sometimes this results in considerable specificity of external control in single-response training. Presumably this happens in pathologic situations as well, giving rise to unusual somatic "symptoms"—Gantt's (1953) idea of "schizokinesis" being not unlike more recent concepts of desynchrony or disregulation. It is now reasonably well established that patterned feedback (two or more conditions to be met before the feedback signal is provided) allows subjects to negate usual subsystem interactions, for example, being able to simultaneously raise heart rate and decrease blood pressure (Schwartz, 1979). As noted previously, specificity of response control is important in biofeedback methodology, because without some demonstration of it, there is no convincing proof that the biofeedback training adds anything new to the usual abilities of the subject to regulate a number of autonomic responses by such voluntary (but indirect) means as sitting quietly, altering one's physical environment, and so on.

Conversely, however, if the consequences of the training are too highly specific then it is difficult to see how they could be clinically useful. This is particularly clear in studies of electromyogram (EMG) feedback, which provide an appropriate illustration even though they do not involve an autonomic response system. The notion of relaxation as a construct suggests a generalized behavioral state, and if we define muscular relaxation in terms of muscle action potentials (EMG levels), we would expect EMG levels recorded from different muscular sites to covary, that is, to correlate within individuals. In fact, for resting subjects who are awake with eyes open, within-subject correlations among frontalis, masseter, forearm, and leg flexor and extensor muscles are quite low (Whatmore, Whatmore, & Fisher, 1981). In studies in which the subjects have been taught to lower frontalis EMG through biofeedback (see Borkovec & Sides, 1979), the generalization to other muscles reported may be due to some subjects achieving the target response by becoming drowsy. This results in marked diminution in action potentials throughout the skeletal musculature. Some subjects may also adopt certain mediational strategies that result in response decrements in other muscles as well as in autonomic responses. But the most general finding is that within-subject analyses of multiple responses do not reveal *general* changes modulated by levels of frontalis EMG activity which have been altered through biofeedback.

When considering patterns of skeletal muscle changes, one should keep in mind that this effector system is anatomically specialized for fine-grained, skilled execution of discrete acts—witness the fine nuances of meaning that can be expressed by flexion and extension of facial muscles. Generalized or total system changes, therefore, might be the exception rather than the rule. In states of high readiness or alarm, however, the organism prepares (as Cannon, 1929, stated) for fight-or-flight, and both preparatory muscular tension and subsequent physical exertion must be served by autonomically mediated adjustments to blood supply and oxygen intake, as well as cessation in feeding, digestion, and other functions not adaptive to the situation. Thus cardiac responses and skin resistance changes always accompany significant motor actions such as escape and avoidance, but the reverse is not necessarily the case. It is little wonder that predictable correlations do not emerge between autonomic changes and overt activities, although dramatic overriding circumstances could well result in between-subject correlations. In neither case are independent "response modes" or systems of behavior indicated.

INTER-RESPONSE STRUCTURE

In this discussion of autonomic responses as functionally interrelated sub-systems, the relationships among autonomic, skeletal muscles, and cognitive events have been briefly considered, while avoiding any assumption that these are *separable* modes of behavior. Another major interaction that could be considered is that between cognitive and motor events. However, the literature on how overt behavior is mediated by covert language and other cognitions is so extensive that it cannot be reviewed here. Suffice it to say that this well-known relationship further contradicts any supposition that cognitive events and overt actions are separate modes of behavior. This view, as I have tried to stress, is a carryover from the dominance of trait theory in assessment. Psychometric principles maintain the fallacy that behaviors are "measures" of more fundamental underlying entities. The behavioral/systems theory expressed here recognizes that response organization is mediated by common underlying mechanisms. Models of response organization thus provide the explanations of the phenomena typically addressed by trait theory. Organization among autonomic responses had been viewed here according to structural networks serving homeostatic needs; some organizational principles for overt motor behaviors need to be considered.

In a review of inter-response relationships (Voeltz & Evans, 1982), we described ways in which response organization within individual repertoires has been conceptualized in basic research. There are a number of functional organizational principles, such as the one in operant theory of response class in which, as mentioned, responses form a cluster because they are all under one common source of contingency control. Any theorizing dealing with more intrinsic organizational principles has been avoided in radical behavioral thinking. In fact, in a provocative essay, Baer (1982) has argued that there are no *necessary* structures to behavior other than trivial ones. That although behaviors can acquire interdependencies these are created by the conditions of the environment rather than being the fundamental properties of any repertoire. One reason, however, that radical behaviorists can sustain this view is that the operant paradigm has not provided suitable empirical designs for investigating response relationships. Similarly the clinical operant literature, by focusing so exclusively on discrete response measurement, has greatly restricted our opportunities for discovering and investigating response interrelationships, despite their obvious prevalence in both clinical report and informal observation (Voeltz & Evans, 1983).

This situation in the basic operant research literature is beginning to show signs of change, however. Dunham (1971) referred to procedures that consider the repertoire of responses in a relatively stable environment as "multiple-response baseline procedures." Using this paradigm, Dunham and Grantmyre (1982) recently demonstrated that if one response in a complex repertoire is punished, the most probable of the unpunished alternative responses will increase in frequency. This "hierarchical" rule holds even if the referent behavior is not reduced by punishment contingencies but rather by removal of opportunity. Furthermore, in their animal subjects, these authors reported a "sequential dependency rule" in which responses that most typically *follow* the referent response will be reduced through reductions in the referent, whether brought about by punishment or by restricting opportunity.

Rachlin and Burkhard (1978) have argued that increases in instrumental responses measured over a lengthy period result from reallocation of time according to a principle of substitutability, and not from response-strengthening, associative processes. Contrary to the so-called "Premack principle," Rachlin and Burkhard (1978) have shown that contingent high-probability responses are not necessarily more effective than contingent low-probability responses in increasing the instrumental level of other responses. The usual Premack effect, if observed at all, is thought to be due to the availability of more time to the subject by deprivation of high-probability responses. Bernstein and Ebbesen (1978) have provided confirmation that for human subjects the same response might substitute very readily for others when these are restricted in the repertoire. The responses that were readily substitutable correlated highly and negatively during the multibaseline period. That *negative* correlations define a response class, is a special feature of any repertoire consisting of mutually incompatible responses. Indeed, Rachlin and Burkhard's (1978) model is based on the situation in which the summed durations of each response equal the total time of the observation period. Of course, this pertains only to molar response categories. As Bernstein and Ebbesen point out:

> The extent of mutual substitution may be a function of the way response classes are defined. In order to break up the continuous stream of behavior into comparable response classes, the characteristics of each class of response must be specified. . . . Whatever the basis for the categories, the system is necessarily somewhat arbitrary, and different systems could produce response repertoires with very different characteristics. Consider a set of typical human activities such as sewing, artwork, reading, and embroidery. If contact with the various objects (e.g., sewing machine, paintbrush, book, and needle) were used to define the response classes, a set of activities that would have a selective substitution pattern would probably result, with sewing and embroidery replacing each other during restriction. On the other hand, if the presence of a negative covariation across days during baseline observations were used to define the response classes, sewing and embroidery would likely become a meta-category, and a hierarchy of activities without substitution would result (p. 252).

This latter observation is yet another instance of the methodological principle mentioned repeatedly in this chapter: Intercorrelations among behaviors, without concern for theoretically based time intervals, do not reveal important relationships. For instance, in ethologic studies of birds, two behaviors such as nest construction and preening, will be mutually exclusive (negatively correlated) at short time intervals because they are topographically incompatible; uncorrelated at intermediate intervals because preening (the higher-frequency response) serves various functions in addition to care of feathers; and positively correlated over longer time periods because both behaviors are closely related to reproductive states (Baerends, 1972). In our studies of response relationships in severely handicapped young children (Evans & Voeltz, 1982), we have used nonexclusionary categories and real-time observation that allows for the measurement of numerous concurrent acts. Even so, the intervals at which the time periods are subsequently "chunked" for statistical analysis of cluster and covariation have a considerable impact upon the type and stability of the clusters that emerge (Evans, Voeltz, Freedland, & Brennan, 1981).

It is my opinion that we are going to need a much more careful analysis of the structural principles underlying response–response relationships. There are various theories that have relevance to this issue: the graphic models of systems theory provide one useful descriptive heuristic (Evans, 1985); Winkler has demonstrated the value of applying economic theory to response interdependencies (Kagel & Winkler, 1972; Winkler, 1980). Even at the simple descriptive level, we require better methodologies. Very few investigators in behavior therapy have reported detailed multiple-baseline analyses of behavior before beginning an intervention. The multiple-baseline control will be recognized as a particularly unsuited experimental design once the inevitability of response interrelationships is appreciated. The design, however, can be reformulated as a concomitant time-series technique for the investigation of prior relationships and their influences on indirect interventions. My colleagues and I have recently provided an illustration of this methodological strategy (Meyer, Evans, Wuerch, & Brennan, 1985); the effect on the distribution of appropriate and inappropriate behaviors of teaching a leisure-time play skill was examined in a small group of severely handicapped adolescents.

CONCLUSION

Social psychologists assure us with a certain perverse delight that people are generally not very good at making judgments of covariation or intuitively estimating correlations (Crocker, 1981; Nisbett & Ross, 1980). In clinical situations, however, we as behavior assessors are very dependent on this apparently questionable skill in our clients, since it is the detection of covariation that provides for the development of one's clinical constructs as well as one's causal hypotheses regarding problematic behavior. Clearly, a source of hypotheses regarding response interrelationships is our set of constructs regarding behavioral organization and certain ideas about how responses are interconnected. It would probably be fair to say that much clinical assessment involves trying to determine ways in which responses in individual repertoires are systematically organized (Evans, 1985).

In this systems view of individual assessment, there are a variety of concepts such as anxiety, assertiveness, social skill, and so on, that serve to summarize related, but physically different responses. To some extent these seem to resemble the trait labels of traditional personality theory. Behavior therapists, however, are probably less prone to attribute causal explanations to these constructs or to assume that they represent invariant characteristics of the individual regardless of situation or circumstances. Clinically, I suspect the majority of behavior therapists are quite comfortable with a world view that assumes that cognitions, psychophysiologic responses, and various overt behaviors all interact in mutually dependent subsystems of individual repertoires. It thus behooves behavioral assessment to focus on these structural interactions and not to rely on the model that these are *alternative* measures of a construct from different "modes" of behavior. This model reflects implicit trait concepts that are not likely to serve us well. Classic psychometric theory pays scant attention to understanding the way responses interact with each other to produce statistical interdependence. We need to develop structural models because the alternative behavioral tradition has been to focus on narrow, isolated, piecemeal, individual responses and deny any response organization. This is a short-sighted view, given that stabilities of response repertoires and their commonalities across individuals (which originally gave rise to trait theory) seem to represent profound features of our psychological experiences. Behavioral assessment represents a promising technology for investigating the structural aspects of behavior. Hopefully, this chapter will serve to further its development by encouraging continued critical examination of some of the conceptual and methodological issues.

REFERENCES

Ainsworth, M. D. S. (1972). Attachment and dependency: A comparison. In J. L. Gewirtz (Ed.), *Attachment and dependency* (pp. 97–137). Washington, DC: V. H. Winston.
Ainsworth, M. D. S., Blehar, M. C., Waters, E., & Wall, S. (1978). *Patterns of attachment: A psychological study of the strange situation.* Hillsdale, NJ: Lawrence Erlbaum.
Baer, D. M. (1982). The imposition of structure on behavior and the demolition of behavioral

structures. In D. J. Bernstein (Ed.), *Nebraska Symposium on Motivation, 1981: Response structure and organization* (pp. 217–254). Lincoln: University of Nebraska Press.

Baerends, G. P. (1972). A model of the functional organization of incubation behavior. In G. P. Baerends & R. H. Drent (Eds.), *The herring gull and its egg. Behaviour Supplement 17*, 261–310.

Beatty, J., & Wagoner, B. L. (1978). Pupillometric signs of brain activation vary with level of cognitive processing. *Science, 199*, 1216–1218.

Bernstein, D. A. (1973). Situational factors in behavioral fear assessment: A progress report. *Behavior Therapy, 4*, 41–48.

Bernstein, D. J., & Ebbesen, E. (1978). Reinforcement and substitution in humans: A multiple-response analysis. *Journal of the Experimental Analysis of Behavior, 30*, 243–253.

Borkovec, T. D. (1976). Physiological and cognitive processes in the regulation of anxiety. In G. E. Schwartz & D. Shapiro (Eds.), *Consciousness and self-regulation: Advances in research* (pp. 261–312). New York: Plenum Press.

Borkovec, T. D., & Sides, J. K. (1979). Critical procedural variables related to the physiological effects of progressive relaxation: A review. *Behaviour Research and Therapy, 17*, 119–138.

Burns, G. L. (1980). Indirect measurement and behavioral assessment: A case for social behaviorism psychometrics. *Behavioral Assessment, 2*, 197–206.

Buss, D. M., & Craik, K. H. (1983). The act frequency approach to personality. *Psychological Review, 90*, 105–126.

Cairns, R. B., & Green, J. A. (1979). How to assess personality and social patterns: Observations or ratings? In R. B. Cairns (Ed.), *The analysis of social interactions: Methods, issues, and illustrations* (pp. 209–226). Hillsdale, NJ: Lawrence Erlbaum.

Campbell, D. T., & Fiske, D. W. (1959). Convergent and discriminant validation by the multitrait-multimethod matrix. *Psychological Bulletin, 56*, 81–105.

Cannon, W. B. (1929). *Bodily changes in pain, hunger, fear and rage*. New York: Appleton-Century-Crofts.

Cone, J. D. (1979). Confounded comparisons in triple response mode assessment research. *Behavioral Assessment, 1*, 85–95.

Corrigan, S. A., & Moskowitz, D. (1983). Type A behavior in preschool children: Construct validational evidence for the Myth. *Child Development, 54*, 1513–1521.

Crocker, J. (1981). Judgment of covariation by social perceivers. *Psychological Bulletin, 90*, 272–292.

Digman, J. M., & Takemoto-Chock, N. K. (1981). Factors in the natural language of personality: Re-analysis, comparison, and interpretation of six major studies. *Mutlivariate Behavioral Research, 16*, 149–170.

Dunham, P. J. (1971). Punishment: Method and theory. *Psychological Review, 78*, 58–70.

Dunham, P. J., & Grantmyre, J. (1982). Changes in a multiple-response repertoire during response-contingent punishment and response restriction: Sequential relationships. *Journal of the Experimental Analysis of Behavior, 37*, 123–133.

Evans, I. M. (1985). Building systems models as a strategy for target behavior selection in clinical assessment. *Behavioral Assessment, 7*, 21–32.

Evans, I. M., & Voeltz, L. M. (1982). *The selection of intervention priorities in educational programming for severely handicapped preschool children with multiple behavior problems*. Final Report, Behavioral Systems Intervention Project, University of Hawaii, Honolulu. (ERIC Document Reproduction Service No. ED 240 765)

Evans, I. M., Voeltz, L. M., Freedland, K., & Brennan, J. M. (1981, April). *Behavioral interrelationships in the design and evaluation of applied intervention research*. Unpublished paper presented at the biennial meeting of the Society for Research in Child Development, Boston.

Eysenck, H. J. (1967). *The biological basis of personality*. Springfield, IL: Charles C. Thomas.

Eysenck, H. J. (1979). The place of theory in the assessment of the effects of psychotherapy. *Behavioral Assessment, 1*, 77–84.

Farkas, G. M., Evans, I. M., Sine, L. F., Eifert, G., Wittlieb, E., & Vogelmann-Sine, S. (1979). Reliability and validity of mercury-in-rubber strain gauge measures of penile circumference. *Behavior Therapy, 10*, 555–561.

Finkboner, J. B. (1982). *A behavioral comparison of two maternal styles: Overprotective and effective.* Unpublished doctoral dissertation, University of Hawaii, Honolulu.

Gantt, W. H. (1953). Principles of nervous breakdown. *Annals of the New York Academy of Science, 56,* 143–163.

Hodgson, R., & Rachman, S. (1974). Desynchrony in measures of fear. *Behaviour Research and Therapy, 12,* 319–326.

Hugdahl, K. (1981). The three-systems-model of fear and emotion—a critical examination. *Behaviour Research and Therapy, 19,* 75–85.

Kagel, J. H., & Winkler, R. C. (1972). Behavioral economics: Areas of cooperative research between economics and applied behavior analysis. *Journal of Applied Behavior Analysis, 5,* 335–342.

Kaloupek, D. G., & Levis, D. J. (1980). The relationship between stimulus specificity and self-report indices in assessing fear of heterosexual social interaction: A test of the unitary response hypothesis. *Behavioral Assessment, 2,* 267–281.

Kaloupek, D. G., & Levis, D. J. (1983). Issues in the assessment of fear: Response concordance and prediction of avoidance behavior. *Journal of Behavioral Assessment, 5,* 239–260.

Kazdin, A. E. (1982). Symptom substitution, generalization, and response covariation: Implications for psychotherapy outcome. *Psychological Bulletin, 91,* 349–365.

Kimmel, H. D. (1967). Instrumental conditioning of autonomically mediated behavior. *Psychological Bulletin, 67,* 337–345.

Kozak, M. J., & Miller, G. A. (1982). Hypothetical constructs versus intervening variables: A re-appraisal of the three-systems model of anxiety assessment. *Behavioral Assessment, 4,* 347–358.

Lacey, J. I. (1967). Somatic response patterning and stress: Some revisions of activation theory. In M. H. Appley & R. Trumball (Eds.), *Psychological stress* (pp. 14–42). New York: Appleton-Century-Crofts.

Lang, P. J. (1968). Fear reduction and fear behavior: Problems in treating a construct. In J. M. Schlien (Ed.), *Research in psychotherapy* (Vol. 3, pp. 90–102). Washington, DC: American Psychological Association.

Lindberg, M. A. (1981). *The educationally achieving child: Convergence of ratings by teachers and direct observation.* Unpublished master's thesis, University of Hawaii, Honolulu.

Mandler, G., Mandler, J. M., & Uviller, E. T. (1958). Autonomic feedback: The perception of autonomic activity. *Journal of Abnormal and Social Psychology, 56,* 367–373.

Masters, J., & Wellman, H. (1974). Human infant attachment: A procedural critique. *Psychological Bulletin, 81,* 218–237.

McFall, R. M. (1982). A review and reformulation of the concept of social skills. *Behavioral Assessment, 4,* 1–34.

Messick, S. (1981). Constructs and their vicissitudes in educational and psychological measurement. *Psychological Bulletin, 89,* 575–588.

Meyer, L. H., Evans, I. M., Wuerch, B. B., & Brennan, J. M. (1985). Monitoring the collateral effects of leisure skill instruction: A case study in multiple baseline methodology. *Behaviour Research and Therapy, 23,* 127–138.

Mischel, W. (1968). *Personality and assessment.* New York: John Wiley & Sons.

Mischel, W. (1981). A cognitive-social learning approach to assessment. In T. V. Merluzzi, C. R. Glass, & M. Genest (Eds.), *Cognitive assessment* (pp. 479–502). New York: Guilford Press.

Nathan, P. E. (1978). Studies in blood alcohol level discrimination. In P. E. Nathan, G. A. Marlett, & T. Loberg (Eds.), *Alcoholism: New directions in behavioral research and treatment* (pp. 161–176). New York: Plenum Press.

Nay, W. R. (1979). *Multimethod clinical assessment.* New York: Gardner Press.

Nelson, R. O. (1977). Methodological issues in assessment via self-monitoring. In J. D. Cone & R. P. Hawkins (Eds.), *Behavioral assessment: New directions in clinical psychology* (pp. 217–254). New York: Brunner/Mazel.

Nelson, R. O., & Hayes, S. C. (1979). Some current dimensions of behavioral assessment. *Behavioral Assessment, 1,* 1–16.

Nisbett, R. E., & Ross, L. (1980). *Human inference: Strategies and shortcomings of social judgment.* Englewood Cliffs, NJ: Prentice-Hall.

Nisbett, R. E., & Wilson, T. C. (1977). Telling more than we can know: Verbal reports on mental processes. *Psychological Review, 84,* 231–259.

Obrist, P. A. (1981). *Cardiovascular psycho-physiology: A perspective.* New York: Plenum Press.

Rachlin, H., & Burkhard, B. (1978). The temporal triangle: Response substitution in instrumental conditioning. *Psychological Review, 85,* 22–47.

Rachman, S. (1978). Human fears: A three systems analysis. *Scandinavian Journal of Behavior Therapy, 7,* 237–245.

Rachman, S., & Hodgson, R. (1974). Synchrony and desynchrony in fear and avoidance. *Behaviour Research and Therapy, 12,* 311–318.

Schachter, S. (1971). *Emotion, obesity and crime.* New York: Academic Press.

Schwartz, G. E. (1979). The brain as a health care system. In G. C. Stone, F. Cohen, & N. E. Adler (Eds.), *Health psychology* (pp. 238–269). San Francisco: Jossey-Bass.

Staats, A. W. (1975). *Social behaviorism.* Homewood, IL: Dorsey Press.

Stark, A. (1981). *Reconceptualizing a clinical construct.* Unpublished master's thesis, University of Hawaii, Honolulu.

Stephens, M. A. P., Norris-Baker, C., & Willems, E. P. (1984). Data quality in self-observation and report of behavior. *Behavioral Assessment, 6,* 237–252.

Stunkard, A., & Koch, C. (1964). The interpretation of gastric motility. *Archives of General Psychiatry, 11,* 74–82.

Voeltz, L. M., & Evans, I. M. (1982). The assessment of behavioral interrelationships in child behavior therapy. *Behavioral Assessment, 4,* 131–165.

Voeltz, L. M., & Evans, I. M. (1983). Educational validity: Procedures to evaluate outcomes in programs for severly handicapped learners. *Journal of the Association for the Severely Handicapped, 8,* 3–15.

Wahler, R. G., & Fox, J. J. (1982). Response structure in deviant child–parent relationships: Implications for family therapy. In D. J. Bernstein (Ed.), *Nebraska Symposium on Motivation, 1981: Response structure and organization* (pp. 1–46). Lincoln: University of Nebraska Press.

Whatmore, G. B., Whatmore, N. J., & Fisher, L. D. (1981). Is frontalis activity a reliable indicator of the activity of other skeletal muscles? *Biofeedback and Self-Regulation, 6,* 305–314.

Winkler, R. C. (1980). Target behavior changes in behavioral economics. In C. M. Bradshaw (Ed.), *Current developments in the quantification of steady-state operant behavior* (pp. 287–298). Amsterdam: Elsevier.

6

BEHAVIOR: ITS UNITS, DIMENSIONS, AND MEASUREMENT

BEATRICE H. BARRETT
W. E. Fernald State School

JAMES M. JOHNSTON
Auburn University

H. S. PENNYPACKER
University of Florida

Descriptions of behavioral assessment have become increasingly diffuse over the past few years (Cone & Hawkins, 1977; Mash, 1979; Mash & Terdal, 1981a; Nelson & Hayes, 1979; O'Leary, 1979). A perusal of recent publications may, for some, provide a déjà vu experience. Has this new field redefined behavior? Redefined it to the extent that behavior now encompasses the hypothetical metalistic activities that behaviorism eschewed decades ago (Skinner, 1938; Watson, 1924)? Or has there emerged a new brand of assessor schooled in traditional procedures and merely applying the popularized label "behavioral" to procedures once called "psychological?" If the latter, then the definition of behavior has, perhaps, remained intact but has merely been overlooked or not thoroughly understood.

Relabeling or creating new or slightly different descriptive vocabulary is not an uncommon way of attracting the professional community. "Schools" of psychotherapy in the 1940s and 1950s were created by, or at least reflected, this conceptual pastime. What practitioners said and wrote about what they did was more different from "school" to "school" than what they really did. From Horney and Alexander to Mowrer, Dollard, and Miller, the major differences were in verbiage. Operations of differently affiliated practitioners were more similar than they were different (Barrett, 1958). But the verbal–conceptual differences became the banners of camp followers whose professional identities became secure in conceptual distinctions often tenuously related to different practices.

"Behavioral assessment" today describes procedures that, by and large, were once called "psychological assessment." A quick glance at a mental testing textbook popular in the 1940s and 1950s (Greene, 1941) provides such a comparison. Although operations listed in today's books and journals (Cone & Hawkins, 1977; Hersen & Bellack, 1976; Mash & Terdal, 1981b) are couched in the language of "specificity," the contents of procedures and concerns have changed so slightly that the oft-reiterated differences seem more apparent than real. Distinguishing characteristics are now said to be more conceptual than methodological (Cone, 1977; Goldfried & Kent, 1972; Mash & Terdal, 1981a; O'Leary, 1979). A recent survey of practitioners is not inconsistent with this interpretation (Swan & MacDonald, 1978).

Amalgamation and the cognitive revolution are fashions of the times—decidedly concordant with "behavioral"-"psychological" equivalence and the conceptual incorporation of some brand of "behavior" into the mainstream of current ideology. The implications of such an amalgam are critical to the viability of behavior science methodology as a major investigative medium in the design of human-service technology. Adoption of "behavioral"-"psychological" equivalence forfeits both the heritage of behavior analysis and the advantages that accrue from its natural science methodology (Johnston & Pennypacker, 1980). The forfeiture returns assessment of human behavior to its prebehavioral status. Readoption of psychometric methods and concerns, so prevalent in today's literature, indicates that the process is well under way. What will be sacrificed if a social science approach to behavior assessment regains its former status?

CURRENT CONCEPTS AND PROCEDURES

Assessment of human behavior purports to examine the functional relations between "meaningful response units and their controlling variables (both current environmental and organismic) for the purpose of understanding and altering behavior" (Nelson & Hayes, 1979, p. 1). Other than the distinction between "altering" and "improving," and the parenthetic recognition of organismic variables, this definition is essentially similar to that of applied behavior analysis by Baer, Wolf, and Risley (1968) in their standard-bearing article. The latter authors sought to distinguish the fledgling field from its laboratory-based heritage. Similarly, the recent literature on behavioral assessment deals repeatedly with its identity as a new field, distinct from traditional "psychological" assessment.

Instead of assuming that behavior is a product of an underlying personality structure resulting from early childhood experiences, behavior assessors treat observed behavior samples as the primary datum, eschewing traits or other unobservables that might encourage a search for consistency of responding in the presence of differing environmental conditions. Absence of interpretive inference confers the epithet "behavioral." Current measurable variables determine behavior. Therefore, assessment should focus directly and objectively on behavior itself in relation to the contemporary observable conditions that account for its maintenance and change.

It follows from these descriptions that behavioral assessment might be expected to approach its subject matter with procedures as distinct as its identity characteristics—procedures designed specifically for functional analysis of human behavior. But that does not appear to be the case. Although direct observation appears in all lists, current literature indicates that interviews are the most frequently used of all behavioral assessment procedures (Haynes & Jensen, 1979; Linehan, 1977; Swan & MacDonald, 1978). Checklists, ratings and rankings by clients and/or others, and self-report questionnaires and inventories are popular methods of quantifying behavior descriptions. Despite its emphasis on specific observable responses and the deterministic role of current environmental variables, behavioral assessment methodology may also include personality inventories (Goldfried, 1977). Moreover, standardized psychometric tests of achievement and intelligence, although routinely classified as nomothetically rather than idiographically oriented, are acceptable (Cone & Hawkins, 1977) if not desirable tools of the behavior assessor (Nelson, 1980).

As long as the obtained responses are treated as behavior samples rather than as signs of inferred causal conflicts or constructs, these conventional tests are admissable in the domain of behavioral assessment (Goldfried, 1977; Nelson, 1980). But behavioral constructs, likened to MacCorquodale and Meehl's (1948) intervening variables, are also admissible, though not considered causal. Behaviors observed in specific situations now define "behavioral" constructs. Their rated presence or absence yields values often summarized in the form of a total score (Linehan, 1980).

Such practices are reminiscent of psychometric efforts to evaluate personality traits or predispositions. Yet behavioral assessors vociferously deny trait theory on the grounds that generality has yet to find convincing empirical support (Cone & Hawkins, 1977). Although a more comprehensive temporal context has recently been argued (Mash & Terdal, 1981a), current measurable variables constitute the general focus of behavioral assessment. Intraindividual variability of responding across different situations is not only the subject matter but a methodologic imperative of behavioral treatment evaluation.

The stated focus of behavioral assessment appears to be inconsistent with the majority of its procedures. To obtain the objective samples of behavior that might reveal the variations of interest requires repeated assessment with instruments that retain sensitivity across repeated applications. Normatively derived tests and devices such as questionnaires, rating scales, and the like are designed for global single-sample inferential assessment of status relative to a standardization or comparison sample. Employed in traditional psychological assessment and associated diagnostic classification, such instruments are not designed to assist in formulation of individualized treatment or ongoing evaluation of its effects. None facilitate identification or analysis of the variables that could be manipulated to alter the behaviors they purport to describe (Skinner, 1953). None are conceived to track the course of individual behavior changes in response to treatment interventions. In short, none are suitable for integration into a self-corrective process of ongoing behavioral treatment evaluation. More importantly, none derive from or are consistent with either the concept of behavior or the methodology that gave rise to behavioral treatment.

ROOTS AND REMNANTS

Behavior analysis brought a new and different methodology to human service—the methodology of the natural sciences. Rooted in the interactions of individual organisms and their environments, its methods are sensitive enough to record individual behavior changes through time and powerful enough to verify treatment effects without recourse to the group statistical tests that had previously masked their presence.

Offering automatic definition of responses, automatically programmed stimuli, and a wealth of contingencies that produce rapid changes in the behavior of individuals, it bypasses human observer error and permits behavior to speak for itself. Its continuous automatic recording shows moment-to-moment fluctuations and the temporal dimensions of treatment effects. Standard response definition and recording units complemented with replicable environmental conditions facilitate comparisons of different effects not only for a given individual but across individuals as well.

Careful design of the behavior–analytic environment provides functional description of deficits in the retarded (Barrett & Lindsley, 1962; Barrett, 1965, 1969, 1975), prosthetics for the handicapped (Lindsley, 1964), analysis of psychotic behavior (Lindsley, 1956, 1960), autistic behavior (Ferster & DeMyer, 1961, 1962), and of functionally defined leadership, cooperation, and competition (Azrin & Lindsley, 1956; Cohen, 1962; Cohen & Lindsley, 1964; Hake & Vukelich, 1973; Hake, Vukelich, & Kaplan, 1973; Hake, Vukelich, & Olvera, 1975; Lindsley, 1966), conditioning history (Weiner, 1964), effects of drugs (Lindsley, 1962a) and depth of anesthesia (Lindsley, Hobika, & Etsten, 1961), and demonstration of contingency control of neurogenic tics (Barrett, 1962) and stuttering (Flanagan, Goldiamond, & Azrin, 1958), fine-tuning of the environment to achieve errorless stimulus

shaping (Sidman & Stoddard, 1966, 1967), and the content-related communication changes during psychiatric interviews (Lindsley, 1969; Nathan,
Schneller, & Lindsley, 1964). The differential reinforcing value of television
program content (Lindsley, 1962b) and the illusive domain of human preference also yield to analysis by these methods (Lockhart, 1979; Morgan &
Lindsley, 1966; Schroeder & Holland, 1969). The latter references afford
ample illustration of the value of functionally defined response classes and
automatic programming over conventional verbal reports (Azrin, Holz, Ulrich, & Goldiamond, 1961) in assessment and analysis of human behavior. In
more recent application, automatic response definition and recording reveals
when palpation of a human breast model detects individual lumps as small as
2 mm in diameter—a standard for training detection of lumps *in vivo* (Adams
et al., 1976; Hall, Goldstein, & Stein, 1977).

Sensitive design of the subject's environment makes complex aspects of
individual behavior accessible to analysis of the variables that compose and
alter them. Temporal dimensions of their natural fluctuations emerge in
permanent tracings drawn directly by response emissions through time.
Wide ranges of individually different behavior patterns demonstrate the
sensitivity of these methods. Yet their basic functionally defined response
classes show lawful variations of human behavior in response to alterations
of its environment and thus affirm the universality of operant principles
revealed by analysis of infrahuman behavior.

The malleability of human behavior demonstrated by these methods
lured clinicians from their psychometrics and group studies. Applications of
procedures derived from the methodology of experimental behavior analysis
became so successful with such a wide-ranging clientele as to change the
complexion of the human service field. But the translation continues to
sacrifice much of both the core methodology and its conceptual foundations (Birnbrauer, Burchard, & Burchard, 1970; Deitz, 1978; Fraley, 1981;
Michael, 1980, 1985; Pennypacker, 1981; Pierce & Epling, 1980; Woods, 1980).

Today's literature refers to the remnants of the parent methodology as
"direct observation"—certainly not attributable to behavior analysis per se.
Distinguished from indirect verbal reports by clients or others, first-hand
observation of clients' behavior in either contrived or natural environments
requires little or no inference. It thus meets the exclusion criterion for a behavioral assessment approach. Substituting for the automatic response de-
finers of the original system are people with coded forms to remind them
what to look at and for. Instead of direct, continuous recording automatically
drawn by occurrences of electromechanically defined behaviors, observers
look and record on intermittent schedules. Post hoc counting of observer
tallies or the checked versus unchecked squares on a recording form now

replaces automatic cumulative counters. Interval timers that once programmed contingencies for the behaver now signal observer behavior.
Elapsed time of the observing period rarely appears in reported data.

Thus response defining is indirect, filtered through human bias and
fatigue; recording is discontinuous; and timing applies not to the behaver's
activity but to the observer's. Replacing online measures of response frequencies, the only measurement of what occurs during an observation
period is a summary total, not of the client's behavior but of the proportion
of observer looks and listens that were checked for seeing or hearing the
behaviors of interest—the number of intervals marked. Reporting then
further removes the available information from retrieval by relating these
counts to the number of intervals used. Only by careful detective work can a
reader sometimes discover how much time went into the observation process. "Goodness" of the observation products depends on another observer's
tallies or checks of what *that* observer saw or heard. Such a standard of
comparison reveals nothing about the accuracy of either observer's records.

Attempts to determine the relative frequency of the observed behaviors
often appear in rating scales denoting levels such as "never," "occasionally,"
"usually," "frequently," and "always." Numerical values usually designate
each position on the scale, and summation yields a quantified subjective
estimate of whatever behavior is being rated (Walls, Werner, Bacon, & Zane,
1977). Today's rating scales purport to focus on "behavior" rather than on
attributes, opinions, or feelings. Unfortunately, revising or relabeling the
content of such scales does not improve the quality of their measured
products. Nor does it bring us anything resembling adequate information for
the stated mission of behavioral assessment. Subjectivity and insensitivity to
anything but gross pre- and post-treatment behavior changes render such
methods inappropriate for a functional analysis of change-inducing variables. These are some of the shortcomings that prototypical behavior assessment methods once put to rest. Alas, only temporarily.

The once-distinctive characteristics of behavior assessment methodology have succumbed to a melding process. From the residuals, there appear
to be three recognizable imprints. First, "behavioral" content appears in
clinical information (Angle, Hay, Hay, & Ellinwood, 1977). Rating scales and
checklists tend to concern what people do rather than how they think or feel,
and descriptive accounts of behavioral assessment reveal varying degrees of
"behaviorese," routinely calling attention to the conceptual distinction between a behavioral versus a psychodynamic interpretive process. Second,
consistent with a basic tenet of applied behavior analysis, self-monitoring
now enjoys considerable status as an assessment technique (Hayes & Cavior,
1980; Mahoney, 1977; Nelson, 1977a, 1977b; Swan & MacDonald, 1978).

Counters and data forms help systematize and objectify its operations in the service of self-control. Third, the time-honored observation process itself is now more "systematic" by virtue of often exhaustively codified behavioral definitions and recording forms designed to increase accuracy and precision of behavior transduction by human observers.

That precision is now a buzzword rather than an accurate description of behavior assessment methods suggest that a cost–benefit analysis would raise major questions about the contribution of current methods to the knowledge base of the field. Expedience and convenience now accompany social validation and consumer decision making, recently recommended as an integral stage in formulating and evaluating human behavior research (Wolf, 1978). Assessment methods reflect growing distance from a natural science concept of behavior. As the discrepancy advances, the methods that emanated from the science of behavior give way to those it once replaced. This cyclic process, so evident in sociopolitical history, has no precedent in the domain of a successful science whose foundations should serve to support its advances. Without successive broadening and strengthening of its fundamental principles and methods, it falls prey to common sense, the source of its original questions. And "common sense . . . seldom is aware of the limits within which its beliefs are valid or its practices successful" (Nagel, 1961, p. 5).

This chapter returns to a natural science concept of behavior. It attempts to clarify a functional definition of behavior and its constituent response classes and to show how methods for quantifying behavior relate to its definition. It views assessment as measurement. And it adopts the position that clients in clinical settings should enjoy at least the methodologic privileges accorded small animals from whom we learned the principles of behavior.

BEHAVIOR: THE SUBJECT MATTER OF ASSESSMENT

While conceptual evanescence tends to reflect contemporary influences, the properties of behavior remain unchanged. Conceptual discrepancies and methodologic inconsistencies are common companions. Drift in one permits vagaries in the other, and failure to acknowledge their interdependence is a costly oversight. In the domain of human behavior assessment, development of maximally effective behavior remediation technology requires essentially the same basic information as does pursuit of its scientific analysis (Johnston, 1982). For this reason, and whatever their conceptual affinity, the investigative methodology of both behavior therapists and their behavior analyst brethren should address the universal properties of the phenomenon they seek to understand—behavior.

DEFINITION

An adequate definition of behavior includes both its interactive and its dynamic properties and, in addition, provides for its accessibility via standard measurement systems of natural science (Johnston & Pennypacker, 1980).

> The behavior of an organism is that portion of the organism's interaction with its environment that is characterized by detectable displacement in space through time of some part of the organism that results in a measurable change in at least one aspect of the environment. (p. 48)

IMPLICATIONS FOR MEASUREMENT

Each component of the definition specifies a characteristic of behavior that should find expression in its measurement. Each implies certain capabilities of a suitable measurement system that distinguishes behavioral from traditional psychological measurement.

Intraindividual Phenomenon.

Consistent with a natural science concept of behavior and its biological significance in adaptation and survival, the science of human behavior, like its progenitor, experimental medicine (Bernard, 1865/1957), views the behavior of individual organisms as the focus of analysis. Variability in an organism's interaction with its environment is the subject matter of the science. To observe it directly, the activities of other organisms are unnecessary. Ample supporting evidence demonstrates that lawful relations emerge from the study of individual organisms interacting with their environments. Recourse to groups cannot describe the behavior of an individual within them, but generalities can and do arise from aggregations of lawfully determined individual behavior.

Sensitivity to the nuances of individual behavior and its interaction with its environment is, then, a principal requirement of a suitable measurement system. Measures designed to describe large samples do not meet the sensitivity prerequisite. Especially exempt are measures derived from either assumed or obtained variability of large samples. Measures that reflect other sources of variation cannot accurately represent variability of individual behavior. Psychometrically derived measures are thus inappropriate. Consistent with definitive statements about behavioral assessment, analysis of intraindividual phenomena provides the methodological approach shared by practitioners and researchers alike. It thus opens the search for lawfulness to participation by both clinic and laboratory.

Movement

"Detectable displacement in space through time" requires movement. Independent states of the behaver attributed to emotional or physiologic conditions such as being anxious or being hungry denote no movement component, nor do static postures such as eye contact, attending, or out of seat. All are capturable in a snapshot. All are prevalent examples potentially reconstructible with a cadaver and well within the skills of a sculptor.

Similarly, independent conditions or changes in the environment that happen to the behaver but require no interactive component fall outside the definitional limits. Examples include being pushed, falling downstairs, and being given a cookie. Being denied access to a meal may not function as a behavioral event until and unless the behaver engages in activity that avoids or escapes such denial.

The environment may be internal or external. The epidermis need not be a barrier to behavior. Thus both visible actions and intraorganism activities such as muscle potential changes and heartbeats qualify. The movement requirement provides for detection by means of public responses or by instruments which convert response occurrences into measurable changes in some aspect of the environment. Thus, gross displacement of objects by some act of the behaver as well as amplified transduction that deflects a needle or changes a display on a monitoring screen both exemplify the movement that makes various forms of behavior accessible to standard scientific measurement. Private events externalized via publicly observable responses are no exception. "The line between public and private is not fixed. The boundary shifts with every discovery of a technique for making private events public" (Skinner, 1953, p. 282).

Continuous Process

In addition to providing for detection, "displacement in space through time" reminds us that behavior is continuous in nature. Discrete static events and states without movement or interactive aspects are not behavioral events. Behavior not only takes time to occur and occurs in time; it also occurs through time. Time is thus a fundamental and universal parameter of behavior. Without temporal dimensions revealing trends and interactions, quantitated description is both incomplete and inappropriate for analysis of behavior and its controlling variables.

The continuous nature of behavior requires repeated observation and measurement. Procedures that sample many behaviors for a snapshot summary are shortcuts that prevent analysis of the continuing interaction of the organism and its environment. Those that focus on a few behaviors but sample them discontinuously also preclude tracking behavior as it changes through time in accord with environmental alterations. Lawfulness emerges not through restricting our range of vision but by expanding it to encompass nature's fullest and richest picture.

Measurable Change in Environment

Behavior and its environment are inseparable. Their relations are our subject matter. By definition, behavior affects the environment. The changes it produces afford our only entry to its measurement. Detection selectively scans the environmental traces of behavior; transduction converts them into measurable form. If we profess to study behavior in its own right, we deal directly with its environmental traces as they occur through time. Automatically transduced events that depress recording pens, or internal changes revealed on a cathode ray tube, or self-recorded private events registered by pushing a switch are examples.

Caveats are in order when the environmental changes produced by behavior become merely symbols of inferred conditions, past or present. Questionnaires, checklists, and the like are examples. In these cases, behavior-produced environmental changes themselves (check marks, encircled numerals) are usually not the subject matter of assessment (except in some educational contexts), even though the stimuli reputed to be controlling them—words on paper—may refer to what an individual did. Inferential measurement is neither conceived for nor designed to provide information about behavior itself.

Irrespective of its diverse conceptual–methodologic embellishments, the language of behavior assessment is the language of measurement. Description, comparison, and prediction underlie all behavior assessment whether undertaken for classification, placement, treatment formulation, prognosis, treatment evaluation, or collection of normative data. The degree to which measurement will accomplish these purposes depends on the fidelity of the correspondence between what is being assessed or analyzed and the measures chosen to represent it.

Variability of the *behaver's* interaction with the environment is the subject matter of both the natural science of behavior and behavior assessment. The spectrum of behavior-descriptive labels, their wide-ranging behavioral referents, and the varying measurement procedures currently applied to them all introduce sources of variation that confound the behavioral phenomena of interest. From the once successful search for lawfulness, behavioral assessment now accepts a state of definitional–methodological anarchy (Cone & Hawkins, 1977). It is, after all, superficially consistent with individualized treatment and with personalized interpretation of the client's behavior. Unfortunately, it is also consistent with the assumption of inherent variability of human behavior—the assumption that originally gave rise to the social sciences' statistically derived concept of human behavior variation.

Practices that distort, mask, or otherwise misrepresent properties of behavior are counterproductive, not only to the development of effective clinical technology, but also to the advancement of the natural science of behavior on which it rests. Sources of such illusory variability, still unrecognized in much of the behavioral assessment literature, lie in decisions regarding the definition of behavior units to be studied, methods for quantitating their properties, and procedures by which they are observed and recorded.

UNITS OF BEHAVIOR ANALYSIS: RESPONSES AND THEIR FUNCTIONAL CLASSES

While various traditional social science approaches may assist in selecting the problem area to be addressed, behavior assessment begins with defining the behaviors selected for measurement during the intervention process. These may include behaviors targeted for development, behaviors designated for management, support behaviors that could serve as alternatives or replacements, and collateral behaviors that may be important to monitor for ancillary or secondary effects.

Measurement accessibility requires dissection of the stream of ongoing behavior–environment interaction into response classes appropriate for quantitative description. To fully represent the properties of behavior discussed earlier, response classes chosen for analysis must consist of movements that produce effects on the environment as they occur. To preserve the functional nature of behavior, response class definition should account for demonstrated controlling antecedent and subsequent environmental variables.

RESPONSE CLASSES IN CONTEMPORARY LITERATURE

Today's cadre of behavioral assessment techniques concerns a widely varied assortment of responses. The more sophisticated classes include physiologically or motorically activated switch operations associated with various replicable environmental conditions. Other less-refined versions include pencil slashes in printed boxes, encircled numerals, and check marks executed by the behaver in response to printed survey or scale items or by an observer/ informant reporting on the behaver/assessee. One of the most prevalent classes of numeral encircling refers to verbal descriptions of remembered events, feelings, or states bereft of any responses. Levels of prompting required for the behaver to execute responses appear in such scales while the behaver's responses themselves remain unmeasured. Even further removed from behavior are observations of clients' stances such as "hands in lap," "in seat," and "on task"—again notated as checks or slashes in time-ruled coded squares. Summation then provides a score connoting an amount of such broadly conceived classes as "appropriate behavior," "assertiveness," "social interaction," or "independence," each defined by its own measures.

As units of behavior analysis, response class definitions must be stable and independent of the units used to measure them; otherwise, variability in the response-class definition will reflect itself as measured variability in the phenomenon under study. Moreover, response classes should represent the interactive property of behavior, specifying what responses do to affect the environment and, ideally, what aspects of the environment control their occurrence. In addition, definition of the classes selected for assessment should be sufficiently molecular to permit measurement of the variability necessary for sensitive analysis and successful treatment. Equating response classes and measurement units and failing to provide a properly sensitive level of analysis obscures the contextual properties of behavior–environment relations which are, after all, the given ingredients of intervention planning.

RESPONSE CLASS FUNCTIONS AND ASSESSMENT

When undertaken for clinical purposes, behavior assessment inventories both the desirable and the aberrant or deficient functional relations of a client's interactions with the environment. Remedial manipulations of the environment then broaden or otherwise modify the client's behavior by recomposing the existing array of selected functional response classes. Tactics to achieve this objective include: (1) altering the conditions under which selected responses occur, (2) providing more complex new functions for existing responses, (3) generating new movements that become functional responses by virtue of the environmental changes they provide, (4) changing some dimensional quantity of an already functional response class such as its frequency, and (5) modifying the topography of a functional response class to produce greater environmental effect. The nature of behavior intervention by definition deals with the functions of responses extant in the client's

repertoire and the manner in which the client's environment sustains presenting problematic behavior.

Response definition most commonly focuses on its form or *topography*, its
most obvious aspect. Speech sounds and dance movements are examples for
which specific criteria are legion. Success—reinforcement—accrues to the
behaver for responses meeting these standards. But when extended to most
response definitions, there appears to be little evidence to indicate an invariant relation between topographically similar or superficially classified behaviors and their functions for the behaver. Thus, on the deviant side of the
inventory, "self-injurious behaviors" designates a socially labeled class selected for intensive treatment due to its aversive effects on most observers
and its frequent life-threatening outcomes which society attempts to prevent. The class encompasses a range of topographies limited only by the
interaction history and/or the creativity of the behaver: eye gouging, rectal
digging, head hitting, nail biting, head banging, screaming, flesh and muscle
chewing, and so on.

All may conceivably serve similar *functions* for the behaver. Moreover,
their functions for the behaver may be quite different from the functions
these behaviors serve for the observer–classifier. Yet neither the label of the
class nor the interventions selected to treat it may reveal the effects such
behaviors achieve for the behaver. Similarly, a single well-defined topography such as head hitting may serve multiple functions by which the behaver
escapes or avoids aversive conditions or obtains social, sensory, or food
reinforcement depending, perhaps, on the antecedent conditions that have
become associated with each of these environmental effects. If topographic
differences and/or societal reactions continue to remain the principal foci of
assessment, the permutations and combinations of behaver-focused environmental effects that may exist across different individuals will present a
melange that defies systematic inquiry.

Lawfulness is more likely to emerge from analysis of response classes
defined in terms of the conditions under which they occur and the effects
they achieve for the behaver than is the case with classes defined by the form
of the movement in question or its effects on third parties (Skinner, 1935).
The class of behaviors knows as imitative emerged from studies of widely
varying topographies which resulted in reinforcement if they matched the
topographies presented by a model. Systematic observation of covarying
topographies during development of imitative behaviors revealed that some
nonconsequated topographies covary with those meeting the matching (imitative) criteria. Thus commonalities of function demonstrated across constituent topographies under a similar set of conditions expanded the imitative
response class (Baer, Peterson & Sherman, 1967).

As an environmental effect or possible treatment technique rather than as a response class emitted by the behaver, contingent imitation of behaver responses by other persons may eventually show lawful relations that define yet other response classes generated by the reciprocal imitations they produce. The different results of reciprocal imitation associated with differing topographies—vocal and motor—(Birnbrauer, 1979) opens the phenomenon to further analysis that should delineate classes associated with the accelerative versus decelerative functions of this environmental effect. In any event, similarities and differences obtained in response to a given environmental antecedent or subsequent event should further clarify the common functional relations of topographically disparate behaviors.

Clearly, a number of topographically different responses showing the same relation to common antecedent and/or subsequent conditions may constitute a functionally homogeneous response class. Such "functional clusters" raise the possibility, indeed the likelihood of altering multiple topographies by manipulating conditions for a single topography within a class (Wahler, 1975). By capitalizing on the empirically substantiated covariance of different response class members, maximum therapeutic gains might be achieved by minimal effort and cost. Moreover, all individuals with a given target sharing a common cluster or response class composition with other individuals might then be treated similarly with expectation of comparable cost-benefit ratios.

Treatment packages involving multiple manipulations as prescriptions for behaviors described only by their topographies preclude this type of assessment. Without empirical verification of the functions served by varying topographies for given individuals under the conditions of their everyday environments, the package risks targeting behaviors that, because they may not share homogeneous functions, could offset or mask whatever effects might otherwise be obtained. Thus an accelerative effect on one class of responses might accompany a decelerative or neutral effect on another class, yet a single topographically defined class may encompass the two functionally different classes.

Such combinations of effect are not predictable, and their likelihood seriously limits both the validity and the generality of package application. The topographical approach retards delineation of functional classes that underlie the vagaries of personal or social linguistic practices. More importantly and for reasons just mentioned, topographical definition may produce illusory variability that is not recognized and therefore not susceptible to either control or analysis.

The purpose of response definition is to derive units of analysis that are accessible to quantification by standard units of measurement. Functionally equivalent events are more likely to share common determinants than are those that resemble each other in superficial or irrelevant respects (Johnston

& Pennypacker, 1980). If behavior assessment defines its unit, the response class, to account for its own relation to antecedent and/or subsequent events, associated measurement procedures will less likely confound irretrievable sources of variability. Orderliness is more likely to appear along the "natural lines of fracture" (Skinner, 1935).

FUNCTIONAL CLASSES, PROGNOSIS, AND
GENERALITY OF TREATMENT

Response classes defined by empirical verification of functional homogeneity across their various topographies constitute the maximally efficient pretreatment assessment baselines from which to select and against which to evaluate the effects of remedial procedures. The likelihood of achieving generality of effect is enhanced by ongoing pretreatment measurement of pertinent functionally related response classes that, by definition, specify at least some of the conditions under which effects will be sustained when treatment terminates (see Birnbrauer, 1981). Pretreatment measurement of functionally defined response classes conducted over a sufficiently long period should display naturally occurring irregularities that may obscure or interact with treatment effects. Such information facilitates adjustment of the temporal dimensions of treatment to override or capitalize on existing response interactions. Optimal reliability and generality should result.

A body of knowledge permitting adequate prognostication of specific and secondary treatment effects would greatly simplify therapeutic endeavors. Treatment protocols could be matched to selected characteristics of presenting problems with a foundation of supporting evidence indicating likely effectiveness. The province of behavior intervention involves altering the functional relations between behaviors and the environment. For this reason, the functions of response classes become the focus of assessment. Given the overwhelming evidence that the environment is orderly and lawful, there is ample reason to postulate lawfulness in the interactive behaviors that it generates and sustains. What society considers aberrant behavior is no exception. When a procedure changes the behavior of an individual, it does so only by controlling the environment that supports such behavior. Therapeutic procedures do not change individuals in any permanent sense, only the environments with which they interact. This applies to pharmacologic interventions in the internal environment, manipulation of the environment outside the epidermis, or a combination. Commonalities in the relations between groups of topographically different responses and their supporting environmental effects will then determine generality of treatment effects across these behaviors. Commonalities in the response class constituents of individuals sharing a similar deviant form of behavior will determine whether cross-subject generality will result from a given environmental alteration. Similarly, commonalities in the cross-setting controlling stimuli of a deviant behavior and/or its targeted alternative(s) will determine the setting generality of the outcome and the suitability of selected alternative topographies.

It is the classification of such response–procedure relations, that is, the commonalities across topographies within response classes, that will facilitate formulation of criteria for optimal response class–treatment matches. In order for such commonalities to emerge, environmental modifications must themselves undergo analysis to sort out those components that are functional for specified response classes from those that are unnecessary or even counteractive to maximal effect.

Elucidating the functional relations shown by pretreatment behavior is a major mission of behavior assessment. It is these relations that are altered in the course of intervention. The interactions between pretreatment behavior and behavior changes during treatment constitute the basic information for development of prognostic indices. These, in turn, depend on evolution of effective, efficient matching of response classes with intervention procedures across clients with diverse behavior topographies, but sharing the common functions that orderly environmental reactions produce. Such an enterprise finds its parallel in bioassays that determine ingredients of a pharmacologic compound most likely to produce the desired effects and least likely to produce simultaneously undesirable side effects. The form of the pill is irrelevant. The job of the behavior assessor is quite similar to that of the bioassayst: to sort out the functions of existing topographies and the manner in which these functional relations change as various elements of a treatment (compound) package are introduced. However, without adequate pretreatment analysis of the functional relations to be altered, there is little hope of discovering the lawfulness of behavior that synthesis of more reliable and more general treatment effects requires.

QUANTIFYING THE DIMENSIONS OF BEHAVIOR UNITS

Determining the functional homogeneity of responses assigned to a class requires repeated measurement of their occurrences under different conditions. Moreover, methods chosen for this purpose should permit quantitative description and direct comparison across conditions and across responses as they occur in time. Selecting the most suitable measure is critical not only for reliability and generality of findings but also for description of the behaviors to which they apply.

Implicit in the choice of measurement is the distinction between sources of variability. As a dynamic organism–environment interaction, any behavior displays its own natural variability. Controlled alterations of environmental conditions during experimentation or treatment impose added variability. It is the business of behavior assessment and analysis to quantitatively distinguish one from the other and to explain the changes in measured behavior resulting from changes in experimenter-imposed conditions.

Sources of variability that are neither a natural property of the organism–environment interaction nor a result of experimental manipulation of that environment are considered to be "extraneous." Intraorganismic physiologic and developmental processes and various aspects of the experimental setting are commonly, though often unfortunately, accepted in this category. However, there is another source of variability that much of current practice fails to recognize. Its illusory source is the measurement process itself. If undetected, the resulting measurement system will confound its own sources of variability with those under analysis. No amount of statistical filtration will rid the data of measurement-produced variability. Dignifying the measurement product as "error variance," a common practice in social science methodology, reflects acceptance of intrinsic variability as a property of the organism rather than as a result of individual organism–environment interaction. Clearly antithetical to a natural science approach, the assumption of variability as an inherent or "given" organismic characteristic supports the statistical social science conception of behavior and obviates functional analysis of independent variables that might control intersubject differences (Johnston & Pennypacker, 1980; Sidman, 1960). A science in its developmental phase can ill afford acceptance of such obvious constraint on its potential knowledge base.

BEHAVIOR PROPERTIES

Quantifying behavior units requires assigning numbers and measurement units to selected dimensions representing fundamental properties of behavior. Accordingly, those properties that are both universal and relevant for adaptive functioning are of primary concern. Since behavior occurs in time, it is always time-referenced. The property of a single instance of behavior describing that point in time when the response occurs is its *temporal locus*. That a response takes time for completion is its universal property of *temporal extent*. Repetition through time, required for functional behavior–environment interaction, is the property of *repeatability*. These properties characterize every instance of behavior. Their dimensions are the subject of behavior measurement.

DIMENSIONAL QUANTITIES OF BEHAVIOR

Quantitative description of a behavior property requires selection of a suitable dimension to be measured. Length and weight are examples of dimensional quantities in the physical sciences; and their associated measurement units, centimeters and grams, are invariably related to each. Similarly, each of the fundamental behavior properties denotes quantifiable aspects. Thus the dimensional quantity representing temporal locus is *latency*, and the dimensional quantity of *duration* represents temporal extent or elapsed time. Repeatability through time, represented by *count*, completes the dimensional quantities of single behavior instances.

Additional dimensional quantities emerge for a series or class of responses, none of which is applicable to single occurrences. For multiple instances, temporal locus and repeatability find expression in the dimensional quantity of *frequency*—the number of responses per unit of time—considered by Skinner to be the fundamental datum of an analysis of freely emitted behavior (1938, 1953). That behavior frequencies change over time requires the dimensional quantity of *celeration* (Lindsley, 1969a)—the combination of temporal locus and repeatability which universally quantifies the dynamic property of behavior-environment interactions. The time interval between responses in a series, quantified as *interresponse time* (IRT), combines the properties of temporal locus and repeatability to represent their analogue in the case of more than one response.

Other dimensional quantities describing patterns of responses, such as quarter life and IRTs per opportunity, may describe serial occurrences of a class of responses. The generality and usefulness of these and other dimensional quantities fashioned for application in particular situations require extensive verification.

MEASUREMENT UNITS: THE REFERENTS FOR
DIMENSIONS OF BEHAVIOR

Quantification of behavior events employs measurement units selected from appropriate scales representing the dimensions chosen for study. Just as standard units (yards, square feet, cubic yards, ounces, and gallons) describe physical dimensions, so standard units represent each of the fundamental dimensions of behavior. Standard *time units* (seconds, minutes, hours, days, weeks, months, years) are absolute and universal descriptors of both latency and duration. Because both are fundamental dimensions of any instance of behavior, time units are basic units of behavior measurement. No quantitative description of behavior is complete without inclusion of at least one temporal referent.

Countability, denoting the recurring property of any unit of behavior analysis, has as its measurement unit the *cycle* which begins with the initiation and ends with the cessation of a single response. *Cycles per unit time* of the counting period describes the frequency dimension of a class of recurring responses. It combines the latency and countability dimensions applicable only to single instances. This compound unit is universally and invariantly descriptive of any repeatable motion. Simple counting determines the value of cycles.

Change in behavior frequency over time simply combines the second time dimension to become *cycles per unit time per unit time*. Such examples as cycles per minute per week and cycles per day per week describe the temporal changes in frequency seen both in skill proficiency growth and in behavior management endeavors. In the case of interresponse times, the cycle under study begins with the cessation of one response and ends with the onset of the next response. Its measurement unit is, then, the *time per cycle*. Table 6-1 summarizes the relations of behavior properties to dimensional quantities and their corresponding measurement units.

CONTROLLING THE CONTROLLABLE: VARIABILITY OF
MEASUREMENT UNITS

Variation in behavioral phenomena, like variation in physical aspects of the environment, requires fixed measurement units for its description. Units of quantitative reference that vacillate from behaver to behaver, from scale to scale, can only confound the true variability of the phenomena being investigated. Use of such evanescent units of measurement not only ensures

TABLE 6-1. Properties, Dimensional Quantities, and Units of Behavioral Measurement

Property	Dimensional Quantity	Unit
Temporal locus	Latency	Time units
Temporal extent	Duration	Time units
Repeatability	Countability	Cycle
Temporal locus and repeatability	Frequency	Cycles/Unit time
Temporal locus and repeatability	Celeration	Cycles/Unit time/Unit time
Temporal locus and repeatability	IRT	Time/Cycle

See Johnston & Pennypacker, 1980, p. 128

limited generality of findings, but liberally bolsters popular assumptions of intrinsic variability beyond the reach of scientific study (Sidman, 1960). If accepted either wittingly or unwittingly, this assumption relegates behavior to prescientific explanatory concepts and precludes refinement of methodology that might reveal the lawful behavior–environment relations upon which a more exact prognostic–prescriptive taxonomy must be based.

Given the numerous sources of uncontrolled variability facing the assessor of human behavior, widespread acceptance of fluctuating measurement units bespeaks inadequate awareness of controllable sources of variability introduced in the measurement process itself. Judicious decision will remove this source of variation if the units included in the measurement system retain constant and universal values throughout the course of study. Such idemnotic units (Johnston & Pennypacker, 1980) reduce replication problems and enhance generality by ensuring direct comparability of measures.

Numerical values attached to time units are universally recognized and apply in any measurement of time. No confusion exists about the amount of time described by t minus 1 at Cape Canaveral or at the various tracking stations around the world. Were it not for the precise uniformity of temporal units, the operations of launching, tracking, and retrieving a space vehicle would be calamitous at best. Nor is there any question whether the value of a second will change from day to day. Time units are thus standard, absolute, and universal, applying to every instance of behavior, every series of repetitions, and every observation/counting/recording period. Similarly, counting conventions are universal. As long as the behavior units being counted retain descriptive stability so that the value or definition of each response remains constant throughout a series of repetitions, the response cycle then has a standard referent. Moreover, given accurate timing devices and an equally accurate description of response cycles, variations emerging from repeated measurement cannot be ascribed to measurement "errors."

UNITLESS VALUES

Contrast the descriptive precision and comparative power of the fixed unit and its standard referent with, for example, the rating scale's numerical values anchored only in verbal descriptions connoting subjectively determined amounts of an assumed dimension of behavior, for example, assertion or anxiety. If we accept *Webster's* (1961) definition of a unit as "a determinate quantity (as of length, time) adopted as a standard of measurement for other quantities of the same kind," and substitute for length one of the dimensions of behavior described above, it becomes immediately apparent that no true measurement units are attached to these values. The referents are indigenous to the scale itself, the respondent's personal interpretation of the accompanying descriptors, and the scale writer's interpretation of the often synthetic dimension represented by the scale. Personal histories and linguistic conventions substituted for standard, absolute units thus render applications of arithmetic inappropriate.

Nonetheless, the common practice of providing greater "sensitivity" by increasing the number of scale points reflects the assumption of intrinsic variability. Thus, presence–absence checklists, when expanded into three-, five-, or seven-point or greater scales, permit greater latitude of response individuality. However, expansion of the scale fails to provide a fixed unit from which to determine individual departure.

Further arithmetic digression occurs in practices such as summing unitless "values" across multiple scales to yield "scores," and in arbitrarily scaling such "scores" into profiles for purposes of comparison. Because a given numerically designated point of one scale is in no way equivalent to or representative of the same point on any other scale, such comparisons are clearly spurious. For the same reason, score or profile comparison across subjects is even less appropriate. Greater disparity of subjective interpretation from respondent to respondent increases the variation in referents for any given numerical "value."

Comparison of repeated measures through time constitutes the basis of scientific validation and, ultimately, prediction and prognosis. However, repeated measures composed of units resulting from unique histories or constraints of the examining situation confound *these* sources of variability with whatever change may appear in obtained scores. Any or all of the factors influencing the original choice of positions on a given scale may vary from one administration to another. A given respondent may attach different interpretations to the labeled points on a scale at different times. For example, a subject's definition of, say, "anxiety" may change from one "testing" to another, especially if treatment intervenes. The result is a shift of unknown quantity in the private "value" of scale points. Thus even the most gross change in scale value cannot reliably represent a true change. Without direct measurement in absolute units, verification is impossible.

INDETERMINATE UNITS

Another version of oscillating, indeterminate, or vaganotic units (Johnston & Pennypacker, 1980) is becoming more prevalent in the literature. Psychological attribute testing and large-scale probability testing of groups now threaten to replace the naturalistic analysis of behavior. Units such as MA, IQ, and scores on achievement tests derive from empirically assessed vari-

ability in the standardization group. As such, they have no standard referents and no absolute values. Puds, purps, and zuds are easily as indeterminate. Similarly, statistical significance testing further reifies indeterminate
units as the "standard" against which to evaluate obtained differences. That
such procedures, by virtue of their dependence on vaganotic units, are
inappropriate for functional analysis of variability should be self-evident.
"The data are asked to perform an impossible task, that of evaluating
themselves against standards that are supplied by their own existence"
(Johnston & Pennypacker, 1980, p. 371).

Alternatives that are consistent with the definition of behavior offered
earlier, that retain the uniqueness of individual behavior values, and that
make use of the standard and absolute idemnotic measures distinguishing
the natural from the social sciences, are explained in detail by Johnston and
Pennypacker (1980).

DIMENSIONLESS QUANTITIES

We have thus far discussed the instability of measures that are widely used
to assess actual or synthetic dimensions of behavior. Their contribution of
variability is indistinguishable from the other sources of variability in the
behavior being studied. Perhaps even more prevalent are quantities bearing
no relation to any real or putative dimensions of behavior. Recommended
for application to opportunity-bound responses (Baer, 1982), the values
associated with a measure such as percentage relate a count representing the subject's behavior, to a count representing the experimenter's or
teacher's behavior in the form of opportunities offered. In calculation, the
attached units of measurement cancel, and the remaining quantity describes
no referent in any natural dimension of behavior. Similarly, relative durations and relative frequencies find no dimensional representation in the
fundamental properties of an organism's behavior. Ratios of this nature
dispense with the units accompanying the original measures; and this essential descriptive information is often unretrievable from published reports.
Even worse, it is impossible to determine sources of variation in a series of
such ratios, for instance, as commonly found in skill acquisition data. Percentage of correct responses may increase due to increased correct responding with the same number of opportunities, correct responding remaining
constant while opportunities decrease, or a combination of these two. The
problem remains identical whenever comparison of any two measures of the
same dimensional quantity takes the form of a ratio that is divided (and
multiplied by 100) to obtain a percentage.

The fact that percentage correct reveals nothing of the temporal characteristics of individual performance permits some deluding and often damaging conclusions. Its use for comparison presents the risk of equating the skills of two individuals who may reach the same percentage score while performing at levels of proficiency disparate enough to place one in the gifted or normal range and the other in the retarded range. Additionally, this property of dimensionless ratios enables habilitators to obtain predetermined and often misleading quantification of progress simply by adjusting the number of response opportunities offered. Multiple examples of differing proficiency in individuals performing at 100% accuracy levels (Barrett, 1979) highlight but a vignette of the variability in basic behavior dimensions that find no expression in the percentage measure. Unfortunate conclusions of skill "mastery" continue to be drawn from a measure that imposes a ceiling that may be exceeded by any of the actual dimensional quantities of response classes. In failing to reveal sources and types of variability, ratios depicting relative measures of the same dimension are sufficiently insensitive to obscure potentially valuable information in the analysis of behavior.

A simple statement retaining the necessary dimensional descriptors would include, at the very least, correct response frequency and error frequency, indicating that the correct response frequency was x times greater than the error frequency. Treating the two frequencies separately acknowledges the reality that *each is free to vary* independently of the other (Barrett, 1980).

CHOICE OF DIMENSIONAL QUANTITIES

Any behavior can be described with each and all of the dimensional quantities mentioned earlier. Ideally, the use of all would yield the maximum potentially valuable information. However, most resources do not permit what could be construed as a measurement luxury. While choices are often necessary, sensitivity and precision are the primary criteria for scientifically suitable selection. Continuous temporal dimensions such as latency and duration are as sensitive as their timing devices, especially when operated automatically. And, although frequency may be limited by the discrete nature of integers used to count response cycles, the temporal parameter of frequency is continuously adjustable to achieve optimal sensitivity for the particular measurement application. The principal consideration is the smallest detectable change, represented by 1/time unit selected. Akin to increasing the power of a microscope or adding finer gradations on a ruler, increasing the length of measurement time increases measurement sensitivity. The longer one looks, the more one sees of the behavior frequency spectrum (Bourie, 1981).

Dimensional quantities may differ in their sensitivity to variations in responding (Springer, Brown, & Duncan, 1981). Appropriate selection is, therefore, a key to the resultant information yield. Counts of correct responses neglect temporal parameters. In addition, simple counting restricts observable variation to the range of response opportunities available to the behaver or to the observer/recorder or both. More restrictive yet are relative counts whose arbitrary ceilings obscure the orderly variation shown by frequency. Temporal dimensions likewise require choice considerations as, for example, if response duration stabilizes while frequency, though unmeasured, undergoes orderly changes. Automatic transduction with continuous direct recording avoids these constraints by retaining each of the dimensional quantities of behavior, thereby presenting more options for analysis. Its use yields the richest and most sensitive quantification of behavior variability.

CONVERTING BEHAVIOR UNITS INTO MEASURABLE NOTATION

The best test of decisions regarding response class definition, dimensional quantities, and units is the completeness and accuracy of information emanating from the measurement of recorded behavior. The stream of ongoing behavior must undergo filtration into defined response classes. Transducing the dimensional quantities of those classes into a recordable form is the process of observation.

Converting the output of observation into permanent notation is the function of recording. These two pivotal processes partly determine the quality of data from which conclusions will be drawn. Decisions affecting the accuracy of their products are therefore critical to the validity of the information obtained from their use. Regardless of what procedures may be chosen, the correspondence between occurrences of selected responses and their recorded representations is the accuracy criterion against which to evaluate their merit. It is essential to rectify sources of inaccuracy in these processes prior to application. Once in use, such contributors to extraneous variability will be inseparable from their recorded products and therefore unavailable for post hoc appraisal.

OBSERVATION

Detecting amounts of dimensional quantities of response classes and transforming them into permanently recordable events makes ongoing behavior amenable to measurement. Performed either by instruments or by people, the transducing function interfaces selected acts of the behaver with the recording procedure. In the case of automated environments, the interface, in addition to activating a recording mechanism, also may activate the environment to respond according to whatever contingencies have been programmed. For the purpose of detection, instrumentation affords sensors responsive to a myriad of behaviors, and current technology offers a wealth of such devices providing capabilities far beyond those of human observers. When calibrated for appropriate sensitivity and designed for stability of response definition, properly selected transducers eliminate fatigue and conditioning history (bias) factors that have long been acknowledged as sources of uncontrolled variability in human observation. More importantly, they assure stable correspondence among occurrences of selected responses and their transmission to recording devices.

Observer/transducer accuracy, whether human or mechanical, electromechanical, or electronic, depends on sensitivity through time to selected dimensions of the response class to be studied. Ideally, each and every emission of a designated response should activate the observing response. The goal of observation is, then, twofold: to create conditions that (1) sensitize the transducer only to those response dimensions selected for recording, and (2) ensure that the transducer reacts appropriately to every occurrence of the selected behaviors. To approximate the accuracy of automatic devices with human observers requires arranging conditions under which the class of behaviors being studied exerts uncontaminated control over the observing response. To the extent that responses are reliably identified and the continuity of ongoing responses directly recordable, standard units of measurement representing dimensional quantities of behavior are applicable. Absence of standard units precludes accuracy comparisons with any dependable estimate of true values.

Response Class Characteristics

A critical source of observational error resides in the clarity and functionality of response class definitions. Any ambiguity will be reflected in inaccurate observing responses. Due to the subjectivity of their definition, hypothetical states elude detection and ensure inexact measurement. As a result, questions of validity inevitably arise. Restricting inquiry to observable events not only provides for detection but also offers the advantage of idemnotic measurement, therefore a closer approximation to true values.

Given that behavior consists of movement in space through time, the observing response should be capable of reacting to each occurrence of specified movement cycles as well as to their temporal distribution. The latter necessitates one or more timing devices coupled with a response-specific sensor, human or otherwise. If the response class is functionally defined, target response emissions *in temporal association with* their related antecedent and subsequent conditions should occasion the observing response. In addition, observation of response class effects in the form of physical products may satisfy the functional definition requirement. Determining one-to-one correspondence between responses and products as well as the authorship of responses may pose problems, especially in group settings. However, response product observation may be useful when on-line observation is not practical. If topographic characteristics define the class of interest, mechanical properties (distance, velocity, inertial force) delineating the specified limits of the class form must be observed and transmitted to the recording mechanism.

Definitional Drift

Establishing one-to-one correspondence between response emissions and activation of the transducer is merely the first step toward ensuring accuracy of the resulting data. Faithful transmission of responding over time is an additional requirement. Drift in accuracy may occur if the observing response fails to track each response, either because it cannot keep pace with a high frequency response class or because it does not filter out other events. The latter is more likely to occur with human observers who, unlike devices, react to subtle changes in response class features. Frequent checks on definitional drift and recalibration of the transducer will help provide the desired definitional stability.

Sensitivity Drift

Both human and automatic sensors require frequent calibration checks to assure that the detection response continues to react selectively only to the events of interest throughout the course of study. Procedures for training and calibrating human observers, including self-observers, are discussed below. For the moment, it should be clear that assuring accuracy of observation is a prerequisite for application of standard measurement procedures.

There are some safeguards for reducing the variability in observer reactions. First, careful selection of observers to rule out obvious biases is a necessity. Second, rigorous training should incorporate the full range of stimulus control technology to achieve accurate reactivity of the observing response. Third, frequent calibration should check and adjust the correspondence between observer behavior and a set of true values. All such observer preparation should take place under carefully controlled conditions with subjects offering the full range of all pertinent response class dimensions. In addition, observer recalibration should take place at intervals throughout the course of study to ensure continued sensitivity to the changing range of values that may result from treatment effects.

Temporal Dimensions of Observation

Another usually undetected source of observational inaccuracy occurs in the temporal programming of the observing response. Just as behavior occurs continuously through time, its observation should track the entire course of its occurence. Continuous and precisely response-synchronized observation will yield the most complete account of naturally occurring fluctuations in behavior. Observation scheduling that departs from the continuous and complete ideal will necessarily produce an intermittent and therefore less than true account of behavior flow. The question becomes one of the extent of observation-imposed "noise" that reduces the accuracy and stability of the obtained data. The more complete the observation of all responses in the class, the more closely will it yield true values of the behavior dimensions being investigated.

Complete observation of all responses in a class is most often not feasible. Empirical analysis should determine the maximally sensitive frequency and duration of observation periods. Since most behavior dimensions vary in response to environmental contingencies, prior analysis of samples under different conditions should reveal the nature of temporal and setting variations in dimensional quantities. An appropriately designed observation schedule can then minimize loss of information while maximizing the representativeness of the sample with respect to periods of relative stability and variability during prestudy probes.

Obviously, frequency of responding will play a major role in observation scheduling, irrespective of which dimensional quantities are being assessed. Low frequency behaviors may demand longer observation periods than behaviors of higher frequency. Whatever sampling schedule is used, the objective is to obtain the best approximation of true parameters of the response class under study. The more continuous the observation, the less likely will there be misrepresentation of naturally occurring temporal variations.

Intermittent sampling within the observation period imposes experimenter-determined but unanalyzed discontinuity on the observation product. In the absence of continuous records as a comparison standard, the extent of error resulting from incomplete observation remains unknown. Yet it is confounded with the natural variability of the behavior being studied as well as with the variability imposed by treatment. The result is reduction in both the accuracy and the generality of conclusions.

Popular forms of incomplete observation include time-sampling with its momentary observations, alternating with relatively longer intervals between observations. Although inter-look intervals may be regularly scheduled, the cumulative observation time within a session may be only a minor fraction of the total session time. The resulting counts describe the number of momentary looks that happen to coincide with the observer's judgment regarding presence or absence of an ongoing behavior.

A variation of time sampling often referred to as interval recording divides the session into a series of temporally contiguous observation intervals. Although it frees the observer to look continuously, it grossly restricts the observation product to checking the presence or absence of behaviors occurring within each interval. Definitional requirements related to the temporal coincidence of the target behavior with observation intervals may complicate the procedure. For example, the behavior of interest may be scored only if it occurs throughout an interval, or it may qualify for checking if it occurs during only part of an interval.

In both interval recording and time-sampling, the passage of arbitrarily determined time intervals rather than the behaver's responses occasion the observing response. Both procedures yield counts of only the number of experimenter-imposed time intervals within observation sessions when the observer's looks and the behaver's actions coincide. Thus, in addition to the problem of definitional slippage, both the continuity and the amount of ongoing behavior remain obscure. Moreover, since both may vary in unexpected directions during treatment, what may appear to be an accurate representation of a subject's behavior during pretreatment assessment cannot be assumed to predict observational adequacy throughout the course of intervention.

Efforts to improve the accuracy and reliability of the human observing response are essentially those that increase its automaticity to make it more closely approximate the precision of nonhuman transducers. A definition of behavior that includes its repeated displacement in space (i.e., its countable cycles) as well as its continuity (i.e., its temporal properties) requires continuous transduction of its response dimensions. Whether human or nonhuman observers are used and regardless of how accurately calibrated they may be, discontinuous procedures preclude continuous transduction and are, therefore, incapable of transmitting the true amount and temporal distribution of the behavior.

None of the discontinuous observation procedures produces accurate information on the number of responses emitted, their duration, their frequency, or their distribution in real time (Binder & Jameson, 1982; Bourie, 1981; Powell, 1984; Powell, Martindale, & Kulp, 1975; Powell, Martindale,

Kulp, Martindale, & Bauman, 1977; Repp, Roberts, Slack, Repp, & Berkler, 1976; Springer, Brown, & Duncan, 1981). Futhermore, *agreement among independent observers using the same schedule of intermittent observation cannot rectify these shortcomings.* The constraints of discontinuous observation thus render it inappropriate for assessing the dimensional quantities of response classes.

RECORDING

Just as behaver responses must occasion observing responses, so must they control recording responses. It is the output of the observation procedure that constitutes the record of what was observed. Due to the intimacy of this relation, sources of variability in the observing response will inevitably reflect themselves in the notation of response emissions and therefore in the accuracy of the data product. Thorough observer training, design excellence, and calibration checks for observer sensitivity will fail to compensate for a notation format and an observation/recording schedule that prevent complete and accurate recording. Conversely, the best recording procedure cannot purge the resulting data of input flawed by imprecise or discontinuously programmed observation.

The nature of the recording response either facilitates or diminishes the accuracy of the resulting data. Its automaticity, like that of the observing response, is a critical factor, for the two must function in fluent coordination to complete the transduction process. Compatibility of the observing and recording components is the objective.

Again, precisely calibrated instrumentation provides the model. When attached to the transducer, the only limit on the latency of the recording response is the operating time of the associated equipment: milliseconds for deflection of an electromechanical recording pen or microseconds for electrooptical, electronic, or magnetic recording media. Given the speed of microprocessing, the upper limits of recording frequency far exceed that of the most fluent human motor responses. In addition, the temporal distribution of all behaver responses can appear as permanent tracings for both on-line and post hoc analysis. If behavior assessors could only become as hooked by current technology as the nation's youth, even obsolescent PacMan could reveal a picture of human behavior assets and liabilities beyond the fantasies of a fatigued army of timer-controlled pencil pushers.

How can the human recording response approach this ideal? Given that it should not interrupt visual observing, the least intrusive recording response should require no visual-motor component. Push buttons or squeeze switches operated merely by fluent finger-thumb opposition with minimal force and excursion provide the simplest and least expensive method of transmitting observed responses to a recording device. Tallying on a blank page or moving a bead on a string offer an approximation for behaver responses below the frequency range of the recording response itself. However, tally marks and slashes in time-ruled squares during intermittent observation are incompatible with maximally accurate observing and recording.

While these tactics may afford a summary record of behavior events, there remains the temporal dimension of recurring responses that reveals the fluctuations of ongoing behavior. Only a continuously operating recording device with a constant time base can portray the continuity of behavior. Automatic recorders are plentiful. If the human recording response is an easily repeatable, relatively nonfatiguing operant, the output can operate such recorders. For example, a small console equipped with five push buttons for each hand provides recording of ten different movement cycles. Adding a toggle switch above each push button permits recording the durations of ten different events. Fluency with such a device requires little practice. Yielding 20 channels of behavior information on a permanent record of response distributions through time, such recording allows uninterrupted observing. With computer readout, frequency distributions and summations are available for whatever measures are desired—all in a choice of the universally recognized standard, absolute measurement units. Today's prices make this a cost-effective buy.

Thus, even without automatic transduction of behaver movements, the observing–recording cycle becomes less cumbersome with assistance from automatic recording devices. Most observation tasks require a dedicated transducer. Therefore, the more automatic the observing–recording chain, the more accurate and complete will be the quantitated portrayal of behavior. Concurrent recording of antecedent and subsequent events along with behaver movement cycles results in permanent records revealing the dynamic interactive property of behavior that defines its functionality—the common focus of both behavior assessment and behavior analysis.

We have stressed both the scientific utility and the application efficiency that result from functionally defined response classes. But functional definition itself requires *functional recording* of the *relations* between behaver movements and their controlling environmental variables, both antecedent and subsequent. For this purpose, transducers that both detect and define selected responses may be arranged so that different antecedents are associated with operation of each. One or more of these antecedent–movement relations may also produce specified subsequent events, thus permitting direct measurement of functional relations between antecedents, responses, and subsequents. Such a system requires a recording channel for each transducer *with respect to each antecedent*. Thus, two antecedents and two transducers require four recording channels. Each channel records from a given transducer only when one of the two antecedents is occurring. Separate recording of the four functionally defined classes facilitates analysis of each class with respect to whatever reinforcement contingencies may be thought useful to study. With such a functional definitional/recording system, each additional transducer necessitates as many recording channels as there are antecedents associated with its operation. Recording of subsequent events occurs in association with whatever antecedent is in effect at the time each is delivered. An automated system that transduces each response emission and subsequent event to a recording mechanism that operates only when specified environmental antecedents are occurring produces a series of permanent tracings of separately recorded antecedent-response-subsequent relational occurrences. This operational definition of functional response classes can be confirmed only by the subject's continuing interaction in the assessing/ analyzing environment. One such system revealed lawful commonalities in functionally defined response classes with demonstrated generality throughout the range of psychometrically defined retardation (Barrett, 1965, 1969, 1973, 1974, 1977; Barrett & Lindsley, 1962). Any definitional vagary in a recording and measurement system of this nature will be due to drift in transducer sensitivity. Frequent calibration checks minimize the problem.

EVALUATING MEASUREMENT PROCEDURES

Appraisal of behavior measurement depends on the extent to which it represents a true portrayal of behavior. All subsidiary criteria derive from the conception of behavior as the fundamental datum of assessment and analysis.

BASIC QUESTIONS

Accordingly, each of the major considerations in designing behavior measurement procedures that follow from a natural science conception of behavior also form a set of criteria for judging measurement adequacy.

- Does it represent the fundamental properties of behavior: movement, the time it takes, its place in time, its continuity through time, and its interactive (measurable) effects on the environment?
- Are its response class definitions unambiguous enough to ensure repeatable and accurate detection, sensitive enough to reveal variability, and functional with respect to controlling antecedent and subsequent events?

- Are the dimensional quantities chosen to represent behavior properties sensitive to the relevant aspects of the behavior being assessed?
- Are the units standard, absolute, and appropriately sensitive to reveal the variability associated with intervention effects as distinct from the variability associated with pretreatment conditions?
- Are its observation procedures exclusively and continually reactive to the dimensional quantities selected for analysis?
- Are its recording mechanisms operating continuously, activated solely by occurrences of selected response classes, and capable of revealing their distribution through real time?

These are questions the behavior assessor might ask of the procedures currently prevalent in the behavior assessment literature. Their answers should reveal the major impediments to replication, generality, and expansion of our knowledge base in behavior assessment and applied behavior analysis.

ACCURACY OF BEHAVIOR PORTRAYAL

The extent to which obtained measures approximate the true values of a naturally occurring phenomenon defines accuracy of measurement. An accurate measurement procedure will provide a one-to-one correspondence between movement cycles and their recorded products. Perfect correspondence (i.e., perfect accuracy) produces true values. The closest approximation to true values results from instruments that are sensitively calibrated to yield the same reading on successive occurrences of the same defined movement cycle. To portray the continuity and temporal distribution of true values requires precise timing and recording devices whose operation is continuous and whose units are appropriate to the task at hand.

If humans perform the functions of detecting and recording, their accuracy may be determined by comparing *each* of their recorded responses with *each* of the same series of responses detected and recorded automatically. For example, training experimentally naive women to detect small lumps in a simulated breast can be brought to high levels of accuracy for lumps as small as 2 mm by comparing reported detection with a continuous automatic recording from pressure-sensitive transducers in each lump (Adams *et al.*, 1976). Simply comparing summations of the responses recorded by the human against those recorded automatically will not suffice. Although summations may be identical, the responses detected by automation may not be those detected by the human observer/recorder. The same logic applies to use of two humans in place of automation. Agreement of one with the other can in no way test the accuracy of the product. This is especially so when neither person has been trained to observe and record accurately the range of response values that may result from treatment effects.

Issues of validity arise only when independently measured true values are not available for comparison with obtained values. If transduction is direct and the recording mechanism responds in one-to-one correspondence with each transduced response through time, the product will be a faithful reproduction of response occurrences, the time they took, their locus in time, and their distribution throughout the recording period.

STABILITY OF MEASUREMENT

In order to reveal relations between behavior and its controlling variables, transduction accuracy must remain stable over time. Of course, a relentlessly accurate measurement procedure meets this criterion by definition. Demonstrating measurement stability over time requires that a succession of constant behavior inputs produce the same values from the instrument or measuring procedure. The greater the number of invariant response repetitions yielding identical recorded values, the more stringent the demonstration and the more confidence one can have regarding the reliability of both the process and its products.

A constant response input will not yield identical values if variability lurks in the measurement units chosen to quantify them. Moreover, absence of standard units precludes comparison with true values. Given demonstrated stability of other components of the measurement process, the universally recognized units denoting countability, duration, latency, frequency, celeration, and IRT remove the unreliability associated with elastic, idiosyncratic units. Accurate timers, continuous automatic recorders, and response-specific transducers make it possible to track the accuracy of a measurement system over time, thereby determining its stability or reliability.

CALIBRATION

Obtaining and maintaining accurate and stable transduction requires calibration—checking and adjusting the measuring system to achieve systematically standardized relations between response class input and recorded output. Initially, calibration procedures vary the sensitivity of the transducer until it operates regularly in perfect correspondence to only the events selected for study. Frequent periodic rechecking and adjustment of sensitivity assures that definitional drift is not occurring and that recording devices are faithfully reproducing what is detected.

Use of automated transducers eliminates the influence of observer fatigue and bias, but it does not replace humans in the calibration process. Although devices may be preferred to detect repeated instances of the same response, frequent observation of their operation is essential for the desired outcome. Astute human observers engaged in periodic concurrent monitoring often supply added sensitivity to the many events that may influence variations in what a transducer is detecting. Human detection of such subtleties could contribute substantially to design refinement that sensitizes transducers to nuances deemed significant.

Just as the operating characteristics of automatic transducers determine their suitability for specific applications, so the personal histories of human observers may play a significant role in their effectiveness as detectors and recorders of specified response classes. Vested interests may create biases that remain unknown unless independently obtained accurate values are available for checking the observing-recording product. Screening and carefully selecting observers is an obvious first step toward achieving the best approximation of accurate recording.

Training observers to perform the observing and recording responses to the highest level of accuracy is akin to sensitizing an automatic transducer to only the response inputs selected for assessment. Stimulus control technology is just as applicable for this purpose as it is for teaching new skills to handicapped people. Shaping is often necessary to reach stable topography of the detecting–transmitting response. Amounts of selected dimensional quantities of the defined response classes must then become discriminative stimuli for the observing response. Once obtained, stimulus control by the appropriate dimensional quantities must retain stability throughout exposure to a wide range of values over repeated observation periods.

Measurement practice sessions with scripted performance by bogus subjects provides known input in the form of behavior episodes with predetermined values of dimensional quantities. Otherwise, videotaping or automatic transduction are useful to provide true values for training criteria. As a precaution against drift, it is important that scripted or otherwise arranged known inputs to observer trainees contain the full range of values that might occur during the course of real treatment.

Once the formal study is underway, frequent periodic checking of observer accuracy against automatically transduced recordings or against products of the subject's responding (calibration) will reveal whether retraining sessions are necessary to adjust selective reactivity to the dimensional quantities under study. Data reporting these calibration checks should replace determinations of interobserver agreement in routine descriptions of behavior assessment methods employing human observers.

Given the advances in detecting and transmitting technology, to say nothing of the recording and analytic capabilities of microcomputers, "the use of unassisted human observers can only be seen as the Stone Age of behavioral observation" (Johnston & Pennypacker, 1980, p. 126).

IMPLICATIONS FOR BEHAVIOR ASSESSMENT

Today's behavioral assessment literature offers a smorgasbord of techniques sufficient to suit nearly anyone's taste. Interpretive orientation rather than methodology distinguishes "behavioral" from other approaches. The result is a verbal veneer superimposed on a set of practices derived from developmental field studies, psychodynamics, and psychometrics, tempered by expedient demands for practicality and pressure for social acceptance. The relation of "behavioral" assessment methodology to any distinct concept of behavior is tenuous at best, and often difficult if not impossible to detect. More specifically, the measurement aspects of "behavioral" assessment appear to reflect something other than behavior as defined in the natural science tradition.

TOWARD CONCEPTUAL-METHODOLOGIC CONSISTENCY

Accepting the label "behavioral" while overlooking both a natural science definition of behavior and its associated measurement procedures leaves behavioral assessment as a field with an identity that is far from obvious—perhaps even obscure. Creating a theoretical superstructure (Lang, 1977) will not heal the very apparent conceptual-methodologic schism. Nor will it create order in the absence of substantiating data. Such an undertaking requires generality of findings for a secure foundation, and generality has not yet emerged from behavioral assessment research. The state of "anarchy" (Cone & Hawkins, 1977) resulting from nonfunctional definitions cannot help but perpetuate itself in the absence of a unifying concept of behavior and methodology that addresses and explicates the properties of that naturally occurring phenomenon.

Reviewing behavior properties and their dimensions should generate instances and noninstances of each. With these categories as guides, a classification of currently measured dependent variables could serve as a starting point for delineating the behavioral aspects of contemporary "behavioral" assessment procedures. Those consistent with a natural science definition, its properties, and dimensions would be the objective of such a survey. Movement cycles and measurement of their effects on the environment through time are necessary elements. Procedures that do not meet the criteria of definitional consistency are not "of or relating to behavior." To retain them under the rubric "behavioral assessment" will only sustain the current level of conceptual-methodologic dissonance. Attendant inconsistencies will inevitably plague the search for generality and thus retard progress toward functional classification and prognostic effectiveness.

IMPROVED SPECIFICATION OF MOVEMENT CYCLES

Having sorted out those measurement practices that are compatible with a natural science concept of behavior, it should become obvious that measuring movements in terms of their effects on the environment invites the use of sensing devices other than human observers. Indeed, such devices now enable physiologic events to be included in the domain of observable behavioral events. Bioelectrical activity and the technology of transduction produce continuous recordings of muscle activity cycles [electromyogram (EMG) and electrocardiogram (EKG)], cycles of electrical activity recorded from the scalp [electroencephalogram (EEG)] and from eye movements [electrooculogram (EOG)]. Heart rate, blood and pulse volume, and respiration are other internal changes now transduced into environmental effects which make them accessible to measurement (Nietzel & Bernstein, 1981). Advances in telemetry now make it possible to obtain measurements of various internal behaviors in natural environments (Rugh & Schwitzgebel, 1977).

By contrast, transducers of observable movement cycles, though more easily obtainable and more straightforward in design, appear infrequently in the literature of behavioral assessment and analysis. A review and classification of some existing devices is available (Schwitzgebel, 1976). Examples include a slouch-transducing device (Arzin, Rubin, O'Brien, Ayllon, & Roll, 1968), a smoking controller (Azrin & Powell, 1968), a urinary accident transducer (Azrin & Foxx, 1971), and a detector of appropriate toileting responses (Azrin, Bugle, & O'Brien, 1971). Other transducers in the literature include those for eye movements (Doran & Holland, 1971), workshop tool usage (Schroeder, 1972), anal sphincter pressure (Kohlenberg, 1973), penile circumference (Laws & Rubin, 1969), blood alcohol concentration (Sobell & Sobell, 1975), multiple tics (Barrett, 1962), duration of speech (Lane, 1964), speech pauses (Ruder, Jensen, & Brandt, 1970), detection of lumps in simulated human breasts (Adams et al., 1976), and private events (Hefferline & Bruno, 1971). The last work began as investigations of electromyographic changes that were demonstrated to be conditionable without "awareness" in the frontier era of human operant conditioning (Hefferline, Keenan, & Harford, 1959). As more sophisticated methods evolved, Hefferline (1962) foresaw the advent of biofeedback and the limitless possibilities for productive interaction between psychophysiologic, clinical-psychological, and behavioristic endeavors:

> Technological advance has been greatly spurred by the crash program directed at telemetering a man in space. Improved transducers, amplifiers, and recorders, developed for use in satellites, are already available commercially at reasonable prices. Obviously such devices can be used efficiently with earthbound . . . subjects. (p. 125)

> Modern instrumentation . . . provides automatic programming of experimental operations too fast or too slow for manual execution and processes voluminous data with superhuman speed and accuracy. With artificial eyes, ears and hands, recording impartially and without lapse of attention, the psychologist, as he [sic] deals with a complex situation, gets a fuller and more trustworthy answer to the question of what is going on. (p. 100)

> With such instrumentation the therapist interested in research can have a consulting room which is at the same time a laboratory. Or any recordings obtained as an adjuvant to therapy can supply data for someone else's scientific use. The feasibility of arrangements of this sort is what leads me to speak of symbiotic relations which could obtain between experimental and clinical psychology. (p. 101)

PARTICIPATION IN A UNIVERSAL MEASUREMENT LANGUAGE

Instrumentation also provides benefits beyond definitional specificity and accuracy. Its recorded output translates continuous behavior–environment interactions into universally recognized idemnotic units of measurement. In so doing, instrumentation affords behavior assessment and analysis a language common not only to its parent science but to other relevant disciplines as well. The need has long been expressed and the impediments recognized (Eiduson, Geller, Yuwiler, & Eiduson, 1964):

> The two central problems in relating biochemistry to behavior are those of quantification and correspondence. Biochemical data are nearly always parametric, consisting of real numbers, real intervals, and a real zero point. In addition, the variable can be expressed in explicit, operationally defined units. Many extremely important behavioral variables, however, are nonparametric, with none of these properties. Indeed some are essentially generic names for a whole class of loosely related behavioral complexes and, as commonly used, are both unitless and dimensionless. . . . Only relatively few . . . have true parametric properties. . . . Response rate is as parametric a measure as any biochemical one and is ideal for crossdisciplinary studies. (pp. 468–469)

> But what of the neurochemist whose discipline presently deals not with the formal composition of the final painting but with the discrete substances that comprise its pigments? . . . His [sic] ultimate goal, of course, is to achieve a point-for-point (or sequence-for-point) correspondence with behavior. . . . It

will be necessary not only to quantify isolated segments snipped off a behavioral complex but also to dissect the entire structure into quantifiable units appropriate to biochemical studies. Not only must the behavioral complex be more rigorously analyzed, but the analysis must be carried out with an eye to the problem of correspondence. Essentially this becomes a search for comparable dimensions and units. (p. 471)

Preparatory to such felicitous cross-science interface, behavior assessment must engage in vigorous efforts at in-house communication. Reproducibility and generality of its findings, the test of its viability, will depend on its awareness and integration of the fundamental functions of measurement: description, comparison, and prediction.

To fulfill any communicative function, quantitative *description* must attach standard units to its obtained values. Idiosyncratic units derived from in-house scales of convenience (e.g., "levels of independence" or "levels of assertiveness") fail to provide standard distinguishing descriptors for their attached numerical values. For this reason, they are useless as quantitative descriptors with any generality beyond the special situations for which they are contrived.

Reproducibility and generality require *comparison* of obtained values both from study to study and longitudinally from condition to condition within intrasubject replications. For this purpose, numbers with vacillating values and vaganotically conceived units are of no use. To find the functional relations between behavior and the environment requires absolute units bearing an invariant relation to the dimension they describe. Without this basic requisite, laws of arithmetic and higher mathematics are inapplicable, generality will remain obscured, and interscience investigations will not be possible.

Prediction requires repeated measurements over time. Unstable units and quantification that neglects the temporal dimensions of individual behavior simply do not provide the information necessary to predict the outcome of measurement of an individual's behavior at a future time. It is well to remember that vaganotically defined phenomena, quantitated by their own empirically determined variability as measured in groups of people, are not the subject matter of behavior assessment or analysis. Similarly, vaganotically conceived units, demonstrating interpretive elasticity and emanating from assumed variability, are not suitable for quantitative description of behavior as a naturally occurring phenomenon (see Cone, 1981). Their origin derives from social science statistical assumptions; their product applies neither to the description or prediction of an individual's behavior over time. For this reason, their application is appropriate only to phenomena that are conceptually consistent with that approach.

Germination and cross-fertilization of experimental and clinical endeavors characterizes the model so successfully applied in the medical sciences for over a century (Bernard, 1865/1957). It cannot be approached without nurture from a medium of discourse that retains its communication function regardless of the purpose for which it is used or the philosophical leanings of its users. Terms of a common language must, therefore, be universal and invariant. Their denotations must be standard across applications. In the reciprocal nurturing process, the vernacular of scientific undertakings and those of clinical exploration and demonstration should be equally precise if for no other reason than to facilitate observation of whatever lawfulness may underlie the phenomenon being studied. Both are concerned with lawfulness or predictability. Neither is likely to advance either the basic science or its technological development if the ingredients of the communication system contain more variability than the behaviors they both address.

To demonstrate generality within its domain as well as productive communication and eventual collaborative investigation with other relevant sciences, behavior assessment and analysis must, at the very least, measure the behaviors it studies in a common language (see Churchman, 1959). Standardization at this level should precede and hopefully would presage standardization at other levels of assessment methodology (Goldfried, 1976, 1979; Kanfer, 1972).

ASSESSING THE AIMS, TECHNIQUES, AND RESULTS OF TREATMENT

It is becoming increasingly popular to engage in the trappings of "behavioral" treatment in order to please—or appease—third parties. Indeed, a recommended procedure for setting treatment goals, choosing behaviors to be altered, selecting procedures for altering them, and determining treatment effectiveness is to submit these decisions for approval by parents, friends, peers, and so on (Kazdin, 1977; Wolf, 1978). As a result, the rating scale is staging a dramatic comeback (Barrett, 1981). Consumers are asked to rate their satisfaction with or approval of all aspects of treatment. If its current rate of growth continues, the rating scale with its unitless values and synthetic dimensions promises to supplant other assessment methods—they will simply be unnecessary accoutrements. Therapeutic decisions and effects will depend on social value judgments. Units of behavior analysis will become inseparable from the linguistic convenience and conditioning histories of rating scale respondents.

If given the chance, standard measurement procedures can halt this regression to prebehavioristic methods. We do not have to revert to the vagaries of societal language to determine what behaviors to change or how much change they need in order to increase the competence of our clients. The *behavior* of skilled classmates, peers, and friends measured as functional response classes can provide unbiased answers to these questions. Quantified performance ranges obtained by measuring the behaviors of competent individuals provide standards for assessing a client's deviations and for determining the aims of intervention (Barrett, 1977; Haughton, 1972; Kunzelmann, 1970; Van Houten, 1979; Walker & Hops, 1976; Willis, 1974). Tailored for each individual's deviant or deficient functional response classes, procedures that produce increasing approximations to these performance standards are, then, the procedures of choice. Determining the response class functions to be altered and selecting the most efficient procedures for doing so require measured behavior for their most effective solution. The measured behavior of choice is the client's. The more standardized the language of measurement we provide, the more precise and enlightening will be the client's answers.

Experimental behavior analysis brought the most sensitive of all measurement systems to the task of quantifying what a behaver does under different environmental conditions. It is an integral component of the operant "preparation" that will facilitate productive collaboration with other disciplines seeking to understand human behavior (Skinner, 1986). From its fruits emerged a methodology that revised the way professionals and others regarded themselves and their troubled brethren. It also revised the way professionals write about what they do. But printed words do not suffice for the progress of either the science of human behavior or its application in improved technology of treatment. Assessment of human behavior must elucidate the written word with measurement—measurement that allowed small animals to produce their own precise recordings—measurement that will permit clients to reveal to investigators the most promising and effective treatments.

ACKNOWLEDGMENT

The authors are grateful to Wayne Robb and Carl Binder for their critical reading and many suggestions.

REFERENCES

Adams, C. K., Goldstein, M. K., Hench, L., Hall, D. C., Madden, M., Pennypacker, H. S., Stein, G. H., & Catania, A. C. (1976). Lump detection in a simulated human breast. *Perception and Psychophysics, 20*(3), 163–167.

Angle, H. V., Hay, L. R., Hay, W. M., & Ellinwood, E. H. (1977). Computer assisted behavioral assessment. In J. D. Cone & R. P. Hawkins (Eds.), *Behavioral assessment: New directions in clinical psychology* (pp. 369–380). New York: Brunner/Mazel.

Azrin, N. H., Bugle, C., & O'Brien, F. (1971). Behavioral engineering: Two apparatuses for toilet training the institutionalized retarded. *Journal of Applied Behavior Analysis, 4,* 249–253.

Azrin, N. H., & Foxx, R. M. (1971). A rapid method of toilet training the institutionalized retarded. *Journal of Applied Behavior Analysis, 4,* 89–99.

Azrin, N. H., Holz, W., Ulrich, R., & Goldiamond, I. (1961). The control of the content of conversation through reinforcement. *Journal of the Experimental Analysis of Behavior, 4,* 25–30.

Azrin, N. H., & Lindsley, O. R. (1956). The reinforcement of cooperation between children. *Journal of Abnormal and Social Psychology, 52,* 100–102.

Azrin, N. H., & Powell, J. (1968). Behavioral engineering: The reduction ot smoking behavior by a conditioning apparatus and procedure. *Journal of Applied Behavior Analysis, 1,* 193–200.

Azrin, N. H., Rubin, H., O'Brien, F., Ayllon, T., & Roll, D. (1968). Behavioral engineering: Postural control by a portable operant apparatus. *Journal of Applied Behavioral Analysis, 1,* 99–108.

Baer, D. M. (1982, May). Some recommendations for a modest reduction in the rate of current recommendations for an immodest increase in the rate of exclusive usages of rate as a dependent measure. Unpublished paper in the symposium, "Is rate of response a universal datum?" Presented at the meeting of the Association for Behavior Analysis, Milwaukee, WI.

Baer, D. M., Peterson, R. F., & Sherman, J. A. (1967). The development of imitation by reinforcing similarity to a model. *Journal of the Experimental Analysis of Behavior, 10,* 405–416.

Baer, D. M., Wolf, M. M., & Risley, T. R. (1968). Some current dimensions of applied behavior analysis. *Journal of Applied Behavior Analysis, 1,* 91–97.

Barrett, B. H. (1958). The role of insight. In J. M. Hadley (Ed.), *Clinical and counseling psychology* (pp. 62–120). New York: Knopf.

Barrett, B. H. (1962). Reduction in rate of multiple tics by free operant conditioning methods. *Journal of Nervous and Mental Disease, 135,* 187–195.

Barrett, B. H. (1965). Acquisition of operant differentiation and discrimination in institutionalized retarded children. *American Journal of Orthopsychiatry, 35,* 862–885.

Barrett, B. H. (1969). Behavioral individuality in four cultural-familially retarded brothers. *Behaviour Research and Therapy, 7,* 79–81.

Barrett, B. H. (1973). *Annual Report:* 1 July, 1972–30 June 1973. Belmont, MA: W. E. Fernald State School of Behavior Prosthesis Laboratory.

Barrett, B. H. (1974). *Annual Report:* 1 July, 1973–30 June, 1974. Belmont, MA: W. E. Fernald State School Behavior Prosthesis Laboratory.

Barrett, B. H. (1975). Course of acquisition: Accuracy and frequency comparisons. In *Instructional Development and Behavior Analysis Program: Annual Report, 1 July 1974–30 June 1975* (pp. 69–74). Belmont, MA: Walter E. Fernald State School, Behavior Prosthesis Laboratory.

Barrett, B. H. (1977). Behavior analysis. In J. Wortis (Ed.), *Mental retardation and developmental disabilities* (Vol. 9, pp. 141–202). New York: Brunner/Mazel.

Barrett, B. H. (1979). Communitization and the measured message of normal behavior. In R. L. York & E. Edgar (Eds.), *Teaching the severely handicapped* (Vol. 4, pp. 301–318). Columbus, OH: Special Press.

Barrett, B. H. (1980, June). From accuracy to fluency with a standard measure. Unpublished paper presented at the meeting of the Association for Behavior Analysis, Dearborn, MI.

Barrett, B. H. (1981, May). Measurement issues. Unpublished paper in the symposium "Progress in Precision Teaching." Presented at the meeting of the Association for Behavior Analysis, Milwaukee, WI.

Barrett, B. H., & Lindsley, O. R. (1962). Deficits in acquisition of operant discrimination and differentiation shown by institutionalized retarded children. *American Journal of Mental Deficiency, 67,* 424–436.

Bernard, C. (1957). *An introduction to the study of experimental medicine.* New York: Dover. (Original work published 1865).

Binder, C. V., & Jameson, D. (1982). An analysis of interval size in a momentary time-sampling procedure. *Journal of Precision Teaching, 3*, 9–15.

Birnbrauer, J. S. (1979). Applied behavior analysis, service and the acquisition of knowledge. *The Behavior Analyst, 2*(1), 15–21.

Birnbrauer, J. S. (1981). External validity and experimental investigation of individual behaviour. *Analysis and Intervention in Developmental Disabilities, 1*, 117–132.

Birnbrauer, J. S., Burchard, J. D., & Burchard, S. N. (1970). Wanted: Behavior analysts. In R. H. Bradfield (Ed.), *Behavior modification: The human effort* (pp. 19–76). San Rafael, CA: Dimensions Publishing Company.

Bourie, C. J. (1981, May). Some dimensions of sampling behavior. Unpublished paper presented at the meeting of the Association for Behavior Analysis, Milwaukee, WI.

Churchman, C. W. (1959). Why measure? In C. W. Churchman & P. Ratoosh (Eds.), *Measurement: Definitions and theories* (pp. 83–94). New York: John Wiley & Sons.

Cohen, D. J. (1962). Justin and his peers: An experimental analysis of a child's social world. *Child Development, 33*, 697–717.

Cohen, D. J., & Lindsley, O. R. (1964). Catalysis of controlled leadership in cooperation by human stimulation. *Journal of Child Psychology and Psychiatry, 5*, 119–137.

Cone, J. D. (1977). The relevance of reliability and validity for behavioral assessment. *Behavior Therapy, 8*, 411–426.

Cone, J. D. (1981). Psychometric considerations. In M. Hersen & A. S. Bellack (Eds.), *Behavioral assessment: A practical handbook* (2nd ed., pp. 38–68). New York: Pergamon.

Cone, J. D., & Hawkins, R. P. (Eds.), (1977). *Behavior assessment: New directions in clinical psychology.* New York: Brunner/Mazel.

Deitz, S. M. (1978). Current status of applied behavior analysis: Science versus technology. *American Psychologist, 33*, 805–814.

Doran, J., & Holland, J. G. (1971). Eye movements as a function of response contingencies measured by blackout technique. *Journal of Applied Behavior Analysis, 4*, 11–17.

Eiduson, S., Geller, E., Yuwiler, A., & Eiduson, B. T. (1964). *Biochemistry and behavior.* New York: Van Nostrand.

Ferster, C. B., & DeMyer, M. K. (1961). The development of performances in autistic children in an automatically controlled environment. *Journal of Chronic Diseases, 13*, 312–345.

Ferster, C. B., & DeMyer, M. K. (1962). A method for the experimental analysis of the behavior of autistic children. *American Journal of Orthopsychiatry, 32*, 89–98.

Flanagan, B., Goldiamond, I., & Azrin, N. H. (1958). Operant stuttering: The control of stuttering behavior through response-contingent consequences. *Journal of the Experimental Analysis of Behavior, 1*, 173–178.

Fraley, L. E. (1981). On the spread of behavior analysis to the applied fields. *The Behavior Analyst, 4*, 33–41.

Goldfried, M. R. (1976). Behavioral assessment. In I. B. Weiner (Ed.), *Clinical methods in psychology* (pp. 281–330). New York: John Wiley & Sons.

Goldfried, M. R. (1977). Behavioral assessment in perspective. In J. D. Cone & R. P. Hawkins (Eds.), *Behavioral assessment: New directions in clinical psychology* (pp. 3–22). New York: Brunner/Mazel.

Goldfried, M. R. (1979). Behavioral assessment: Where do we go from here? *Behavioral Assessment, 1*, 19–22.

Goldfried, M. R., & Kent, R. N. (1972). Traditional versus behavioral personality assessment: A comparison of methodological and theoretical assumptions. *Psychological Bulletin, 77*, 409–420.

Greene, E. B. (1941). *Measurements of human behavior.* New York: Odyssey Press.

Hake, D., & Vukelich, R. (1973). Analysis of the control exerted by a complex cooperative procedure. *Journal of the Experimental Analysis of Behavior, 19*, 3–16.

Hake, D., Vukelich, R., & Kaplan, S. J. (1973). Audit responses: Responses maintained by access to existing self or coactor scores during non-social, parallel work, and cooperation procedures. *Journal of the Experimental Analysis of Behavior, 19*, 409–423.

Hake, D., Vukelich, R., & Olvera, D. (1975). The measurement of sharing and cooperation as equity effects and some relationships between them. *Journal of the Experimental Analysis of Behavior, 23*, 63–79.

Hall, D., Goldstein, M. K., & Stein, G. H. (1977). Progress in manual breast examination. *Cancer, 40*, 364–370.

Haughton, E. C. (1972). Aims—Growing and sharing. In J. B. Jordan & L. S. Robbins (Eds.), *Let's try doing something else kind of thing* (pp. 20–39). Seattle, WA: Special Child Publications.

Hayes, S. C., & Cavior, N. (1980). Multiple tracking and the reactivity of self-monitoring: II. Positive behaviors. *Behavioral Assessment, 2*, 283–296.

Haynes, S. N., & Jensen, B. J. (1979). The interview as a behavioral assessment instrument. *Behavioral Assessment, 1*, 97–106.

Hefferline, R. F. (1962). Learning theory and clinical psychology—An eventual symbiosis? In A. J. Bachrach (Ed.), *Experimental foundations of clincial psychology* (pp. 97–138). New York: Basic Books.

Hefferline, R. F., & Bruno, L. J. (1971). The psychophysiology of private events. In A. Jacobs & L. B. Sachs (Eds.), *The psychology of private events* (pp. 164–192). New York: Academic Press.

Hefferline, R. F., Keenan, B., & Harford, R. A. (1959). Escape and avoidance conditioning in human subjects without their observation of the response. *Science, 130*, 1338–1339.

Hersen, M., & Bellack, A. S. (Eds.). (1976). *Behavioral assessment: A practical handbook.* Elmsford, NY: Pergamon Press.

Johnston, J. M. (1982, May). Behavior technology in the year 2000: What do we want it to look like? Invited address presented at the meeting of the Association for Behavior Analysis, Milwaukee, WI.

Johnston, J. M., & Pennypacker, H. S. (1980). *Strategies and tactics of human behavioral research.* Hillsdale, NJ: Lawrence Erlbaum.

Kanfer, F. H. (1972). Assessment for behavior modification. *Journal of Personality Assessment, 36*, 418–423.

Kazdin, A. E. (1977). Assessing the clinical or applied importance of behavior change through social validation. *Behavior Modification, 1*, 427–452.

Kohlenberg, R. J. (1973). Operant conditioning of human anal sphincter pressure. *Journal of Applied Behavior Analysis, 6*, 201–208.

Kunzelmann, H. P. (Ed.). (1970). *Precision teaching.* Seattle, WA: Special Child Publications.

Lane, H. (1964). Differential reinforcement of vocal duration. *Journal of the Experimental Analysis of Behavior, 7*, 107–115.

Lang, P. J. (1977). Physiological assessment of anxiety and fear. In J. D. Cone & R. P. Hawkins (Eds.), *Behavioral assessment: New directions in clinical psychology* (pp. 178–195). New York: Brunner/Mazel.

Laws, D. R., & Rubin, H. B. (1969). Instructional control of an autonomic sexual response. *Journal of Applied Behavior Analysis, 2*, 93–99.

Lindsley, O. R. (1956). Operant conditioning methods applied to research in chronic schizophrenia. *Psychiatric Research Reports, 5*, 118–139.

Lindsley, O. R. (1960). Characteristics of the behavior of chronic psychotics as revealed by free-operant conditioning methods. [Monograph]. *Diseases of the Nervous System, 21*, 66–78.

Lindsley, O. R. (1962a). Operant conditioning techniques in the measurement of psychopharmacologic response. In J. H. Nodine & J. H. Moyer (Eds.), *Psychosomatic medicine: The first Hahnemann symposium* (pp. 373–383). Philadelphia: Lea & Febiger.

Lindsley, O. R. (1962b). A behavioral measure of television viewing. *Journal of Advertising Research, 2*(3), 2–12.

Lindsley, O. R. (1964). Direct measurement and prosthesis of retarded behavior. *Journal of Education, 147*, 62–81.

Lindsley, O. R. (1966). Experimental analysis of cooperation and competition. In T. Verhave (Ed.), *The experimental analysis of behavior* (pp. 470–501). New York: Appleton-Century-Crofts.

Lindsley, O. R. (1969a). Personal communication.

Lindsley, O. R. (1969b). Direct behavioral analysis of psychotherapy sessions by conjugately programmed closed circuit television. *Psychotherapy: Theory, Research and Practice, 6*, 71–81.

Lindsley, O. R., Hobika, J. H., & Etsten, B. E. (1961). Operant behavior during anesthesia recovery: A continuous and objective method. *Anesthesiology, 22*, 937–946.

Linehan, M. M. (1977). Issues in behavioral interviewing. In J. D. Cone & R. P. Hawkins (Eds.), *Behavioral assessment: New directions in clinical psychology* (pp. 30–51). New York: Brunner/Mazel.

Linehan, M. M. (1980). Content validity: Its relevance to behavioral assessment. *Behavioral Assessment, 2*, 147–159.

Lockhart, K. A. (1979). Behavioral assessment of human preference. *The Behavior Analyst, 2*(2), 20–29.

MacCorquodale, K., & Meehl, P. E. (1948). On a distinction between hypothetical constructs and intervening variables. *Psychological Review, 55*, 95–107.

Mahoney, M. J. (1977). Some applied issues in self-monitoring. In J. D. Cone & R. P. Hawkins (Eds.), *Behavioral assessment: New directions in clinical psychology* (pp. 241–254). New York: Brunner/Mazel.

Mash, E. J. (1979). What is behavioral assessment? *Behavioral Assessment, 1*, 23–29.

Mash, E. J., & Terdal, L. G. (1981a). Behavioral assessment of childhood disturbance. In E. J. Mash & L. G. Terdal (Eds.), *Behavioral assessment of childhood disorders* (pp. 3–76). New York: Guilford Press.

Mash, E. J., & Terdal, L. G. (Eds.). (1981b). *Behavioral assessment of childhood disorders*. New York: Guilford Press.

Michael, J. (1980). Flight from behavior analysis. *The Behavior Analyst, 3*(2), 1–22.

Michael, J. (1985). Fundamental research and behaviour modification. In C. F. Lowe, M. Richelle, D. E. Blackman, & C. M. Bradshaw (Eds.), *Behaviour analysis and contemporary psychology* (pp. 159–164). London: Lawrence Erlbaum.

Morgan, B. J., & Lindsley, O. R. (1966). Operant preferences for stereophonic over monophonic music. *Journal of Music Therapy, 3*, 135–143.

Nagel, E. (1961). *The structure of science*. New York: Harcourt, Brace & World.

Nathan, P. E., Schneller, P., & Lindsley, O. R. (1964). Direct measurement of communication during psychiatric admission interviews. *Behaviour Research and Therapy, 2*, 49–57.

Nelson, R. O. (1977a). Methodological issues in assessment via self-monitoring. In J. D. Cone & R. P. Hawkins (Eds.), *Behavioral assessment: New directions in clinical psychology* (pp. 217–240). New York: Brunner/Mazel.

Nelson, R. O. (1977b). Assessment and therapeutic functions of self-monitoring. In M. Hersen, R. M. Eisler, & P. M. Miller (Eds.), *Progress in behavior modification* (Vol. 5, pp. 263–308). New York: Academic Press.

Nelson, R. O. (1980). The use of intelligence tests within behavioral assessment. *Behavioral Assessment, 2*, 417–423.

Nelson, R. O., & Hayes, S. C. (1979). Some current dimensions of behavioral assessment. *Behavioral Assessment, 1*, 1–16.

Nietzel, N. T., & Bernstein, D. A. (1981). Assessment of fear and anxiety. In M. Hersen & A. S. Bellack (Eds.), *Behavioral assessment: A practical handbook* (2nd ed., pp. 215–245). New York: Pergamon Press.

O'Leary, K. D. (1979). Behavioral assessment. *Behavioral Assessment, 1*, 31–36.

Pennypacker, H. S. (1981). On behavior analysis. *The Behavior Analyst, 4*, 159–161.

Pierce, W. D., & Epling, W. F. (1980). What happened to analysis in applied behavior analysis? *The Behavior Analyst, 3*(1), 1–9.

Powell, J. (1984). On the misrepresentation of behavioral realities by a widely practiced direct observation procedure: Partial interval (one-zero) sampling. *Behavioral Assessment, 6*, 209–219.

Powell, J., Martindale, A., & Kulp, S. (1975). An evaluation of time-sample measures of behavior. *Journal of Applied Behavior Analysis, 8*, 463–469.

Powell, J., Martindale, B., Kulp, S., Martindale, A., & Bauman, R. (1977). Taking a closer look: Time sampling and measurement error. *Journal of Applied Behavior Analysis, 10*, 325–332.

Repp, A. C., Roberts, D. M., Slack, D. J., Repp, C. F., & Berkler, M. S. (1976). A comparison of frequency, interval, and time-sampling methods of data collection. *Journal of Applied Behavior Analysis, 9,* 501–508.

Ruder, K. F., Jensen, P. J., & Brandt, J. F. (1970). An apparatus and procedure for the perceptual study of speech pauses. *Journal of the Experimental Analysis of Behavior, 14,* 287–290.

Rugh, J. D., & Schwitzgebel, R. L. (1977). Instrumentation for behavior assessment. In A. R. Ciminero, K. S. Calhoun, & H. E. Adams (Eds.), *Handbook of behavioral assessment* (pp. 79–113). New York: John Wiley & Sons.

Schroeder, S. R., & Holland, J. G. (1969). Reinforcement of eye movements with concurrent *Applied Behavior Analysis, 5,* 523–525.

Schroeder, S. R., & Holland J. G. (1969). Reinforcement of eye movements with concurrent schedules. *Journal of the Experimental Analysis of Behavior, 12,* 897–903.

Schwitzgebel, R. L. (1976). Behavioral technology. In H. Leitenberg (Ed.), *Handbook of behavior modification and behavior therapy* (pp. 604–626). Englewood Cliffs, NJ: Prentice-Hall.

Sidman, M. (1960). *Tactics of scientific research.* New York: Basic Books.

Sidman, M., & Stoddard, L. (1966). Programming perception and learning for retarded children. In N. R. Ellis (Ed.), *International review of research in mental retardation* (Vol. 2, pp. 151–208). New York: Academic Press.

Sidman, M., & Stoddard, L. T. (1967). The effectiveness of fading in programming a simultaneous form discrimination for retarded children. *Journal of the Experimental Analysis of Behavior, 10,* 3–15.

Skinner, B. F. (1935). The generic nature of the concepts of stimulus and response. *Journal of General Psychology, 12,* 40–65.

Skinner, B. F. (1938). *The behavior of organisms.* New York: Appleton-Century-Crofts.

Skinner, B. F. (1953). *Science and human behavior.* New York: Macmillan.

Skinner, B. F. (1986). Some thoughts about the future. *Journal of the Experimental Analysis of Behavior, 45,* 229–235.

Sobell, M. B., & Sobell, L. C. (1975). A brief technical report on the MOBAT: An inexpensive portable test for determining blood alcohol concentration. *Journal of Applied Behavior Analysis, 8,* 117–120.

Springer, B., Brown, T., & Duncan, P. K. (1981). Current measurement in applied behavior analysis. *The Behavior Analyst, 4,* 19–31.

Swan, G. E., & MacDonald, M. L. (1978). Behavior therapy in practice: A national survey of behavior therapists. *Behavior Therapy, 9,* 799–807.

Van Houten, R. (1979). Social validation: The evolution of standards of competency for target behaviors. *Journal of Applied Behavior Analysis, 12,* 581–591.

Wahler, R. G. (1975). Some structural aspects of deviant child behavior. *Journal of Applied Behavior Analysis, 8,* 27–42.

Walker, H. M., & Hops, H. (1976). Use of normative peer data as a standard for evaluating classroom treatment effects. *Journal of Applied Behavior Analysis, 9,* 159–168.

Walls, R. T., Werner, T. J., Bacon, A., & Zane, T. (1977). Behavior checklists. In J. D. Cone & R. P. Hawkins (Eds.), *Behavioral assessment: New directions in clinical psychology* (pp. 77–146). New York: Brunner/Mazel.

Watson, J. B. (1924). *Behaviorism.* Chicago: University of Chicago Press.

Webster's third new international dictionary. Springfield, MA: Merriam, 1961.

Weiner, H. (1964). Conditioning history and human fixed-interval performance. *Journal of the Experimental Analysis of Behavior, 7,* 383–385.

Willis, B. (1974, July). *Project report IV of State of Washington's child service demonstration programs for precise educational remediation for managers of specific learning disabilities programs.* Tacoma, WA: Intermediate School District No. 111.

Wolf, M. M. (1978). Social validity: The case for subjective measurement or how applied behavior analysis is finding its heart. *Journal of Applied Behavior Analysis, 11,* 203–214.

Woods, T. S. (1980). On the alleged incompatibility of analysis and application: A response to Pierce and Epling. *The Behavior Analyst, 3*(2), 67–69.

7

THE CONTINUING SEARCH FOR UNITS OF ANALYSIS IN PSYCHOLOGY: BEYOND PERSONS, SITUATIONS, AND THEIR INTERACTIONS

RICHARD M. McFALL
ELIZABETH C. McDONEL
Indiana University—Bloomington

One of the most hotly debated questions in psychology over the past 15 years has been: "What should the primary units of analysis be in psychological theories aimed at describing, predicting, and explaining human behavior?" Some authors have argued that the primary units should be the attributes of persons. Others have argued they should be the attributes of situations. Still others have argued that they should be the interactions of persons and situations. This controversy over the proper units of analysis, which has become known as the "person–situation debate," has led to the publication of numerous books and articles in recent years; in many ways, however, the more that has been written on the topic, the further away the debate has seemed to be from resolution!

In writing the present chapter, we tried to steer a delicate course between two outcomes we considered equally undesirable. On the one hand, we saw little value in providing yet another comprehensive account of the person–situation debate, with its list of players and their various claims and counterclaims, attacks and counterattacks. On the other hand, we wanted to avoid merely fanning the flames of the old controversy or adding new noise to the existing confusion without contributing something new of value.

Our purpose in writing this chapter was threefold. First, we wanted to distill, as best we could, the essence of the psychological puzzle that the various arguments in the person–situation debate have been attempting to solve. Second, we hoped to gain a clearer understanding, through logical and empirical analysis, of the reasons why none of the proposed solutions to the puzzle has worked thus far. And third, we tried to develop an integrative, fresh perspective on the puzzle—one that might contribute to progress toward an eventual solution.

A SYNOPSIS OF THE PRESENT DEBATE

THE PERSONOLOGICAL PERSPECTIVE

Until the 1960s, the dominant conceptual perspective in clinical/personality psychology was the individual differences or personological approach. This was expressed in a variety of different forms, such as psychoanalytic theory, neoanalytic theories, and trait theory; but the common underlying principle was that human beings could best be described, predicted, and understood in terms of a critical set of specific attributes within each person. While the different theorists disagreed strongly about which intrapsychic attributes were critical, they all agreed that the critical attributes were intrapsychic. Notable exceptions to this consensus were provided by Kurt Lewin (1935) and Egon Brunswik (1956).

In principle, personological theories held that once the critical attributes of an individual were ascertained, it should be possible to use this information to derive valid descriptions, predictions, and explanations concerning that individual's behavior. In practice, however, most theories encountered insurmountable problems when it came to deciding on the critical attributes and ascertaining the extent of their presence in a person. Psychoanalytic theory, for example, offered a long list of intrapsychic states that were believed to affect behavior; but the methods for detecting the existence of these states in individuals were unreliable, and the functional links between these states and observable behavior were indirect and virtually untestable. Psychoanalytic theory had enjoyed considerable popularity on the basis of its strengths as a rich, colorful, and robust descriptive and post hoc explanatory system; but by the 1960s, its utter failure as a predictive system had sent most empirically oriented psychologists in search of better theories.

In terms of predictive utility and testability, the most promising personological theories were the various trait theories and their cousins in the area of mental abilities. They not only identified the personal attributes that should affect behavior, but they specified how the effects should be expressed in behavior, and tried to provide reliable methods for assessing both the attributes and their effects. Sophisticated quantitative methods were used to test the validity of predictions derived from these theories. The trait theories also had some value as descriptive systems, although they lacked the colorful language of the more dynamic theories. Trait theories were least valuable as explanatory systems. There is something unsatisfying about the conclusion, for example, that individuals play football because they are high on the trait of aggression. Moreover, it is virtually impossible to make strong causal inferences since trait attributes cannot be manipulated experimentally, and thus the best research evidence can be only correlational.

There are several reasons why empirically oriented psychologists might have been willing to sacrifice rich description and the promise of causal explanations for the increased predictive utility of a trait approach. One major factor was that clinical/personality psychologists had begun to concentrate on the tasks of diagnosis, clinical prediction, and personality assessment, and these activities demanded the more formal, quantitative, and "objective" methods available in the trait approach. The American psychologist's sympathy for functionalism, coupled with a growing commitment to empiricism, demanded testable predictions (Boring, 1957). In addition, the trait approach brought with it some bonuses. The so-called "objective" measures, involving self-reports of behavior or experience as assessed by paper-and-pencil questionnaires, permitted the collection of large amounts of data on large numbers of individuals at minimal expense. These data could be coded and quantified readily and reliably. And, best of all, they could be analyzed quickly in complex ways by a newly emerging tool—the computer! In fact, the computer made it relatively easy to apply factor-analytic techniques to large samples of data in the hope of discovering the "true" units of personality, even when an investigator began a research project with no good ideas about which personal attributes were most important (e.g., see R. B. Cattell, 1957).

In summary, the stage was set for the current edition of the person-situation debate.[1] The personological perspective was dominant, with the trait approach being the only representative of this perspective that was both sufficiently testable to be considered scientifically acceptable and sufficiently practical to be considered useful in diagnosis, clinical prediction, and research.

The Consistency Issue

There was one pivotal issue that eventually led to widespread disillusionment with the trait approach. An explicit assumption underlying the concept of traits is that they are enduring response predispositions that manifest themselves in a consistent fashion across time and across situations. Before we can explain how this assumption caused problems, we need to elaborate on the idea of consistency.

There were at least three ways in which trait theorists might have meant that they expected an individual to behave consistently (Magnusson, 1976):

1. By "current edition," we are referring to the debate over the past 15 years. At earlier points in the history of psychology, similar debates occurred; but they will not be the focus of this chapter.

1. A person's behavior might show *absolute* temporal and cross-situational consistency. For example, an individual might show the same degree of aggressiveness at all times and in all situations.

2. A person's behavior might show *relative* consistency when compared to the behaviors of other individuals across time and situations. That is, within a group, a person's rank order on a trait dimension would stay the same, even though the absolute level may vary for the whole group as a function of the particular situation. For example, if person "A" were higher than person "B" on the trait of aggression, then we would expect "A" to show more aggression than "B" in all situations, even though the absolute levels of aggression for both may be high in one situation and low in another.

3. A person's behavior might show logical or *internal* consistency, even though it may appear to be inconsistent in an absolute or relative sense. That is, a person's behavior may be organized in a coherent fashion. Once we understand that organization, we should be able to make specific predictions about the occurrence, strength, and topography of particular behaviors. The organization might take any of a number of forms. For example, if persons "A" and "B" were equally high on the trait of aggression, but "A" was high on the trait of dependency while "B" was low on dependency, then we might predict that "A" and "B" would behave equally aggressively in asocial tasks, but that "A" would behave less aggressively than "B" in social tasks. In a somewhat different example, an individual might be consistently more aggressive than others under certain circumstances, such as when there were threats to the person's self-esteem, but otherwise be consistently less aggressive than others.

It is unlikely that trait theorists meant to imply that people would show the *absolute* type of consistency; we know from common experience, as well as from research evidence, that people simply do not behave that consistently. It also seems improbable that most trait theorists were thinking of the *internal* type of consistency; the methods used in most trait research (e.g., correlational analyses of "true score" estimates based on subjects' responses to many items sampled from common trait domains) simply are not appropriate for studying the extent to which an individual's behavior is logically consistent or structurally coherent. Clearly, most trait theorists were predicting that people would manifest *relative* consistency in their behavior across time and situations; most theoretical discussions about traits and most research methods used to assess them have pointed to this type of consistency.

In summary, then, the preeminence of the personological perspective was based heavily on the strength of trait theories; and they, in turn, were founded on the assumption of relative consistency. But this was a very precarious arrangement: If negative research evidence were to undercut the idea of relative consistency, then the major support for trait theories and for the personological perspective would have been seriously damaged, and the entire structure then would be in jeopardy of collapse.

That is what happened. By 1968, the *zeitgeist* for a paradigm shift (Kuhn, 1962) led to the publication of two extremely influential books, both of which provided compelling logical and empirical criticisms of the trait approach to personality and advocated as an alternative the social-learning approach (Mischel, 1968; Peterson, 1968). There were important differences between the authors of these two books (e.g., Mischel was not trained as a trait theorist; Peterson was trained as a trait theorist and had devoted 10 years of research to the approach); nevertheless, both used the wealth of accumulated correlational research evidence to make a very convincing case against the trait assumption that human behavior is characterized by its relative consistency. With a few notable exceptions, such as cognitive and ability measures, the evidence revealed that consistency coefficients seldom exceeded, and usually were below, the .30 or .40 level. This meant that, at best, trait consistency accounted for only 10–15% of the cross-situational variance in behavior. Both authors concluded that this was not good enough. In retrospect, these two books seem to have been responsible for bringing the person–situation debate to a boil.

It is beyond the aim and scope of this chapter to review in detail the research evidence and arguments for and against trait theories. Interested readers are referred to any of a large number of existing reviews and discussions (Alker, 1972; Allport, 1958, 1966; Argyle & Little, 1972; Bem, 1972; Bem & Allen, 1974; Bem & Funder, 1978; Bowers, 1973; Ekehammar, 1974; Endler, 1973; Endler & Magnusson, 1976; Epstein, 1979, 1980; Magnusson, 1976; Magnusson & Endler, 1977; McReynolds, 1979; Mischel, 1968, 1969, 1971, 1973, 1979; Pervin & Lewis, 1978; Peterson, 1968; Sells, 1963; Vernon, 1964; Wachtel, 1973a,b; Wallace, 1966, 1967). For our present purposes, it is both fair and sufficient to report that many psychologists were dismayed to discover that people are far more *in*consistent than consistent, and that the measured amount of relative consistency is too trivial to support an entire theory. Furthermore, although the results of trait studies sometimes achieved statistical significance, they rarely yielded results that would have a significant practical impact on psychologists' efforts to describe, predict, and understand human behavior.

Of course, one can never prove the null hypothesis. Thus, it is always perfectly legitimate for investigators to discount negative evidence and hold to the belief that their position will be vindicated by tomorrow's research. In this vein, some investigators have persisted in their search for traits, undaunted by the negative evidence. They claim to be encouraged by the fact that existing trait measures can predict behavior across situations at a level beyond chance. They seem to feel that "where there is smoke, there is fire." They argue logically that there must be consistency in behavior; otherwise, it would be random. If it were random, people could not interact because behavior would be unpredictable. If only they could develop better trait constructs, build more sensitive measures, perform more sophisticated analyses, and create more complex models of higher-order trait structures, then perhaps the trait approach might overcome the damage it has sustained on the issue of consistency (e.g., see Alker, 1972; Allport, 1966; Block, 1968, 1977; Bowers, 1977; Epstein, 1977; Stagner, 1976). They are persuaded both by their own experiences and by the prevalence of trait concepts in common language that there is relative consistency in individual behavior, and that psychologists simply have failed thus far to build theories and measures capable of reflecting the implicit trait theories that laypeople use effectively in their everyday interactions.

Consistency in the Eye of the Beholder

Although many trait theorists are convinced by their subjective experiences that people behave consistently, Mischel (1968, 1973) and Jones and Nisbett (1971) have presented evidence to suggest that our subjective experiences of consistency in the behaviors of the people around us often may be illusory. That is, when we observe the behavior of others, we sometimes have a natural bias toward perceiving consistency where it does not, in fact, exist. There are several reasons for this perceptual bias. First, humans often tend to be more sensitive to information that is consistent with their preconceptions than to disconfirming information (Tversky & Kahneman, 1974; for possible exception, see Reyes, Thompson, & Bower, 1980). If we selectively attend to and recall consistent information, we are bound to believe that the world is more consistent than it is.

Second, human observers are subject to sampling biases that promote the subjective appearance of consistency. Ordinarily, we observe other persons behaving in only a limited number of roles and situations; thus, we tend to see a restricted and repetitive sample of their total behavior. This leads us to draw the erroneous conclusion that these individuals behave consistently in general.

Third, human observers tend to ignore the homogenizing influence that they themselves exert on the behavior of others. To the extent that the observer functions as a consistent stimulus for the behavior of another person, then the observer will tend to evoke from that person a restricted sample of behavior that will appear consistent to the observer.

Fourth, the layperson observer ordinarily is not concerned with making specific, falsifiable predictions about the behavior of other persons; instead, the layperson uses perceived trait constructs to make only the most global and unfalsifiable type of generalizations about others. Thus, the layperson seldom has a good opportunity to test empirically the validity of the notion that people behave consistently. In the absence of a critical test, the assumption persists. Of course, the psychologist ordinarily is concerned with making specific, falsifiable predictions. As already noted, the empirical evidence from such predictions suggests that trait constructs are inadequate for such purposes.

Finally, there is an information processing bias toward construing other people in simplistic, consistent ways. For the practical purpose of everyday functioning, the layperson's simplistic system of classifying other persons on trait dimensions probably is both sufficient and cost-effective. From an information processing point of view, it probably would be too costly, with too little gain in practical utility, for the layperson to employ more complex systems of classifying and predicting other persons (Miller, 1956). But the psychologist usually is interested in achieving the highest possible level of predictive accuracy, and simplicity and efficiency are only secondary considerations. Thus, the fact that trait constructs are sufficient for the layperson's purpose does not mean that they are sufficient for the psychologist's purposes. In short, the layperson's naive belief in behavioral consistency and reliance on trait constructs does not provide very convincing support for the perpetuation of the trait approach in psychology.

The New Search for Consistency

Since the decline of the trait approach was brought about by negative evidence on the consistency issue, some investigators have reasons that the trait approach can be rescued by finding new positive evidence on this issue. At least three separate efforts to find consistency are worth discussing.

1. Consistency through aggregation. Epstein (1977, 1979, 1980) has argued that traits have only appeared to be inconsistent because they have not been measured properly. Previous attempts to assess cross-situational consistency were methodologically flawed, he asserted, because they failed to sample the trait behaviors adequately. Small samples are notoriously unreliable due to a large error of measurement; however, error of measurement can be reduced and the stability of sample means for behavioral observations can be increased (both within subjects and across subjects) simply by increasing the number of observations comprising an assessment sample.

To illustrate this point, Epstein (1979, 1980) reported four studies in which the stability of trait scores increased simply as a function of the number of observations contributing to each subject's score. For example, in one study, 28 subjects were assessed on a number of self-reported trait variables each day for a month. In a between-subject analysis, the correlation between trait scores, as assessed on two different days, averaged below .30. However, when the mean trait scores were averaged across all odd days and were correlated with the scores averaged across all even days, the resulting split-half reliability typically exceeded .70 and sometimes exceeded .90. A similar pattern was found for within-subject split-half analyses. In general, the four studies "demonstrated that when single events are examined, there is little evidence for stability, but that when averaging is done over a sufficient sample of events, there is strong evidence for stability" (Epstein, 1979, p. 1121). Epstein claimed that this was true for self-report measures, global ratings of behavior by others, and direct observations of objective behaviors.

Part of Epstein's argument is well-founded. The only fair test of trait consistency is one in which the trait measures employed are as reliable as is practically feasible. Since the reliability of a measure sets an upper limit on its potential validity, a trait construct cannot be tested fairly with unreliable measures. Furthermore, as we know from the law of sampling distributions, the reliability of an estimate of a population parameter is a function of sample size; the larger the sample, the more reliable the estimate. Using the Spearman-Brown formula, for example, we can compute what magnitude of increase in reliability will result from a given increase in the size of a particular sample. Thus, Epstein is correct in asserting that estimates of traits will be more stable if based on sufficiently large samples, and that stable estimates of traits will permit better empirical tests of the validity of trait constructs.

The remainder of Epstein's (1979, 1980) argument is critically flawed in at least four respects.[2] First, he has confused the matter of measurement stability, or reliability, with the matter of cross-situational consistency. The important difference between the two is clearly reflected in Mischel's (1968) distinction between reliability and validity: Reliability has to do with the agreement between measures taken under maximally *similar* conditions. Validity has to do with the agreement between measures taken under maximally *dissimilar* conditions. As Mischel (1979) has noted, most of the data summarized by Epstein (1979) addressed the important issue of measurement stability (i.e., reliability), but ignored the issue of cross-situational consistency (i.e., validity). When Epstein administered the same measures to the same subjects in the same settings each day for a month, and then performed a split-half correlational analysis of the data, he was assessing

2. Mischel and Peake (1982) have raised similar criticisms of Epstein's work in an article published after the present chapter had been written. The reader is encouraged to see Mischel and Peake's article for an extended discussion on the topic of consistency.

reliability, not validity. Of course, reliability is a *sine qua non* for validity, but a measure can be reliable without being valid. To establish the validity of his trait constructs, Epstein needed to control for method variance by using at least two dissimilar methods of measuring the same trait (Campbell & Fiske, 1959), and needed to control for situational variance by administering these measures under at least two dissimilar circumstances (Mischel, 1968). His measures of the *same* trait, obtained with different methods under different circumstances, should have shown a meaningful pattern of convergence; his measures of different traits, however, even when obtained with the same method under similar circumstances, should have shown a clear pattern of divergence (see Campbell & Fiske, 1959).

In only one of the four studies reported by Epstein (1979) were scores from personality trait inventories systematically compared with the scores from criterion measures. The results of these analyses failed to provide convincing evidence for the validity of the trait constructs. All measures were based on subjects' self-reports, so one important source of bias toward consistency was uncontrolled. For 14 consecutive days, not including weekends, undergraduate students rated themselves on two types of criterion variables: subjective emotional states and objective events. By excluding weekends, the possible variability due to situational influences was reduced, thereby increasing the opportunity for person variables to exert the dominant influence.

Overall, the resulting correlations (Epstein, 1979, p. 1118, Table 5) failed to demonstrate a convincing pattern of either convergent or discriminant validity. Specifically, analyses of relationships between subjects' self-ratings on several subjective personality trait measures (e.g., anxiety, hostility, extroversion) and their daily self-ratings on several subjective emotional dimensions yielded a correlation matrix in which virtually every variable was indiscriminately correlated with every other variable at a moderate (.29–.59) and significant level. The pattern of intercorrelations failed to show adequate discriminant validity. Analyses of relationships between the subjective personality trait measures and daily ratings of objective behavioral events, however, yielded a correlation matrix in which very few variables were significantly correlated. This pattern of intercorrelations failed to show adequate convergent validity.

Finally, the most consistent and strongest correlate of the criterion measures was not the personality inventories, but was subjects' responses, obtained on only *one* occasion, to a series of simple, straightforward questions about the typical frequency or intensity of each of the criterion variables. This finding is ironic, indeed. Epstein (1979) presented this study in an effort to argue the case that trait measures can be useful predictors of criterion behaviors if the criterion variables are reliably assessed on the basis of adequately large samples of observations. Yet his own data indicate that a single, well-conceived behavioral question (*not* based on a large aggregated sample) consistently proved to be a better predictor both of subjective and of objective events than were the personality trait measures. For example, subjects' ratings on a five-point scale (from "almost never" to "very often") of how much time they typically spent studying was the best predictor (.80) of subjects' self-reported number of hours per day actually spent studying, averaged over the 14 days. In general, then, this study may have demonstrated that the reliability of measuring criterion variables could be improved by aggregating data over a 14-day sample, but it failed to demonstrate that this increase in reliability led to a significant improvement in the cross-situational consistency, or validity, of personality trait measures.

There is another serious problem with Epstein's (1979, 1980) proposed solution to the search for cross-situational consistency. He has suggested that the best way to demonstrate stable response dispositions is to aggregate behavior across a large sample of diverse situations. The resulting average, in turn, should be highly related to the average of a similar aggregation of behaviors across a similar sample of situations. However, this solution requires a questionable tradeoff: cross-situational stability is achieved only at the expense of predictive utility. As Vernon (1964) noted some time ago, "the broader one's trait construct (as a result of averaging behavior in many different situations), the less predictive can it be in any one situation" (p. 238).

Epstein admitted that his solution was useful only for predicting average behavior, but he argued that such actuarial predictions were useful because they show "that in the long run, we can depend on people behaving true to character" (1979, p. 1123). But Meehl (1978) has challenged the utility of theories that cannot be subjected to a very "risky test" because they only make general predictions about a person's average behavior. "A theory that can only predict that it will rain in April, for example, is not very impressive; but a theory that can correctly predict how much it will rain on any particular day has some measure of verisimilitude" (Meehl, 1978, p. 818).

To illustrate the costs and benefits of aggregating data over large samples, consider the problems involved in attempting to forecast the local precipitation on, say April 1st. First, we might aggregate and average the local precipitation records for April 1st over the past 50 years. This should give us a very stable estimate; we should be able to compare the average rainfall for odd versus even years, over that period, and obtain an extremely high correlation.[3] Of course, our 50-year average will not be particularly

---

3. To compute this correlation, of course, we would determine the mean rainfall for each of the 365 days of the year and assess the degree to which differences between the daily means were consistent from one sample to another.

useful for predicting the actual rainfall on the next April 1st. We might conclude that our predictive inadequacy is due to "error of measurement," and decide instead only to predict the average April 1st rainfall over the next 50 years. Chances are, the means for our two 50-year samples would be almost perfectly correlated.[3] But we should not be fooled by our success. We still have not learned how to predict the rainfall on a specific April 1st. It is misleading to assume that our inability to predict rainfall on a particular day is always due to measurement error. In fact, our assessment of rainfall on a given day might be highly reliable, as shown by the agreement of data taken from several rain gauges. This would suggest that we are measuring true variability, not "error." Therefore, our predictive failure would be due to our lack of knowledge about the determinants of rainfall, not to a lack of measurement precision.

A mean based on aggregated data from large samples may be stable, but it tells us little about the factors that produce variability around the mean. To predict rainfall on a particular date, we must understand what causes precipitation and be able to apply this knowledge to the specific local circumstances on a given date. With such knowledge, we will be able to predict more accurately than we could merely on the basis of aggregated averages.

Obviously, the issue of predictive utility hinges on the level of generality of the question being asked. If we are interested in knowing only the most general characteristics of people (or weather), then averages based on large samples may be useful. But if we want specific knowledge about the behavior of a particular person (or the precipitation on a particular day), then averages based on large samples will not be useful. Since clinical/personality psychologists typically are interested in making specific predictions, the search for consistency through aggregation will not provide much help.

Finally, there are two logical flaws in Epstein's (1977, 1979, 1980) arguments. First, whereas the lack of evidence for behavioral consistency seriously undermines the status of trait theory, a demonstration of behavioral consistency, by itself, does not confirm the existence of traits. Studies showing high split-half reliabilities on a measure should not be interpreted as proof that "traits are alive and well" (Epstein, 1977). Not all stability is due to traits. For example, a person's food preferences, blood pressure, or physical strength, all of which tend to be consistent, are not usually construed as proof of personality traits.

Second, the average of a given sample, no matter how stable it may be, does not necessarily reflect some true essence of the sample from which the average was derived. Take, for example, a large sample of paint chips drawn from a population composed of 50% white chips and 50% black chips. The mean reflectance of the sample will be a middle gray; moreover, with sufficiently large samples, the middle gray average should be a highly reliable finding. But the stability of the average does not mean that we have captured the essence of the population of paint chips. It takes more than the demonstration of stable averages to make a convincing case for trait theory.

In summary, then, the search for consistency through aggregation is correct in its stress on the importance of reliable measurement, but it confuses reliability with validity, it sacrifices predictive utility for stability, and it erroneously assumes that a stable average both captures the essence of a phenomenon and proves the existence of traits.

2. Consistency through moderator variables. Another proposed explanation for the apparent inconsistency in human behavior (e.g., Alker, 1972) is that previous attempts to demonstrate relative consistency have been too simplistic. They have treated all subjects as though they were homogeneous except in regard to the particular trait dimensions being assessed, rather than recognizing that the behavioral manifestations of traits may be moderated by the influences of other variables on which subjects also differ. For example, subjects' sex, age, socioeconomic status, and IQ may exert an important, but often overlooked moderating influence on the expression of traits. In fact, the expression of certain traits may be moderated by the person's standing on one or more other trait dimensions. By dividing a sample of subjects into more homogeneous subgroups on the basis of these and other possible moderating variables, the complex interactions among traits and moderator variables may become apparent. By taking these interactions into account, strong evidence of cross-situational consistency may be revealed at last.

In principle, the search for consistency through the analysis of moderator variables seems reasonable. Clearly, if traits did not exert their influence in a simple, independent, and additive fashion, then more complex methods would be required to measure them, assess their validity, and evaluate their predictive utility. The call for greater methodological complexity, however, introduces several potential problems.

First, the complex interactions among trait measures and moderator variables must be firmly established through careful cross-validation before they may be offered as valid explanations for behavior (Bem, 1972; Mischel, 1968). It is too easy, with today's sophisticated and computerized statistical techniques, to engage in fishing expeditions, in which all possible interactions among many traits and a multitude of moderator variables are analyzed, with no preconceptions about how all the variables will be related. The significant interactions "discovered" through this post hoc procedure must be replicated before they can be interpreted with any confidence. Even then, one can never be sure about inferring the directionality of mediating influences. Ideally, the relationships between traits and moderator variables should be predicted on the basis of trait theory, rather than being discovered;

however, if an unexpected relationship is discovered and replicated, either it should be integrated with the existing trait theory or the theory should be modified to accommodate it.

The second problem with the moderator approach is that the type of interactions it hypothesizes tend to convey a false sense of theoretical precision, are difficult to refute, and usually are too complex to be grasped intellectually (Nisbett, 1977). The potential complexity of the moderator approach can become a trap. Because the investigator is looking for complex interactions, rather than simple main effects, the hypotheses generated by the approach give the illusion of being more precise. Yet the complexity actually makes it more difficult to specify expected outcomes and to determine whether the hypotheses have been disconfirmed by a given set of results. The list of all possible moderator variables seems almost endless. By the time that four or five such variables are included in an analysis of one or more traits, the presence of higher-order interactions makes the results virtually uninterpretable. Findings that are uninterpretable are essentially useless.

A third problem is that an analysis of moderator variables need not be limited to person variables. Situational factors also might function as moderators. "Mischel's (1968) observation that behavioral consistencies are situationally specific can be translated into the assertion that individual differences are themselves a function of situational moderators" (Bem, 1972, p. 21). If the moderator approach is to become more than a vague restatement of the general proposition that behavior is a function of the complex interaction of person and situational variables, its advocates first must specify precisely which moderator variables will have what effects on which traits, and then provide compelling evidence to support their predictions.

Finally, the search for consistency through the analysis of moderator variables is complicated to an extreme degree by the possibility that not all individuals may respond to a given moderator variable in the same way. The effects of moderator variables may be idiographic. In this case, we could detect consistency in an individual's behavior only after analyzing the unique structure of each person's responses to relevant moderator variables.

In summary, it is one thing to claim that previous trait research failed to find evidence of cross-situational consistency because the role of moderator variables was overlooked; it is another thing to provide a list of the overlooked variables and demonstrate that their inclusion yields trait-relevant behavioral consistency. Although the moderator approach is feasible in principle, its utility remains to be demonstrated in practice.

3. Consistency through idiographic assessment. The third proposed solution to the search for consistency is not particularly new, nor is it always advanced in an attempt to resurrect trait theory. But it does represent a

different approach than those discussed thus far, and deserves attention as a possible method for predicting behavior across situations on the basis of person variables.

Bem and his colleagues (Bem, 1972; Bem & Allen, 1974; Bem & Funder, 1978) have suggested that higher cross-situational correlations might be obtained if we took an idiographic, as opposed to a nomothetic approach to personality assessment. That is, it may be that certain personality dimensions are relevant for classifying some individuals, but not other individuals. Furthermore, it may be that these personality dimensions are relevant for classifying the behavior of some individuals only in certain types of situations. For example, persons "A" and "B" may show a relatively high degree of personal consistency in their aggressive behavior across situations, while person "C" may show a low degree of personal consistency. In addition, person "A" may become highly aggressive only in one situation, such as when interacting with "authority figures," while person "B" may become moderately aggressive in response to several types of situations.

A typical nomothetic assessment of these persons on the trait of aggression would fail to provide evidence of *relative* consistency across situations. In some situations, "A" would score higher than "B"; in other situations, "B" would score higher than "A"; and in all situations, the scores for "C" would appear to fluctuate randomly. But an idiographic assessment of these three persons on the dimension of aggression should enable us to predict the unique patterns of aggression likely to be shown by persons "A" and "B" while allowing us to state that the behavior of person "C" cannot be predicted on the dimension of aggression.

To illustrate this approach, Bem and Allen (1974) asked subjects to indicate whether they were cross-situationally consistent on the trait dimensions of friendliness and conscientiousness. On a number of self-report, observational, and unobtrusive measures across several situations, the subjects who classified themselves as consistently friendly showed significantly less variability than the subjects who described themselves as inconsistent. The results for the dimension of conscientiousness were less clear-cut.

No doubt, the reader will recognize Bem's approach as one that assumes that behavior will be internally consistent, or coherently organized, rather than absolutely or relatively consistent. On the whole, most trait theorists have not adopted this approach, although Allport (1961), one of the leading proponents of trait theory, insisted that traits must be assessed idiographically. It has been more characteristic of psychodynamic theorists (e.g., Wachtel, 1973a,b), cognitive theorists (e.g., Kelly, 1955), and social learning theorists (e.g., Staats, 1975) to analyze the contribution of person variables to behavior in terms of their unique organization within each individual.

Psychologists who have taken this approach to the study of personality typically have encountered problems on at least three fronts. First, they have had difficulty in deciding what units of analysis to use for describing or categorizing the critical person variables. Although their goal has been to capture the uniqueness of each personality in a way that would allow them to predict and explain the behavior of specific individuals, they could not avoid the need to generate, at some level, a common set of conceptual units with which to construe persons. A unique language system simply could not be created each time a new person was being assessed. Perhaps a general set of common conceptual units like those in the periodic table of chemical elements could be created to guide the analysis of personality composition and structure in individuals. With a finite number of elements organized into a coherent system, chemists can account for all matter. But what should be the psychological equivalents of the units in the periodic table? How might we create such units, or select among the many possibilities?

The second problem is an extension of the first. Since this approach is interested in analyzing the unique structure, or organization, of each individual's personality, it must provide some theoretical framework for conducting structural analysis. Again, this requires a general set of conceptual tools with which to describe and analyze the structural arrangements of the more basic units. What are the possible ways in which personalities might be organized? And what are the implications of these different organizations? Of course, ultimately, the system used to analyze personality structure should lead to valid, useful, and falsifiable predictions.

This raises the third problem. How shall we measure the basic units, analyze the structure, and test the predictions? To answer these questions, we need a measurement model that is congruent with our theoretical approach, and we need to develop specific assessment methods that are congruent with our measurement model. The methods must accurately capture the units that have been selected as most important, must reveal the structural features that are theoretically significant, and must make it possible to test the degree to which personality is coherent as predicted.

So far, no theoretical orientation has managed to solve all three of these problems satisfactorily. Nevertheless, the idea of continuing to search for consistency in personality through the assessment of idiographic coherence seems to be appealing primarily on logical, intuitive, or aesthetic grounds. The number of ways that personality might be construed within this approach seems almost limitless, and the number of ways that have been systematically explored thus far is small. Very little research on idiographic assessment procedures had been reported prior to the publications by Bem and his colleagues (Carlson, 1971). Without a great deal of additional effort, the potential of this approach will not have been fairly tested. Until someone comes forth with more convincing evidence on the utility of this approach, however, it is not unreasonable for other investigators to opt in favor of looking elsewhere for alternative approaches to describing, predicting, and explaining human behavior.

THE SITUATIONAL PERSPECTIVE

The burgeoning interest in the situational perspective can be attributed in part to the spreading disenchantment with the personological perspective. For this reason, it is useful at the outset to draw a heuristic distinction between two general types of situationists. Some clearly recognize the great need for research aimed at building, testing, and refining theoretical models and assessment procedures that will systematically take into account the contribution of situational or environmental influences on human behavior. Others seem to have concluded on the basis of faulty syllogistic reasoning that, by default, the validity of the situational perspective already has been established. They apparently reason as follows:

> The two major determinants of behavior are person variables and situation variables.
> Traits are person variables.
> Trait measures have seldom accounted for more than 10% of the total variance in behavior.
> Therefore, by subtraction, situation variables must account for nearly 90% of the variance in behavior.

Confident in the logic of their inference, they apparently see little need for research to confirm the obvious.

Overview

It is virtually impossible to find an example of a pure situationist—someone who claims that behavior is determined exclusively by situational variables— just as it is virtually impossible to find examples of pure personologists. However, there are psychologists who believe that, at this stage of development in the science, the most fruitful approach to the description, prediction, and explanation of behavior is to analyze the situations in which behavior occurs. Situationists are fond of pointing out that when persons are in church they behave church, when in restaurants they behave restaurant, when at cocktail parties they behave party, and so forth. The implication is that there is greater similarity in the behavior of different individuals within the same situation than in the behavior of the same individual across different situations. This amounts to the prediction that different situations will elicit a pattern of *relative* consistency when behavior is assessed across persons. In effect, this is the inverse of the trait prediction of cross-situational consistency. If one wants to predict behavior, according to this perspective, it is more informative to know details about the situations in which the person will be behaving than it is to know details about the personality of the person who will be behaving.

Attempts to study situational influences have followed three general lines to date. First, some investigators have been interested in studying situations per se, with little concern for tracing the uniqueness of the individuals who are passing through those situations. Although these investigators recognize the existence of individual differences within situations, they tend to regard such variation as "noise" to be reduced by averaging across the behavior of many individuals in order to get a stable estimate of "true" situational influences. Obviously, this research strategy is the same one employed by the personologists who attempt to get a stable estimate of "true" personality factors by averaging one person's behavior across many different situations. As one might expect, this approach is associated with many of the same problems as were discussed previously in the section on the personological use of the aggregation strategy. The major difference between the situationists and personologists who use this research strategy is simply that one group's independent variable is the other group's "error"; one group's "figure" is the other's "ground."

Some of the leading investigators in this approach to the study of situational influences have been Argyle (Argyle, Furnham, & Graham, 1981), Barker (1968; see also Barker & Wright, 1955), Goffman (1967, 1971), Harré and Secord (1972), Moos (1968, 1973), and Sells (1963). By and large, the most influential investigators in this area have not identified themselves with the mainstream of research in clinical/personality psychology, but have thought of their work more in terms of such labels as "social psychology," "ecological psychology," "environmental psychology," or "ethology." (Argyle et al., 1981, have provided a helpful discussion of the distinctions among such labels and their methodological implications.)

In general, the theoretical and empirical work of these investigators is essentially descriptive and is based primarily on a methodology of naturalistic observation. Beyond these similarities and their common focus on situational influences, these investigators often show considerable divergence. For example, they disagree on how situations should be conceptualized. Some investigators construe situations as structural units with specific physical parameters (e.g., places like elevators, bars, restaurants, schools); others construe them as functional units (e.g., situations evoking embarrassment, calling for assertion, or provoking aggression). There also is divergence in how these investigators believe situations should be measured. Sometimes situations simply are treated quantitatively (e.g., the frequency or duration of behavior in different settings is counted); other times situations are treated more qualitatively (e.g., narratives of within-situation behavioral sequences are recorded in the hope of eventually uncovering situation-bound patterns or rules). There is considerable variation in the degree to which these investigators employ systematic coding systems in their observations. There is virtually no standardization of coding categories for the classification of situations. Investigators also differ widely in their willingness to manipulate the environment to assess situational influences experimentally.

Perhaps the most fundamental unresolved problem in this general line of research is that investigators have not yet developed a generally-agreed-upon taxonomy for situations (see Frederiksen, 1972), and it is not even clear how they should go about devising such a taxonomy (McReynolds, 1979). Situationists are at a disadvantage, relative to personologists, because the physical boundaries and identities of persons, as units of analysis, are so much more clear-cut than the boundaries and identities of situations. This contrast is especially accentuated when behavior is studied over time. We easily recognize the same person from one occasion to the next, but it is not such a simple matter to decide whether the same situation exists from one occasion to another. This ambiguity is even worse when situational variability is not under experimental control, as when naturalistic observations are the major source of data. Until these taxonomic and methodological problems are solved, this approach to the study of situational influences may be intriguing, but its full potential cannot be gauged.

A second general line of research into situational influences has been carried out by learning theorists, social behaviorists, and operant psychologists. While there are many theoretical and methodological disagreements among these investigators, they share the general belief that behavior is controlled primarily by its environmental antecedents and consequences. In an attempt to achieve precision, operationally defined environmental events (stimuli) are manipulated experimentally and their influences on operationally defined behaviors (responses) are assessed. No doubt, the reader is familiar with numerous examples of carefully controlled experiments, involving both human subjects and human–analogue subjects, in which "lawful" relationships among antecedent stimuli, responses, and contingent reinforcing stimuli have been demonstrated. It is this type of research that has received the brunt of the criticism against the situational perspective (e.g., Bowers, 1973).

While they recognize the existence of individual differences in persons' responses to situations, these situationists have attempted to demonstrate experimentally that such differences can be explained on the basis of subjects' differential learning histories. Thus, what appear to be personality influences on behavior can be reduced, in principle, to the accumulated influences of environmental variables. Since learning is ongoing, these theorists would not expect the same degree of consistency across time as trait theorists would.

One of the major points of disagreement among these situationists concerns the extent to which it is useful or necessary to discuss accumulated environmental influences in terms of organismic changes that mediate subsequent stimulus effects. At the extreme, Skinner (1953) sees no gain in speculating about such mediating processes. Staats (1975) feels there is value in considering organismic processes (e.g., motivation), as long as one bears in mind that they are shaped by one's learning history. Bandura (1977) and Rotter (1966) assign a central role to person variables, like "self-efficacy" and "perceived locus of control," while merely presuming that an individual's standing on such variables arises from one's learning history. In a way, then, some investigators who regard themselves as learning theorists and situationists almost seem to have come full circle to the point where they are interested in assessing "situationally determined" personality characteristics.

The strength of the learning approach, of course, is that it lends itself nicely to the development of controlled experiments in which situational factors are manipulated and the effects of these independent variables on dependent variables are assessed. As long as the investigator relies on operational definitions of situational variables, and as long as these variables can be controlled by the investigator, this is a strong approach. However, it begins to encounter difficulties outside the controlled environment. Once again, the lack of an adequately precise language for isolating and classifying "stimuli" in the natural environment is a major obstacle (Frederiksen, 1972). Furthermore, there is not a satisfactory methodology for assessing the naturally occurring determinants of a specific individual's behavior. Outside the laboratory, the situationist must rely on correlational methods to infer causality—as must the personologist—but lacks an array of assessment tools comparable to the personologist's personality tests.

A third line of research by situationists has been concerned with the behavioral effects of situations as they are perceived by individuals (Kelly, 1955; Mischel, 1973, 1979). According to this approach, the reason two persons behave differently in ostensibly the same situation is that they construe the situation differently. Presumably, if they construed it more similarly, they would respond more alike. This line of work places as much emphasis on the individual as it does on the situation, since the ultimate meaning of any situation depends on the meaning imposed on it by each individual. This is the most complicated of the situational approaches to the assessment and prediction of behavior. It is difficult enough to classify situations when they are perceived from only one point of reference (e.g., the investigator's); it seems almost impossible to classify situations after they have been filtered through the perceptual and interpretive processes of a large number of different individuals. Not the least of the problems involves the creation of a reliable and valid method of assessing how each individual construes all of the events surrounding him or her at a particular point in time. Of course, even if it were possible to do this, it would beg the question of what factors determine how different individuals construe the same situation. Even if it were possible to determine that two persons perceived a given situation similarly, it still might be reasonable to expect that the two persons would respond differently for other reasons.

Critique

None of the three situational approaches outlined above has been developed thus far to the point of providing a coherent theoretical and methodological framework for the description, prediction, and explanation of human behavior. The first approach, with its focus on average behavior within a situation, is of little value to clinical psychologists concerned with understanding and predicting the behavior of specific individuals.

The second approach, with its emphasis on experimentally controlled demonstrations of situational influences, is of little practical value beyond the artificial circumstances controlled by the experimenter. The clinician is given no general assessment tools with which to predict the behavior of a particular person in a particular situation. The clinician is able to make only "low-risk" predictions, first observing the individual's behavior in a given situation and then predicting that in similar future situations the individual will behave similarly. Of course, since no two situations are ever exactly alike, and since no formal system is provided for classifying situations as similar or different, this tends to lead to vague and unfalsifiable predictions. In addition, since the reinforcers for behavior are unknown, except when they are controlled by the investigator, this approach offers only post hoc explanations of an individual's naturalistic behavior.

The third approach, with its focus on situations as subjectively perceived by each individual, almost seems to be a personological approach in disguise. As such, it suffers from the problems of both the personological and the situational perspectives. Perhaps its major contribution, thus far, has been that it has represented an effort to overcome the dualism that has characterized the thinking behind the person–situation debate. It has highlighted the importance of considering possible interactions between situational factors and person variables.

Situational Specificity

The evidence reviewed thus far has indicated that a person's behavior in a particular situation cannot be predicted very accurately either on the basis of trait-type personality variables or on the basis of classifications of situational variables. Mischel (1968, 1973) has interpreted this evidence to mean that behavior therefore is "situation specific." By this, he apparently meant that each individual displays a unique pattern of responses across situations. To predict a given individual's behavior in a specific situation, one must conduct an idiographic assessment of that individual's unique behavior pattern within that situation.

To understand and evaluate this concept of situational specificity, it is helpful to see that it actually consists of two parts: It is both a description of a problem and a prescription of how to solve that problem. Descriptively, the concept merely represents an admission that neither the personological nor the situational perspective has proven wholly adequate; on this point, there is general agreement. Prescriptively, the concept represents an assertion that an idiographic assessment of the person-by-situation interaction is necessary if we are to predict behavior; on this point, the empirical support is not so clear-cut. We turn now to an examination of the interactional perspective.

THE INTERACTIONAL PERSPECTIVE

According to an interactional perspective, "behavior is a function of a continuous process of multidirectional interaction or feedback between the individual and the situations he or she encounters" (Magnusson & Endler, 1977, p. 4). This perspective is not merely a compromise, or middle ground position between the personological and situational perspectives. On the contrary, it is offered as a new and distinctive approach that attempts to achieve a synthesis of the two previous perspectives. It assumes that the whole is greater than the sum of its parts, and that the determinants of behavior cannot be broken down into separate or independent components representing persons and situations. Behavior can be understood only by analyzing the behavior of a person in a context.

The interactive relationships between persons and situations are complex and difficult to analyze. To begin with, not all situations are equally relevant or significant in the lives of all persons. That is, to a considerable extent, individuals are able to choose the situations they will encounter. When two individuals enter the same situation, they do so with different personal histories; as a consequence, they are likely to perceive and be affected by the situation differently. This also means that they are likely to respond to it differently. In turn, their responses will alter the situation differentially, so that it will no longer be the same situation for both persons. In other words, persons shaped their own environments, and individualized environments shape unique persons. The relationship is reciprocal and dynamic. Viewed in this way, it is meaningless to ask, "Which is the most important determinant of behavior—the person or the situation?" Instead, we should be concerned with analyzing the *process* by which the person and the situation interact in a dynamic, ongoing way (Magnusson & Endler, 1977).

The interactional perspective is not really new, having been proposed in various forms as early as the 1920s (Kantor, 1924) and 1930s (Lewin, 1935; Murray, 1938); however, it has attracted increased attention in recent years. According to Ekehammar (1974), one major reason for the late emergence of the interactional perspective is that appropriate methodological and statistical techniques were not available previously. In fact, as we shall see, appropriate techniques still are not readily available. This suggests that the current interest in the interactional perspective may be in reaction to a growing awareness of the inadequacies of the personological and situational perspectives.

The units of analysis and statistical techniques used in trait research or in social–learning experiments cannot be adapted readily to the requirements of the interactional perspective. Specifically, analysis of variance statistical procedures are inappropriate for analyzing the dynamic processes involved in interactions (Alker, 1977; Olweus, 1977). Ironically, research using analysis of variance (ANOVA) procedures has been widely cited in support of the interactionist approach and has helped to stimulate interest in it. Bowers (1973), for instance, summarized the results of 11 studies in which the proportions of variance accounted for by persons, situations, and their interaction were assessed in analysis of variance designs. The results consistently showed that the interaction term accounted for more variance than either the person or the situation variables alone. Results such as these have been offered as proof of the superiority of the interactional perspective (e.g., see Bowers, 1973; Magnusson, 1976); actually, such results fail to provide evidence one way or the other about the value of this perspective (Olweus, 1977).

Confusion has arisen from the fact that the word "interaction" has been used in two very different ways, with two incompatible meanings (Lazarus & Launier, 1978; Magnusson & Endler, 1977; Olweus, 1977; Pervin & Lewis, 1978; Sameroff & Chandler, 1975). On the one hand, it has been used to refer to a statistical relationship within a data matrix; on the other hand, it has been used to refer to a conceptual model aimed at describing and explaining the dynamic process by which persons, situations, and behaviors are interrelated and integrated. Some important distinctions between these two uses are as follows: The statistical use involves the partitioning of variance into independent component parts; the conceptual use is concerned with the process by which inseparable components function together as a whole. The statistical use typically involves samples obtained at static points in time; the conceptual use is interested in the interactive process as it unfolds over time. The statistical use is of little value in answering the question of *how* variables interact, which is the question of primary interest in the conceptual use.

ANOVA procedures may help answer specific questions within a study, but they will never be able to provide a final resolution to the general question of whether the person, the situation, or their interaction exerts the greatest influence on behavior. This is because a clever investigator can always arrange the experimental conditions, intentionally or otherwise, to produce an outcome favorable to any one of the three possibilities. To demonstrate that the situation is most influential, for example, the investigator can always select an extremely homogeneous sample of subjects and assess their behavior across a very heterogeneous series of situations. The investigator also can select person variables for study that are poorly conceived, imprecisely specified, and unreliably measured. And the investigator can select dependent variables that are differentially sensitive to the influences of situations, as opposed to persons. Of course, the investigator who wants to demonstrate that person variables are more influential can simply reverse these sources of bias. The essential point here is that the proportion of variance due to persons, situations, or their interaction is not a constant, but is always a function of the particular questions being asked in an experiment, the details of the experimental arrangements, and the characteristics of the populations, situations, and measures employed. Thus, the question of which type of variable is most influential in intrinsically unresolvable.

If ANOVA techniques are inappropriate for studying the interactional perspective, then what alternative techniques are appropriate? Pervin and Lewis (1978) have stressed the need for using more descriptive research methods, complaining that "much of the research to date has involved a freezing of behavior rather than a witnessing of the unfolding of behavior" (p. 18). Lazarus and Launier (1978) also have advocated the use of descriptive methods to capture the continuous interplay between persons and situations. Fiske (1977) and Olweus (1977) have emphasized the need to study sequences of behavior over time. Familiar methods such as multivariate analysis, regression analysis, factor analysis, and cluster analysis will be of limited value in achieving these research objectives. Alternative methods such as time-series analysis, Markov process analysis, and the analysis of conditional probabilities (e.g., Gottman, 1979, 1981; Raush, 1972; Schlundt, 1982a,b) will be more valuable.

Unfortunately, research based on an interactional perspective has only recently begun to employ appropriate methods for capturing the true sequential and transactional nature of social behavior (e.g., Argyle *et al.*, 1981; Duncan & Fiske, 1977; Gottman, 1979, Raush, 1977; Schlundt, 1982a, 1982b; Trower, 1980). Better methods, consistent with the basic assumptions and interests of the perspective, still need to be developed.

Even after the methodological problems have been solved, difficult conceptual problems will remain. The most basic problem involves the choice of conceptual units of analysis. That is, how will the flow of events be "chunked" to capture the important transactional processes underlying the behavior of persons within situations across time? The interactional perspective is more complex than either of the two preceding perspectives. If the "unit" problem was not satisfactorily solved in either of the simpler perspectives, it should be even more difficult to solve in the interactional perspective. Thus far, few investigators have paid much attention to this problem, and no satisfactory solutions have been demonstrated (see McFall, 1982).

Although the interactional perspective has been characterized as the zeitgeist of current research in clinical/personality psychology (Ekehammar, 1974), empirical support for the perspective has been slow to emerge. New methods of analysis and new conceptual units of analysis must be developed and applied before this picture will change. Until then, the interactional perspective will remain merely a tantalizing, but unproven, approach to studying human behavior.

BEYOND THE CURRENT DEBATE

Based on our synopsis of the person–situation debate, it appears that so far none of the three perspectives has emerged as clearly superior to any other. Of course, it is possible that future research based on one of the perspectives may eventually settle the issue; toward that end, we have attempted to summarize some of the major conceptual and methodological problems that need attention within each perspective. It is also possible, however, that in the long run the debate will be resolved by approaching the underlying issue from yet another perspective—one that rises above the polemics and dualistic thinking that have characterized the debate thus far.

In the present section, we search for just such an alternative perspective. We begin by tracing some of the historical roots of the current debate. After all, the history of psychology is essentially the story of a search for units of analysis with which to describe, predict, and explain behavior. Hopefully, the cool detachment provided by a historical perspective enables us to distill the controversy to its essential elements and to perceive an alternative path toward an eventual solution.

THE PERSONAL EQUATION

In his history of psychology, Boring (1957) told the story of the Greenwich astronomer named Maskelyne who noticed in 1795 that his assistant, Kinne-brook, was making serious and consistent errors of nearly 1 second in his observations of the times of stellar transits. Kinnebrook was informed of his "error," but was unable to correct it, so Maskelyn dismissed him. An account of the incident, published in 1816, attracted the attention of Bessel, an astronomer at Konigsberg, who thought that Kinnebrook's "error" might have been involuntary and set out to see whether similar "errors," or individ-ual differences in observation, occurred among more experienced observers. He compared his own observations to those of another observer and found a consistent average discrepancy of more than 1 second. The results of his investigations, published in 1822, stimulated considerable research interest in this phenomenon, which was referred to as the "personal equation." Research aimed at measuring, explaining, and correcting the personal equa-tion flourished into the 1860s and even continued into the 1880s, although the chronograph and other methods aimed at eliminating observer error had been developed by the 1850s.

   One line of investigation that grew out of the personal equation re-search was concerned with studying reaction time differences associated with different sensory and stimulus modalities. In fact, when Wundt estab-lished the world's first psychology laboratory in 1879, he carried out such reaction time experiments for the purpose of studying indirectly the struc-ture of consciousness (Boring, 1957). Wundt was not particularly interested in the personal equation, or in reaction time differences between subjects, but was interested in stimulus effects. This led him to regard between-subject differences merely as "error" to be controlled by averaging reaction times to a given stimulus across many trials with many subjects.

   In 1883, an American student, James McKeen Cattell, became Wundt's laboratory assistant. He observed that subjects in Wundt's experiments seemed to show consistent individual differences in reaction times, with some subjects responding more quickly than others regardless of the partic-ular stimulus modality being tested. In effect, Cattell revived interest in the personal equation. Because he was fascinated with individual differences among subjects, he averaged each subject's reaction times across many trials with different stimuli. He relied on the correlational methods in these studies, rather than the experimental method, since he could not manipulate subjects' personal characteristics, which were the independent variables of primary interest. According to Boring (1957), Cattell spent three very productive years at Leipzig, publishing over half a dozen articles "about reaction times or about individual differences. Some of these papers are now classic. The excitement about the reaction experiment as a tool for mental measurement was then at its height, and Cattell combined his conventional interest in reaction times with his unconventional concern about the individual, so that some of his papers were contributions to both topics" (Boring, 1957, pp. 533–534).

"Cattell's psychology is, however, something more than mental tests and reaction times and statistical method and the resultant objective judgments that are not introspections. It is a psychology of human *capacity*. It is motivated by the desire to determine how well men [sic] can do in this or that situation. It is concerned little with an analysis of capacities into conscious causes, and only a little more with the physiological causes. It seeks a description of human nature in respect of its range and variability. . . . This psychology of capacity is, of course, functional psychology" (Boring, 1957, p. 539).

In light of the current person–situation debate, it is especially interesting that Cattell somehow managed to carry out two types of reaction time research—correlational studies of individual differences and experimental studies of stimulus effects—without sensing any inherent incompatibility or conflict between them. How could he do this? Was he simply too naive, given the newness of psychology as a discipline, to be aware that the two types of research, like oil and water, were not supposed to mix? Or did he have an integrated perception of his research that we have overlooked? Perhaps he had not yet fallen into the trap of conceptualizing human behavior in a dualistic, polarized fashion.

Binet, another pioneer in the area of individual differences, also managed to carry out two types of research—correlational studies of intelligence and experimental studies of memory and judgment—with no apparent conflict. In their historical account of developmental psychology, Cairns and Ornstein (1979, in Hearst's *The first century of experimental psychology*) explained how Binet and his colleagues viewed the relationship between these two approaches to psychology:

> For Binet both levels of analysis are vital because they subserve different aims and functions. On the one hand, global assessment precedures (such as the intelligence scale) are addressed to the question of diagnosis: how effectively a child can adapt to particular settings and problems. They can be used for both individual analysis and for practical judgments and predictions. On the other hand, experimental strategies are addressed to the questions of determination:

how differences in adaptation arise, and how they are influenced in the course of development. Problems develop when either: (1) assessment devices are used to answer questions about determination; or (2) experimental techniques are used as diagnostic tools. It is regrettable that this insight has yet to penetrate present-day controversies. . . . (p. 481)

What can be learned from these historical examples? First, the current schism between the personological and situational perspectives is not inevitable; there was a time when psychologists employed both perspectives without feeling compelled to choose between them. Second, investigators previously were able to integrate the two approaches by viewing them as complementary, rather than competitive; they realized that each served a particular function, addressed different questions. Instead of becoming trapped in a false dichotomy, these investigators used the two perspectives in combination to triangulate on a problem, knowing that this strategy could be far more revealing than if they had operated from only one perspective. Finally, these investigators seemed to realize that the subject matter of psychology is too big, complex, and diverse to be captured by any one conceptual or methodological framework. Perhaps because the discipline of psychology was still so new, the earlier investigators were willing to settle for the short-range and modest goals of describing, predicting, and explaining particular phenomena within specific contexts, rather than trying to develop one explanatory system to cover everything.

TWO SCIENCES OF MODERN PSYCHOLOGY

By 1957, the schism between correlational studies of individual differences, on one side, and experimental studies of stimulus effects, on the other, had grown so wide that Cronbach complained that psychology essentially had become two distinct scientific disciplines, each with its own conceptual and methodological foundations. He deplored this separation, claiming that it impeded the progress of psychological research, and called for a rapprochement aimed at building a unified science. To unify the "two sciences," he proposed the development of a hybrid discipline in which the correlational and experimental approaches would be crossbred to produce a science of Aptitude X Treatment interactions (ATIs). Eighteen years later, Cronbach's views had changed dramatically as a result of his unsuccessful attempts to develop the ATI hybrid:

When ATIs are present, a general statement about a treatment effect is misleading because the effect will come or go depending on the kind of person treated. When ATIs are present, a generalization about aptitude is an uncertain basis for prediction because the regression slope will depend on the treatment chosen. Having said this in 1957, I was shortsighted not to apply the same argument to interaction effects themselves. An ATI result can be taken as a general conclusion only if it is not in turn moderated by further variables. If Aptitude X Treatment X Sex interact, for example, then the Aptitude X Treatment effect does not tell the story. Once we attend to interactions, we enter a hall of mirrors that extends to infinity. However far we carry our analysis—to third order or fifth order or any other—untested interactions of a still higher order can be envisioned. [Cronbach, 1975, p. 119]

Cronbach (1975) went on to say that traditional psychology, modeled as it is after the physical sciences, has aspired "to amass empirical generalizations, to restructure them into more general laws, and to weld scattered laws into coherent theory" (p. 125). However, given the inherent problems of complex interactions, Cronbach concluded that psychology's aspirations are unrealistic: "enduring systematic theories about man in society are not likely to be achieved" (p. 126). He proposed that psychology abandon its preoccupation with developing and testing nomothetic propositions and concentrate instead on the intensive local observation, description, and interpretation of effects in a context.

Cronbach's suggestion that psychology abandon (for the foreseeable future) its search for a single, unifying perspective is provocative, almost heretical; but other authors have come to similar conclusions. For example, Scriven (1969) and Fiske (1979) have asserted that the field of psychology is too complex, too multifaceted to be studied by a single paradigm or viewed from a single perspective. In effect, this conclusion amounts to a rediscovery of the wheel, since it represents a return to the position taken by J. M. Cattell, Binet, and other early psychologists.

CONSTRUCTIVE ALTERNATIVISM

Over a decade ago, investigators in the area of psychotherapy-outcome research were embroiled in a controversy over the global question, "Which is the best psychotherapy technique?" The controversy was resolved when the adversaries realized that they were fighting over an unanswerable question. Kiesler (1966) and Paul (1969) pointed out that it was futile to search for a single therapeutic solution to all psychological problems for all people, and suggested that investigators set their sights instead on answering the more focused and realistic question: When administered in this way and evaluated by these measures, "what treatment, by whom, is most effective for this individual with that specific problem, under which set of circumstances, and how does it come about?" (Paul, 1969, p. 44). Although psychologists saw the value of this reconceptualization for psychotherapy research, they apparently failed to see that the person–situation debate could benefit from a similar reconceptualization.

The decision to abandon the immediate goal of a unified science of psychology transforms the person–situation debate into a meaningless feud over a pseudo-issue. It implies that there is no single answer to the question, "What are *the best* units of analysis with which to describe, predict, and explain human behavior?" Instead of seeking all-purpose answers to such a global question, it is more fruitful to look for specific answers to delimited questions, such as: "What is the utility of construing these phenomena in this way, in this particular context, for this purpose, as evaluated by these criteria?" A particular construction about human behavior may have utility for certain purposes, but not others. It may be relevant for certain contexts, but not others. Or it may appear useful when judged by certain criteria, but not others. In short, there are many alternative ways of construing human behavior—the personological, situational, and interactional perspectives being only three, very general possibilities—and the merit of any one alternative can only be evaluated in relation to a specified purpose and set of conditions. This perspective is what Kelly (1955) has called "constructive alternativism."

Viewing the person–situation debate from this alternative perspective, we can see that much of the past disagreement has resulted from miscommunication and misunderstanding. The disputants frequently have arrived at discrepant conclusions on the basis of the same evidence simply because they evaluated the evidence in terms of different purposes and against different criteria. Reflecting on our earlier discussion of trait theories, for example, we now can see that there is research evidence to support the utility of Epstein's (1979, 1980) constructions for predicting a person's mean response as sampled across many different situations, but not for predicting specific responses in a specific situation. Whether one is impressed by Epstein's constructions will depend on whether their utility is relevant to the particular questions one hoped to answer. Similarly, research by Block (1977) and Stagner (1976) indicates that their constructions are useful for predicting from one type of indirect trait measure to another, but not for predicting to actual behavior in specific naturalistic tasks. Again, one may or may not find these constructions useful for one's own purposes.

Constructions derived from the situational or interactional perspective can be reexamined in the same way. For example, Barker's (1968) constructions about environmental settings as determinants of behavior may be useful for predicting the characteristic response patterns of many individuals in specific situations, but not for predicting the idiographic responses of a particular person in a situation.

To minimize miscommunication and misunderstanding, it is the responsibility of the investigator who proposes a particular construction to specify clearly what its aim, purpose, and referents are. Furthermore, the onus is on the proposer to provide evidence of a construction's utility, as proposed. Finally, the proposer is obligated to label as speculation any generalizations beyond the specific conditions represented in the research design.

When more than one construction has been offered for a particular purpose, the question is not, "Which is true?" but "What are the relative benefits and drawbacks of each construction?" Only when two constructions have essentially equal utility for a specified purpose does it become appropriate to consider other factors, such as parsimony, elegance, comprehensiveness, or interrelatedness to other constructions for other phenomena.

A MULTIFACETED PSYCHOLOGY

Once we stop insisting on a single, unifying perspective in psychology and accept the current reality of diversity, this actually fosters the development of psychology as a scientific discipline—albeit a multifaceted one. It is more practical to assess the utility of many separate constructions, each explicitly tied to a limited range of local phenomena and serving a specific purpose, than it is to choose among a few grand theoretical systems.

The acceptance of diversity also may encourage us to be more creative in our constructions. This chapter has focused on the classic dichotomy between personological and situational determinants of behavior, as though these two factors, or some combination of them, were the only ways to slice up our subject matter. Obviously, there are other ways of slicing things— ways that have tended to get lost in our urgency to settle on a single perspective. In fact, it is possible to discern many facets to the domain of psychology, and we should explore what might be gained by using these alternative constructions.

Fiske (1979), for example, has proposed that psychological phenomena can be divided into two broad and contrasting categories: attributes of persons and behaviors. Interestingly, in our discussion thus far, we have considered the problems involved in classifying persons and situations, but we have not even considered the problems involved in classifying behaviors! Behaviors have been treated here as though they were always dependent variables, but they also can function simultaneously as independent and dependent variables, such as in person–person interactions, where one person's response becomes the stimulus for the next person's response, which becomes a stimulus for the first person's response, and so on. An alternative to studying the effects of personality and situational variables on behavior, according to Fiske (1979; see also Duncan & Fiske, 1977), is studying the relationships between behaviors in face-to-face interactions, with the aim of uncovering a structure of conditional probabilities from which one might infer the operation of social rules.

Another pair of potentially useful conceptual facets is revealed by the distinction between research that examines phenomena at static points in time and research that studies sequences of events as they unfold over time. Most of the discussion in this chapter has focused on the static type of constructions, but the inclusion of *time* as another dimension of analysis introduces many interesting new possibilities (Fiske, 1977). Ironically, time was considered a fundamental unit of analysis in the research of the earliest psychologists, but its utility for construing psychological phenomena seemed to get overlooked along the way. Today's investigators in the area of social interaction research have resurrected time as an important facet in their work (e.g., Duncan & Fiske, 1977; Gottman, 1979; Raush, 1977, Schlundt, 1982a).

These are only a few of the many different dimensions along which psychologists might construe their subject matter. The reader no doubt can add others to the list, such as cognitive phenomena, physiological phenomena, and observer and measurement effects. And there are still others waiting to be created. For now, the field of psychology should encourage the development of such a multifaceted discipline, while becoming more stringent about requiring that the specific, limited utility of each particular construction be demonstrated before it is granted the status of a "local, contemporary truth" (Cronbach, 1975); and that the limits of generalization for a given "truth" be specified.

MULTIFACETED ASSESSMENT, UNCERTAINTY, AND CHOICE

According to "Heisenberg's uncertainty principle," all measurement unavoidably involves some elements of uncertainty and choice. In physics, for example, a given particle's position at a specific moment cannot be predicted exactly; at best, the particle's position is an uncertainty that can be determined only probabilistically. Furthermore, the act of measuring one variable, such as a particle's momentum, precludes the possibility of simultaneously measuring certain other variables, such as the particle's position. In other words, the decision to measure one variable implies a choice not to measure certain other variables at the same time.

Something analogous to the Heisenberg principle seems to be operating in psychological assessment, as well. First, it seems that a certain level of measurement uncertainty is inevitable in our assessment of social behavior. For example, we simply may not be able to predict precisely what a given individual will do at a specific moment in a given interaction; probabilistic predictions may be the best that we can do. Second, it seems that our assessment decisions always imply choices. When we decide to focus on the assessment of person variables, for example, we usually must sacrifice some degree of control over situational variables in the process. Similarly, when we decide to chunk the flow of behavior into discrete units and then sort these units into behavioral categories, we invariably are forced to ignore the temporal and sequential aspects of social behavior. In fact, the decision to measure anything at all involves an implicit choice not to measure some alternative possibilities. The selection of a particular measurement target necessarily results in the nonmeasurement of other things. Those things that we do not measure, we simply call "error."

Figure 7-1 provides a simplified example of a multifaceted conceptual model for possible use in behavioral assessment. It is a three-dimensional model in which persons and situations, behavior and time, and measurement and error, respectively, are the pairs of opposing facets that make up the three orthogonal dimensions of this six-sided conceptual cube. In this particular model, the "error" facet would always remain on the bottom (as shown), and the cube would rotate only on the horizontal plane. No more than three sides of the cube would be visible at any one time, one of which would always be the "measurement" facet.

If you imagine rotating this cube, you will notice that you cannot decide to bring one facet into view without forcing another facet to disappear, at least momentarily, from your view. For example, if you decide to focus on measuring persons over time, the facets of situation and behavior will no longer be exposed to view. In this simple model, there are four combinations of facets that can be brought into focus together; however, it is conceivable that more complex, multidimensional models would offer many more combinations and require many more decisions.

Regardless of their level of complexity, the basic implications of such multifaceted assessment models are essentially the same: It is impossible to perceive all facets of the whole model all at once; choices are unavoidable; and some degree of uncertainty, due to our inability to perceive the whole, is inevitable. The whole is greater than what is reflected in the particular facets being examined at a given moment. We must resist the temptation to overgeneralize about the whole on the basis of what we can see of it at a given moment. If we decide to study person variables, for example, then we should be aware that our choice of focus has moved situation variables temporarily into the background. This awareness should help us resist the temptation to overemphasize the importance of the particular variables we happen to be studying.

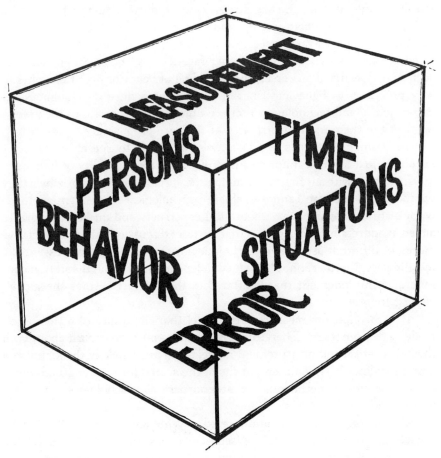

FIG. 7-1. Simplified example of a multifaceted conceptual model for possible use in behavioral assessment.

ASSESSMENT IMPLICATIONS

What are the assessment implications of our discussion of constructive alternativism and a multifaceted discipline of psychology? It seems clear that investigators should stop arguing about the absolute truth of particular theoretical perspectives and concentrate instead on building, testing, and refining limited theoretical models that will have utility in relation to a specific set of phenomena. Each theoretical model, in turn, will require the parallel development of its own appropriate measurement model. For example, if one's theory takes situational factors into account, then one must develop some system for classifying or assessing situations in theoretically relevant ways. If one's theory stresses the importance of certain person variables, then one must develop some system for classifying or assessing the theoretically relevant aspects of persons. Similarly, investigators interested in theories that emphasize other facets of psychological phenomena, such as transactional processes, the unfolding of behavior over time, physiologic processes, or behavior–behavior relationships, must develop measurement models and technologies that are uniquely appropriate to the assessment of the theoretical constructs that they are proposing.

Assessment methods are like tools, designed to serve very specific purposes. Just as one cannot meaningfully evaluate the utility of hammers, saws, or pliers without first determining the specific purposes for which they will be used, one also cannot evaluate psychological assessment methods without first knowing what theoretical constructs and questions they are aimed at addressing. This implies that abstract discussions about the relative merits of different assessment techniques or methodologies are essentially meaningless. Merits cannot be judged independent of some theoretical context, and any judgment that is offered in the abstract betrays the judge's implicit theoretical framework.

It is through the measurement model that the utility of a theoretical model is demonstrated. Therefore, investigators must be explicit about both their theoretical and measurement models, and must specify the logical and inferential links between them. In short, the search for meaningful, theory-based assessment methods is an integral part of psychology's search for useful theories.

The implications of a multifaceted psychology can be illustrated by considering three representative issues in behavioral assessment: (1) the importance of idiographic versus nomothetic assessment, (2) the importance of establishing stable baselines before assessing within-subject changes, and (3) the importance of including representative samples of relevant situations in the assessment tasks.[4]

Idiographic Versus Nomothetic

Behavioral assessors typically advocate taking an idiographic approach toward assessment; however, on closer examination, any sharp distinction between idiographic and nomothetic approaches can be seen as a false dichotomy. All assessments inevitably involve elements of both the idiographic and nomothetic approaches. On the one hand, all assessment is

4. We thank our editors, Rosemery O. Nelson and Steven C. Hayes, for suggesting these particular sample issues.

inherently idiographic in that it is aimed at differentiating among events. On the other hand, the process of differentiation necessarily involves the use of nomothetic devices such as abstractions, classifications, generalizations, and theories. Each event may be unique, but it would be impossible to apprehend and communicate about an event without the aid of taxonomies, which treat certain events *as though* they were alike.

The critical question, therefore, is *not* whether idiographic or nomothetic assessment is best. The key question is: What nomothetic units of analysis will be most useful for describing, predicting, and explaining the particular unique events of interest to us? This latter question, of course, is the central theme of this chapter and is at the very heart of scientific psychology.

Stable Baselines

A methodological tenet in behavioral assessment is that a stable baseline must be established before within-subject changes can be meaningfully assessed. Viewed from the perspective of a multifaceted psychology, this is generally sound methodological advice, but it is not an inviolable principle. For instance, there are times when the phenomenon of interest is intrinsically "unstable," showing a high degree of variability across repeated measurement occasions. A rigid insistence on achieving a stable baseline in such cases would be inappropriate and unnecessarily restrictive. The expectation of baseline stability implicitly assumes the operation of a "steady-state" model that satisfies the following conditions: (1) the controlling variables are known, (2) these variables are being held constant across measurement occasions, and (3) as long as the controlling variables are held constant, the dependent variable will not change. Obviously, all three of these assumptive conditions may not be met in every assessment situation. Alternatives to the steady-state model need to be developed, along with appropriate methodological and measurement tools for applying these alternatives to particular assessment problems. One example of a promising alternative is the time-series model (e.g., Gottman, 1981), which starts from a different set of assumptions, raises different expectations regarding baseline performance, and uses different methods to analyze within-subject change.

The conceptual units of analysis we choose for examining a phenomenon carry with them certain implicit and explicit assumptions, and these dictate the measurement approach that is most appropriate. When we change conceptual models, the tenets underlying our assessment methods may also need to change. In some cases, it may be neither necessary nor desirable to establish a stable baseline before assessing within-subject change.

Again, the critical question is, what units of analysis and allied assessment methodologies will be most useful for describing, predicting, and explaining the specific phenomena of interest to us?

Including Representative Situations in the Assessment Task

Most behavioral assessors are adamantly opposed to taking a "sign" approach to assessment, and are insistent that an adequate assessment task must capture a representative "sample" of the target behavior in its natural context (e.g., see Goldfried & Kent, 1972). Unfortunately, the "sign versus sample" debate has tended to obscure a more fundamental truth about *all* assessment; namely, the ultimate criterion by which any assessment procedure is to be judged is its *utility*. In other words, if a novel "sign"-based assessment procedure were able to provide better predictions and explanations than any existing "sample"-based procedure, then we should welcome the new procedure—even if it does not include a representative sample of relevant situations as part of the assessment task.

Behaviorists' advocacy of sample-based assessment actually represents little more than a forecast that this assessment approach eventually will prove to be the most fruitful one. This forecast is based, in part, on the relative failure, to date, of sign-based assessments to demonstrate their utility in psychology. To a lesser extent, the forecast is based on encouraging results recently obtained with specific sample-based assessments. For the most part, however, our ability to describe, predict, and explain behavior is still at a fairly primitive stage of development, and thus it would be premature to decide either that sign-based assessment procedures have *no* utility and should *never* be used, or that sample-based procedures are *always* superior. It is easy to think of examples of successful sign-based assessment methods in other disciplines (e.g., the litmus test in chemistry; the Wasserman test in medicine); it is not difficult to imagine how similar sign-based assessments might prove useful for certain prediction tasks in psychology.

Having argued against the absolute supremacy of sample-based assessments, we hasten to add that some of the apparent failures of sample-based methods in the past *may* have been due to inadequacies in sampling. Behavioral assessors characteristically have not been sufficiently attentive to the potential importance of measuring behaviors within a representative sample of their natural contexts. We suspect that this inattention to sampling considerations reflects the fact that psychological theorists have not yet come up with a satisfactory taxonomy for situations. In the absence of well-defined units of analysis for situations, it is difficult to determine what constitutes an appropriate and representative sample of situations for inclusion in an assessment task. Once again, we see how the continuing search for units of analysis plays a crucial role in the progress of our science.

EPILOGUE

Interestingly, investigators in the area of abilities research spent many years embroiled in a debate known as the "nature–nurture controversy." It concerned the degree to which abilities, such as intelligence, are determined by genetic or constitutional factors, on the one hand, and by environmental influences, on the other. There are some enlightening parallels between that controversy and the one that was the center of focus in this chapter. As in the person–situation debate, advocates of both the "nature" and "nurture" sides acknowledged in moments of candor that abilities are not determined solely by one factor or the other; yet they still seemed obsessed with demonstrating that one factor or the other was the dominant influence. Logical arguments and empirical evidence were accumulated by both sides in support of their respective positions. Meanwhile, an interactionist position emerged as an alternative to the first two, and its supporters searched for an appropriate methodology for demonstrating their position's superiority. Studies in which analysis of variance designs were used to partition variance into "nature," "nurture," and "interaction" components initially seemed promising, but experience with this strategy revealed that the size of the resulting components varied from study to study as a function of the particular details of the study and the particular abilities being examined. On closer inspection, investigators even found it difficult to delineate a clear boundary between what was "nature" and what was "nurture." It also became apparent that such studies were not actually assessing dynamic and reciprocal interactive influences since, by definition, these "transactional" processes could not be partitioned into separate components. Eventually, most investigators realized that the nature–nurture controversy was inherently unresolvable; there could be no single absolute answer. With this realization, the global controversy slowly dissipated and the distinction between constitutional and environmental variables became only one of many facets that investigators might find useful to examine in connection with a particular set of phenomena. It still might be useful, for example, to conduct research in the area of behavioral genetics, but the research would need to address specific questions about specific phenomena in specific contexts, and results would need to be treated as "local, contemporary truths."

History tends to repeat itself. Certainly, the parallels between the nature–nurture controversy and the person–situation debate are striking. It is our hope that psychologists will see that the person–situation debate, like the nature–nurture controversy before it, is inherently unresolvable. Once the debate has been laid to rest, perhaps psychology will have more success in its search for meaningful units with which to describe, predict, and explain human behavior.

REFERENCES

Alker, H. A. (1972). Is personality situationally specific or intrapsychically consistent? *Journal of Personality, 40,* 1–16.

Alker, H. A. (1977). Beyond ANOVA psychology in the study of person–situation interactions. In D. Magnusson & N. S. Endler (Eds.), *Personality at the crossroads: Current issues in interactional psychology* (pp. 243–256). Hillsdale, NJ: Lawrence Erlbaum.

Allport, G. W. (1958). What units shall we employ? In G. Lindzey (Ed.), *The assessment of motives* (pp. 239–260). New York: Rinehart.

Allport, G. W. (1961). *Pattern and growth in personality.* New York: Holt, Rinehart & Winston.

Allport, G. W. (1966). Traits revisited. *American Psychologist, 21,* 1–10.

Argyle, M., Furnham, A., & Graham, T. A. (1981). *Social situations.* Cambridge, England: Cambridge University Press.

Argyle, M., & Little, B. R. (1972). Do personality traits apply to social behavior? *Journal for the Theory of Social Behavior, 2,* 1–35.

Bandura, A. (1977). Self-efficacy: Toward a unifying theory of behavioral change. *Psychological Review, 84,* 191–215.

Barker, R. G. (1968). *Ecological psychology.* Stanford, CA: Stanford University Press.

Barker, R. G., & Wright, H. F. (1955). *The Midwest and its children.* Evanston, IL: Row, Peterson.

Bem, D. J. (1972). Constructing cross-situational consistencies in behavior: Some thoughts on Alker's critique of Mischel. *Journal of Personality, 40,* 17–26.

Bem, D. J., & Allen, A. (1974). On predicting some of the people some of the time: The search for cross-situational consistencies in behavior. *Psychological Review, 81,* 506–520.

Bem, D. J., & Funder, D. C. (1978). Predicting more of the people more of the time: Assessing the personality of situations. *Psychological Review, 85,* 485–501.

Block, J. (1968). Some reasons for the apparent inconsistency of personality. *Psychological Bulletin, 70,* 210–212.

Block, J. (1977). Advancing the psychology of personality: Paradigmatic shift or improving the quality of research? In D. Magnusson & N. S. Endler (Eds.), *Personality at the crossroads: Current issues in interactional psychology* (pp. 37–64). Hillsdale, NJ: Lawrence Erlbaum.

Boring, E. G. (1957). *A history of experimental psychology* (2nd ed.). New York: Appleton-Century-Crofts.

Bowers, K. S. (1973). Situationism in psychology: An analysis and a critique. *Psychological Review, 80,* 307–338.

Bowers, K. S. (1977). There's more to Iago than meets the eye: A clinical account of personal consistency. In D. Magnusson & N. S. Endler (Eds.), *Personality at the crossroads: Current issues in interactional psychology* (pp. 65–82). Hillsdale, NJ: Lawrence Erlbaum.

Brunswik, E. (1956). *Perception and the representative design of psychological experiments.* Berkeley: University of California Press.

Cairns, R. B., & Ornstein, P. A. (1979). Developmental psychology. In E. Hearst (Ed.) *The first century of experimental psychology* (pp. 459–510). Hillsdale, NJ: Lawrence Erlbaum.

Campbell, D. T., & Fiske, D. W. (1959). Convergent and discriminant validation by the multitrait-multimethod matrix. *Psychological Bulletin, 56,* 81–105.

Carlson, R. (1971). Where is the person in personality research? *Psychological Bulletin, 75,* 203–219.

Cattell, R. B. (1957). *Personality and motivation: Structure and measurement.* Yonkers-on-Hudson, New York: World Book.

Cronbach, L. J. (1957). The two disciplines of scientific psychology. *American Psychologist, 12,* 671–684.

Cronbach, L. J. (1975). Beyond the two disciplines of scientific psychology. *American Psychologist, 30,* 116–127.

Duncan, S., & Fiske, D. W. (1977). *Face to face interaction: Research, methods, and theory.* Hillsdale, NJ: Lawrence Erlbaum.

Ekehammar, B. (1974). Interactionism in personality from a historical perspective. *Psychological Bulletin, 81,* 1026–1048.

Endler, N. S. (1973). The person versus the situation—a pseudo issue? A response to Alker. *Journal of Personality, 41,* 287–303.

Endler, N. S., & Magnusson, D. (1976). Toward an interactional psychology of personality. *Psychological Bulletin, 83,* 956–974.

Epstein, S. (1977). Traits are alive and well. In D. Magnusson & N. S. Endler (Eds.), *Personality at the crossroads: Current issues in interactional psychology* (pp. 83–98). Hillsdale; NJ: Lawrence Erlbaum.

Epstein, S. (1979). The stability of behavior. I. On predicting most of the people much of the time. *Journal of Personality and Social Psychology, 37,* 1097–1126.

Epstein, S. (1980). The stability of behavior. II. Implications for psychological research. *American Psychologist, 35,* 790–806.

Fiske, D. (1977). Personologies, abstractions, and interactions. In D. Magnusson & N. S. Endler (Eds.), *Personality at the crossroads: Current issues in interactional psychology* (pp. 273–286). Hillsdale, NJ: Lawrence Erlbaum.

Fiske, D. (1979). Two worlds of psychological phenomena. *Ameican Psychologist, 34,* 733–740.

Frederiksen, N. (1972). Toward a taxonomy of situations. *American Psychologist, 27,* 114–123.

Goffman, E. (1967). *Interaction ritual: Essays on face to face behavior.* Chicago: Aldine Publishing.

Goffman, E. (1971). *Relations in public: Microstudies of the public order.* New York: Basic Books.

Goldfried, M. R., & Kent, R. N. (1972). Traditional vs. behavioral assessment: A comparison of methodological assumptions. *Psychological Bulletin, 77,* 409–420.

Gottman, J. M. (1979). *Marital interaction: Experimental investigations.* New York: Academic Press.

Gottman, J. M. (1981). *Time series analysis: A comprehensive introduction for social scientists.* Cambridge, England: Cambridge University Press.

Harré, R., & Secord, P. (1972). *The explanation of social behaviour.* Oxford: Blackwell.

Jones, E. E., & Nisbett, R. E. (1971). *The actor and the observer: Divergent perceptions of the causes of behavior.* Morristown, NJ: General Learning Press.

Kantor, J. R. (1924). *Principles of Psychology* (Vol. 1). Bloomington, IN: Principia Press.

Kelly, G. A. (1955). *The psychology of personal constructs.* New York: Norton.

Kiesler, D. J. (1966) Some myths of psychotherapy research and the search for a paradigm. *Psychological Bulletin, 65,* 110–136.

Kuhn, T. S. (1962). *The structure of scientific revolutions.* Chicago: University of Chicago Press.

Lazarus, R. S., & Launier, R. (1978). Stress-related transactions between person and environment. In L. A. Pervin & M. Lewis (Eds.), *Perspectives in international psychology* (pp. 287–327). New York: Plenum Press.

Lewin, K. A. (1935). *A dynamic theory of personality.* New York: McGraw-Hill.

Magnusson, D. (1976). The person and the situation in an interactional model of behavior. *Scandinavian Journal of Psychology, 17,* 253–271.

Magnusson, D., & Endler, N. S. (Eds.) (1977). *Personality at the crossroads: Current issues in interactional psychology.* Hillsdale, NJ: Lawrence Erlbaum.

McFall, R. M. (1982). A review and reformulation of the concept of social skills. *Behavioral Assessment, 4,* 1–33.

McReynolds, P. (1979). The case for interactional assessment. *Behavioral Assessment, 1,* 237–247.

Meehl, P. E. (1978). Theoretical risks and tabular asterisks: Sir Karl, Sir Ronald and the slow progress of soft psychology. *Journal of Consulting and Clinical Psychology, 46,* 806–834.

Miller, G. A. (1956). The magical number seven, plus or minus two: Some limits of our capacity for processing information. *Psychological Review, 63*, 81–97.

Mischel, W. (1968). *Personality and assessment*. New York: John Wiley & Sons.

Michel, W. (1969). Continuity and change in personality. *American Psychologist, 24*, 1012–1018.

Mischel, W. (1971). *Introduction to personality*. New York: Holt, Rinehart & Winston.

Mischel, W. (1973). Toward a cognitive social learning reconceptualization of personality. *Psychological Review, 80*, 252–283.

Mischel, W. (1979). On the interface of cognition and personality: Beyond the person–situation debate. *American Psychologist, 34*, 740–754.

Mischel, W., & Peake, P. K. (1982). Beyond Déjà Vu in the search for cross-situational consistency. *Psychological Review, 89*, 730–755.

Moos, R. H. (1968). Situational analysis of a therapeutic community milieu. *Journal of Abnormal Psychology, 73*, 49–61.

Moos, R. H. (1973). Conceptualizations of human environments. *American Psychologist, 28*, 652–665.

Murray, H. A. (1938). *Explorations in personality*. New York: Oxford University Press.

Nisbett, R. E. (1977). Interactions versus main effects as goals of personality research. In D. Magnusson & N. S. Endler (Eds.), *Personality at the crossroads: Current issues in interactional psychology* (pp. 235–242). Hillsdale, NJ: Lawrence Erlbaum.

Olweus, D. (1977). A critical analysis of the "modern" interactionist position. In D. Magnusson & N. S. Endler (Eds.), *Personality at the crossroads: Current issues in interactional psychology* (pp. 221–234). Hillsdale, NJ: Lawrence Erlbaum.

Paul, G. L. (1969). Behavior modification research: Design and tactics. In C. M. Franks (Ed.), *Behavior therapy: Appraisal and status* (pp. 29–62). New York: McGraw-Hill.

Pervin, L. A., & Lewis, M. (1978). Overview of the internal-external issue. In L. A. Pervin & M. Lewis (Eds.), *Perspectives in interactional psychology* (pp. 1–22). New York: Plenum Press.

Peterson, D. R. (1968). *The clinical study of social behavior*. New York: Appleton-Century-Crofts.

Raush, H. L. (1972). Process and change—A Markove model for interaction. *Family Process, 11*, 275–298.

Raush, H. L. (1977). Paradox levels and junctures in person–situation systems. In D. Magnusson & N. S. Endler (Eds.), *Personality at the crossroads: Current issues in interactional psychology* (pp. 287–304). Hillsdale, NJ: Lawrence Erlbaum.

Reyes, R. M., Thompson, W. C., & Bower, G. M. (1980). Judgmental biases resulting from differing availabilities of arguments. *Journal of Personality and Social Psychology, 39*, 2–12.

Rotter, J. B. (1966). Generalized expectancies for internal versus external control of reinforcement: *Psychological Monographs, 80* (Whole No. 609).

Sameroff, A. J., & Chandler, M. J. (1975). Reproductive risk and the continuum of caretaking casualty. In F. Horowitz, M. Hetherington, S. Scarr-Salapatek, & G. Siegel (Eds.), *Review of Child Development Research, 4*, 187–244.

Schlundt, D. G. (1982a). An observational study of the behavioral components of social competence: The rules of topic management, speaking turn regulation, and communication affect in heterosexual dyadic interaction. Unpublished doctoral dissertation, Indiana University, Bloomington.

Schlundt, D. G. (1982b). Two PASCAL programs for managing observational data bases and for performing multivariate information analysis and log-linear contingency tables analysis of sequential and non-sequential data. *Behavior Research Methods and Instrumentation, 17*, 51–52.

Scriven, M. (1969). Psychology without a paradigm. In L. Breger (Ed.), *Clinical–cognitive psychology: Models and integrations* (pp. 9–24). Englewood Cliffs, NJ: Prentice-Hall.

Sells, S. B. (1963). An interactionist looks at the environment. *American Psychologist, 18*, 696–702.

Skinner, B. F. (1953). *Science and human behavior*. New York: Macmillan.

Staats, A. W. (1975). *Social behaviorism*. Homewood, IL: Dorsey Press.

Stagner, R. (1976). Traits are relevant: Theoretical analysis and empirical evidence. In N. S.

Endler & D. Magnusson (Eds.), *Interactional psychology and personality* (pp. 109–124). New York: John Wiley & Sons.

Trower, P. (1980). Situational analysis of the components and processes of behavior of socially skilled and unskilled patients. *Journal of Consulting and Clinical Psychology, 48,* 327–339.

Tversky, A., & Kahneman, D. (1974). Judgment under uncertainty: Heuristics and biases. *Science, 185,* 1124–1131.

Vernon, P. E. (1964). *Personality assessment: A critical survey.* England: Methuen.

Wachtel, P. L. (1973a). Psychodynamics, behavior therapy and the implacable experimenter: An inquiry into the consistency of personality. *Journal of Abnormal Psychology, 82,* 324–334.

Wachtel, P. L. (1973b). On fact, hunch and sterotype: A reply to Mischel. *Journal of Abnormal Psychology, 82,* 537–540.

Wallace, J. (1966). An abilities conception of personality: Some implications for personality measurement. *American Psychologist, 21,* 132–138.

Wallace, J. (1967). What units shall we employ? Allport's question revisited. *Journal of Consulting Psychology, 31,* 56–64.

8

BEHAVIORISM WITH A PERSONALITY: THE PARADIGMATIC BEHAVIORAL ASSESSMENT APPROACH

ARTHUR W. STAATS

University of Hawaii

Since some of what is presented herein represents criticism of existing behavioral approaches, some introduction seems to be appropriate. The analysis to be presented derives from a very large and comprehensive behaviorism, which has been called variously social behaviorism and, more recently paradigmatic behaviorism (Staats, 1981, 1983, 1984). This is a third-generation behaviorism in that it is built in part upon the knowledge provided by the first generation of behaviorism of Pavlov, Thorndike, and Watson, and the second-generation of behaviorism of Skinner, Keller, and Schoenfeld, as well as Hull, Spence, Osgood, Mowrer, and Neal Miller. Paradigmatic behaviorism is a third-generation development because it has selected only parts of preceding traditions, rejecting other parts, and because it has introduced wide-ranging, new developments. Thus, while this approach has much content overlap with radical behaviorism, as an example, it also has different characteristics at each of its levels of interest. It includes a different philosophy of science (Staats, 1983a), a different basic learning theory (Staats, 1970, 1975), a different way to approach the study of personality (Staats, 1971b, 1975), a different theory of abnormal behavior (Staats, 1975; Staats & Heiby, 1985), a different approach to clinical treatment (Evans, in press; Staats, 1972, 1975), and a different conception of behavioral assessment (Burns, 1980; Staats, 1975).

To continue, the second generation of behaviorism began with a struggle for precedence among the various theories of Hull, Tolman, Guthrie, and Skinner (see MacKenzie, 1977; Staats, 1983a). The survivor of that struggle was Skinner's operant behaviorism. It is important to realize that the resolution of that second-generation competition has left a legacy in behavioral psychology, that is, the idea that the best behaviorism has won, and that we need look no longer for other varieties of behaviorism. In the present view, expressed in various works of paradigmatic behaviorism (e.g., Staats, 1975), it is necessary to reject that conclusion. It is true that operant (radical) behaviorism has made and will continue to make a great contribution to behavioral psychology and that it contains elements that will be part of any behaviorism. In addition, operant behaviorism has changed over the past several decades, adopting characteristics that it did not at first have, including characteristics that conflict with its original principles. Moreover, operant behaviorism is still capable of a certain amount of basic change. But there are some changes it will resist, and others it cannot absorb. And there are many needed developments that operant behaviorism by its nature cannot instigate. Ultimately a new behaviorism will replace it, and I would suggest that paradigmatic behaviorism provides a much more advanced framework theory for behavioral psychology.

This is the reason why differences from radical behaviorism will not be softened in the present chapter. When criticism occurs, however, the suggestion is not that we retreat to some traditional view, as some of the new cognitive approaches seem to suggest, but that we move ahead to a third-generation behaviorism. In addition to the specific ideas that are presented in this chapter, there is thus a general behaviorism involved that has heuristic implications on a very broad basis by which to guide the development of the field. The editors of the present volume have set the goal of dealing with the *conceptual* foundations of behavioral assessment. The largest conceptual consideration is that of the basic behaviorism that is to be employed by the field, and that choice is a primary concern of the present chapter.

THE PERSONALITY/BEHAVIORISM SCHISM

One of the central ways that paradigmatic behaviorism differs from other behavioristic approaches concerns its treatment of the topic of personality. Psychology is beset by a number of conceptual schisms that, along with its competitive methods and theories and divisive organization, maintain it as a disunified, disorganized science (Staats, 1983a)—which incidently prevents it from being recognized as a full science. One of the fundamental schisms that fragments psychology concerns the concept of personality. On the one hand, there has been a traditional view that there are internal processes or structures of a personal nature that determine the individual's external behavior. Individuals are seen to display characteristic behavior over a variety of situations, and over widely spaced time intervals, because the same internal personality trait pertains across those variations. It is important to realize that a general conceptual position such as this has important effects upon the scientists who hold the view. In the present case, if one accepts the cause of human behavior to be some internal personality process or structure, then the indicated path in the study of behavior is the description and measurement of personality. As we know, a large part of psychology has been devoted to those tasks.

On the other hand, one of the features of Watson's behaviorism was the rejection of that conceptual framework. Dismayed by the many mentalistic concepts that abounded, concepts that had poor empirical definition, Watson proposed that psychology restrict itself to the study of observables, to stimuli and responses. Personality, according to Watson, is only behavior (1930, p. 274), not some internal something. This position had the general effect of turning behaviorists away from the consideration of theories of personality and from the methods, findings, and concepts established in the field of psychological measurement. One development of the behavioristic position was to question some of the facts upon which the concept of personality was based—for example, that individuals exhibit consistency of behavior across situations. This challenge to the concept of the general personality trait came from several studies. Hartshorne and May (1928, 1929) conducted an extensive study of children's "moral'" character using a number of different behavioral tests of such characteristics as deception, self-control, helpfulness, persistence, and so on. Children were observed for behaviors like cheating in the classroom and on a take-home test, cheating in a game and on records of athletic performance, stealing money, and lying. Hartshorne and May found a low correlation between the various tests of character (less than .30). Their conclusion was that there are specific habits, but not traits that are general. In another study, Newcomb (1929) kept daily records of boys at summer camp on such behaviors as verbosity and ascendancy–submission, as indices of the trait of extroversion and introversion. There was little consistency of the specific behaviors across situations, and there was little intercorrelation among the various specific behaviors that were supposed to index the trait.

As Bem and Allen (1974) point out, these studies were joined by others of that era that used paper-and-pencil tests to assess the generality of traits, which again produced correlations of less than .30. These various results supported the behavioristic viewpoint that behavior was determined by the environment, by the situation, and thus was specific to the situation. Thus, as Bem and Allen indicate, the trait-environment question posed a lively controversy in the 1930s. In general, it may be added, it is typical for such conflicts eventually to subside, not because the opposing positions have been unified, but because the grounds for the controversy at that point have been exhausted of interest. The issue then lies dormant until the advocates of one of the positions takes up the cudgels once again (Staats, 1983a), and so on in an endlessly repeated cycle.

In the present case, the contemporary issue was renovated by the social learning theory analysis of Mischel (1968). He again took the position that there are not consistencies of behavior across situations, of the type that would be demanded by the concept of the personality trait. Mischel's major argument was based on the review of the previously conducted studies. The resuscitation of the issue has again resulted in a flurry of articles, some in support of the trait position that there is consistency to behavior, and others in criticism of the concept, suggesting that there is little consistency and that the situation is the primary determinant of behavior (Bem & Allen, 1974; Block, 1971, 1977; Epstein, 1979; Endler & Magnusson, 1976; Kenrick & Stringfield, 1980; Magnusson & Endler, 1977; Olweus, 1972, 1974, 1977a,b; Rushton, Jackson, & Paunonen, 1981). Block (1971), for example, had judges rate individuals on various personality variables over widely separated periods in their lives through interviews and using records of their childhood development taken from the Berkeley longitudinal studies. Block found considerable evidence for personality consistency. He also had judges observe children during their fourth-, sixth-, and eighth-grade progression, for 3 hours a day for 5–9 months. Again, Block found considerable consistency.

Olweus (1972, 1974, 1977a,b) had classmates rate boys in the sixth grade and ninth grade on aggressive behavior such as starting fights. The correlations were substantial, .66, and, when rater unreliability was adjusted, increased to .80. In another study, Olweus (1977b) found that teacher ratings, self-ratings, and peer ratings of aggressive behaviors were all highly correlated. Since observations of the children in different situations were involved, this again provides evidence of a trait of aggression.

Epstein (1979) has reviewed the large number of studies that provide evidence of the extent of consistency in individuals' behavior over time and across different situations. He concludes that "there is enough cross-situational stability in everyday life so that useful statements about individual behavior can be made without having to specify the eliciting situations. This, of course, is the way a trait is usually defined, and the findings demonstrate the utility of such a concept" (Epstein, 1979, p. 1122).

THE PERSON-SITUATION ISSUE: WAGES OF
THE SIN OF SCHISMATIC SEPARATISM

It has been said that one of the characteristics of psychology that prevents it from advancing to the state of a unified science involves the existence of broad schismatic positions (Kimble, 1984; Staats, 1983a), like the situation–personality argumentation described above. A typical way to quiet such a controversy when it has raged for awhile is to say that both sides are correct, which resolves nothing but can produce temporary peace. That is what has happened in the contemporary case. The overt controversy began again with

Mischel's (1968) assertion that there was no consistency to behavior, and thus the concept of the personality trait should be rejected. That opened the gates, and a host of articles addressed to the issue appeared. Then the second phase began, during which it was suggested that both sides are correct, that behavior is a function both of personality and the situation (Endler & Magnusson, 1976). This interactionist position rests upon other studies that suggest there are personality–causal variables and situational–causal variables, as well as an interaction between the two which is also seen as a causal variable in the analysis of variance experimental designs used in these studies (see Staats, 1980). For example, Gilmore and Minton (1974) found that, under a success situation, internal-locus-of-control personalities (those who attribute their behavior to themselves) attributed success to internal factors more than did external-locus-of-control subjects; but such attribution was reversed under failure. The interaction term of the experiment predicted the most variance of the dependent variable.

The wages of sin involved in this type of debate, in the present view, involve the great investment of time and energy into research and theory that is frequently not valuable in and of itself, when the significance of the work for gaining precedence in the controversy is subtracted. In the present view, the theoretical framework that gives impetus to such investments is at fault. This theoretical framework separates interests into competitive fragments that dispose studies to be conducted in an antagonistic manner, even though both sides are interested in important areas of research that could be brought together in a unified manner. The interactionist view is positive in the sense that it removes the antagonism. But interactionism is ecclectic; it combines but does not unify. Interactionism has not indicated how personality and learning (situationism) are to be interwoven to produce a heuristic theory structure. Interactionism has left vague what personality consists of, how personality affects behavior, and what the principles are by which the environment (situation) affects the individual's behavior (Staats, 1980).

What is needed is a theory framework that directs psychology to study the important types of causation of the behavior in which the field is interested. This framework—unlike the personality view, the situationist view, or the interactionism view—must be specific. Rather than studies that attempt to resolve the question of whether there is personality, situation, or interaction causation in general, what is needed is specification of what the elements of personality are and how personality affects behavior according to specific principles. Rather than studies that show grossly that behavior can differ in different situations, what is needed is the specification of what environmental circumstances produce what behaviors, according to specific principles. Moreover, how the situation interacts with personality must be specified (see Staats, 1980).

The present view is that Watson's radical behaviorism did not provide a framework theory with respect to the concept of personality that inspired theoretical–empirical analysis of the events involved. What behaviorism did inspire was criticism of traditional conceptions of personality, of the methods of studying personality, and of the findings that resulted. Radical behaviorism also set the original stage for much effort spent in trying to disprove the traditional view, and works of this type inevitably brought further studies aiming to disprove the radical behavioristic position. In adopting many of the elements of radical behaviorism, social learning theory took on antipersonality theory characteristics in contemporary times, renewing the consistency-specificity (the personality–situationism) issue. In the present author's view, the personality–situationism issue, and the time and effort devoted to it, have not contributed much to understanding better the important events involved in this realm of study, in a manner that would be productive for the field of behavioral assessment or any other field that would draw upon such a contribution. A better framework theory is available, as the following sections attempt to outline.

A BEHAVIORISTIC THEORY OF PERSONALITY: THE BASIC BEHAVIORAL REPERTOIRES

It should be noted that the focus of the work of the second-generation behaviorists was in the animal laboratory. Skinner's behaviorism, for example, while suggesting that his operant approach extends broadly to human behavior, did not utilize the relevant empirical knowledge that has been found in the various areas of human behavior (see, as examples, Skinner, 1953, 1957). The implicit focus of all the behaviorisms has been on constructing a basic animal learning theory, on the assumption that this theory would explain all types of human behavior. None of the behaviorisms did much in the way of constructing theories that used the products of study obtained by other approaches in the other areas of human psychology. Rather, nonbehavioral knowledge has been rejected or excluded.

EARLY PARADIGMATIC BEHAVIORISM AND BEHAVIORAL ASSESSMENT

Paradigmatic behaviorism, while arising in the context of the first two generations of behaviorism, did not employ that "exclusionary" principle, developed to a high degree in radical behaviorism. Rather, paradigmatic behaviorism developed a basic theory construction methodology by which to integrate nonbehavioral knowledge into its structure. While recognizing that much traditional theory was not acceptable according to behavioristic criteria, and recognizing that many statements of traditional psychology were incorrect, paradigmatic behaviorism considered study of the traditional areas of knowledge also to reveal much that is productive. Characteristic of paradigmatic behaviorism has been its own elaboration of behavioral principles, concepts, and methods of analysis, while at the same time considering traditional knowledge in the various areas for its productive empirical elements and empirically based conceptual elements.

Thus, as an example, paradigmatic behaviorism played a role in the development of behavior modification, behavior analysis, and behavioral assessment. Nevertheless, the present author, even during his graduate clinical training, had had contact with the field of personality theory and personality testing and had seen that this area of knowledge included a positive contribution, along with many invalid conceptions. Very clearly, as an example of the latter, it was clear that the traditional concept of personality was not defined by antecedent conditions (either learning or biological conditions, although personologists usually gravitate to the latter view). Moreover, the traditional definitions of personality itself are poorly specified. Intelligence is a good example; psychologists gave up long ago trying to say what intelligence is, being satisfied with measuring it. But the poor understanding of what personality is, what it derives from, and how it works its effects does not detract from the fact that there are many valuable observations of human behavior in the field of personality theory and personality testing. Moreover, there is much human behavior that requires study and explanation that has not been dealt with within the principles of conditioning. There *are* individual differences in behavior for people in the same situation. There are consistencies in behavior over time, some of them stipulated by personality tests—for example, children high in intelligence and low in intelligence tend to remain in their relative positions. There are consistencies in behavior across situations that can be recognized in naturalistic observations as well as in formal studies.

Based on this view, at the same time that paradigmatic behaviorism was involved in early behavior modification and behavioral assessment developments, this approach was also involved in constructing a general theory of human behavior that included a theory of personality. My first personality concepts were clearly behavioral in character: for example, the concept of the reinforcer system. The concept is that, naturally and through learning, a large number of stimuli become reinforcing for the individual. We may speak of these stimuli as constituting the individual's reinforcer system, for one thing, because each individual differs in the elements of this system. Moreover, this concept constitutes a bridging theory, because it enables us to join this behavior analysis with knowledge from the field of personality testing, as the following statement indicates.

> Perhaps the function of certain types of "tests" used by the applied psychologist is at least in part to assess the reinforcers that are effective for an individual or a group. Such tests might consist of items that control the appropriate verbal behaviors with respect to the reinforcing value of stimulus objects and events, such as the behavior of others and various activities. For example, more than half the items on the Strong Vocational Interest Blank . . . ask the subject to state whether he likes, dislikes, or is indifferent to various occupations, school subjects, amusements, activities, and characteristics of people. This may be considered to involve a simple listing of reinforcers for the individual. (Staats, 1963, p. 305)

Thus, the analysis introduced an early and central personality concept— the reinforcer system—in behavioral terms, in a manner showing how some traditional personality tests were behaviorally legitimate, and in this way providing a framework for later development. For example, a behavioral assessment instrument, called the Pleasant Events Schedule (MacPhillamy & Lewinsohn, 1971) was later constructed that measured the individual's positive reinforcers, a behavioral assessment instrument to measure the reinforcer system. In addition, however, the early statement of paradigmatic behaviorism also involved a conceptual framework for the analysis of behavior problems (abnormal behavior) and their treatment. Within this conceptualization, there was a further indication of the need for behavioral analysis (see Staats, 1963, pp. 459–460) as well as behavioral assessment in clinical practice, as the following indicates.

> Perhaps a rationale for learning psychotherapy will also have to include some method for the assessment of behavior. In order to discover the behavioral deficiencies, the required changes in the reinforcing system, the circumstances in which stimulus control is absent, and so on, evaluational techniques in these respects may have to be devised. Certainly, no two individuals will be alike in these various characteristics and it may be necessary to determine such facts for the individual prior to beginning the learning program of treatment.
>
> Such assessment might take a form similar to some of the psychological tests already in use. It is possible, however, that a general learning rationale for behavior disorders and treatment will itself suggest techniques of assessment. (Staats, 1963, pp. 508–509)

The cautious language employed above was the result of an editor's reservation, since this was the first call for behavioral assessment, and there was no evidence or other behaviorism at that time to support the statements. However, the implications for the field of behavioral assessment were clear. Unlike the treatment of the field of personality by radical behaviorism, the above-stated rationale provided a basis for an interest in assessment of complex behavior for applied purposes. This opening was extended in subsequent works that were also seminal. Thus, Kanfer and Saslow (1965) presented an approach to clinical diagnosis that was based upon behavioral analyses, including the measurement of the individual's reinforcer system as a central area of concentration. Mischel (1968) wrote a specialized book that presented essentially a radical behaviorist view of the field of personality, but also described the area of assessment in a manner that helped stimulate the development of the field of behavioral assessment. An important point to emphasize here, however, is that paradigmatic behaviorism, even in its earlier forms, began the elaboration of a conception of personality that was productive for behavioral developments. Moreover, the conception was the beginning of a theoretical development that incorporates aspects of traditional psychology within its behavior principles, in a manner that can fulfill the interests of personologists as well as behavioral psychologists.

THE DEVELOPING THEORY

There had been other behaviorally oriented psychologists who attempted to incorporate a concept of personality into their learning theories. Tolman (1951) includes the term as an unspecified intervening variable in his theory, as did Rotter (1954). Dollard and Miller (1950) attempted to join learning principles with a psychoanalytic view; but the conception of personality was not clear and specified, and the implications of the conception were similarly vague. Mowrer (1950) attempted the same combination, but with even less specification and little direct bridging of the separate theoretical bodies of psychoanalysis and animal learning principles.

The intervening variable methodology consisted of observing relationships between complex stimulus and response events and then proposing a series of intervening variables as logical terms to help one systematize the complex relationships. The intervening variable, thus, did not stand for any event itself, but as a means of depicting the relationship between events. To illustrate, the intervening variable called learning was used to name the relationship between conditioning variables and the strength of behavior. In the standard view, an intervening variable, such as personality, was not considered to be anything real, but merely be a name for a type of relationship between a class of environmental events and a class of behavioral events.

This was never the view of paradigmatic behaviorism. Personality was considered to be something substantive, not a term for a relationship. The individual's reinforcer system, for example, was seen to be constituted of substantive events, the actual stimuli that can serve a reinforcing function for the individual. The concept of the reinforcer system was based upon observations of the vast differences between individuals in what constituted positive and negative reinforcers for them. As is indicated below (see the "Emotional-Motivational Repertoire" section), the concept of the reinforcer system was not speculative, but was based upon a series of experiments and theoretical developments whose purpose was to study this aspect of personality. Centrally, this development was always carried forth within the confines of a behavioristic theory-construction methodology, albeit not an operant behaviorism methodology. The methodology was behavioral in that it required stipulation of what personality is in behavioral terms, as well as stipulation of how personality comes about, and how it has its effects.

In describing this development, let us begin with the statement of the key concept in the theory, the concept of the basic behavioral repertoire. There are radical behaviorists who have begun to employ the concept of the repertoire. It is important to note that the significant development of the concept has been made in paradigmatic behaviorism (see Staats, 1963, 1968a, 1968b, 1975; Staats, Staats, Heard, & Finley, 1962). In paradigmatic behaviorism, personality is composed of basic behavioral repertoires. The theory states that the individual from birth on begins to learn a complex system or repertoire of behaviors in three general areas. The areas are not independent and wholly separated, and do not involve differences in principle. The separation is functional, nevertheless, in providing a conceptual basis for treating the various phenomena of concern. The three areas of personality are the language–cognitive, the emotional–motivational, and the sensory–motor repertoires (see Staats, 1975). In a nutshell, what is being said is that individuals learn complex repertoires of behavior (or learn to respond to a multitude of stimuli) in a manner that affects behavior in later situations. The elements of these repertoires can be elicited directly by those later situations, and they can also indirectly serve a role in mediating response to those situations. In doing so, these repertoires play the role of a personal cause in the determination of the individual's behavior in that situation. Let us take a child who has learned to make a number of specific motor responses to specific verbal stimuli (forming a repertoire of verbal–motor units), and who thus can "follow instructions." That child, with this rich verbal–motor repertoire, will learn better in many situations than will a child with serious deficits in that repertoire, because most learning requires following directions. That "personality" repertoire will thus determine the individual differences in learning between those children. We must thus study such aspects of personality, how they are learned, and how they function in later situations to affect the individual's later experience, learning, and behavior. When we do so, we find we are studying the subject matter of personality and that some of the knowledge of personology can be useful.

To continue, the theory says that the infant begins to learn elements, units, in each of the personality repertoires according to the basic principles of instrumental and classical conditioning, in a cumulative-hierarchical process, one repertoire being necessary for the acquisition of later repertoires. (The basic learning theory, unlike that of operant behaviorism, considers the two types of conditioning to be interrelated, Staats, 1970, 1975.) Once the child has acquired elements in his or her personality repertoires, however, the child is no longer the same as before. Before the child has personality repertoires, we can explain the child's behavior simply by the relevant classical conditioning and reinforcement conditions in the situation. Increasingly, as the child acquires basic behavioral repertoires, what the child experiences and learns, and how the child responds, in any situation will be determined typically to a larger and larger extent by what the child brings to the situation rather than the conditions in the situation itself. To predict how a person will behave in a situation demands knowledge of that person's basic behavioral repertoires. To solve an individual's problems of life adjustment may also require being able to change the individual's basic behavioral repertoires, *not just intervention into the life situation.* This theoretical conception is diagrammed in abstract form in Figure 8-1. In this diagram, S_1 refers to the original learning situation in which the individual acquires his or her basic behavioral repertoires, BBR_1. S_2 represents the individual's present situation, including the conditioning circumstances that are involved in this situation. B represents the behavior of the individual in this situation. The figure diagrams the proposition that the individual learns personality repertoires, and that, in later situations, the individual's behavior is a function of the particular situation, but also of the repertoires he or she brings to the situation. The diagram also shows that the individual's behavior produces effects, denoted by S_3 and by BBR_2. In the first instance, those behaviorally produced effects

FIG. 8-1. The individual learns his or her personality repertoires (BBR_1) from the past environmental circumstances (S_1), and these repertoires in conjuction with the present environmental circumstances (S_2) determine the individual's behavior (B), which in turn affects further personality repertoire development (BBR_2) and the later environmental circumstances (S_3) that will together produce yet later behavior.

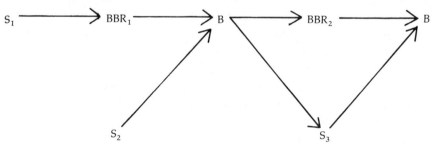

can be new stimulus circumstances. For example, when one individual behaves offensively to another, the latter will later not act in a friendly manner,
as a consequence, thus the result is a changed social stimulus. In the second
case, an individual's behavior may also result in the acquisition of new basic
behavioral skills, for example, the behavior of selecting and reading a textbook may produce an additional verbal repertoire that will result in better
performance later when the subject is enrolled in a college course. These
latter effects indicate that the "personality development" processes involved
are never fixed, once and for all, but rather involve continued development
and interaction among the various elements of the basic behavioral repertoires.

We can see from this abstract representation that personality in this
theory is not an intervening variable, an empty term, or calculational device.
Personality consists of something of substance: repertoires of behavioral
elements. However, for this theory to have substance, these basic behavioral
repertoires must be specified, and much of the work of social behaviorism
has involved that specification (e.g., see Staats, 1963, 1968a, 1968b, 1971a,
1975), as will be indicated. The schematization of the theory of personality, it
should be emphasized, also stipulates the sites of investigation that must be
of concern to the behavior modifier and the behavioral assessor, as well as to
the personality theorist. That is, with reference to the theory schematized in
Figure 8-1, specification is relevant to the several sites of interest. Very
centrally, in the task of establishing the necessary knowledge base, we also
need a full description of what composes the BBRs of normal and not-
normal people, a very special province of behavioral assessment. The following discussion elaborates the several sites of study described, and indicates
their significance for behavioral assessment.

PERSONALITY DESCRIPTION

It is important to indicate that the definitional description and diagram of the
purview of study as depicted in Figure 8-1 represents only a general conception. One's general conception is not without significance, however; even in
summary form, it can indicate the nature of the task, the general areas
which one will study. But there is a very large difference between such a
general conception and a full theory structure that indicates the specific
elements in the general conception, that provides the content for the various
empirical studies and clinical practices that are based upon the specific
statements of the theory, and so on. As an example of a general conception,
Lewin's general theory (1935) has been analyzed in behavioral terms
(Spence, 1944) as consisting of laws interrelating the environmental situa-

tion variables, the person or personality variables, and the behavior variables of the individual. Bandura (1978) presents the same position, with the environment, the person, and the person's behavior interacting with one another. However, in both of these cases, specification is lacking to varying degrees for the three basic elements involved in the conception. The person in Bandura's theory is said to be the individual's "cognitive and other internal events that can affect perceptions and actions" (1978, p. 345), in a manner that resembles Lewin's statements. But what those cognitive and other internal events are is not specified, nor is the process by which those characteristics are acquired or how and by what principles these events, in interaction with the environment, produce the individual's behavior, and so on (Staats, 1980). Without this specification, there can be a general conception; but it cannot constitute a specifically heuristic theory that indicates, for example, what conditions must occur for the creation of desirable personality characteristics or the change of undesirable characteristics and, hence, for solving problems of behavior.

The importance of the paradigmatic behaviorism approach is that it has been built upon stipulated, extensive analysis and research. And the value of the schematized conception in Figure 8-1 as an heuristic theory for behaviorists, resides in that stipulation. That means, however, that the interested practitioner, researcher, or theorist must consult the works that present that stipulation if the theory is to be employed in research or practice. It is not possible to present that specification in one chapter; the present work can only attempt to provide key references and enough material to suggest what is involved, and to indicate some of the significance of the approach. Moreover, it must be emphasized that much research is necessary to add to the specification. With respect to the diagram in Figure 8-1, the theory of the basic behavioral repertoires constitutes one of the essential elements that requires stipulation, which begins with the description of the three general areas of the personality (basic behavioral) repertoires: the language–cognitive repertoire, the sensory–motor repertoire, and the emotional–motivational repertoire or system.

THE LANGUAGE–COGNITIVE REPERTOIRE

It is important to note that developing paradigmatic behaviorism's theory of personality was not an armchair exercise. Moreover, it was not formed in other traditional ways, for example, solely through clinical observations or test construction, where elementary principles of behavior are not of interest. Paradigmatic behaviorism's approach has involved what has been called multilevel theory construction (Staats, 1981, 1983a). The elementary principles of conditioning are taken as basic. But the approach was to develop these principles in a series of levels, so that more advanced topics of the study of human behavior could be successfully considered in all of their complexity, but with behavioral stipulation. The following discussion will illustrate this multilevel theory development in the language–cognitive area, as this is relevant to behavioral assessment.

Paradigmatic behaviorism began its general program with the investigation of human problem solving and reasoning (Staats, 1956, 1957b). Employing the standard behaviorism methodological strategy, a sample of problem solving was used that could be considered in terms of simple conditioning concepts. The present author concluded from this work, however, that the strategy of jumping directly from the basic conditioning principles to such a complex type of human behavior was inappropriate. It necessitated selecting a sample of problem solving and reasoning that was so simple that it was not representative of the cognitive behavior of humans in which we are interested. This has been the classic behavioristic approach to researching cognitive phenomena; which we can see in Hullian works (Hull, 1930; Judson, Cofer, & Gelfand, 1956; Maltzman, 1955) as well as Skinnerian works (see Long & Holland in Skinner, 1961; Epstein, 1984).

It became the paradigmatic behaviorism position, however, that successful extension of conditioning principles to complex cognitive phenomena demands a different strategy or methodology, one that involves advancement in a series of steps or levels. To illustrate, further analysis indicated to the author that such cognitive phenomena as problem solving and reasoning depend upon the language skills of the individual. Before understanding such cognitive phenomena, therefore, it is necessary to understand language, what it is, how it is acquired, and how it functions. The language level of study is more basic than the study of problem solving. Moreover, it is language that can be directly related to the elementary level of study in this multilevel analysis. That is, language acquisition itself can be seen to take place via the more basic principles of conditioning. Mowrer (1954), Osgood (1953), and Skinner (1957), and a number of other behaviorists (see Cofer, Foley, 1942; Razran, 1939a,b; Watson, 1930) had analyzed aspects of language or language-related phenomena in the context of conditioning. Paradigmatic behaviorism utilized aspects of this preceding work, in developing a new theoretical formulation, and was the first to begin the systematic experimental study of both classical and instrumental conditioning, and how the principles interact, in the learning of functional language skills. This was done in laboratory research and also by what has been called experimental-longitudinal research which involved specified, but naturalistic, research with the author's own children—beginning in infancy—and the systematic extension of the findings to other children (see Staats, 1968a; Staats,

Brewer, & Gross, 1970). The aim of the experimental–longitudinal research was to produce language development—since functional skills were involved—as well as to study the process of that development. The work with the author's own children began at the very earliest stages of language development and continued for years, through more advanced repertoires such as learning reading, writing, and number concepts. Since the training circumstances were variegated, the method developed was that of observing and recording every stimulus presentation, each response, and each reinforcer. Surprisingly, although it is generally thought that psychology knows something about language development, the normal learning input and the response output in the process of language development has still not generally become a focus of systematic study. Paradigmatic behaviorism, however, provides the prototypical methodology.

To continue, the various experimental methodologies—group methods, single-subject methods, and experimental–longitudinal methods—were employed in the study of the language repertoires, employing both classical conditioning and reinforcement principles (e.g., see Finley & Staats, 1967; Harms & Staats, 1978; Staats, 1957a,b, 1961, 1963, 1964, 1968a, 1971b; Staats, Brewer, & Gross, 1970; Staats & Butterfield, 1965, Staats, Finley, Minke, & Wolf, 1964; Staats & Hammond, 1972; Staats, Minke, & Butts, 1970; Staats, Minke, Finley, Wolf, & Brooks, 1964; Staats, Minke, Martin, & Higa, 1972; Staats & Staats, 1958, 1975; Staats, Staats, & Biggs, 1958; Staats, Staats, & Crawford, 1962; Staats, Staats, Schutz, & Wolf, 1962; Staats & Warren, 1974). On the basis of these experimental studies and the conceptual analyses involved, it was possible to set forth a general theory of language and the manner in which language is learned (Staats, 1968a). In brief, this theory states that language consists of a complex of interrelated repertoires that can be isolated and described, and to some extent have been in other behaviorists' works as well as in the author's work. For example, the child must learn, according to reinforcement principles, a large repertoire of motor response units that are controlled (elicited) by single-word stimuli (like verbs, adverbs, and adjectives) and word combinations. This is called the verbal–motor repertoire. Procedures for training a child in such a repertoire have been described (Staats, 1968a, 1971a). Through the same basic principles, the child learns to make vocal responses that produce language stimuli—for example, in learning a very large labeling repertoire, a verbal imitation repertoire, a letter-and-word-reading repertoire, and so on. The controlling stimuli for these vocal responses may be verbal or nonverbal. Classical conditioning is equally important in language acquisition, as in the formation of the verbal–emotional repertoire. This repertoire consists of a large number of words that as stimuli will elicit a positive emotional response in the individual, and a large number of words that will elicit a negative emotional response. As will be indicated in the section on "The Emotional-Motivational Repertoire," this repertoire is centrally important because such words also function as reinforcing stimuli (Harms & Staats, 1978; Staats, Gross, Guay, & Carlson, 1973) and as directive—or discriminative or incentive—stimuli (Staats & Burns, 1982; Staats & Warren, 1974). This repertoire of single words provides the elements for the infinitely large number of combinations of words in language that have emotional-reinforcing-incentive properties. This repertoire of words, as is later indicated in the emotional-motivational section, also provides the basis for the measurement of the individual's reinforcers (and emotional and directive stimuli) by the means of verbal tests and assessment instruments.

Now, one of the central new characteristics of paradigmatic behaviorism's theory of language was its concern not only with the learning of language but also with the *functions* that language performs in affecting the way the individual behaves. This represents the next level of the theory development, and was exemplified in paradigmatic behaviorism's early concern with how language was the mechanism by which such cognitive phenomena as reasoning and problem solving and communication occurred (Staats, 1956, 1957a,b, 1963). The functions of language were thus studied in systematic theoretical and empirical works concerned with formulating the theory of language. The best example that can be given here is of the extension of the theory of language into the consideration of intelligence and intelligence testing, as is briefly indicated below.

Paradigmatic behaviorism began its development of a theory of intelligence, (Staats, 1963) with the conception that intelligence is composed of various skills that are very important because they make the individual a better learner. Take the verbal–motor repertoire that has already been mentioned, which consists of the various words that singly and in combination elicit single motor responses and complex combinations of motor responses. The verbal–motor repertoire constitutes the basic behavioral repertoire that enables the individual to follow instructions. A child who has not learned a good number of units in this repertoire cannot follow instructions. Such a child is severely handicapped, because following instructions is involved in almost every human activity. And it is heavily involved in being successful in school. Every task the teacher presents involves giving instructions that must elicit the appropriate responses in the child, if the child is to learn. Having a verbal–motor repertoire thus makes the child a far superior learner to the child without that repertoire.

The next theory level advance in the development being described was to analyze intelligence systematically in terms of this theory of language. For example, it might be expected that if the verbal–motor repertoire was so important to learning in the classroom that the assessment of this repertoire would appear on intelligence tests. After all, intelligence tests were constructed to predict the goodness of the child's school learning. This expectation receives strong support. When intelligence test items are analyzed systematically, it is found that the ability to follow directions is involved to varying degrees on every item (see Staats, 1971a). The richness of the child's verbal–motor repertoire is thus a central aspect of intelligence measurement (Staats, 1968a, 1971a; Staats & Burns, 1981).

But the level-by-level theory development does not stop there. When one has made an analysis of intelligence in terms of language repertoires, and the language repertoires have already been analyzed in terms of basic conditioning principles, and when the theory development has included procedures by which to produce those language repertoires through training, then one has a theory structure by which things can be done. This type of theory states that if we train a child in certain language repertoires that the child has not yet learned, then the child will be more intelligent. Moreover, the theory will tell us in just what ways the child will be more intelligent. This projection was verified in a gross way in earlier studies (see Staats, 1968a) and a recent trilogy of experiments (see Staats & Burns, 1981) has extended that empirical stipulation. In the first study Staats and Burns showed that intelligence, as measured by the Wechsler Preschool and Primary Scale of Intelligence (WPPSI) Mazes and Geometric Design subtests (Wechsler, 1967), was improved when children had been trained to learn certain basic behavioral repertoires that are in traditional conceptualizations considered to be quite different from the types of intelligence measured by those subtests. Moreover, the same basic behavioral repertoires of language were shown to underlie both of the WPPSI subtests, although these are usually thought to measure different aspects of intelligence. This is an important point, because the result shows that the theory and research involved provide a better understanding of what intelligence is than the traditional conceptions and tests of intelligence. In a second study Staats and Burns (1981) showed the same supportive results in the area of conceptual ability, as this is measured on children's intelligence tests, and in the third study this was extended to the various number-related items that appear in abundance on intelligence tests.

What this means for the development of behavioral assessment can be seen at least in part on the basis of this example. Paradigmatic behaviorism has a theory of intelligence that is stated in explicit behavioral terms. That theory provides knowledge by which one may train children to be intelligent, and by which to understand what intelligence is as well as how it should be assessed. Discussion returns to this topic, after the other parts of the present approach have been treated. What has been said is intended to illustrate that paradigmatic behaviorism includes extensive theoretical–empirical stipulation of the language–cognitive aspects of personality in the advancing multi-level theory-construction program. While the matter cannot be developed here, it should be noted that the theory of language and language function has special meaning for a paradigmatic behavior therapy (or paradigmatic behavioral analysis), since language is posed as a fundamental method of conducting therapeutic behavior and personality change (Staats, 1972).

THE SENSORY–MOTOR REPERTOIRE

There has been very little study of the sensory–motor skills that are important to human behavior, and that characterize the individual in a manner that we term personality. This is because there has not been a theory framework that projects this area as an important concern. The behavior modification framework has tended to have a narrow clinical focus, that is, to be concerned only about behavioral development that is a problem. Paradigmatic behaviorism states, however, that there are basic behavioral repertoires of a sensory–motor nature that individuals learn that are foundations for further learning, and that to understand human behavior we have to know about those repertoires of skills through stipulated, systematic assessment and research.

Let us take, as an example, the fact that much human learning takes place on the basis of imitation. Proponents of social learning theory very productively conducted a number of studies showing how children learned through imitations or modeling (Miller & Dollard, 1941; Bandura, 1969). However, social learning theory considered modeling to involve new basic principles, on the same level as the elementary conditioning principles (Bandura & Walters, 1963). This does not provide a framework for the analysis of what modeling is composed of, or how the ability to model comes about (for not all children model). To illustrate the type of analysis that is necessary, on the Geometric Design test of the WPPSI, children are asked to draw a geometric figure that they are shown. Some children can make a drawing that is sufficiently similar to the model to be considered intelligent. Some children cannot. What enables some children to be intelligent, to imitate, on this test? How is that something acquired? Why does the skill (item) involved contribute to intelligence? These are questions posed in the paradigmatic behaviorism approach, that do not arise in a less stipulated theory.

Again, paradigmatic behaviorism developed its analysis of the imitation skills of which modeling and other characteristics are composed in a level-by-level manner. One aspect of language that was analyzed in terms of the basic conditioning principles was that of writing. Writing involves the manual production of verbal stimuli, rather than the vocal production of such stimuli. Writing as a response must come under complex stimulus control, that of the various verbal stimuli that are provided by others or by oneself. To illustrate, the child must learn to write a particular letter when auditorily given the name of that letter. However, learning the repertoire of letter-writing responses involves the use of another type of controlling stimulus, that is, the visually presented letters themselves. The child must first learn a repertoire of copying, or imitational writing responses. If we are interested in understanding the various skill repertoires involved in learning to write, we must study them specifically, in detail. It is strange that this was not done, by educationists, by personality theorists, by developmental psychologists, by behaviorists, or by social learning theorists. Yet some very central imitation repertoires are involved. In a series of experiments, paradigmatic behaviorism research has provided training to children in the acquisition of writing repertoires in which every stimulus and every response of the children has been stipulated and recorded. Whereas traditional developmental psychology has considered such motor skills to be a matter of maturation, it was shown rather that the skill is standardly acquired according to instrumental conditioning principles employing reinforcement (Staats, 1968a; Staats, Brewer, & Gross, 1970; Staats & Burns, 1981). It takes from 500 to 1000 training trials for the child to acquire a copying and writing repertoire for the uppercase letters of the alphabet. Although the training varies in difficulty, all children with normal language can attain the same final performance level, under good training conditions.

One of the important things this research indicates is that imitation, modeling, takes place on the basis of previously learned basic behavioral repertoires. A child can only imitate, that is, copy a letter if the child has previously learned the behavioral repertoire in question. It is certainly important to establish that the child can learn through imitation, as various learning orientations have indicated (Bandura & Walters, 1963; Miller & Dollard, 1941; Skinner, 1953; Staats, 1963). But that only treats one aspect of the study. We must ask what modeling is composed of, rather than leaving it as a catch-all category, as has occurred in social learning theory (see Woll, 1978). There are various kinds of acts of modeling, and they rest upon different repertoires. When we make an analysis, we must ask how those repertoires are learned. And then in the next level of development, we must ask how those repertoires function to produce differences in human behavior, differences that frequently lead to the description of personality differences.

To illustrate this, the previously described study by Staats and Burns (1981) of Geometric Design and Mazes intelligence involves this last level of analysis. That is, analysis of the Geometric Design and Mazes tests revealed that a prominent aspect of the skills necessary to be considered intelligent was that of copying line drawings. There are attentional skills involved, holding-the-pencil skills, the skill of making lines with intent, the skills involved in drawing a bit and comparing as one goes along, and so on. These are sensory–motor skills. Moreover, they are sensory–motor skills of exactly the type that had been studied in children learning to write the letters of the alphabet. Analysis of letter-writing and the Geometric Design and Mazes intelligence subtests revealed great overlap in the skills required. This explains, in good part, why some children are intelligent as measured by their performance on the Mazes and Geometric Design parts of the WPPSI intelligence test. They are the fortunate children who have received learning experiences such as learning to write the letters of the alphabet! As a result they are prepared to copy new line figures easily, and to learn them.

It is not possible to indicate more here concerning the sensory–motor aspects of the basic personality repertoires. Paradigmatic behaviorism has systematically studied in experimental–longitudinal investigation how children have learned such essential skills as visual tracking in the infant, standing, walking, catching a ball, swimming, toileting skills (this analysis, it should be noted, has been propedeutic to well known behavior analyses of others), and so on, as indicated in some of the author's general works (Staats, 1963, 1968a, 1971a, 1975). However, there is a vast amount of research necessary to specify this realm of events (the sensory–motor skills important to adjustment), and the paradigmatic behaviorism framework and its prototypical methodology can serve as a foundation for projecting this study as a goal of the field of behavioral assessment and related endeavors. To construct behavioral assessment instruments of this repertoire requires knowledge of its contents. Our framework must direct us to seek that type of knowledge.

THE EMOTIONAL-MOTIVATIONAL REPERTOIRE

From the beginning, in the early development of paradigmatic behaviorism's basic learning theory, both the principles of the classical conditioning of emotional responses and the instrumental conditioning of motor responses were studied in the context of the learning of functional human behaviors (Staats, 1957a,b; Staats & Staats, 1957, 1958). This is a central area in which paradigmatic behaviorism differs basically from radical behaviorism. To elaborate, the very first experiment of the author, albeit in the naturalistic situation, was conducted while he was a graduate student in the early 1950s. The experiment tested the expectation that words come to elicit an emotional response when they are paired with stimuli that already elicit that emotional response—through classical conditioning. My subject was a pet cat, the conditioned stimulus was the word "No," and the negative emotion-eliciting stimulus was a mild spanking when the animal was apprehended during or after having been incontinent in the house. Through this treatment, the word did acquire a behavioral "meaning" for the animal. Several years later, this experiment was replicated in laboratory formality with human subjects, where a word was paired with a mild electric shock or loud noise (Staats, Staats, & Crawford, 1962). The emotional response (a galvanic skin response) was conditioned to the word. It was also found that the experimental subjects who had been conditioned rated the word to be unpleasant—showing additionally that verbal rating can be used to measure the emotional and other behavioral properties of a stimulus.

This research took the elementary principle of classical conditioning and applied it to a significant type of human behavior. The research is important for understanding the emotional functions of language, for human languages contain a very large number of words that elicit positive or negative emotional responses, as we can conclude from Osgood's extensive work (see Snider & Osgood, 1969). Moving on to the next level of the theory development, we must ask what is the behavioral importance of such words in the language. In answer, in the basic learning theory of paradigmatic behaviorism, stimuli that elicit emotional responses are considered also to be capable of making other stimuli have emotional value. This is central. Because of language, the human being has an extensive set of stimuli available at all times by which to make other stimuli of all kinds become positive or negative emotional stimuli, for someone else or for oneself. This also means that one can create reinforcing and directive (incentive) stimuli via language, for the emotional-reinforcing-directive properties of stimuli are linked together. If this theoretical analysis is true, then language should have extensive behavioral functions, for there are multitudes of emotional words and an infinite set of word combinations—not just the few, such as praise, that have been considered as conditioned reinforcers in operant behaviorism. To see what these functions are, however, requires extensive theoretical and experimental behavioral analysis, which has been one of the goals of paradigmatic behaviorism. One series of studies employed the author's language conditioning methods to show that words that evoke emotional responses can be paired with other stimuli to make the latter emotional also (Staats & Staats, 1957, 1958). Another series of experiments showed that emotion-eliciting words would function as reinforcing stimuli (Finley & Staats, 1967; Harms & Staats, 1978; Staats et al., 1973). Another series of studies showed that emotional words function as directive or discriminative stimuli (Staats & Burns, 1982; Staats & Warren, 1974). Among these studies were experiments that investigated the motivational principles involved in the theory—namely, that deprivation–satiation operations would affect the emotional-

reinforcing-directive functions of the word stimuli. The experimental procedures used food words, on the basis of the analysis that in the natural
environment food words have been paired with foods many times and thus
have come to be conditioned stimuli for the emotional response foods elicit.
One study showed that human subjects deprived of food salivated more to
the sound of food words than nondeprived subjects (Staats & Hammond,
1972). Another experiment showed that food words were stronger reinforcing stimuli for deprived subjects than nondeprived subjects (Harms & Staats,
1978), and the third showed that food words were stronger directive (discriminative) stimuli for an approach response with food-deprived subjects than
for nondeprived subjects (Staats & Warren, 1974).

These developments anchor an essential basic theory. It is this theoretical–empirical structure that provided the basis for projecting the theory of
the emotional–motivational aspects of personality. This structure also provides the foundation for understanding how verbal test instruments in
behavioral assessment and psychological testing measure the emotional-
reinforcing-directive stimuli that are functional for individuals. Let us continue to elaborate what is involved in these developments, however. The
personality theory of emotion–motivation states that there are many stimuli
that elicit emotional responses for humans on a biological basis, but that
people are capable of infinitely extensive learning in this respect. Much of
this learning occurs on a verbal level. There are, thus, a great multitude of
stimuli that come through the individual's conditioning history (including
language experience) to elicit an emotional response, and hence are capable
of serving as reinforcing and incentive stimuli. Moreover, this constellation
differs for each individual on the basis of the multitudinous past conditioning
circumstances associated with family, ethnic, cultural, professional, personal,
and other differences, as well as on the basis of deprivation–satiation differences. These emotional–motivational differences result in individuals later
learning different behaviors, even when exposed to the same situations. For
example, the individual who has a positive emotional response to symphonic
music will have a different learning experience when attending a concert
than will the individual with no such emotional response, and their behavior
during the concert and later on will reflect that difference. It is because of
such reasons that traditional personality tests such as the Strong Vocational
Interest Blank (1952), the Allport-Vernon-Lindzey Study of Values (1951),
and the Edwards Personal Preference Schedule (1953) are predictive of
behavior as shown in their validation studies. When we know about the
individual's emotional–motivational system, we know things that are important to the individual's behavior. In the present author's first analysis of this
area, he stated that the Strong interest test was a "simple listing of reinforcers for the individual" (Staats, 1963, p. 305). Some years later, a behav-

iorally oriented schedule was composed that embodied this behavioral analysis (MacPhillamy & Lewinsohn, 1971). Although different terminology is used on this behavioral assessment instrument, it measures the same types of things as do the traditional personality tests that deal with motivational factors. Thus, it makes no sense to neglect using the extensive work done on the traditional instruments. It is very important that from the standpoint of Skinner's analysis of verbal tests (1969, pp. 77–78), neither type of instrument is valuable; from the viewpoint of paradigmatic behaviorism analysis, both are. This latter position does not rest upon a general rejection of psychological tests, on the basis of the general rejection of the concept of personality, in the manner of radical behaviorism. Rather, the position rests upon a stipulated behavioral analysis advanced in a step-by-step manner from the basic conditioning principles up to the specific analysis of the tests. Furthermore, the position includes experimental investigation of the verbal tests of the emotional-reinforcing-directive system. One set of three studies (Staats *et al.*, 1973) showed that the Strong Vocational Interest test actually measured reinforcement value; that is, items from the test that individuals had rated positively were employed as reinforcing stimuli applied in a response-contingent manner to strengthen a particular response. Such items were also shown to be capable of making a stimulus, with which they were paired in a classical conditioning procedure, come to elicit a positive emotional response. And in the third experiment, which is described in the next section, it was found that choice-making behavior of subjects was determined by the subject's "interest" in the alternatives available.

Again, a vast amount of work is needed to specify and measure the emotional–motivational system of humans in a manner that can be employed to solve problems of human behavior. But before that work is undertaken, it is necessary to have a framework theory that indicates what is necessary. In simple terms, the efforts of the field of behavioral assessment depend upon the investigators knowing the content of what is to be assessed, which must be specifically indicated. Paradigmatic behaviorism offers to the field of behavioral assessment a framework theory that provides that content, in a way not provided by the other behaviorism theories. Part of the above-mentioned content consists of stipulating and measuring the three basic behavioral repertoires.

THE PERSONALITY–BEHAVIOR CONNECTION

Traditional personality theory has been weak in specifying what events determine personality as well as what constitutes personality. Similarly, traditional personality theory does not systematically specify how and by what principles personality exerts its effects upon the individual's behavior. This ambiguity can give rise to conflicting interpretations and expectations, and is one of the reasons traditional concepts of personality have been unacceptable to behaviorists. For example, we really cannot know whether personality trait theory is supported by evidence of the consistency of behavior until we know what behavior a particular type of personality is supposed to determine. To elaborate, there is a traditional personality concept of "interest," and there are personality tests to measure individuals' interests. Moreover, these tests have predictive value for later performance. But what are interests, and how do interests affect behavior? The statement of the personality theory is too vague to answer such questions, and traditional theorists have given up trying to define interests or how they have their affects. As another example, we have a concept of the religious personality, and there is a personality test that measures religious values (Allport et al., 1951). But what are the behaviors displayed by a person who has high religious values, and what are the principles by which religious values as an aspect of personality have their affects on behavior?

Standard behaviorism has not been concerned with such matters, because it rejects the concept of personality as a determinant of behavior. To illustrate, Watson's position that personality is the total of the individual's behavior cannot indicate how personality is a determinant of the individual's behavior. Social learning theory—only just beginning to introduce a concept of personality in its theory (Bandura, 1977a,b, 1978)—has not indicated that it aims for any more specificity in this regard than does traditional personality theory.

Let us examine the paradigmatic behaviorism theory as shown in Figure 8.1, using the example of religious values as part of the personality trait of religiosity. To begin, religious values may be considered to constitute part of the individual's total emotional–motivational system. The emotional–motivational system is characterized generally by the myriad stimuli that elicit positive or negative emotional responses in the individual. In the present specific case, a person with a strong religious personality can be seen to be someone who, among other things, has strong positive emotional responses to "religious" stimuli, that is, those stimuli that are part of religious practices, events, objects, and conceptions. Now, the Allport-Vernon-Lindzey study of values is a personality test that, among other things, measures religious values. Using the present terms, this test measures the strength of emotional response to a sample of religious stimuli relative to the strengths to samples of other stimuli, for example, economic and political stimuli.

This is a very explicit analysis of the concept of religious values and of the personality test. It says that, for the religious person, religious stimuli elicit a positive emotional response (among other effects). Now, the important thing is that the theory then specifies the principles by which the individual's personality trait of religiousness affects the individual's behavior. Remember that the basic theory involved says that a stimulus that elicits a positive emotional response is also a positive reinforcer. Thus, for the religious person, and not for the nonreligious person, religious stimuli are reinforcing. Religious and nonreligious types of individuals would be expected to learn differently, hence, in any situation in which religious stimuli are made contingent upon some behavior: the religious person would be conditioned to make the response, the nonreligious person would not. Moreover, religious stimuli will have different incentive value for the two types of individuals. Situations that include religious stimuli will act as incentives (directive stimuli) to the religious person, who will approach them. But this will not pertain for the nonreligious person. The principles by which the religious personality (emotional-motivational system) works its effects are thus quite explicitly stated by the theory.

The specificity of this statement provides a basis for testing specifically and experimentally whether there is an effect of religious personality on behavior. This has been demonstrated in a study that involves the precise control of the laboratory. Groups of subjects were selected to be either low or high on the Allport-Vernon-Lindzey scale of religiousness. They were then presented with a discrimination task in which they had to learn to make an approach response (pulling one class of stimuli toward them) or an avoidance response (pushing another class of stimuli away). One class of stimuli was composed of religious words, the other class of stimuli was composed of words designating common vehicles. An apparatus was employed that measured the interval of time between the presentation of each stimulus and the occurrence of the individual's response, to the thousandth of a second. Over a number of trials, the experiment showed that religious subjects made the approach response to religious stimuli faster than nonreligious subjects, and this was reversed for the vehicle words. Also, the religious subjects approached the religious stimuli faster than they did the nonreligious stimuli, and the reverse was true of the nonreligious subjects. The religious subjects avoided the religious stimuli more slowly than they did the nonreligious words, and this relationship was in the opposite direction for the nonreligious subjects. The results were explicit, and detailed, and they showed clearly the principles involved in the conception. That is, to a greater extent for people with religious personalities than for people with nonreligious personalities, religious stimuli had positive directive (discriminative or incentive) value. This was a controlled laboratory study, but we would expect that the principles would result in the same types of effects with various types of behavior in real life. Situations like deciding in favor of (approaching) or opposition to (avoiding) abortion laws, the teaching of creationism in school, practicing contraception, the legalization of prostitution, voting for a political candidate who is religious versus one who is not, the teaching of sex education, going to a religious movie, subscribing to a secular versus religious magazine, tuning in to a secular versus religious television program, and so on, can be expected to be affected by the religious component of the individual's emotional–motivational system. This theory, thus, predicts consistency of behavior, in very specific and verifiable principles that can be shown in a general and experimental way. Of course, other variables may control the individual's behavior in addition to the religious emotional–motivational system, and these require stipulation also. This specification of prediction is possible because the aspect of personality involved is made explicit, because there are measures of that aspect of personality, *and because the principles by which the personality differences affect behavior are explicitly stated.*

Another experiment has been conducted that is a closer approximation to a real-life situation involving the emotional–motivational system. This experiment concerned (vocational) interests, defined precisely as occupationally related stimuli that have positive or negative emotion-eliciting value—hence constituting part of the more general emotional-motivational system. Staats *et al.*, (1973) selected subjects on the basis of their occupational interests, employing the Strong Vocational Interest Blank, to constitute different groups—for example, subjects with high interests in chemistry and low interests in music, or the reverse. The subjects were then placed in a situation where they could select one of two magazine articles to read, the articles being labeled as pertaining to music or chemistry. The labels given the magazine articles were selected, on the basis of knowledge of the individual's emotional–motivational system provided by the Strong interest inventory, to elicit either a positive or negative emotional response in the subject. This knowledge thus provided a means of predicting what the subject's choice response would be. The predictions were perfect for the subjects, indicating that the principles were strong enough to determine individual behavior precisely. In terms of the consistency–specificity issue, it should be noted, the results showed that when exposed to the *same* situation subjects with different personality characteristics, in terms of measured interests, responded *differently.* The situation (specificity) did not determine the subjects' behavior; their personality (their emotional–motivational systems) did. Importantly, what is being described is also a unification of psychometric and behavioral methods. In this specific case, the psychometric test is being validated using paradigmatic behavioral theory to generate experimental behavioral studies.

Granted that personality tests can measure the emotional–motivational personality system, a question that has arisen from the radical behaviorist position is "could not the same information be obtained from observing the person's behavior?" It is important to realize that this question arises on a theoretical basis, because the basic operant theory separates classical conditioning and operant conditioning and makes the latter centrally important and the former relatively unimportant. Skinner (1975) has stated that emotions have nothing to do with motor behavior, in a causal sense, and the works of operant behaviorists have not systematically elaborated the significance of classical conditioning for its affects on behavior. In the present view, the question above should be answered by recourse to findings, not by the theoretical position of operant behaviorism. Extensive research in paradigmatic behaviorism shows that behavior in a stimulus situation can be changed by contingent reinforcements, yes, but also by change in the emotional response elicited by the situation. The emotional response can be the proximal cause of behavior. If one wants to change the behavior, the emotional response can be changed. Frequently the easiest and the most direct way to change behavior is through changing the emotional response, and this can be done through language (see Hêkmat, in press; Staats, 1972). Furthermore, especially significant in an analysis for behavioral assessment, the easiest and most direct way of measuring the individual's behavioral proclivities may be to measure the individual's emotional responses (through ratings). It is thus important to stress that operant behaviorists should make contact with the literature of paradigmatic behaviorism because it provides information on the importance of emotional responding for behavior, as well as information on how to measure emotional responding and how to change emotional responding. Paradigmatic behaviorism's basic theory and its elaborations open additional, behaviorally appropriate possibilities, without closing those we have already found. To attain those benefits it is necessary to switch from the basic learning theory of operant behaviorism (Skinner, 1938) to the basic learning theory of paradigmatic behaviorism (Staats, 1970, 1975).

PERSONALITY CONSISTENCY AND THE PARADIGMATIC BEHAVIORISM ANALYSIS OF THE PERSONALITY–BEHAVIOR RELATIONSHIP

Earlier in this chapter, in the "Person-Situation Issue" section, it was said that the consistency–situationism controversy was stated on such a general level that it did not direct us toward the study of what is needed to understand complex human behavior. For one thing, the traditional view has not indicated specifically how traits are supposed to determine behavior. That makes it difficult to know when expectations have or have not been met. Mischel (1968) has rather generally taken the position that the situation determines behavior—but rather than specification of how, his position is a criticism of the traditional view of personality causation. Thus, neither position gives us the knowledge we need. Without specification and analysis, only gross statements are possible, and these will be in error frequently.

Let me give an example. As has been indicated already, Staats and Burns (1981) trained one of two groups of preschool children in letter-writing and reading skills. The paradigmatic behaviorism analysis indicated that the basic behavioral repertoires learned in this process were very much like the skills needed for success on the Geometrics Design and Mazes subtests of the WPPSI intelligence test. Thus, a consistent increase of performance was expected across the two intelligence testing situations, for children receiving the training. And that is what occurred. It is important to realize that the expectation from the traditional intelligence testing view was that the two subtests measure different kinds of intelligence. On the contrary, however, learning the same basic behavioral repertoire increased performance on both subtests. Moreover, the finding of generality of performance across the two subtest situations cannot be expected within a situationist position, or an interactionist position. The message is that only by analysis of the specific personality and situational variables can we understand and deal with and measure what are the determinants of human behavior.

DEVELOPING THE BASIC BEHAVIORAL REPERTOIRES

The situationist position, even when it recognizes that the past learning history of the individual is to be considered, tends to place the emphasis upon the study of how the present situation affects behavior. Behavioral psychology has tended in general to focus upon the present situation. In the first place, the artificial simplicity of the animal laboratory has meant the selection of responses for study precisely because they are isolated and not greatly influenced by individual differences in prior conditioning history. And the rejection of traditional psychotherapies (that looked for causes of psychopathology in psychoanalytically significant events of childhood) led behavior therapists to reject also a concern with the effects of past learning. For example, it was stated that "All treatment of neurotic disorders is concerned with habits existing at *present*; their historical development is largely irrelevant" (Eysenck, 1960, p. 11). This position has also been urged within operant behavior modification approaches (Lovaas, 1966).

The paradigmatic behaviorism position is quite different in this respect. A very central element that must be understood is that, while every learning and behavioral situation involves basic conditioning principles, the learning process also depends upon characteristics the individual has *already* learned. Human learning is unique for its duration and for its *building* nature. The child may begin life with few repertoires that have any important effects on the basic characteristic of the child's learning. But that state is lost progressively, as the child acquires behavioral skills of an emotional–motivational, language–cognitive, and sensory–motor type *that become themselves determinants of the learning that is to follow.*

This is true for each of the three basic behavioral repertoires. In fact, this process is an essential reason why the term basic behavioral repertoires was introduced—because the repertoires are basic to later learning. To illustrate, when the child gets to school, the child's learning will be determined by the conditioning variables that are present in the school. Some teachers are sophisticated and will manipulate reinforcement conditions effectively, for example, and others will not. It has been appropriate for our behavior modification work to be concerned with such variables. But cumulative–hierarchical learning principles are yet more central than conditioning variables in producing the differences in school success that children display. It must be realized that each learning task the teacher presents requires that the students will have reached an appropriate place in their cumulative–hierarchical learning, for the child will not be able to succeed at the task unless he or she has the necessary basic behavioral repertoires. For example, when children are introduced to the task of learning to read, they are at a point in a cumulative–hierarchical learning sequence that in successful cases will have involved a vast prior learning accomplishment. When that cumulative–hierarchical learning has not occurred, the child will be a poor learner in this task. It is then easy to conclude in traditional views that the child has some learning disability, some inherited weakness in the ability to learn. For the standard behaviorist, such learning difficulties are considered in terms of inadequate conditions of learning (reinforcement) provided by the teaching procedures. But the difficulty may be, and usually is (see Collette-Harris & Minke, 1978; Ryback & Staats, 1970; Staats & Butterfield, 1965; Staats, Minke, & Butts, 1970) deficits in cumulative–hierarchical learning.

But is this not obvious? The answer is no. While we have a general realization that children must have certain skills before they can profit from certain additional types of learning, this knowledge and the principles and implications involved are so poorly specified that they are generally ignored in terms of explaining problems of learning and behavior and development. And this is not restricted to traditional psychology. As an example, social learning theory has not known how to consider its own central principles of imitation (modeling). Bandura (1969, 1971) has considered modeling as a third type of basic principle of learning, on a par with classical and instrumental conditioning. This conception makes imitation part of the individual's biological inheritance. This theory has not included the principles of cumulative–hierarchical learning, and the realization that *modeling itself involves repertoires that have been learned*, on the one hand, but are basic to additonal learning, on the other—which is the paradigmatic behaviorism position (see Staats, 1963, 1968a, 1971a, 1975). Modeling principles are not basic; they are derived, a part of cumulative–hierarchical learning.

To continue, however, there is little recognition of the significance of the cumulative–hierarchical learning in the field of behavioral assessment, if we are to judge by the utilization of the principles in constructing assessment devices. Traditional psychology, it should be noted, has constructed instruments that measure personality characteristics over progressive age groups. That was an original aspect of intelligence testing and remains a prominent feature of such tests. However, because of the underlying conception that intelligence tests are indexes of biologically based, mental entities, there has been no attempt within traditional psychology to consider the items of intelligence tests as samples of the basic behavioral repertoires *as they are learned* at certain ages in the cumulative–hierarchical learning process (see Staats & Burns, 1981). In the paradigmatic behaviorism theory of intelligence, it is considered important that tests such as the Stanford-Binet measure samples of basic behavioral skills at the different age levels that half the children at the particular age will have learned. *It is because the skills are essential in the child's further learning that the intelligence test results are predictive of how well the child will do in further schooling* (Staats, 1968a, 1971a; Staats & Burns, 1981).

Paradigmatic behaviorism considers that what is needed, centrally, is a functionally complete description of the age-graded development of the basic behavioral repertoires as the basis for constructing behavioral assessment instruments measuring intelligence. But this description must include the specification of the cumulative–hierarchical learning that is involved in the development of the basic behavioral repertoires. That is the necessary knowledge by which *to do* something about the matter when a child is found who is falling behind. The research conducted within paradigmatic behaviorism has attempted to provide that type of knowledge in the areas with which it has dealt, for example, the development of language and intelligence, reading, writing, number concepts, and so on. That is not to say the knowledge is complete. But these works provide a methodology and theory framework that suggests a large number of additional works, which will yield the type of knowledge generally lacking in understanding personality, in this case intelligence (Staats, 1971a; Staats & Burns, 1981).

This statement is not based upon armchair theorizing, it should be noted. As an example, it has already been said that intelligence tests actually assess important aspects of the child's basic behavioral repertoires. Paradigmatic behaviorism has stipulated that psychology has the task of specifying what those repertoires are as well as the conditions of learning that result in the development of those repertoires. It is also important to study analytically how training in particular repertoires affects the child's intelligence repertoires, as measured by intelligence tests. The study in which training in copying and reading the letters of the alphabet raised the children's intelligence measurements on the Geometrics Design and Mazes subtests of the WPPSI has already been described. Another experiment revealed that children who had learned the appropriate vocabulary (i.e., had learned to label the objects that were relevant) were better on concept-type intelligence test items that require the indication of why things are similar, how families of objects should be classified together, and the indication of the concept-names of families of objects. An additional experiment studied the repertoires underlying the various number–concept items that occur with profusion on intelligence tests. Children trained in certain basic behavioral repertoires concerning the discrimination of numbers, the counting of objects, and so on, achieved higher intelligence scores, on items that were of a different nature than those involved in their learning experience (Staats & Burns, 1981).

On the one hand, traditional approaches that measure intelligence but do not stipulate what it is or how it is acquired can tell us little about how to remediate problems of intelligence. On the other hand, it may also be said that in this sphere that the situationism, behavior-problem-focused framework that is employed by many behavioral researchers is insufficient. We do need to know the conditions of reinforcement in the classroom, and how to correct problems of reinforcement for the nonattending, acting out, or hyperactive child. Frequently, however, the problem of disruptive classroom behavior is not that of changing the contingencies for the "symptomatic" behavior itself, with a focus on removing the undesirable behavior. Rather, the child's *lack* of the basic behavioral repertoires of intelligence that prevent the child from learning, along with all the resulting behavioral concomitants, constitute the problem. To be able to assess the child's primary—as opposed to secondary—problem requires the ability to assess the basic language-cognitive repertoires involved. To be able to remediate the fundamental problem requires provision of training to the child that will produce the basic behavioral repertoires (rather than trying to remove or decrease the more salient undesirable behavior). It is thus necessary for the theory to indicate the principles and conditions of learning involved in the acquisition of the personality repertoires. And it is necessary to indicate the cumulative–hierarchical learning sequences that are involved. These areas of knowledge constitute the necessary content for the framework theory that is to be useful both to behavioral assessment and behavior therapy. Paradigmatic behaviorism provides that framework theory in prototypical form, pointing the way toward what must be done more generally in this sphere.

CUMULATIVE–HIERARCHICAL LEARNING AND CONSISTENCY

Finally, it is possible to address the question of consistency within this context as it is generally stated. The major point is that cumulative–hierarchical learning contributes consistencies in the personality development of the child over time. Advantageous development of the language–cognitive repertoires, for example, provides a basis for continued advantageous learning—which helps account for the consistency in intelligence measurements over time. Deficits in the learning of these language–cognitive repertoires will normally lead to a "downward cycle" of development, because the repertoires are necessary for that development (Staats, 1971a, 1975). A major point here is that the types of correlational studies on which much of the consistency–specificity (situationism-vs.-personality) issue is based deal only in generalities. To establish, for example, that IQ scores tend to be consistent for groups of children over time—that consistency is shown by most children, but not by all—does not indicate what is involved in the cases that are consistent or in the cases where inconsistency occurs. To establish that achievement motivation typically shows low correlations in longitudinal studies, for example, while it may be used as support for the general situational–specificity argument (Mischel, 1968), does not tell us what achievement motivation consists of, how it is learned, how it has its effects upon the individual's behavior and further personality development, or indeed what is involved when some individuals show consistency over time and situations and others do not. Behavioristic positions, thus, as well as traditional theories can be too general and "theoretical," in this sense, to be useful as guides to specific analysis. What is necessary for the development of the fields of behavior assessment and behavior modification are works that provide the analytic areas of knowledge of the type being described, as additional discussions also suggest. This is why paradigmatic behaviorism's program requires analyses of the basic behavioral repertoires and how they are learned (e.g., see Herry & Leduc, 1981; Leduc, 1984; Staats, 1963, 1968a, 1971a, 1975; Staats, Brewer, & Gross, 1970; Staats & Burns, 1981). Such types of studies should be employed as the foundation of a field of behavioral assessment that attempts to establish the *particular elements* that are causative in the behavior problems of the clinic, educational institution, and so on, as a basis for treating the problems.

THE PRESENT SITUATION-BEHAVIOR SITE OF
BEHAVIORAL ASSESSMENT

The manner in which the individual learns his or her basic behavioral repertoires and what the repertoires consist of have been indicated as sites of concern to behavioral assessment. The manner in which the "situation" enters into these interests involves the original learning of the basic personality repertoires. However, the situation enters into the determination of differences in human behavior at another point, as indicated in Figure 8-1. When individuals encounter a later situation, the behavioral variables in that situation also will help determine performance. To illustrate, entering a large university will entail environment differences for many high school graduates. Large classes, for example, will remove the immediate social reinforcement for classroom preparation that in high school was provided by the personal reinforcement of teachers and peers. The student's preparation under the new conditions may weaken and deteriorate. This situational condition may interact with students' basic behavioral repertoires, in the sense that some students' work behaviors may have been more under the influence of that source of reinforcement than will have been the case for other students, whose reinforcement may come from what is commonly called interest, a personality characteristic that has already been defined herein in the "Personality-Behavior Connection" section. We may see consistent work behaviors, and consistent performance, in the latter type of student over the change of situations, whereas we may see a deteriorating change in work and performance in the student whose behavior has formerly been maintained by personal reinforcement.

It is clear that knowledge of the situation can be important in planning for intervention to improve the individual's adjustment, as can knowledge of the individual's personality repertoires. If one knew that direct social reinforcement was very important for a student, to follow the above example, one might not advise enrollment in a large state university. Such assessment has been a function of traditional personality tests, interest tests being a prime example, even though personality theory could not describe the events in analytic, or behaviorally acceptable, terms. The IQ test is also employed in this manner when test results are used as a means of placing students into classes or colleges to harmonize with the difficulty level of the demands the students will meet. Special education classes may be seen as an attempt to suit the situation to the student's intelligence (basic behavioral repertoires). For such situational manipulation to be maximally effective, however, using this example, it must be based upon a detailed knowledge of the language–cognitive repertoires such that educational situations may be designed to be appropriate for students with different levels of advancement. Present-day intelligence tests have not been constructed with that knowledge at hand, and as a consequence manipulation of special classes to adjust the situation of the student may be considered gross in nature. When we know the specific repertoires the child lacks, special training can be applied that will be specifically remedial, as illustrated in the already described training that resulted in enhancement of the children's intelligence.

Behavior assessment efforts have also concentrated attention on the situation–behavior site of concern (see Fernandez-Ballesteros, 1983, for an excellent account, albeit in Spanish). In general, the attempt is to determine what the nature of the problem behavior is and to establish those circumstances that maintain the behavior, as a basis for projecting changes that will remedy the problem behavior. The present author described the importance of the situation in the first general behavioral analysis or taxonomy of behavioral problems (Staats, 1963, Chapter 11) as well as ways to alter the situation to produce benign behavior modification. Goldfried and Sprafkin's (1976) "SORC" model may be used as another example (although in the present view this is not a developed analytic framework). The S stands for the situational contributors to the problem. (The R stands for the behavior, or response itself. The C stands for the reinforcement consequences of the behavior that maintain the behavior, which actually should be considered to be part of the situational variables. And the O stands for any organismic variables that may be involved—but this organismic concept has not been developed theoretically or experimentally, and what it is intended to encompass cannot be indicated. It is thus not a substitute for the basic behavioral repertoire theory, which is specified theoretically and empirically. Moreover, the framework does not include classical conditioning, and so on.) Kanfer and Saslow (1965) present another model that is based on analysis of the situational conditions involved in the maintenance of problematic behavior. They include analysis of (1) the features of the problem, especially as others see it, (2) the reinforcers that are involved, (3) any sociological problems, (4) the client's interpersonal relationships, and (5) a general analysis of the social-cultural-physical environment. This, too, is oversimplified and exhibits the weaknesses of its basic theoretical foundation of operant behaviorism.

Another traditional interest in behavioral assessment has been the objectification of the effects of therapeutic treatment (Goldfried & Sprafkin, 1976; Kanfer & Saslow, 1965; Staats, 1963). Single-organism research with animals, for example, had utilized designs that involved presenting experimental conditions and withdrawing them or changing them, to see their effects on behavior. Early behavior modification efforts developed such methods for assessing the effects of treatments on human behavior (see Hart, Allen, Buell, Harris, & Wolf, 1964; Staats, Staats, Schutz, & Wolf, 1962). Using such methods, the value of treatment can be assessed by objective observation of the effects upon the behavior of the single subjects in various ways that have been formulated (Hersen & Barlow, 1977). Various types of measuring instruments can be employed. The major point of this brief mention is that therapy may be considered to be a situation that has a causative effect upon the behavior of the individual—and it has been conceived of in somewhat similar terms within the context of behavioral assessment (Ciminero, Calhoun, & Adams, 1977; Cone & Hawkins, 1977; Haynes, 1978; Hersen & Bellack, 1976).

In conclusion, behavioral assessment must be interested in analysis and assessment of the effects of the present life situation on the individual's behavior, and that includes assessment of the characteristics of therapy procedures. It is very significant that both of these interests have been recognized in traditional approaches to working with problems of human behavior, in both clinical and educational settings. It may thus be said that, unlike some of the other sites of interest indicated in paradigmatic behaviorism's theory as schematized in Figure 8-1, traditional psychology as well as standard behavioral approaches to assessment are interested in the effects of the individual's situation on his or her behavior. Ability to analyze the situation, however, depends upon the goodness of the theory used, that is, the extent to which it says what aspects of the situation have important effects on behavior. Paradigmatic behaviorism and operant behaviorism differ in this respect. For example, paradigmatic behaviorism specifies that classical conditioning variables in the situation are important determinants of the individual's overt behavior, in ways not recognized in radical-behaviorism-based approaches.

THE BEHAVIOR-PERSONALITY AND BEHAVIOR-ENVIRONMENT SITES OF STUDY

This is not elaborated, but Figure 8-1 indicates that there are additional sites of study suggested by the paradigmatic behaviorism model. In terms of the behavior–personality interaction, we can see readily that the way the individual behaves in certain ways will have important effects upon the nature of the individual's experience, learning, and further personality development. The study of Staats et al. (1973) has already been described whereby subjects with certain interests selected certain types of reading matter, in a two-choice situation. Thus, these subjects' choice making behavior determined what they read, and the experience they thereby received. Such experience produces new learning that results in the formation of new elements of the individual's basic behavioral repertoires. In the experiment, subjects high in chemistry interests, as an example, chose articles to read that would produce further information about chemistry (langauge–cognitive development), as well as condition the subjects to positive emotional responses to topics in the field of chemistry. It is clear that these effects are examples of how personality, through the behaviors it determines, results in consistencies in personality development. The study showed that people who have interests in chemistry have choice behaviors that enhance those interests, and this applies to many other aspects of the emotional–motivational personality system. Personality theory and the field of behavioral assessment must be concerned with this site of study, that is, the manner in which the individual's behavior produces further personality development. Interactional psychologists (Bowers, 1973; Wachtel, 1973) have supported this conception that individuals create for themselves stable environments, but the present position has been that the principles involved require specific behavioral stipulation and study, and that a general statement is not enough (Staats, 1980).

The same is true of the way that behavior affects the environment. Paradigmatic behaviorism was the first behavioral approach to abstract the behavior–environment interaction for consideration (Staats, 1963, 1968a, 1971a, 1975), and in recent years this principle has been adopted by the new social learning theory interest in interaction (Bandura, 1968; Mischel, 1973, 1977). As paradigmatic behaviorism has indicated, however, the mere statement that behavior affects the environment does not complete the task. It is necessary to indicate specifically how, and how this affects the individual's later personality development and behavior. Paradigmatic behaviorism has been specific in indicating the manner in which such interactions occur, but the present point is that this is a site for systematic study that should become an interest in behavioral assessment. Early examples of behavior–environment lines of causation have included description of the manner in which the individual's self-concept, which includes the individual's self-descriptions, influence how others respond to the individual (Staats, 1963, pp. 260–266), and the manner in which the parent's treatment of the child's behavior determines that behavior in a manner that in turn helps determine the parent's love for the child (Staats, 1963, pp. 411–414). Staats and Butterfield (1965) treat the language–cognitive problems of a child whose personal history is described as involving a downward cycle of development: The child's deficits in language–cognitive skills result in the receipt of aversiveness from the school environment which in turn conditions the child to have negative emotional responses to the school that later mediate overt destructive behaviors such as vandalizing the school, a behavior that in turn results in the severe environmental circumstance of being placed in a reform institution. These principles of behavioral interaction (Staats, 1971a) have been generalized in the context of explaining how severe abnormal personality defects can arise through learning (Staats, 1975, pp. 272-276). And the manner in which social interactions and person–institution interactions can be involved in developing severe abnormal behavior has been generally described (Staats, 1975, pp. 276-280). Again, these are areas for systematic research in behavioral assessment and behavior analysis and behavior therapy generally.

PARADIGMATIC BEHAVIORISM'S ABNORMAL PSYCHOLOGY

There is not space in this chapter to do justice to this topic. But it is essential to indicate, even by mention, what is involved. That is, in addressing the present topics, the general concepts of the basic behavioral repertoires and of cumulative–hierarchical learning have been indicated. The concepts apply to personality in general, that is to say to normal personality. It is also important to extend the present approach to the consideration of the concerns of psychopathology. In the present view, a psychology of abnormal behavior is needed in behavioral psychology to provide the broad theory that can serve as a foundation for the conceptual, empirical, and clinical interests of behavioral assessment and behavior therapy. The author's first general paradigmatic behaviorism work (Staats, 1963) included an incipient abnormal psychology, at a time when behavior therapy and behavior modification had begun but still lacked a conceptual framework. Eysenck had already proposed that abnormal behavior involves "deficient conditional reactions" and "surplus conditional reactions" (1960, p. 7). I used this simple principle in developing behaviorism's first abnormal psychology. In a chapter entitled "Behavior Problems and Treatment" (Staats, 1963), the various problems of abnormal psychology were analyzed and found to consist of behavioral deficits, inappropriate behaviors, inappropriate behaviors resulting from behavioral deficits, inadequate or inappropriate stimulus control, defective discriminative stimulus control of behavior, and inadequate or inappropriate reinforcing (incentive) systems. This classification system was employed by Bandura (without reference to either Eysenck's concept or Staats's abnormal psychology), under the title of "A social learning theory interpretation of psychological dysfunctions" (Bandura, 1968). This classification system was considered by Goldfried and Sprafkin (1976) to be fundamental in the development of the field of behavioral assessment. It is significant to note that Skinner's behaviorism provided no basis for the development of the field of behavioral assessment. On the other hand, the paradigmatic behaviorism analysis provided a behavioral taxonomy, the concept of behavioral assessment, and established the need for devising behavioral assessment instruments for use with behavioral treatment methods (see Staats, 1963, pp. 465–511). Kanfer and Saslow's (1965) account may be considered as an important elaboration of this approach that also has been seen as a seminal work in the development of the field of behavioral assessment (Fernandez-Ballesteros, 1983). Other works have since organized the behavioral literature in the context of abnormal psychology (Ullmann & Krasner, 1969). Such efforts remained within the radical behaviorism approach and have not served to provide a new heuristic theory for projecting new analyses of the psychopathologies, beyond that of the taxonomy described above.

Paradigmatic behaviorism, however, in developing its concepts of personality, of cumulative–hierarchical learning, and other concepts and principles such as that of behavioral competition, the antilearning repertoire, personality repertoire interaction, and other types of interactions, has constructed an abnormal psychology in summary form that, it is suggested, can provide the basis for a new and basically founded abnormal psychology (Staats, 1975, Chapter 8; Staats & Heiby, 1985). By this is meant an abnormal psychology that can serve as a heuristic *guide* to the fields of behavior modification and behavioral assessment—rather than one that is just a *repository* of the findings that have been made in these two behavioral fields.

The basis of the abnormal psychology is the model presented in Figure 8-1, with the elaborations that are necessary for the new concerns to be dealt with. Figure 8-2 schematizes paradigmatic behaviorism's abnormal psychology, in simplified, summary form.

The approach states that the various sites of concern of the paradigmatic behaviorism model require development as the basis for a complete abnormal psychology. There are two types of deviation that can produce problems of human behavior. The two types, called deficit and inappropriate, apply not just to the individual's behavior, but also to personality repertoires, to the conditions that originally produced the personality repertoires, to the situation in which the abnormal behavior occurs, and indeed to all of the other sites that have been proposed to be of concern in the present approach to the field of behavioral assessment.

This theoretical model indicates what the interests of this abnormal psychology (and of the fields based upon the abnormal psychology) must be. Unlike positions that have taken an ahistorical view of behavioral applications, the paradigmatic behaviorism view is that deficits and inappropriate aspects of the basic behavioral repertoires arise in childhood and in the periods that follow. While Lovaas (1966) has stated, for example, that it is

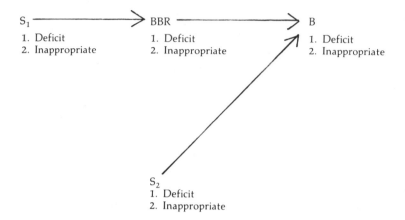

FIG. 8-2. There are several sites of concern in the study of abnormal behavior. The individual's past life history (S_1) may have been deficient or inappropriate in various ways. Such circumstances will produce deficits or inappropriate aspects of the learned personality repertoires (BBR). The present life circumstances (S_2) will interact with the individual's personality repertoires to produce the behavior exhibited (B). Although not diagrammed, this is a continuing interaction. That is, the individual's behavioral deficits and inappropriate behaviors result in producing abnormal conditions in later situations, which in turn result in the formation of further deficient and inappropriate aspects of personality repertoire development, and so on.

useless to be concerned with the parent's role in the etiology of childhood schizophrenia, paradigmatic behaviorism deems this a central area of study. And it will be central for behavioral assessment to make behavioral analyses that will ascertain what are the deficits and inappropriate aspects in the learning conditions that produce the deficient and inappropriate development of the child's personality repertoires that produce deficient and inappropriate behaviors in later situations. Such assessment knowledge is essential if intervention programs are to be begun early in the child's life, to remedy developments that if unchecked would lead to the severe cases labeled childhood schizophrenia or to other abnormal states.

The same thing is true for the abnormal basic behavioral repertoires themselves. What are the abnormalities in the personality repertoires that constitute depression? homosexuality? learning disabilities? schizophrenia? We should understand, firmly, as an example, that setting up a token economy where schizophrenic patients are reinforced for self-care and simple work behaviors—important as success in these things might be—is not the same as investigation that establishes in terms acceptable to a behavioral approach what schizophrenia *consists of*. In the paradigmatic behaviorism view, schizophrenia consists of deficits in the language–cognitive repertoires, the emotional–motivational system, and the sensory–motor repertoires, and inappropriate developments in these personality repertoires as well (Staats, 1975). This has been indicated in summary form—but a great deal must be done to turn this conceptual framework into the substantive body that is needed (see, for example, Staats & Heiby, 1985). It may be noted that Leduc and Dumais (in press) have set up a ward in a mental hospital, based on paradigmatic behaviorism theory. Treatment involves training chronic hospital patients, many of them schizophrenic, in the three personality repertoires. The theory and the treatment procedures derived from the theory are relevant for all types of abnormal personality.

Again, there is also the task of specifying the life-situational effects upon the person with abnormal personality repertoires. A life situation may be deficient or inappropriate for such a person although the situation would not involve these problems for the individual with normal basic behavioral repertoires. For example, the life situation may not insure the presence of social relationships for the retiring schizophrenic, and thus constitutes isolation (a deficit) that exacerbates the problem. The normal person may not be bothered by the isolation, or may actively change the situation. Study of the interactions of personality and situation requires much greater systematic stipulation and assessment. It should be understood that actions in the treatment of problems of abnormal psychology frequently rest upon such knowledge, and the inadequacy of such knowledge insures that many errors will occur. We have a contemporary example in the policy of returning hospitalized psychotics to the community. This policy has resulted in additional misery for individuals not able to cope with the outside world, and for the community as well, and a high rate of return to the hospital situation (Serban, 1980). In reviewing the evidence of this problem it has been said that "Unquestionably, there has been a need for a fresh look at the life situation of the schizophrenic patient as he re-enters the community, for a reconsideration of the nature and limitations of his adaptive capabilities" (Silverstein, 1981, p. 599). This need is stipulated in the paradigmatic behaviorism model, projected in 1975 (see Staats, 1975), and it remains a focus of study for behavioral assessment of the future.

In addition, the personality repertoires relevant to abnormal classifications require systematic specification. As example in this important area, the Staats-Heiby theory of depression (Heiby & Staats, in press; Staats & Heiby, 1985) describes two individuals who have each lost a central loved person. The result for one individual—who has no other strong affective-reinforcer-incentive stimuli in work, recreation, interpersonal, or other areas—is a catastrophic loss in happiness and in the maintenance of effective behavior, that is, a clinical depression. For the person with a richly endowed emotional-motivational personality system, the loss is a tragedy, but other affective-reinforcer-directive stimuli in work, recreation, social, and other spheres maintain behavior and insure that the individual continues to experience liberal positive emotional circumstances. This individual does not develop a clinical depression.

As another focus of study, the abnormal behaviors (symptoms) of the individual produce effects on the social (and physical) environment that constitute additional causes in the individual's personality development. This site of causation is very important in the development of abnormal personality characteristics (see Staats, 1975, Chapter 8, for additional examples of this principle) because the deficits and inappropriate aspects of behavior usually produce deficient and inappropriate environmental circumstances, sometimes in a continuing, downward cycle (Staats, 1975). The conception of abnormal psychology includes additional sites of interest and principles for analysis.

It is the case that concentrated, systematic investigation of these principles and sites of interest must be conducted. And that indicates a centrally important feature of the paradigmatic behaviorism approach. The field of behavioral psychology (as is generally the case) needs a theoretical framework that serves as a guide in the sense of indicating what areas of knowledge must be developed to continue the field's basic and applied progress. Neither operant behaviorism or social learning theory has systematically provided that framework, and it is paradigmatic behaviorism's objective to do so. Many of the sites of study that paradigmatic behaviorism's framework indicates should become of central interest are in the area of behavioral assessment, or are in areas that are basic to behavioral assessment. Behavioral assessment needs an analytic abnormal psychology to serve as a foundation for constructing its assessment instruments.

One further point should be emphasized. The present conception (see Staats, 1975, Chapter 8; Staats & Heiby, 1985) constitutes, in outline form, a new theory of psychopathology. This theory analyzes the different categories of psychopathology within a framework that is explanatory and, moreover, that relates the different psychopathologies to each other. This is done in a behavioral way that is distinct both from the traditional model of different mental diseases and from the standard behavioristic model of separated behavior problems. The potential for elaboration of this theoretical framework and the heuristic value of that elaboration have been shown by the Staats-Heiby theory of depression (Staats & Heiby, 1985). The theory unifies knowledge of depression that has been gained in the context of different and competitive approaches. The theory makes a more profound and differentiated analysis of depression than is otherwise available, indicating that the one category of psychopathology has different explicit subtypes (see also Heiby & Staats, in press). And the theory provides the basis for experimental, clinical, and measurement works of various kinds (see Kameoka, Heiby, & Staats, 1985), all within a methodology that is strictly behavioral.

A BEHAVIORISM IS A BACKGROUND THEORY
WITH HEURISTIC IMPLICATIONS

We can isolate at least three conceptual bodies, with at least a basis in behavioral principles, that have attempted to be general in scope. The oldest is also the most developed internally (whose potential has already been most fully expended), because it has had the greatest number of individuals working on it, for the greatest length of time. It is also the most organized in terms of member scientists, journals and other publications, organizations, and so on. Its age also has meant that it has basic characteristics that derive from the context of problems current at the time of its development some forty to fifty years ago. Many of these characteristics are no longer advantageous. This approach has been called variously operant conditioning, operant behaviorism, radical behaviorism, the experimental analysis of behavior, and so on. A new behaviorism, paradigmatic behaviorism, has incorporated some characteristics of the operant version, while also contributing features to the development of the human aspects of operant behaviorism. There is also a third orientation, called social learning theory, that must be included, because it has utilized behavioristic principles as basic, and because, along with the others, it has contributed a good deal to the growth of behavior modification, although it has hybrid characteristics some of which are not fundamentally behavioristic.

It is not the purpose of the present chapter to characterize these three approaches. It is important to suggest, however, that the different theories are frameworks that notwithstanding much commonality nevertheless have different implications, suggest different problems for study, and indicate different avenues of advancement to be followed in such areas as behavioral assessment. Thus, for example, the contemporary consistency-specificity issue sprang from the social learning theory framework of the late 1960s, not from operant or paradigmatic behaviorism. Following behaviorism's original rejection of the concept of personality, the social learning theory analysis went further to question whether there were actually any data in the field of personality measurement that justified the concept of the personality trait. Operant behaviorism, in contrast, over the years since Watson, had followed the characteristic of ignoring the fields of personality and personality measurement. Paradigmatic behaviorism never accepted the latter position from the beginning, holding instead that there was knowledge in the fields of personality and personality measurement that had to be incorporated into behaviorism (Staats, 1963; Staats, Staats, Heard & Finley, 1962), and for the same reason also found the situationism orientation to be lacking. The important point is that large theoretical frameworks have characteristics—sometimes implicit—that provide impetus for development in the fields to which the frameworks are relevant. When one is immersed in one orientation, many of these characteristics are implicit. While the characteristics guide and limit the work done in the field, in the absence of contrasting the characteristics to those of another approach, there is no evaluation of those characteristics. When one apprises oneself of only one approach, it may seem as though there is no other way things can be done.

The field of behavioral assessment is dominated now primarily by the operant or radical behaviorism framework. That framework guides the work of the field in certain ways to do certain types of things, and it also places restrictions on what is done. Such a guide could be as completely successful as the science involved could manage at the particular time. However, the framework could also be incorrect at points and be giving misleads in its guidance. The framework could also have restrictions and lacunae and give faulty and erroneous guides. Paradigmatic behaviorism says that there are various weaknesses of this kind in the operant behaviorism framework, for the field of behavioral assessment as well as for other areas of psychology. Paradigmatic behaviorism is suggested also as a framework theory that, while behavioristic in the fundamental sense, has many characteristics that in their difference from operant behaviorism provide different guides to the development of behavior assessment and behavior therapy and other areas of study, ranging from its different philosophy of science, its different basic "learning theory," and on to its approach to the study of human behavior and the treatment of human problems.

The present chapter attempts to say in the most general sense that the field of behavioral assessment must consider its background theories, what they are, what their characteristics are, and what those characteristics provide as guides for the various works in the field. The framework theories should be compared for their characteristics and for the implications those characteristics have for the development of the field as Minke, in press, has indicated. Although such analyses have not been focal, they are as important as the specific works that take place in the field, because the work in behavioral assessment and in psychology generally depends in good part upon the framework theory that is employed.

A comparative analysis of the three general frameworks mentioned is not possible in the present work, although this has been envisaged in the present approach. The active behavioral psychologist, however, should compare the works of Skinner—since that is the basic theory employed for radical behaviorists—with the works of the present author, to see which provides the better theoretical foundation for projecting needed developments and new directions (see Minke, in press, for an example). A few implications may be indicated on this topic, since several general areas are involved.

METHODOLOGICAL IMPLICATIONS

Skinner has said that behavior and the variables of which it is a function must be directly observed, and this cannot be circumvented by using the subject's statements as data "because the subject cannot correctly describe either the probability that he will respond or the variables affecting such a probability" (1969, pp. 77–78). Mischel has said also that the "specificity of behavior suggests that sample predictor behavior should be as similar as possible to the behavior used on the criterion measure" (1972, p. 323). "One of the basic assumptions underlying behavioral assessment is that the behavioral sample measures nothing beyond itself (Goldfried & Sprafkin, 1974; Mischel, 1968, 1972). The logical outcome of this assumption is that there is no theoretical rationale for the employment of an indirect sample of behavior (interviews, self-report inventories, standardized tests, etc.) to make decisions about another non-sampled population of behaviors" (Burns, 1980, p. 197). Burns has outlined the contrast between the behavioral assessment view based upon direct measurement with the framework posed by paradigmatic behaviorism. Even though behavioral assessment may employ indirect measurement devices, this is inconsistent with its basic position stated above. In the paradigmatic behaviorism view, following from its specificity characteristics, whatever measurement devices are employed require close derivation from the framework theory employed. Thus, when a type of measurement proves to be useful, this finding disproves the theory that cannot justify that usefulness. The above-mentioned inconsistency is a case in point. There are indirect verbal personality tests, such as intelligence tests and interest tests, that predict with useful accuracy behavioral performance (such as school grades) that differs from that which has been measured.

The point should be made more generally. That is, it has been the methodology of radical behaviorism to reject traditional concepts and areas of empirical evidence out of hand, without systematic consideration. Following Watson's original position, something can be labeled "mentalistic," and thereby be totally discredited and ignored. This methodology cannot be rationalized within general scientific method, at least from the standpoint of paradigmatic behaviorism's philosophy of science (see Staats, 1983a; in press). For rejection of empirical evidence, and theoretical formulations as well, require the same "due process" as does acceptance of evidence and theory.

One of the criteria by which to evaluate a behavioral assessment approach that is supposed to be general in its scope is its ability to account for such findings as the utility of personality tests in prediction. Paradigmatic behavioral assessment accepts that challenge, and in doing so provides justification for some of the traditional verbal testing methods of measurement. Let us take interest tests as an example. Studies have been conducted that show that words can be conditioned to elicit a positive or negative emotional response, as has been indicated herein. Such a word will have positive or negative reinforcement value, and the word will also have directive (discriminative) value for either approach or avoidance responses. One type of approach or avoidance responding is that of verbal evaluation—whether one uses a seven-point rating scale, like–dislike scoring, or any of the others that have been employed. Furthermore, when an actual stimulus event (or situation, person, or what-have-you) has emotional-reinforcing-directive value, the word or words denoting that event will also have that same value. The series of studies (Harms & Staats, 1978; Staats *et al.*, 1973; Staats & Warren, 1974) with food words mentioned earlier showed this conclusively. The body of research and theory that justifies these statements also shows why verbal items can be employed to assess the stimulus functions of emotional stimuli (such as reinforcement value) and why such tests tell us important things about human behavior. That is why interest tests can be useful—they involve assessment of the stimuli that have emotional-reinforcing-directive functions for the individual. In this respect, thus, paradigmatic behaviorism takes a position completely opposite Skinner's statement (1969, p. 77–78) that humans cannot verbally indicate, in response to verbal items on a personality test, what the stimuli are of which their behavior would be a function in the presence of those stimuli. For one of the tasks of *paradigmatic behavioral assessment* is establishing through behavioral research the "goodness" of traditional tests and types of test items.

To continue, there are methods of assessment employed by those who have constructed intelligence tests for which paradigmatic behaviorism also provides a behavioral derivation. Hence, these methods, as well as the instruments composed by the methods, are said to be valuable in understanding human behavior. In short, paradigmatic behaviorism's theory has methodological implications of a very general sort, implications that cannot be dealt with here (Staats, 1968a, 1975, 1977, 1981, 1983a, 1983b; Staats, Brewer, & Gross, 1970; Staats & Burns, 1981). A large body of knowledge is involved that must be consulted specifically for those implications. It may only be said in the present context that paradigmatic behaviorism has consistently opened methodological pathways to be explored, outside of the orthodoxy that operant behaviorism constitutes. About 1960, for example, I recall having one of my early articles introducing the token reinforcement (economy) system, returned by the editor of an operant behaviorism journal because the response I employed in the study was not a "free-operant." The experimental analysis of behavior then restricted researchers to the operant chamber/cumulative record methodology. It was necessary to break out of that methodological restriction to conduct the other types of behavior modification studies that advanced the field. The same is true today, and will always be true in science. Each conceptual advance, no matter how productive, contains features that are restrictive of other advances, features that must be set aside later on.

THEORETICAL IMPLICATIONS

There are many heuristic implications to be derived from paradigmatic behaviorism's theoretical body that cannot be derived from the two other behavioral approaches. The study of Leduc and Dumais (in press) is a case in point. It was found that the condition of chronic mental ward patients, a majority of whom were schizophrenic, could be improved considerably, in some cases to the point of successful discharge, through learning experiences aimed at repairing deficits in their personality repertoires. The potentialities for the repair of deficit personality repertoires (see also Leduc, 1985; Staats & Burns, 1981) have not yet been exploited, however, only demonstrated.

It should be noted that such developments will require the construction of new instruments with which to assess the state of the personality repertoires. The Staats-Heiby theory (1985), for example, calls for multifaceted development of assessment instruments. It is one thing to suggest that traditional tests of personality can measure important parts of personality repertoires, and another thing to suggest that traditional tests presently fulfill the needs for the measurement of personality repertoires. The field of personality theory has not provided a theoretical basis for the measurement of personality repertoires any more than operant behaviorism or social learning theory have. The various approaches have not produced theories of the constituents of the language–cognitive repertoires, the emotional–motivational repertoires, and the sensory–motor repertoires. These approaches thus do not provide theories to serve as the basis for the construction of instruments to measure these personality repertoires. Paradigmatic behaviorism has certainly not completed the development of the theory of personality involving the three repertoires. But it has provided the prototypical, framework theory (see, for example, Staats, 1968a, 1971a). And this framework calls for the extensive work that is necessary to stipulate specifically of what the personality repertoires, both normal and abnormal, consist. Amassing these data is a large theoretical (and empirical) task that remains to be done. Moreover, paradigmatic behaviorism calls for the stipulation of the other sites of study indicated in Figures 8-1 and 8-2, that is, stipulation of the conditions of the original learning of the personality repertoires, the present situation, the behavioral characteristics, and the stipulation of the effects that behavior has on the individual's social environment and on later behavior. Large theoretical and empirical efforts lie ahead in this type of study, and the products of those efforts will be meaningful for psychology in general, especially if they are unified as in paradigmatic behaviorism.

EMPIRICAL IMPLICATIONS

It is now recognized that a particular approach (or paradigm) in science legitimizes various activities of the scientists who practice within the approach—including what types of problems the scientists consider appropriate and important for study (Kuhn, 1962; Staats, 1983). When the experimental analysis of behavior was being followed, for example, it legitimized a focus on studying behavior in the operant chamber as a function of reinforcement schedules. This work occupied a great proportion of basic research, much of which had no value in advancing behavioral psychology. Nevertheless, the approach constituted a model for applications. Thus, when psychotic behavior was the object of study, the operant chamber was employed and the interest was in how the subjects responded to schedules (Lindsley, 1956). When mental retardates were the objects of study, the interest was in whether or not the responding of these subjects to schedules of reinforcement was similar to the performance one would expect from basic animal learning study (Bijou, 1957). A further extension of this approach in the 1960s, about which the present author only heard second-hand accounts, involved an experiment where a human subject was put into a large "living-quarters" operant chamber, where bar-pressing was necessary for securing all of the subject's wants such as food, drink, entertainment, and so on, toward the goal of studying general human behavior. The teaching machine/programmed instruction work involved a similar methodological technology that defined a set of acceptable problems. Some of these extensions were valuable in contributing to the demonstration that conditioning principles applied to different types of subjects. But the study of human behavior was very much restricted by the framework. For our entrance into the empirical work of behavior modification and behavioral assessment, I saw it to be necessary to break out of the mold (set by the technological problem definition of the operant approach of that vintage), in a manner that was first considered heretical.

The characteristics of every approach set the characteristics of the empirical problems that are legitimized. As paradigmatic behaviorism differs from operant behaviorism and social learning in its theory (and in its philosophy of science), in the methodology it has used and innovated, in the findings of others that it employs in building its structure, it projects different lines of empirical, methodological, and theoretical work that are to be pursued. Basic operant behaviorism heavily legitimized the study of schedules in the operant chamber with a large variety of subjects. Social learning theory emphasized the study of how learning occurs through imitation in a large variety of subjects, situations, and behaviors. And paradigmatic behaviorism likewise has contributed to the formation of contemporary behavioral work and has had its impact on empirical developments in various areas of psychology many of which have been incorporated into and are now considered part of radical behaviorism and social learning theory.

In the field of behavioral assessment, a few projections have already been made in this chapter. A few additional examples can be given. One area in which work has already begun involves studies intended to explain *why* the indirect measures that are used are legitimized within the approach, since radical behaviorism has not done this. Although verbal reports and ratings (see MacPhillamy & Lewinsohn, 1971) are employed in behavioral assessment, we have seen that some investigators in behavioral psychology take the position that such indirect measures are not appropriate. It is thus necessary to show, in basic studies, why the items on indirect measures do index behavioral processes important to the individual's behavior. We cannot rest solely with *opinions* in this issue. Paradigmatic behaviorism calls for empirical–theoretical analysis of the *methods* of personality measurement. It is also necessary to similarly investigate tests that have been constructed within traditional personality approaches. That is, behavioral analysis should be made of all personality tests with the goal of seeing what it is that is measured, in behavioral terms, and why it is important to do so. This is a large research area.

As another example, paradigmatic behaviorism sets the goal of unifying behavioral and traditional knowledge on a yet broader basis. As has been indicated, within the traditional personality concepts of interests, values, intelligence, and so on, there are important aspects of the basic behavioral repertoires. Tests of these personality concepts according to the tenets of paradigmatic behaviorism have involved empirical manipulation of these basic behavioral repertoires, in a manner that is not available in other fields of psychology, including in the field of behavioral assessment. Such empirical specification must be extended very generally to the field of personality, with the aim of producing theories that lend themselves to behavioral assessment and behavior modification manipulation. For example, the Staats-Heiby theory of depression has been the basis for formulating a research project that involves both experimental studies and the development of behavioral assessment instruments (see Kameoka, Heiby, & Staats, 1985). The combination of the paradigmatic behavioral analysis and the knowledge found in the traditional field of personality yields a conceptual body richer than that found in either body of knowledge considered separately. The call for research is clear—we need many studies to specify the personality repertoires, how they are learned, and how they function—and paradigmatic behaviorism has prototypical examples already (Staats, 1971a, 1975; Staats & Burns, 1981, 1982; Staats et al., 1973).

CONCLUSION

The purpose of the present chapter has been to acquaint the audience of behavioral assessors with paradigmatic behaviorism, at least in a beginning way. Presently, many behavioral researchers take their leads only from operantly oriented or social learning theory works. I have stressed that a major framework theory is involved that is different from the radical behaviorism framework theory or the framework theory of social learning. Moreover, the framework theory that paradigmatic behaviorism constitutes contains many projections and guides to further study. Such products cannot be recognized or realized without making a study of the framework theory and its findings, methods, and implications. This framework theory in its formative works contributed important elements to the development of behavioral assessment. This framework theory has continued to develop and now has sufficient research, theory, and method to contribute to various areas of study in behavioral psychology. This framework theory constitutes a behaviorism, as clearly as radical behaviorism. However, it has a much broader horizon, and it legitimatizes types of study and types of knowledge not envisaged in radical behaviorism.

If behaviorism is a science requiring the objective comparison and evaluation of theoretical bodies that have different characteristics but that apply to the same realm of events, then the field of behavioral assessment must invest part of its energies in such efforts, because such different theoretical bodies do exist. In the 1950s, Laffal, Lenkoski, and Ameen (1956) presented a psychodynamic interpretation of a schizophrenic's bizarre language, in which they stated that learning approaches had nothing to offer in considering such clinical problems—a generally accepted position of that time. In making the first behavioral analysis of schizophrenic language, one of the present author's objectives was to show the error of this position. He thus concluded this analysis by saying that the learning (behavioral) approach had much to offer in dealing with clinical problems and that the approach could "no longer be ignored" (Staats, 1957, p. 269). Two years later the first United States behavior modification studies of the modern era began to appear, one of the most influential done by two behaviorist colleagues, closely associated with early paradigmatic behaviorism (Ayllon & Michael, 1959). In the early 1970s the present author (Staats, 1972) outlined why verbal psychotherapy (called "language behavior therapy" and "cognitive behavior therapy" in the analysis) had an important role to play in behavior therapy and behavior analysis. Although radical behaviorists strongly criticized this analysis (see Tryon, 1974) and later ignored it, within a few years the field of cognitive behavior modification became a vigorously active part of our field, unfortunately using an eclectic approach instead of the real behaviorism.

The message today is similar: A conceptual-empirical-methodological structure exists in paradigmatic behaviorism that projects important new lines of development. This structure is presently shut out in the same way the general behavioral approach was shut out by psychodynamic psychology in the 1950s. Whether the newer behavioral structure has important things to contribute to various behavioral areas can only be established through systematic examination, by behavioral psychologists who have invested an appropriate effort in learning to use the structure. We have the beginnings of a paradigmatic behavioral abnormal psychology (see Staats, 1975, Chapter 8; Staats & Heiby, 1985; Kameoka et al., 1985), of a paradigmatic behavior therapy (see Evans, in press; Leduc, 1984; Staats, 1972; 1975, Chapters 9, 10, 11; 1979), and of a paradigmatic behavioral assessment (see Burns, 1980; Staats, 1975, Chapter 12; Staats & Burns, 1981, 1982; Staats et al., 1973). It is now time to say again—and a major objective of this chapter is to say it—this behavioral approach should no longer be ignored.

ACKNOWLEDGMENT

The author wishes to express appreciation to Donald M. Topping, Director of the Social Science Research Institute, for support that enabled this chapter to be written.

REFERENCES

Allport, G. W., Vernon, P. E., & Lindzey, G. (1951). *Study of values* (rev. ed.). Boston: Houghton-Mifflin.

Allyon, T., & Michael, J. (1959). The psychiatric nurse as a behavioral Engineer. *The Journal of Experimental Analysis of Behavior, 2,* 323–334.

Bandura, A. (1968). A social learning interpretation of psychological dysfunctions. In P. London & D. Rosenhan (Eds.), *Foundations of abnormal psychology*. New York: Holt, Rinehart & Winston, pp. 293–344.

Bandura, A. (1969). *Principles of behavior modification*. New York: Holt, Rinehart & Winston.

Bandura, A. (1971). *Psychological modeling*. Chicago: Aldine-Atherton.

Bandura, A. (1977a). *Social learning theory*. Englewood Cliffs, NJ: Prentice-Hall.

Bandura, A. (1977b). Self-efficacy: Toward a unifying theory of behavioral change. *Psychological Review, 84,* 191–215.

Bandura, A. (1978). The self-system in reciprocal determinism. *American Psychologist, 33,* 344–358.

Bandura, A., & Walters, R. (1963). *Social learning and personality*. New York: Holt, Rinehart & Winston.

Bem, D. J., & Allen, A. (1974). On predicting some of the people some of the time: The search for cross-situational consistencies in behavior. *Psychological Review, 81,* 506–520.

Bijou, S. W. (1957). Patterns of reinforcement and resistance to in young children. *Child Development, 28,* 47–54.

Block, J. (1971). *Lives through time*. Berkeley, CA: Bancroft Books.

Block, J. (1977). Advancing the psychology of personality: Paradigmatic shift or improving the quality of research. In D. Magnusson and N. S. Endler (Eds.), *Personality at the crossroads: Current issues in interactional psychology* (pp. 37–63). Hillsdale, NJ: Lawrence Erlbaum.

Bowers, K. S. (1973). Situationism in psychology: An analysis and a critique. *Psychological Review, 80,* 307–336.

Burns, G. L. (1980). Indirect measurement and behavioral assessment: A case for social behaviorism psychometrics. *Behavioral Assessment, 2,* 196–216.

Ciminero, A. R., Calhoun, K. S., & Adams, H. R. (Eds.) (1977). *Handbook of behavioral assessment*. New York: John Wiley & Sons.

Cofer, C. N., & Foley, J. P. (1942). Mediated generalization and the interpretation of verbal behavior. I. Prolegomena. *Psychological Review, 49,* 513–540.

Collette-Harris, M., & Minke, K. A. (1978). A behavioral experimental analysis of dyslexia. *Behaviour Research and Therapy, 16,* 291–295.

Cone, J. D., & Hawkins, R. P. (Eds.) (1977). *Behavioral assessment: New directions in clinical psychology*. New York: Brunner/Mazel.

Dollard, J., & Miller, N. E. (1950). *Personality and psychotherapy*. New York: McGraw-Hill.

Edwards, A. (1953). *Edwards Personal Preference Schedule*. New York: Psychological Corporation.

Endler, N. S., & Magnusson, D. (1976). Toward an interactional psychology of personality. *Psychological Bulletin, 83,* 956–974.

Epstein, R. (1984). Simulation research in the analysis of behavior. *Behaviorism, 12,* 41–59.

Epstein, S. (1979). The stability of behavior: I. On predicting most of the people much of the time. *Journal of Personality and Social Psychology, 37,* 1097–1126.

Evans, I. (Ed.) (in press). *Paradigmatic behavior therapy*. New York: Springer.

Eysenck, J. J. (1960). *Behaviour therapy and the neuroses*. New York: Pergamon Press.

Fernandez-Ballesteros, R. (1983). *Evaluacion conductual*. Madrid, Spain: Piramide.

Finley, J. R., & Staats, A. W. (1967). Evaluative meaning words as reinforcing stimuli. *Journal of Verbal Learning and Verbal Behavior, 6,* 193–197.

Gilmor, T. M. & Minton, H. L. (1974). Internal versus external attribution of task performance as a function of locus of control, initial confidence and success-failure outcome. *Journal of Personality, 42,* 159–174.

Goldfried, M. S., & Sprafkin, J. N. (1974). Behavioral personality assessment. *Behavioral approaches to therapy*. Morristown, NJ: General Learning Press.

Harms, J. Y., & Staats, A. W. (1978). Food deprivation and conditioned reinforcing value of food words: Interaction of Pavlovian and instrumental conditioning. *Bulletin of the Psychonomic Society, 12,* 294–296.

Hart, B. M., Allen, K. E., Buell, J. S., Harris, F. R., & Wolf, M. M. (1964). Effects of social reinforcement on operant crying. *Journal of Experimental Child Psychology, 1,* 145–153.

Hartshorne, H., & May, M. A. (1928). *Studies in the nature of character: Vol. 1. Studies in deceit*. New York: MacMillan.

Hartshorne, H., & May, M. A. (1929). *Studies in the nature of character: Vol. 2. Studies in service and self-control.* New York: MacMillan.

Haynes, S. N. (1978). *Principles of behavioral assessment.* New York: Gardner Press.

Heiby, E. M., & Staats, A. W. (in press). Classification of depression. In I. Evans (Ed.), *Paradigmatic behavior therapy: Critical perspectives on applied social behaviorism.* New York: Springer.

Hekmat, H. (in press). Language behavior therapy of anxiety disorders. In I. Evans (Ed.), *Paradigmatic behavior therapy.* New York: Springer

Herry, M., & Leduc, A. (1981). The principle of higher-order instrumental conditioning in Staats learning theory. *International Newsletter of Social Behaviorism, 1,* 5-13.

Hersen, M., & Barlow, D. (1977). *Single case experimental designs.* New York: Pergamon Press.

Hersen, M., & Bellack, A. S. (Eds.). (1976). *Behavioral assessment: A practical handbook.* New York: Pergamon Press.

Hull, C. L. (1930). Knowledge and purpose as habit mechanisms. *Psychological Review, 37,* 511-525.

Judson, A. J., Cofer, C. N., & Gelfand, S. (1956). Reasoning as an associative process: II. "Direction" in problem solving as a function of prior reinforcement of relevant responses. *Psychological Reports, 2,* 501-507.

Kameoka, V. A., Heiby, E. M., & Staats, A. W. (1985). Vulnerability for depression in a high risk population. Research grant application Department of Health and Human Services, Public Health Service.

Kanfer, F. H., & Saslow, G. (1965). Behavioral analyses. *Archives of General Psychiatry, 12,* 529-538.

Kenrick, D. T., & Stringfield, D. O. (1980). Personality traits and the eye of the beholder: Crossing some traditional philosophical boundaries in the search for consistency in all of the people. *Psychological Review, 87,* 88-104.

Kimble, G. A. Psychology's two cultures. (1984). *American Psychologist, 39,* 833-839.

Kuhn, T. S. (1962). *The structure of scientific revolutions.* Chicago: University of Chicago Press.

Laffal, J., Lenkoski, L. D., & Ameen, L. (1956). "Opposite Speech" in a schizophrenic patient. *Journal of Abnormal and Social Psychology, 52,* 409-413.

Leduc, A. (1984). *Recherches sur le behaviorisme paradigmatique ou social.* Quebec: Behaviora.

Leduc, A. (1985). Accelerated socialization of a "Wild Child." Invited address presented at the annual convention of the Association for Behavioral Analysis, Columbus, Ohio.

Leduc, A., & Dumais, A. (in press). Applications of social behaviorism in psychiatric institutional settings. In I. Evans (Ed.), *Paradigmatic behavior therapy.* New York: Springer.

Lewin, K. (1935). *A dynamic theory of personality.* New York: McGraw-Hill.

Lindsley, O. R. (1956). Operant conditioning methods applied to research in chronic schizophrenia. *Psychiatric Research Reports, 5,* 140-153.

Lovaas, O. I. (1966). A behavior therapy approach to the treatment of childhood schizophrenia. In J. P. Hill (Ed.), *Minnesota symposium on child psychology* (Vol. I, pp. 108-159). Minneapolis: University of Minnesota Press.

MacKenzie, B. D. (1977). *Behaviorism and the limits of scientific method.* Atlantic Highlands, NJ: Humanities Press.

MacPhillamy, D. J., & Lewinsohn, P. M. (1971). *Pleasant Events Schedule.* Unpublished manuscript, University of Oregon, Engers, Oregon.

Magnusson, D., & Endler, S. (1977). Interactional psychology: Present status and future prospects. In D. Magnusson and N. S. Endler (Eds.), *Personality at the crossroads: Current issues in interactional psychology* (pp. 3-31). Hillsdale, N.J.: Lawrence Erlbaum.

Maltzman, I. (1955). Thinking: From a behavioristic point of view. *Psychological Review, 62,* 275-286.

Miller, N. E., & Dollard, J. (1941). *Social learning and imitation.* New Haven: Yale University Press.

Minke, K. A. (in press). A comparative analysis of modern general behaviorisms: Unification by generational advance. In A. W. Staats and L. P. Mos (Eds.), *Annals of theoretical psychology* (*Vol. 5*). New York: Plenum.

Mischel, W. (1968). *Personality and assessment.* New York: Holt, Rinehart & Winston.

Mischel, W. (1972). Direct versus indirect personality assessment: Evidence and implications. *Journal of Consulting and Clinical Psychology, 38*, 319–324.

Mischel, W. (1973). Toward a cognitive social learning reconceptualization of personality. *Psychological Review, 80*, 252–283.

Mischel, W. (1977). On the future of personality measurement. *American Psychologist, 32*, 246–254.

Mowrer, O. H. (1950). *Learning theory and personality dynamics*. New York: Ronald Press.

Mowrer, O. H. (1954). The psychologist looks at language. *American Psychologist, 9*, 660–694.

Newcomb, T. M. (1929). *Consistency of certain extrovert–introvert patterns in 51 problem boys*. New York: Columbia University Teachers College, Bureau of Publications.

Olweus, D. (1972). Personality and aggression. In J. K. Cole & D. D. Jensen (Eds.), *Nebraska symposium on motivation* (Vol. 20, pp. 261–321). Lincoln: University of Nebraska Press.

Olweus, D. (1974). Personality factors and aggression: With special reference to violence within the peer group. In J. de Wit & W. W. Hartup (Eds.), *Determinants and origins of aggressive behavior* (pp. 535–565). The Hague, Netherlands: Mouton.

Olweus, D. (1977a). A critical analysis of the "modern" interactionist position. In D. Magnusson & N. S. Endler (Eds.), *Personality at the crossroads: Current issues in interactional psychology* (pp. 221–233). Hillsdale, NJ: Lawrence Erlbaum.

Olweus, D. (1977b). Aggression and peer acceptance in preadolescent boys. *Child Development, 48*, 1301–1313.

Osgood, C. E. (1953). *Method and theory in experimental psychology*. New York: Oxford University Press.

Razran, G. H. (1939a). A quantitative study of meaning by a conditioned salivary technique (semantic conditioning). *Science, 90*, 89–90.

Razran, G. H. (1939b). The nature of the extinctive process. *Psychological Review, 46*, 337–365.

Rotter, J. (1954). *Social learning and clinical psychology*. Englewood Cliffs, NJ: Prentice-Hall.

Rushton, J. P., Jackson, D. N., & Paunonen, S. V. (1981). Personality: Nomothetic or ideographic? A response to Kendrick and Stringfield. *Psychological Review, 88*, 582–589.

Ryback, D., & Staats, A. W. (1970). Parents as behavior therapy-technicians in treating reading deficits (dyslexia). *Journal of Behavior Therapy and Experimental Psychiatry, 1*, 109–119.

Serban, G. (1980). *Adjustment of schizophrenics in the community*. New York: SP Medical and Scientific Books.

Silverstein, M. L. (1981). Schizophrenics—From the back ward through the revolving door. *Contemporary Psychology, 26*, 599–601.

Skinner, B. F. (1953). *Science and human behavior*. New York: MacMillan.

Skinner, B. F. (1957). *Verbal behavior*. New York: Appleton-Century-Crofts.

Skinner, B. F. (1969). *Contingencies of reinforcement*. New York: Appleton-Century-Crofts.

Skinner, B. F. (1975). The steep and thorny way to a science of behavior. *American Psychologist, 30*, 42–49.

Snider, J. G., & Osgood, C. E. (1969). *Semantic differential technique*. Chicago: Aldine.

Spence, K. W. (1944). The nature of theory construction in contemporary psychology. *Psychological Review, 51*, 47–68.

Staats, A. W. (1956). A behavioristic study of verbal and instrumental response hierarchies and their relationship to human problem solving. Unpublished doctoral dissertation, University of California, Los Angeles.

Staats, A. W. (1957a). Learning theory and "opposite speech." *Journal of Abnormal and Social Psychology, 55*, 268–269.

Staats, A. W. (1957b). Verbal and instrumental response hierarchies and their relationship to problem solving. *American Journal of Psychology, 70*, 442–446.

Staats, A. W. (1961). Verbal habit families, concepts, and the operant conditioning of word classes. *Psychological Review, 68*, 190–204.

Staats, A. W. (with contributions by C. K. Staats) (1963). *Complex human behavior*. New York: Holt, Rinehart & Winston.

Staats, A. W. (1964). *Human learning*. New York: Holt, Rinehart & Winston.

Staats, A. W. (1968a). *Learning, language, and cognition*. New York: Holt, Rinehart & Winston.

Staats, A. W. (1968b). Social behaviorism and human motivation: Principles of the attitude-reinforcer-discriminative system. In A. G. Greenwald, T. C. Brock, & T. M. Ostrom (Eds.), *Psychological foundations of attitudes* (pp. 33–66). New York: Academic Press.

Staats, A. W. (1970). A learning-behavior theory: A basis for unity in behavioral-social science. In A. R. Gilgen (Ed.), *Contemporary scientific psychology* (pp. 183–239). New York: Academic Press.

Staats, A. W. (1971a). *Child learning, intelligence and personality*. New York: Harper & Row.

Staats, A. W. (1971b). Linguistic-mentalistic theory versus an explanatory S-R learning theory of language development. In D. I. Slobin (Ed.), *The ontogenesis of grammar* (pp. 103–150). New York: Academic Press.

Staats, A. W. (1972). Language behavior therapy: A derivative of social behaviorism. *Behavior Therapy, 3*, 165–192.

Staats, A. W. (1975). *Social behaviorism*. Homewood, Il: Dorsey Press.

Staats, A. W. (1977). Experimental-longitudinal methods in assessment, research and treatment. *Journal of Abnormal Child Psychology, 5*, 323–332.

Staats, A. W. (1979). The three-function learning theory of social behaviorism: *Learning and Behavior, 2*, 13–38.

Staats, A. W. (1980). 'Behavioral interaction' and 'interactional psychology' theories of personality: Similarities, differences, and the need for unification. *British Journal of Psychology, 71*, 205–220.

Staats, A. W. (1981). Paradigmatic behaviorism, unified theory, unified theory construction methods, and the zeitgeist of separatism. *American Psychologist, 36*, 239–256.

Staats, A. W. (1983a). *Psychology's crisis of disunity: Philosophy and method for a unified science*. New York: Praeger.

Staats, A. W. (1983b). Paradigmatic behaviorism: Unified theory for social–personality psychology. In L. Berkowitz (Ed.), *Advances in experimental social psychology* (pp. 126–179). New York: Academic Press.

Staats, A. W., Brewer, B. A., & Gross, M. C. (1970). Learning and cognitive development: Representative samples, cumulative-hierarchical learning, and experimental-longitudinal methods. *Monographs of the Society for Research in Child Development, 35*, (8, Whole No. 141), 1–85.

Staats, A. W., & Burns, G. L. (1981). Intelligence and child development: What intelligence is and how it is learned and functions. *Genetic Psychology Monographs, 104*, 237–301.

Staats, A. W., & Burns, G. L. (1982). Personality specification and interaction theory. *Journal of Personality and Social Psychology, 43*, 873–881.

Staats, A. W., & Butterfield, W. H. (1965). Treatment of nonreading in a culturally-deprived juvenile delinquent: An application of reinforcement principles. *Child Development, 26*, 925–942.

Staats, A. W., Finley, J. R., Minke, K. A., & Wolf, M. M. (1964). Reinforcement variables in the control of unit reading responses. *Journal of the Experimental Analysis of Behavior, 7*, 139–149.

Staats, A. W., Gross, M. C., Guay, P. F., & Carlson, C. C. (1973). Personality and social systems and attitude-reinforcer-discriminative theory: Interest (attitude) formation, function, and measurement. *Journal of Personality and Social Psychology, 26*, 251–261.

Staats, A. W., & Hammond, O. W. (1972). Natural words as physiological conditioned stimuli: Food-word-elicited salivation and deprivation effects. *Journal of Experimental Psychology, 96*, 206–208.

Staats, A. W., & Heiby, E. (1985). Paradigmatic behaviorism's theory of depression: Unified, explanatory, and heuristic. In S. Reiss & R. Bootzin (Eds.) *Theoretical issues in behavior therapy*. New York: Academic Press.

Staats, A. W., Minke, K. A., & Butts, P. (1970). A token-reinforcement remedial reading program administered by black instructional technicians to backward black children. *Behavior Therapy, 1*, 331–353.

Staats, A. W., Minke, K. A., Finley, J. R., Wolf, M. M., & Brooks, L. O. (1964). A reinforcer system and experimental procedure for the laboratory study of reading acquisition. *Child Development*, *35*, 209–231.

Staats, A. W., Minke, K. A., Martin, C. H., & Higa, W. R. (1972). Deprivation-satiation and strength of attitude conditioning: A test of attitude-reinforcer-directive theory. *Journal of Personality and Social Psychology*, *24*, 178–185.

Staats, C. K., & Staats, A. W. (1957). Meaning established by classical conditioning. *Journal of Experimental Psychology*, *54*, 74–80.

Staats, A. W., & Staats, C. K. (1958). Attitudes established by classical conditioning. *Journal of Abnormal and Social Psychology*, *57*, 37–40.

Staats, A. W., Staats, C. K., & Biggs, D. A. (1958). Meaning of verbal stimuli changed by conditioning. *American Journal of Psychology*, *71*, 429–431.

Staats, A. W., Staats, C. K., & Crawford, H. L. (1962). First-order conditioning of a GSR and the parallel conditioning of meaning. *Journal of General Psychology*, *67*, 159–167.

Staats, A. W., Staats, C. K., Heard, W. G., & Finley, J. R. (1962). Operant conditioning of factor analytic personality traits. *Journal of General Psychology*, *66*, 101–114.

Staats, A. W., Staats, C. K., Schutz, R. E., & Wolf, M. M. (1962). The conditioning of reading responses using "extrinsic" reinforcers. *Journal of the Experimental Analysis of Behavior*, *5*, 33–40.

Staats, A. W., & Warren, D. R. (1974). Motivation and three-function learning: Deprivation-satiation and approach-avoidance to food words. *Journal of Experimental Psychology*, *103*, 1191–1199.

Strong, E. K., Jr. (1952). *Vocational interest blank for men: Manual*. Stanford, Ca: Stanford University Press.

Tolman, E. C. (1951) The intervening variable. In M. H. Marx (Ed.), *Psychological theory* (pp. 87–102). New York: MacMillan.

Tryon, W. W. (1974). A reply to Staat's language behavior therapy: A derivative of social behaviorism. *Behavior Therapy*, *5*, 273–276.

Ullmann, L. P., & Krasner, L. (1969). *A psychological approach to abnormal behavior*. Englewood Cliffs, NJ: Prentice-Hall.

Wachtel, P. L. (1973). Psychodynamics, behavior therapy and the implacable experimenter: An inquiry into the consistency of personality. *Journal of Abnormal Psychology*, *82*, 324–334.

Watson, J. B. (1930). *Behaviorism*. (rev. ed.) Chicago: University of Chicago Press.

Wechsler, D. (1967). *Wechsler Preschool and Primary Scale of Intelligence*. New York: Psychological Corporation.

Woll, S. (1978). The best of both worlds? A critique of cognitive social learning. Unpublished manuscript, California State University, Fullerton, California.

9

PHYSIOLOGIC VARIABLES

DONALD A. WILLIAMSON
WILLIAM F. WATERS
MIKE F. HAWKINS
Louisiana State University

"Nothing is more certain than that our behavior is a product of our nervous system" (Bower & Hilgard, 1981, p. 745). This statement is so widely accepted in psychology that it is often considered to be a truism. Yet, as Bower & Hilgard (1981) have noted, throughout the history of psychology there has been a consistent bias against neurophysiologic explanations of behavior. This bias has been especially strong within the conceptual framework of radical behaviorism (Skinner, 1950, 1974). As Skinner (1950) pointed out, many earlier physiologic theories of behavior were based more upon the "conceptual nervous system" than the central nervous system (CNS).

Despite this apparent bias, behaviorism has in many respects always based much of its framework within the physiologic and biological domain. The inclusion of physiologic events in behavioral theory is especially obvious within the paradigm of classical conditioning (Hall, 1966, Pavlov, 1927, Razran, 1961). However, even in operant conditioning the potential importance of physiologic processes has never been denied. As Skinner (1974) has noted, the objection of behaviorism to physiologic explanations has been more methodological than philosophical. Only recently, has technology advanced to the point that events "within the skin" can be measured reliably. For this reason, Skinner (1974) acknowledged the need for inclusion of physiologic variables in a comprehensive analysis of behavior.

Following the lead of their experimental colleagues, early behavior therapists tended to focus almost exclusively on the assessment of overt motor behavior (Kazdin, 1978). Although several early behavioral studies did include psychophysiologic assessment (e.g., Paul, 1969; Paul & Trimble, 1970; Waters, McDonald, & Koresko, 1972), the emphasis of the 1960s and early 1970s was clearly upon assessing behavior, not physiology. A slight shift in emphasis has been apparent from the mid-1970s to the present. The increased interest of behavior therapists in the assessment of physiologic and biological variables was spurred by the dramatic growth of behavioral medicine during the late 1970s. In general, as behavior therapists became more involved in treating medical and health problems, the assessment of biological and behavioral responses relevant to these problem areas began to receive more attention (Russo, Bird, & Masek, 1980).

A review of the behavioral literature indicates only a few attempts to integrate biological and behavioral conceptualizations for specific pathologic conditions, for example, for migraine headaches (Cinciripini, Williamson, & Epstein, 1981; Williamson, 1981) and for hypertension (Schwartz, Shapiro, Redmond, Ferguson, Ragland, & Weiss, 1979). The purpose of this chapter is to propose a general biobehavioral model of human behavior that can be used as a conceptual framework for behavioral assessment in a variety of medical and psychiatric disorders. Before discussing this model, an overview of basic neuroanatomy and physiology is presented for purposes of review. A later subsection, a biobehavioral model of human behavior, discusses assessment in terms of this conceptual model.

BASIC NEUROANATOMY AND PHYSIOLOGY

THE NEURON

The human nervous system comprises more than 10 billion neurons (Ganong, 1975). A neuron is an individual nerve cell with the specialized function of responding to a variety of stimuli through the transmission of nerve impulses. Neurons respond by releasing neurotransmitters into the junction between neurons, which is called the synapse. Neurotransmitters influence adjacent neurons by changing the neurons' membrane permeability to sodium and potassium ions. If the exchange of ions is sufficiently large, the result is depolarization of the postsynaptic neural membrane and the generation of an action potential at the axon. This action potential is propagated along the axon of the neuron, resulting in the release of neurotransmitters into the next synapse and continuation of the neural signal. There are probably many neurotransmitters, including acetylcholine; the biogenic amines, for example, norepinephrine, dopamine, and serotonin; the neuropeptides, for example, the enkephalins and substance P; and the amino acids, for example, glycine (Ganong, 1975; Krieger & Martin, 1981; Snyder, 1980). In general, some neurotransmitters facilitate neural transmission, while others inhibit neural transmission.

ANATOMY AND PHYSIOLOGY OF THE NERVOUS SYSTEM

The nervous system is commonly divided into two divisions: central and peripheral. The CNS is composed of the neurons enclosed within the skull and spinal column. The peripheral nervous system is made up of the neurons outside these bony structures. The peripheral nervous system is commonly subdivided into the autonomic nervous system (ANS) and the somatic nervous system. Both of these divisions contain specialized receptor neurons for senses such as somatosensory, visual, auditory, olfactory, and taste receptors, as well as the receptors for internal stimuli, that is, interoceptors and proprioceptors. The sensory systems are responsible for transforming energy from the external and internal environments into a neural signal that can be deciphered by the CNS.

The ANS regulates the glands, cardiac muscle, and the smooth muscle in the blood vessels and visceral organs. The ANS can be subdivided into two systems: sympathetic and parasympathetic. The sympathetic division of the ANS can be considered a catabolic system because its activation increases the body's use of energy. Stimulation of the sympathetic nervous system produces a constellation of effects that the pioneering physiologist Walter B. Cannon (1945) described as preparing the animal for "fight or flight." These effects include increased heart rate, respiration, blood sugar, and sweating. The parasympathetic division is an anabolic, rather than a catabolic, system. Parasympathetic activity is associated with such energy-saving responses as decreased heart rate, respiration, and metabolic rate, and increased digestion and salivation. Therefore, the sympathetic and parasympathetic nervous systems activate smooth muscles, cardiovascular tissue, and glands to produce opposing responses. The dynamic interaction of these responses maintains the balance of the body's internal milieu.

Major biological systems necessary for the maintenance of life are innervated by the sympathetic and parasympathetic divisions of the ANS. Furthermore, with the possible exceptions of the blood vessels in the lungs, kidneys, gastrointestinal tract, and brain, and the sweat glands, all of the major organs and glands are innvervated by both sympathetic and parasympathetic branches of the ANS (Ganong, 1975). Therefore, measurement of the activity of these systems can be conceptualized as indirect measurement of basic ANS activity (Kallman & Feuerstein, 1977).

The somatic division of the peripheral nervous system innervates the striated (skeletal) musculature. These muscles control voluntary movement and posture. When muscle tissue is stimulated via the motor pathways, muscle fibers respond by contracting. The electrical activity associated with muscle contraction can be recorded with electromyography (Basmajian, 1962).

For a more complete discussion of the nervous system, the reader may wish to refer to basic physiology texts such as Ganong (1975) or Guyton (1976).

A BIOBEHAVIORAL MODEL OF HUMAN BEHAVIOR

As indicated in the preceding section, research and knowledge concerning the physiologic basis of behavior have been expanding rapidly. Though numerous texts of physiologic psychology (e.g., Brown & Wallace, 1980; Kalat, 1980) and behavioral psychology (e.g., Bandura, 1977; Skinner, 1974) have discussed their respective areas of research in great detail, there has been no attempt to draw together this information in a manner that integrates both behavioral and physiologic principles within the context of behavioral assessment. The purpose of this chapter is to present a biobehavioral model of human behavior that integrates behavioral and biological principles. The utility of this biobehavioral model is that it forms the basis for a conceptual framework by which the assessment of physiologic variables fits within the traditional "SORC" model of behavioral psychology Stimulus-Organism-Response-Consequence (Kanfer & Phillips, 1970). It should be noted that this model is an elaboration of the current model for behavioral assessment (Nelson & Barlow, 1981; Nelson & Hayes, 1979) in that it expands upon the physiological component of the triple-response system of motor behavior, cognitive–verbal behavior, and physiologic–emotional behavior.

Figure 9-1 summarizes this biobehavioral model. The format for the model is as follows. Physiologic systems and responses are enclosed within the box and thus should be regarded as organismic variables and responses. Outside the organism are the traditional components of the behavioral model, that is, situational variables or antecedent conditions, overt motor behavior, and the consequences of behavior. Lines with arrows refer to the interactions among biological systems, environmental conditions, and overt behavior. Situational variables within this model refer to antecedent conditions that are external to the organism. These stimuli are received by exteroceptors and teleceptors. Likewise, internal stimuli are received by interoceptors and proprioceptors. This sensory information is then processed by the higher integrative systems which in turn activate the effector systems, that is, the somatic nervous system and/or the ANS. These effector systems produce specific biological responses that then stimulate the interoceptors and proprioceptors that serve the function of an internal feedback loop. As shown in Figure 9-1, all of the biological systems can be influenced by the current condition of the organism, which may be either permanent

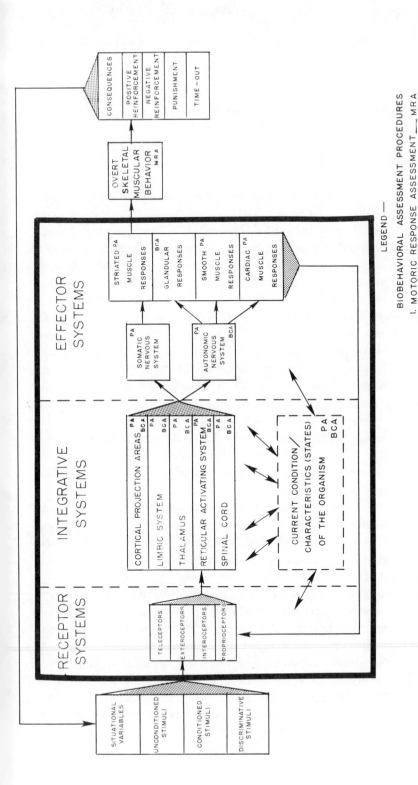

FIG. 9-1. A biobehavioral model of human behavior.

301

characteristics or temporary states. Striated muscular responses may produce overt skeletal muscular behavior that results in certain types of consequences that may be external to the organism, for example, altering the
environment, or internal, for example, reducing ANS activity. These consequences form the basis of response-produced external or internal feedback.

SITUATIONAL VARIABLES

Though perhaps a trivial point, it must be recognized that before the occurrence of any behavior, a set of antecedent conditions always exists. As has
been pointed out by many behavioral (Skinner, 1974) and personality (e.g.,
Mischel, 1973) theorists, these antecedent or situational variables can have a
significant influence upon the individual's behavior. In the most general
sense, these situations can be categorized as either stimulus conditions that
elicit behavior, or stimulus conditions that set the occasion for behavior.

Situations or stimulus conditions that elicit behavior include unconditioned stimuli or conditioned stimuli. The common characteristic of these
types of antecedent conditions is that presentation of the stimulus or situation reliably produces an occurrence of behavior. The behavior may be either
autonomic or somatic. Also the association between the stimulus and response may be innate, as in the case of reflexive behavior (unconditioned
responses), or it may have been conditioned, as in the case of classically
conditioned behavior (conditioned responses). Conditioned or unconditioned
stimuli can elicit a wide array of responses. For example, presentation of food
cues can elicit salivation. Presentation of particular sexual stimuli can elicit
penile tumescence in males and increased vaginal blood flow in females
(Barlow, 1977). Also, conditioned and unconditioned stimuli can function as
stressors, (e.g., dangerous stimuli), or as the antecedents of anxiety, (e.g.,
phobic stimuli). In such cases, the conditioned response or unconditioned
response is said to be a conditioned or unconditioned stress response or a
conditioned or unconditioned emotional response.

Situations or stimulus conditions that set the occasion for behavior have
typically been labeled discriminative stimuli in the operant conditioning
literature (Millenson & Leslie, 1979). Discriminative stimuli are antecedent
conditions that function as a signal for the contingency between behavior
and probable consequences, such as reinforcement and punishment. According to traditional behavioral theory, discriminative stimuli can be differentiated from stimuli that elicit behavior. That is, discriminative stimuli do
not reliably produce behavior unless the stimulus is highly correlated with
either the availability of either environmental reinforcement or punishment.

From a biobehavioral perspective, distinguishing between discriminative stimuli and conditioned or unconditioned stimuli is much more difficult. For all three types of stimuli, both CNS or ANS responses are usually elicited, for example, in the case of the orienting response, and often skeletal muscular behavior occurs, which in turn has specific consequences. Therefore, technically speaking, it is very difficult to distinguish one type of stimulus from another in terms of elicited versus emitted behavior. Instead, the biobehavioral model proposes a behavior–analytic approach by which stimulus–response relationships can be observed or assessed from a variety of levels ranging from cellular to organismic response changes. This behavior–analytic approach obviates the necessity for proposing two or more types of learning or even two types of behavior, for example, operant versus reflexive. We believe that this approach is both more parsimonious and more in line with current biological and behavioral research (Miller, 1978; Williamson & Blanchard, 1979a,b).[1]

One widely observed phenomenon in the learning literature is that despite the fact that most situational variables are a complex of stimuli that vary in terms of physical characteristics, sensory modality, time, and many other dimensions, only certain elements of the situation are related to the production of behavior (Levine, 1975; Reynolds, 1961). Most current theorists have proposed that the learning of this type of stimulus control is mediated by the mechanisms of selective attention (Rösler, 1981), which themselves are altered by changes in stimulation and by learning (Waters & Wright, 1979).

Changes in situational variables are monitored by receptors of various types. This information is then relayed to the CNS where it is integrated to allow effectors to initiate a coordinated response. The following section describes the types of receptors with which humans are equipped, how the CNS integrates sensory information, and what effector responses can result.

RECEPTOR SYSTEMS

Information about our external and internal environments is monitored by neuronal cells that are specialized to detect and convert energy. These specialized cells are the sensory receptors. Receptors have the ability to transduce a wide variety of energies into the electrochemical "language" of

1. It should be noted that other behavioral theorists (e.g., Guthrie, 1935; Hall, 1966) have also questioned the distinction between classical and operant conditioning. However, their reservations have been based on paradigmative rather than neurophysiological bases.

the nervous system. They differ from one another in the type of energy to which they are maximally sensitive. For example, the receptors in the retina respond most readily to light energy while others, such as those in the skin and some in the brain itself, are more sensitive to changes in temperature. However, these differences in sensitivity are relative rather than absolute. That is, even though a sensory receptor responds maximally to one type of energy, it will also respond to other forms of energy if the strength of the stimulus is sufficiently great (Carpenter, 1978, Guyton, 1976). Sufficient pressure on the closed eyelid, for example, will stimulate the photoreceptors of the retina and produce a sensation of spots of light. Similarly, all receptors that have been identified to date can be stimulated with electrical current.

Changes in the external environment are monitored by receptors for vision, hearing, smell, taste, and the various skin senses such as pressure, pain, and temperature. Receptors of this type are classified as teleceptors or as exteroceptors depending upon the distance from the body of the source of stimulation. Teleceptors respond to stimuli that originate at a greater distance. The receptors in the eyes, ears, and nose are teleceptors. Exteroceptors are responsive to external stimuli closer to the body. Examples include receptors for taste, and for the skin senses.

In addition to our ability to monitor changes in the external environment, we also possess interoceptors and proprioceptors which are sensitive to internal stimuli (Carpenter, 1978). Interoceptors are located in organs of the body. These include, but are not limited to, such organs as the gastrointestinal tract, heart, blood vessels, and lung. Interoceptors monitor the activities of various functions such as digestion, blood pressure, and respiration. Proprioceptors provide information about the position and movement of the body in space. They are located in the muscles, tendons, and joints, and in the semicircular canals of the inner ear.

While all of the receptors that register changes in external stimuli produce perceptible sensations, some changes in internal events are not commonly perceived despite the fact that these changes are detected by interoceptors or proprioceptors. Examples include changes in muscle length and tension, blood pressure, and the chemical composition of blood perfusing the brain. Several theories of biofeedback training have suggested that external biofeedback may produce improved ability to discriminate these internal stimuli (Brener, 1974; Williamson & Blanchard, 1979b).

Information from all sensory receptors is transmitted to the CNS (the brain and spinal cord). The sensation that one experiences ultimately depends upon the part of the brain to which the sensory fibers are projected. For example, in vision, stimulation of the optic nerve will produce the sensation of light, whether or not light has actually stimulated the retina. Similarly, stimulation of any portion of the optic tract from its origin at the optic chiasm, through relay nuclei of the thalamus, to its termination in the occipital cortex, will produce the same sensation. This phenomenon applies to all of the sensory modalities and is known as the doctrine of specific nerve energies. It was first proposed by the 19th-century German physiologist, Johannes Müller (1842). Müller's doctrine remains one of the fundamental laws of physiology, and it illustrates the importance of CNS integration of sensory information.

INTEGRATIVE SYSTEMS

Neural information from sensory receptors reaches the CNS via the cranial nerves or the spinal nerves. The cranial nerves carry impulses from the so-called "special" senses; that is, from sensory receptors located in the head. The special senses and their associated cranial nerves (c.n.) are as follows: smell (c.n. 1), sight (c.n. 2), taste (c.n. 7, 9, and 10), and hearing (c.n. 8). There are a total of 12 pairs of cranial nerves. In addition to information from the special senses, these nerves also transmit impulses from other types of sensory receptors. These senses include pain, temperature, and touch receptors in the head and neck. The tenth cranial nerve (the vagus nerve) also provides sensory information from receptors in the thoracic and abdominal viscera. Many of the cranial nerves also carry information back to sense organs that permits adjustments for optimizing sensation.

Sensory input from the rest of the body enters the CNS through the spinal cord via 31 pairs of spinal nerves. These nerves enter the spinal cord through the dorsal surface and transfer the sensory message either to fiber tracts which relay the signal to the brain or to motor neurons that transfer a "command" message back to the body. This type of spinal cord integration is responsible for the single reflexes. The fiber tracts that ascend the spinal cord are highly segregated according to the type of receptor information they transmit and the location of the receptor in the body. This segregation represents the anatomic basis of the doctrine of specific nerve energies. That is, the sensation one experiences depends on which path the information takes. The doctrine holds because the information from different receptors is transmitted to different parts of the brain. This type of segregation of information based on location of the receptor is known as topographic representation. It is a basic principle of sensory integration and is found in all sensory modalities.

All sensory information that reaches the cerebral cortex, with the exception of olfaction, is relayed through the thalamus. The thalamus contains a variety of nuclei that receive sensory input and transmit it to the correct portion of the cerebral cortex. Therefore the topographic representation of the information is maintained. For example, the postcentral gyrus of the parietal lobe is the primary receiving cortex for sensory information from the body. This information is organized along the gyrus in a highly specific manner. Sensory information from the feet and legs is represented on the medial surface, the trunk and arms are represented more laterally, and information from the head and face is projected to the most lateral portions. Furthermore, the size of the cortical receiving area is proportional to the number of sensory receptors in a particular part of the body. The cortical representation for receptors from the hands and face, for example, is much larger than that for the trunk and back because the hands and face contain many more receptors. Other sensory information is projected from various parts of the thalamus to particular areas of the cortex. For example, visual stimulation is projected to the occipital cortex.

Neural impulses from the sensory systems are also relayed via collateral pathways to the ascending reticular activating system (ARAS) in the brain stem. It has been known for a long time that stimulation of the ARAS by a sensory stimulus produces the conscious, alert state that makes perception of the stimulus possible (Moruzzi & Magoun, 1949). Since all ascending sensory tracts project collateral fibers to the ARAS and the ARAS projects diffusely to the cerebral cortex, this system is not specific to any sensory modality and thus is thought to serve as one of the neurologic substrates of attention and sleep.

Sensory pathways from external and internal sources also project to a phylogenetically old part of the CNS called the limbic system. This system consists of a primitive type of cortex around the hilus of the cerebral hemispheres and a group of subcortical structures, such as the amygdala, the hippocampus, and the septal nuclei. Activation of the limbic system has been associated with strong emotional states such as fear and rage, motivational states, and activation of the ANS.

The general function of these and other CNS structures is the integration of sensory information and the generation of neural "commands" to the effector systems. In the case of motor behavior, these "commands" are thought to have primary origin in the motor cortex and are coordinated by the cerebellum. In the case of autonomic behavior, the "commands" are thought to be coordinated by a series of midbrain and brain stem structures including the hypothalamus, the limbic system, and the medulla.

Evaluation of the integrative systems of the CNS is one of the least well-developed methodologies of neurologic and behavioral assessment. Indirect measurement of these functions via neuropsychological assessment can be accomplished, although a considerable degree of inference is involved in this type of assessment. Direct measurement of cortical electrical activity can be accomplished via recording the electroencephalogram and evoked cortical potentials. Further discussion of these procedures will be presented in the section on Psychophysiologic Assessment, below.

CURRENT CONDITION OF THE ORGANISM

The processing and integration of sensory information, as well as the output of the integrative system can be influenced by a variety of biological characteristics. These could include inherited characteristics, such as genetic predispositions for certain disorders (Rosenthal, 1970), an underdeveloped CNS, or an overly responsive ANS (Eysenck & Rachman, 1967), as well as environmentally induced or self-induced physiologic states like those that accompany prolonged stress or the ingestion of drugs. Occasionally, these characteristics produce measurable behavioral sequelae (e.g., mental retardation, motor ataxia) that exist as long as the biological condition persists. In the case of permanent neurologic impairment, as occurs in brain trauma, for example, the changes in the state of the organism over time may occur very slowly and be of minimal magnitude. In the case of transient states that are due to the effects of drugs, the most remarkable behavioral effects typically diminish in direct proportion to the half-life of the chemical agent. However, long-term ingestion of certain chemicals (e.g., alcohol, narcotics, and minor tranquilizers) is thought to produce some relatively long-term changes in cellular functioning that can produce a host of withdrawal symptoms and addictive behaviors (e.g., Davis & Walsh, 1970; Petursson & Lader, 1981; Snyder, 1977).

From a conceptual perspective, biological characteristics can best be regarded as moderator variables. That is, it is assumed that these characteristics will have a very general effect upon behavior, emotions, and cognitions. Thus, these biological characteristics should have rather widespread effects upon behavior that are similar across persons with the biological characteristic. It is presumed that these similarities should enable clinical researchers to identify certain behavioral disorders or syndromes, for example, affective disorders and schizophrenia, which have a specific biological basis. However, the biobehavioral model proposes that behavior is determined not only by biological characteristics but also by the interaction of behavior with the person's environment. For example, a person suffering from endogenous depression usually experiences a sleep disturbance and has a very low activity level, which has the consequences of chronic fatigue and low rates of positive reinforcement. The implication of this formulation is that diagnosis of endogenous depression using a dexamethasone suppression test (Stokes,

Stoll, Mattson, & Sollod, 1976) does not indicate that treatment should be limited to treatment via antidepressant medication. Preferably, pharmacologic treatment should be combined with behavior therapy in order to increase positive activities (Lewinsohn, 1975) and to modify faulty cognitions (Beck, 1976). Thus, the biobehavioral model proposes that assessment of both biological and behavioral determinants of these disorders is essential for proper treatment planning.

EFFECTOR SYSTEMS

After sensory information has been integrated in the CNS, the body can respond to this information with two basic types of effectors: muscles and glands. Control of these effectors is mediated by two divisions of the peripheral nervous system: the somatic nervous sytem and the ANS.

Muscle fibers are divided into three categories based upon anatomic and functional differences: striated muscle, cardiac muscle, and smooth muscle. Approximately 40% of the body mass is striated muscle while smooth and cardiac muscle account for 5–10%.

Striated muscle is named for the fact that, when magnified, it has a striped or striated appearance. It is usually attached with tendons to a skeletal bone at each end of its length and contraction of the muscle moves the bones relative to one another. Striated muscle is occasionally called "voluntary muscle" because it is this type of muscle that is activated in various voluntary movements such as writing or running. However, this type of muscle is also responsible for several reflexive behaviors, such as flinching, which are not under voluntary control.

Cardiac muscle, as its name suggests, is found exclusively in the heart. While cardiac muscle does have a striped appearance, the arrangement and function of the fibers is quite different from striated muscle. One of the primary differences between the two types of muscle is that cardiac muscle fibers are connected to one another in such a way that excitation of one fiber is transmitted to all of the fibers associated with it. Therefore, cardiac muscle contracts as a unit and produces the rhythmic pulsation characteristic of the heart.

Smooth muscle is the so-called "involuntary muscle" of the body. Contraction of this muscle is not normally associated with conscious control. Smooth muscle fibers do not have the striped appearance of striated fibers (hence the name) and are approximately 20 times smaller in diameter and thousands of times shorter in length. Smooth muscle is found at the base of hairs, in major blood vessels, in the eye, and in the walls and sphincters of most of the visceral organs of the body.

Smooth muscle at the base of hairs is responsible for erection of hairs (piloerection) in humans and subhumans. These muscles also produce "goose bumps" in humans due to the fact that we have lost most of our furry pelage in the course of evolutionary development. Smooth muscle in blood vessels controls the diameter of the vessels and, therefore, affects blood pressure and the amount of blood that perfuses a given area. In the eye, smooth muscle controls the diameter of the pupil in response to light and other stimuli, and the shape of the lens to allow visual accommodation for distance. Smooth muscles in the walls and sphincters of visceral organs regulate the movement of these organs and therefore contribute to such processes as peristalsis, digestion, and secretion by certain glands.

Glandular responses represent the second major class of effectors. While the muscle cells have specialized in the ability to contract when stimulated, glandular cells have evolved the ability to secrete. Another difference also exists in the nature of the response of these two types of effectors. Muscular contraction tends to be rapid and localized. Glandular secretions, on the other hand, produce a more prolonged and generalized response by releasing hormones either into the bloodstream or via ducts to a specific organ.

There are two types of glands: exocrine and endocrine. Both types begin to develop as invaginations of epithelial tissue. Whether the gland is classified as exocrine or endocrine depends upon whether or not it maintains contact with the epithelial tissue from which it is derived. Exocrine glands are also known as "duct glands" because they have maintained contact with the epithelium via an elongated tube through which they secrete their products. Exocrine literally means "outside secreting" and these glands secrete their contents onto the surface of the body or into the hollow viscera. Examples include the lacrymal (tear), sweat, sebaceous (oil), and salivary glands, the gallbladder, pancreas, seminal vessicles, and prostate.

Endocrine, or "inside secreting," glands, on the other hand, do not maintain a continuity with the epithelial surface. Instead they separate themselves from the epithelium and secrete hormones into the tissue around them. Therefore, the endocrine glands are also known as "ductless glands." The secreted hormone enters the bloodstream through a nearby capillary or enters the lymphatic system. Examples of endocrine glands include the pituitary, adrenal, thyroid, parathyroid, ovaries, and the testes. The pancreas also has an endocrine component that secretes insulin.

In addition to direct neural control described below, glandular secretion is also regulated by humoral (blood-borne) factors. For example, calcium metabolism is controlled by the parathyroid gland, and hormonal secretion from the parathyroid is regulated by the amount of calcium in the blood. But the most important example of humoral regulation of hormonal secretion is the mechanism by which the pituitary modulates the activity of the other endocrine glands. The pituitary is divided anatomically and functionally into an anterior and posterior section. The posterior pituitary secretes two hormones, oxytocin and vasopressin, into the bloodstream which affect milk secretion from the breast and water retention by the kidney, respectively. These effects are exerted on target organs like other endocrine secretions and do not contribute to the regulation of other endocrine glands. The anterior pituitary, however, secretes several hormones whose function it is to control the secretory activity of the other endocrine glands. Thus the anterior pituitary is a major controller of the endocrine system and is therefore frequently referred to as the "master gland" (Guyton, 1976).

Measurement of glandular activity and other biochemical changes can be assessed using a variety of assay methods. These procedures will be discussed in more detail in the section "Biochemical Assessment," below.

Both muscles and glands are also controlled by neural mechanisms. This innervation is provided by one of two divisions of the peripheral nervous system, that is, the somatic nervous system or the ANS. As noted earlier, striated muscles are innervated by the somatic division. Neural "commands" from the motor system stimulate motor neurons which cause the contraction of muscle fibers via the release of the neurotransmitter acetylcholine. The electrical activity of muscle contraction can be measured by electromyography. Motoric behavior produced by the contraction of muscle units and the resulting force upon the joints can be measured using behavioral assessment procedures. These procedures will be discussed in more detail in the section on assessment from a biobehavioral perspective.

CONSEQUENCES/FEEDBACK

From a biobehavioral perspective, all effector responses produce some type of afferent feedback or environmental consequence. As shown in Figure 9-1, striated muscle responses, smooth muscle responses, and glandular responses all provide afferent feedback which is monitored by receptors. For example, some of these receptors might respond to the pressure produced by arterial blood pressure or inflation of the lungs, while others might respond to the chemical constituents of the blood plasma such as oxygen content or pH. In addition, proprioceptors detect changes in body posture and limb movement via muscle spindles and Golgi tendon organs (Ganong, 1975). The feedback from these various receptors is utilized in feedback loops to maintain homeostasis. For example, when the temperature of the blood perfusing the brain decreases, various endocrine and vasomotor effectors respond in ways that result in increased body temperature (Myers, 1974). Thus, afferent feedback modulates future biological responses in order to maintain homeostatic balance within the system.

In a similar fashion, overt motoric behavior produces afferent feedback which can be detected via teleceptors and exteroceptors. This feedback may be in the form of perceptible changes in body or limb position or may represent changes in the external or internal environment. As noted by Adams (1976), the consequences of motor behavior can be conceptualized as providing both information feedback as well as incentives or motivation to behave in a certain manner.

Motor skills research (e.g., Bilodeau & Bilodeau, 1969) has consistently shown that information feedback has a significant influence upon the learning of complex motor skills. Furthermore, this research has shown that immediate feedback of a precise nature produces rapid acquisition and optimal control of a motor response. As noted by Williamson and Blanchard (1979a,b), this same type of feedback has been found to optimize biofeedback learning of autonomic control.

The motivational aspects of behavioral consequences can best be understood in terms of operant principles of positive and negative reinforcement, punishment, and time-out. From a strict operant framework, the consequences of behavior must be defined in terms of objective environmental events. However, from a biobehavioral perspective, consequences can be conceptualized and defined objectively in terms of external and internal environmental events. For example, eating behavior can be regarded as positively reinforced by the consumption of food as well as negatively reinforced by the reduction of hunger. Similarly, the avoidance of or escape from a phobic stimulus is negatively reinforced by reduction of sympathetic arousal elicited by the phobic stimulus. Pain-related behavior may be elicited by an unconditioned or conditioned stimulus, and also reinforced by the provision of analgesic medications and attention of family members and/or the health-care professional. Thus, a biobehavioral model expands upon the traditional behavioral model in that it provides a conceptual framework for identifying and measuring biological events which may serve as either antecedent conditions or consequences for overt behavior.

ASSESSMENT FROM A BIOBEHAVIORAL PERSPECTIVE

In general, a biobehavioral perspective on behavioral assessment has similar features and assumptions it shares with traditional behavioral assessment (e.g., Ciminero, 1977; Hersen & Bellack, 1976). More precisely, a biobehavioral perspective assumes that: (1) biological or behavioral responses are samples of behavior, (2) these responses are usually assumed to be situationally determined, (3) assessment involves direct measurement of responses, (4) assessment must include both the antecedent conditions, as well as the consequences of behavior. Also, the functions of assessment from a biobehavioral perspective are similar to traditional behavioral assessment in that both types of assessment are used for description in behavioral–analytic terms, selection of treatment, and evaluation of treatment outcome (Ciminero, 1977). The major differences between assessment from a biobehavioral perspective and traditional behavioral assessment are: First, behavioral measures are conceptualized in terms of physiologic systems, for example, overt behavior is conceptualized as striated muscular behavior, electroencephalography measures CNS behavior, and so on, rather than in terms of qualitatively different classes of behavior, for example, emotion, cognition, and overt behavior. Second, physiologic indices of response changes are emphasized over self-report and indirect assessment procedures. Third, assessment is directed more precisely at measuring the pathophysiology of many disorders, for example, assessment of the blood pressure for measuring hypertension, electromyography for measuring muscle pain, or assessment of sphincter muscle pressure in the case of various bowel disorders.

Like traditional behavioral assessment, assessment from a biobehavioral point of view relies primarily upon direct measurement of biological or behavioral responses, and inferences concerning the determinants of behavior are minimized. Instead, biobehavioral concepts can be operationalized in terms of stimulus-response patterns. For example, psychophysiologic responses of heart rate acceleration, lowered skin resistance, peripheral vasoconstriction, and increased muscle tension produced by a stimulus or situation might be defined as a sympathetic arousal response, a component of the stress response. The stimulus thus might be inferred to be a stressor. It would be less inferential, however, to indicate that the stimulus is simply arousing. One area of assessment that does require a higher degree of inference is assessment of CNS functions. This higher degree of inference is especially true in the case of traditional neuropsychological assessment (e.g., Boll, 1981; Lezak, 1976; Walsh, 1978). Because neuropsychological assessment is more inferential, it will not be discussed in detail in this chapter. However, it should be recognized that neuropsychological assessment does involve measurement of discrete behavioral responses in the context of specific tasks and therefore is best conceptualized as falling somewhere between the extremes of direct behavioral observation, which minimizes inference, and more traditional psychological assessment, which requires a higher degree of inference.

Several psychometric issues that have recently been addressed in the general area of behavioral assessment are especially important when assessment is viewed biobehaviorally. These issues are reliability, validity, and standardization of assessment procedures. As noted by Russo et al. (1980), many biological and behavioral assessment procedures can be criticized on grounds of reliability and validity. For example, skinfold thickness measures of adiposity have been found to be unreliable unless certain precautionary measures are taken, for example, taking careful measurements to ensure that the same skinfold site is measured each time and using the same persons for measurement at each assessment period (Johnson & Stalonas, 1977). Also, the test–retest reliability of psychophysiologic assessment has not been well studied. Most psychophysiologic researchers have assumed, based upon earlier work concerning response specificity and stereotopy (Lacey, Bateman & Van Lehn, 1953; Lacey & Lacey, 1958; Malmo & Shagass, 1949), that consistent stimulus or task conditions should produce reliable psychophysiological response patterns. However, empirical evidence of test–retest reliability has not been demonstrated for psychophysiologic assessment procedures that are commonly used in behavioral medicine research, for example, stress tests (Andrasik, Blanchard, Arena, Saunders, & Barron, 1982; Arena, Blanchard, Andrasik, Cotch, & Myers, 1983; Cohen, Williamson, Monguillot, Hutchinson, Gottlieb, & Waters, 1983) and during relaxation or biofeedback sessions (Cohen, McArthur, & Rickles, 1980; Cohen et al., 1983). This deficiency may account for some of the conflicting results concerning the pathophysiology of various psychophysiologic disorders (see Cohen et al., 1983). The same concerns may be said to apply to human biochemical assessment as well (see Russo et al., 1980).

An issue in behavioral assessment is the lack of standardization for many assessment procedures. As was the case for many early behavioral assessment procedures, assessment of biological functions has often been tailor-made for evaluating a single patient or for use in a single experiment. Standardized psychophysiologic assessment procedures have only recently been reported (Schiffer, Hartley, Schulman, & Abelman, 1976). Although standardization of assessment procedures will be important for comparing experimental results across laboratories, exclusive reliance upon standardized assessment procedures may unduly restrict the flexibility of applying behavioral assessment principles to the unique characteristics of individual subjects. Such inflexibility must be avoided if behavior therapy is to remain within the paradigm of behavioral analysis, which places a premium upon establishing assessment and treatment strategies for individual subjects (Ciminero, 1977).

The following three sections will describe the three major types of assessment for a biobehavioral perspective so that the potential uses of these types of assessment can be elucidated. Abbreviations for relevant assessment procedures for each of the major component of the biobehavioral model are shown in the right-hand upper corners of each component in Figure 9-1.

ASSESSMENT OF MOTORIC BEHAVIOR

In the context of a biobehavioral model, behavioral assessment of motoric behavior is the assessment of movement produced by the contraction of striated muscle. Assessment of motoric behavior involves use of the concepts and principles that are primary subject areas of this volume and other handbooks of behavioral assessment (Ciminero, Calhoun, & Adams, 1977; Hersen & Bellack, 1976). In addition to traditional relationships among the "triple-response" systems (see Chapter 5, this volume), for a biobehavioral perspective the relationship between motoric and biological responses are also of great significance. Though these relationships have only recently begun to attract much interest among behavioral researchers, we might expect greater interest in biobehavioral relationships as the interactions of physiology and behavior become more well established.

    Good examples of research concerning relationships between behavior and physiology are provided by recent studies of physiologic changes as a function of the type A behavior pattern. These studies have examined the psychophysiologic (Krantz, Schaeffer, Davis, Dembroski, McDougall, & Schaffer, 1981; MacDougall, Dembroski, & Krantz, 1981; Schaeffer, 1981) and biochemical (Glass, Krakoff, Contrada, Hilton, Kehoe, Mannucci, Collins, Snow & Elting, 1980) reactions to a variety of behavioral tasks which involve competition, social interaction or stress. As noted in a review by Matthews (1982), most of these studies have shown that male type A subjects exhibit elevated cardiovascular and catecholamine responses in comparison to control subjects.

    Thus, behavioral assessment from a biobehavioral model involves the same basic methodology and principles used in traditional behavioral assessment. However, assessing correlated biological responses is often included in many cases.

PSYCHOPHYSIOLOGICAL ASSESSMENT

Psychophysiologic assessment involves the measurement of physiologic variables in reference to environmental, psychological, or behavioral events (Kallmann & Feuerstein, 1977). In most patients, psychophysiologic assessment involves electronic amplification and conditioning of a bioelectric response, as in the case of recording the electrocardiogram, the electromyogram (EMG), and the electroencephalogram (EEG). In other patients, indirect measurement procedures must be used. For example, assessment of the vasomotor response involves measurement of the amount of light reflected from (or penetrating) a vascular bed via photoplethysmography. Also, the measurement of many physiologic responses can be achieved by recording physical pressure or electrical resistance changes produced by the response, for example, in the cases of respiration, penile tumescence, skin temperature, and skin resistance. For more complete descriptions of the technical details of psychophysiologic recording, the reader may wish to refer to any of the excellent texts on this subject (Greenfield & Sternback, 1972; Venables & Martin, 1967).

As illustrated in Figure 9-1, psychophysiologic assessment can provide information concerning a variety of biological systems. For example, electroencephalography and the averaging of EEG responses, called cortical evoked potentials, can provide assessment information concerning the functioning of the cortex and, in a more general sense, the functioning of the brain. These measures have been most widely used in research concerning sleep (Coates & Thoresen, 1981) cognitive processing (Donchin, Ritter, & McCallum, 1978), attention (Hillyard, Picton, & Regan, 1978), and seizures (Mostofsky, 1981). These areas of research are now quite well established and have led to some exciting developments in the treatment of related disorders.

For example, in research on seizure disorders, Sternman and Friar (1972) established that certain seizure patients showed abnormally low sensory-motor rhythm in their EEG. Based upon this finding, they developed an EEG biofeedback procedure for increasing the amount of sensory-motor rhythm EEG which had the effect of reducing the frequency of seizures. Later research (Sternman, MacDonald, & Stone, 1974) suggested that abnormal EEG frequencies in seizure patients were not isolated to just the sensory-motor rhythm. Based upon this finding, Sternman and MacDonald (1978) were able to develop a more generalized EEG biofeedback procedure for "normalizing" the EEG of seizure patients and producing significant seizure reduction in six of eight patients.

The measurement of autonomic responses is very important in psychophysiologic assessment because of the strong relationships among ANS activity, emotions, psychophysiologic disorders, and stress reactions. Psychophysiologic assessment of autonomic activity has been used for objectively measuring emotional arousal for quite some time (Paul, 1969; Paul & Trimble, 1970). Earlier behavioral researchers tended to use only one or a very few psychophysiologic responses, such as heart rate or skin resistance, as indicators of emotional states like anxiety. More recently, behavioral researchers have begun to draw upon basic research showing that individuals vary with regard to the pattern of psychophysiologic responses to external stimuli, that is, individual response specificity and stereotypy (Lacey et al., 1953; Lacey & Lacey, 1958). Therefore, concurrent measurement of a number of psychophysiologic responses is necessary in order to reliably

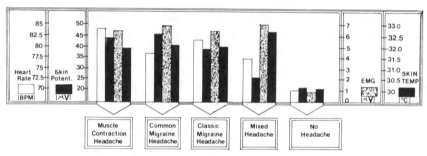

FIG. 9-2. Psychophysiological response patterns for four headache groups and a no-headache control group during a period of rest–relaxation. Reprinted from Cohen et al. (1983), with permission from Plenum Publishing Corp.

detect generalized activity of the ANS. Unfortunately, this strategy has only recently been utilized in the behavioral assessment literature pertaining to emotional arousal or stress-related disorders.

A good example of multiresponse recording is provided by a recent study from our laboratory (Cohen *et al.*, 1983). This study was designed to evaluate differences in psychophysiologic response patterns for four headache groups, muscle-contraction, common migraine, classic migraine, and mixed headache, in comparison to a no-headache control group.[2] Stimulus conditions which differentiated the groups were a rest or relaxation condition and a stress test involving an oral "intelligence test." Figure 9-2 illustrates the response pattern differences for the rest/relaxation condition. Discriminant analysis of these data indicated that a no-headache control group could be perfectly differentiated (i.e., 100% hit rate) from the headache groups based upon the psychophysiologic response profile shown in Figure 9-2.

The results for the stress test are shown in Figure 9-3. Discriminant analysis of these data indicated the no-headache control group could be differentiated from all the headache groups except for common migraine. In addition, the stress test reliably differentiated among the headache groups. Correct classification of the muscle-contraction (hit rate = 72.7%) and the classic migraine (hit rate = 72.2%) groups was especially high. These data suggest that psychophysiologic assessment can be a powerful diagnostic tool for headaches. In fact, the classification of subjects using psychophysiologic assessment was found to be more reliable (67.4% agreement) than that of secondary diagnoses by the subjects' personal physicians (59.6% agreement).

A final area of psychophysiologic assessment is measurement of neuro-

2. Diagnoses were based on specific sets of symptoms for each class of headache. For the details of these diagnostic criteria, refer to Cohen et al. (1983).

muscular activity via EMG recording (Basmajian, 1963). Surface EMG recording is especially important for assessing treatment options and outcome for neuromuscular disorders such as spastic torticollis and muscle dystonia (Bird, Cataldo, & Parker, 1981).

In summary, psychophysiologic assessment is a relatively new area within the general framework of behavioral assessment. Psychophysiology provides a fairly broad-based set of procedures which allows for objective evaluation of many "events within-the-skin," for example, emotional reactions, stress reactions, brain functions, and neuromuscular functions. Because of the breadth of potential psychophysiologic applications, we expect these procedures to receive increasing attention from researchers with a biobehavioral orientation.

BIOCHEMICAL ASSESSMENT

The biochemical properties of human tissue and fluid samples can be assessed by a variety of assay techniques. These biochemical properties can then be used as indices of psychological events. Biochemical assessment represents a relatively new set of procedures for assessment in behavior therapy and behavioral medicine. However, a review of the recent literature in these areas indicates that biochemical assessment is being used much more frequently than was the case even 5 years ago. For example, the amount of

FIG. 9-3. Psychophysiological response patterns for four headache groups and a no-headache control group during a stress test. Reprinted from Cohen et al. (1983), with permission from Plenum Publishing Corp.

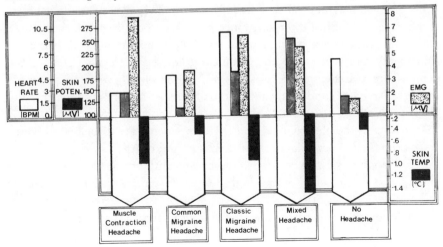

epinephrine and norepinephrine in blood plasma has been used as an index of ANS activity after relaxation training (Hoffman, Benson, Arns, Stainbrook, Landsberg, Young, & Gill, 1982) and after stressing type A and type B individuals (Glass *et al.*, 1980). Biochemical assessment has also been extensively used in attempts to differentiate clinical populations of psychiatric patients. Many excellent reviews of this literature are available to the interested reader (Usdin, Sourkes, & Youdim, 1980; van Praag & Verhoeven, 1980).

In general, any particular neurotransmitter, hormone, ion, metabolite, drug, or neuropeptide may be measured using one of dozens of biochemical assay techniques. A complete description of these techniques is beyond the scope of the present chapter, but a brief overview of four of the most frequently used assays follows; these are electrophoresis, chromatography, spectroscopy, and radioimmunoassay (RIA). For a more detailed description of these and other procedures, the reader may wish to consult a specialized text such as Morris and Morris (1976).

Electrophoresis

The assay technique of electrophoresis is based on the fact that the movement of charged molecules in an electric field depends upon the size of the particles and the magnitude of the particles' charge. Therefore, if the viscosity of the medium through which the molecule passes and the voltage applied to the medium are held constant, a sample can be separated into its components based upon their size and electrical charge.

The procedure in applying this technique begins by selecting some inert substance which will support the liquid conducting medium. A sheet of filter paper may be used (paper electrophoresis), but the most common support substance is a polymer gel such as polyacrylamide [polyacrylamide gel electrophoresis (PAGE)]. Either substance provides a porous network through which the conducting medium may pass. The support substance is then thoroughly moistened with the conducting liquid and the two ends of the support are placed in reservoirs. In each reservoir, there is an electrode immersed in more conducting liquid so that when a current is supplied to the electrode, voltage may be passed across the support substance. A sample is then placed in the electric field and the components are dispersed in bands across the field in accordance with their size and charge.

Electrophoresis can be used to assay any number of biochemicals, including plasma proteins, with a high degree of sensitivity. For example, as little as 5–10 μg (1 μg $= 1 \times 10^{-6}$ g) of protein can be detected (Bohinski, 1979). In general, this technique can be used to separate any molecule that carries a charge. Examples would include, amino acids, nucleic acids, peptides, and inorganic ions.

Chromatography

The method of chromatography derives its name from the fact that it was first used in the 19th century to analyze mixtures of dyes (Orten & Neuhaus, 1975). It was found that when a drop of dye mixture was placed on a piece of blotting paper, it would separate into its component colors. Today, chromatography retains its name despite the fact that it is used to separate a wide variety of uncolored substances. With modifications, chromatography has proved to be extremely valuable and is probably the most frequently used separation procedure.

There are many chromatographic techniques which are described in detail elsewhere (Morris & Morris, 1976). However, all of these techniques have in common the fact that they employ some stationary substance across which is passed a mixture of gas or liquid containing the sample to be analyzed. Separation occurs because of the differential interaction of components of the sample with the stationary substance. Depending upon the type of interaction, separation can be achieved due to such things as the size, charge, or solubility of the molecular components.

One of the most common chromatographic techniques is column chromatography in which a hollow tube of virtually any length is packed with a matrix of stationary material. This material is frequently composed of porous gel particles which act like sieves to slow the passage of some molecules while allowing others to pass unimpeded. By passing a solvent containing the sample through the column, the smaller molecules are slowed because they must pass through each of the gel particles they encounter. The larger molecules, however, can flow around the particles and travel through the column more quickly. Thus the sample is separated and the components are collected from the effluent emerging from the end of the column. This process can be greatly accelerated by applying high pressure to the solvent mixture. The technique of high-pressure liquid chromatography (HPLC) currently is gaining in popularity because a separation that would require hours with conventional chromatography can be accomplished in minutes with HPLC.

Chromatography is widely used for many reasons. Not only is the technique fairly inexpensive and simple to use but it also can be employed to separate a wide variety of substances. Chromatographic procedures can be used to assay sugars, lipids, amino acids, neurotransmitters, inorganic ions, steroid hormones, and barbiturates. The advantage of this technique over electrophoresis is that the substance to be assayed need not possess an electrical charge.

Spectroscopy

Basically, spectroscopic techniques identify a substance or measure its quantity based upon how much electromagnetic radiation it absorbs. When visible electromagnetic radiation (i.e., light) or invisible electromagnetic radiation (e.g., x-rays or ultraviolet rays) pass through a substance, a certain amount of the radiation is absorbed in the form of energy. Devices called spectrophotometers can measure what kind of energy and how much energy is absorbed and thereby identify the sample.

The energy of electromagnetic radiation is inversely related to its wavelength. That is, the higher the wavelength, the lower the energy. So, in the visible spectrum, for example, red light has a longer wavelength and a lower energy than violet light. When visible light is passed through a substance, only certain wavelengths (colors) will be absorbed based upon the particular structure of the substance. This phenomenon is known as the absorption spectrum, and it can be considered as a molecular "fingerprint." A slight alteration in the conformation of a molecule will make it absorb a different set of wavelengths. Additionally, the amount of a particular wavelength or set of wavelengths that is absorbed is directly proportional to the quantity of the molecule present in the sample. As the quantity of the substance increases so does the amount of absorption. Therefore, spectrophotometers allow us to measure which wavelengths and how much of these wavelengths are absorbed, and thus tell us which molecules are present and in what quantity.

A variation on this procedure uses a device called a spectrofluorometer. This device operates on the principle that when some molecules absorb energy from electromagnetic radiation, they emit light (fluorescence) of a wavelength peculiar to their structure. This emission ray can be measured, and its wavelength determined to identify the molecule.

The advantages of spectroscopic techniques are that they can be highly refined and automated, and an extremely small sample can be used (Williams & Wilson, 1975). These techniques can be employed to assay sugars, proteins, carbohydrates, amino acids, peptides, enzymes, metals, and a variety of other substances.

Radioimmunoassay

Radioimmunoassay is one of the most sensitive and specific assay techniques currently available (Bohinski, 1979). Radioimmunoassay was originally developed by R. S. Yalow and colleagues to isolate insulin in human plasma. However, it has since been found to be an extremely valuable assay for any substance that can be made radioactive and for which an antibody can be prepared (Yalow, 1978). The significance of this technique is attested by the fact that Yalow was awarded the Nobel Prize in 1977 for its discovery. The possibilities for its application in the future appear to be virtually unlimited (Orten & Neuhaus, 1975).

The basic technique of RIA relies upon the competition between a radioactively labeled and an unlabeled antigen for binding to a limited amount of antibody. Let us use insulin as an example. First, human insulin (the antigen) would be injected into another animal such as a rabbit or goat. The animal's immune system then develops a highly specific antibody to defend against the foreign antigen. This antibody can be extracted from the animal's blood plasma and used in the assay procedure. A known quantity of the antibody is combined with a known quantity of human insulin, which has been labeled with radioactivity. This combination is then added to a sample suspected of containing human insulin. The labeled and the unlabeled insulin will then compete with one another to bind with the antibody. The greater the amount of unlabeled insulin in the sample, the less the radioactive insulin will be able to bind and vice versa. After a given period of time the excess unbound insulin is separated from the bound insulin and the radioactivity of the bound fraction is measured; the higher the radioactivity, the lower the concentration of insulin in the test sample.

Radioimmunoassay assay techniques have the advantages of extreme specificity and sensitivity. These techniques can also be automated. As stated previously, RIA can be employed with any substance which can be made radioactive and for which an antibody can be produced. Therefore, minute amounts of steroid hormones, peptides, neurotransmitters, proteins, metabolites, and various drugs can be detected. This technique offers an extremely broad range of potential applications in both basic and clinical research.

Although any one of these assays may be used for assessing any number of biochemicals, a common practice is to use a combination of the procedures in order to provide very accurate measurements. A good example of this approach is provided by Glass *et al.* (1980). In this study, epinephrine and norepinephrine were assayed using a series of techniques. First blood samples were collected and spun in a centrifuge to extract the plasma. A radioactive label was then added to the plasma in the presence of an enzyme which would attach the label to epinephrine and norepinephrine. After this reaction, the plasma was subjected to a chromatographic procedure to separate the two neurotransmitters. Then the amount of radioactivity emitted by the two samples, and therefore the quantity of neurotransmitter, was measured with a spectrometer.

To summarize, biochemical assessment provides an objective method for measuring any number of biochemical levels or responses that may be related to health or behavioral phenomena. Although these techniques have not been widely used in behavioral assessment, it might be expected that as the procedures become more popularized, their utilization will increase.

AN EMERGING BIOBEHAVIORISTIC FRAMEWORK

As noted above, the interfaces between psychology and related disciplines such as neurophysiology, neurochemistry, neuroendocrinology, and others (collectively known as the neurosciences) have been expanding at a rapid rate. This has occurred in the absence of an explicit, unifying conceptual framework. Terms such as biological psychology, psychobiological sciences, and biobehavioral science convey the message of interdisciplinary fusion. However, they do not represent a conceptual framework, a manner of approaching the investigation and understanding a class of phenomena. Behaviorism is such a conceptual framework, but it needs to be broadened to encompass the biological–psychological interfaces. The "black box" of physiologic process has been acknowledged in modern behaviorism, but not embraced, at least not formally. In this chapter, a model for conceptualizing the assessment of human behavior was described that is philosophically compatible with traditional behaviorism. This paradigm, biobehaviorism, attempts to integrate the best of both biological and behavioral psychology.

Biobehaviorism is, essentially, an extension of traditional behaviorism. It implies a materialistic, deterministic, molecular, probabilistic, and operational approach. However, none of these principles preclude concepts of choice, integrated or holistic response, organism growth, or organism-initiated behavior. The description "probabilistic" refers to the tenet that a response, whether it is release of a neurotransmitter or swinging a baseball bat, is multiply determined and that all of the determinants may not be known. In fact, some of the determinants may be chance events. The emission of a response is a probability statement that is complexly but completely determined. By operational, we mean simply that a concept is only as good as the material referents by which it is defined. To the extent that a concept has many quantifiable and relatively objective referrents, it is a useful one. In biobehaviorism, but not in some earlier forms of behaviorism, the referents may be biological, and often must be biological. Concepts such as attention, imagery, or thought that have rather weak behavioral referents may (should) have stronger biological referents and, as such, are likely to be more acceptable in a biobehavioristic framework than in a traditional behavioristic one.

As noted earlier, a biobehavioristic approach to psychology utilizes an SORC model. Basically, the O stands for Organism a complex array of physiologic systems composed of units such as receptors and effector cells that operate on an S-R basis. The simplest unit in this melange, the neuron, behaves in ways that are traceable to multiple interacting stimuli that determine the probability of a response. The functioning of an organ, subsystem, or system is quite similar: response probability is determined by multiple inputs to its components. One no longer talks about a function such as fine motor control being "located in the cerebellum." Instead, one refers to a functional system that includes the cerebellum. What this understanding implies is that, in the wider view, a response such as reaching for a doorknob is not a simple S-R function. It is a wonderfully complicated array of integrated S-R phenomena beginning with the cochlear transduction of air pressure waves stemming from a knock on the door. By complicated we mean not only that many systems are involved, but that the state of each of these systems before, during, and after the knock on the door is a variable to be considered. That is, the response of some physiologic unit is not only a function of the immediate stimulus, but also of the preexisting condition of the organism.

By now, it should be apparent that from a biobehavioral perspective, stimuli can have both external and internal sources. For example, the binding of norepinephrine to the proper receptor on a neural dendrite is a stimulus that cause adenyl cyclase to be activated (a response). Adenyl cyclase is a stimulus that causes adenosine triphosphate to produce adenosine monophosphate (a response), and so on through the entire sequence of the action potential, eventually leading to neurotransmitter release and binding to other receptors. This sequence is no less S-R than the cochlear transduction of air pressure waves. Stimuli are causes of responses, and these responses are stimuli that are causes of other effects.

Physiologic stimulus and response and organismic stimulus and response are analogous. Both are determined and probabilistic. Both are subject to excitatory, inhibitory, and modulatory phenomena. Both are integrative and feedback sensitive. Each determines the other. The essential difference lies in the units of analysis used by the observer. Whether we examine the stimulation and response of dopaminergic neurons or of overt motor behavior, analogous processes are involved. The fact that we must study human behavior at different levels of complexity using different units of behavior does not preclude unifying principles of behavior, nor does it preclude a unifying conceptual framework. Rather, it demands them.

Thus, a biobehavioristic model is best regarded as a multilevel conceptual framework that allows for objective assessment of biological and behavioral variables that are associated with what has generally been assumed to be complex psychological phenomena. Though a biobehavioristic framework does not reduce this complexity, it does provide a conceptual model from which objective measurement procedures can be designed to evaluate the phenomenon at levels ranging from molecular to molar. From this perspective, it should be possible to understand human behavior more completely and to design specific interventions for dysfunction at any level of analysis.

SUMMARY

In this chapter we have attempted to describe the conceptual foundations for assessing human behavior from the integrated perspective of biological and behavioral psychology. This framework is the logical extension of earlier behavioral models into the realm of biological science. A biobehavioral framework is both methodologically and philosophically congruent with traditional behaviorism. However, by extending the behavioral model in the direction of biological science, the power for objective measurement of events "within-the-skin" can be greatly increased. In this era of cognitivism (Sampson, 1981) and increased clinical interest in assessing and modifying internal events (Mahoney, 1974), perhaps an alternative framework that relies very heavily upon direct, objective measurement will enable applied behavioral science to broaden its scope without losing its objectivity.

REFERENCES

Adams, J. A. (1976). *Learning and memory: An introduction.* Homewood, IL: Dorsey Press.

Andrasik, F., Blanchard, E. B., Arena, J. G., Saunders, N. L., & Barron, K. D. (1982). Psycho-physiology of recurrent headache: Methodological issues and new empirical findings. *Behavior Therapy, 13,* 407–429.

Arena, J. G., Blanchard, E. B., Andrasik, F., Cotch, P. A., & Myers, P. E. (1983). Reliability of psychophysiological assessment. *Behavior Research and Therapy, 21,* 447–460.

Bandura, A. (1977). *Social learning theory.* Englewood Cliffs, NJ: Prentice-Hall.

Barlow, D. H. (1977). Assessment of sexual behavior. In A. R. Ciminero, K. S. Calhoun, & H. E. Adams (Eds.). *Handbook of behavioral assessment.* New York: John Wiley & Sons.

Basmajian, J. V. (1962). Electromyography comes of age. *Science, 176,* 603–609.

Beck, A. T. (1976). *Cognitive therapy and the emotional disorders.* New York: International Universities Press.

Bilodeau, E. A., & Bilodeau, I. M. (1969). *Principles of skill acquisition.* New York: Academic Press.

Bird, B. L., Cataldo, M. F., & Parker, L. (1981). Behavioral medicine for muscular disorders. In S. M. Turner, K. S. Calhoun, & H. E. Adams (Eds.), *Handbook of clinical behavior therapy* (pp. 406–466). New York: John Wiley & Sons.

Bohinski, R. C. (1979). *Modern concepts in biochemistry* (3rd ed.). Boston: Allyn and Bacon.

Boll, T. J. (1981). Assessment of neuropsychological disorders. In D. Barlow (Ed.), *Behavioral assessment of adult disorders* (pp. 45–86). New York: Guilford Press.

Bower, G. H., & Hilgard, E. R. (1981). *Theories of learning.* Englewood Cliffs, NJ: Prentice-Hall.

Brener, J. (1974). A general model of voluntary control applied to the phenomenon of learned cardiovascular change. In P. A. Obrist, A. H. Black, J. Brener, & L. V. DiCara (Eds.), *Cardiovascular psychophysiology* (pp. 365-391). Chicago: Aldine.

Brown, T. S., & Wallace, P. M. (1980). *Physiological psychology.* New York: Academic Press.

Cannon, W. B. (1945). *The way of an investigator.* New York: W. W. Norton.

Carpenter, M. B. (1978). *Human neuroanatomy* (7th ed.). Baltimore: Williams & Wilkins.

Ciminero, A. R. (1977). Behavioral assessment: An overview. In A. R. Ciminero, K. S. Calhoun, & H. E. Adams (Eds.). *Handbook of behavioral assessment* (pp. 3-13). New York: John Wiley & Sons.

Ciminero, A. R., Calhoun, K. S., & Adams, H. E. (1977). *Handbook of behavioral assessment.* New York: John Wiley & Sons.

Cinciripini, P. M., Williamson, D. A., & Epstein, L. H. (1981). Behavioral treatment of migraine headaches. In J. M. Ferguson & C. B. Taylor (Eds.), *The Comprehensive Handbook of Behavioral Medicine* (Vol. 2, pp. 207-228). Jamaica, NY: Spectrum Press.

Coates, T. J., & Thoresen, C. E. (1981). Treating sleep disorders: Few answers, some suggestions, and many questions. In S. M. Turner, K. S. Calhoun, & H. E. Adams (Eds.). *Handbook of clinical behavior therapy* (pp. 240-289). New York: John Wiley & Sons.

Cohen, M. J., McArthur, D. L., & Rickles, W. H. (1980). Comparison of four biofeedback treatments for migraine headache: Physiological and headache variables. *Psychosomatic Medicine, 40,* 344-354.

Cohen, R. A., Williamson, D. A., Monguillot, J. E., Hutchinson, P. C., Gottlieb, J., & Waters, W. F. (1983). Psychophysiological response patterns in vascular and muscle-contraction headaches. *Journal of Behavioral Medicine, 6,* 93-107.

Davis, V. E., & Walsh, M. J. (1970). Alcohol, amines, and alkaloids: A possible biochemical basis of alcohol addiction. *Science, 166,* 1005-1007.

Donchin, E., Ritter, W., & McCallum, W. C. (1978). Cognitive psychophysiology: The endogenous components of the ERP. In E. Callaway, P. Tueting, & S. H. Koslow (Eds.), *Event-related potentials in man* (pp. 349-441). New York: Academic Press.

Eysenck, H. J., & Rachman, S. (1967). *The causes and cures of neurosis.* San Diego, CA: Robert R. Knapp.

Ganong, W. F. (1975). *Review of medical physiology.* Los Altos, CA: Large Medical Publications.

Glass, D. C., Krakoff, L. R., Contrada, R., Hilton, W. F., Kehoe, K., Mannucci, E. G., Collins, C., Snow, B., & Elting, E. (1980). Effect of harassment and competition upon cardiovascular and plasma catecholamine responses in Type A and Type B individuals. *Psychophysiology, 17,* 453-463.

Greenfield, N. S., & Sternback, R. A. (1972). *Handbook of psychophysiology.* New York: Holt, Rinehart & Winston.

Guthrie, E. R. (1935). *The psychology of learning.* New York: Harper.

Guyton, A. C. (1976). *Textbook of medical physiology* (5th ed.). Philadelphia: W. B. Saunders.

Hall, J. F. (1966). *The psychology of learning.* New York: J. B. Lippincott.

Hersen, M., & Bellack, A. S. (1976). *Behavioral assessment: A practical handbook.* Oxford: Pergamon Press.

Hillyard, S. A., Picton, T. W., & Regan, D. (1978). Sensation, perception, and attention: Analysis using ERPs. In E. Callaway, P. Tueting, & S. H. Koslow (Eds.), *Event-related potentials in man* (pp. 223-347). New York: Academic Press.

Hoffman, J. W., Benson, H., Arns, P. A., Stainbrook, G. L., Landsberg, L., Young, J. B., & Gill, A. (1982). Reduced sympathetic nervous system responsivity associated with the relaxation response. *Science, 215,* 190-192.

Johnson, W. G., & Stalonas, P. (1977). Measuring skinfold thickness—A cautionary note. *Addictive Behavior, 2,* 105-107.

Kalat, J. W. (1980). *Biological psychology.* Belmont, CA: Wadsworth.

Kallman, W. M., & Feuerstein, M. (1977). Psychophysiological procedures. In A. R. Ciminero, K. S. Calhoun, & H. E. Adams (Eds.), *Handbook of behavioral assessment* (pp. 329-364). New York: John Wiley & Sons.

Kanfer, F. H., & Phillips, J. S. (1970). *Learning foundations of behavior therapy.* New York: John Wiley & Sons.

Kazdin, A. E. (1978). *History of behavior modification.* Baltimore: University Park Press.

Krantz, D. S., Schaeffer, M. A., Davis, J. E., Dembroski, T. M., MacDougall, J. M., & Shaffer, R. T. (1981). Extent of coronary atherosclerosis, Type A behavior, and cardiovascular response to social interaction. *Psychophysiology, 18,* 654–664.

Krieger, D. T., & Martin, J. B. (1981). Brain peptides (first of two parts). *The New England Journal of Medicine, 304*(5), 876–885.

Lacey, J. I., Bateman, D. E., & Van Lehn, R. (1953). Autonomic response specificity: An experimental study. *Psychosomatic Medicine, 15,* 8–21.

Lacey, J. I., & Lacey, B. C. (1958). Verification and extension of the principle of autonomic response-stereotypy. *American Journal of Psychology, 71,* 51–73.

Levine, M. (1975). *A cognitive theory of learning: Research on hypothesis testing.* New York: John Wiley & Sons.

Lewinsohn, P. M. (1975). The behavioral study and treatment of depression. In M. Hersen, R. Eisler, & P. Miller (Eds.), *Progress in behavior modification* (Vol. 1, pp. 19–64). New York: Academic Press.

Lezak, M. D. (1976). *Neuropsychological assessment.* New York: Oxford University Press.

MacDougall, J. M., Dembroski, T. M., & Krantz, D. S. (1981). Effects of types of challenge on pressor and heart rate responses in Type A and B women. *Psychophysiology, 18,* 1–9.

Mahoney, M. J. (1974). *Cognition and behavior modification.* Cambridge, MA: Ballinger.

Malmo, R., & Shagass, C. (1949). Physiologic study of symptom mechanisms in psychiatric patients under stress. *Psychosomatic Medicine, 11,* 25–29.

Matthews, K. A. (1982). Psychological perspectives on the Type A behavior pattern. *Psychological Bulletin, 91,* 293–323.

Millenson, J. R., & Leslie, J. C. (1979). *Principles of behavioral analysis.* New York: Macmillan.

Miller, N. E. (1978). Biofeedback and visceral learning. *Annual Review of Psychology, 29,* 373–404.

Mischel, W. (1973). Toward a cognitive social learning reconceptualization of personality. *Psychological Review, 80,* 252–283.

Morris, C. J. O. R., & Morris, P. (1976). *Separation methods in biochemistry.* New York: John Wiley & Sons.

Moruzzi, G., & Magoun, H. W. (1949). Brain stem reticular formation and activation of the EEG. *Electroencephalography and Clinical Neurophysiology, 1,* 455–473.

Mostofsky, D. I. (1981). Recurrent paroxysmal disorders of the central nervous system. In S. M. Turner, K. S. Calhoun, & H. E. Adams (Eds.), *Handbook of clinical behavior therapy* (pp. 447–474). New York: John Wiley & Sons.

Müller, J. (1842). *Element of physiology.* London: Taylor & Walton.

Myers, R. D. (1974). *Handbook of drug and chemical stimulation of the brain.* New York: Van Nostrand Reinhold.

Nelson, R. O., & Barlow, D. H. (1981). Behavioral Assessment: Basic strategies and initial procedures. In D. H. Barlow (Ed.), *Behavioral assessment of adult disorders* (pp. 13–43). New York: Guilford Press.

Nelson, R. O., & Hayes, S. C. (1979). Some current dimensions of behavioral assessment. *Behavioral Assessment, 1,* 1–16.

Orten, J. M., & Neuhaus, O. W. (1975). *Human biochemistry* (9th ed.). St. Louis: C. V. Mosby.

Paul, G. L. (1969). Inhibition of physiological response to stressful imagery by relaxation and hypnotically suggested relaxation. *Behavior Research and Therapy, 7,* 249–256.

Paul, G. L., & Trimble, R. W. (1970). Recorded vs. "live" relaxation training and hypnotic suggestion: Comparative effectiveness for reducing physiological arousal and inhibiting stress response. *Behavior Therapy, 1,* 285–302.

Pavlov, I. P. (1927). *Conditioned reflexes.* London: Oxford University Press.

Petursson, H., & Lader, M. H. (1981). Benzodiazepine dependence. *British Journal of Addiction, 76,* 133–145.

Razran, G. (1961). The observable unconscious and the inferable conscious in current social psychophysiology: Interoceptive conditioning, semantic conditioning, and the orienting reflex. *Psychological Review, 68,* 81–147.

Reynolds, G. S. (1961). Contrast, generalization, and the process of discrimination. *Journal of the Experimental Analysis of Behavior, 4*, 289–294.

Rosenthal, D. (1970). *Genetic theory and abnormal behavior.* New York: McGraw-Hill.

Rösler, R. (1981). Event-related brain potentials in a stimulus-discrimination learning paradigm. *Psychophysiology, 18*, 447–455.

Russo, D. C., Bird, B. L., & Masek, B. J. (1980). Assessment issues in behavioral medicine. *Behavioral Assessment, 2*, 1–18.

Sampson, E. E. (1981). Cognitive psychology as ideology. *American Psychologist, 36*, 730–743.

Schiffer, F., Hartley, H. L., Schulman, C. L., & Abelman, W. H. (1976). The quiz electrocardiogram: A diagnostic and research technique for disease. *The American Journal of Cardiology, 37*, 41–47.

Schwartz, G. E., Shapiro, A. P., Redmond, D. R., Ferguson, D. C. E., Ragland, D. R., & Weiss, S. M. (1979). Behavioral medicine approaches to hypertension: An integrative analysis of theory and research. *Journal of Behavioral Medicine, 2*, 311–363.

Skinner, B. F. (1950). Are theories of learning necessary? *Psychological Review, 57*, 193–216.

Skinner, B. F. (1974). *About behaviorism.* New York: Alfred Knopf.

Snyder, S. H. (1977). Opiate receptors and internal opiates. *Scientific American, 236*, 44–56.

Snyder, S. H. (1980). Brain peptides as neurotransmitters. *Science, 209*, 976–983.

Sternman, M. B., & Friar, L. (1972). Suppression of seizures in an epileptic following sensorimotor EEG feedback training. *Electroenceophalography and Clinical Neurophysiology, 33*, 89–95.

Sternman, M. B., & MacDonald, L. R. (1978). Effects of central cortical EEG feedback training on incidence of poorly controlled seizures. *Epilepsia, 19*, 207–222.

Sternman, M. B., MacDonald, L. R., & Stone, R. K. (1974). Biofeedback training of sensorimotor electroencephalogram rhythm in man: Effects on epilepsy. *Epilepsia, 15*, 395–416.

Stokes, P. E., Stoll, P. M., Mattson, M. R., & Sollod, R. N. (1976). Diagnosis and psychopathology in psychiatric patients resistant to dexamethasone. In B. J. Sachar (Ed.), *Hormones, behavior, and psychopathology* (pp. 225–229). New York: Raven Press.

Usdin, E., Sourkes, T. L., & Youdim, M. B. H. (1980). *Enzymes and neurotransmitters in mental disease.* New York: John Wiley & Sons.

van Praag, H. M., & Verhoeven, W. M. A. (1980). Neuropeptides: A new dimension in biological psychiatry. *Progress in Brain Research, 53*, 229–252.

Venables, P. H., & Martin, I. (1967). *Manual of psychophysiological methods.* Amsterdam: North Holland.

Walsh, K. W. (1978). *Neuropsychology: A clinical approach.* New York: Churchill Livingstone.

Waters, W. F., McDonald, D. G., & Koresko, R. L. (1972). Psychophysiological responses during analgesic systematic desentization and non-relaxation control procedures. *Behavior Research and Therapy, 10*, 381–393.

Waters, W. F., & Wright, D. C. (1979). Maintenance and habitation of the phasic orienting response to competing stimuli in selection attention. In H. D. Kimmel, E. H. Van Olst, & J. F. Orlebecke (Eds.), *The orienting reflex in humans* (pp. 101–121). Hillsdale, NJ: Lawrence Erlbaum.

Williams, B. L., & Wilson, K. (1975). *Principles and techniques of practical biochemistry.* London: Edward Arnold.

Williamson, D. A. (1981). Behavioral treatment of migraine and muscle-contraction headaches: Outcome and theoretical explanations. In M. Hersen, R. M. Eisler, & P. M. Miller (Eds.), *Progress in behavior modification* (Vol. 2, pp. 163–201). New York: Academic Press.

Williamson, D. A., & Blanchard, E. B. (1979a). Heart rate and blood pressure biofeedback. I. A review of the recent experimental literature. *Biofeedback and Self-Regulation, 4*, 1–34.

Williamson, D. A., & Blanchard, E. B. (1979b). Heart rate and blood pressure biofeedback. II. A review and integration of recent theoretical models. *Biofeedback and Self-Regulation, 4*, 35–50.

Yalow, R. S. (1978). Radioimmunoassay: A probe for the fine structure of biologic systems. *Science, 200*, 1236–1245.

III
THE PURPOSES OF
BEHAVIORAL ASSESSMENT

10

SELECTION OF TARGET BEHAVIORS

ROBERT P. HAWKINS

West Virginia University

Before intervening to change the behavior of a client, student, employee, consumer, or other learner, it is usually necessary to select ("target" as a verb) the behaviors to be changed.[1] This chapter discusses the conceptual foundations for such targeting. The emphasis here is on clinical services and research, but it should be pointed out that in many ways the discipline of education is ahead of the clinical disciplines. For example, the Individualized Education Program required for the last several years in educating handicapped children—by the Education for All Handicapped Children Act of 1975, Public Law 94-142—must state, among other things, the long-range goals for the child, the short-term instructional objectives or target behaviors (in measurable terms), the specific procedures to be used in teaching, and the methods for evaluating progress. The concept of criterion-referenced (as opposed to norm-referenced) tests was developed in education and the term coined by Robert Glaser in 1963 (Livingston, 1977) in regard to educational assessment. And learning hierarchies—the skill accumulation in which acquisition of one skill is highly dependent upon the presence of particular prerequisite skills—have been the subject of educational research for several years (e.g., Resnick, Wang, & Kaplan, 1973). All of these developments, and others, are highly relevant in a behavioral approach to targeting.

To place selection of "target" (an adjective here) behaviors in context, consider the "behavioral assessment funnel" described elsewhere (Hawkins, 1979) as a metaphor for the successive phases of clinical, educational, and other assessments. In the first phase, the scope of information gathered and the range of options considered are very broad. This is the screening and general disposition phase of assessment. In the second phase—definition and general quantification—the focus is narrower, as are the decision options. The outcome in this phase—often accompanied by a classificatory labeling of

---

1. Or, in some cases, no behavior of the referred client is appropriate to target, but rather another person's behavior (or some other environmental characteristic), as when the "expectations" of (contingencies applied by) persons in the learner's environment are unfair or unrealistic (see Goldiamond, 1984).

the client, student, or trainee—is usually placement at a certain level in a curriculum, in a certain type of clinical service, on a certain psychotropic medication, or in a certain training or maintenance program.

Phase three of the funnel is where the behavioral assessor pinpoints specific behaviors as the targets for intervention and designs that intervention. Here the focus becomes narrowest, ending in the straight, narrow "neck" of the funnel. The fourth phase is that of monitoring progress, generally with a consistent narrow focus (thus the straight, thin "neck"); and the fifth phase is follow-up, which may still be narrow or may be somewhat broader, to assess collateral effects, as suggested by Voeltz and Evans (1982). These third, fourth, and fifth phases are a familiar part of behavioral assessment, but are seldom done in nonbehavioral assessment. The third phase is the topic of the present chapter and the following chapter: the targeting of specific behaviors and the design of an intervention.

This chapter begins with a review of the general characteristics that tend to differentiate a behavioral perspective on targeting from other perspectives, including limited inference, emphasis on effective (competent) performance, emphasis on specific situations or tasks, individualization of target (here a noun) selection, the use of direct observation, and an emphasis on the functions performed by the current and alternative behaviors. This review identifies some of the historical streams that have led to the current views among behavioral assessors regarding selection of target behaviors.

The chapter then identifies and discusses some of the unsettled issues among behavioral assessors regarding target behavior selection. The issues identified are a "constructional" versus "eliminative" emphasis, the selection of indirect target behaviors rather than the ultimate behavior change desired, the utility of hypothetical constructs as targets for change, the relevance of various functional relations between behaviors, the relevance of social validation of target selection, the relative places of ideographic versus nomothetic approaches in targeting, prioritizing among target behaviors, and whether accurate targeting is actually critical.

CHARACTERISTICS AND HISTORY OF A BEHAVIORAL APPROACH TO SELECTION OF TARGET BEHAVIORS

It took a few years before the applied behavior analysis and behavior therapy movements, which began their current growth in the late 1950s (Martin & Pear, 1983), seriously addressed issues of targeting (e.g., Goldfried & D'Zurilla, 1969; Hawkins, 1975; Winett & Winkler, 1972). The old assessment concepts were clearly inappropriate, as were most of the methods, but it was not clear what should take their place. The focus of attention was initially on proving simply that a technology based on learning theory could be effective in improving learners' lives. During this phase of our field's development, we often moved rather quickly from the vague complaints of clients (or other referring agents) to a listing of behaviors to be changed, operating on an intuitive manner and with little conception of the process that we used or its assumptions (Baer, 1982a), except that it was critical to specify outcomes in terms of measurable behavior change. Sometimes we even left selection of target behaviors completely to others, including laypersons such as parents (e.g., Walder, Cohen, & Daston, 1967) or teachers (see Winett & Winkler, 1972). Increasingly, however, we have taken responsibility for targeting, and it has been recognized that "This discipline needs to know . . . how to translate any complaint into behaviors to be changed, which, if changed, will end the complaining behaviors to the satisfaction of the complainer" (Baer, 1982b, p. 286). In fact, Ullmann and Krasner (1965, p. 28) and Nelson and Barlow (1981) consider identification of target behaviors to be the first goal of behavioral assessment. In practice, however, it is questionable that one can separate targeting of specific behaviors from the design of alternative interventions, because the functional analysis involved in targeting includes hypotheses regarding the environmental variables which control current performance or could control alternative performance, or both. Such hypotheses imply the kinds of interventions that should produce the desired behavior change, as will become particularly evident later in discussing the behavior analytic approach of Goldiamond and colleagues (Goldiamond, 1974; Goldiamond, 1984; Goldiamond & Dyrud, 1967; Schwartz & Goldiamond, 1975).

A behavioral perspective on targeting can be characterized on several related dimensions. Probably most assessors who identify themselves as behavioral would agree generally with these characterizations, though there would be much less agreement on their implications, as is discussed below. Each of these characteristics of a behavioral perspective is discussed with reference to some of the primary researchers involved in identification of the characteristic, or in development of related assessment technology.

LIMITED INFERENCE

As Goldfried (1977; see also Goldfried & Kent, 1972) pointed out:

> The basic difference between traditional and behavioral assessment procedures is best reflected in a distinction originally made by Goodenough in 1949, when she drew the comparison between a *sign* and *sample* approach to the interpretation of tests. When test responses are viewed as a sample, one assumes that they paralleled the way in which a person is likely to behave in a non-test

situation. Thus, if a person responds assertively on a test, one may assume that this or similar assertive behaviors also occur in other situations as well. When test responses are viewed as signs, an inference is made that the performance is an indirect or symbolic manifestation of some other characteristic. An example would be a predominance of Vista responses on the Rorschach . . . such responses presumably indicate the person's ability for self evaluation and insight. For the most part, traditional assessment has employed a sign as opposed to sample approach to test interpretation. In the case of behavioral assessment, only the sample approach makes sense. [p. 17]

The sign approach—in which the observed behavior is an indirect index of some unobserved, usually internal, "personality" construct—is a natural outgrowth of a medical model of maladaptive behavior. The observed behavior is considered only a symptom or sign of some underlying process or structure which is the real problem and the cause of the observed behavior. This approach, in which hypothetical constructs are treated as the primary causes of behavior, has also pervaded personality research and theory that deals with normal behavior. Often the hypothesized variable is very global and diffuse, such as "dependency," "hostile feelings," or "self-concept."

Though such vague definitions of problems may not be optimally helpful to clients and students, because they do relatively little to facilitate the design of an individualized teaching/treatment procedure, they are understandably persistent for several reasons. Krumboltz (1966) pointed out three of these reasons: (1) the abstractness of the goals facilitates individual interpretations of them to meet the individual clinician's personal preferences; (2) vague goals permit an illusion of agreement between parties discussing them—clinicians, educators, professionals talking with clients, and so forth— thus avoiding aversive disagreements; and (3) abstract goals can be developed that *appear* applicable to numerous clients or other learners (e.g., self-actualization, improved self-esteem), thus simplifying one's conception of both assessment and treatment. Further advantages are that (1) the statement of a precise objective is more likely to be followed by a request for a thorough rationale than is the statement of a vague one, thus punishing precise statements; (2) precise objectives leave the clinician or other professional more open to evaluation, more readily accountable, in that success or failure are easily detected; (3) vague personality terms have a history of being moderately useful as *predictors* of a wide range of performances, given the illusion of also explaining those performances, and thus appear more fundamental than do the performances themselves; (4) vague terms and terms referring to constructs at another level of analysis often sound profound, insightful, explanatory, or even poetic, which is likely to produce various forms of confirmation, awe, deference, and other social reinforcers from colleagues and clients; and (5) vague and hypothetical terms usually require less knowledge and less effort to generate than does a careful analysis of existing and alternative functional relations.

The sample approach that characterizes behavioral assessors is a natural outgrowth of behaviorism's origins in the animal laboratory, where scientific caution and parsimony are highly valued, and mentalism generally avoided. To the behavioral assessor, the observable behavior is seen as a problem or asset *in itself* rather than a sign of some other, less tangible entity or process. The assessor's task is seen as selecting which behaviors to change and then which environmental factors to manipulate in order to achieve that change.

Several authors have pointed out that behavioral assessors' interest in observable behaviors themselves, rather than inferred entities and processes, does not relieve us from having to deal with issues regarding the validity, reliability, procedural standardization, and normative standardization of our assessment devices (e.g., Cone, 1977; Goldfried, 1977; Hartmann, 1976; Linehan, 1977). However, it should also be recognized that the psychometric issues involved in behavioral assessment are not the same as those faced by traditional assessment (Cone, 1981). When one is directly interested in the behavior being assessed, there should be no question whether it is a valid measure of an inferred, hypothetical characteristic or dimension, as one must be concerned with in traditional assessment. Of course, there can be a question whether a particular response functions in a particular way for a particular individual, or even for some proportion of the population. Thus, one may question whether an angry-sounding "Go to hell" from a teenager to his or her parent is validly called a coercive response, in that it functions to punish the parent's demanding something of the youth. But no hypothetical construct is involved, and thus there is no "validation inference"—using Goldfried and Kent's (1972) term—to another level of conception. In this sense, one could say that validity questions are not "vertical," in that they involve no inference to another level. Instead, when one is assessing at the same level as one is conceptualizing the behavior, as has typified behavioral assessment (perhaps with the exception of cognitive behavioral assessment and anxiety assessment), the validity questions could be characterized as "horizontal." They are questions that traditional assessment has seldom addressed, because it was preoccupied with the difficult task of developing devices that showed satisfactory vertical validity. Horizontal validity questions are ones like the functional question just presented, or whether a client's verbal description is an adequate account of his or her behavior and environmental events, whether performance in a contrived simulation test represents typical performance, whether performance in the presence of an observer represents performance elsewhere, whether the behavior changes accomplished adequately addressed the referral problem (Hawkins, 1979), whether the hypothesized functional relations within the behavioral "system" receive support by the occurrence of the predicted "ripple effect" of the intervention (Evans, 1985; Goldiamond, 1984); and so on (see Cone & Hawkins, 1977).

EMPHASIS ON EFFECTIVE PERFORMANCE

In 1969, Goldfried and D'Zurilla pointed out that although "the behavioral model is an eminently reasonable way in which to conceptualize human functioning, it has failed thus far to address itself to any clear definition of what behavioral patterns may be considered 'adaptive' and 'nondeviant'" (p. 158). They then defined adaptiveness or competence as effective responding to specific "problem situations," "situations which, by virtue of their novelty or conflicting demands, present circumstances that involve the failure of previously effective responses" (p. 159). And they defined an effective response to such a situation as "a response or pattern of responses to a problem situation which alters the situation so that it is no longer problematical, and at the same time produces a maximum of other positive consequences and a minimum of negative ones" (p. 158). By their reference to "previously effective responses," they, like other behaviorists, acknowledge that there is nothing unusual about maladaptive behaviors; they were in fact adaptive at one point, in that the environment taught them. Furthermore, Goldfried and D'Zurilla pointed out that the adaptiveness of a behavior pattern is to be evaluated by the positive and negative outcomes it produces.

Goldfried and D'Zurilla then described a series of steps by which an assessor could discover the more difficult problem situations in a particular context—such as being a freshman or sophomore on a university campus— and develop a type of test to determine how well a particular individual was prepared for adaptive functioning in that context, that is, how competent the person was for that environment. Briefly, their method involved the following:

1. The assessor conducts a *situational analysis*, in which problem situations are identified by persons who are very familiar with the context of interest. In the authors' project, their primary method for identifying problem situations for undergraduate students at school was to have them list and describe the ones they noticed each day for several days. An alternative approach, which the authors made some use of, is direct observation by the assessor or questioning an indigenous observer.

2. The assessor then conducts a response *enumeration*, in which a wide variety of responses to the situation are described, responses ranging from very effective to very ineffective. Again, these alternative response descriptions can be obtained from the subjects or from observers.

3. In the *response evaluation* step, each response is judged by "significant others" who have frequent contact with the kind of subject to whom the assessment will be applied, who normally play a role in judging the adequacy of such subjects' performance, and whose opinions are likely to be respected by others, especially the subjects.

4. The assessor then goes through the *development of a measurement format*. The content of situations and scoring criteria, developed in steps 1 through 3, are then converted into a series of situations to be simulated, questions to be asked, or whatever the assessor judges to be sufficiently valid and feasible, and a method for scoring responses.

5. Finally, the resulting assessment device is applied to real subjects in an *evaluation of the measure*, applying appropriate criteria for validity and reliability.

Goldsmith and McFall (1975) appear to have been the first to apply the Goldfried and D'Zurilla model. They used it to develop a social skills treatment program for psychiatric inpatients in a Veterans Administration Hospital. First, they obtained ratings and interviews from a group of psychiatric outpatients,[2] identifying the situational contexts that they found uncomfortable (e.g., dating, job interviews) and the critical moments that were problematic within those contexts.[3] They chose the five most frequently mentioned critical moments—such as initiating or terminating interactions, responding to rejection, and being assertive, which might be called "specific tasks"—and they developed 55 vignettes in which problem situations were presented, by audiotape, that included these critical moments. Then eight "normals" (hospital staff) demonstrated how they would respond to each situation. These eight alternative responses were each evaluated as to how effective they seemed to each of five judges (child care workers, psychiatrist, and so forth), thus providing a social validation (see Kazdin, 1977; Van Houten, 1979; Wolf, 1976, 1978). The judges also provided explanations as to what made each response relatively effective or ineffective, and these explanations were then restated by the experimenters as principles of effective responding to each situation.

The experimenters used the resulting material as the basis for a social skills training program, in which the principles of effective responding were used in coaching patients how to respond and why. The principles were also used in developing scoring criteria for evaluating patient performance.

2. It is assumed that they asked outpatients because the goal was to teach the inpatients skills that would be especially useful when they left the hospital, as recommended in Ayllon and Azrin's (1968) "relevance of behavior rule."

3. They also asked about the participants and the purposes (potential patient reinforcers?) of the interactions. Assumedly, these were included in subsequently developed vignettes.

The Goldfried and D'Zurilla model provides a method for developing an assessment device or system by which deficits in competence can be discovered and targeted for remediation, either as primary prevention or as treatment. Although the discarding of problem situations that were reported by only a few persons makes the resulting assessment system somewhat normative and there is overemphasis on verbal report, the careful, empirical analysis of effective performance could be extremely useful in selection of target behaviors for individual treatment; and the system could provide effective screening of potential clients without labeling the clients as deviant. The method for developing the analyses of effective responding is apparently very time-consuming and expensive, but research of this general sort could be quite useful to behavioral assessment.

EMPHASIS ON SPECIFIC SITUATIONS OR TASKS, AND CLASSES THEREOF

It will have been evident from the preceding description that behavioral assessors generally take seriously the situation-specificity of behavior (Mischel, 1968; Peterson, 1968), while still recognizing that many particular situations can have the same function—forming a stimulus class—in regard to some behavior of interest. The situations in which the effectiveness of a person's behavior is evaluated can be characterized as tasks; McFall (1982) has pointed out that daily living consists of multiple, interrelated, and temporally concurrent or overlapping tasks.

Borrowing from Ossorio (1982), one might break life tasks arbitrarily into six levels of scope: (1) specific movements such as smiling or reaching, (2) individual actions such as saying "Hello" or shaking hands, (3) short-term activities such as carrying on a conversation or planning a trip, (4) long-term projects such as courting or getting through graduate school, (5) life-long enterprises such as maintaining a marriage or being active in a career, and (6) way-of-life tasks such as being trusted or contributing to society. The higher levels have nested within them a variety of tasks of lesser scope; thus, they are more complex, they generally take longer to accomplish, and their accomplishment is more difficult to measure.

It should also be noted that the list of tasks presented here is a mixture of performances and outcomes (effects), as is typical in casual conversation. But if all tasks are described in terms of outcomes, it is evident that each is a specification of reinforcers to be obtained (or punishers to be avoided). Analysis of what it takes to achieve such a reinforcer is called task analysis, though such a term is generally applied to only tasks at approximately level 3.

Although task analysis has received little attention in clinical work, except in work with behaviorally retarded persons, it is quite familiar in industry and education. Elsewhere I have suggested the relevance of task analysis to clinical targeting and intervention (Hawkins, 1976), and many researchers have used task analysis quite effectively without mentioning the concept.

There are four advantages of talking about tasks and the sequences of behavior required to perform them competently. First, it tends to keep the assessor's focus on observable outcomes and thus on developing skills to perform clearly specified, useful functions. Second, it provides a form of clarity that often leads the assessor to consider a wide range of intervention options, even including changing the desirability (reinforcing function) of the outcome. Third, it encourages the assessor to approach targeting and design of interventions in a "constructional" (Goldiamond, 1974), repertoire-expanding manner, rather than in an "eliminative," repertoire-contracting one, as is discussed below. Fourth, it involves breaking a task into parts, thus promoting development of interventions that build skills in small, readily achieved steps.

Through task analysis, behavioral assessors select relatively specific behaviors for change. Although very broad, inclusive goals may be selected initially—such as "to be more assertive" or "to get along well with her boss"—they are broken down into much more specific, teachable goals and objectives.

Not only are the behaviors relatively specific, but so are the situations in which they are to occur. To a behavioral assessor, the ideal statement of a behavioral target might be similar to that used by Mager (1975) in describing instructional objectives in general:

> 1. Performance. An objective always says what a learner is expected to be able to *do*.
> 2. Conditions. An objective always describes the important conditions (if any) under which the performance is to occur.
> 3. Criterion. Wherever possible, an objective describes the criterion of acceptable performance by describing how well the learner must perform in order to be considered acceptable (p. 21).

Thus, the behavioral assessor will tend to specify, relatively exactly, how the task is to be performed.

However, as McFall (1982) and Gilbert (1978) indicate, there may often be excessive cost and even risk in assuming that a *particular* task analysis is the *only* way for the client to perform competently. McFall (1982) points out that most goals or outcomes can be achieved in a variety of ways (and with roughly comparable side effects). On the one hand, this appears to have been recognized by Goldfried and D'Zurilla (1969) in that they did not treat performance as dichotomous in effectiveness but rather varying along a continuum; and Goldsmith and McFall (1975) recognized it by developing their "principles of effective responding" rather than by adopting a fixed pattern as "the correct" one for their patients to learn. Similarly, Gilbert (1978) pointed out that in some circumstances one can simply define clearly the outcome to be achieved by the learner and then let him or her practice until his or her behavior becomes proficient in achieving that outcome, regardless what particular topography of behavior that involves. However, one should note that Yeaton and Bailey's (1978) task analysis of safe street-crossing involved a relatively fixed series of behaviors under consistent stimulus control; but that is probably quite appropriate, because the skills were being taught to young children and involved their physical safety.

Another issue involved in conceptualizing targeting as task analysis is how large a task to select for analysis. As mentioned earlier, level 3 of Ossorio's (1982) description is common. But, as McFall (1982) points out, even twitching an eyelid or lifting a finger can be an important task (to be analyzed) if one is conducting physical rehabilitation of, say, stroke victims. It also seems to be the case that macroscopic tasks can be chosen profitably for analysis, even in clinical cases, as when one helps an adolescent choose a career or a married couple decide what kind of relationship they wish to have. Existential therapy tends to address macroscopic tasks; there seems no reason why behavior therapists cannot do so and have the added flexibility of moving to whatever level of scope appears productive. However, when behavior therapists lump numerous tasks together and label the related skills "social skills," closely approximating a trait conception, the definitional problems experienced by Arkowitz (1981) seem inevitable. The role of task analysis is discussed later as a current issue.

INDIVIDUALIZATION OF TARGETING

As Krumboltz (1966), Goldfried and Sprafkin (1976), and others have pointed out, the behavioral assessor is less likely than other clinicians to set the same few goals for all clients, goals such as improved self-esteem, self-actualization, or ego strength. As Goldfried and Sprafkin put it:

> Unlike the insight-oriented therapist, the behavior therapist tailor-makes the therapy goals to suit each client's problems. The specific goals chosen depend on the problematic behaviors, the factors maintaining them, and the relative seriousness of each problematic behavior. Accordingly, the behavior therapist requires assessment techniques that enable him to specify this information. [p. 19]

Thus, the behaviors selected, the conditions or situations in which they are to occur, and the criteria by which adequacy of performance will be judged are, ideally, all made individual to the particular learner. This means that the behavioral assessor will take into account the learner's current natural environment, probable future environment (see Goldiamond, 1984; Hawkins & Hawkins, 1981), the remainder of his or her repertoire (e.g., assets, liabilities, reinforcers, stimulus control), and such factors as physical attractiveness, age, income, and health.

This individualization is evidenced in the compendium of questions that Kanfer and Saslow (1969) suggested for behavior therapists to consider in attempting to analyze clinical problems functionally. Their questions included, for example, "Who objects to or appreciates these behaviors?" "What are important reinforcers and punishers for this client?" "Who exerts consequence control over the client's behavior?" "What reinforcers would be lost if treatment succeeded?" and "What are the norms in this client's environment?" Similar individualization is evident in the constructional approach described by Goldiamond (1974) and Schwartz and Goldiamond (1975), which adds an ongoing, continuous individualization by setting weekly assignments based on current performance and environmental conditions. More is said below about the constructional approach.

USE OF DIRECT OBSERVATION OF BEHAVIOR OR ITS PRODUCTS

Direct observation is defined here as the untransmuted sensing of behavior and its environmental context by a trained observer who is either the professional himself or herself or is serving as the professional's agent. In the behavioral assessment literature (e.g., Cone & Hawkins, 1977, pp. xx–xxii; Mash & Terdal, 1976, pp. 261–278), direct observation typically also implies precise, quantitative recording of the behaviors of interest, but that implication is not necessarily intended here.[4]

Sometimes behavior need not be directly observed because it produces effects on the environment that leave physical, sometimes permanent, products that are a source of information not readily obtained from direct observation of the behavior itself. Manufactured products, lists of planned tasks, writing on restroom walls, completed school tasks, sound specto-

---

4. Also typically implied is that any recordings be made immediately, though this is not denoted by the term "direct observation." Because one can imagine an observer's intentionally postponing some fairly simple recording until after leaving the observation setting, in order to minimize a learner's reactivity to observation, immediate recording does not seem a critical dimension of direct observation, provided the observer is a trained agent of the professional.

grams, and diaries are all transmutations of behavior, products that can be inspected to discover potential target behaviors or criteria for adequate performance.

Although systematic, direct observation has a long history (Hartmann & Wood, 1982), its use in clinical assessment appears to have flourished only with the advent of applied behavior analysis and behavior therapy (Mash & Terdal, 1976, p. 261). As I have already discussed, a behavioral perspective defines adjustment problems as problems of behavior (especially observable) in the presence of certain tasks, not problems of "personality" traits. Both the behaviors and the tasks are recognized as highly individual to persons and their environments. Furthermore, the behavioral perspective includes appreciation for the control exerted over behavior by the current environment, including the stimuli of the moment. Thus, it seems inevitable that behavioral assessors would make extensive use of direct observation of behavior and its products, whether that observation is in the presence of naturally occurring tasks—the natural environment—or in a controlled environment or simulation. Both of these are discussed below.

Observation in the Natural Environment

Perhaps the most influential research regarding direct observation in natural environments has been that of Bijou and colleagues. Bijou, Peterson, and Ault (1968; see also Bijou, Peterson, Harris, Allen, & Johnston, 1969) outlined two methods for directly observing and immediately recording the behavior of children and others in their preschool or other natural setting. The first of these is relatively open-ended, yet systematic, and is sometimes called ABC recording, referring to antecedents, behaviors, and consequences. It involves descriptively noting antecedent stimuli in the left of three columns on a recording sheet, noting the ensuing specific response of the subject in the middle column, and noting any observed consequences in the right column. A time notation is made in the margin every few minutes. The clinician or teacher making or reviewing such records may detect potential problems of stimulus control, response frequency, consequence control, and so on. Further, ABC recording keeps observers themselves more alert to nuances of behavior and its environment than more casual, impressionistic observation, and thus may lead to detection of adjustment problems.

The second type of recording suggested by Bijou et al. (1968) was interval recording (see Hall, 1974; Hawkins, 1982), which Arrington (1932, 1943) had previously included as a form of time sampling. During successive 10-second intervals, the observer records, in spaces specified for each particular interval, a symbol for each of the behaviors or other events occurring during those intervals. Unlike ABC recording, the observer uses a code that lists and defines the behaviors or other events of current interest. The quantitative data from these interval records are of scientific quality and have certain advantages (Baer, 1982b; Hawkins, 1982). Although they do have shortcomings (Hartmann & Wood, 1982; Johnston & Pennypacker, 1980), they have been used often in applied research. But, more relevant here, these data can be used to identify behaviors of unusually high or low rates, duration, stimulus control, and so forth, and thus potential target behaviors.

These two observation methods were used, in the laboratory preschool where they were developed, to target and monitor many different problems of small children (e.g., Allen, Hart, Buell, Harris, & Wolf, 1964; Allen, Henke, Harris, Baer, & Reynolds, 1967; Buell, Stoddard, Harris, & Baer, 1968; Harris, Wolf, & Baer, 1964). They were also applied in a home environment (Hawkins, Peterson, Schweid, & Bijou, 1966).

Observation in a Controlled, Simulation Environment

Direct observation in the natural environment appears to have been used most with children. Though use with adult problems should be explored further, it may be less necessary because adults are usually better observers and reporters of the events around them; it may be less useful because adults and those in their natural environments may be much more reactive to being observed; and it may be more expensive because adults are so mobile.

The alternative that still permits direct observation of specific behaviors is observation during simulations contrived by the assessor to resemble real-life tasks. Usually these simulations take place in an office or laboratory and involve repeated presentations of lifelike situations of a particular type. Such simulations or analogues are not only less costly and less likely to produce negative social effects for the client, but they also permit the assessor to optimize the frequency and nature of the task, standardize tasks, and use special equipment or personnel that may be difficult to place in the natural environment (Cone & Hawkins, 1977).

As McFall (1977) points out, assessment in simulated situations has a history going back at least to World War II, where it was used in selecting candidates for an overseas intelligence operation conducted by the Office of Strategic Services (OSS). Although the assessment was based on task analyses of the jobs to be performed and the assessment was quite extensive, taking 3 days, the OSS unfortunately reduced the resulting performance data to 11 trait scores that proved of little predictive validity (and training value).

It is hoped that today's behavioral assessor would use the performance data themselves. Certainly that is the plan proposed in Goldfried and D'Zurilla's (1969) "behavioral–analytic model for assessing competence," described earlier, and the procedure followed by Goldsmith and McFall (1975) in applying this model to assessing interpersonal skills of psychiatric inpatients.

The Role of Direct Observation Data in Selection of Target Behaviors

It is important to recognize that the data obtained by direct observation do not automatically identify target behaviors, although some textbooks seem to imply this (e.g., Martin & Pear, 1983; Schwartz & Johnson, 1981). Blindly measuring even several behaviors in a particular situation would, at best, only identify as problematic those behaviors observed and those situations sampled. Clearly, what is often needed in clinical and educational services is a somewhat iterative approach, in which cruder data from interviews, tests, informal observations, and the like are used to determine in what situations to measure what behaviors; and from these results even more precise measurement or more interviewing may be needed before target behaviors are selected and a functional analysis hypothesized (see Hawkins, 1979).

It is already evident from what has been said that behavior therapists strive to define their goals in measurable terms. Many behavior therapists insist upon measurement of countable movement cycles (e.g., Cone, 1981; Johnston & Pennypacker, 1980; White, 1977), though many other assessment devices are also used (Cone & Hawkins, 1977; Mash & Terdal, 1976), even personality inventories (Swan & MacDonald, 1978). What is not clear is how routinely direct observation is actually used in providing human services. Though behavioral assessment literature, particularly that which is presented in behavior analysis (operant behavior) terms, gives the impression that direct observation is a routine part of service delivery, this may not be the case except where research or university training is being conducted in conjunction with service delivery. The tasks of developing a useful, reliable behavior code and training observers are formidable and expensive to date. It is uncertain whether even the most committed behavior analysts and therapists typically conduct precise measurement through direct observation when they are working in community mental health centers, private practice, private schools, and other services not closely affiliated with a university.

This is not to say that such measurement is not, or could not be made, cost-effective. Perhaps with continued use of direct measurement in university services—as exemplified by the work of Lovitt (e.g., Lovitt, 1967; Lovitt, 1977; Lovitt & Hansen, 1976), Haynes (1978), and Forehand (Forehand & McMahon, 1981; Forehand, Reed, Roberts, McMahon, Griest, & Humphreys, 1978)—cost-effective procedures will be developed for an increasing range of problems. This seems a desirable goal, particularly in the case of observation in the natural environment. The real benefits of direct observation, as compared to any other source of information (verbal report, test, and so forth), are not only the objectivity and comprehensiveness of information regarding the learner's *behavior*, but also the objectivity and comprehensiveness regarding the *stimulus context* in which the behavior occurs: the physical and social environment, the specific cues, and the consequences. This information is likely to affect one's intervention plan dramatically, because the behavior is seen embedded in a system.

EMPHASIS ON THE FUNCTIONS PERFORMED BY CURRENT AND ALTERNATIVE BEHAVIORS

Kanfer and Saslow (1969) presented a guide for the clinician to use in gathering information for a thorough functional analysis of clinical problems. Based on Lindsley's (1964) approach—involving the stimulus (S), response (R), contingency (K), and consequence (C)—Kanfer and Saslow added variables of the organism's (O) biological condition, yielding SORKC as an acronym for the five classes of variables about which information might be needed for a functional analysis (see also Kanfer & Phillips, 1970). Goldfried and Sprafkin (1976) later omitted the contingency (K) from the list of variables and included among the organismic variables not only physiological, neurological, genetic, and biochemical factors but also private self-statements or thoughts, standards for evaluation, and feelings. The controversial nature of these additions is discussed later.

Hawkins (1975) also emphasized functional relations in behavioral assessment and pointed out that selection of what behavior to teach is not, as sometimes suggested (Wilson & O'Leary, 1980), a value decision. The relevance or "functional validity" of a targeted behavior can be experimentally evaluated by testing the effects of its acceleration or deceleration on the learners' adjustment. This is discussed later, under "Current Issues in Targeting."

The Nature of a Functional Analysis

In a functional analysis—a term used here to mean a conceptual analysis of functional relations between stimuli and responses, or between responses alone—behavior is described as embedded in functional relations. The functional relations describe what the current relevant behaviors gain and lose for the person and under what specific stimulus and contextual conditions. The analysis should also identify other, alternative functional relations that promise to reap more benefits and fewer costs to the person or others.

The terms used in a functional analysis are of profound importance, both for theoretical reasons and for practical ones. They are not a special set of concepts developed and used only in the area of specialization involved—

be it clinical psychology, psychiatric nursing, education, rehabilitation, or some other field—as is typical of most clinical and other applied terminology. They are the same terms employed in the rest of the natural science of behavior, terms commonly called "learning principles," but more accurately identified as general behavior principles (Bijou, 1979).

Such an embedded, natural science description of behavior in its hypothesized current functional relations, and of alternative behavior in its prospective functional relations, yields clear implications for several altnerative interventions that might directly or indirectly change the behavior or functions that define it as problematic.

Types of Functional Relations

Bandura (1968) proposed a system for classifying deviant behaviors that really constitutes a typology of functional relations, involving fairly specific segments of individual repertoires, a far cry from the classification of *persons* that has typified clinical assessment and much of educational assessment, as illustrated by such terms as manic-depressive, hysteric, and learning-disabled. In abbreviated form, the classes were as follows[5]:

I. *Difficulties in the stimulus control of behavior*
   A. *Defective stimulus control.* The response, while appropriate in some contexts, occurs in contexts where it is not appropriate.
   B. *Inappropriate stimulus control.* The response is never appropriate, such as head-banging, but it occurs in some contexts.
II. *Aversive self-reinforcing systems.* Standards for one's own performance are set too high.
III. *Deficient behavioral repertoires.* There is a simple lack of skill, often with complex repercussions.
IV. *Aversive behavioral repertoires.* The person demonstrates an excess of some behavior that is aversive to others.
V. *Difficulties with incentive systems (reinforcers)*
   A. *Defective incentive systems in individuals*
      Reinforcers (and assumedly punishers) are insufficiently effective to produce normal behavior.
   B. *Inappropriate incentive systems in individuals.*
      Stimuli are serving as reinforcers that should not do so (e.g., drugs, child sex objects).
   C. *Absence of incentives in environment.* The environment fails to provide needed, appropriate consequences.

5. Mager and Pipe (1970) offered a similar analysis that was less specific to clinical problems.

D. *Inappropriate incentives in environment.* This class was added by Goldfried and Sprafkin (1976) to Bandura's list. It refers to the social environment's labeling some behavior as problematic and yet reinforcing it.

This scheme is certainly more complex than the common practice of organizing problems into simply behavior excesses and deficits (e.g., Ross, 1974) or into the three groups used, for example, by Martin and Pear (1983): excesses, deficits, and inappropriate stimulus control. But subsequently, Kanfer and Grimm (1977) offered an even more extensive scheme. In outline form, it was as follows:

I. *Behavior deficits*
   A. *Information:* inadequate base of knowledge for guiding behavior
   B. *Interpersonal interaction:* failure to engage in acceptable social behaviors due to skill deficits
   C. *Self-directing skills:* inability to supplement or counter immediate environmental influences and regulate one's behavior through self-directing responses
   D. *Self-reinforcement:* deficiencies in self-reinforcement for performance
   E. *Self-monitoring:* deficits in monitoring one's own behavior
   F. *Self-control:* inability to alter responses in conflict situations
   G. *Deficits in the range of reinforcers:* limited behavior repertoire due to restricted range of reinforcers
   H. *Skills:* deficits in cognitive and/or motor behaviors necessary to meet the demands of daily living
II. *Behavior excesses*
   A. *Anxiety:* conditioned inappropriate anxiety to objects or events
   B. *Self-monitoring:* excessive self-observational activity
III. *Problems in environmental stimulus control*
   A. *Stimuli that elicit inappropriate emotional reactions:* affective responses to stimulus objects or events leading to subjective distress or unacceptable behavior
   B. *Restrictive environments:* failure to offer support or opportunities for behaviors appropriate in a different milieu
   C. *Inefficient arrangements of controlling stimulus for daily activities:* failure to meet environmental demands or responsibilities, arising from inefficient organization of time
IV. *Inappropriate self-generated stimulus control*
   A. *Self-labeling:* self-descriptions serving as cues for behaviors leading to negative outcomes
   B. *Covert behaviors:* verbal or symbolic activity serving to cue inappropriate behavior
   C. *Discrimination of internal cues:* faulty labeling of internal cues

V. *Inappropriate contingency arrangement*
  A. *Adequate behavior not followed by positive consequences:* failure of the environ-
     ment to support appropriate behavior
  B. *Beneficial effects of inappropriate behavior:* environmental maintenance of
     undesirable behavior
  C. *Reinforcement surplus:* excessive use of positive reinforcement for desir-
     able behavior
  D. *Noncontingent reinforcement:* delivery of reinforcement independent of
     responding

Although other groupings of problems are certainly possible, and some
behavioral assessors would quarrel with the utility of such concepts as
"anxiety" (Hawkins, 1976), self-reinforcement (Catania, 1976; Goldiamond,
1976a,b), or self-control (Brigham, 1980), it should be noted that ineffective
behavior patterns are generally presented by Kanfer and Grimm (1977) as
problems of inadequate antecedent stimulus control or consequence contingencies, thus making them readily susceptible to direct intervention. It is this
character—the use of the same concepts by which we analyze behavior of
other kinds in other contexts, and by which we subsequently design interventions—that gives a functional analysis its power, its pragmatic (and
theoretical) value. A functional analysis that describes behavior in terms of
the control exerted by current and very recent observable stimuli, using as
descriptors only the terms from a natural science of behavior, immediately
suggests possible interventions. The reason is that the principles named in
the analysis were derived from an *experimental* science, a science in which
behavior control (learning and maintenance) has been repeatedly demonstrated through systematic manipulation of environmental variables ("teaching," in its broadest sense).

The Constructional Approach

A particularly interesting approach to functional analysis and intervention in
clinical problems is the "constructional" one developed by Goldiamond (1974)
and colleagues. This approach—presented relatively clearly in Schwartz and
Goldiamond (1975)—gets its name from the fact that its "solution to problems is the construction of repertoires (or their reinstatement or transfer to
new situations) rather than the elimination of repertories" (Goldiamond,
1974, p. 14). Goldiamond points out that "The prevalent approach at present
focuses on the alleviation or *elimination* of distress through a variety of means
which can include chemotherapy, psychotherapy, or behavior therapy"
(p. 14), and he designates these approaches as pathology-oriented, as eliminative (one might say "contractive" as opposed to "expansive"). Extinction,

punishment, and desensitization procedures would be part of such a patho-logic, eliminative focus, a focus found by Wilson and Evans (1983) to be common among behavior therapists in targeting child behaviors for inter-vention. The constructional approach, in contrast, increases the client's options or flexibility as suggested by Myerson and Hayes (1977). In effect, it augments the client's freedom.[6]

The constructional approach can only be sketched here. The approach is modeled after programmed instruction and contains these four elements in common with it:

1. The statement of a target or outcome in observable terms. This outcome must be something to be established or constructed.

2. Description of the entering repertoire that is relevant to such con-struction.

3. Specification and use of change procedures that will expand the entering repertoire so as to produce the outcome through steps involving continual success.

4. Use of existing maintaining variables rather than extrinsic rein-forcers. According to Schwartz and Goldiamond's (1975) definition of the approach, "What keeps the client going through the program is getting what he came for. Accordingly, the approach is highly individualized" (p. 72), though it could be argued that this is not an essential ingredient, particularly for work with children and others who are not eagerly seeking help.

In the constructional approach defined by Schwartz and Goldiamond (1975) the client, with the therapist's help, analyzes what consequences are maintaining the current, maladaptive (costly) behavior pattern and then determines a less costly avenue to acquire that same reinforcer. That is, the client and therapist use the same motivation that creates the problem to solve the problem. Also, the approach requires that clients identify their own assets—the "entering repertoire"—which doubtless adds to the positive char-acter of the approach.

Other major characteristics have to do with how the problem is solved. The client leaves each session with an assignment that is highly individual-ized to his or her current skills and other resources, including performance on past assignments, which has been recorded by way of a log. The assign-ments may be aimed directly at building some skill or may be aimed more indirectly, such as at changing someone else's behavior so as to change "potentiating variables," the antecedent motivating factors that affect the

6. Recently, Goldiamond (1984) has presented a further analysis, in which interventions are characterized also along the dimensions of "linear–nonlinear" and "topical–systemic." As I understand the analysis, eliminative interventions would typically be relatively linear (direct) and topical (addressed rather exclusively at the complaint).

current potency of a consequent stimulus, as does food deprivation or the presence of very loud noise. Later, the place of a constructional approach is discussed as a current issue, and illustrations are given.

CURRENT ISSUES IN TARGETING

A behavioral perspective on assessment is relatively new and radically different from most of what has preceded, especially in assessing for intervention in clinical problems. Furthermore, this perspective is not really one unitary, coherent view. Clinical tradition, behavior therapy, and applied behavior analysis are discernable streams of history and thought regarding behavior and thus regarding assessment and behavior change (see Martin & Pear, 1983). Thus, at this early stage of development, there are several issues in assessment on which agreement between behavioral assessors is far from complete, either because of basically differing perspectives or simply because behavioral assessment is in its infancy. Some of those issues are presented here, and my own biases are doubtless evident. However, in order to conceptualize some of the issues, I would first like to define the goal of clinical (and other educational) intervention.

A DEFINITION OF ADJUSTMENT AND MALADJUSTMENT

Any clinical, educational, or vocational assessment or intervention implies a conception of adjustment, habilitation, mental health, and competence (here meaning effectiveness, not the social judgment thereof, as suggested by McFall, 1982) and thereby also of maladjustment, pathology, inadequacy, mental illness, and incompetence. Defining adjustment and maladjustment has been difficult for psychology and related fields (see Scott, 1958), and we are far from a consensus. For example, on the one hand, Knopf (1979) deals with the issue by defining abnormal behaviors as "those that persistently deviate from cultural and developmental norms in either extremes of frequency and intensity, and that are evidenced by impairment in one or more of the following areas of human functioning: intellectual and cognitive, emotional expression and control, and interpersonal relationships" (p. 32). On the other hand, Schwartz and Johnson's (1985) book on psychopathology in children appears to avoid the issue, while Lahey and Ciminero (1980) offer a definition of maladaptive behavior as "any pattern of thought, feeling, or action that is harmful to the individual or others" (p. 4).

Lahey and Ciminero's (1980) use of the term "maladaptive behavior" is not simply an aesthetic preference over the terms "abnormal behavior" or "psychopathology." As behaviorists, they no doubt wished to emphasize that it is the adaptiveness, functionality, or effectiveness of behavior that define its value, *not its deviance* from norms, though norms can affect functionality and no doubt correlate with effectiveness to a significant degree. Probably they also wished to avoid the implied "psyche" in "psychopathology," and they may have found it advantageous theoretically to have available the concept of a continuum from "adaptive" to "maladaptive" rather than the simplistic dichotomy of "pathological" versus "normal."

It does appear that, among behavior therapist and behavior analysts, a consensus may now be possible in defining adaptive and maladaptive behavior, or more accurately, in defining the *adaptiveness of behavior*, because neither the person nor any specific behavior can be considered dichotomously as adaptive or maladaptive. The resulting definition would resemble the one given by Lahey and Ciminero (1980), a conception proposed by Ferster (1965), and a definition of social skill by Libet and Lewinsohn (1973). The definition of adaptiveness or adjustment (adapted from Hawkins, 1984) might be something like this:

> Adjustment (habilitation, adaptation, competence) is the degree to which the repertoire maximizes short- and long-term reinforcers, for the person and for others, and minimizes short- and long-term punishers. The adaptiveness of any particular behavior in the repertoire—or perhaps more accurately, any functional relation between the environment and the repertoire—is the degree to which it contributes to this maximization of the benefit/cost or reinforcer/ punisher ratio for the individual and others in the present and future.

Or, in plainer terms, the more people maximize their own and others' benefits and minimize their own and others' costs in an environment, the better adjusted they are to that environment. The adaptiveness of any particular response or response complex would be the degree to which it maximizes the benefits and minimizes costs. Goldiamond (1984) provides a systematic method of analyzing the benefit/cost matrix for a clinical problem in a particular person–environment system.

This definition has several advantages. First, it uses concepts that are already a familiar part of the basic scientific principles utilized by many investigators, a desirable situation for purposes of parsimony and continued interaction between applied and basic behavioral sciences. Second, it defines the task of treatment—and other education, habilitation, or prevention— fairly clearly and in potentially measurable terms: to change the functional relations between the environment and the repertoire so as to increase the "income" and maintenance of reinforcers for the learner, or others, or to decrease the "income" and maintenance of punishers. Third, it is applicable to all habilitative activities, whether one is parenting a 3-month-old infant, treating an alcoholic, rehabilitating a stroke victim, training a machinist,

352 PURPOSES OF BEHAVIORAL ASSESSMENT

teaching history to a high school student, or teaching a delinquent youth to tell the truth. Fourth, it deals with both the individual's needs—which have been emphasized almost exclusively by clinicians and by most definitions of abnormality, pathology, or maladjustment—and the needs of the rest of society (see Myerson & Hayes, 1977). Fifth, it does not overemphasize social judgments or social norms, as do many definitions; instead it leaves them as one factor that influences occurrence of punishers or reinforcers. Sixth, it treats adjustment as a continuum and does not emphasize pathology, as many definitions have in the past (Goldiamond, 1974). Seventh, it does not categorize *persons* as adjusted or maladjusted; rather, it calls specific *performances* more or less adaptive. And finally, it is culturally and situationally relative; it incorporates the fact that what is adaptive in China will differ from what is adaptive in California, and what is adaptive with a spouse will differ from what is adaptive with a clerk.

This definition carries many implications (see Hawkins, 1984; Hawkins & Hawkins, 1981), several of which will be evident when considering some of the following unresolved issues in behavioral targeting.

CONSTRUCTIONAL VERSUS ELIMINATIVE TARGET SELECTION

The constructional approach described earlier suggests that we make every reasonable attempt to expand repertoires rather than contract them. This seems a promising and ethically safe preference, although it is not yet clear how thoroughly one can adhere to it in some kinds of problems, especially such as the self-injurious behavior often seen in severely developmentally disabled clients. Also, those who see "anxiety" as a significant causal factor in many adjustment problems (e.g., see Levis & Boyd, 1979; Wolpe, 1969, 1979) and who choose the very popular desensitization, an eliminative procedure, as an intervention, may find a thoroughgoing constructional approach unappealing. Nevertheless, the constructional approach appears worthy of persistent effort, not only because of its ethical and freedom-enhancing character, but also because it demands skillful and creative functional analyses by the clinician, analyses that can lead to valuable reconceptualizations of a variety of behavioral problems and assets.

The flexible, creative character of the constructional approach comes largely from the fact that numerous points of intervention are revealed by a serious functional analysis and that one is often forced to consider unusual alternatives in order to remain constructional. To clarify this, I will suggest a theoretical scheme that I have heretofore used only in my teaching, then use that scheme in some illustrations of possible constructional solutions to problems.

Concepts Useful in a Functional Analysis

In this discussion, I borrow part of the concept of setting events from Kantor (1959), as presented in Bijou and Baer (1978); the concept of potentiating variables—termed thus because they govern the potency of consequent stimuli as reinforcers or punishers—from Goldiamond and colleagues (Goldiamond & Dyrud, 1967; Schwartz & Goldiamond, 1975); and most of the remaining concepts from Keller and Schoenfeld (1950) and Skinner (1953, 1969). As the starting point, I offer the following sketch of factors governing behavior. Rather than the familiar three-term contingency (Skinner, 1969), it involves six terms. The first three terms are antecedent to the behavior and include contextual cues, motivating operations, and specific discriminative stimuli. The fourth, fifth, and sixth terms are the response itself, the contingent relation between the response and its consequences, and the consequent stimuli themselves. Only the first two terms should require explanation here, the others being very familiar.

Contextual cues, as used here, are the stimuli that serve as ambient, often subtle and distal, cues affecting the current probability of a particular response. For example, when I am at a convention attended by friends from Western Michigan University, where I used to teach, I am likely to make the error of referring to the place where I now teach as "Western," while I rarely make that error when in West Virginia. Similarly, it is more difficult to recall a person's name when you see that person in an unusual context. Contextual cues appear to be one part of what Bijou and Baer (1978) mean by setting events or setting factors. Many of the changes in our behavior that we attribute to the "atmosphere," "mood," or "tone" of a particular environment or situation—such as a physician's office, boxing match, or a nightclub—are a result of such contextual cues. Sometimes the cues arising from our own previous responses in the situation serve such a contextual role in relation to our subsequent responses, even though other, more salient and readily specifiable cues exert more obvious influence.

The second term consists of motivating operations, which include both potentiating and what I will call "depotentiating" operations, events or conditions that affect the power of a consequent stimulus.[7] The most familiar potentiating variables from the laboratory are water deprivation, food deprivation, and the presence of loud noise or electric shock. Each affects the

7. Michael (1982) calls these "establishing operations," a term used briefly by Keller and Schoenfeld (1950), in which are included the factors earlier called "drive," but which goes further than that concept without having its disadvantages as a hypothetical construct. Bijou and Baer (1978) include such operations in their concept of the "setting event" or "setting factors," showing the influence of Kantor (1959). I have used the term "motivating operation" (Hawkins, 1977).

power of a particular type of event as a consequence; water presentation, food presentation, noise reduction, or shock reduction become reinforcers (or more powerful ones) under these conditions. But there are several other classes of motivating variables. Salt intake affects the power of water presentation or termination; illness can depotentiate food presentation as a reinforcer, even potentiate it as a mild punisher; events that elicit anger seem also to depotentiate painful stimuli as punishers and even increase the reinforcing power of seeing someone else become angry (though the emotion cannot be said to cause this effect but only to correlate with it); and the feeling of an unlighted cigarette in the mouth makes seeing a flame reinforcing of a smoker's match-striking behavior, even though the presence of flame had not been an effective reinforcer 10 seconds earlier. One can consider reinforcer sampling (Ayllon & Azrin, 1968; Martin & Pear, 1983) as another motivating operation. Even the establishment of a conditioned reinforcer through a more gradual learning process would be such an operation. Thus, I have enumerated at least five types of manipulations that could serve as motivating operations and might thus be available for manipulation in a program to change a targeted behavior: chemical, health, emotional, precurrent stimuli, and learning (even "reminding").

Illustrations Applying the Constructional Approach to Clinical Targeting

A few clinical examples briefly illustrate constructional targeting using these six factors. Each is necessarily simplified, to illustrate a single application. Use of contextual cues is illustrated by Schwartz and Goldiamond's (1975) case of a depressed man who was overworking, neglecting his family (whom he enjoyed and valued greatly), and, as a result, jeopardizing his marriage, his health, and his children's development. The authors might have conjectured, among other things, that the man was afraid of (avoiding) failure at his work and then might have applied an eliminative procedure such as desensitization. Instead they used, as one of their interventions, the man's taking his wife on "dates" more frequently, thus putting himself under the influence of contextual cues for purely social, nonwork interaction. They also set a goal of "Do all work at the office," which should improve his efficiency at work (for which "Do no work at home" might be less effective), and perhaps having him receive at least as many professionally relevant reinforcers as he had been receiving by working inefficiently on weekends. A second example might involve a client who does not fall asleep readily at night. That client might arrange contextual cues by having a certain ritual before bedtime, such as reading a novel for at least 30 minutes while sipping warm milk.

Use of motivating operations is illustrated in a case of my own, a 14-year-old, socially and linguistically deficient youth who did a variety of strange or mildly aggressive things at home and school—teasing the cat, squeaking, burping, remaining mute when questioned, and so on—all of which were followed by attention and often agitation on the part of his mother and other family members. Although I could have used extinction and punishment procedures to eliminate these behaviors, instead I had his parents read stories with him frequently, thus partially satiating him for attention and, at the same time, expanding his linguistic skill and store of social information. Similarly, Glenn (1983) describes the case of a passive-resistant boy whose mother barraged him with instructions and commands, to such an extent that the mother's approval may have lost much of its reinforcing power for the boy and her disapproval or distress shifted from a punisher to a reinforcer, a common effect accompanying anger. Glenn suggested that the best way to break this vicious circle might be to target first the mother's commanding behavior, on the grounds of its motivational effect.

Use of discriminative stimulus control might be illustrated by one's teaching a client to make daily "to do" lists, thus creating discriminative stimuli (S^Ds) that are durable (unlike "remembering") and reviewable as a complete set, so that more efficient prioritizing of activities occurs. Also, the familiar method of prompting skillful performance and gradually shifting stimulus control to the normal S^Ds exemplifies a constructional strategy. A third example would be one of bringing adequate S^Ds closer to the behavior, as when a student learns to review notes shortly before a test, or a salesperson rehearses a sales pitch just before using it.

Some constructional interventions emphasizing the nature of the response itself are quite familiar, especially those involving shaping. Here the form of the response is gradually changed through shifts in the reinforcement and extinction contingencies. For example, voice loudness in shy adolescents has been increased in order to make the youngsters more effective in accessing social and socially mediated reinforcers (Jackson & Wallace, 1974; Schwartz & Hawkins, 1970).

Constructional use of consequent stimuli is very familiar in behavior analysis and therapy. School children have been motivated to perform well academically (e.g., Redd, Ullmann, Stelle, & Roesch, 1979), youngsters have begun picking up forest litter (Burgess, Clark, & Hendee, 1972), and many other favorable behavior changes have been wrought simply by the addition of new consequences for adaptive behavior. When there is existing maladaptive (high-cost) behavior, the constructional approach emphasizes studying the function(s) that it performs for the person and then constructing new performances to achieve that same end. For example, Hawkins and Hayes (1974) decided that a schoolgirl's reading errors were being reinforced by extra teacher attention and therefore made that attention differentially contingent upon correct responses, which greatly improved the youngster's accuracy. Similarly, Goldiamond (1984) reported a case in which a young woman effectively quieted her "noisy" Mexican in-laws through a behavior pattern similar to Gilles de la Tourette syndrome, which involved beating her chest while vigorously turning her head, grimacing, and voicing a four-letter expletive. The solution included teaching her alternative ways to keep the relatives quieter.

A constructional intervention that manipulated the contingent relation between a targeted response and a consequence might involve enriching the schedule of a spouse's expressed appreciation of housekeeping achievements or providing a learning-disabled child with more immediate feedback about academic performance.

Another habilitative procedure involving the contingent relation alone, with no substantial change in the target behavior, is simply making the existing repertoire effective by "prosthetic" interventions (Lindsley, 1964). Here the contingency, or behavioral requirement, is changed so that the existing behavior achieves the reinforcer. For example, in order to make the existing (or readily learned) responses of a cerebral palsied or severely retarded learner adequate for achieving the consequences of getting his or her clothes on, one can use pants with elastic waistbands, Velcro fastenings, large arm openings, and so on. Eating utensils, games, ambulation devices, and other aspects of the physical environment can be devised or adapted to meet the skills that are present or readily attainable by persons with various handicaps. Sometimes the inadequacy of one skill can be compensated for by developing a compensatory behavior, such as writing notes to oneself to compensate for poor recall. And sometimes the compensatory behavior may be in another repertoire, as when we choose a partner for some team activity (even marriage) who has skills that compensate for some of our deficits.

Though all of these examples have involved a constructional behavior-analytic approach, it must be acknowledged that a behavior analytic approach can also be eliminative. Thus one may target directly a client's sexual arousal at the sight of an attractive child and punish that behavior or attempt to reduce the reinforcing effectiveness of sexual contact with children through pairing child pictures with aversive stimuli. Similarly, one may punish self-injurious behaviors of an autistic child or stealing in a delinquent adolescent. Eliminative targeting and intervention often appears to be more direct and more quickly effective, but it sometimes is based on a very superficial functional analysis or none at all. Elsewhere, I have illustrated this with the following real example.

A behavior analyst was given responsibility for the case of a young man with a Ph.D. in biology who had developed hysterical blindness and lost his university teaching position. The behavior analyst was particularly interested in studying the aversive control of behavior, so he constructed some laboratory apparatus with which he could make electric shock contingent upon the young man's failure to make an avoidance response that required a gross visual discrimination. Then, as the subject became proficient at avoiding the shock under one discrimination problem, the problem was made more subtle and complex.

This may sound reasonable until we look at more facts of the case. The biologist had great difficulty getting through graduate school, the teaching job he had lost was his first position, he had held it only a few months when he became "blind," he had demonstrated a high level of anxiety about his work, and he had always shown an unusual amount of dependent behavior.

It would seem that the man's problem was much more than hysterical blindness, and involved such things as his job competency, his own evaluation of his job performance, the achievement goals he set for himself, and certain kinds of dependent behavior under stress. [Hawkins, 1975, pp. 196–197]

A constructional approach to targeting would have analyzed such variables.

Supportive Research

Carr and Durand (1985) recently reported research that supports and further illustrates the constructional approach, as applied to autistic children. They measured several disruptive behaviors while the children were working on tasks, then they separately manipulated the difficulty of the task and the amount of attention given the child while working on the task. They found that for some children an increase or decrease in task difficulty had little or no effect on their disruptive behavior, while a change in the amount of attention had a substantial effect. They conceived of these children's disruptive behaviors as communicating "How do you like my work?" a response that is maintained by contingent adult attention. This group might be called the attention-seeking group.

For other children, Carr and Durand found that changes in adult attentiveness had little or no effect on their disruptive behavior, while a change in the difficulty of the task had a substantial effect. They conceived of these children's disruptive behaviors as communicating "This is too hard for me" a response that is controlled by the consequence of task termination or adult assistance. This group might be called the task-relief group.

Carr and Durand then taught one of two verbal responses to individuals from each group: "How do you like my work?" or "This is too hard." The former was followed by adult attention/approval and the latter by adult assistance. When members of the attention-seeking group were taught to say "How do you like my work?" their disruptive behavior declined substantially, but when they were taught "This is too hard" no such improvement ensued. Similarly, when members of the task-relief group were taught to say "This is too hard" their disruptiveness declined, while teaching them "How do you like my work?" had no effect or actually increased the disruptive behavior (to which the experimenter's response was something like "You're doing wonderful, now do *more*"). In both cases, by teaching the child a skill that would obtain an outcome that apparently was currently functional as a reinforcer, these researchers circumvented the disruptive behaviors that were immediately costly to the teacher and ultimately costly to the child.

It is not yet clear how consistently the constructional approach can be applied, nor whether it is as efficient as a more direct approach, when the problem is a behavioral excess. It does appear worthy of thorough exploration, and behavioral assessors should probably be biased in its favor because of its freedom-enhancing nature.

THE VALUE-JUDGMENT VERSUS EMPIRICAL APPROACH

Although it has been common for behavior therapists to say that "choosing therapeutic objectives (targets) is a matter of value judgment" (Wilson & O'Leary, 1980, p. 285; parentheses mine), this can be debated. The appropriateness of a particular goal seems to be an empirical question, fundamentally (Hawkins, 1975). The issue is what responses at what levels will improve the effectiveness (reinforcer/punisher ratio) of the learner's repertoire. As I illustrated above, with the case of the young PhD biologist who was hysterically blind, some target behaviors are better choices than others. I would agree that those choices can be empirically evaluated, and to a limited degree they are being evaluated every time we conduct research on an intervention and measure a target behavior. Let me provide an illustration of this point. Suppose that a clinician is faced with a freshman who is unhappy and questioning the meaning of life, a type of problem that therapists may find difficult because the client mentions neither a behavior nor a specific situation. The clinician may hypothesize that the student's report of malaise is a way of describing a drastic reduction in the rate of his or her social behaviors and/or receipt of social and socially mediated reinforcers, which often results from leaving a home environment where many well-established social relationships existed. If the clinician then helps the client establish new rewarding relationships and the report of malaise ends, this is suggestive evidence that the functional analysis that targeted social interactions was correct for that client. If, however, the clinician had targeted the client's verbal behavior regarding a philosophy of life and had obtained no improvement in the report of malaise, this would suggest that such target selection was incorrect for that client.

Of course these hypothetical assessments and treatments, as described here, are not scientifically adequate, though they are the kind of process that constitutes the "professional experience" upon which a clinician or educator must often rely. A better basis for judgment would be the kind of systematic, documented experience that we call science. For example, a group of researchers on several college campuses might apply each of three reasonable assessment hypotheses to a series of clients in a well-controlled experiment, perhaps the above social relationship hypothesis, the verbal philosophy of life hypothesis, and a study skills hypothesis. The researchers would document that the social, verbal, or study behaviors they addressed were actually changed and would measure the client's reports of malaise, plus whatever other dependent variables seemed particularly relevant (e.g., achievement, social involvement, rating of life satisfaction). They would probably find that each assessment hypothesis was valid (effective) to some *degree* for certain clients and to a lesser degree for others. They would also find that one hypothesis was more valid for more *clients* than another. If the clients involved were representative of subsequent freshmen voicing similar complaints, the clinicians would then have an empirically based, prioritized list of three assessment hypotheses to apply to these subsequent clients.

A related issue is who should select targets for intervention: the professional or the learner. In schools, of course, we readily accept the fact that the behaviors to be learned are to be selected primarily by the professional, though parents often have significant involvement, either directly or through an elected school board. But in the clinic we may go so far in the other direction as to say that "choosing therapeutic objectives . . . ought to be determined primarily by the client" (Wilson & O'Leary, 1980). Yet Barlow, Reynolds, and Agras (1973) did not accept a transsexual's judgement that a sex-change operation would be the most beneficial outcome for him. Instead they taught him to behave in a more masculine manner—thus expanding his repertoire, augmenting his options—and his judgement about a sex-change operation changed as a *result*. Also, the mis-targeting described in my previous illustration involving the PhD biologist was at least agreeable to the client, though it proved invalid. In fact, I have often found the observational, verbal, and problem-solving skills of clients and students— especially children, delinquents, retarded persons, and poorly educated adults—to be quite inadequate for the task of identifying targets, even with considerable "leading" by the clinician or teacher.

This is not to say that the client's judgement is irrelevant. If the clinician-scientists conducting the above hypothetical study of unhappy college freshmen were to look for predictors of the relative effectiveness of the three assessment hypotheses, they might find that the clients' own preference for one hypothesis over another was a very good predictor of the effectiveness of the hypothesis. At the very least, clinicians working with adult outpatients—who can readily choose not to comply with treatment instructions or even to continue in treatment—must attend to the client's own hypotheses. But I believe that the clinician cannot avoid responsibility for the choice of assessment hypotheses and that he or she is typically more competent than the client in choosing that hypothesis. One great advantage that the client has is extended and intimate experience in the network of environmental contingencies and personal responses that make up the problem, and the clinician's task during assessment is to sample enough of this same information to arrive at a promising selection of targets for intervention. The client's own reaction to one or more such selections, and the rationales for them, may help the clinician decide whether enough of the right kinds of information has been gathered and considered in arriving at the assessment hypothesis.

We behavior therapists have often been remiss in presenting our assessment hypotheses, perhaps partly because we are not yet sufficiently skilled at formulating such functional analyses. For example, Bailey and Lessen (1984) found that even the applied behavior analysis literature seldom provides adequate rationales or empirical justification for the intervention targets selected, and Emery and Marholin (1977) found virtually no rationales in the delinquency literature. Some researchers have also complained that we often target the behavior of the referred client when it might be more adaptive in the long run to target aspects of that client's environment (Holland, 1978; Morris, 1978; Winett & Winkler, 1972). But we are gradually becoming more sensitive to our responsibilities for target selection and even beginning to build an applied empirical base for that task (e.g., Carr & Durand, 1985; McKnight, Nelson, Hayes, & Jarrett, 1984; Voeltz & Evans, 1982; Wilson & Evans, 1983).

It should be recognized that applied research is not the only empirical basis on which target selection is founded. All behavioral science is potentially relevant, and particularly relevant are those laws and procedures described by Bijou (1979) as "general behavior principles." These principles have made possible a kind of analysis that consistently describes an individual's behavior in terms of the functions performed by the environment for that individual and that behavior. The power of such an analysis comes from the fact that not only are the principles founded on thousands of studies but also the behavior is described in terms of environmental variables that can be directly *manipulated*, giving the clinician or educator immediate and usable cues regarding possible interventions. Persons in all clinical, educational, and other applied disciplines would be well advised to learn thoroughly this behavior analytic approach, and it should be recognized that such learning is not accomplished by only a course or two in behavior modification, behavior therapy, or behavior theory (see Michael, 1980).

In addition, much further applied research is needed, and the direction that such research might take should be evident from a discussion of the relevance of task analysis, skill hierarchies, and other functional relations.

THE RELEVANCE OF TASK ANALYSIS, SKILL HIERARCHIES, AND OTHER FUNCTION RELATIONS

Task Analysis

As mentioned earlier, task analysis has received little explicit attention in clinical work. Thus, the potential benefits of this approach have yet to be explored adequately. It appears that concepts like "social skills," "assertiveness," and "impulsivity" could be approached more effectively by behavioral assessors using a task analysis perspective than the traitlike perspective that one sometimes finds.

In conducting a task analysis, one attempts to discover how a task is performed competently—that is, a situation responded to effectively or adaptively—so that this performance can be taught to persons who are not competent at the task (thus, it might be called "skills analysis"). The overall performance is broken into component steps to make clear the various effects (outcomes, reinforcers) that must be produced enroute to the terminal goal (reinforcer) for which the task is named. Thus, if one has already selected as a goal, teaching a child to make friends with others, one's first job is to define the desired outcomes, the functional relations implied by "friendship." These might include, for example, "the client child's attention, approval, admiration, and even presence will serve as reinforcers for the other child" and "the client child's verbal behavior will contain or lead to many reinforcers for the other child ('He's fun,' 'He helps us win,' and so on)." The next job is to analyze the task of achieving these functional relations, perhaps using some form of "template matching" (Bem & Funder, 1978) to find out what the learner's particular environment will reinforce and punish. In the friend-making analysis, one might decide that some important component skills are approaching other children, initiating play, discovering the other person's interests, showing interest in what the other party says and does, talking about (thus knowing about) topics that interest the other party, and so on.

Usually task analyses specify sequential performance, like this friendship-making example sounds thus far, but they can also specify concurrent and alternative performance. Thus, one might specify that the child approaches the peer "in a relaxed manner" or that the suggestion of a joint activity be "accompanied by a smile or other positive facial expression." It will be noted that even though concurrent performances are being specified here, the analysis thus far still reveals a response chain. In specifying that chain, it is probably best to focus first on the enroute *effects* to be accomplished, such as "first get her positive attention," rather than focus on the behavioral topography or movements to be emitted. This focus on effects should maximize the contingency-shaping, by "natural reinforcers" (Ferster,

1972), of the fine-grain performance as the learner practices *in vivo* (see Meadowcroft, 1978). Otherwise, the behavior may be so rule-governed (Skinner, 1969) or rote as to appear stilted and be insufficiently effective.

In addition to linear sequences or chains, there may be many alternative behaviors at various points in interacting. Thus, when the child's peer is having difficulty accomplishing some job, the child might *either* offer to help physically or offer advice (but probably not call the other person inept, unless the contingency shaping between them has developed such a remark as a friendly joke). Or, when the child first approaches the other person, the child might *either* introduce himself or herself, or invite the other person to play, or ask where the other person lives. Sometimes various alternative responses will be roughly equal in effect. At other times, antecedent stimuli should evoke only a narrow range of alternative responses, as when a stranger says "Hi, I'm Patty," which should evoke a very similar response from the client.

With some tasks, particularly in industry or education, there may be an accepted sequence in which the responses are to be performed—as in performing long division problems—or an accepted set of concurrents or alternatives. But it should not be assumed that the sequence or concurrents that are accepted are the most *functional* in achieving the goals, as Kazdin (1977) pointed out. Thus, although Goldsmith and McFall (1975) obtained the judgments of normal hospital personnel regarding how certain community-living tasks could be performed competently by mental hospital patients, such social validation is only a convenient (perhaps often necessary) substitute for an experimental validation, as will be discussed later. By focusing attention constantly on the terminal effects and the en route effects to be produced, what begins as a rule-governed performance based on the accepted sequence or concurrencies may be shaped into an increasingly effective one, especially if variations are explicitly encouraged and extensive practice is arranged.

Some degree of task analysis is usually found in behavioral assessors' selection of general and specific target behaviors, though it appears that greater awareness of this would yield much more thorough and empirically based task analyses, thus contributing more to our applied science.

Skill Hierarchies

Some skills cannot be acquired, or at least are very difficult to acquire, until other skills are already in place. This phenomenon seems particularly obvious in the learning of mathematical skills (see Resnick, *et al.*, 1973), but it is also clear that a person must be skilled at grasping before learning to hammer effectively, must attend to positive feedback in order for the relevant behavior to be reinforced by that feedback, and must respond appropriately to (understand) oral language before learning to follow someone's oral instructions. It has been suggested (Lovaas, Schreibman, Koegel, & Rehm, 1971) that autistic children's learning is delayed by their "stimulus overselectivity," which implies that one might target broader stimulus-scanning as a "keystone" skill (see Voeltz & Evans, 1982) that is prerequisite to (or at least facilitative of) the learning of numerous other skills (Koegel, Egel, & Dunlap, 1980).[8]

We currently know very little about skill hierarchies involved in such problems as depression, alcoholism, hyperactivity, delinquency, anorexia, and the many other adjustment problems addressed by clinicians daily, and the necessary empirical evidence may take several decades to develop. Meanwhile, the practitioner can speculate rationally, use the speculations of other experts, and perhaps use normal development as a suggestive guide (Hawkins, 1975; White, 1980). As Hunt and Azrin (1973) suggest regarding alcoholism, instead of asking "Why is this man an alcoholic?" we might ask "Why isn't everyone an alcoholic?" and thereby investigate the behavioral development and conditions that seems to promote nonalcoholic performance. This would, of course, be consistent with the constructional approach discussed earlier, and it would contribute to preventive programs immensely.

Access Behaviors

Some behaviors are important because of their relevance to gaining or maintaining access to an environment that is either rich in rewards or effective in teaching needed skills. The rich environment would directly improve the client's reinforcer/punisher ratio (adjustment); while the teaching environment would improve the client's adjustment in the longer run.

An example of gaining access to a reinforcer-rich environment is the deinstitutionalization of hospitalized clients. Any behavior targeted because it will facilitate successful deinstitutionalization would likely be habilitative due to this effect alone, even if that behavior is not habilitative in the shorter run, in the institution itself. The client may be taught to sit without rocking, to say "Thank you" appropriately, to ask for help when needed, and to select clothing appropriately so that others will accept the person into their midst more readily and perhaps even seek him or her out.

8. Actually, such an approach may be just as inefficient as the teaching of "sequencing" to learning disabled students or the teaching of geometric formboard assembly to retarded learners. These assumed underlying skills are probably most efficiently learned incidental to learning skills that are directly useful (see Brown, Branston, Hamre-Nietupski, Pumpian, Certo, & Gruenwald, 1979; White, 1980).

An example of targeting behavior that gains or maintains access to an important learning environment would be selection of a student's compliance with rules so that he or she may stay in school. Similarly, a socially withdrawn boy's learning some facts about baseball, learning to play a musical instrument, learning to initiate conversations, or simply learning to bathe and groom himself may be part of a plan to gain him access to social environments that will teach him the numerous additional skills necessary for more complete social effectiveness (and may, at the same time, be rich in reinforcers). Of course, all such targeting, when it directly addresses the client's behavior rather than the behavior of those in the learning environment, accepts the status quo of that environment's contingencies, as Winett and Winkler (1972) complained regarding teaching school youngsters to "be still, be quiet, be docile." An indirect alternative is to modify that environment, as when one tries to make a father more tolerant regarding his daughter's choice of clothing or make the general public more tolerant of harmless talking-to-self.

Behaviors Functioning as Contextual Stimuli or as Motivating Operations

When a husband shows admiration for his wife's performance at work, he probably makes it more likely that she will later agree with his suggestion that they throw a dinner party for his boss. When a father plays a game with his daughter, it probably becomes more likely that she will then clean her bedroom cheerfully. And when a student enters the schoolroom with a friendly greeting and smile for his teacher, the teacher is probably less prone to scold him for minor misbehavior later. These behaviors that provide contextual cues, often quite distant in time from the behaviors they affect, can be very relevant targets, as Wahler and Fox (1981) imply.

Other behaviors may be selected for their motivational effect, their effect on the power of particular consequences for the client or others. Earlier I discussed briefly the task analysis of friendship-making, pointing out that one result of such interactions is the enhancement of certain client behaviors, and even presence, as social reinforcers. Somewhat similarly, Wahler (1969) found that a mother's approval gained value as a reinforcer when he taught her to punish effectively. Finally, a supervisor's effectiveness with supervisees might be enhanced by getting to know them as individuals and showing some interest in their personal lives.

Several other functional relations between behaviors could be discussed such as the importance of do-say and say-do correspondence (Karlan & Rusch, 1982) or generalized imitation (Wahler & Fox, 1981) in acquisition of numerous other skills or in access to various environments; but the examples presented already should suffice to illustrate the general phenomenon. The degree to which such behavioral functions are considered seems to vary dramatically from one behavioral assessor to another. At our present level of development, much research and conceptual analysis will be needed before careful functional analyses can be expected routinely of behavioral assessors.

DIRECT VERSUS INDIRECT TARGETS

It should be evident from the preceding that functional analysis often results in an indirect form of targeting. For example, the assessor may select some behavior to be decelerated as the *ultimate* target, such as the costly behavior of obsessive thinking about death, yet address that problem by selecting other behaviors to construct, ones that might be called *intermediate* target behaviors because they mediate between the current status and the desired status. These intermediate behaviors may even be those of some person other than the client. But this functional analytic approach must be differentiated from indirect targeting that is not based on a functional analysis, such as teaching children who read poorly to crawl on all fours, walk a balance beam, or discriminate geometric patterns, on the questionable assumption that these skills are necessary for learning to read (see Lovitt, 1967, 1977). Brown and colleagues (e.g., see Brown et al., 1979) have addressed this issue as it relates to the education of severely handicapped persons, pointing out that such skills as putting pegs in a pegboard or passing a beanbag to the next person in a circle are not nearly as functional and justifiable, in terms of preparation for daily living in the community, as are inserting proper coins in a vending machine or selecting the correct public restroom for their gender. Much of the treatment of delinquents has been similarly wasteful and ritualistic (Emery & Marholin, 1977).

HYPOTHETICAL CONSTRUCTS AS TARGET BEHAVIORS

Private ("Cognitive") Events

A further form of indirectness of targeting is to select unobservable behaviors or entities for modification. It is currently popular in some circles to conceptualize adjustment problems in terms of such unobservable constructs as thoughts, beliefs, perceptions, feelings, attributions, or expectations and in terms of the processes that are hypothesized to affect such things, processes such as selective abstraction, repertoire search, interpretation, arbitrary inference, and all-or-none thinking (e.g., Beck, 1976; Hollon & Bemis, 1981; McFall, 1982). This popularity is evidenced even among many who are identified with behavioral assessment and behavior therapy. Although these cognitive behavior therapists are "a rather broad assortment of strange bedfellows" (Meichenbaum & Cameron, 1982, p. 313; see also Zettle & Hayes, 1982)—showing differences in theoretical concepts, assessment procedures, general style of intervention, selection of target behavior, selection of interventions, and so on—they share the assumption that much, perhaps even all, maladaptive behavior is at least partly a result of maladaptive cognitions. The central role given cognitions is illustrated by Meichenbaum and Cameron when they say that the point for intervention is somewhere "in the cognition-affect-behavior-consequence complex" (p. 312) and by Meichenbaum's (1977) statement that "The clinician's concern is with the . . . 'why' and 'how' rather than *merely* the performance outcome" (p. 236, italics added), suggesting that the real causes of behavior are the hypothesized private structures and processes termed "cognitive." The scientific defensibility and ultimate utility of such cognitive accounts of behavior may be the greatest area of disagreement today among psychologists in general and behavioral assessors in particular.

An opposing viewpoint, one arising from basic research rather than a clinical tradition, would argue for conceptual parsimony and reluctance to insert seemingly unnecessary constructs into the causal chain of which overt behavior is a part (e.g., Jones, 1977; Moore, 1981; Skinner, 1953; Skinner, 1977). For example, Morris, Higgins, and Bickel (1982) provide evidence that, despite claims by some cognitivists to the contrary, the subjective inference that characterizes mentalism is also very evident in cognitive accounts of behavior. They point out that because scientists, as members of the general culture, have a long-standing and shared history of reinforcement involving extrascientific, mentalistic explanation of behavior, and because manipulation of words is so much easier than seeking empirical answers to difficult questions, it is very tempting to explain behavior by reference to hypothesized cognitive entities and processes. This is particularly tempting when immediate controlling stimuli are not obvious and where the observed stimulus control is not one that was directly taught. It can even be argued that "cognitive *behavioral* assessment" is a nonsense term because cognitive science often uses the mentalism and the physiologic reductionism that modern behaviorism has generally eschewed (see Bijou, 1979).

It should be acknowledged that objections to cognitive conceptions of maladjustment focus primarily on the scientific merits of such a conception of behavior rather than the practical merits. It seems possible, at least in the short term, that some cognitive conceptions of problems may be useful because they may lead most clinicians to effective interventions more readily than will the terms of a natural science, which are less familiar to most clinicians. For example, if a child's father proudly describes dealing with his

14-year-old son's smoking in a very authoritarian manner, a clinician might conclude something like "He thinks (believes, assumes, and so on) that a good father is a macho father," or even something like "He *has* the belief that . . . ," which reifies a hypothesized entity: belief (see Hineline, 1983). The clinician might then plan to intervene to modify the father's *verbal* behavior about the stimulus equivalence of "good father" and "macho father." This may well prove to be effective, especially in combination with some other interventions. Though it would be affirming the consequent, and thus erroneous logic, to say that such a favorable outcome firmly validates the clinician's verbal conception of the functional relations, the clinician's conception may still facilitate effective intervention. The targeting may be relatively invalid as science, in that there is no "belief" or "thought" causing the father's behavior; yet the targeting may be acceptably functional in that it promotes relatively effective intervention for that clinician. Only extensive research could show whether certain cognitive conceptions commonly promote more effective interventions than noncognitive conceptions, and for what clinicians and kinds of problems. Thus far the evidence is not impressive (e.g., Rosenthal, 1982, p. 348; Zettle & Hayes, 1980, 1982).

Emotions

But cognitive events are not the only constructs that may be questioned. Clinical psychology has for many decades emphasized emotions as intrinsic to adjustment problems (though the definition of adjustment that I offered earlier certainly carries no such implication), as the term "emotional disturbance" vividly illustrates. Anxiety has been particularly emphasized and has generally been construed to have a causal role, most notably in Freudian psychology, but often in behavior therapy as well. For example, poor performance on tests, in public speaking, in approaching members of the opposite sex, in joining activities held in small rooms, and myriad other skills is often attributed to anxiety. The anxiety is then targeted for intervention, commonly through desensitization, while the performance problem itself is often left to change as an indirect result of the change in anxiety.

But anxiety is a construct invented by humankind. One cannot point to or count one anxiety (see Johnston & Pennypacker, 1980) as one can a correct test answer, a spoken word, entering an elevator, an approach to a member of the opposite sex, or leaving one's house. Instead, anxiety is identified as an inconsistent collection of physiologic responses, verbal reports, and numerous possible motor responses ranging from escaping a stimulus to speaking dysfluently for a moment. This strange and varying assemblage of behaviors, some of which appear to be respondent and some of which are *clearly* operant, does not seem a likely candidate for a target "behavior." Even if one

addressed separately the social performance deficits, the physiologic correlates, and the verbal report of dread or helplessness, as proposed by Lang
(1977), the primary excuse for such an approach seems to be the clinician's
assumption that these poorly correlated responses constitute a single entity,
a drive or similar construct (Cone, 1979).

The popularity of the anxiety conception and anxiety targeting among
behavior therapists appears to be attributable, at least in part, to six factors:
(1) It is consistent with the way our general verbal community describes
various problems; thus it fits the conception we have been taught since
childhood. (2) It is similarly consistent with verbal tradition in clinical psychology, psychiatry, and social work, thus it is seldom questioned and often
reinforced. (3) It is a targeting for which most clinicians probably have a
ready treatment, often systematic desensitization. (4) Targeting anxiety,
rather than the various performance problems presented by individual persons in individual environments provides the same simple answer to each
assessment problem, saving the assessor much effort. (5) The systematic
desensitization that is implied, for many clinicians, is a method that Wolpe
(1958) described with unusual precision, as Wilson and O'Leary (1980) point
out, thus making it relatively easy to carry out. (6) Furthermore, most
therapies for anxiety (including desensitization), like the assessment that
leads to the targeting of anxiety, is conveniently carried out in the clinician's
comfortable, familiar office and requires only the clinician and client to be
present. By contrast, targeting performance problems directly suggests such
varied, inconvenient, demanding, sometimes expensive procedures as bringing in other parties or going out into the client's natural environment.

Not only is the construct anxiety questionable in terms of its theoretical
parsimony, the importance of anxiety in some human adjustment problems
has failed to receive experimental support. This is illustrated in Wilson and
O'Leary's (1980) discussion of fears and phobias and their treatment. Phobias have generally been conceived as being caused or at least maintained by
anxiety, which is conceptualized as a drive (Mowrer, 1939) or as conditional
emotional stimulation, reduction of which is a reinforcer (e.g., Levis & Boyd,
1979). Thus, the phobic's maladaptive avoidance and escape behavior is considered to be reinforced by reduction in another behavior: anxiety. But, as
Wilson and O'Leary point out, "The decisive factor governing the extinction
of phobias is the systematic nonreinforced exposure to the anxiety-arousing
stimulus conditions; that is, arranging for phobic clients to confront the
source of their anxieties without experiencing the catastrophic consequences
neurotics typically anticipate. *In vivo* exposure is more effective than imaginal
exposure" (p. 163). Though Wilson and O'Leary might not agree with the
following rephrasing of this passage, I would state it thus: "The reestablish-
ment of behavior that has disappeared—due to punishment, to reinforce-

ment of an alternative response, to a shift in antecedent stimuli or motivating variables, or to a combination of these—is most effectively accomplished by simply arranging for the behavior to occur repeatedly and be followed by reinforcing events." The fact that desensitization does, at least, work better than a placebo control (Paul, 1966) is not inconsistent with this more parsimonious account. Desensitization is probably a powerful form of instruction and a potentiation of the therapist's approval and of other stimuli that subsequently will be contingent upon performance. It is neither necessary nor parsimonious to attribute improved performance—as do Wilson and O'Leary (1980, p. 104), consistent with Bandura (1977)—to modification of clients' "expectations of self-efficacy," "beliefs that they can cope with formerly feared situations," or "sense of efficacy." These appear to be unnecessary, hypothetical, mentalistic constructs that are no more defensible theoretically than anxiety.

While I cannot subscribe to the targeting of anxiety, I do not discount the importance of targeting some of the behaviors often considered to be components of anxiety. Thus, I assume that gastrointestinal activity does contribute to ulcers, that some aspects of muscle tension or correlated responses contribute to headache or even to cardiovascular disease, and so on. In such cases, these subtle behaviors, many of them called physiologic responses (e.g., see Lang, 1977), may well be the most appropriate targets. But this does not imply targeting a hypothetical construct such as anxiety.

THE RELEVANCE OF SOCIAL VALIDITY

Wolf (1976, 1978) has made a case for social validation of behavior changes in clients, and Kazdin (1977) reviewed and discussed several studies applying various forms of social validation. In general, as it relates to targeting, social validation has involved obtaining verbal opinion statements about the applicability of targeted *behaviors* to the more general problem of the client or the appropriateness and adequacy of behavior *changes* attained through intervention. These verbal reports may be obtained from the client, as suggested by Myerson and Hayes (1977) and Williams (1977); from persons who control important contingencies for the client (parent, spouse, teacher, judge, potential employer, and so forth), as exemplified by Goldfried and D'Zurilla (1969) or Werner, Minkin, Minkin, Fixsen, Phillips, and Wolf (1975); from persons for whom the client controls important contingencies (subordinates), as shown by Willner, Braukmann, Kirigin, Fixsen, Phillips, and Wolf (1977); from representative members of the general social community (especially appropriate in the field of public education); or from relevant professional experts, as shown by Goldsmith and McFall (1975).

Although the increased use of social validation in behavior therapy and behavior analysis is a welcome movement toward accountability, there is a tendency to lose sight of the fact that the goal of intervention is to optimize the client's and others' benefits and minimize their costs; that is, to develop a repertoire that is optimally *functional*. Another person's evaluative reaction to a particular behavior, and particularly their *verbal* evaluation of that behavior is not necessarily a good index of the functionality of the behavior for that individual or for others, particularly in the long run. For example, a clinician might ask a parent (or group of parents, developmental psychologists, and the like) to evaluate how adequately the clinician had taught a previously aggressive, demanding child client to approach the parent and politely request some privilege. The parent (or others) may report that the child now does this extremely well, much better than before intervention. Yet the parent may now be giving the child far fewer privileges than earlier and may have become brave enough to impose new deprivations and punishers that were previously avoided because the child used effective counterpunishers for the parent. Similarly, as I have indicated elsewhere (Hawkins, 1984), asking taxpayers for social validation of educational goals for a severely retarded learner can readily overlook some important short-term and long-term personal and societal functions (see also Baer, 1981). By the same token, basing a school curriculum on what students think they should learn would probably have a seriously deterimental effect on their learning and, ultimately, on the culture (though such data are certainly not irrelevant). As a final, clinical example, a group of coeds may report that a clinician has greatly improved a young male's skill at behaviors designed to get a date, but this verbal judgment does not necessarily mean that their agreeing to a date will be more probable; the two behaviors are not under the same control.

Furthermore, it often seems to be assumed that all adjustment is *social* adjustment and thus that others' reactions—whether verbal judgments or other reactions—are the important or only criterion of competence. For example, Ross (1974) defined psychological disorders in children thus:

> A psychological disorder is said to be present when a child emits behavior that deviates from a discretionary and relative social norm in that it occurs with a frequency or intensity that authoritative adults in the child's environment judge, under the circumstances, to be either too high or too low. [p. 14]

But many of the skills that are appropriate to target are not behaviors for which social reactions are the primary function. For example, planning meals, budgeting, stopping smoking, controlling one's alcohol consumption, completing a job application, and finding one's way through a city are all skill groups that are very useful, but their primary usefulness is not in obtaining desirable social reactions from others, and particularly not verbal judgments of the learner's skill.

This is not to say that such verbal judgments are irrelevant or useless in targeting or evaluating interventions. It is simply to say that social validity, as generally described in the literature, is not *functional validity* (habilitative validity) but rather an inexpensive, indirect index of functional validity. This was partially acknowledged by Kazdin (1983) when he wrote:

> Presumably, if the target children differ from their peers prior to treatment and are brought to within normative levels after treatment, clinically significant changes have been achieved. However, such evidence does not necessarily attest to the relevance of the target behaviors. The behaviors that are brought to within normative levels may not be critical to the adjustment of the children in everyday life. For example, at this point, it is unclear that increases in eye contact, initiation of requests, voice volume, and other behaviors effectively treated are consistently related to *social interaction* in everyday situations or to child adjustment as reflected in child, parent, or teacher ratings. [pp. 92–93, italics added]

Verbal reports, norms, comparisons of known groups, and such are useful and probably often relatively valid indices of the functionality of behavior. But only if assessors remain aware that *social* validity is a substitute for or supplement to functionality, or habilitative validity, will social validity measures avoid some of the pitfalls into which many other indirect measures have fallen.

IDIOGRAPHIC VERSUS NORMATIVE, NOMOTHETIC,
OR NOMOLOGIC TARGETING

Implicit in much of what I have already said is the assumption that the functions which one will discover in an individual case will be quite unique, individual, or idiographic. This seems inevitably true because all of the factors that determine current behavior—genetic and current physical variables, personal history of interaction with the environment, and current environmental conditions—are different from one person-environment combination to the next. Carr and Durand's (1983) research is but one demonstration of this, and Bem and Funder (1978) pointed out how individual the "template" of contingencies is from one environment to another. For this reason, we might question the use of norm-based assessment devices, such as IQ tests, standardized academic tests, and even empirically derived behavioral checklists from which items have been dropped because only a few people exhibit that particular problem. But some behavioral assessors find certain uses for normative data in relation to targeting (e.g., Hawkins, 1975; Kazdin, 1977; Nelson & Bowles, 1975; Van Houten, 1979). First, norms can help to identify potential clients. For example, a mother who complains that her 7-year-old son peeked at her undressing might be reassured that this is

normal, and a woman who is concerned about her husband's sexual adjustment because he expresses interest in more than one position for coitus may
be similarly reassured and may become a client herself. Second, norms—or
at least comparative data from competent persons—can also be useful in
identifying behaviors that would probably be functional in performing a
particular task, as Goldsmith and McFall (1975) did, in a limited sense, using
the Goldfried and D'Zurilla (1969) method to determine both the problematic tasks and promising behaviors for hospital inpatients. Third, these same
kinds of norms can be used to identify criterion levels of performance, levels
that suffice to achieve the effects desired. Finally, normative behavior can be
critical in gaining social acceptance (even though that is sometimes its only
function), which is why Lent (1968) observed the dressing habits of young
women in the community in order to determine what he should teach
institutionalized clients before sending them into that environment.

In addition to norms, some behavioral assessors find at least one nomothetic or classificatory scheme useful, the *Diagnostic and statistical manual of
mental disorders* (3rd ed.) (*DSM III*) (American Psychiatric Association, 1980).
Nelson and Barlow (1981) seem to argue in favor of using *DSM III* in
behavioral assessment on three grounds. First, the various behavioral criteria listed under each classification are somewhat empirically based. Second,
when a clinician meets the criteria, the clinician's attention will be drawn to
behaviors (or environmental "stressors") that might have otherwise gone
unexamined (see also Taylor, 1983). And third, the nomenclature of *DSM III*
provides a common language for communication among clinicians. The last
two of these arguments refer to actual utility of *DSM III*, while the first
simply provides a basis for such utility.

To illustrate the room for disagreement, I might contend that the
second value of *DSM III* identified by Nelson and Barlow (1981) would be
better achieved by a nonclassificatory scheme, an inductive, open-ended
table of behavioral correlations that makes no assumptions regarding syndromes or labels and is thus free of the limiting biases of diagnostic tradition
and theory. It might also be noted that functional analysis consists of
identifying relations between *stimuli* and *responses*, while *DSM III* draws attention primarily to the latter. Furthermore, I might contend that the third
value which Nelson and Barlow (1981) see in *DSM III* is actually an impediment to progress toward a functional-analysis approach, because it perpetu-
ates the status quo and tends to label the client as basically different from the
clinician and from others.

Nathan's (1981) arguments favoring use of *DSM III* are different. He
points out that the reliability of classification using *DSM III* appears to be
much higher than the reliability of functional analyses of a problem, due to
the absence of guidelines as to how the latter are to be derived. He further

argues that the utility of classification is roughly equivalent to the utility of functional analysis. Though he does seem to feel that in the hands of a behavioral clinician a functional analysis is more useful, he also points out that, with the psychoses, functional analysis has made little progress and the *DSM III* classification probably leads to a more effective treatment, namely, an appropriate psychotropioc drug. Taylor (1983) also takes this position.

Again, illustrating the room for argument, I might point out that the reliability contest posed by Nathan (1981) and Taylor (1983) is not a fair one. In the behavioral assessment funnel (Hawkins, 1979), diagnostic labeling falls at the second level: definition and general quantification of the problem. At this level, norm-referenced tests and other assessments have their greatest utility, because the assessor is doing a rather crude sorting of whole persons. But a functional analysis of a complex repertoire is a far more precise process that belongs at the third level down in the funnel: pinpointing and design of intervention.

A functional analysis—or "case formulation," which Turkat and Maisto (1983) describe as quite different from classificatory diagnosis—might be considered a fine-grain sorting of behavior–environment functional relations. The number of alternative functional analyses of clinical cases is infinite, and even the number of accurate (effective) functional analyses of a particular case is probably often quite large. In contrast, the number of alternative *DSM III* classifications is small. If one is sorting whole persons into general groupings—such as those to be treated with drug A versus drug B, C, or D—a general label such as a *DSM III* classification may be sufficient. But if one is planning a teaching kind of intervention, a crude sorting of persons will be inefficient at best. The number of alternative interventions already available to the skillful behavior analyst or behavior therapist far exceeds the number of interventions available to nonbehavioral clinicians, and an efficient, individualized intervention probably should be based on a functional analysis.

Kazdin (1983), without focusing exclusively on *DSM III*, also endorses the use of nomothetic—or at least classificatory—systems. Though his analysis emphasizes *DSM III*, he also points out that alternative systems are being developed. These alternatives may start from more objective, behavioral assumptions than *DSM III*, may use profiles rather than simple labels, and may be highly empirical in their development (e.g., Achenbach, 1982; Edelbrock & Achenbach, 1980). Kazdin argues that in behavior therapy we have no standardized means of describing our clients in terms of problem severity, breadth, chronicity, onset, and various contextual factors (environmental, behavioral, and physical). He feels that behavior therapists' reports of treatment results "will continue to be dismissed mistakenly by many who view the lack of information about the client/patient population as implicit evidence that the persons are not impaired or are analogue populations" (p. 94). He further argues—as have Hawkins, Fremouw, and Reitz (1982) regarding repertoire characteristics, demographics, and environmental characteristics—that classification can serve as a predictor of treatment outcome, but only if such classification is practiced. Finally, Kazdin notes that behavioral researchers could contribute greatly to the identification and quantification of relevant dimensions of dysfunctions, but only if they are involved in such an effort. Kazdin's arguments, particularly when they are focused on more basic issues than the use of *DSM III* or even, necessarily, nomothetic classification as such, seem quite provocative. The exact roles of norms, dimensional classification, labels, and such in behavioral assessment will no doubt be evolving over the next several years.

PRIORITIZING AMONG TARGET BEHAVIORS

Probably most clinical and other educational goals involve learning several concurrent or sequential responses. Sometimes all of these target responses cannot effectively be addressed at the same time, and many times it is reasonable to expect that modifying one behavior will lead to multiple other changes, favorable or unfavorable. Thus, prioritizing is often appropriate. However, guidelines for prioritizing are not yet clear in behavioral assessment; thus it is included here as a current issue.

Among the factors that might serve as guidelines in prioritizing, Nelson and Hayes (1979) have enumerated four.

> Several guidelines have been offered: (a) alter the behavior that is most irritating to the mediator involved (Tharp & Wetzel, 1969); (b) alter a behavior that may be relatively easy to change (O'Leary, 1972); (c) alter behaviors which will produce therapeutically beneficial response generalization; or (d) when responses exist as part of a longer chain, alter responses at the beginning of the chain. [Angle, Hay, Hay, & Ellinwood, 1977, p. 7]

A few others might be added, some of which overlap considerably with the four already listed. First, one should modify behaviors lower in a skill hierarchy—the "keystone," "pivotal," or "foundation" skills—before modifying those higher in the skill hierarchy if there is, indeed, good evidence that one does depend upon the other. This was why I questioned a graduate student who targeted cursive writing skills in children who could not yet read, print, or reliably discriminate letters of the alphabet (Hawkins, 1975). Similarly, establishment of say-do correspondence (i.e., keeping promises, see Karlan & Rusch, 1982; Williams & Stokes, 1982) may be critical to establishing instructional control over the behavior of a small child, a delinquent, or an adult who fails to follow his or her own plans or promises. Second, one should give priority to behaviors that promise to have very general utility. For example, skill at decision making or problem solving is useful daily in all aspects of life, and a client whose specific complaint results partly from a deficit in this set of behaviors should probably have that deficit remedied early in the intervention. Third, construction of repertoires should take precedence over elimination, as described earlier. Fourth, behaviors that gain (or deny) the client access to natural environments where a variety of important behaviors will be taught or reinforcers made available should receive high priority. For example, a modicum of personal cleanliness habits are critical to gain access to friendships and social groups where much incidental learning occurs and many reinforcers are available. Similarly, certain conduct is necessary for a student to stay in school. Fifth, behaviors given priority by the client should tend to be preferred, on the basis of the client's more extensive and intimate experience with the contingencies in his or her life. Sixth, some behavior changes are urgent in the sense that the opportunity for a certain intervention may pass, the behavior may pose a serious risk to someone, or some temporally scheduled consequence of major importance (e.g., school expulsion) may be imminent. Seventh, when a response chain is involved, one must sketch out alternative intervention plans and decide whether forward chaining or backward chaining appears more promising, and thus whether the first response or the last receives top priority.

HOW CRITICAL IS ACCURATE TARGETING?

It is generally accepted and often stated by behavioral assessors that an accurate selection of ultimate target behaviors is necessary, along with an accurate analysis of the functions of which those behaviors are a part. These, in turn, may lead to selection of intermediate target behaviors, behaviors that will facilitate the learning and performance of the ultimate target behaviors. But this insistence upon accurate targeting (and intervention) may be overly optimistic and somewhat illusory.

First, it should be recognized that at any point in time it is normally impossible to determine how a particular performance was *acquired*. Morse and Kelleher (1966) demonstrated this with lower animals, and Haughton and Ayllon (1965) with a psychiatric patient.

Furthermore, I do not believe we can typically do better than make educated formulations about the *current functional relations* that derive from the original etiology. There are at least partial exceptions, as when Abel, Blanchard, Barlow, and Mavissakalian (1975) presented audiotaped descriptions of various stimulus situations to a client who reported a sandal fetish but was found to show greater sexual arousal to girls' feet than to sandals. But in most clinical practice, it would be impractical or impossible to vary systematically the relevant antecedent and consequent stimuli sufficiently to discover their actual functional relations to various behaviors. Through interviewing, direct observation in natural and simulated situations, and use of rating scales, tests, and physiologic recordings, one can arrive at a *tenable* list of ultimate target behaviors, a *tenable* functional analysis of these behaviors in relation to the environment, and perhaps a list of intermediate target behaviors suggested by the functional analysis.

Finally, I suspect that in many cases, little will be lost by certain inaccuracies in the functional analysis and the resulting selection of target behaviors. At least in the case of clients whose own benefit/cost ratio is the primary problem, the environmental contingencies usually exist already that will support more adaptive behavior once it is emitted regularly for a period of time. Almost anything that "shakes up" the repertoire has a chance of being therapeutic: more effective behavior may appear, be reinforced, and become durable.

This may be why there is often a placebo effect in psychological intervention (Shapiro & Morris, 1978). Behavior therapists may obtain particularly favorable placebo effects because, in presenting their treatment rationales, they may include some of the components that Kazdin and Krouse (1983) found to augment people's verbal prediction of treatment effectiveness: explanation that it is new, improved, widely tested, and based on scientific research; that it affects thoughts and feelings as well as more obvious behaviors; and perhaps that it has been successful with several cases with whom the behavior therapist has worked. Furthermore, behavior therapists are relatively directive and give specific "homework" assignments, arrange for effective stimulus control, and arrange for consequences, so that some kind of behavior change is very likely. Some of the new behavior may make contact with natural contingencies and produce habilitative change, even if it was not through the process planned by the therapist.

CONCLUSION

The selection of targets in behavioral assessment can range from very simple to extremely complex. As indicated by Kazdin (1983, p. 93), for some problems the referring complaint may directly identify the target behavior and little further analysis may be needed. For example, analysis of the variables that originally caused or currently control self-injurious behavior in a child may be unnecessary. But more complexly controlled behaviors—such as aggressive behavior toward peers, avoidance of peers, or taking a lethal dose of pills—may require considerable data gathering and several iterations of functional analyses. Even when the ultimate general goal is quite obvious—such as "to stop her attempting suicide," "to teach him to speak fluently," or "to get my studying done on time"—one functional analysis may reveal a very different set of intermediate targets from another functional analysis. Although we have guidelines about what variables may be involved in a functional analysis and we have several methods for obtaining data, there is no comprehensive set of guidelines for either gathering the data or integrating the data into a functional analysis (Nathan, 1981). Nor is there a generally accepted terminology for a functional analysis. Some clinicians who identify themselves as behavioral emphasize unobserved, hypothesized cognitive and emotional constructs in their accounts, and largely ignore directly verifiable functional relations. Others restrict themselves to observable variables; while still others fall between the two extremes. At present, it appears that the best tool available is a thorough understanding of behavior theory.

If we are to advance in our ability to select target behaviors effectively—or to conduct behavioral assessment in general—we need to continue both basic and technological development. We need basic research, such as Sidman and Tailby's (1982) on stimulus equivalence, or Catania, Matthews, and Shimoff's (1982) on rule-governance of behavior; longitudinal research on populations at risk for various disorders, so that we can observe disorders as they develop (or fail to); research on the unplanned effects of some interventions and on other interrelationships between behaviors (Wahler & Fox, 1981); evaluations of clinical interventions based on differing functional analyses; and many other kinds of studies. At the same time, we must continue conceptualizing the process of targeting and improving our procedures so as to make the selection of target behaviors maximal in effect and minimal in cost.

ACKNOWLEDGMENT

The author wishes to thank Drs. John Cone and Philip Chase for their very helpful comments on a draft of this chapter.

REFERENCES

Abel, G. G., Blanchard, E. B., Barlow, D. H., & Mavissakalian, M. (1975). Identifying specific erotic cues in sexual deviations by audiotaped descriptions. *Journal of Applied Behavior Analysis, 8,* 247–260.

Achenbach, T. M. (1982). A normative-descriptive approach to assessment of youth behavior. In A. J. McSweeny, W. J. Fremouw, & R. P. Hawkins (Eds.), *Practical program evaluation in youth treatment* (pp. 96–115). Springfield, IL: Charles C Thomas.

Allen, K. E., Hart, B. M., Buell, J. C., Harris, F. R., & Wolf, M. M. (1964). Effects of adult social reinforcement on isolate behavior of a nursery school child. *Child Development, 35,* 511–518.

Allen, K. E., Henke, L. B., Harris, F. R., Baer, D. M., & Reynolds, N. J. (1967). Control of hyperactivity by social reinforcement of attending behavior. *Journal of Educational Psychology, 58,* 231–237.

American Psychiatric Association. (1980). *Diagnostic and statistical manual of mental disorders* (3rd ed.). Washington, DC: Author.

Angle, H. V., Hay, L. R., Hay, W. M., & Ellinwood, E. H. (1977). Computer assisted behavioral assessment. In J. D. Cone & R. P. Hawkins (Eds.), *Behavioral assessment: New directions in clinical psychology* (pp. 369–380). New York: Brunner/Mazel.

Arkowitz, H. (1981). Assessment of social skills. In M. Hersen & A. S. Bellack (Eds.), *Behavioral assessment: A practical handbook* (2nd ed.) (pp. 296–327). New York: Pergamon Press.

Arrington, R. E. (1932). *Interrelations in the behavior of young children.* New York: Columbia University Press.

Arrington, R. E. (1943). Time sampling in studies of social behavior: A critical review of techniques and results with research suggestions. *Psychological Bulletin, 40,* 81–124.

Ayllon, T., & Azrin, N. (1968). *The token economy: A motivational system for therapy and rehabilitation.* New York: Appleton-Century-Crofts.

Baer, D. M. (1981). A hung jury and a Scottish verdict: "Not proven." *Analysis and Intervention in Developmental Disabilities, 1,* 91–97.

Baer, D. M. (1982a). Applied behavior analysis. In G. T. Wilson & C. M. Franks (Eds.), *Contemporary behavior therapy: Conceptual and empirical foundations* (pp. 277–309). New York: Guilford Press.

Baer, D. M. (1982b). Some recommendations for a modest reduction in the rate of current recommendations for an immodest increase in the rate of exclusive usages of rate as a dependent measure. In S. Graf (Chair), *Is rate of response a universal datum?* Symposium presented at the Association for Behavior Analysis convention, Milwaukee, WI.

Baer, D. M. (1982c). The imposition of structure on behavior and the demolition of behavioral structures. In D. J. Bernstein (Ed.), *Nebraska symposium on motivation, 1981: Response structure and organization* (pp. 217–254). Lincoln: University of Nebraska Press.

Bailey, S. L., & Lessen, E. I. (1984). An analysis of target behaviors in education: Applied, but how useful? In W. L. Heward, T. E. Heron, D. S. Hill, & J. Trap-Porter (Eds.), *Focus on behavior analysis in education* (pp. 162–176). Columbus, OH: Charles E. Merrill.

Bandura, A. (1968). A social learning interpretation of psychological dysfunctions. In P. London & D. Rosenhan (Eds.), *Foundations of abnormal psychology* (pp. 293–344). New York: Holt, Rinehart & Winston.

Bandura, A. (1977). Self-efficacy: Toward a unifying theory of behavioral change. *Psychological Review, 84,* 191–215.

Barlow, D. H., Reynolds, J., & Agras, W. S. (1973). Gender identity change in a transexual. *Archives of General Psychiatry, 28,* 569–576.

Beck, A. T. (1976). *Cognitive therapy and the emotional disorders.* New York: International Universities Press.

Bem, D. J., & Funder, D. C. (1978). Predicting more of the people more of the time: Assessing the personality of situations. *Psychological Review, 85,* 485–501.

Bijou, S. W. (1979). Some clarifications on the meaning of a behavior analysis of child development. *The Psychological Record, 29,* 3–13.

Bijou, S. W., & Baer, D. M. (1978). *Behavior analysis of child development.* Englewood Cliffs, NJ: Prentice-Hall.

Bijou, S. W., Peterson, R. F., & Ault, M. H. (1968). A method of integrating descriptive and experimental field studies at the level of data and empirical concepts. *Journal of Applied Behavior Analysis, 1,* 175–191.

Bijou, S. W., Peterson, R. F., Harris, F. R., Allen, K. E., & Johnston, M. S. (1969). Methodology for experimental studies of young children in natural settings. *The Psychological Record, 19,* 177–210.

Brigham, J. A. (1980). Self-control revisited: Or why doesn't anyone actually read Skinner anymore? *The Behavior Analyst, 3,* 25–33.

Brown, L., Branston, M. B., Hamre-Nietupski, S., Pumpian, I., Certo, N., & Gruenwald, L. (1979). A strategy for developing chronological age appropriate and functional curricular content for severely handicapped adolescents and young adults. *Journal of Special Education, 13,* 81–90.

Buell, J., Stoddard, P., Harris, F. R., & Baer, D. M. (1968). Collateral social development accompanying reinforcement of outdoor play in a preschool child. *Journal of Applied Behavior Analysis, 1,* 167–173.

Burgess, R. L., Clark, R. N., & Hendee, J. C. (1972). The development of anti-litter behavior in a forest campground. *Journal of Applied Behavior Analysis, 5,* 1–5.

Carr, E. G., & Durand, V. M. (1985). Reducing behavior problems through functional communication training. *Journal of Applied Behavior Analysis, 18,* 111–126.

Catania, A. C. (1976). The myth of self-reinforcement. In T. A. Brigham, R. Hawkins, J. Scott, & T. F. McLaughlin (Eds.), *Behavior analysis in education: Self-control and reading.* Dubuque, IA: Kendall/Hunt.

Catania, A. C., Matthews, B. A., & Shimoff, E. (1982). Instructed versus shaped human verbal behavior: Interactions with nonverbal responding. *Journal of the Experimental Analysis of Behavior, 38,* 233–248.

Cone, J. D. (1977). The relevance of reliability and validity for behavioral assessment. *Behavior Therapy, 8,* 411–426.

Cone, J. D. (1979). Confounded comparisons in triple response mode assessment research. *Behavioral Assessment, 1,* 85–95.

Cone, J. D. (1981). Psychometric considerations. In M. Hersen & A. S. Bellack (Eds.), *Behavioral assessment: A practical handbook* (2nd ed.). New York: Pergamon Press.

Cone, J. D., & Hawkins, R. P. (Eds.). (1977). *Behavioral assessment: New directions in clinical psychology.* New York: Brunner/Mazel.

Edelbrock, C. S., & Achenbach, T. M. (1980). A typology of Child Behavior Profile patterns: Distribution and correlates for disturbed children aged 6–16. *Journal of Abnormal Child Psychology, 8,* 441–470.

Emery, R. E., & Marholin II, D. (1977). An applied behavior analysis of delinquency: The irrelevancy of relevant behavior. *American Psychologist, 32,* 860–873.

Evans, I. M. (1985). Building systems models as a strategy for target behavior selection in clinical assessment. *Behavioral Assessment, 7,* 21–32.

Ferster, C. B. (1965). Classification of behavioral pathology. In L. Krasner & L. P. Ullmann (Eds.), *Research in behavior modification: New developments and implications.* New York: Holt, Rinehart & Winston.

Ferster, C. B. (1972). Clinical reinforcement. *Seminars in Psychiatry, 4,* 101–111.

Forehand, R. L., & McMahon, R. J. (1981). *Helping the noncompliant child: A clinician's guide to parent training.* New York: Guilford Press.

Forehand, R., Peed, S., Roberts, M., McMahon, B., Griest, D., & Humphreys, L. (1978). *Coding manual for scoring mother–child interactions* (3rd ed.). Unpublished manuscript, University of Georgia.

Gilbert, T. F. (1978). *Human competence: Engineering worthy performance.* New York: McGraw-Hill.

Glenn, S. (1983, May). *Behavior analysis of complex cases: Some overlooked relations in clinical intervention.* Paper presented at the Association for Behavior Analysis convention, Milwaukee, WI.

Goldfried, M. R. (1977). Behavioral assessment in perspective. In J. D. Cone and R. P. Hawkins (Eds.), *Behavioral assessment: New directions in clinical psychology* (pp. 3–22). New York: Brunner/Mazel.

Goldfried, M. R., & D'Zurilla, T. J. (1969). A behavioral-analytic model for assessing competence. In C. D. Spielberger (Ed.), *Current topics in clinical and community psychology* (Vol. 1) (pp. 151–196). New York: Academic Press.

Goldfried, M. R., & Kent, R. N. (1972). Traditional versus behavioral personality assessment: A comparison of methodological and theoretical assumptions. *Psychological Bulletin, 77,* 409–420.

Goldfried, M. R., & Sprafkin, J. N. (1976). Behavioral personality assessment. In J. T. Spence, R. C. Carson, & J. W. Thibaut (Eds.), *Behavioral approaches to therapy*. Morristown, NJ: General Learning Press.

Goldiamond, I. (1974). Toward a constructional approach to social problems: Ethical and constitutional issues raised by applied behavioral analysis. *Behaviorism, 2*, 1–85.

Goldiamond, I. (1976a). Self-reinforcement. *Journal of Applied Behavior Analysis, 9*, 509–514.

Goldiamond, I. (1976b). Fables, armadyllics, and self-reinforcement. *Journal of Applied Behavior Analysis, 9*, 521–525.

Goldiamond, I. (1984). Training parent trainers and ethicists in nonlinear analysis of behavior. In R. J. Dangel and R. A. Polster (Eds.), *Parent training: Foundations of research and practice* (pp. 504–546). New York: Guilford Press.

Goldiamond, I., & Dyrud, J. E. (1967). Some applications and implications of behavior analysis for psychotherapy. In J. Schlien (Ed.), *Research in psychotherapy* (Vol. 3) (pp. 54–89). Washington, DC: American Psychological Association.

Goldsmith, J. B., & McFall, R. M. (1975). Development and evaluation of inter-personal skill-training program for psychiatric inpatients. *Journal of Abnormal Psychology, 84*, 51–58.

Goodenough, F. L. (1949). *Mental testing*. New York: Rinehart.

Hall, R. V. (1974). *Behavior modification: Vol. 1. The measurement of behavior*. Lawrence, KS: H & H Enterprises.

Harris, F. R., Wolf, M. M., & Baer, D. M. (1964). Effects of adult social reinforcement on child behavior. *Young Children, 20*, 8–17.

Hartmann, D. P. (1976, September). *Must the baby follow the bathwater? Psychometric principles— behavioral data*. Paper presented at the American Psychological Association convention, Washington, DC.

Hartmann, D. P., & Wood, D. D. (1982). Observational methods. In A. S. Bellack, M. Hersen, and A. E. Kazdin (Eds.), *International handbook of behavior modification and therapy*. New York: Plenum Press.

Haughton, E., & Ayllon, T. (1965). Production and elimination of symptomatic behavior. In L. P. Ullmann & L. Krasner (Eds.), *Case studies in behavior modification* (pp. 94–98). New York: Holt, Rinehart & Winston.

Hawkins, R. P. (1975). Who decided *that* was the problem? Two stages of responsibility for applied behavior analysts. In W. S. Wood (Ed.), *Issues in evaluating behavior modification* (pp. 195–214). Champaign, IL: Research Press.

Hawkins, R. P. (1976, December). The role of assessment in behavioral intervention: Cut the umbilical cord, but save the baby. In M. R. Goldfried (Chairperson), *Issues in behavioral assessment*. Symposium presented at the Association for Advancement of Behavior Therapy convention, New York.

Hawkins, R. P. (1977). Behavior analysis and early childhood education: Engineering children's learning. In H. L. Hom, Jr. & P. A. Robinson (Eds.), *Psychological processes in early education* (pp. 99–131). New York: Academic Press.

Hawkins, R. P. (1979). The functions of assessment: Implications for selection and development of devices for assessing repertoires in clinical, educational, and other settings. *Journal of Applied Behavior Analysis, 12*, 501–516.

Hawkins, R. P. (1982). Developing a behavior code. In D. P. Hartmann (Ed.), *Using observers to study behavior*. New directions for methodology of social and behavioral science, No. 14. San Francisco: Jossey-Bass.

Hawkins, R. P. (1984). What is "meaningful" behavior change in a severely/profoundly retarded learner?: The view of a behavior analytic parent. In W. L. Heward, T. E. Heron, D. S. Hill, & J. Trap-Porter (Eds.), *Focus on behavior analysis in education*. Columbus, OH: Charles E. Merrill.

Hawkins, R. P., Fremouw, W. J., & Reitz, A. L. (1982). A model useful in designing or describing evaluations of planned interventions in mental health. In A. J. McSweeny, W. J. Fremouw, & R. P. Hawkins (Eds.), *Practical program evaluation methods in youth treatment*. Springfield, IL: Charles C Thomas.

Hawkins, R. P., & Hawkins, K. K. (1981). Parental observations on education of severely retarded children: Can it be done in the classroom? *Analysis and Intervention in Developmental Disabilities, 1,* 13–22.

Hawkins, R. P., & Hayes, J. E. (1974). The School Adjustment Program: A model program for treatment of severely maladjusted children in the public schools. In R. Ulrich, T. Stachnik, & J. Mabry (Eds.), *Control of human behavior: Vol. 3. Behavior modification in education* (pp. 197–208). Glenview, IL: Scott, Foresman.

Hawkins, R. P., Peterson, R. F., Schweid, E., & Bijou, S. W. (1966). Behavior therapy in the home: Amelioration of problem parent–child relations with the parent in a therapeutic role. *Journal of Experimental Child Psychology, 4,* 99–107.

Haynes, S. N. (1978). *Principles of behavioral assessment.* New York: Gardner Press.

Hineline, P. N. (1983). When we speak of knowing. *The Behavior Analyst, 6,* 183–186.

Holland, J. G. (1978). Behaviorism: Part of the problem or part of the solution? *Journal of Applied Behavior Analysis, 11,* 163–174.

Hollon, S. D., & Bemis, K. M. (1981). Self-report and the assessment of cognitive functions. In M. Hersen & A. S. Bellack (Eds.), *Behavioral assessment: A practical handbook* (2nd ed.). New York: Pergamon Press.

Hunt, G. M., & Azrin, N. H. (1973). A community-reinforcement approach to alcoholism. *Behaviour Research and Therapy, 11,* 91–104.

Jackson, D. A., & Wallace, R. F. (1974). The modification and generalization of voice loudness in a fifteen-year-old retarded girl. *Journal of Applied Behavior Analysis, 7,* 461–471.

Johnston, J. M., & Pennypacker, H. S. (1980). *Strategies and tactics of human behavioral research.* Hillsdale, NJ: Lawrence Erlbaum.

Jones, R. R. (1977). Conceptual vs. analytic use of generalizability theory in behavioral assessment. In J. D. Cone & R. P. Hawkins (Eds.), *Behavioral assessment: New directions in clinical psychology.* New York: Brunner/Mazel.

Kanfer, F. H., & Grimm, L. G. (1977). Behavioral analysis: Selecting target behaviors in the interview. *Behavior Modification, 1,* 7–28.

Kanfer, F. H., & Phillips, J. S. (1970). *Learning foundations of behavior therapy.* New York: John Wiley & Sons.

Kanfer, F. H., & Saslow, G. (1969). Behavioral diagnosis. In C. M. Franks (Ed.), *Behavior therapy: Appraisal and status.* New York: McGraw-Hill.

Kantor, J. R. (1959). *Interbehavioral psychology.* Granville, OH: Principia Press.

Karlan, G. R., & Rusch, F. R. (1982). Correspondence between saying and doing: Some thoughts on defining correspondence and future directions for application. *Journal of Applied Behavior Analysis,* 151–162.

Kazdin, A. E. (1977). Assessing the clinical or applied importance of behavior change through social validation. *Behavior Modification, 1,* 427–452.

Kazdin, A. E. (1983). Psychiatric diagnosis, dimensions of dysfunction, and child behavior therapy. *Behavior Therapy, 14,* 73–99.

Kazdin, A. E., & Krouse, R. (1983). The impact of variations in treatment rationales on expectancies for therapeutic change. *Behavior Therapy, 14,* 657–671.

Keller, F. S., & Schoenfeld, W. N. (1950). *Principles of psychology.* New York: Appleton-Century-Crofts.

Knopf, I. J. (1979). *Childhood psychopathology: A developmental approach.* Englewood Cliffs, NJ: Prentice-Hall.

Koegel, R. L., Egel, A. L., & Dunlap, G. (1980). Learning characteristics of autistic children. In W. Sailor, B. Wilcox, and L. Brown (Eds.), *Methods of instruction for severely handicapped students* (pp. 259–301). Baltimore: Paul H. Brookes.

Krumboltz, J. D. (1966). Behavioral goals for counseling. *Journal of Counseling Psychology, 13,* 153–159.

Lahey, B. B., & Ciminero, A. R. (1980). *Maladaptive behavior: An introduction to abnormal psychology.* Glenview, IL: Scott, Foresman.

Lang, P. J. (1977). Physiological assessment of anxiety and fear. In J. D. Cone & R. P. Hawkins

(Eds.), *Behavioral assessment: New directions in clinical psychology* (pp. 178–195). New York: Brunner/Mazel.

Lent, J. R. (1968). Mimosa Cottage: Experiment in hope. *Psychology Today*, 2, pp. 157–163.

Levis, D. J., & Boyd, T. L. (1979). Symptom maintenance: An infrahuman analysis and extension of the conservation of anxiety principle. *Journal of Abnormal Psychology, 88*, 107–120.

Libet, J. M., & Lewinsohn, P. M. (1973). Concept of social skill with special reference to the behavior of depressed persons. *Journal of Consulting and Clinical Psychology, 40*, 304–312.

Lindsley, O. R. (1964). Direct measurement and prosthesis of retarded behavior. *Journal of Education, 147*, 304–312.

Linehan, M. M. (1977). Issues in behavioral interviewing. In J. D. Cone & R. P. Hawkins (Eds.), *Behavioral assessment: New directions in clinical psychology* (pp. 30–51). New York: Brunner/Mazel.

Livingston, S. A. (1977). Psychometric techniques for criterion-referenced testing and behavioral assessment. In J. D. Cone & R. P. Hawkins (Eds.), *Behavioral assessment: New directions in clinical psychology* (pp. 308–329). New York: Brunner/Mazel.

Lovaas, O. I., Schreibman, L., Koegel, R. L., & Rehm, R. (1971). Selective responding by autistic children to multiple sensory input. *Journal of Abnormal Psychology, 77*, 211–222.

Lovitt, T. C. (1967). Assessment of children with learning disabilities. *Exceptional Children, 34*, 233–239.

Lovitt, T. C. (1977). *In spite of my resistance I've learned from children.* Columbus, OH: Charles E. Merrill.

Lovitt, T. C., & Hansen, C. L. (1976). Round one—placing the child in the right reader. *Journal of Learning Disabilities, 9*, 347–352.

Mager, R. F. (1975). *Preparing instructional objectives* (2nd ed.). Belmont, CA: Fearon-Pitman.

Mager, R. F., & Pipe, P. (1970). *Analyzing performance problems: Or "You really oughta wanna."* Belmont, CA: Lear Siegler, Inc./Fearon.

Martin, G., & Pear, J. (1983). *Behavior modification: What it is and how to do it* (2nd ed.). Englewood Cliffs, NJ: Prentice-Hall.

Mash, E. J., & Terdal, L. G. (Eds.). (1976). *Behavior therapy assessment: Diagnosis, design, and evaluation.* New York: Springer.

McFall, R. M. (1977). Analogue methods in behavioral assessment. In J. D. Cone and R. P. Hawkins (Eds.), *Behavioral assessment: New directions in clinical psychology* (pp. 152–177). New York: Brunner/Mazel.

McFall, R. (1982). A review and reformulation of the concept of social skills. *Behavioral Assessment, 4*, 1–33.

McKnight, D. L., Nelson, R. O., Hayes, S. C., & Jarrett, R. B. (1984). Importance of treating individually assessed response classes in the amelioration of depression. *Behavior Therapy, 15*, 315–335.

Meadowcroft, P. (1978, May). Beyond the experience of inner learning (as in inner skiing). Paper presented at the Midwestern Association for Behavior Analysis, Chicago.

Meichenbaum, D. (1977). *Cognitive-behavior modification: An integrative approach.* New York: Plenum Press.

Meichenbaum, D., & Cameron, R. (1982). Cognitive-behavior therapy. In G. T. Wilson & C. M. Franks (Eds.), *Contemporary behavior therapy: Conceptual and empirical foundations.* New York: Guilford Press.

Michael, J. (1980). Flight from behavior analysis. *The Behavior Analyst, 3*, 1–22.

Michael, J. (1982). Distinguishing between discriminative and motivational functions of stimuli. *Journal of the Experimental Analysis of Behavior, 37*, 149–155.

Mischel, W. (1968). *Personality and assessment.* New York: John Wiley & Sons.

Moore, J. (1981). On mentalism, methodological behaviorism, and radical behaviorism. *Behaviorism, 9*, 55–77.

Morris, E. K. (1978). A brief review of legal deviance: References in behavior analysis and delinquency. In D. Marholin II (Ed.), *Child behavior therapy* (pp. 214–238). New York: Gardner Press.

Morris, E. K., Higgins, S. T., & Bickel, W. K. (1982). Comments on cognitive science in the experimental analysis of behavior. *The Behavior Analyst, 5*, 109–125.

Morse, W. H., & Kelleher, R. J. (1966). Schedules using noxious stimuli. I. Multiple fixed-ratio and fixed-interval termination of schedule complexes. *Journal of the Experimental Analysis of Behavior, 9*, 267–290.

Mowrer, O. H. (1939). A stimulus-response analysis of anxiety and its role as a reinforcing agent. *Psychological Review*, 553–565.

Myerson, W. A., & Hayes, S. C. (1977). Controlling the clinician for the client's benefit. In J. E. Krapfl and E. A. Vargas (Eds.), *Behaviorism and ethics* (pp. 243–260). Kalamazoo, MI: Behaviordelia.

Nathan, P. E. (1981). Symptomatic diagnosis and behavioral assessment: A synthesis. In D. H. Barlow (Ed.), *Behavioral assessment of adult disorders* (pp. 1–11). New York: Guilford Press.

Nelson, R. O., & Barlow, D. H. (1981). Behavioral assessment: Basic strategies and initial procedures. In D. H. Barlow (Ed.), *Behavioral assessment of adult disorders* (pp. 13–43). New York: Guilford Press.

Nelson, R. O., & Bowles, P. E., Jr. (1975). The best of two worlds: Observations with norms. *Journal of School Psychology, 13*, 3–9.

Nelson, R. O., & Hayes, S. C. (1979). Some current dimensions of behavioral assessment. *Behavioral Assessment, 1*, 1–16.

O'Leary, K. D. (1972). The assessment of psychopathology in children. In H. C. Quay & J. S. Werry (Eds.), *Psychopathological disorders of childhood* (pp. 234–272). New York: John Wiley & Sons.

Ossorio, P. G. (1982, August). An approach to "cognition." In T. Knapp (chairperson), *Contemporary views of cognition*. Symposium presented at the American Psychological Association convention, Washington, DC.

Paul, G. L. (1966). *Insight versus desensitization in psychotherapy*. Stanford, CA: Stanford University Press.

Peterson, D. (1968). *The clinical study of social behavior*. New York: Appleton-Century-Crofts.

Redd, W. H., Ullmann, R. K., Stelle, C., & Roesch, P. (1979). A classroom incentive program instituted by tutors after school. *Education and Treatment of Children, 2*, 169–176.

Resnick, L. B., Wang, M. C., & Kaplan, J. (1973). Task analysis in curriculum design: A hierarchically sequenced introductory mathematics curriculum. *Journal of Applied Behavior Analysis, 6*, 679–709.

Rosenthal, T. L. (1982). Social learning theory. In G. T. Wilson & C. M. Franks (Eds.), *Contemporary behavior therapy: Conceptual and empirical foundations* (pp. 339–363). New York: The Guilford Press.

Ross, A. O. (1974). Psychological disorders of children: A behavioral approach to theory, research, and therapy. New York: McGraw-Hill.

Schwartz, A., & Goldiamond, I. (1975). *Social casework: A behavioral approach*. New York: Columbia University Press.

Schwarz, M. L., & Hawkins, R. P. (1970). Application of delayed reinforcement procedures to the behavior problems of an elementary school child. *Journal of Applied Behavior Analysis, 3*, 85–96.

Schwartz, S., & Johnson, J. H. (1985). *Psychopathology of childhood* (2nd ed.). New York: Pergamon Press.

Scott, W. A. (1958). Research definitions of mental health and mental illness. *Psychological Bulletin, 55*, 29–45.

Shapiro, A. K., & Morris, L. A. (1978). The placebo effect in medical and psychological therapies. In S. L. Garfield & A. E. Bergin (Eds.). *Handbook of psychotherapy and behavior change* (2nd ed.) (pp. 369–410). New York: John Wiley & Sons.

Sidman, M., & Tailby, W. (1982). Conditional discrimination vs. matching to sample: An expansion of the testing paradigm. *Journal of the Experimental Analysis of Behavior, 37*, 5–22.

Skinner, B. F. (1953). *Science and human behavior.* New York: Macmillan.

Skinner, B. F. (1969). *Contingencies of reinforcement: A theoretical analysis.* Englewood Cliffs, NJ: Prentice-Hall.

Skinner, B. F. (1977). Why I am not a cognitive psychologist. *Behaviorism, 5*, 1–10.

Swan, G. E., & MacDonald, M. L. (1978). Behavior therapy in practice: A national survey of behavior therapists. *Behavior Therapy, 9*, 799–807.

Taylor, C. B. (1983). DSM-III and behavioral assessment. *Behavioral Assessment, 5*, 5–14.

Tharp, R. G., Wetzel, R. J. (1969). *Behavior modification in the natural environment.* New York: Academic Press.

Turkat, I. D., & Maisto, S. A. (1983). Functions of and differences between psychiatric diagnosis and case formulation. *The Behavior Therapist, 6*, 184–185.

Ullmann, L. P., & Krasner, L. (1965). Introduction. In L. P. Ullmann & L. Krasner (Eds.), *Case studies in behavior modification* (pp. 1–63). New York: Holt, Rinehart & Winston.

Van Houten, R. (1979). Social validation: The evolution of standards of competency for target behaviors. *Journal of Applied Behavior Analysis, 12*, 581–591.

Voeltz, L. M., & Evans, I. M. (1982). The assessment of behavioral interrelationships in child behavior therapy. *Behavioral Assessment, 4*, 131–165.

Wahler, R. G. (1969). Oppositional children: A quest for parental reinforcement control. *Journal of Applied Behavior Analysis, 2*, 159–170.

Wahler, R. G., & Fox, J. J. (1981). Setting events in applied behavior analysis: Toward a conceptual and methodological expansion. *Journal of Applied Behavior Analysis, 14*, 327–338.

Walder, L. O., Cohen, S. I., & Daston, P. G. (1967). *Teaching parents and others principles of behavior control for modifying the behavior of children* (Progress report No. 32-31-7515-5024). Washington, DC: U.S. Office of Education.

Werner, J. S., Minkin, N., Minkin, B. L., Fixsen, D. L., Phillips, E. L., & Wolf, M. M. (1975). Intervention package: An analysis to prepare juvenile delinquents for encounters with police officers. *Criminal Justice and Behavior, 2*, 55–83.

White, O. R. (1977). Data-based instruction: Evaluating educational progress. In J. D. Cone & R. P. Hawkins (Eds.), *Behavioral assessment: New directions in clinical psychology* (pp. 344–368). New York: Brunner/Mazel.

White, O. R. (1980). Adaptive performance objectives: Form versus function. In W. Sailor, B. Wilcox, & L. Brown (Eds.), *Methods of instruction for severely handicapped students* (pp. 47–69). Baltimore: Paul H. Brookes.

Williams, J. A., & Stokes, T. F. (1982). Some parameters of correspondence training and generalized verbal control. *Child and Family Behavior Therapy, 4*, 11–32.

Williams, J. L. (1977). Commentary. In J. E. Krapfl & E. A. Vargas (Eds.), *Behaviorism and ethics* (pp. 261–264). Kalamazoo, MI: Behaviordelia.

Willner, A. G., Braukman, C. J., Kirigin, K. A., Fixsen, D. L., Phillips, E. L., & Wolf, M. M. (1977). The training and validation of youth-preferred social behaviors with child-care personnel. *Journal of Applied Behavior Analysis, 10*, 219–230.

Wilson, F. E., & Evans, I. M. (1983). The reliability of target-behavior selection in behavioral assessment. *Behavioral Assessment, 5*, 15–32.

Wilson, G. T., & O'Leary, K. D. (1980). *Principles of behavior therapy.* Englewood Cliffs, NJ: Prentice-Hall.

Winett, R. A., & Winkler, R. C. (1972). Current behavior modification in the classroom: Be still, be quiet, be docile. *Journal of Applied Behavior Analysis, 5*, 499–504.

Wolf, M. M. (1976, September). Social validity: The case for subjective measurement or how applied behavior analysis is finding its heart. Paper presented at the American Psychological Association convention, Washington, DC.

Wolf, M. M. (1978). Social validity: The case for subjective measurement or how applied behavior analysis is finding its heart. *Journal of Applied Behavior Analysis, 11*, 203–214.

Wolpe, J. (1958). *Psychotherapy by reciprocal inhibition.* Stanford, CA: Stanford University Press.

Wolpe, J. (1969). *The practice of behavior therapy.* Oxford: Pergamon Press.

Wolpe, J. (1979). The experimental model and treatment of neurotic depression. *Behaviour Research and Therapy, 17,* 555–565.

Yeaton, W. H., & Bailey, J. S. (1978). Teaching pedestrian safety skills to young children: An analysis and one-year follow-up. *Journal of Applied Behavior Analysis, 11,* 315–329.

Zettle, R. D., & Hayes, S. C. (1980). Conceptual and empirical status of rational–emotive therapy. In M. Hersen, R. M. Eisler, & P. M. Miller, (Eds.), *Progress in beahvior modification* (Vol. 9). New York: Academic Press.

Zettle, R. D., & Hayes, S. C. (1982). Rule-governed behavior: A potential theoretical framework for cognitive-behavioral therapy. In P. C. Kendall (Ed.), *Advances in cognitive–behavioral research* (Vol. 1) (pp. 73–118). New York: Academic Press.

11

THE DESIGN OF INTERVENTION PROGRAMS

Illinois Institute of Technology

Assessment prior to treatment initiation is a fundamental component of the behavioral intervention process. It is used for diagnosis, for the identification of specific behavior deficits and excesses, for the selection of intervention targets, for the identification of the determining or controlling variables of problem behaviors, for the design of intervention programs, and as a basis for the evaluation of intervention effects (Ciminero, Calhoun, & Adams, 1977; Cone & Hawkins, 1977; Haynes, 1978; 1983; Haynes & Wilson, 1979). Furthermore, assessment is necessary for the continuing examination and refinement of behavioral construct systems.[1]

Although this chapter focuses on one particular function of behavioral assessment—the design of intervention programs—the interdependence of the various assessment functions should be apparent. Intervention program design can be influenced by the diagnostic categorization of the client,[2] identified problem behaviors, etiologic factors, and the results of ongoing outcome evaluations.

This chapter addresses the conceptual and methodological aspects of intervention design. The first section, entitled "The Assessment–Interventional Relationship," reviews the conceptual basis for the relationship between assessment and intervention and notes the variance in that relationship across construct systems. The following section, "Dimensions of Intervention Decisions," discusses the interdependence of assessment and

1. The term "behavioral construct systems" refers to the theoretical models for understanding behavior and behavior problems that emphasize neobehavioristic methods and concepts (see Bandura, 1969; Kanfer & Phillips, 1970). The plural form reflects the conceptual diversity of these paradigms which may emphasize operant, social-learning, cognitive–behavioral, or classical conditioning operations.

2. The terms "client" or "target subject" are used interchangeably to refer to the consumers of behavioral interventions. They may include individual adults or children, families, school systems, couples, or community organizations.

intervention in behavioral construct systems and examines some of the determinants of that relationship. The criteria on which intervention decisions are made and the determinations of those decisions are then outlined. The last section of the chapter, "Issues in the Design of Intervention Programs," considers some of the conceptual and methodological issues associated with the design of intervention programs.

THE ASSESSMENT–INTERVENTION RELATIONSHIP

Intervention systems (such as psychoanalysis, psychopharmacology, and behavior therapy) are based upon complex and interrelated assumptions about behavior and its determinants. Each intervention system stresses the importance of particular *phenomena* (such as intrapsychic events or neurotransmission), focuses on specific *determinants* of behavior, and promotes particular *methods* of understanding and modifying behavior (Hersen, Kazdin, & Bellack, 1983; Wolman, 1965). Thus, while psychoanalysis emphasizes early psychosexual conflicts as one cause of behavior problems and free association as a method of assessing such determinants, psychopharmacology emphasizes the importance of biogenic amines or neurotransmitter dysfunctions as causes[3] of the same behavior problems and advocates biochemical assessment procedures as the preferable method of assessment.

These conceptual and methodological assumptions have a profound impact on the role of assessment in the design of intervention programs. For many intervention systems such as gestalt, client-centered, or transactional therapies, intervention begins with the first contact between therapist and client—assessment is an ongoing but informal and unsystematic process integrated within the intervention process (Hersen & Goldstein, 1984). Other intervention systems, particularly the behavior therapies, while recognizing the potentially therapeutic aspects of assessment, more frequently include a systematic assessment phase prior to initiating intervention. While assessment continues throughout intervention in behavioral systems, initial intervention strategies are more frequently determined by the results of a preintervention assessment phase (Cooke & Meyers, 1980; Goldfried & Sprafkin, 1976; Haynes & Wilson, 1979; Hersen, 1981; Lahey, Vosk, & Habif, 1981; Mash & Terdal, 1981).

Despite the importance attached to preintervention assessment in behavioral construct systems, there is significant variability in the degree to

3. The terms "etiologic" and "causal" are used interchangeably and do not have historical or exclusionary implications. They refer to variables that reliably control the parameters of targeted behaviors. The fact that one variable has a causal relationship to a target behavior does not preclude other variables from having such a relationship.

which behavioral intervention programs are dependent on or reflect the results of preintervention assessment. The sources of this variance are examined in the following two subsections.

CONCEPTUAL DETERMINANTS OF THE
ASSESSMENT–INTERVENTION RELATIONSHIP

Each intervention construct system includes a number of assumptions about behavior which influence the role of assessment in the intervention program and, in particular, the role of assessment in the design of intervention strategies (Haynes, 1978). The most important assumptions concern presumed differences in etiology between and within behavior disorders and individual differences in response to treatment (Haynes, 1984).

One assumption that strongly affects the role of preintervention assessment in the design of intervention programs is the degree to which determinants are presumed to vary across behavior problems (Haynes, 1979). If it is assumed that different behavior problems share a common etiology, intervention programs can be designed independently of preintervention assessment. For example, if different behavior problems are ascribed to common determinants such as "psychosexual conflicts" or "unmet dependency needs," intervention programs will target those presumed determinants and will be minimally influenced by preintervention assessment.

In contrast, behavioral construct systems more frequently assume that there are significant differences in causal factors across behavior problems. It is assumed that there are differences in the determinants of depression, migraine headaches, and childhood hyperactivity. Because etiologic factors are often targeted for intervention, behavioral intervention programs are likely to vary across these disorders as a function of causal factors identified during preintervention assessment.

A more important determinant of the role of assessment in intervention design is the presumed degree of homogeneity of causality *within* behavior problem categories. In many construct systems, a nonvariant etiology is assumed to be associated with a particular behavior problem or diagnostic category and intervention strategies are fairly homogeneous within that category. Examples of univariate causal models might include biogenic amine dysfunction for depression (Mendels, 1975), dependency in asthma (Alexander, 1981), hostility in hypertension (Alexander, 1950), or sexual identity conflicts in paranoia (Haynes, in press). In construct systems assuming such etiologic homogeneity, intervention strategies are automatically identified when behavior problems are identified or classified.

Behavioral construct systems assume considerable variance in topographical and etiologic factors within as well as between behavior disorders. Individuals may become "depressed" as a consequence of numerous permutations of possible causes such as social and assertive skill deficits, social anxiety, cognitive ruminative and self-depreciatory behaviors, learned helplessness, recent changes in stimulus–control conditions, or decrements in reinforcement rate (Seligman, Klein, & Miller, 1976). In addition, depressed individuals may manifest different verbal, motoric, cognitive, and physiologic symptom clusters.

Because of this presumed heterogeneity, problem identification or diagnosis alone is insufficient to indicate intervention strategies. Assessment of the idiosyncratic determinants of depression, as well as the idiosyncratic pattern of depressive behaviors, will have a significant impact on intervention decisions. Intervention programs for a depressed individual may involve various combinations of social skills training, in vivo or systematic desensitization, cognitive restructuring, marital and family therapy, assertion training, and/or pharmacologic intervention (Seligman et al., 1976).

The importance of preintervention assessment in behavioral construct systems also reflects the presumed degree of individual differences in response to treatment (Jeffrey, Wing, & Stunkard, 1978; Ollendick, Shapiro, & Barrett, 1981). It is assumed that individuals placed in similar diagnostic categories and with similar topographical and causal characteristics can react differently to the same intervention program. Therefore, preintervention assessment of variables that mediate or predict response to intervention becomes important.

In summary, the emphasis on preintervention assessment in the design of behavioral intervention programs is a function of three primary tenets of a behavioral construct system: (1) there are individual differences in topography and determinants across behavior problems, (2) there are individual differences in topography and determinants across individuals within the same class of behavior problem, and (3) there are individual differences in response to treatment.

Despite this relative emphasis on variance in topographical and etiologic factors, univariate causal models for behavior problems frequently can be noted in the behavioral literature. Examples of such models include parental contingencies as the determinant of child behavior problems, reinforcement loss as the determinant of depression, elevated cephalic muscle contraction as the determinant of tension headache, learning parameters and contingencies as the determinants of classroom performance, behavioral exchanges as the determinant of marital distress, eating patterns as the determinant of obesity, and conditioned fear responses as the determinant of phobias

(Adams & Sutker, 1981). While such hypothesized causal relationships may be valid and even heuristic, invoking them in an exclusively univariate causal model will necessarily limit the power and generalizability of behavioral construct systems and the intervention programs based on them. The etiologic conceptualization of and intervention with behavior problems will be significantly enhanced by invoking more complex multivariate models of causality. Such models are becoming more prevalent (Cooke & Meyers, 1980; Haynes, 1981; Hersen, 1981; Jacobson & Margolin, 1979; Jeffrey & Knauss, 1981; Karoly, 1981; McFall, 1982; Vincent, 1980; Voeltz & Evans, 1982; Wahler, Berland, & Coe, 1979; Youkilis & Bootzin, 1981).

The role of preintervention assessment in the design of behavioral intervention programs also varies as a function of the homogeneity of classification categories, the power of a particular intervention, the social significance of the target behavior, and the presumed relationship between etiology and treatment. These factors are considered in greater detail in the following subsection.

BEHAVIORAL ASSESSMENT IN THE DESIGN OF INTERVENTION PROGRAMS—A CLOSER LOOK

Preintervention assessment has been one of the defining methodological characteristics of behavioral interventions (Bandura, 1969; Kanfer & Phillips, 1970). However, it is expensive, time-consuming, and delays the initiation of treatment. Therefore, its utility and impact on intervention outcome should be carefully considered.

A random selection of recently published case studies suggests that there is considerable variability in the use of preintervention assessment.[4] In many studies (e.g., Barmann & Murray, 1981; Egel, 1981), interventions were designed prior to client selection and were not influenced by preintervention assessment. In other studies (e.g., Jackson & King, 1981; Piersel & Kratochwill, 1981), preintervention assessment had a significant impact on the intervention design. Although the purpose of the intervention (such as comparative evaluation of intervention programs of testing causal hypotheses) accounts for some of the variance, there remains significant variation in the degree to which intervention programs are influenced by preintervention assessment. Several factors influence that variation: (1) diagnostic homogeneity, (2) intervention power, (3) the significance of the target behavior, and (4) the etiology–intervention relationship.

4. I would like to express my appreciation to Karen Clark for her help with this review.

Diagnostic Homogeneity

Diagnostic systems [such as the *Diagnostic and Statistical manual of the American Psychiatric Association* (Vol. 3) (*DSM III*), American Psychiatric Association, 1980] are intended to provide categories that are internally homogeneous in topography, etiology, and/or response to treatment. The actual degree of homogeneity of those categories determines the role of assessment beyond that necessary for diagnosis (Haynes, 1979). If individuals placed in a particular classification category (such as "childhood autism" or "erectile dysfunction") are homogeneous on dimensions of topography, etiology, and response to treatment, categorization is sufficient for description and intervention design, and the benefits of additional preintervention assessment are reduced. Within-category variance on those dimensions, however, suggests that additional assessment is necessary to design intervention strategies.

Levels of homogeneity are not constant across the diagnostic categories encountered by behavior analysts. Some behavior problem categories, such as "schizophrenia, paranoid type," include very diverse behaviors and hypothesized determinants. Other behavior categories, such as "head banging," "tantrums," or "agoraphobia" involve less topographical and etiologic diversity. Although from a behavior analytic perspective, all behavior problems may require assessment beyond that necessary for classification, a general intervention program format can more easily be designed for some than for other classes of behavior problems.

Intervention Power

Intervention power—the degree to which a particular intervention results in clinically meaningful changes when applied to a particular target problem—interacts with diagnostic homogeneity to influence the role of preintervention assessment. "Intervention power" has several possible operational definitions. It may be indexed by average improvement scores across recipients, the proportion of recipients manifesting significant improvement, or efficiency (speed, cost, number of client contacts required). Adjunctive measures of intervention power include side effects, remission rate, and indices of generalization.

The use of preintervention behavioral assessment is primarily predicated on the assumption that it will increase the probability or degree of intervention effectiveness. Therefore, if a particular intervention program has been demonstrated to be effective for a particular class of behavior problems, assessment beyond that necessary for problem identification or classification may not significantly affect the probability of success or degree of effectiveness or may not be cost efficient. In such a case, problem identification or classification would be sufficient to indicate an effective intervention.

For some behavior problems (e.g., tension headaches) but not for others (e.g., depression), interventions have been developed that seem to be effective, regardless of topographical or etiologic variance within the category (Nathan, 1981). In such cases, the impact of preintervention assessment is reduced.

The proliferation of standardized treatment programs for disorders, such as headaches (Haynes, 1981), marital distress (Stuart, 1980), insomnia (Youkilis & Bootzin, 1981), social skills deficits (McFall, 1982), sexual dysfunctions (Heiman & Hatch, 1981), and aggressive child behaviors (Patterson, Cobb & Ray, 1973), is based on an important assumption: The degree of heterogeneity of these problem behaviors (individual differences within problem areas) is not sufficient to significantly affect intervention outcome. Therefore, extensive preintervention assessment for the purpose of intervention design is assumed to be unnecessary.

Despite statistical indices that such standardized programs are effective, their proliferation and noncontingent application may be premature. Several observations suggest caution in adopting standardized intervention programs: (1) they are frequently based upon unvalidated univariate models of causality, (2) indices of outcome are frequently compromised by measurement and methodological inadequacies, (3) side effects, temporal generalization, and situational generalization are seldom adequately assessed, and (4) they are frequently evaluated on restricted populations.

In summary, there is an inverse relationship between the power of an intervention with a particular behavior problem and the utility and/or impact of preintervention assessment. With powerful interventions, the probability or degree of intervention success may not be significantly increased by preintervention behavioral assessment. In other cases, preintervention assessment may increase the probability or degree of successful intervention but may prove to be unwarranted if judged via cost–benefit analysis. Although standardized intervention programs have been found to be effective across recipients with some disorders, adoption of such programs may be premature.

Social and Personal Significance of the Behavior Problem

The social and personal significance of the targeted behavior must be considered when utilizing a cost–benefit analysis to determine the utility of preintervention assessment. There are qualitative as well as quantitative components of the "benefit" component: The social and personal significance of benefits associated with preintervention assessment varies across behavior problems. A 10% failure rate for a standardized intervention program for nail biting may not warrant extensive preintervention assessment to design individualized intervention programs that would reduce the failure rate to 5%. However, more extensive preintervention assessment may be warranted by a proportionate increase in the effectiveness of interventions for suicidal, self-mutilatory, or socially violent behaviors.

These considerations further suggest that a qualitative and/or quantitative *cost–benefit analysis* may influence the assessment–intervention relationship. Behavior analysts make subjective determinations of whether the benefits to be derived from preintervention assessment (primarily in terms of increased treatment efficacy) warrant the increased cost (primarily in terms of time, delayed treatment, effort, and expense).

The Etiology–Intervention Relationship

The importance of preintervention behavioral assessment to intervention design is based on the assumption that etiologic variables identified by the assessment are frequently targeted for modification. However, intervention programs vary in the degree to which they target etiological variables. For example, analgesics such as aspirin can modify many minor pain disorders regardless of the pain location, the degree of involvement of skeletal musculature, or sources of eliciting or exacerbating stress (Haynes, Cuevas, & Gannon, 1982). In this case, further attention to causal variables would probably not be associated with clinically signficant increases in the effectiveness of aspirin. Similarly, programmed learning environments can be used to teach verbal and motor skills to individuals with organic dysfunctions even though learning contingencies were not responsible for the targeted deficiencies. Therefore, more extensive preintervention assessment may be necessary for interventions that do than for those that do not target etiologic variables.

Summary

Although the use of assessment to design behavioral intervention programs is one of the traditional defining characteristics of behavioral construct systems, the utility of preintervention assessment varies as a function of a number of dimensions. These include diagnostic homogeneity, intervention efficacy, the social and personal significance of the targeted behavior, and the degree to which etiologic variables are targeted in the intervention program. When planning assessment strategies, behavior analysts must carefully consider the proportion of individuals who would not be successfully treated with the application of a standardized program, the significance of the untreated problem behaviors, and the overall cost-effectiveness of the assessment process.

The points delineated above addressed the role of assessment in the design of intervention programs. However, there are many other functions of behavioral assessment which suggests its utility, independent of its role in intervention design. In particular, the empirical rigor, validity, and efficacy of behavioral interventions and their underlying construct systems are contingent upon the integration of systematic assessment efforts within intervention programs. Rote application of prepackaged programs in the absence of assessment procedures will diminish the conceptual and methodological advances that have been characteristic of behavioral construct systems.

DIMENSIONS OF INTERVENTION DECISIONS

Many intervention decisions are required in the assessment–intervention process: deciding whether or not to intervene, selecting or designing specific intervention programs, selecting components within intervention programs, deciding when an ongoing intervention should be modified, deciding when to terminate intervention, and deciding when to initiate follow-up interventions. Another major decision—selecting target behaviors—is covered in Chapter 10 of the present volume.

DECIDING WHETHER OR NOT TO INTERVENE

Initially, a behavior analyst must decide whether or not to intervene with a particular client and whether or not to target a particular referral problem. Several factors influence these decisions.

Expected Probability and Degree of Success

Because of the time and financial investments required and the potentially negative ramifications of failure, the decision to intervene or not is affected by the degree of expected success. This consideration is particularly germane when alternative intervention strategies may be more effective; behavior analysts are ethically bound to insure that clients receive the intervention having the greatest probability of success. Our Medical Psychology Laboratory at Southern Illinois University applied behavioral intervention strategies with stress-related psychophysiologic disorders. We have declined to treat several individuals requesting treatment of cancer-related pain, hypertension, and asthma; instead, we referred them to physicians. In each case, our impact on the client, derived from a preintervention assessment, was estimated to be insufficient to warrant intervention; and we decided that there was a greater probability of benefit with pharmacologic intervention. The time and financial commitment that would have been required of us and the client did not seem warranted by the expected probability and degree of success; and we decided the clients would be better served if they were referred for alternative interventions. Decisions about whether or not to intervene based on estimated impact are also influenced by available resources. The probability of intervention success may have a stronger influence on intervention decisions when there are limited resources (e.g., available staff, time, funds).

Etiologic Considerations

Because determinants of behavior problems vary in their amenability to modification through behavioral interventions, the expected probability of successful intervention is often influenced by etiologic considerations. Although intervention programs need not involve manipulations of hypothesized etiologic factors, etiologic considerations often influence decisions about the appropriateness of a particular intervention for a client.

Etiologic indices can sometimes suggest a more appropriate method of intervention. Elevated blood pressure in response to vasopressor medication, organically caused dyspareunia, migraine headache associated with estrogen fluctuations, amphetamine-induced paranoia, and asthmatic responses to specific allergins (Haynes & Gannon, 1981), are examples of behavior problems whose etiologies reduce the expected probability of successful behavioral intervention and suggest alternative (in these cases pharmacologic) intervention strategies.

Ethical Considerations

The goals of clients are not always consistent with those of behavior analysts. A request by educational or institutional staff for training in more powerful methods of aversive behavior control would require cautious consideration. Similarly, requests by parents and teachers for intervention with children sometimes reflect inappropriate expectations of the adult more than the behavior problems of the child.

The ethics of behavior change is an extremely complex issue which has been addressed in a number of reviews (e.g. Begelman, 1975; Craighead, Kazdin, & Mahoney, 1976). It is important to emphasize that behavior analysts who apply behavioral interventions are not value free. Behavior analysts should be sensitive to their own value systems and the ethical issues inherent in their professional behavior.

Mediating Factors

Factors that mediate intervention outcome, particularly *cooperation* by the client or by significant individuals in the client's social environment, can also influence the decision of whether or not to intervene. While negative mediational indices do not preclude intervention, they influence the expected probability of success. Interventions with uncooperative court-referred clients, a client experiencing marital distress with an uncooperative spouse, or medical/psychological dysfunctions (such as hypertension or asthma) with an uncooperative primary physician are examples where mediational factors may limit intervention success.

SELECTION AND DESIGN OF INTERVENTION PROGRAMS

The selection and design of an intervention program are the most complex and difficult intervention decisions facing a behavior analyst. The complexity of these decisions is a function of the individual differences among clients in behavior problem topography, etiology, and response to intervention, and the multitude of intervention programs and strategies available to the behavior analyst.

The particular intervention strategies selected will be influenced by a number of factors such as client mediational variables, social–environmental variables, and variables associated with the therapist and intervention process. These are discussed more fully in the section "Determinants of Intervention Program Design," below.

SELECTING INTERVENTION PROGRAM COMPONENTS

Not only must an overall intervention program be designed, but components within that program must be selected. Intervention programs include components such as targeted behaviors and behavior chains, reinforcing and punishing stimuli used in contingency manipulation programs, instructional variables, homework assignments, stimulus and response hierarchies, and situational stimuli. These components must be selected to maximize intervention effectiveness and to promote generalization. For example, in a home-based contingency management program with an aggressive child (Patterson *et al.*, 1973), the behavior analyst must select generalized, back-up,

and social reinforcers for the child and for the parents, reinforcement schedules, time-out stimuli and procedures, temporal parameters, methods of
didactic interaction with the parents, and the most effective method of
facilitating program adherence. Similarly, the design of a social skills training
program (McFall, 1982) requires the selection of components such as specific
role-play scenarios, response prompts, a graduated chain of behaviors upon
which to focus, modeled behaviors, specific homework assignments, methods of self-monitoring, and specific behaviors and scenes for a cognitive
restructuring program.

MODIFICATION, ENHANCEMENT, AND TERMINATION
OF INTERVENTION

The data acquired through systematic assessment throughout the intervention process provide information about the effects of the intervention and
can indicate when modifications of the intervention program are warranted.
Most intervention programs require continual monitoring and intermittent
modification (Hersen & Barlow, 1976). These modifications may involve
instituting a new intervention program, changing components of an ongoing
program, changing target behaviors, initiating further discussion of the
program rationale with the client, and/or instituting follow-up intervention
sessions.

In a recent marital therapy case, a couple's overall level of marital
satisfaction and their satisfaction with communication was not enhanced
after several weeks of communication training, although behavioral indices
of communication behaviors from analogue discussions suggested improvement. Further assessment revealed that dissatisfaction and the communication deficits were more situation-specific than the initial assessment had
suggested. Training and homework assignments were changed to focus on
those specific topics of dissatisfaction with a consequent increase in the
couple's overall marital satisfaction and satisfaction with communication.

Similarly, termination of an intervention program is frequently contingent upon indices of satisfactory and stable changes in targeted behaviors
and etiological factors. Follow-up interventions (booster sessions) are usually
contingent on indices of or a high probability of recidivism.

SUMMARY

The behavior analyst must make a number of intervention decisions: whether
or not to treat a client, whether or not to target specific behaviors for
intervention, which intervention strategies to apply, the selection of pro-

gram components, when and how to modify an ongoing intervention program, when to terminate an intervention program, and when to institute
follow-up interventions.

The most complex and challenging intervention decisions are those
involving the selection and design of intervention programs. The following
section examines more closely the factors that affect program design.

DETERMINANTS OF INTERVENTION PROGRAM DESIGN

The previous sections examined the role of behavioral assessment in the
intervention process, the conceptual bases for the assessment–intervention
relationship and the types of intervention decisions that are made. In this
section a number of factors that influence the design of intervention programs are considered. These include diagnosis, target behavior characteristics, client mediational variables, task analysis, intervention history, social-
environmental variables, intervention variables, and assumptions from
behavioral construct systems. These factors influence all intervention decisions but are particularly salient considerations in the design of intervention
programs.

DIAGNOSIS

The concept of diagnosis was discussed earlier in this chapter ("Diagnostic
Homogeneity") and refers to any system of classification or labeling of
behavior problems or behavior syndromes. As noted earlier, diagnosis is
sufficient to specify intervention strategies when there is homogeneity of
topography or determinants within the diagnostic class. Diagnostic classes
which do not possess sufficient homogeneity are less useful in identifying
intervention strategies because of within-class variance in the factors which
influence intervention decisions.

As noted previously (Haynes, 1979), the utility of diagnosis for intervention design is also influenced by the situational or temporal stability of
the targeted syndromes. If a behavior problem such as "unassertiveness,"
"agoraphobia," or "enuresis" does not manifest situational or temporal covariance (i.e., is emitted randomly or inconsistently), assessment of situational variables will not facilitate the design of intervention programs.
However, most behavior problems manifest stimulus control or situational
control (Kazdin, 1982) and behavior problems that manifest reliable cross-
situational variance require situational assessment.

To reiterate, diagnostic classification also implies homogeneity of topography and etiology. Although many of the changes from the *Diagnostic and*

statistical manual of mental disorders (Vol. 2) (DSM II) to *DSM III* reflect an increased emphasis on within-category topographical homogeneity (Nathan, 1981), categorical homogeneity cannot be assumed in most diagnostic systems. Current classification systems do not provide sufficient within-class homogeneity to serve as the primary index for selecting intervention strategies.

Regardless of the difficulties with classification or labeling systems, behavior analysts should be familiar with the empirical treatment literature relevant to commonly used diagnostic classes (American Psychiatric Association, 1980; Endicott & Spitzer, 1978) and use diagnostic classification to generate hypotheses about etiology intervention and as a stimulus for additional assessment (Haynes, 1984). Diagnostic labels can also be a rich source of hypotheses about covarying behaviors and mediational variables.

TARGET BEHAVIOR CHARACTERISTICS

One of the most powerful determinants of intervention program design is the behaviors targeted for intervention. Target behavior characteristics such as rate, directionality of desired change, topography, variability, the operant-versus-nonoperant nature of the behavior, the degree of situational control, and underlying physiologic mechanisms can impact upon intervention strategies. Behaviors may be targeted by the client, by mediators in the client's environment (such as parents, teachers, or institutional staff) or by the behavior analyst.

There is an impressive and expanding literature on the effects of behavioral interventions on a wide range of target behavior problems (see Hersen, Eisler, & Miller, *Progress in Behavior Modification* series). Identificaiton of target behaviors is a form of classification and can usually point to previously developed intervention strategies. These programs are frequently based upon etiologic assumptions drawn from a behavioral construct system and the characteristics of the problem behavior. A familiarity with the etiologic and intervention research relevant to a particular disorder is mandatory for competent program design.

Unfortunately, there are many behavior problems for which behavioral interventions have not been extensively investigated or developed (Adams & Sutker, 1984). Methodological considerations, particularly the restricted populations used in previous research, can also limit the utility of previously published intervention studies.

The task of designing intervention programs is also complicated by the fact that most clients present multiple behavior problems. For example, Wittlieb, Eifert, Wilson, and Evans (1978) reviewed 36 single-case child behavior therapy studies and found that there was more than one presenting

problem in 67% of the cases. Intervention programs can usually be constructed for each presenting problem, but concurrent intervention with
many target behaviors is complex, time-consuming and, perhaps, less likely
to succeed.

The selection of initial target behaviors from an array of presenting
problems is influenced by a number of considerations. These include: (1) the
degree of danger associated with the behavior to the target subject or others,
(2) the degree to which the behavior mediates other problem behaviors,
(3) the degree to which the behavior is amenable to intervention, (4) the
social valence (aversiveness, desirability) associated with particular target
behaviors and goals, (5) the position of the behavior in a behavior chain, and
(6) its rate of covariation with other problem behaviors (Karoly, 1981; Voeltz
& Evans, 1982; Wahler *et al.*, 1979; Wittlieb *et al.*, 1978). Target behavior
selection is considered in greater detail in Chapter 10 of this volume.

CLIENT MEDIATIONAL VARIABLES

All behavioral intervention programs require clients or individuals in their
environment to perform prescribed behaviors. For example, family intervention strategies for child behavior problems sometimes require that parents
emit prescribed intervention procedures such as positive point delivery,
time-out, and/or contingency contracting (Patterson *et al.*, 1973). Similarly,
interventions for some stress-related psychosomatic disorders require that
target subjects practice relaxation exercises, identify and monitor sources of
stressful stimuli in their environment, and/or practice cognitive mediational
behaviors (Haynes & Gannon, 1981). These *behavioral prescriptions* derive from
an *interactionist* or *reciprocal determinism* philosophy of behavioral construct systems—individuals are assumed to be active agents in their environment and
capable of modifying environmental variables that function as determinants
of behavior problems (Bandura, 1969).

Intervention effectiveness is a partial function of the degree of compliance to behavioral prescriptions and a number of variables influence the
probability or degree of compliance. An important task of the behavior
analyst is to identify, evaluate, and sometimes modify these mediating factors. The following is a discussion of target subject factors that can affect
clients' adherence to intervention program prescriptions.

Motivation and Resistance

Motivation is a complex construct related to other mediating factors (Cofer
& Appley, 1964) and in the context of an intervention program refers to the
probability of an individual emitting the behaviors necessary for successful

intervention. An individual who is "motivated" is more likely to attend therapy sessions on time, complete homework assignments, follow prescribed schedules of self-reinforcement, complete self-monitoring tasks, and verbalize to the behavior analyst a desire for behavior change. Clients who are unmotivated or "resistant" (Chamberlain, Patterson, Kavanagh, & Forgatch, 1982) are those who emit negative verbalizations to behavior analysts about the intervention process, who do not emit prescribed behaviors, and who behave in other ways to impede the intervention process. These behaviors both predict and mediate program outcome.

Motivation and resistance have multiple determinants. One major determinant is the *expected ratio of gains and losses associated with a successful intervention program*. For example, some husbands who attend marital intervention sessions are in a traditional sex role-stereotyped marital relationship: they make most of the decisions, derive more reinforcement than their wives from a job and extramarital activities, and have few household responsibilities. It is not surprising that many are resistant to intervention that may result in a more egalitarian division of input into decisions and household responsibilities and a modification of extramarital activities. Resistance behaviors such as being late for sessions, objecting to suggested exercises, failure to participate in homework assignments, and "forgetting" to self-monitor would not be unexpected in view of the loss of reinforcement these clients anticipate will be associated with the intervention process.

Additional operant analyses suggest other possible determinants of motivation and resistance. Resistance behaviors may be emitted to punish the therapist, to punish others in the client's environment, and to avoid emitting behaviors that the individual finds aversive. Also, resistance may reflect attributions or other cognitions that are incompatible with the behavioral intervention process (such as beliefs that children should behave out of a "sense of responsibility" rather than because of external rewards).

Compliance with early assessment requirements (such as self-monitoring, return of completed questionnaires, participant observation, and session attendance) may be a measure of motivation (Keefe, Kopel, & Gordon, 1978). Most importantly, failure of clients to engage in the behaviors necessary for effective intervention is a cue that instructional, cognitive, or contingency variables have not been adequately addressed in the preintervention assessment.

Goals

Most applied behavior analysts have encountered clients whose goals were incongruent with those of the intervention process and, as noted earlier, client goals can sometimes determine whether or not intervention is appropriate. Clients' goals can be limited to establishing a supportive relationship with a therapist, identifying historical determinants of behavior, identifying "intrapsychic" processes, or laying "blame" on another individual. Clients may also verbalize behavioral goals that, although consistent with a behavioral philosophy, are inconsistent with the outcome of the functional analysis (e.g., clients who want desensitization for apparently operantly controlled behaviors). Obviously, client goals (frequently indicated in the target problem referral) are an important determinant of program design and should be carefully evaluated.

Social Validity

The perception by clients or their social mediators of the social validity (desirability, appropriateness, value) of intervention goals, procedures, and causal attributions inherent in the intervention process, can affect their degree of participation in the intervention program (Kazdin, 1977; Wolf, 1978). Clients who object to the use of external reinforcers, to the quantification of behavior, to assuming personal responsibility for behavior change, or to assumptions of environmental determinism are unlikely to adhere to the requirements of behavioral intervention programs. Frequent and systematic assessment of clients' perceptions of the intervention methods and goals can help in the early identification of perceptions that are likely to impede the intervention process.

Resources

Intellectual, financial, educational, cognitive, physiologic, and behavioral resources can also influence intervention program design as well as the probability and degree of intervention effectiveness (Karoly, 1981; Kendall & Hollon, 1981; Nelson, 1980). Clients with developmental disabilities, organic impairments, or additional deficits who have other limitations in their behavioral or cognitive repertoires represent special problems for behavior analysts. Often, standardized intervention programs can be applied with these individuals only after substantial modifications to meet their special requirements. Although individuals with such deficits can still be effectively involved in behavioral intervention programs, a more fine-grained shaping process may be required.

Competing Behavior Problems

The probability of successful intervention with a targeted behavior may be diminished because of competing behavior problems. This can occur when the competing behavior problems interfere with adherence to behavioral prescriptions inherent in the intervention process. For example, marital distress might reduce the effectiveness of "pleasuring exercises" in sex therapy for some couples. It may also reduce the between-parent cooperative and communicative behaviors necessary for home-based child behavioral intervention programs. Similarly, the attentional deficits characteristic of some psychotic disorders may reduce the effectiveness of desensitization, relaxation training, or other cognitive intervention strategies.

In summary, motivation, goals, program perceptions, resources, and competing behavior problems are a few of the possible client mediational variables which may influence intervention effectiveness. These variables most frequently impact on the prescriptive behaviors that are inherent in behavioral intervention programs. The potential impact of these mediating variables emphasizes the importance of their preintervention assessment as well as their continued assessment during program implementation.

Despite its apparent importance, little research has been conducted on the impact of client mediational variables. As pointed out by Johnson, Wildman, and O'Brien (1980), an impediment to the analysis and modification of these mediational variables has been a failure to measure adherence to program prescriptions. As a result, correlates of program adherence have not been extensively investigated.

The impact of these mediating variables can be addressed in two ways: (1) intervention programs can be adjusted to lessen the impact of adverse mediational variables, and (2) the mediational variables can be modified. As an example of the first approach, client objections to intervention methods or goals can be addressed by substituting other methods or labeling intervention processes in a manner that is more congruent with client expectations.

Many mediational variables are under contingency and/or informational control and can sometimes be modified by the behavior analyst. For example, a client's concern about his or her "right" to behave assertively would likely influence adherence to an assertion training program. Such a concern could be addressed through readings and discussions about how to be assertive while still maintaining a sensitivity to the rights and feelings of others (Cotler & Guerra, 1976). Similarly, the probability of intervention success can be enhanced by discussing with clients (or their social mediators) their perceptions of program goals, motivational issues, and their perceptions of intervention procedures prior to beginning intervention. Also, indices of motivation may be altered by contingency manipulations (e.g., therapist-delivered social or financial reinforcement for completing behavioral prescriptions).

Mediational variables may be the initial targets of the intervention program. For example, marital intervention might precede intervention with parent–child interactions or sexual enhancement training (Stuart, 1980). Or, contingency systems operating for institutional staff may require modification to provide sufficient reinforcers for their participation in complex behavioral intervention programs.

To reiterate, the *assessment and, when necessary and appropriate, modification of variables that mediate intervention effectiveness should be an integral part of and precede every behavioral intervention program*. Failure to address mediational variables satisfactorily can significantly increase the probability of failure in behavioral intervention programs.

The philosophy underlying these efforts emphasizes the importance of an explicit discussion between the behavior analyst and client. The rights of clients to object to intervention strategies and goals should be respected. Clients' concerns about intervention programs should be addressed, not only because they can influence intervention effectiveness, but also because it is the client's right to be informed about these issues and to object to any aspect of the assessment–intervention process. While behavior analysts should clearly communicate their perceptions of the assessment–intervention process, they do not have the right to proceed in a manner inconsistent with the values of the clients.

TASK ANALYSIS AND BEHAVIORAL SKILLS

Task analysis (sometimes referred to as *component* or *criterion analysis*) refers to the specification of response components and sequences in a complex chain or array of behaviors (Gagne, 1962; Karoly, 1981; Mullinix & Galassi, 1981). Behavioral goals such as effective marital communication, heterosocial skills, writing skills, shoe tying, cooperative sibling interaction, effective coping with environmental stressors, and increased utilization of community resources are composed of multiple, sequentially arranged response elements. These elements may be limited to discrete behaviors but frequently involve response–response and stimulus–response chains, clusters, and hierarchies, along with considerable situational variability (Karpowitz & Johnson, 1981; Kazdin, 1979; 1982; Voeltz & Evans, 1982).

A task analysis of the desired end product will influence the design of intervention strategies because it will identify goal components and sequences and a client's skill level on those components. Individuals with the same goals will differ in their skills in mastering the various elements of those goals and intervention procedures will vary accordingly. While most task analyses are conducted subjectively, more valid methods of task analysis involve social validity impact or between-group comparisons (Kazdin, 1982; McFall, 1982; Mullinix & Galassi, 1981). Examples of empirically based task analyses include comparing the problem-solving behaviors of distressed and nondistressed marital couples, the social interaction behaviors of socially active and socially inactive college students, or the cognitive coping strategies of clients with and without psychosomatic disorders (Barlow, 1981; Haynes & Gannon, 1981).

INTERVENTION HISTORY

Clients' perceptions of or participation in behavioral intervention programs can be influenced by their previous experience with interventions. For example, this author had difficulty in beginning token programs at two psychiatric institutions because of previous experiences by ward personnel with similar programs. The previous programs had apparently been administered in an unsystematic and autocratic manner, without sufficient staff incentives and with insufficient supervision of or consultation with staff. Naturally, ward staff were reluctant to begin an intervention program similar to one that had been inappropriately administered. We have had similar difficulty in instituting home-based contingency management programs for children because families had been involved in previous behavioral programs that focused on the use of aversive control procedures, that did not sufficiently attend to the goals of the parents, or in which behavior analysts failed to continue with the program after the end of the academic term.

Problems also arise with clients who have had previous experience with nonbehavioral interventions. These clients sometimes expect a specific "therapeutic process" from the intervention, a specific type of interaction with the behavior analyst, and/or a specific program focus. These expectations are frequently inconsistent with the goals or methods of behavioral construct systems.

As with other client mediational factors, clients' previous experience with interventions and expectations based on those experiences should be evaluated carefully during preintervention assessment. The intervention program can then be modified to address some of the clients' concerns or they may be addressed directly through discussions with the client.

SOCIAL-ENVIRONMENTAL VARIABLES

One defining characteristic of behavior construct systems is the emphasis on social-environmental determinants of behavior (Bandura, 1969; Kanfer & Phillips, 1970; Mash & Terdal, 1981; Nelson & Hayes, 1979). Social-environmental variables are presumed to function as *discriminitive stimuli* for behavior (stimuli indicating the conditional probabilities of contingencies for specific behaviors), as *consequences* that maintain behavior (such as parent-delivered rewards), and as stimuli that *elicit* behavior (such as classicially conditioned environmental stressors).

Because environment covariation *can* reflect a causal relationship, one of the most important goals of preintervention assessment is the identification of environmental sources of behavioral variance: The behavior analyst must determine if, and to what extent, target behaviors demonstrate covariation with environmental events. This information has a significant impact on the selection of intervention strategies and on the selection of components of these strategies because environmental "controlling" stimuli are often imbued with causal properties and are targeted for modification.

There are several interdependent classes of environmental events that can affect behavior occurrence or topography. These include antecedent events, consequent events, social mediational variables, social supports, and other environmental, organizational, and resource constraints.

Antecedent Events

The probability of occurrence of target behaviors may vary across antecedent environmental events (this is known as *situational specificity*—see Karpowitz & Johnson, 1981; Kazdin, 1979). As noted by Messick (1981) and Mischel (1981), the degree of situational control varies among behaviors. Therefore, the importance to the assessment process of situational analyses will vary. Types of antecedent events that may affect the probability of occurrence of behavior include informational cues (such as instructions), the presence or absence of specific individuals, temporal factors (such as time since last meal), modeling or social facilitation effects (such as the behavior of peers), changes in reinforcement schedules (such as contrast effects and reinforcement decrements), changes in internal states (such as modifications in estrogen or blood sugar levels), exposure to classically conditioned stimuli (such as conditioned fear stimuli), self-generated stimuli (such as behavior chains), and cognitive events (such as thoughts of previous aversive experiences).

These events are important assessment targets because they sometimes influence the *conditional probability* of behavior (the probability of occurrence of the target behavior given the occurrence of a specific antecedent event compared to the noncontingent probability of the target behavior) and of contingencies. Therefore, the identification of antecedent sources of behavioral variance can assist in the identification of etiologic variables.

Identified antecedent sources of behavioral control can affect intervention design in several ways: (1) they can indicate the differential operation of contingencies that might be maintaining the target behavior (such as differences in contingencies delivered to a child by each parent); (2) they can indicate hierarchies of antecedent stimuli controlling respondent target behaviors (such as the stimuli associated with agoraphobic fear responses or erectile dysfunction, which might be included in *in vivo* desensitization programs); (3) they can suggest methods of behavioral self-control (such as modification of diet, relaxation training, or cognitive restructuring); (4) they can suggest strategies for coping with environmental events (such as modification by the client of environmental sources of psychophysiologic stress); and (5) they can provide information that facilitates other behavioral intervention programs (such as minimizing environmental complexity in working with some hyperactive, learning-disabled children).

Contingencies

One major contribution of behavioral construct systems has been to document the importance of contingencies in the control of behavior. Contingency theory and contingency manipulation subsumes a major portion of most behavioral intervention textbooks (Bandura, 1969; Kanfer & Phillips, 1970; Rimm & Masters, 1979), particularly those with an operant emphasis (Catania & Brigham, 1980; Kazdin, 1980), and accounts for much of the published behavioral intervention literature.

There is considerable variation across behavior problems in the role of social–environmental contingencies. For example, although social–environmental contingencies have been hypothesized (Lachman, 1972; Ullmann & Krasner, 1976) to influence the manifestation of psychophysiologic disorders such as headache or hypertension, on the one hand, there is currently little evidence that such factors play a clinically meaningful role in these disorders; and successful intervention programs have been developed that do not include contingency manipulation (Haynes & Gannon, 1981). On the other hand, social–environmental contingencies appear to be important etiologic factors in other medical/psychological disorders such as chronic pain, and are important components of intervention programs (Fordyce, 1976).

Despite variance across behavior problems in the causal role of contingencies, the identification of environmental contingencies, particularly social contingencies, that may account for the occurrence, topography, or other characteristic of targeted behaviors is an important goal of preintervention assessment. This task is complicated by the fact that many targeted behavior problems (such as deficient academic or social skills) can be due to the absence of, as well as the occurrence of, particular contingencies.

Many classes of contingencies have been implicated in the etiology of behavior disorders. These contingency relationships include termination of avoidance of aversive situations, reciprocal exchanges of reinforcers and punishers, omission of appropriate reinforcement or punishment, intrinsic reinforcement (such as that associated with heroin or alcohol intake), inappropriate reinforcement or punishment parameters (timing, type, intensity, frequency), self-reinforcement and punishment, and reinforcement of undesirable behaviors. Specific reinforcing and punishing stimuli encompass a wide range of verbal, visual, attentive, social, physiologic, self-delivered, sexual, motor, and cognitive events.

Despite the emphasis on contingencies, documentation of their role in the development or maintenance of behavior problems is indirect. Although some experimental psychopathology research with animals (Maher, 1970) has demonstrated that behavior disorders could be produced through contingency manipulation, inferences about the etiologic role of contingencies are primarily derived from intervention studies with behavior problems. These studies have shown that many targeted behaviors can be modified by manipulation of the contingencies presumed to control them.

Although such behavior modification demonstrations have *functional utility* for the behavior analyst, the derivation of causal inferences from them is unwarranted. Successful modification of a behavior problem through manipulation of a variable is not sufficient to indicate that the manipulated variable had an etiologic function for the targeted behavior. For example, successful intervention with problem behaviors such as organically caused speech impediments, autistic behavior, or hyperactive behavior, through contingency manipulation does not necessarily imply that contingencies functioned as etiologic variables for those behaviors.

Given the inferential constraints noted above, one of the most heuristic assumptions that a behavior analyst can make in designing intervention programs is that *behavior pays off*. This seemingly simplistic assumption must be tempered with the knowledge that contingency factors are multiple, complex, interrelated, interacting, idiosyncratic, frequently difficult to identify, and sometimes irrelevant.

The preintervention assessment of contingency factors has an impact on intervention design in many ways: (1) it can suggest methods of modifying intrinsicially reinforcing effects of problem behaviors (such as disulfiram administration for alcoholics), (2) it can identify reinforcing stimuli for use in an intervention program (such as social interactions that may be reinforcing for a child or prescribing "activity" as a reinforcer for a hyperactive child), (3) it can suggest reinforcers useful in contingency contracting (such as the exchange of pleasing events between spouses or other family members), (4) it can identify reinforcers useful in self-control programs (such as increased television time or positive self-statements for increased academic performance or social behavior), (5) it can suggest back-up reinforcers appropriate for large-scale contingency systems (such as back-up reinforcers for institutional token systems), (6) it can identify environmental events that may be maintaining problem behaviors (such as family or institutional staff attention to verbalizations of pain or discomfort), (7) it can suggest appropriate contingency parameters (such as the timing, intensity, or amount of a specific contingency), (8) it can suggest punishing stimuli that may be effective with minimal adverse side effects (such as time-out procedures in a home-based child intervention program), (9) it can identify alternatives to cognitive contingencies maintaining behavior disorders (such as substituting effective cognitive coping strategies when a socially anxious individual experiences social rejection), and (10) it can identify contingency deficits that may account for targeted deficits (such as insufficient reinforcement for the use of community resources or energy conservation). Perhaps most importantly, preintervention assessment of contingency and antecedent factors results in an increasingly sophisticated understanding of the determinants of behavior problems which ultimately may be applied in preventative paradigms.

Social Mediational Variables

Because of an emphasis on behavior change in the natural environment and the etiologic importance of social stimuli, many behavioral intervention programs involve participation by members of a client's social environment. Participation by persons in the natural environment can mediate program effectiveness, the generalization of behavior change to the natural environment, and long-term maintenance of the behavior change. Involvement of those in the client's social environment, focusing particularly on the behavior of family members, is typical in interventions with marital problems (spouses; see Stuart, 1980), depression (family and friends; see Seligman et al., 1976), chronic pain (family; see Fordyce, 1976), alcoholism (family; see Miller & Foy, 1980), psychotic behavior (family, staff; see Kazdin, 1980), sexual dysfunctions (sexual partner; see Heiman & Hatch, 1981), and community agencies (staff and administrators; see Nietzel, Winett, MacDonald & Davidson, 1977). Because so many behavioral intervention programs rely on persons in the natural environment, their mediation potential must be carefully evaluated.

The factors that influence the behavior of social mediators are similar to those affecting clients' mediation potential and were previously discussed. In particular, the ability of social mediators to carry through with behavioral prescriptions (such as reinforcement delivery or prompts) should be carefully evaluated.

As with all mediational factors, assessment and, when necessary, modification of the behavior of social mediators should be an early element in an assessment/intervention program. Intervention programs instituted with uncooperative, skeptical, or untrained persons in the natural environment are less likely to be successful. Although the hypothesized mediational functions of the social environment have not always been supported, a careful assessment of social mediators can suggest the desirability and methods of modifying their behavior or of modifying the intervention program to enhance the probability of intervention success.

Social Supports

Social supports of the client may also influence treatment outcome in intervention programs that do not involve other persons as formal components (Cooke & Meyers, 1980; Wahler, 1981). Intervention programs such as those focusing on eating control, cessation of smoking, habit change, parent–child interaction, social skill acquisition, and interpersonal communication may be affected by the behavior of significant individuals in the client's natural environment.

Many behavioral intervention programs involve public behaviors, such as weight charting, self-monitoring, and the application of contingencies to children in restaurants and stores, which are particularly sensitive to social contingencies. Even when behavioral prescriptions do not involve public behaviors, many clients discuss their intervention programs with friends and family and their reactions can affect the degree of adherence to intervention programs. Spouses, extended family members, and friends can facilitate or inhibit positive behavior change and their probable reactions toward clients should be evaluated. Indications that the behavior of these individuals may not facilitate prescribed behavior changes suggests the need for intervention in the social environment or for teaching the client strategies for coping with the behavior of these persons.

Organization Resources and Other Environmental Constraints

Other constraints may influence the design of intervention programs. Some institutions have strict guidelines about allowable types of interventions, the types of reinforcers that may be controlled, or the types of aversive stimuli that may be used (Kazdin, 1980). Also, financial constraints limit the choice of reinforcers, and time constraints limit the types of intervention programs that may be instituted for many clients. For example, Maher (1981) noted that because of the extensive time commitment associated with kidney dialysis, intervention or assessment programs with dialysis patients must be designed to minimize the consumption of their remaining free time. Similarly, space and privacy issues are frequently important when doing family therapy with large families or in small homes.

In summary, the multitude of social–environmental factors that influence behavior and that affect intervention programs suggest the adoption of a *systems perspective* (Cromwell & Peterson, 1981; Haynes, 1984; McFall, 1982; Vincent, 1980). Behavior problems cannot be viewed in isolation from the complex interactions and variations in situational factors, maintaining contingencies, social mediational variables, and environmental constraints. The cost of adopting a systems perspective is a much more complex preintervention assessment task. However, the benefits are increasingly powerful intervention programs and a conceptual system which incorporates a greater proportion of relevant causal and mediational variables.

Behavioral construct systems have traditionally subsumed a narrow domain of presumed controlling variables. Through frequent exposure to conceptual and methodological elements of behavioral construct systems, most behavior analysts have learned to focus selectively on particular social–environmental events as the most likely controlling factors for behavior disorders. Although such a priori biases have been rewarded by the development of a useful behavior change technology, *they have also served to reduce the permeability of the behavioral construct systems to new etiologic concepts.* Because of an emphasis on empiricism, elements in behavioral construct systems are easily tested and refined. However, new elements are not readily incorporated. For example, heuristic concepts such as "insularity" (Wahler, 1981) or "resistance" (Chamberlain *et al.*, 1982) as important mediators of behavioral intervention outcome are infrequently introduced and slowly assimilated. The behavior analyst can avoid contributing to the conceptual isolation of behavioral construct systems by searching for behavioral chains, behavior–environment relationships, and controlling and mediating factors that are not part of current behavioral lore. The preintervention behavioral assessment is a particularly fertile process for the development of new hypotheses.

INTERVENTION VARIABLES

The previous sections have considered the influence on intervention design of diagnosis, target behavior characteristics, target subject variables, and social–environmental factors. These dimensions point to the importance of topographical characteristics and controlling variables of behavior problems and are particularly important determinants of the goals of behavioral intervention. However, frequently several intervention methods may be used to achieve those goals, and the behavior analyst must design an intervention program from an array of possible strategies. For example, assessment of a distressed marital couple might suggest a low rate of exchange of positive behaviors as one determinant of their distress. Procedures to increase their exchange of positive behaviors might include readings, in-session modeling, didactic discussions with the behavior analyst, self-monitoring of positive events, participant monitoring of the spouses' positive behaviors, token exchanges contingent on positive behavior, training to develop more positive communication skills, and negotiated contracts to increase positive exchanges (Jacobson, 1979; Stuart, 1980).

A number of evaluative dimensions associated with intervention methods should be considered when selecting from an array of intervention procedures. These include demonstrated efficacy or power, cost-efficiency, side effects, and the viability of alternative interventions.

Power

Intervention power refers to indices of outcome and may be measured by the average improvement for groups of subjects, the proportion of individuals significantly improved, the degree to which behavior changes approximate socially validated norms, the generalizability of effects, or remission rates. Intervention power is the most important dimension upon which intervention strategies should be evaluated. However, indices of efficacy do not always generalize across populations or settings, and evaluations of behavioral interventions have frequently been confined to narrow populations of environments.

Cost-Efficiency

Assuming that several applicable intervention strategies do not significantly differ in expected efficacy, considerations of cost-efficiency become important (Karoly, 1981). Those interventions that are effective but less costly (in time, money, and/or effort) are preferable. Considerations of cost-efficiency are particularly relevant when issues of effectiveness have been addressed satisfactorily. However, the resources of the behavior analysts and clients are not unlimited and there may be cases in which less effective interventions are selected over more effective but more costly ones.

Side Effects

Most intervention procedures have effects in addition to those on the main target behaviors (Epstein & Martin, 1977; Kazdin, 1982; Voeltz & Evans, 1982). In some individuals, these side effects may be positive (such as generalized relaxation skills sometimes accompanying relaxation training for insomnia). In others, they may be sufficiently undesirable to preclude the use of an intervention strategy. Undesirable side effects may include an increased probability of alternative undesirable target behaviors, unwanted generalization, aggression, or overly restrictive environments. Adoption of a systems approach suggests that particular care should be taken to evaluate possible side effects. It is illogical to assume that the modification of primary targets such as aspects of a client's life, the interaction between family members, or the administrative structure of an organization will have effects limited to those targets.

Intervention Alternatives

Selection of an intervention procedure should also take into consideration the efficacy, cost efficiency, and side effects of alternative interventions. The most effective and least aversive intervention strategies should be selected.

VARIABLES ASSOCIATED WITH THE BEHAVIOR ANALYST

Ideally, all behavior analysts (or other interventionists such as institutional staff) would be well trained in all behavioral intervention strategies. Unfortunately, this condition is seldom approached, and the selection of intervention programs must sometimes reflect the specialized competencies of the behavior change agent. The competence of the behavior change agent is an important determinant of outcome in all interventions.

One disadvantage of behavioral interventions is that they sometimes erroneously appear simple to apply. As a result, individuals with insufficient training sometimes apply behavioral intervention programs without adequate understanding of their controlling parameters. For example, the outcome of a seemingly simple procedure such as time-out is affected by parameters such as the time-out stimulus selected, its schedule of application, the duration of time-out, the target subject's previous experience with time-out, procedures for removal from time-out, instructional variables, and the environment from which the subject is removed.

The values of the behavior analyst also influence intervention decisions. The selection of goals, target behaviors, and intervention procedures, as well as the degree of informed consent and explicit communication between the behavior analyst and client reflect the values of the behavior analyst. One task of the behavior analyst is to be aware of his or her value system and, when necessary, communicate those values to the client. Clients have the right to make intervention decisions, including the decision to seek another therapist, based upon a clear communication from the behavior analyst concerning those issues. The values of the behavior analyst are particularly important in the use of aversive procedures, sexual reorientation training, providing institutional or educational staff with more effective methods of behavioral control, and in the modification of sex role patterns of family members.

ASSUMPTIONS UNDERLYING A BEHAVIORAL CONSTRUCT SYSTEM

Conceptualizations of behavior characteristics, etiology, and the intervention procedures based on those conceptualizations are only reflections of a heuristic but unstable and evolving construct system. Like all construct systems, behavioral construct systems suggest events upon which to focus, which variables are most likely to function as behavioral determinants, and which intervention strategies are most likely to be effective (Haynes, 1978). Thus, the behavior of the behavior analyst is strongly influenced by previous exposure to and reinforcement for employing a particular conceptual paradigm. The strength of these conceptual biases is a function of the methods by which they were taught and the reinforcement associated with their use.

In effect, behavior analysts presume an understanding of behavior causality prior to initial assessment of a problem behavior. We each possess a subjective hierarchy of potential determinants, and potentially effective intervention strategies and intervention programs are frequently designed on the basis of these a priori conceptualizations without the benefit of empirical evaluation. In our review of 41 cases published in 1981, 65% instituted programs to modify hypothesized controlling variables without attempting an empirical or qualitative evaluation of the validity of those hypothesized etiologic factors (see footnote 4, p. 390). Care must be exercised to avoid a myopic or unquestioning adoption of the tenets of any construct system.

A subjective appraisal of the evolution of the various psychological construct systems over the past several decades suggests three important concepts: (1) the proportion of behavioral variance accounted for by behavioral construct systems is increasing over time, (2) most alternative construct systems (biopsychological systems are an exception) are weak and unevolving, and (3) we know very little about the determinants of behavior. Therefore, it is the *methodology* associated with a behavioral construct system which should be maintained; behavior analysts should not become irrevocably tied to particular conceptualizations or models of behavior.

In summary, intervention programs are sometimes determined less by the characteristics of the client, environmental variables, and intervention power than by our a priori conceptualizations of them. The functional utility of those conceptualizations varies across clients, behaviors, environments, and intervention strategies.

SUMMARY

There are a number of factors influencing the selection of behavioral intervention programs. These include diagnosis, target behavior characteristics, client mediational variables, task analysis, intervention history, social–environmental variables, intervention variables, variables associated with the behavior analyst, and assumptions underlying the behavioral construct system. These factors do not act in isolation but interact to influence intervention decisions.

The factors that influence intervention decisions have important implications for assessment methods. First, traditional methods of psychological assessment do not provide the type of information necessary for the design of behavioral intervention programs. The inferences derived from such assessment methods tend to be nonspecific, nonoperationalized, higher-order abstractions based upon trait assumptions. For optimal utility in intervention decisions, assessment methods must provide specific, minimally inferential, and situationally specific information. Furthermore, the assessment methods must incorporate a systems focus and take into account the interactional nature of variables.

Two major deficiencies stand out: First, there are no systematic or empirically based methods of deriving most of the information necessary for program design. Such determinants of intervention design as client and social–environmental mediation potential, the analysis of the client's goals, and the skills of the behavior analyst are frequently evaluated informally and/or unsystematically. Second, there is no systematic method of integrating the acquired data for the purpose of program design. The conceptualization or *functional analysis* phase of assessment remains obscure and only recently has been the focus of empirical study. These deficiencies partially account for the dearth of published studies in which the development of intervention programs is based on a multimethod, multimodel, preintervention behavioral assessment. Despite its impact on the design of intervention programs, the identification of etiologic relationships in behavioral assessment has also been infrequently explicated. The following section outlines the assumptions and methods associated with the derivation of causal inferences.

DERIVING ETIOLOGIC INFERENCES

Behavioral intervention programs frequently manipulate hypothesized controlling variables, and one important goal of preintervention assessment is the identificaiton of those variables. There are several methods of deriving causal inferences, but most involve examination of the *conditional probabilities* or *covariation* among events (Sellitz, Wrightsman, & Cook 1976). If two events are causally related, the probability of occurrence (or other characteristics such as intensity or duration) of one must be at least a partial function of the occurrence (or other characteristic) of the other. Stated differently, causality may be inferred only when the probability of an event is significantly different in association with the causal factor (conditional probability) from its unconditional probability. Thus, statistical association is a prerequisite for inferring causality.

Inferences of causality from conditional or covarying relationships must be drawn with caution. Conditional probabilities or covariation do not necessarily indicate causality and can indicate other relationships—such as control by a common mediator (Sellitz *et al.*, 1976). Therefore, demonstrations of statistical association are insufficient to warrant assumptions of causality. However, behavior analysts do make preintervention causal inferences based only on weak indices of conditional probability or covariation between events. Interview questions such as "In what situations do you tend to get headaches?" or "How do you respond when your daughter gets out of bed during the night?" are attempts to develop causal hypotheses by the informal identification of conditional probabilities.

Consistent with the conceptual biases noted earlier, the impact of these observed or inferred relationships upon causal inferences is a function of their congruence with assumptions inherent in a behavioral construct system. Conditional probabilities and covariations that are consistent with etiologic assumptions within the construct system are weighted heavily; those that are inconsistent with such assumptions are typically given less importance. The deleterious impact of such a causal deduction system on the evolutional quality of any construct system is obvious.

All assessment procedures (such as interviews or naturalistic observation) can be used to identify causal relationships, and the resulting data can be examined with several data-analytic structures. Perhaps the most powerful nonmanipulation method of causal analysis is through time-lagged sequential correlational analyses (Glass, Wilson, & Gottman 1975). This method involves repetitive and concurrent measurement of two events (such as a target behavior and a hypothesized controlling variable) across time. Correlation coefficients can then be calculated on the basis of several levels of precedence or time lags. For example, daily measures of "state anxiety" and nightly measures of sleep-onset latency, if taken for 1 month, can be used to examine the degree to which variance in nightly sleep-onset latency is associated with variance in the previous day's level of state anxiety. Additional information on the *direction* of the causal relationship can be gained by comparing the derived coefficients with the coefficients of association between each night's sleep-onset latency and state anxiety measured the following day.

Other correlational models used for causal inference involve *multiple linear regression* (Horne, Yang, & Ware, 1982), normative comparisons (Hayes, 1978), and causal modeling (Asher, 1976). Regression procedures, including discriminate function analysis, are designed to account for variance in a criterion variable through reference to predictor variables. It is assumed that causal relationships will be manifested by significant levels of common variance. In normative comparisons, the rate of hypothesized predictor (or its level of covariation with target behaviors) is compared with norms from a general or comparison population. For example, if the rate or degree of negative reciprocity of aversive behaviors is higher for a dysfunctional family than would be expected on the basis of normative data, we are more likely to assume that negative reciprocity plays a causal role in the family interaction patterns than if the negative reciprocity rate did not significantly differ from that of comparison groups.

Causal modeling refers to a class of statistical methods for evaluating possible paths of causation and facilitates the derivation of causal inferences in nonexperimental situations in which measures have been taken on many variables. It can also help detect the operation of mediational variables by examining the pattern of intercorrelations among a set of variables acting on a phenomenon; in this case, causal modeling helps estimate the strength of each variable in predicting the phenomenon (Asher, 1976).

As noted earlier, regression, normative, and causal modeling procedures are correlational methods of causal analysis that cannot be used to *affirm* causal hypotheses. However, they are useful methods of *deriving* causal hypotheses and can provide strong disconfirmatory data. Hypothesized etiologic relationships that are not manifested in expected time-lagged, multiple regression, normative, or causal modeling coefficients must be suspect.

Perhaps the most powerful method of evaluating causality is through systematic *manipulation* of the hypothesized controlling variables. This is the investigative method most frequently used in experimental analysis of behavior and applied behavior analysis and is illustrated in most articles published in the *Journal of Applied Behavior Analysis* and the *Journal of the Experimental Analysis of Behavior*. If sources of experimental confound are carefully controlled (Hersen & Barlow, 1976; Kazdin, 1982; Kratochowill, 1978), systematic modification of the parameters of an hypothesized etiologic variable can support causal inferences if these manipulations are reliably associated with expected changes in the dependent variable.

Manipulation is frequently used in intervention studies but infrequently used in assessment (Haynes, 1984). For example, the potential efficacy of various reinforcers can be examined through their systematic manipulation in an analogue reinforcement program. Also, eliciting stimuli can be presented in an analogue psychophysiologic assessment situation to help evaluate the impact of specific environmental events on psychophysiologic arousal.

Despite the importance of causal inferences in the design of intervention programs, systematic, preintervention causal analyses are seldom undertaken. They are very time-consuming and many behavior analysts consider them unnecessary. More importantly, causal relationships are frequently inferred on the basis of qualitative and subjective rather than quantitative analyses of relationships. A more systematic and quantitative approach (such as the derivation of conditional probabilitive from time-series designs) would increase confidence in inferred causal realtionships and would contribute to the validity and evolution of behavioral construct systems.

The derivation of causal inferences is further complicated by the fact that most targeted behaviors have multiple interacting determinants and by the fact that different assessment methods and data analytic systems provide different indices of causality. The behavior analyst attempts to integrate these inferential and sometimes conflicting data in a *functional analysis*. As noted in the following section, the decision-making processes that are part of the functional analysis remain subjective and largely unidentified.

ISSUES IN THE DESIGN OF INTERVENTION PROGRAMS

The design of intervention programs is a complex and insufficiently understood process and many issues remain to be addressed. Particularly relevant are issues concerning the utility and psychometric characteristics of the assessment instruments, the role of the functional analysis in intervention design, and problems with the underlying behavioral construct systems.

THE APPLICATION AND CLINICAL UTILITY
OF BEHAVIORAL ASSESSMENT PROCEDURES

A number of authors (Emmelkamp, 1981; Haynes, 1983, 1984; Jacobson, 1985; Margolin, 1981; Swan & MacDonald, 1978; Wade, Baker, & Hartmann, 1979) have noted that behavioral assessment procedures have more empirical than clinical utility. For example, Wade *et al.* (1979) found that many behavior therapists formulate intervention plans solely on the basis of structured interviews and traditional, trait-oriented assessment instruments [such as the Minnesota Mulitiphasic Personality Inventory (MMPI)] and that the systematic assessment methods recommended in this and other volumes on behavioral assessment are less frequently used in applied settings. Emmelkamp (1981) and Swan and MacDonald (1978) also noted discrepancies between the types of assessment procedures used in research and in clinical applications. The low rate of clinical application of many behavioral assessment procedures is a function of their characteristics, the professionals who apply them, and the contingency systems within which they are applied.

First, many behavioral assessment procedures have restricted clinical utility because of the cost associated with their application. Behavioral assessment procedures are frequently time-consuming and can sometimes delay intervention (Bloom & Fischer, 1982). This is a particularly salient characteristic of observations and self-monitoring measures that may involve data collection over a number of days. Second, many behavioral assessment procedures are expensive to apply and/or require extensive training. For example, the application of observation coding systems to assess marital interaction often requires many hours of training for several coders who then must spend considerable time observing, coding, and reducing data (Margolin, 1981).

The training required to administer behavioral assessment instruments can also hinder their clinical application. Many professionals, particularly those from traditional clinical training programs, are insufficiently trained in the application of behavioral assessment procedures (Bloom & Fischer, 1982) and are appropriately reluctant to use them.

The clinical utility of behavioral assessment instruments is also limited because the information they provide is not always relevant to clinical decision making (Jacobson, 1985). Behavioral assessment is a set of procedures particularly useful for designing and evaluating behavioral intervention programs. It can be useful in a variety of other decision-making situations encountered by clinicians, such as measuring academic or intellectual achievement, differentiating functional from organic etiologies, or diagnosing patients for statistical purposes (Barlow, 1981). However, in many cases, there are alternative assessment strategies that are more specifically designed and more useful for these purposes.

The clinical utility of behavioral assessment procedures is further limited because no validated instruments have been developed to address many clinically relevant areas. For example, valid behavioral assessment instruments have not yet been developed for the assessment of many aspects of psychosomatic, paranoid, schizophrenic, depressive, hypochondriacal, antisocial, addictive, and postdivorce behavior problems (see Barlow, 1981).

Perhaps most significantly, the contingency systems associated with service delivery are often not conducive to the use of extensive assessment procedures. Many mental health institutions receive funds on a "fee for service" basis or on the basis of client contact hours and many assessment procedures do not maximize chargeable client contact time (Haynes, Lemsky & Sexton-Radek, 1986). Also, many private practitioners may hesitate to charge clients for extensive assessment procedures and may be unwilling to accept the reduced client contact time and resultant fee reductions associated with the use of behavioral assessment instruments.

The clinical utility of behavioral assessment procedures can be enhanced by: (1) developing and validating assessment instruments to address a broader range of problem behaviors, (2) developing assessment instruments that are less expensive and time-consuming to administer, (3) providing additional pre- and postdoctoral training for applied psychologists in behavioral assessment concepts and procedures, and (4) modifying the financial contingencies that inhibit the use of behavioral assessment instruments in applied settings.

PSYCHOMETRIC CHARACTERISTICS OF BEHAVIORAL ASSESSMENT INSTRUMENTS

Because intervention decisions are based on data derived from behavioral assessment instruments, error variance in the data obtained or threats to the validity of the instruments can affect the validity of the resultant interventions (Haynes, 1983; Nelson & Hayes, 1979). One significant source of variance in assessment is method variance—different assessment procedures applied to the same target frequently provide different data. Inferences about target behavior characteristics, etiology, situational controls, and co-varying behaviors and the intervention decisions based upon these inferences will, therefore, vary as a function of the particular assessment instrument used.

Because of the important role of assessment instruments in clinical decision making, their psychometric properties require close scrutiny (Foster & Cone, 1980; Goldfried, 1979; Haynes, 1978; Haynes & Wilson, 1979; Kanfer, 1979; Russo, Bird & Masek, 1980). Behavioral assessment instruments have historically been developed and evaluated solely on the basis of face validity. Only recently have the psychometric qualities of assessment instruments, such as generalizability (Coates & Thoresen, 1978), reliability and validity (Haynes, 1978), factorial structure (Galassi & Galassi, 1980), and sensitivity (Bloom & Fischer, 1982) been systematically addressed.

One result of the investigation of the psychometric properties of behavioral assessment instruments is an enhanced understanding of their common and idiosyncratic sources of error. Threats to validity such as reactivity (Baum, Forehand, & Zegoib, 1979; Haynes & Horn, 1982), demand factors (Rosenthal, 1966), observer drift and bias (Kratochwill & Wetzel, 1977), variance in sampling parameters (Powell, Martindale, & Kulp, 1975), and subject expectations (Briddell & Wilson, 1976) are becoming better understood and controlled.

The psychometric analysis of behavioral assessment instruments and the identification of their associated sources of error will have a positive effect on the development of intervention programs. Data derived will more accurately and comprehensively reflect the constructs being measured, and thus more valid intervention-relevant inferences can be drawn.

VALIDITY OF THE FUNCTIONAL ANALYSIS

The integration of information derived from preintervention behavioral assessment into a conceptual model of the target client is a complex process. This functional analysis must take into account multiple problem behaviors, multiple mediational variables, other individuals in the client's social environment, complex response–response and response–environment stimulus chains, situational elements, client cognitions, response classes, and multiple, interacting etiologic factors. The functional analysis is the conceptual model from which intervention strategies are derived, and thus is one of the most important aspects of behavioral assessment.

Despite its central role in intervention design, the functional analysis is most frequently achieved through an informal, subjective, and unsystematic process and has not been subjected to empirical analysis. It is a major source of potential error because the application of valid assessment instruments does not preclude the derivation of an invalid conceptualization of the client. As noted by Emmelkamp (1981), Goldfried (1979), Haynes (1984), Karoly (1981), and Mash and Terdal (1981), the reliability (or stability) of the functional analysis requires examination. Other than an analog study of Felton & Nelson (1984) there are no data on the stability of functional analyses (or the resultant intervention designs) across behavior analysts examining the same assessment data for a client or for the reliability of functional analyses from separate assessments of the same client. Similarly, there are no data on the degree to which different assessment procedures result in different functional analyses.

The *conceptual validity* of functional analyses and the validity of resultant intervention programs have been examined only indirectly. For example, the etiologic hypotheses that are components of a functional analysis are usually subjected to indirect validation only through intervention studies: The hypothesized etiologic relationships are assumed to be valid if intervention procedures aimed at modifying them result in predicted changes in targeted behaviors. Similarly, the validity of treatment strategies derived from functional analyses have been subjected to the same indirect validation. Demonstrations of treatment effects in predicted directions can be considered validation of etiologic hypotheses and intervention design only when alternative explanations for observed effects are excluded—a condition seldom met.

The clinical utility of functional analyses also remains to be demonstrated. Because functional analyses require the integration of complex assessment data, it must be shown that: (1) a functional analysis increases the probability or degree of intervention success beyond that which would be achieved with the application of standardized intervention programs, and (2) the increased probability or degree of improvement warrants the time expenditure. As noted in the section on "The Assessment-Intervention Relationship," the contribution of a functional analysis to treatment outcome is inversely related to the power of the intervention and directly related to the etiologic and topographical diversity of the targeted problem behavior.

EXTENDING THE FOCUS OF BEHAVIORAL ASSESSMENT

The validity and clinical utility of behavioral assessment for the design of intervention programs is tied to the construct system upon which it is based. As with all newly formulated construct systems, there are conceptual and methodological limitations with behavioral construct systems that reduce the applicability of behavioral assessment. These limitations are relevant for the design of intervention programs because intervention program design is especially sensitive to the conceptual and methodological characteristics of a construct system. Two major deficits of behavioral construct systems have been noted: an emphasis on intervention rather than etiology, and a focus on a narrow range of etiologic variables.

A number of authors (Freedman, Rosenthal, Donahoe, Schlundt, & McFall, 1978; Goldfried, 1979; Haynes, 1983, 1984; Keefe et al., 1978) have noted that treatment research is proceeding at a much faster pace than research on the etiology of behavior disorders. In effect, behavioral construct systems are becoming more technological but less conceptually based. As a result, interventions are frequently designed on the basis of unsubstantiated a priori assumptions about the etiology of a particular disorder. For example, frontal electromyographic (EMG) biofeedback for tension headaches was based on an unsubstantiated assumption that tension headaches were caused by elevated muscle tension in the frontal region, and stimulus–control interventions with insomnia were based upon unsubstantiated assumptions that the insomniacs' sleep-onset difficulties were attributable to their presleep behavior patterns (Haynes & Gannon, 1981). However, treatment validity is tied to the validity of underlying etiologic conceptualizations, and the importance of etiologic research should not be underestimated.

Based, in part, on a historical rejection of traditional models of clinical psychology and an emphasis on methodological behaviorism, behavioral construct systems have tended to focus on a small domain of variables, particularly observable operant events in close temporal relationships, and have tended to minimize the potential relevance of other variables. More recently, a broader range of variables such as subjective perceptions (Wolf, 1978), physiologic responses (Haynes & Gannon, 1981), and cognitive events (Kendall & Hollon, 1981) have been included in both intervention and conceptual models. This represents a significant expansion from the previous exclusive focus on observable operant behaviors. Assuming that such events have significance for understanding behavior disorders, more powerful, efficient, and generalizable intervention programs will be the result.

The restricted focus has also extended to relationships among variables. Behavior analysts have focused on temporally contingent variables and have ascribed less etiologic credence to relationships involving more extended temporal dimensions. For example, most behavioral observation coding systems are used to examine relationships among behaviors occurring within a 1-hour period and usually within a 1-minute period. However, many determinants may occur days, weeks, or months prior to the targeted behavior (Margolin, 1981). Both the difficulty in assessing such relationships and the potential impact of their assessment on intervention programs are apparent.

As noted throughout this chapter, it is no longer sufficient to focus assessment efforts exclusively on discrete behaviors or environmental elements. It is difficult to account satisfactorily for behavior through reference only to discrete situational and/or consequent stimuli. It is necessary to assume a systems conceptualization of behavior (Vincent, 1980) and attend to behavior chains (Kazdin, 1982), and complex behavior interrelationships (Voeltz & Evans, 1982). It is becoming increasingly apparent that patterns, sequences, hierarchies, and other dimensions of behavioral covariance are important predictors and determinants of behavior.

SUMMARY

Assessment is an integral part of the behavioral intervention process and one of its most important functions is to facilitate the design of intervention programs. The close assessment–intervention relationship is a result of assumptions of individual differences in topography and determinants within and between behavior problems and in response to treatment. In spite of these underlying concepts, however, univariate models of causality and the use of prepackaged standardized intervention programs are commonly found in the behavioral literature, and there is considerable variability in the degree to which intervention programs are based on preintervention assessment.

The importance of preintervention assessment to the design of behavioral intervention programs is a function of a number of factors. These include the homogeneity of the diagnostic or problem behavior categories, the power of the intervention, the social and personal significance of the targeted behavior problem, and the degree to which the intervention program targets hypothesized etiologic factors. Because of the financial and time expense involved in preintervention assessment, these factors must be carefully considered before instituting the assessment process. However, there are other reasons for stressing the importance of assessment. In particular, the empirical rigor and cybernetic quality of the behavior construct systems are dependent upon an emphasis on assessment.

The behavior analyst must make many types of intervention decisions. These include whether or not to intervene with a client, which behaviors to target, which intervention strategies to apply, and which intervention components to select, when and how to modify an ongoing intervention program, and when to terminate or strengthen an intervention program. The most complex and important of these is the initial design of intervention programs.

There are many factors influencing the design of intervention programs and the selection of their components. These include diagnosis, target behavior characteristics, client mediational variables (motivation and resistance, goals, social validity, resources, and competing behavior problems), task analysis, and intervention history. Other factors affecting intervention design include social–environmental variables (antecedent events, contingencies, social mediational variables, social supports, and other environmental constraints), intervention variables (power, cost-efficiency, side effects, and intervention alternatives), variables associated with the behavior analyst, and assumptions underlying a behavioral construct system. These factors suggest the importance of a specific, multimethod, multimodal behavioral assessment that adopts a systems perspective.

Many behavioral intervention programs are designed to manipulate hypothesized controlling variables for the targeted behavior. Several nonmanipulation methods of isolating etiologic factors are available, but all involve observing conditional probabilities or covariance between events. Manipulation is another possible but infrequently used method of deriving etiologic hypotheses. None of these methods can be assumed to identify etiologic relationships in a valid way; however, they can be used to derive etiologic hypotheses and to provide disconfirmatory data.

The discussion of behavioral assessment in the design of intervention programs raises several issues. First, behavioral assessment instruments and procedures appear to be infrequently used in nonresearch situations. This deficiency in clinical utility may be a function of the cost associated with their use, deficient training of professionals, and of the contingencies surrounding the delivery of psychological services. Second, the psychometric characteristics of behavioral assessment instruments have only recently been investigated, and there likely are significant sources of error variance that have not been identified. Third, the reliability, validity, and utility of the functional analysis has not been sufficiently investigated. Finally, the focus of behavioral construct systems has been traditionally limited to observable operant factors operating within a limited time frame. More recently, behavior analysts have begun to examine the role of a wider range of interacting variables operating in an extended time frame.

ACKNOWLEDGMENT

I would like to express my appreciation to Linda Gannon, C. Chrisman Wilson, Rosemery Nelson, and Steven C. Hayes for their comments on earlier drafts of this chapter.

REFERENCES

Adams, H. E., & Sutker, P. B. (1984). Comprehensive handbook of psychopathology. New York: Plenum Press.

Alexander, A. B. (1981). Asthma. In S. N. Haynes & L. Gannon (Eds.), Psychosomatic disorders: A psychophysiological approach to etiology and treatment (pp. 322–358). New York: Praeger.

Alexander, F. (1950). Psychosomatic medicine, its principles and applications. New York: W. W. Norton.

American Psychiatric Association. (1980). The diagnostic and statistical manual of the American Psychiatric Association (Vol. 3). Washington, DC: Author.

Asher, H. B. (1976). Causal modeling. Beverly Hills, CA: Sage Publications.

Bandura, A. (1969). Principles of behavior modification. New York: Holt.

Barlow, D. (Ed.). (1981). Behavioral assessment of adult disorders. New York: Guilford Press.

Barmann, B. C., & Murray, W. J. (1981). Suppression of inappropriate sexual behavior by facial screening. Behavior Therapy, 12, 730–735.

Baum, C. G., Forehand, R., & Zegoib, L. E. (1979). A review of observer reactivity in adult-child interactions. Journal of Behavioral Assessment, 1, 167–177.

Begelman, D. A. (1975). Ethical and legal issues of behavior modification. In M. Hersen, R. M. Eisler, & P. M. Miller (Eds.), Progress in behavior modification, 1975 (pp. 159–190). New York: Academic Press.

Bloom, M., & Fischer, J. (1982). Evaluating practice: Guidelines for the accountable professional. Englewood Cliffs, NJ: Prentice-Hall.

Briddell, D. W., & Wilson, G. T. (1976). The effects of alcohol and expectancy set on male sexual arousal. Journal of Abnormal Psychology, 85, 225–234.

Catania, A. C., & Brigham, T. A. (Eds.) (1980). *Handbook of applied behavior analysis, social and instructional processes.* New York: Irvington Press.

Chamberlain, P., Patterson, G. R., Kavanagh, K., & Forgatch, M. (1982). *Client resistance: An empirical analysis.* Unpublished manuscript.

Ciminero, A. R., Calhoun, K. S., & Adams, H. E. (Eds.). (1977). *Handbook of behavioral assessment.* New York: John Wiley & Sons.

Coates, T. J., & Thoresen, C. E. (1978). Using generalizability theory in behavioral observation. *Behavior Therapy, 9,* 157–162.

Cofer, C. N., & Appley, M. H. (1964). *Motivation: Theory and research.* New York: John Wiley & Sons.

Cone, J. D., & Hawkins, R. P. (Eds.) (1977). *Behavioral assessment: New directions in clinical psychology.* New York: Brunner/Mazel.

Cooke, C. J., & Meyers, A. (1980). The role of predictor variables in the behavioral treatment of obesity. *Behavioral Assessment, 2,* 59–69.

Cotler, S. B., & Guerra, J. J. (1976). *Assertion training.* Champaign, IL: Research Press.

Craighead, W. E., Kazdin, A. E., & Mahoney, M. J. (1976). *Behavior modification: Principles, issues and applications.* Boston: Houghton Mifflin.

Cromwell, R. E., & Peterson, G. W. (1981). Multisystem-multimethod assessment: A framework. In E. E. Filsinger & R. A. Lewis (Eds.), *Assessing marriage: New behavioral approaches* (pp. 38–54). Beverly Hills, CA: Sage Publications.

Egel, A. L. (1981). Reinforcer variation: Implications for motivating developmentally disabled children. *Journal of Applied Behavior Analysis, 14,* 345–350.

Emmelkamp, P. M. G. (1981). The current and future status of clinical research. *Behavioral Assessment, 3,* 249–253.

Endicott, J., & Spitzer, R. L. (1978). A diagnostic interview: The schedule for affective disorders and schizophrenia. *Archives of General Psychiatry, 35,* 837–844.

Epstein, L. H., & Martin, J. E. (1977). Compliance and side-effects of weight regulation groups. *Behavior Modification, 1,* 551–558.

Felton, J. L., & Nelson, R. O. (1984). Inter-assessor agreement on hypothesized controlling variables and treatment proposals. *Behavioral Assessment, 6,* 199–208.

Fordyce, W. E. (1976). *Behavioral methods for chronic pain and illness.* St. Louis: C. V. Mosby.

Foster, S. L., & Cone, J. D. (1980). Current issues in direct observation. *Behavioral Assessment, 2,* 313–338.

Freedman, B., Rosenthal, L., Donahoe, C., Schlundt, D., & McFall, R. A. (1978). A social-behavioral analysis of skills deficits in delinquent and nondelinquent adolescent boys. *Journal of Consulting and Clinical Psychology, 46,* 1448–1462.

Gagne, R. M. (1962). The acquisition of knowledge. *Psychological Review, 69,* 355–365.

Galassi, M. D., & Galassi, J. P. (1980). Similarities and differences between two assertion measures: Factor analyses of the College Self-Expression Scale and the Rathus Assertiveness Inventory. *Behavioral Assessment, 2,* 43–57.

Glass, G. V., Wilson, V. L., & Gottman, J. M. (1975). *Design and analysis of time-series experiments.* Boulder: University of Colorado Press.

Goldfried, M. R. (1979). Behavioral assessment: Where do we go from here? *Behavioral Assessment, 1,* 19–22.

Goldfried, M. R., & Sprafkin, J. N. (1976). Behavioral personality assessment. In J. T. Spence, R. C. Carsons, & J. W. Thibaut (Eds.), *Behavioral approaches to therapy* (pp. 194–223). Morristown, PA: General Learning Press.

Haynes, S. N. (1985). Paranoia. *Behavior Therapy,* In press.

Haynes, S. N. (1978). *Principles of behavioral assessment.* New York: Gardner Press.

Haynes, S. N. (1979). Behavioral variance, individual differences and trait theory in a behavioral construct system: A reappraisal. *Behavioral Assessment, 1,* 41–49.

Haynes, S. N. (1981). Muscle contraction headache. In S. N. Haynes & L. R. Gannon (Eds.), *Psychosomatic disorders: A psychophysiological approach to etiology and treatment* (pp. 447–484). New York: Praeger.

Haynes, S. N. (1983). Behavioral assessment. In M. Hersen, A. Kazdin, & A. Bellack (Eds.), *The clinical psychology handbook* (pp. 397–426). New York: Pergamon Press.

Haynes, S. N. (1984). Behavioral assessment of adults. In M. Hersen & G. Goldstein (Eds.), *Handbook of psychological assessment* (pp. 369–404). New York: Pergamon Press.

Haynes, S. N., Cuevas, J., & Gannon, L. R. (1982). The psychophysiological etiology of muscle-contraction headache. *Headache, 22,* 122–132.

Haynes, S. N., & Gannon, L. R. (1981). *Psychosomatic disorders: A psychophysiological approach to etiology and treatment.* New York: Praeger.

Haynes, S. N., & Horn, W. F. (1982). Reactive effects of behavioral observation. *Behavioral Assessment, 4,* 443–469.

Haynes, S. N., Lemsky, C., & Sexton-Radek, K. (1985). The scientist-practitioner: An alternative model. In J. R. McNamara & M. A. Appel (Eds.), *Critical issues in professional psychology.* New York: Praeger. In press.

Haynes, S. N., & Wilson, C. C. (1979). *Behavioral assessment: Recent advances in methods and concepts.* San Francisco: Jossey-Bass.

Heiman, J. R., & Hatch, J. P. (1981). Conceptual and therapeutic contributions of psychophysiology to sexual dysfunction. In S. N. Haynes & L. R. Gannon (Eds.), *Psychosomatic disorders: A psychophysiological approach to etiology and treatment* (pp. 222–268). New York: Praeger.

Hersen, M. (1981). Complex problems require complex solutions. *Behavior Therapy, 12,* 15–29.

Hersen, M., & Barlow, D. H. (1976). *Single-case experimental designs: Strategies for studying behavior change.* New York: Pergamon Press.

Hersen, M., Eisler, R. M., & Miller, P. (1973–1986). *Progress in Behavior Modification.* New York: Academic Press.

Hersen, M., & Goldstein, G. (Eds.). (1984). *Handbook of psychological assessment.* New York: Pergamon Press.

Hersen, M., Kazdin, A., & Bellack, A. (Eds.). (1983). *The clinical psychology handbook.* New York: Pergamon Press.

Horne, G. P., Yang, M. C., & Ware, W. B. (1982). Time series analysis for single-subject designs. *Psychological Bulletin, 91,* 178–189.

Jackson, H. J., & King, N. J. (1981). The emotive imagery treatment of a child's trauma-induced phobia. *Journal of Behavior Therapy and Experimental Psychiatry, 12,* 325–328.

Jacobson, N. S. (1985). Uses versus abuses of observational measures. *Behavioral Assessment, 7,* 323–330.

Jacobson, N. S. (1979). Behavioral treatment for marital discord: A critical appraisal. In M. Hersen, R. M. Eisler, & P. M. Miller (Eds.), *Progress in behavior modification* (pp. 169–206). New York: Academic Press.

Jacobson, N. S., & Margolin, G. (1979). *Marital therapy: Strategies based on social learning and behavior exchange principles.* New York: Brunner/Mazel.

Jefferey, D. B., & Knauss, M. R. (1981). The etiologies, treatments and assessments of obesity. In S. N. Haynes & L. R. Gannon (Eds.), *Psychosomatic disorders: A psychophysiological approach to etiology and treatment* (pp. 269–308). New York: Praeger.

Jeffrey, R. W., Wing, R. R., & Stunkard, A. J. (1978). Behavioral treatment of obesity: The state of the art 1976. *Behavior Therapy, 9,* 189–199.

Johnson, W. G., Wildman, H. E., & O'Brien, T. (1980). The assessment of program adherence: The Achilles' heel of behavioral weight reduction? *Behavioral Assessment, 2,* 297–301.

Kanfer, F. H. (1979). A few comments on the current status of behavioral assessment. *Behavioral Assessment, 1,* 37–39.

Kanfer, F., & Phillips, J. (1970). *Learning foundations of behavior therapy.* New York: John Wiley & Sons.

Karoly, P. (1981). Self-management problems in children. In E. J. Mash & L. G. Terdal (Eds.), *Behavioral assessment of childhood disorders* (pp. 79–126). New York: Guilford Press.

Karpowitz, D. H., & Johnson, S. M. (1981). Stimulus control in child-family interaction. *Behavioral Assessment, 3,* 161–171.

Kazdin, A. E. (1977). Assessing the clinical and applied importance of behavior change through social validation. *Behavior Modification, 1,* 427–452.

Kazdin, A. E. (1979). Situational specificity: The two edged sword of behavioral assessment. *Behavioral Assessment, 1,* 57–75.

Kazdin, A. E. (1980). *Behavior modification in applied settings.* Homewood, IL: Dorsey Press.

Kazdin, A. E. (1982). Symptom substitution, generalization, and response covariation: Implications for psychotherapy outcome. *Psychological Bulletin, 91,* 349–365.

Keefe, F. J., Kopel, S. A., & Gordon, S. B. (1978). *A practical guide to behavioral assessment.* New York: Springer.

Kendall, P. C., & Hollon, S. D. (Eds.). (1981). *Assessment strategies for cognitive–behavioral intervention.* New York: Academic Press.

Kratochwill, T. R. (Ed.). (1978). *Single subject research: Strategies for evaluating change.* New York: Academic Press.

Kratochwill, T. R., & Wetzel, R. J. (1977). Observer agreement, credibility, and judgment: Some considerations in presenting observer agreement data. *Journal of Applied Behavior Analysis, 10,* 133–139.

Lachman, S. (1972). *Psychosomatic disorders: A behavioristic interpretation.* New York: John Wiley & Sons.

Lahey, B. B., Vosk, B. N., & Habif, V. L. (1981). Behavioral assessment of learning disabled children: A rationale and strategy. *Behavioral Assessment, 3,* 3–14.

Maher, B. (1970). *Introduction to research in psychopathology.* New York: McGraw-Hill.

Maher, B. (1981). Psychological intervention in hemodylasis. Invited address at Southern Illinois University, Carbondale, November.

Margolin, G. (1981). Practical applications of behavioral marital assessment. In E. E. Filsinger & R. A. Lewis (Eds.), *Assessing marriage, new behavioral approaches* (pp. 90–111). Beverly Hills, CA: Sage Publications.

Mash, E. J., & Terdal, L. G. (Eds.). (1976). *Behavior therapy assessment: Diagnosis, design and evaluation.* New York: Springer.

Mash, E. J., & Terdal, L. G. (1981). *Behavioral assessment of childhood disorders.* New York: Guilford Press.

McFall, R. M. (1982). A review and reformulation of the concept of social skills. *Behavioral Assessment, 4,* 1–33.

Mendels, J. (1975). *The psychobiology of depression.* New York: Spectrum Publications.

Messick, S. (1981). Constructs and their vicissitudes in educational and psychological measurement. *Psychological Bulletin, 89,* 575–588.

Miller, P. M., & Foy, D. W. (1980). Substance abuse. In S. M. Turner, K. S. Calhoun, & H. Adams (Eds.), *Handbook of clinical behavior therapy* (pp. 191–213). New York: John Wiley & Sons.

Mischel, W. (1981). *Introduction to personality.* New York: Holt.

Mullinix, S. D., & Galassi, J. P. (1981). Deriving the content of social skills training with a verbal response components approach. *Behavioral Assessment, 3,* 55–66.

Nathan, P. (1981). Symptomatic diagnosis and behavioral assessment: A synthesis. In D. H. Barlow (Ed.), *Behavioral assessment of adult disorders* (pp. 1–12). New York: Guilford Press.

Nelson, R. O. (1980). The use of intelligence tests within behavioral assessment. *Behavioral Assessment, 2,* 417–423.

Nelson, R. O., & Hayes, S. C. (1979). Some current dimensions of behavioral assessment. *Behavioral Assessment, 1,* 1–16.

Nietzel, M. T., Winett, R. A., MacDonald, M. L., & Davidson, W. S. (1977). *Behavioral approaches to community psychology.* New York: Pergamon Press.

Ollendick, T. H., Shapiro, E. S., & Barrett, R. P. (1981). Reducing stereotypic behaviors: An analysis of treatment procedures utilizing an alternating treatments design. *Behavior Therapy, 12,* 570–577.

Patterson, G. R., Cobb, J. A., & Ray, R. S. (1973). A social engineering technology for retraining families of aggressive boys. In H. E. Adams & I. P. Unikel (Eds.), *Issues and trends in behavior therapy* (pp. 234–251). Springfield, IL: Charles C Thomas.

Piersel, W. C., & Kratochwill, T. R. (1981). A teacher-implemented contingency management package to assess and treat selective mutism. *Behavioral Assessment, 3*, 371–382.

Powell, J., Martindale, A., & Kulp, S. (1975). An evaluation of time-sampling measures of behavior. *Journal of Applied Behavior Analysis, 8*, 463–469.

Rimm, D. C., & Masters, J. C. (1979). *Behavior therapy, techniques and empirical findings.* New York: Academic Press.

Rosenthal, R. (1966). *Experimenter effects in behavior research.* New York: Appleton-Century-Crofts.

Russo, D. C., Bird, B. L., & Masek, B. J. (1980). Assessment issues in behavioral medicine. *Behavioral Assessment, 2*, 1–18.

Seligman, M. E., Klein, D. C., & Miller, M. R. (1976). Depression. In H. Leitenberg (Ed.), *Handbook of behavior modification and behavior therapy* (pp. 168–210). New York: Appleton-Century-Crofts.

Sellitz, C., Wrightsman, L. S., & Cook, S. W. (1976). *Research methods in social relations.* New York: Holt.

Stuart, R. B. (1980). *Helping couples change.* New York: Guilford Press.

Swan, G. E., & MacDonald, M. L. (1978). Behavior therapy in practice: A national survey of behavior therapist. *Behavior Therapy, 9*, 799–807.

Ullmann, L. P., & Krasner, L. (1976). *A psychological approach to abnormal behavior.* Englewood Cliffs, NJ: Prentice-Hall.

Vincent, J. P. (1980). *Advances in family intervention, assessment and theory.* Greenwich, CT: JAI Press.

Voeltz, L. M., & Evans, I. M. (1982). The assessment of behavioral interrelationships in child behavior therapy. *Behavioral Assessment, 4*, 131–165.

Wade, T. C., Baker, T. B., & Hartmann, D. P. (1979). Behavior therapists' self-reported views and practices. *The Behavior Therapist, 2*, 3–6.

Wahler, R. (1981). Insularity. Invited address presented at Southern Illinois University, Carbondale, October.

Wahler, R. G., Berland, R. M., & Coe, T. D. (1979). Generalization processes in child behavior change. In B. B. Lahey & A. E. Kazdin (Eds.), *Advances in clinical child psychology* (Vol. 2) (pp. 301–334). New York: Plenum Press.

Wittlieb, E., Eifert, G., Wilson, F. E., & Evans, I. M. (1978). Target behavior selection in recent child case reports in behavior therapy. *The Behavior Therapist, 1*, 15–16.

Wolf, M. M. (1978). Social validity: The case for subjective measurement, or how applied behavior analysis is finding its heart. *Journal of Applied Behavior Analysis, 11*, 203–214.

Wolman, B. B. (Ed.). (1965). *Handbook of clinical psychology.* New York: McGraw-Hill.

Youkilis, H. D., & Boutzin, R. R. (1981). A psychophysiological perspective of the etiology and treatment of insomnia. In S. N. Haynes & L. R. Gannon (Eds.), *Psychosomatic disorders: A psychophysiological approach to etiology and treatment* (pp. 179–221). New York: Praeger.

12

ASSESSING THE EFFECTS OF THERAPEUTIC INTERVENTIONS

STEVEN C. HAYES
University of Nevada-Reno

ROSEMERY O. NELSON
University of North Carolina at Greensboro

This chapter examines the use of behavioral asssessment in the evaluation of treatment outcome. The evaluation of treatment impact in formal research settings overlaps with previous chapters, and raises issues (e.g., research design) that go well beyond the scope of the present text and have been the subject of many others. For this reason, we intend to focus our discussion on the actual clinical environment—that is, the evaluation of professional services delivered to clients.

DISTINGUISHING RESEARCH AND EVALUATION

Society has always been ambivalent about science. The pursuit of knowledge can be frightening because it implies a willingness to take us into unknown and perhaps undesirable places. Knowledge is a genie that once let out of the bottle, cannot readily be returned.

These human worries are reflected in our folklore and common culture. In the biblical story of creation, humankind's fall from grace is caused by eating from the tree of knowledge; in countless horror movies, grave danger is produced by "mad scientists" who pursue knowledge despite conflicts between this pursuit and human values; in our newspapers today, it is commonplace to read of the risks of computers, genetic engineering, test tube babies, and so on.

The same kinds of concerns are seldom associated with treatment per se. Therapists are viewed as being motivated by the desire to help persons in pain. As an easy check on the difference in attitude, note the nature of restrictions on research with human subjects versus those with clients. Whereas the researcher is confronted with forms, questions, and hurdles when manipulating independent variables, the therapist is left much more on his or her own when implementing treatment strategies. At its extreme, the private practitioner may have little accountability at all.

Treatment evaluation can be confusing because it mixes these two areas. Before we can objectively examine the costs and benefits of evaluation, we must first distinguish it from formal treatment research on the one hand and therapy on the other. We will then need to delineate the different levels of evaluation that are possible, because there are distinct plusses and minuses to each type.

THE COMPATIBILITY OF "RESEARCH" AND THE CLINICAL ENVIRONMENT

Dictionaries define "research" as the careful hunting for facts or the truth. This sense of "research" is clearly quite compatible with treatment. After all, successful treatment involves a kind of investigation of the world of the particular client.

Over the years, "research" has also come to mean a search for objective facts in which regard for the welfare of the subjects of the research may be secondary to the development of scientific knowledge. Perhaps because of dramatic instances of abuse (particularly in medicine), guidelines have been developed to protect research subjects. This sense of the word "research" is often not compatible with professional practice. Clients are not necessarily subjects; and research that puts knowledge first and the client second is, by definition, distinct from the normal activities of a practitioner.

In common language, people usually call something "research" on the basis of the formal or structural characteristics of the activity. For example, if systematic data are collected, or if a hypothesis can be specified, or if presentable data result, the activity is likely to be considered to be "research," regardless of the goal of the activity.

Treatment evaluation has many of the structural aspects of formal research; but, on functional grounds, treatment research and treatment evaluation seem quite distinct. Their goals and purposes are different. The goal of science is to develop better organized statements of relations between events; in other words, the goal is a better rule or law. A major goal of treatment evaluation is to improve client functioning. When the two goals are mixed, confusion can result, unless careful distinctions are made.

DIFFERENT LEVELS OF EVALUATION

At least six activities seem distinguishable (see Table 1). In unevaluated treatment, the goal is improved client outcome. Because there is no evaluation, formal or systematic measures are not taken. Treatment is specified

TABLE 12-1. Factors Distinguishing Various Levels of Evaluation

Levels of Evaluation	Primary Goals	Secondary Goal	Activities		
			Measurement	Treatment Specification	Evaluation Designs
Pure research	Better scientific statements	—			Being used
Treatment research		Improved client outcome	Systematic, comprehensive, frequent	Sufficient to enable replication	deliberately
Formal treatment evaluation	Improved client outcome	Better scientific statements			Being recognized or used deliberately in the service of improved outcome
Informal treatment evaluation			Somewhat systematic	Sufficient to enable consistency within the treatment program	No attempt to identify or to use evaluation designs
Anecdotal case reports		—	Unsystematic		
Unevaluated treatment					

only to the degree required by record keeping, or by the ability of the therapist to behave more or less consistently. Typically, much of what the therapist does will not be written down in any way. There is no attempt to identify, much less to use deliberately, sequences of changes in intervention. At a slightly higher level, unsystematic, anecdotal case reports are usually characterized by slightly more information about the client or about treatment, but the measures are still unsystematic.

The third level is informal treatment evaluation. At this level, the word "evaluation" finally begins to seem appropriate. The root words of evaluation mean "out" and "worth"; that is, to bring out or to figure out the worth of something. In informal treatment evaluation, the goal of evaluation is almost entirely to determine treatment worth so as to improve client functioning. Measures may begin to be more systematic, broader in spectrum, and sometimes more frequent. Treatment specification, however, is still weak because there is no intent to develop and pass on knowledge, but simply to make sure our analysis of the case is confirmed by client progress. For this purpose, treatment need only be consistent, not necessarily sufficiently specified that others can do it. Also, in informal treatment evaluation, little consideration is given to design issues. Many well-done "case reports" are actually best thought of as informal treatment evaluation.

Formal treatment evaluation is the first level that begins to mix therapeutic and scientific goals. The overriding goal is still improved client outcome; as a secondary goal, however, the practitioner would like to say some things about treatment, such as whether the client improved due to treatment; what the real problem was; what about treatment was helpful; whether this client responded like similar clients, and so on. Formal treatment evaluation thus is designed so that knowledge can be passed on. Measures are clearly systematic, frequent, and comprehensive. Treatment must be sufficiently specified that it can be replicated by others. Evaluation designs are either recognized as being implicitly part of the normal delivery of treatment, or are used deliberately to better ask and answer questions relevant to client progress. Importantly, however, the goal of formal evaluation is only to determine the worth of active attempts to help the client, that is, the knowledge sought is only knowledge about the first goal of treatment: client improvement.

In treatment research, the goal is primarily the generation of better organized scientific statements. Client improvement is always hoped for, but it is secondary. A specific client's needs are to be accommodated to the research project, if possible; but the individual client's needs did not start the sequence of events and are not the central issue.

Finally, in pure research on applied problems, client improvement is not even a secondary goal in any immediate sense. Survey research or research in experimental psychopathology would be an example.

It is harder to see the goals of an activity than it is to see its form; yet, it is in the easy-to-see formal or structural areas (e.g., Are data collected?) that research and evaluation are similar. They differ in functional areas that are more difficult to discern (e.g., Why are you collecting data?). Thus, on the surface, research and evaluation look quite similar. An empirical practitioner could easily and mistakenly be accused of "doing research on clients"; it could falsely be said that clients are being used as guinea pigs, and so on. For this reason, the benefits of formal and informal treatment evaluation, as compared with treatment or treatment research, must be distinguished clearly.

Society has generated a large number of rules to protect human subjects. These include procedural protections, such as the submission of research proposals to human subjects committees, as well as specific mandated activities on the part of a researcher, such as the acquisition of informed and written consent from the subjects. Quite apart from the formal legal requirements that surround the term "research," there are a number of informal requirements as well. These include the ethical practices in a particular applied profession (such as the standards set forth by the American Psychological Association), and the individual, idiosyncratic application of ethical and moral guidelines to research activities. Thus if treatment evaluation is equated with research, we can predict that treatment evaluation will rarely be done. By way of contrast, if it can be shown that routine evaluation improves treatment outcome, then *neglect* of routine evaluation could be considered to be unethical.

WHY DO EVALUATION?

Evaluation is important to the client because treatment almost always involves meaningful client goals, costs, and risks. A maximally successful treatment should accomplish therapeutic goals at low cost and with low risk. Evaluation sets the stage for this by identifying the ongoing costs and benefits of treatment. Both formal and informal evaluation have as their primary goal the improvement of individual client outcome, and thus seek to complement the purpose of treatment more generally.

The possible benefits of evaluation occur in at least three major areas: feedback to client and to therapist, enhancement of clinical science, and accountability.

FEEDBACK

Clinical decisions informed by systematic evaluation (or challenged by single case designs in the case of formal evaluation) seem more likely to be correct and productive than uninformed decisions due to the feedback that evaluation provides. Many of our clinical hypotheses are undoubtedly wrong. Unfortunately, there is a strong tendency to miss errors for at least four reasons: first, it seems to be a basic psychological law (demonstrable from pigeons to people) that signals of negative outcomes are avoided (Dinsmoor, 1983). Simply put, we would rather not know we are failing. Second, we tend to overemphasize events that confirm our previous views. Third, there are strong social pressures on "being right"; once we have conceptualized something, we have an investment in avoiding being wrong about our guesses. Finally, the client may look to the therapist as an expert who "knows"; to the extent that the therapist is influenced by this impression, it may be more desirable to hold to a position than to treat the client successfully. It is for these reasons that science itself is such a fragile, but critically important, human strategy. Evaluation tends to ward off our own tendency toward self-deception by allowing the data to decide the rightness or wrongness of our views.

This does not necessarily mean that evaluation must improve client outcome. It could be (as some therapists claim) that conceptualizing a case sufficiently well to evaluate it tends to make us insensitive to its subtle aspects. This is an empirical question that no one has addressed directly up to now. Yet, our experience in many other areas of human effort seems to show major benefits as intuition gives way to science; for example, while craftsmen could build suitable structures based on feelings and intuition, only well-trained engineers and architects could design skyscrapers, or massive tunnels and bridges. Clinical "feel" is probably adequate for some tasks, but inadequate for many others.

The feedback provided by both formal and informal evaluation also seems naturally to lead to a great degree of involvement in a case and to a more systematic approach. It is very easy to become sloppy in clinical work. Quite apart from the output of evaluation, the evaluation process itself seems to inoculate the clinician against careless or haphazard practices. Again, this is ultimately an empirical question—so we must presently view it only as a probable effect of evaluation.

Both formal and informal evaluation can also provide feedback to the client. Clients often have a hard time identifying progress they have made (or problems they have) when changes are incremental. Through systematic evaluation, it is possible to show clients their own progress. A large body of literature suggests that feedback alone can often modify behavior in beneficial ways (Fellner & Sulzer-Azaroff, 1984).

To accomplish this feedback goal, one category of measures that can and should be collected during the course of therapy are relevant measures of the client's progress. Ideally, these measures are taken prior to the initiation of treatment, repeated at regular intervals as therapy progresses, and taken at the conclusion of treatment and again at follow-up. The advantage of collecting measures throughout the course of therapy is that feedback is provided to the therapist and client of client progress while therapy is still ongoing. If the outcome measures reveal that the treatment plan is producing desirable changes in the client's behavior, then the therapist can pursue the plan with renewed confidence. Conversely, if the outcome measures reveal that the treatment plan is not producing changes in the client's behavior, or is producing undesirable changes, the therapist has the opportunity to modify the plan. Timely modification can occur before too much therapist and client time and effort and client fees have been expended, or before too many unwanted effects have occurred (e.g., client's prematurely terminating treatment, or client's behavior worsening).

Another category of measures that can and should be collected during the course of therapy are measures that the treatment plan is being adequately implemented within efficacious parameters. Such evaluations of the treatment plan have been labeled, respectively, as evaluations of treatment integrity and of treatment strength (Yeaton & Sechrest, 1981). If client outcome measures do not show desirable changes, a potentially (but not presently) effective treatment plan may be prematurely discarded. This type of error might be prevented if therapy procedures are independently evaluated to determine if treatment is being implemented as planned and at an efficacious strength.

Some examples of measuring treatment integrity or the adequacy of treatment implementation follow; others are provided by Barlow, Hayes, and Nelson (1984) and by Peterson, Homer, and Wonderlich (1982). If a portion of the treatment procedure includes a client practicing relaxation training at home, different relaxation tapes could be prepared with different key words embedded in different places on the tapes; the client could be asked to report the word (e.g., "turtle," "raincoat") and its approximate location on the tape to provide greater assurance that the client practiced the relaxation exercises (Collins, Martin, & Hillenberg, 1982). If a therapist were attempting to contrast the relative effectiveness of two different treatments for the same client by randomly assigning the treatments to different therapy sessions, the integrity of the treatments could be evaluated by taping the therapy sessions and asking an independent judge to corroborate which treatment was in effect for each session. If a parent were asked to respond to particular child behaviors with differential consequences, the parent could be asked to record in a diary not only the child's behaviors, but also his or her response to them; a second adult in the home could be asked to take reliability data, perhaps one hour per day, on both the child's behavior and the parent's response to provide some assurance that the treatment plan was being implemented.

Measuring the strength of treatment, along with client outcome and treatment integrity, could also serve a useful purpose. Even if present client outcome does not appear to be successful, more desirable outcomes might be obtained by modifying the strength of the treatment, rather than changing the treatment plan per se. Presently, there are no adequate and generally useful quantitative measures of treatment strength (Yeaton & Sechrest, 1981). Treatments that lend themselves to quantification can be evaluated for strength by quantifying the parameters of treatment. For example, if time-out is unsuccessful in modifying behavior, the solution may be to increase the length of time-out. To do this it would be important to have measured the length of time-out actually delivered. For treatments that are not easily quantified, it may be possible to use ratings of dimensions of strength. For example, if covert sensitization were being used, the aversiveness of the delivery of the scenes could be evaluated and modified if necessary.

ADVANCEMENT OF CLINICAL SCIENCE

Another certain benefit of formal evaluation is that the knowledge base of the field expands. Therapists are working with many thousands of clients every day, yet the results with only an infinitesimal fraction will ever be shared with the professional community. Ultimately, this must slow the growth of the clinical sciences. There are at least two major ways that formal evaluation can contribute to the advancement of knowledge. First, it can lead to new insights about the nature of psychological disorders and their treatment. Second, it can assess the generality (external validity) of effects of known treatments across clients. To see this, formal evaluation must be discussed in a bit more detail.

Formal Evaluation

Professionals are often told to assess their clients systematically, to design specific treatments for their clients, and to make sure the intervention has produced a beneficial effect. These common practical guidelines parallel very closely the essential elements of formal evaluation. In some sense it can be argued that good practitioners are already doing evaluations of potential scientific value with most clients they see, if they follow fully the guidelines required for good professional practice. For example, the practical requirement that the professional systematically assess the client is translated into the requirement that systematic, relevant, and repeated measurements be taken of the client's actual problems. The practical suggestion that specific treatments be designed for the client is modified in formal evaluation methodology only by the requirement that treatments be specified in such a way as to be replicable. Finally, the practical recommendation that clinicians determine whether their treatments are actually benefiting the client is translated into the requirement that evaluators recognize the design strategies that they are using and use design elements appropriately so as to demonstrate and replicate significant effects.

In the on-line clinical environment, formal evaluation of an individual case is made possible by time-series methodology (Barlow et al., 1984). The fundamental core of this methodology is systematic, relevant, comprehensive, repeated measurement of the individual client over time.

Establishment of the Degree of Intraclient Variability

An estimate of the degree of variability in the client's behavior (as repeatedly measured) is critical in single case methodology. In the context of this estimate, determinations are made about the level and trend in the behavior, and predictions are drawn about the future course of the behavior. Measures need only be stable enough to see effects, should they occur. The target problem and probable effects of intervention bear heavily on issues of stability. For example, if a total reduction of a behavior is anticipated, extreme variability would present no problem. Conversely, if measurement variability could not allow any treatment effect to be seen, then it would be foolish to proceed. This methodological advice dovetails nicely with clinical realities, however. For example, a client showing infrequent, nondestructive outbursts of anger would probably not be treated for anger control if the frequency of the outbursts would be indistinguishable from what was expected after treatment.

When the client's behavior is excessively variable, several actions can be taken. First, the clinician can simply wait until patterns become clearer. Often variability is temporary (for example, it may be caused by the initial effect of entering treatment), and it is frequently better to wait than to plunge ahead unnecessarily.

Second, if at times the client is behaving well and at times badly, the practicing clinician will probably begin to search for factors that account for these differences. For example, if a client's anxiety is high some weeks and low others, the clinician may search for reasons accounting for it. Finding that the client's anxiety is high only on weeks containing arguments or conflict might lead to a treatment program of social skills training or therapy around the issue of rejection. Further, the previously unstable measures might now be quite stable when organized into times following or not following social conflict.

A third strategy is to examine the temporal unit of analysis. Often measures are collected in particular units for convenience (e.g., clients are often asked to self-record in daily blocks). If the actual phenomena may be better seen in larger units, then the data may be blocked (or intraclient averaged). For example, a clinician working with a marital couple might find that daily records of arguments reveal extremely variable behavior, some days there are no arguments, and on others there are several. This may be expected, since all couples have some good days and some bad. More clinically important may be, for example, the average number of arguments in a week. When the data are blocked by weeks, stability may emerge. Some of the detail is lost, but this is always true. Organizing events by day disguises hourly variability; organizing them by hour disguises minute-by-minute effects. Part of good clinical skill seems to involve knowing when to ignore individual trees in order to see the forest.

Estimates of variability, level, and trend are then used in the determination of the impact of treatment. This guideline merely formalizes rules of good clinical practice. Practical clinical guides often exhort clinicians to "examine regularly and consistently whether therapy is being helpful" (Zaro, Varach, Nedelmann, & Dreiblatt, 1977, p. 157). Similarly, no good practitioner would be satisfied with only one or two assessments of a client. Systematic measures are needed over the time period that included both the determination of client needs, and the design, implementation, and conclusion of treatment.

Particular measures of applied interest must be taken under consistent conditions. Any condition that might reasonably be expected to influence the measure cannot be allowed to covary with treatment. Usually the best way to protect against this is to keep the measurement procedure as standard as possible on such dimensions as the time of assessment, the assessor, the assessment situation, implicit demands on the client, and the like. Measures must also be sensitive and comprehensive. The impact of treatment must be examined broadly and with quality measures because it is well known that treatment effects tend to be diverse and, at times, iatrogenic.

A critical component of any formal evaluation is the degree to which "the techniques making up a particular . . . application are completely identified and described" (Baer, Wolf, & Risley, 1968, p. 95). Any deficiencies in this step will threaten an ability to replicate effects that are achieved. One way to think about this is to distinguish between behavior controlled by rules versus by direct experience. While direct experience can produce highly effective clinical behavior, in formal evaluation we can only give away the knowledge obtained if we can in fact describe the functionally important characteristics of treatment—that is, formulate a treatment rule.

The specification of treatment is not a matter of endless listing of all conditions present in the intervention. Rather, it should summarize the apparently critical components of the intervention that professionals can use as a guide. If the rule is inadequate, this will become clear in future attempts to replicate the treatment. This is also the way that the adequacy of the rule is determined; quite simply, there is no way to know if an intervention has been adequately specified until the long process of replication has occurred.

Finally, time–series designs must be used to evaluate the impact of treatment. All time–series analyses can be organized into a few core elements by the nature of their estimates of stability and the logic of their data comparisons. These core elements can then be creatively combined to contribute to good clinical decision making. There are three general types of elements: within, between, and combined series (Barlow et al. 1984; Hayes, 1981). Within-series strategies rely on changes seen within a series of data points (in a single measure or homogeneous set of measures) organized by the time of their collection. There are two subtypes: the simple phase change and the complex phase change.

The simple phase change consists of (1) the establishment of stability, level, and trend within a series of data points across time, taken under similar conditions; (2) a change in the conditions impinging on the client; and (3) examination of concomitant changes in the stability, level, or trend in a series of data points taken under the conditions. It is a within-series strategy in that it is systematic changes seen within a series of data points across time that are examined.

A common example of the simple phase change is the A/B design. If the stability, level, or trend shown in A suddenly changes when B is implemented, our confidence increases that B is responsible for that change. Often there are possible alternative explanations for the effect (e.g., maturation, the effect of measurement, coincidental external events; see Barlow & Hersen, 1984; Campbell & Stanley, 1963; Kratochwill, 1978), and usually the effect must be replicated before our confidence in the effect is sufficiently high. One way is to repeat the phase change in reverse order (the A/B/A design). If the behavior tracks the change once again, our confidence increases further. This simple phase change process can be repeated indefinitely, each sequence forming a new completed design (e.g., A/B/A/B; B/A/B). Two treatments can be compared in the same manner (e.g., B/C/B; C/B/C/B). All of these are merely specific applications of the logic of the simple phase change, allowing us to ask questions such as, Does treatment work? and, Which treatment is better?

The simple phase change can also be coordinated into a more complex series of phases. Each of the complex phase change strategies specifies an overall integrative logic. An interaction element is a series of phase changes in which a treatment or treatment component (B) is alternately added or subtracted from another treatment or treatment component (C). A number of specific sequences are possible (e.g., B/B+C/B; C/C+B/C; B+C/C/B+C). The interaction element asks the question, "What is the combined effect of two treatment components compared to one alone?"

Complex phase changes can address other issues, such as the relative effects of two separate treatments. A simple phase change comparing two treatments does not make sense unless it is known that either works relative to baseline. If this is not known, the design must compare them with baseline as well as with each other by combing simple phase change strategies for determining their effectiveness. For example, the sequence A/B/A/C/A combines an A/B/A with an A/C/A. This allows us to ask whether B and C are effective. It also allows a comparison of the two treatments, but it is weak, because order effects are possible and noncontiguous data are being compared (the data in the B phase with those in the C phase). To strengthen this comparison, other subjects might receive an A/C/A/B/A sequence. If the conclusions are the same, then the believability of the treatment comparison is strengthened.

In contrast with the within-series elements, in which changes within a series of data points are compared, the between-series strategies compare two or more series of data points across time. The comparisons are repeatedly made *between* these series. The most useful type of pure between-series element is the alternating treatments design. The logic of this design (Barlow & Hayes, 1979) is based simply on the rapid and random (or semirandom) alternation of two or more conditions, in which there is one potential alternation of condition per measurement opportunity. Since a single data point associated with one condition may be preceded and followed by measurements associated with other conditions, there is no opportunity to estimate stability, level, and trend within phases. Rather, these estimates are obtained within conditions by collecting measurements associated with a condition each into a separate series. If there is a clear separation between such series, differences among conditions are inferred. For example, suppose a clinician wishes to examine the relationship of therapist self-disclosure to client self-disclosure. At the beginning of some sessions (randomly determined), the therapist makes a self-disclosure; in the other sessions, no self-disclosure is used. Tape recordings of the sessions are rated. If the series of data points created by connecting the values found for the self-disclosure sessions is associated with more client self-disclosure than the other sessions, we determine that the manipulation had an effect.

This design strategy is often combined with other design elements (e.g., a baseline), though it is not required. It is particularly useful for the comparison of two or more treatments or when measurement is cumbersome or lengthy (e.g., an entire MMPI). Only four data points are absolutely needed (two in each condition). Each data point may incorporate many treatment sessions; the rapid alternation refers only to the rate of treatment alternation relative to the rate of measurement. On the other extreme, alternations might be made several times per session (e.g., Hayes, Hussian, Turner, Anderson, & Grubb, 1983).

This design is also valuable when difficult assessment decisions are presented. Suppose, for example, that a client is presenting with social deficits. The clinician may have a difficult time determining if the client is more likely to respond to anxiety management procedures or social skills training procedures. Rather than guess, the clinician might do both in an alternating treatments fashion. The better treatment may quickly be revealed, and all treatment effort could then go in this direction.

Finally, several design elements in time series experimentation borrow from both of the previously described strategies. These combined-series elements utilize coordinated sets of comparisons made both between and within series of measurements. Undoubtedly the most familiar combined-series element is the multiple baseline. Its logic is intended to correct for major deficiencies of a simple phase change (say, an A/B). In an A/B, any changes between the two phases could be due to coincidental extraneous events: maturation, cyclical behavior, baseline assessment, and so on. The multiple baseline solves these problems by replicating the A/B but with different lengths of baseline for each replication, such that an effect is seen in the interrupted series before a change is made in the uninterrupted series (a strategy that controls for the amount of baseline assessment of mere maturation) and with the actual time of the phase change arbitrarily altered (to reduce the possibility of correlated extraneous events).

The opportunity to use the multiple baseline element in clinical practice is extensive. Multiple baselines often form naturally across behaviors due to the tendency for practicing clinicians to tackle subsets of problems sequentially rather than all at once. Multiple baselines across settings are less common but also naturally occur when clinicians treat problem behavior shown in one specific condition first rather than treating the problem all at once (e.g., Hayes & Barlow, 1977). The multiple baseline across people is probably one of the clearest examples of natural design elements that arises in clinical practice. Nothing could be more natural to clinical work than an A/B. To form a multiple baseline, all the clinician need do is save several A/B analyses with similar problems and the same treatment. Individual clients will inevitably have different lengths of baseline, often widely so, due to case complexities or to matters of convenience. Thus, sequential cases usually lead to natural multiple baseline across people (Hayes, 1985).

Through the use of these three elements—systematic measurement, treatment specification, and time–series designs—formal evaluation allows two major contributions to be made to clinical science. First, many new findings in the literature have resulted from such an approach. Thus, with this approach, it is possible to show the impact of an innovative treatment, to show the validity of a creative clinical analysis, to identify the impact of previously unrecognized variables, and so on. Second, it is also possible, to use this methodology to show the generality of treatment by clinical replication. In clinical replication (Barlow et al., 1984), a series of clients with well-specified problems is given a particular, well-specified treatment (e.g., Beck's cognitive therapy for depression; Beck, Rush, Shaw, & Emery, 1979). Clients are assessed carefully and repeatedly. Successes, partial successes, and failures are carefully identified; and attempts are made to relate treatment outcome to particular characteristics of the client, treatment, and so on. Clinical replication series of this sort have had an enormous impact on the clinical sciences (e.g., Masters & Johnson, 1970; Wolpe, 1958). The primary value of clinical replication series is to show the generalizability or external validity of given treatments across various client characteristics. This is an enormously important area because it addresses the core question of an empirical approach to treatment ("which treatment will work best for this given client with these given characteristics?"; Paul, 1969). Regardless of its importance, without the inclusion of practicing clinicians in the evaluation effort, it is hard to see how clinical replication can ever be a major part of our clinical knowledge base.

Process Measures

Included in the scientific enterprise are hypothesis testing and theory building. These components are enhanced if clinicians collect a third type of measure in addition to outcome measures and measures of treatment integrity. This third type of measure checks on process or the effect of the experimental manipulation (Kazdin, 1980). To illustrate, let us suppose that a clinician is testing the efficacy of Beck's cognitive therapy for depression (Beck et al., 1979). The clinician ensures that the cognitive therapy is adequately implemented and measures the client's depression at various stages of therapy. To conclude, however, that the effective mechanism in Beck's therapy is alteration in maladaptive cognitions, these cognitions would need to be assessed separately, by the Dysfunctional Attitude Scale (Weissman & Beck, 1979), or by the Automatic Thoughts Questionnaire (Hollon & Kendall, 1980), for example. As another illustration, let us suppose that a clinician hypothesizes that relaxation training works for tension headaches because relaxation promotes increased peripheral blood flow. The clinician ensures that the relaxation training is adequately implemented, and that client records of headache pain are obtained. To conclude, however, that blood flow made a notable contribution to the efficacy of relaxation for headache pain, changes in actual blood flow for individual clients would need to be assessed separately. These measures are often not taken when the treatment seems "obviously" related to a given process; this has sometimes led to years of unfruitful research because false explanations are mistakenly taken to be proven by beneficial outcome alone. Occasionally, the reverse is true, when measures are taken only of process and not outcome. For example, the assumption that being on-task leads to increased academic output led to programs to increase on-task behavior. It was only years later that it was realized that even successful attempts of this type did *not* necessarily increase academic performance (Hay, Hay, & Nelson, 1977). Thus, measures of both outcome and process are important.

These intermediate or process measures (also called checks on the experimental manipulation) are useful in hypothesis testing and theory building. They also allow a post hoc data analysis, examining the outcome data of subjects who failed to respond to the experimental manipulation (Kazdin, 1980). Moreover, these intermediate measures help test the clinician's formulation of the client's problems. For example, if the clinician believed that a client's job dissatisfaction was due largely to poor social skills, it would be wise to measure both social skills (as a process measure) and job satisfaction (as an outcome measure).

In order to assess the effect of therapy process, it may also be important at times to measure the behavior of the therapist, not just the client, and to relate the two (Barlow et al., 1984). This presents no new methodological issues because in principle the behavior of the therapist is as measurable as that of the client.

ACCOUNTABILITY TO PATIENTS AND THIRD PARTY PAYERS

Another reason that clinicians should perform evaluations and collect objective outcome data on their clients' progress is for accountability purposes. Are patients or their third-party payers receiving the treatment benefits for which they are paying? Mental health treatment costs $15 billion annually in the United States (Pines, 1982) or about 15% of all health care costs (Klerman, 1983).

Insurance carriers (as well as private citizens) are searching for ways to curtail these costs. Alternatives include placing a ceiling on benefits accorded an individual recipient, instituting a copayment feature, placing some services outside the boundaries for reimbursement, limiting providers who are eligible for reimbursement, and reimbursing only effective therapeutic procedures (McGuire & Frisman, 1983; Stricker, 1979). This last alternative to cost curtailment is currently the most popular, as evidenced by the following two examples.

The Civilian Health and Medical Program of the Uniformed Services (CHAMPUS) contracted with the American Psychological Association and the American Psychiatric Association to devise an internal and national peer review system to evaluate outpatient psychological services provided under its coverage. As part of the review process, each provider is asked to submit at designated review points (after 8, 24, 40, and 60 sessions) a CHAMPUS Out-Patient Psychological Treatment Report. This form asks for information about the patient's problem, the therapist's goals and planned intervention, and an estimate of progress since the last form was submitted. As noted by Stricker (1979),

> The progress report on the [form] must relate to the specific treatment goals and must contain a clear justification when progress is not of reasonable magnitude. Both the therapist and the patient will make independent judgments as to the extent of progress since the last review point. [p. 121)

Obviously, objective measures collected by the therapist facilitate estimates of client progress required by CHAMPUS. The CHAMPUS requirements are presented in detail because it is the largest health insurance plan and because it is thought to be a prototype of the type of accountability to be required by other insurance companies and third-party payers (Craighead, 1978; Rodriguez, 1983; Stricker, 1979).

A second example of the movement toward accountability was the establishment in 1978 of the National Center for Health Care Technology. An important component of the center's work was to advise the Medicare program as whether particular technologies should be reimbursed (Banta & Saxe, 1983). Although this center was eliminated as an administrative agency by Reagan administration budget cuts in 1981, its work regarding the evaluation of psychotherapies was to have proceeded in two stages. The first stage was the development of criteria by which all psychotherapies could be assessed. The second stage was an application of these criteria to various forms of psychotherapy for the various disorders for which they were indicated (Perry, 1983).

The trend, then, to curtail the costs of health care is by reimbursing only effective treatments. One way to help establish effectiveness is by treatment evaluation, including the collection of objective measures of patient progress. It is probably particularly important that these measures be of known quality. Treatment process and outcome can often be evaluated, for example, by measures developed specifically for an individual client, but it is not surprising that third-party payers may not know how to evaluate some of these measures. This is one area of difficulty for behavioral assessors. There seem to be several solutions: (1) to rely on measures that have high face value, (2) to use standardized measures when available, and (3) to use multiple measures.

GUIDELINES FOR COLLECTING MEASURES

The following suggestions may provide guidelines for using behavioral assessment to collect evaluation measures during clinical practice.

   1. *Clinical problem(s) must be stated in specific terms.* Most clinicians, both in their clinical practice and research, communicate with each other in terms of the Diagnostic and Statistical Manual of Mental Disorders (DSM-III; American Psychiatric Association, 1980). These diagnoses may be used in making a referral or in referring to *Psychological Abstracts* or in publishing a clinical research article.

   While these diagnoses are useful for communication purposes, among others, they are too broad to serve as targets of therapeutic intervention or as outcome measures. Instead, client's problem behaviors and desired therapeutic objectives should be defined with clear behavioral referrents (Mischel, 1968).

   Clients and some therapists may initially conceptualize presenting problems in global terms, such as a poor self-concept or nervousness. Various strategies can be useful in behavioral specification. The specific operational or diagnostic criteria for each disorder in DSM-III may provide valuable suggestions for therapeutic goals. During the intake session(s), the client can be asked about acceptable evidence that his or her problems had improved. For example, the client could be asked how he or she would know if self-concept had improved or if nervousness had been reduced. Another strategy is to ask the client to specify what it is they would like to have different in their lives. For example, if any three of the client's wishes could be granted, what would they be? Or the therapist might ask the client for examples or illustrations—for example, "You say that you are feeling depressed. Can you explain that by giving an example of something you say or do that shows that you are depressed?" Still another strategy is to ask the client to describe a typical day currently, and a day as he or she would like it to be. The latter can help delineate specific therapeutic goals.

   2. *Specify several problem behaviors.* Most disorders are sufficiently complex that several intervention goals can readily be identified. For each goal or aspect of the problem, a measure or measures should be constructed. Sometimes the particular, multiple problems that a client presents match the diagnostic criteria of DSM-III. Even though certain behaviors are characteristic of certain disorders, it is not certain that these behaviors covary or

change at the same rate in each individual client. Therefore, measures of each behavior should be obtained. In other cases, the combination of intervention goals is idiosyncratic. For example, Humphreys and Beiman (1975) describe a case in which six problem areas were identified: uncertain vocational goals, inadequate social skills, unassertiveness, marital difficulties, fear of crowded places, and public speaking phobia. Quantified measures are needed of each goal.

Another reason for measuring multiple behaviors is to assess response covariation (Voeltz & Evans, 1982). It is sometimes feared that improvements in target behaviors may produce unwanted changes in nontreated behaviors. An example of this undesirable covariation is symptom substitution. It is sometimes hoped that improvements in target behaviors may be generalized and produce desirable changes in other nontreated behaviors. In either case, broad-spectrum measurement of a variety of behaviors can assess desirable or undesirable response covariation.

3. *Obtain multiple measures for each problem.* Not only is it advisable to measure several different behaviors per client, but it is also advisable to obtain several different measures for each problem or goal. The main reason for multiple measurement is that a single valid measure of a disorder is rare.

This concept has become familiar in two ways: (1) through the psychometric notion of construct validity, and (2) through the idea of the triple response system. By definition, there is no one ideal measure of a construct. Instead, data from several measures converge to assess a construct. Instead, data from several measures converge to assess a construct. Campbell and Fiske (1959) have proposed the multitrait–multimethod matrix to help establish construct validity. At least two "traits" (types of behaviors) are assessed by at least two methods across a number of individuals. To help establish construct validity of the measures, dissimilar measures of the same trait should converge, and similar measures of different traits should diverge. In any case, multiple measures are needed to assess a construct.

The concept of the triple response system has been most developed in relation to the assessment of anxiety (Lang, 1968) and of sexual responses (Barlow, 1977). The basic idea is that response covariation among motor, verbal–cognitive, and physiological measures cannot be assumed. Therefore, each type of behavior must be independently assessed. While these points raise conceptual problems (e.g., Evans, Chapter 5, this volume), the more general point seems well taken: it should not be assumed that a single measure portrays an adequate picture of client change.

Moreover, even if there were agreement among different measures in one client at a particular point in time, there is no guarantee that synchrony would be maintained as treatment progressed. For example, in one study, no consistent relationship during treatment was found between simultaneous measures of heart rate and approach behavior in nine phobic cases (Leitenberg, Agras, Butz, & Wincze, 1971). The independent variable of treatment may affect different behaviors in different ways. Multiple measures are needed to obtain converging evidence of treatment progress.

4. *Select measures that are sensitive and meaningful.* Measures should be selected that are sensitive to the intervention being employed. Perhaps, in past research, related manipulations produced change in these measures (Kazdin, 1980). Measures that are sensitive to treatment or other interventions typically allow a sufficiently broad range of responding, that is, have a low floor and a high ceiling (Kazdin, 1980).

On a molecular–molar dimension, more molecular measures of behavior have a greater probability of change in the face of an intervention. Molar measures, conversely, may be less sensitive but may be more meaningful. To illustrate, molecular measures of social skills may include smiling and latency to verbal reply, while molar measures of social skills may include peer ratings of skill on a one to seven rating scale. Since it is unlikely that one measure can fill both roles, it is advisable to use both types of measures: molecular measures that can be measured precisely and that are sensitive to therapeutic change, and molar measures that are meaningful or high in construct validity.

Molar measures also relate to two other important assessment concepts, both related to the meaningfulness, or substantive or clinical significance of behavior change. One is the use of normative data. For some molar measures, there are published data (means, standard deviations) for particular samples of subjects. Such normative data can provide a useful comparison for an individual client's (subject's) data. Before treatment, the norms help to gauge the severity of the presenting problem; after treatment, the norms help to gauge the degree of improvement, in comparison with a "normal" sample (Kazdin, 1977; Nelson & Bowles, 1975).

Molar measures are also related to the concept of social validation (Kazdin, 1977; Wolf, 1978). In social validation, a relevant community group is asked to rate behavioral performances generally pre- and posttreatment. These molar ratings help to establish the meaningfulness of behavior change.

5. *Collect measures early in the course of treatment.* In many cases, reasonable hypotheses about the nature of the presenting problem can be derived during the initial or intake session. Measures related to those hypotheses can begin to be collected immediately. The assessment phase can be concluded with a substantial baseline already completed, thereby preventing delays prior to treatment intervention (Hayes, 1981). It is advisable to collect data initially on a rather large number of possible measures. As assessment and intervention proceed, and hypotheses are tested, refined, and discarded, only the relevant measures can be retained.

6. *Take the same measures repeatedly.* Repeated measures taken prior to, during, and following treatment are superior to only pre–post measures for three reasons. First, repeated measurement provides feedback to the therapist about treatment effectiveness at an opportune time. Second, inadequacies of measurement (e.g., variability in applying the measure) can be separated from therapeutic change. Third, a closer link between independent and dependent variables can be established through repeated measurement. Changes or variability in the data can be noted. Some changes may be correlated with planned interventions. This helps establish a causal link between treatment and behavior change. Other changes may be due to unplanned events. Such variability permits the scientist–practitioner to formulate or to refine hypotheses about independent variables or factors that are contributing to the client's problem.

Every effort should be made to take follow-up measures as well. These follow-up measures can be used not only to assess maintenance of treatment effects, but to test hypotheses about maintenance versus relapse. To illustrate, greater maintenance of therapeutic gains might be predicted if a significant other was also involved in the therapy than if none was involved.

7. *Collect data on the same measure under similar conditions.* Valid comparisons can be made across repeated measurements only if the measures are obtained under similar stimulus conditions. The principle here is that behavior tends to be situation specific (Mischel, 1968). Not only can treatment produce changes in the dependent measures, but so can alterations in the measurement situation. If a client is asked to provide a daily global rating of his or her depression, it should be made at the same time each day. Unplanned changes in the assessment situation that influence the data have traditionally been labeled measurement error.

8. *Obtain inconvenient measures less frequently than convenient measures.* Although it is recommended that several different types of measures be taken of several different client problems, it is not necessary to obtain all measures with the same frequency. It is permissable to take convenient measures more often than inconvenient measures. For example, in a case study reported by Katell, Callahan, Fremouw, and Zitter (1979), an overweight client completed a daily food diary in which she recorded certain facts about her eating. On a weekly basis, the client was asked to eat a meal in a small on-campus dining area while being videotaped; her eating behavior was subsequently coded from the videotapes. Also on a weekly basis, an observer entered the home and coded her eating behavior during a family supper. Presumably, self-monitoring was a more convenient measure and hence was done daily, while the less convenient analogue and naturalistic observations were done weekly.

9. *Select measures of high quality.* There is a controversy among behavioral assessors on the criteria to use in evaluating the quality of a behavioral

measure. This controversy is elaborated in Chapter 13 by Hayes, Nelson, and Jarrett in this volume. Suffice it to say here that the controversy focuses on the appropriateness of psychometric criteria in evaluating the quality of behavioral measures. Some believe that these time-tested, traditional criteria are appropriate for behavioral assessment (e.g., Curran & Mariotto, 1980; Goldfried & Linehan, 1977). Others believe that new criteria should be devised that are more compatible with behavioral assumptions (e.g., Cone, 1981; Nelson, 1983). Alternative criteria that have been proposed include measurement accuracy (Foster & Cone, 1980); idiographic approaches to measurement (Cone, 1981); identification of variables that contribute to measurement variability (Nelson, 1983); and identifying assessment devices and strategies that enhance treatment effectiveness (Nelson & Hayes, 1979). These issues are discussed in Chapter 13.

10. Graph the data. If repeated measures are taken of several client behaviors, it is especially advisable that the data be graphed as they are collected to facilitate interpretation (Barlow & Hersen, 1984; Parsonson & Baer, 1978). Time from baseline through treatment and follow-up is indexed on the abscissa; the measure is indexed on the ordinate.

When several measures are taken, it is useful to summarize their data on the same graph so that comparisons across measures can be made. The same abscissa can be used for all types of measurement. Different ordinates will probably be necessary, since the different types of measures will have different units of measurement.

Another item to enter on the data graphs is any significant event that might account for alterations or variability in the data. Planned significant events include the introduction of and alterations in treatment. Unplanned significant events include other notable life events, such as changes in relationships or in health status.

WHAT KINDS OF MEASURES?

Measures may be considered within several contexts. First, the same measures may be used to assess independent variables (i.e., whether or not the treatment is being adequately implemented), process or intermediate dependent variables (i.e., whether or not the treatment is affecting the processes that it is hypothesized to be affecting), and outcome dependent variables (i.e., whether or not the treatment produced therapeutic improvement in the patient's problems). Second, some measures are collected by the therapist; others, by the client; and still others, by significant others of the client or by hospital or clinic personnel. Third, some measures are obtained in the clinic, hospital, or other treatment setting, whereas other measures are obtained in the client's natural environment (e.g., work setting or home). Fourth, different measures focus on different aspects of the triple response system (originally proposed by Lang, 1968, in relationship to anxiety). Some measures focus on the client's overt motor behavior; others focus on the client's cognitive or verbal behavior; others focus on physiological responses. Finally, the procedure of behavioral assessment has been likened to a funnel (Hawkins, 1979). There is an initial assessment during which a broad range of information is collected for the purpose of selecting suitable target behaviors. The assessment funnel then narrows, and more specific information is sought; the variables controlling the target behavior are determined and a treatment is selected. Assessment then continues to determine whether the treatment is adequately implemented and whether the predicted changes in the process and outcome measures occur. Different behavioral assessment techniques are useful at different stages of the funnel progression. The measures presented now may be considered within these several different contexts.

SELF-REPORT MEASURES

Self-report measures can be provided by the client for each of the three behavioral content systems (Cone, 1978). To illustrate, a person can provide reports of his or her motor activity (motor content, such as, "I don't do as much housework as I used to"), physiological activity (physiological content, such as, "My heart frequently races"), and cognitive activity (cognitive content, such as, "I think I'm worthless").

While direct measures of motor and physiological content do not always agree with self-report measures (direct measures of cognitive content are not possible; Cone, 1978; Lang, 1968), this lack of agreement does not lessen the importance of self-report measures. Verbal reports simply provide different measures of behavior; and not inferior measures of behavior (Barlow et al., 1984). What clients think about their own problems is important.

Interviews

Interviews are very helpful in the earliest stages of behavioral assessment when a broad range of information is being gathered. They are useful not only because of the content of the client's self-report, but also as an opportunity for the clinician to perform a mental status examination, or to observe aspects of the client's appearance and behavior (e.g., rate and quality of speech, mannerisms, affect, clothing; Nelson & Barlow, 1981). While many interviews are unstructured, which enhances their flexibility, it is easier to quantify structured interviews, for example, the Schedule for Affective Disorders and Schizophrenia (Endicott & Spitzer, 1978), or the Duke computerized behavioral assessment interview (Angle, Ellinwood, Hay, Johnsen, & Hay, 1977). These structured interviews may be repeated at least on a pre–posttreatment basis as a broad-gauge measure of client progress.

Questionnaires

Questionnaires differ in their degree of specificity, ranging from broad questionnaires that assess a wide variety of life areas, to those with a more specific focus. Broad questionnaires are useful in the early stages of the behavioral assessment funnel to help determine the client's problems areas. They may also be used on a pre–posttreatment basis to evaluate overall client progress. Examples of broad questionnaires include the Minnesota Multiphasic Personality Inventory (Hathaway & McKinley, 1951); the Symptom Checklist with 90 items (SCL-90; Derogatis, cited by Hargreaves, Atkinson, & Sorensen, 1977, and by Clifford, 1981); and the Denver Community Mental Health Questionnaire (Ciarlo & Reihman, cited by Hargreaves et al., 1977, and by Clifford, 1981).

More specific questionnaires are useful during the early stages of the behavioral assessment funnel to identify specific problematic situations (e.g., Fear Survey Schedule II, Geer, 1965, reprinted in Mash & Terdal, 1976), specific target behaviors (e.g., the Marital Pre-Counseling Inventory, Stuart & Stuart, 1972), and possible reinforcers (e.g., Reinforcement Survey Schedule, Cautela & Kastenbaum, 1967, reprinted in Mash & Terdal, 1976). Questionnaires assessing specific responses are also useful during the narrow portion of the behavioral assessment funnel. These may be administered repeatedly to measure both process and outcome dependent variables. To illustrate, the Beck Depression Inventory (Beck, Ward, Mendelson, Mock, & Erbaugh, 1961) could be periodically readministered to determine whether a client's depression was improving, while the Automatic Thoughts Questionnaire (Hollon & Kendall, 1980) could be periodically readministered to determine whether a hypothesized change in dysfunctional cognitions was mediating the change in depression (Beck et al., 1979).

Self-Ratings

To obtain measures of a client's subjective state, the client may be asked to rate his or her own moods or feelings. Such self-ratings may occur either in the natural environment or in the clinic. They may be cued either temporally or by a specific stimulus. An example of a temporally cued self-rating in the natural environment was provided by Sirota and Mahoney (1974), who asked an asthmatic client to rate her own level of muscular tension cued by a variable-interval 30-minute timing device. An example of self-rating in the clinic cued by a specific stimulus is provided by Foa, Steketee, and Milby (1980) who had obsessive–compulsive washers self-rate their levels of discomfort on a 1–100 point scale when in the presence of their most feared contaminant.

Card Sorts

Another measure of subjective states, usually used within the clinic setting, is the card-sort procedure. Individualized scenes or situations that produce a particular subjective state, for example, fear or sexual arousal, are typed on index cards. The client is asked to imagine each scene as vividly as possible and to either sort the cards into stacks representing various feeling levels or to rate each card as to the feeling it generates. For example, scenes depicting appropriate and deviant sexual behavior were prepared for sexual deviants who were then asked to imagine each scene and to rate their degree of sexual arousal on a 0–4 point scale (Brownell, Hayes, & Barlow, 1977). The card-sort procedure would be administered to the client repeatedly during the course of therapy to provide a measure of change.

PSYCHOPHYSIOLOGICAL MEASURES

Psychophysiological measures tend to be used more in formal research settings than in on-line clinical research. Even in the clinic setting, however, these measures may be useful, particularly for anxiety problems (e.g., the manual recording of pulse to measure heart rate, Kanter & Goldfried, 1979), for the measurement of sexual responses (e.g., the penile strain gauge to measure male sexual arousal to appropriate and deviant sexual stimuli, Brownell et al., 1977), and for the measurement of medically related problems (e.g., electomyograph recordings during reported tension headaches, Epstein & Abel, 1977). These psychophysiological recordings would be obtained repeatedly during the course of therapy, but possibly on a less frequent basis than more convenient measures. These recordings could be used to measure either outcome variables (e.g., to measure reductions in essential hypertension, treated by anxiety management training, Bloom & Cantrell, 1978) or process variables (e.g., in the earlier example by Epstein and Abel, 1977, the outcome measure of headaches was a self-report measure, but the headaches were hypothesized to be mediated by muscular tension, measured psychophysiologically).

OBSERVATIONAL MEASURES

Observational measures usually focus on motor behavior. They may be obtained in the natural environment or in the treatment setting. In both settings, either naturally occurring behavior can be observed or a particular stimulus can be introduced to generate a contrived observational setting. The observer may be the client, significant others of the client, or treatment personnel, including the therapist. To increase the probability of accurate observational data, at least occasionally a second observer should simultaneously but independently collect observational data.

Self-Monitoring or Self-Recording

In self-monitoring, a client notices and records occurrences of his or her own problem behaviors as they are occurring, usually in the natural environment. During the early stages of the behavioral assessment funnel, the client may be asked to keep a diary of problematic responses and the circumstances surrounding their occurrence. This type of diary may help the clinician in formulating hypotheses about appropriate target behaviors and controlling variables. Further on in the behavioral assessment funnel, the client may monitor more specific responses. At this time, frequency counts or duration are appropriate measures. In an example of a frequency count, a 10-year-old girl referred for stomachaches with no known organic basis recorded on a Girl Scout calendar each time she said her stomach hurt (Miller & Kratochwill, 1979). In an example of a duration measure, obsessive–compulsive patients with washing rituals were asked to record the duration of their own washing and cleaning behavior (Foa et al., 1980).

As a method of data collection, self-recording offers several advantages. First, if the client complies with the self-monitoring instructions, an inexpensive and practical source of data is provided. Second, for some behaviors, especially those that are covert or private by societal convention, self-monitoring is the only available source of data. Third, self-monitoring may contribute to the therapeutic process because the reactive changes in behavior that it generates are usually in a therapeutic direction (Nelson, 1977).

Several suggestions, many of them research-based, have been offered to improve clients' compliance with self-monitoring instructions and to enhance the chances that accurate data will be collected (Barlow et al., 1984; McFall, 1977; Nelson, 1977). Among these suggestions are (1) make sure that the client is fully trained in the self-recording procedure; (2) have a second observer occasionally take data at the same time that the self-recorder does, and make the self-recorder aware that this will be done periodically; (3) have clients initially record only a single response and at an uncluttered time if possible; and (4) reward the client for accurately recorded data (determined by comparing the second observer's data with the self-recorder's data).

Observations in the Natural Environment

The collection of data in the natural environment has the advantage of measuring behavior in the criterion situation in which therapeutic change is ultimately desired. Naturalistic data collection frequently requires the cooperation of a client's friends or relatives. For example, the granddaughter of an 82-year-old heart patient monitored his compliance with a regimen consisting of exercise, diet, and medication; another family member also recorded these data on occasion so that the accuracy of the data could be estimated (Dapcich-Miura & Hovell, 1979).

As an alternative to observational data collected in naturally occurring situations, stimuli may be deliberately arranged to provide the client with the opportunity to display the problematic response or progress toward correcting it. For example, exhibitionists underwent a temptation test in which an attractive female confederate purposely placed herself in a situation that had a high probability of eliciting exposing behavior (Maletsky, 1974).

Finally, the therapist may also occasionally collect data in the natural environment—for example, agoraphobics were instructed to leave their homes and to remain outside until feelings of tenseness or discomfort occurred; the therapist remained in the house and recorded the duration of time that the client spent outside (Emmelkamp, 1974).

Observations in the Treatment Setting

When observational data are collected in the treatment setting, the client's behavior can be quantified immediately, or the client's behavior can be audio- or videotaped for later quantification. In an example of the former, during the therapy sessions themselves, an observer behind a one-way mirror counted the number of words per 30-second interval used by a depressed man with a very slow speaking rate (Robinson & Lewinsohn, 1973). In an example of the latter, the conversational skills of formerly hospitalized male psychiatric patients were assessed in 8-minute conversations with female personnel of the mental health center; the tapes of these conversations were subsequently scored for the number of times the patient asked questions about the partner, disclosed positive information about himself, and complimented the partner (Kelly, Urey, & Patterson, 1980).

Sometimes, direct observation is done in the clinic in naturally occurring situations, while at other times, a particular stimulus is deliberately introduced (contrived observation). In an example of the former, before the treatment session began, a secretary surreptitiously quantified the gender-specific motor behavior of a transsexual arriving and waiting in the reception area by using a checklist for sex-role motor behavior (Barlow, Hayes, Nelson, Steele, Meeler, & Mills, 1979; Barlow, Reynolds, & Agras, 1973). In an example of the latter, patients with obsessional slowness were asked to perform three tasks: a real-life task that ordinarily took the patient a long time to complete (e.g., shaving, combing hair), a standard task (crossing out all fours on a page of digits), and a series of arithmetic problems. The measures were duration to completion of each task and subjective discomfort (Rachman, 1974).

A special type of contrived situation used to observe interpersonal behaviors is role-playing. For example, in the clinic maritally distressed couples were asked to discuss topics that had been selected as being problematic for that couple (Bornstein, Bach, Heider, & Ernst, 1981). These role-played interactions occurred on a pre–posttreatment basis, and were quantified from videotape by using a variation of the Marital Interaction Coding System (Hops, Wills, Patterson, & Weiss, 1971). As an alternative to a client's role-playing with a significant other, the client may be asked to role-play with a staff member. In an example of this technique, a staff person role-played an employer and conducted job interviews with formerly hospitalized patients (Kelly, Laughlin, Claiborne, & Patterson, 1979).

Indirect Measures

Indirect measures are not measures of the problem responses as they are occurring, but are rather indications that the problem responses have already occurred. Indirect measures can be used either as measures in their own right or as ancillary measures to validate more direct response measures.

One type of indirect measure is the behavioral byproduct. To return to an earlier example, compliance with a medical regimen by an elderly heart patient was assessed by measuring behavioral byproducts: the amount of orange juice remaining in a special calibrated plastic container was taken to indicate the amount of orange juice consumed by the patient; the number of pills remaining in the prescription bottle was taken to indicate the number of pills consumed by the patient (Dapcich-Miura & Hovell, 1979).

A second type of indirect measure is archival records. In an illustration of the use of such records, municipal, county, and state police records were examined during treatment and follow-up to determine if any charges were filed or convictions obtained against the sexual offender clients (Maletzky, 1980).

CONCLUSION

The practicing clinical environment has been all but ignored as a source of information for clinical science. The modal number of career publications by PhD clinicians continues to be zero. Clinicians report that most of their knowledge comes from experience, not from research publications. Behavioral assessment could allow the evaluation of routine clinical work to assume a role in the development of clinical knowledge, as well as in the provision of feedback about client progress and in accountability. The critical tools are single-subject designs and quantified dependent measures.

REFERENCES

American Psychiatric Association (1980). *Diagnostic and statistical manual of mental disorders* (3rd ed.). Washington, DC: Author.

Angle, H. V., Ellinwood, E. H., Hay, W. M., Johnsen, T., & Hay, L. R. (1977). Computer-aided interviewing in comprehensive behavioral assessment. *Behavior Therapy, 8,* 747–754.

Baer, D. M., Wolf, M. M., & Risley, T. R. (1968). Some current dimensions of applied behavior analysis. *Journal of Applied Behavior Analysis, 1,* 91–97.

Banta, H. D., & Saxe, L. (1983). Reimbursement for psychotherapy: Linking efficacy research and public policy-making. *American Psychologist, 38,* 918–923.

Barlow, O. H. (1977). Behavioral assessment in clinical settings: Developing issues. In J. D. Cone & R. P. Hawkins (Eds.), *Behavioral assessment: New directions in clinical psychology* (pp. 283–307). New York: Brunner/Mazel.

Barlow, D. H., & Hayes, S. C. (1979). Alternating treatments design: One strategy for comparing the effects of two treatments in a single subject. *Journal of Applied Behavior Analysis, 12,* 199–210.

Barlow, D. H., Hayes, S. C., & Nelson, R. O. (1984). *The scientist–practitioner: Research and accountability in clinical and educational settings.* New York: Pergamon.

Barlow, D. H., Hayes, S. C., Nelson, R. O., Steele, D. L., Meeler, M. E., & Mills, J. R. (1979). Sex role motor behavior: A behavioral checklist. *Behavioral Assessment, 1,* 119–138.

Barlow, D. H., & Hersen, M. (1984). *Single case experimental designs: Strategies for studying behavior change* (2nd ed.). New York: Pergamon.

Barlow, D. H., Reynolds, E. J., & Agras, W. S. (1973). Gender identity change in a transsexual. *Archives of General Psychiatry, 28,* 569–576.

Beck, A. T., Rush, A. J., Shaw, B. F., & Emery, G. (1979). *Cognitive therapy of depression.* New York: Guilford.

Beck, A. T., Ward, C. H., Mendelson, M., Mock, J., & Erbaugh, J. (1961). *Archives of General Psychiatry, 4,* 561–571.

Bloom, L. J., & Cantrell, D. (1978). Anxiety management training for essential hypertension in pregnancy. *Behavior Therapy, 9,* 377–382.

Bornstein, P. H., Bach, P. J., Heider, J. F., & Ernst, J. (1981). Clinical treatment of marital dysfunction: A multiple-baseline analysis. *Behavioral Assessment, 33,* 335–343.

Brownell, K. S., Hayes, S. C., & Barlow, D. H. (1977). Patterns of appropriate and deviant sexual arousal: The behavioral treatment of multiple sexual deviations. *Journal of Consulting and Clinical Psychology, 45,* 1144–1155.

Campbell, D. T., & Fiske, D. W. (1959). Convergent and discriminant validation by the multitrait-multimethod matrix. *Psychological Bulletin, 56,* 81–105.

Campbell, D. T., & Stanley, J. C. (1963). *Experimental and quasi-experimental designs for research*. Chicago: Rand-McNally.

Cautela, J. R., & Kastenbaum, R. A. (1967). Reinforcement Survey Schedule for use in therapy, training, and research. *Psychological Reports, 29*, 1115–1130.

Clifford, D. (1981). Instruments of measuring outcomes in mental health program evaluation: Results of a survey. *Evaluation News, 2*, 54–58.

Collins, F. L., Martin, J. E., & Hillenberg, J. B. (1982). Assessment of compliance with relaxation instructions: A pilot validation study. *Behavioral Assessment, 4*, 219–223.

Cone, J. D. (1978). The Behavioral Assessment Grid (BAG): A conceptual framework and a taxonomy. *Behavior Therapy, 9*, 882–888.

Cone, J. D. (1981). Psychometric considerations. In M. Hersen & A. S. Bellack (Eds.), *Behavioral assessment* (pp. 38–68). New York: Pergamon.

Craighead, W. E. (1978). Report of task force for treatment evaluation and third party payment. *The Behavior Therapist, 1* (2), 9–10.

Curran, J. P., & Mariotto, M. J. (1980). A conceptual structure for the assessment of social skills. In M. Hersen, R. M. Eisler, & P. M. Miller (Eds.), *Progress in behavior modification: Vol. 10* (pp. 1–37). New York: Academic.

Dapcich-Miura, E., & Hovell, M. F. (1979). Cointingency management of adherence to a complex medical regimen in an elderly heart patient. *Behavior Therapy, 10*, 193–201.

Dinsmoor, J. A. (1983). Observing and conditioned reinforcement. *Behavioral and Brain Sciences, 6*, 693–728.

Emmelkamp, P. M. G. (1974). Self-observation versus flooding in the treatment of agoraphobia. *Behaviour Research and Therapy, 12*, 229–237.

Endicott, J., & Spitzer, R. L. (1978). A diagnostic interview: The schedule for affective disorders and schizophrenia. *Archives of General Psychiatry, 35*, 837–844.

Epstein, L. H., & Abel, G. G. (1977). An analysis of biofeedback training effects for tension headache patients. *Behavior Therapy, 8*, 37–47.

Fellner, D. J., & Sulzer-Azaroff, B. (1984). A behavioral analysis of goal-setting. *Journal of Organizational Behavior Management, 6*, 33–51.

Foa, E. B., Steketee, G., & Milby, J. B. (1980). Differential effects of exposure and response prevention in obsessive-compulsive washers. *Journal of Consulting and Clinical Psychology, 48*, 71–79.

Foster, S. L., & Cone, J. D. (1980). Current issues in direct observation. *Behavioral Assessment, 2*, 313–338.

Geer, J. H. (1965). The development of a scale to measure fear. *Behaviour Research and Therapy, 3*, 45–53.

Goldfried, M. R., & Linehan, M. M. (1977). Basic issues in behavioral assessment. In A. R. Ciminero, K. S. Calhoun, & H. E. Adams (Eds.). *Handbook of behavioral assessment* (pp. 15–46). New York: Wiley.

Hargreaves, W. A., Atkinson, C. C., & Sorensen, J. E. (Eds.). (1977). *Resource materials for community mental health program evaluation*. Rockville, MD: National Institute of Mental Health.

Hathaway, S. R., & McKinley, J. C. (1951). *MMPI Manual*. New York: Psychological Corporation.

Hawkins, R. P. (1979). The functions of assessment: Implications for selection and development devices for assessing repertoires in clinical, educational, and other settings. *Journal of Applied Behavior Analysis, 12*, 501–516.

Hay, W. M., Hay, L. R., & Nelson, R. O. (1977). Direct and collateral changes in on-task and academic behavior resulting form on-task versus academic contingencies. *Behavior Therapy, 8*, 431–441.

Hayes, S. C. (1981). Single case experimental design and empirical clinical practice. *Journal of Consulting and Clinical Psychology, 49*, 193–211.

Hayes, S. C. (1985). Natural multiple baselines across persons: A reply to Harris and Jenson. *Behavioral Assessment, 7*, 129–132.

Hayes, S. C., & Barlow, D. H. (1977). Flooding relief in a case of public transportation phobia. *Behavior Therapy, 8,* 742–746.

Hayes, S. C., Hussian, R. A., Turner, A. E., Anderson, N. B., & Grubb, T. D. (1983). The effect of coping statements on progress through a desensitization hierarchy. *Journal of Behavior Therapy and Experimental Psychiatry, 14,* 117–129.

Hollon, S. D., & Kendall, P. C. (1980). Cognitive self-statements in depression: Development of an automatic thoughts questionnaire. *Cognitive Therapy and Research, 4,* 383–395.

Hops, H., Wills, T. A., Patterson, G. R., & Weiss, R. L. (1971). *Marital interaction coding system.* (Available from NAPS, c/o Microfiche Publications, 305 E. 46th Street; New York, New York 10017)

Humphreys, L., & Beiman, I. (1975). The application of multiple behavioral techniques to multiple problems of a complex case. *Journal of Behavior Therapy and Experimental Psychiatry, 6,* 311–315.

Kanter, N. J., & Goldfried, M. R. (1979). Relative effectiveness of rational restructuring and self-control desensitization in the reduction of interpersonal anxiety. *Behavior Therapy, 10,* 472–490.

Katell, A., Callahan, E. J., Fremouw, W. J., & Zitter, R. E. (1979). The effects of behavioral treatment and fasting on eating behaviors and weight loss: A case study. *Behavior Therapy, 10,* 579–587.

Kazdin, A. E. (1977). Assessing the clinical or applied importance of behavior change through social validation. *Behavior Modification, 1,* 427–452.

Kazdin, A. E. (1980). *Research design in clinical psychology.* New York: Harper and Row.

Kelly, J. A., Laughlin, C., Claiborne, M., & Patterson, J. (1979). A group procedure for teaching job interviewing skills to formerly hospitalized psychiatric patients. *Behavior Therapy, 10,* 299–310.

Kelly, J. A., Urey, J. R., & Patterson, J. T. (1980). Improving heterosocial conversational skills of male psychiatric patients through a small group training procedure. *Behavior Therapy, 11,* 179–188.

Klerman, G. L. (1983). The efficacy of psychotherapy as the basis for public policy. *American Psychologist, 38,* 929–934.

Kratochwill, T. R. (1978). *Single-subject research: Strategies for evaluating change.* New York: Academic.

Lang, P. J. (1968). Fear reduction and fear behavior: Problems in treating a construct. In J. M. Schlien (Ed.), *Research in psychotherapy: Vol. 3.* Washington, DC: American Psychological Association.

Leitenberg, H., Agras, W. S., Butz, R., & Wincze, J. (1971). Relationship between heart rate and behavioral change during the treatment of phobias. *Journal of Abnormal Psychology, 78,* 59–68.

Maletzky, B. M. (1974). "Assisted" covert sensitization in the treatment of exhibitionism. *Journal of Consulting and Clinical Psychology, 42,* 34–40.

Maletzky, B. M. (1980). Self-referred versus court-referred sexually deviant patients: Success with assisted covert sensitization. *Behavior Therapy, 11,* 306–314.

Mash, E. J., & Terdal, L. G. (Eds.). (1976). *Behavior therapy assessment.* New York: Springer.

Masters, W. H., & Johnson, V. E. (1970). *Human sexual inadequacy.* Boston: Little, Brown.

McFall, R. M. (1977). Parameters of self-monitoring. In R. B. Stuart (Ed.), *Behavioral self-management: Strategies, techniques, and outcomes.* New York: Brunner/Mazel.

McGuire, T. G., & Frisman, L. K. (1983). Reimbursement policy and cost-effective mental health care. *American Psychologist, 38,* 935–940.

Miller, A. J., & Kratochwill, T. R. (1979). Reduction of frequent stomachache complaints by time out. *Behavior Therapy, 10,* 211–218.

Mischel, W. (1968). *Personality and assessment.* New York: Wiley.

Nelson, R. O. (1977). Assessment and therapeutic functions of self-monitoring. In M. Hersen, R. M. Eisler, & P. M. Miller (Eds.), *Progress in behavior modification: Vol. 5.* New York: Academic.

Nelson, R. O. (1983). Behavioral assessment: Past, present, and future. *Behavioral Assessment*, 5, 195–206.

Nelson, R. O., & Barlow, D. H. (1981). An overview of behavioral assessment with adult clients: Basic strategies and initial procedures. In D. H. Barlow (Ed.), *Behavioral assessment of adult disorders*. New York: Guilford.

Nelson, R. O., & Bowles, P. E. (1975). The best of two worlds—observations with norms. *Journal of School Psychology*, 13, 3–9.

Nelson, R. O., & Hayes, S. C. (1979). Some current dimensions of behavioral assessment. *Behavioral Assessment*, 1, 1–16.

Parsonson, B. S., & Baer, D. M. (1978). The analysis and presentation of graphic data. In T. R. Kratochwill (Ed.), *Single subject research: Strategies for evaluating change* (pp. 101–165). New York: Academic.

Paul, G. L. (1969). Behavior modification research: Design and tactics. In C. M. Franks (Ed.), *Behavior therapy: Appraisal and status* (pp. 29–62). New York: McGraw-Hill.

Perry, S. (1983). The National Center for Health Care Technology: Assessment of psychotherapy for policymaking. *American Psychologist*, 38, 924–928.

Peterson, L., Homer, A. L., & Wonderlich, S. A. (1982). The integrity of independent variables in behavior analysis. *Journal of Applied Behavior Analysis*, 15, 477–492.

Pines, M. (1982, May 4). Movement grows to create guidelines for mental therapy. *The New York Times*, p. C1.

Rachman, S. (1974). Primary obsessional slowness. *Behaviour Research and Therapy*, 12, 9–18.

Robinson, J. C., & Lewinsohn, P. M. (1973). Behavior modification of speech characteristics in a chronically depressed man. *Behavior Therapy*, 4, 150–152.

Rodriguez, A. R. (1983). Psychological and psychiatric peer review at CHAMPUS. *American Psychologist*, 38, 941–947.

Sirota, A. D., & Mahoney, M. J. (1974). Relaxing on cue: The self regulation of asthma. *Journal of Behavior Therapy and Experimental Psychiatry*, 5, 65–66.

Stricker, G. (1979). Criteria for insurance review of psychological services. *Professional Psychology*, 10, 118–122.

Stuart, R. B., & Stuart, F. (1972). *Marital pre-counseling inventory*. Champaign, IL: Research Press.

Voeltz, L. M., & Evans, I. M. (1982). The assessment of behavioral interrelationships in child behavior therapy. *Behavioral Assessment*, 4, 131–165.

Weissman, A. N., & Beck, A. T. (1979). *The Dysfunctional Attitude Scale*. Unpublished master's thesis, University of Pennsylvania, Philadelphia.

Wolf, M. M. (1978). Social validity: The case for subjective measurement or how applied behavior analysis is finding its heart. *Journal of Applied Behavior Analysis*, 11, 203–214.

Wolpe, J. (1958). *Psychotherapy by reciprocal inhibition*. Stanford: Stanford University Press.

Yeaton, W. H., & Sechrest, L. (1981). Critical dimensions in the choice and maintenance of successful treatments: Strength, integrity, and effectiveness. *Journal of Consulting and Clinical Psychology*, 49, 156–168.

Zaro, J. S., Barach, R., Nedelmann, D. J., & Dreiblatt, I. S. (1977). *A guide for beginning psychotherapists*. Cambridge: Cambridge University Press.

IV
EVALUATING
BEHAVIORAL ASSESSMENT

13

EVALUATING THE QUALITY OF BEHAVIORAL ASSESSMENT

STEVEN C. HAYES

University of Nevada-Reno

ROSEMERY O. NELSON

University of North Carolina at Greensboro

ROBIN B. JARRETT

University of Texas Health Science Center at Dallas

A decade ago, behavioral assessment first began to be recognized as a distinct area. At first, behavioral assessment was seen merely as a subarea of the *content* of traditional psychological assessment. The whole field of assessment, for example, might have been said to include personality assessment, intellectual assessment, and behavioral assessment, as if behavior was just another of many areas to be assessed. Later, behavioral assessment began to be defined as a specific set of assessment techniques. In this view, a subject's performance on the Minnesota Multiphasic Personality Inventory (MMPI) might be called "nonbehavioral" while self-monitoring or direct observation was considered "behavioral." Both views remain strong in behavioral assessment and psychology more generally.

Viewing behavioral assessment as a content subarea, or as a set of techniques, however, has created problems for the field. First, it has hampered the development of behavioral assessment as a comprehensive alternative to a traditional approach to assessment. Obviously, if behavioral assessment is merely a *sub*area or a *sub*set of techniques, it must be *sub*ordinate to a more comprehensive approach. A second and related effect in some ways has been more damaging. If behavioral assessment is a subset of traditional assessment, to be of value it must show its ability to meet the standards of "quality" set by traditional assessment. Its success or failure, in other words, is dependent on the success achieved in meeting traditional criteria, regardless of the intellectual consistency between these criteria and behavioral assessment.

This latter view, we will argue, has been adopted by many behavioral assessors themselves, with a resultant cost in terms of disillusionment and dissatisfaction. We will attempt to show that behavioral assessment must adopt its own standards of quality or risk a loss of the unique opportunity it presents to the clinical community.

A DEFINITION OF BEHAVIORAL ASSESSMENT

Behavioral assessment is the identification of meaningful response units and their controlling variables for the purposes of understanding and of altering behavior. The purposes of behavioral assessment are: (1) to select target behaviors, (2) to devise an intervention program, and (3) to evaluate treatment outcome (Nelson & Hayes, 1979). There are several aspects of this definition that deserve comment. First, behavioral assessment attempts to measure "meaningful response units." "Responses" need not be overt, but in line with both radical behavioral (Skinner, 1945) and some current methodological behavioral views (Mahoney, 1974), they must be observable, at least by one person. Specifically rejected is the measurement of hypothetical entities, unobservable to anyone. In traditional assessment, the goal is often the measurement of inferred states, which no one (not even the client) may be able to observe directly. A higher level of inference in interpreting assessment results is required by the traditional view than by the behavioral view (Goldfried & Kent, 1972). Thus, behavioral assessment cannot be a content subarea of traditional assessment because personality, intelligence, and so on are rejected as hypothetical entities and are reinterpreted in behavioral terms. That is, some of the same actual behaviors are assessed by both approaches, but different assumptions are brought to the interpretation of these behaviors.

Second, behavioral assessment seeks also to measure the "controlling variables" of these response units. Far from measuring just behaviors, behavioral assessment encompasses both what humans do and *why* they do it. These controlling variables might include antecedents, consequences, physiologic states, learning history, or states of reinforceability which are thought to influence responding.

Third, identification of meaningful response units and their controlling variables is designed to meet a specified purpose, namely, understanding and altering behavior. Behavioral assessment seeks to aid in the selection of target behaviors and effective treatment evaluation.

Note that, by this definition, behavioral assessment is not a content subarea, nor is it a set of techniques. It is an assessment approach (Nelson, 1983) with its own set of assumptions and goals.

DISTINGUISHING BETWEEN BEHAVIORAL AND
TRADITIONAL ASSESSMENT

The nature and assumptions of traditional assessment differ markedly from those of behavioral assessment. Because other chapters in the present volume also examine this distinction, we will summarize it only briefly. The differences between traditional and behavioral lie more in their respective assumptions about behavior and its assessment than in specific techniques (Hartmann, Roper, & Bradford, 1979). In fact, the two approaches share several assessment strategies, for example, roleplaying, interviews, and questionnaires. Even the *Diagnostic and statistical manual of mental disorders,* Third edition (DSM-III) (American Psychiatric Association, 1980), mental status examinations, and intelligence tests can be used within a behavioral framework (Nelson, 1980; Nelson & Barlow, 1981). Traditional views typically emphasize personologism, that is, behavior is thought to result from relatively stable intraorganismic (usually intrapsychic) causal variables. Hence, during assessment, behavior is interpreted as a *sign* of these underlying variables (Goldfried & Kent, 1972; Goodenough, 1949). The focus of assessment is on what the person *has* (Mischel, 1968).

Conversely, most modern behaviorists have adopted an interactionist view that behavior is a function both of organismic variables such as one's physiologic state and learning history (which are due to remote environmental and biological influences) and the current environment. In this view, behavior is interpreted as a *sample* of behavior that is likely to occur in repetitive or similar situations. The focus of assessment is on what the person *does,* in a given situation.

Viewed from a behavioral perspective, the traditional view does not seem to attend to the controlling variables surrounding behavior, because the controlling variables it seeks to measure (stable traits) are themselves behaviors to be explained. For example, hostility might be measured, not as a behavior to be explained in its own right but as a cause of other behavior (e.g., aggression). For this reason, situational, consequential, and physiologic variables are typically not measured. Assessment is concluded when an adequate assessment is made of the nature and interconnections between various traits and tendencies.

Because in this view controlling variables are themselves likely to be behaviors, the treatment implications of traditional assessment are not necessarily obvious. Therapists can *directly* manipulate only the variables that control the behavior of others, not that behavior itself. This is a necessary extension of the fact that therapists are (and can only ever be) part of the client's environment. Therefore, knowledge of a behavior–behavior relationship (so often the output of a traditional approach) cannot be of use, unless the therapist already knows how to alter the first behavior. Often this is not known, and consequently traditional assessment need not have therapeutic implications. The intrapersonal causes of behavior, having been identified, often imply more about the nature of a person's difficulty (diagnosis and classification) and likely future responses than they do about immediate courses of action, therefore, traditional assessment focuses more on diagnosis and classification. Since behavioral assessment seeks to find more proximal and manipulable causes, there seems to be a stronger link between behavioral assessment and the resultant treatment program than between traditional assessment and treatment. Perhaps for the same reason, traditional assessment frequently ceases when intrapsychic causes have been identified, whereas behavioral assessment often involves repeated measures of objective dependent variables before, during, and after treatment (Goldfried & Pomeranz, 1968; Hartmann et al., 1979).

Another dissimilarity between the two approaches is their assumptions about similarities and differences in behaviors that are simultaneously measured from the same person. In behavioral assessment, few assumptions are made about which responses are likely to covary. This is thought to depend largely on similarity in the functional relationships between behavior and the environment. Thus, when behavioral theorists divide behavior into different types, such as the division between motor, physiologic, and verbal behavior (labeled by behaviorists as the triple-response system; Cone, 1979), the assumption is that the responses are likely to be asynchronous. The sources of control over response covariation is thus an assessment area in its own right. From a traditional point of view, responses that are thought to reflect the same underlying internal cause should covary; responses that are manifestations of imcompatible internal entities should not. If two measures are thought to be manifestations of the same hypothesized cause, their covariation is then to be one indication of the quality of the measures.

Finally, the two approaches differ in the degree to which idiographic or nomothetic approaches are used in assessment. Traditional assessment has often been based on theoretical systems that suggest which intraperson states are important, and how they relate to behavior. Since these states are thought to have similar effects across people, assessment tends to be nomothetically oriented. In behavioral assessment, the goal is often to measure the specific behavioral patterns of an individual. Few theoretical assumptions are made about the nature and role of a given behavior. Thus, assessment tends to be relatively idiographic, even to the point of developing new devices to measure the behavior of an individual (e.g., Shapiro, 1966, 1970). Behavioral assessment tends to be done repeatedly, across time and within an individual.

Traditional assessment tends to be based on single measurements across many individuals.

THE HONEYMOON PERIOD OF BEHAVIORAL ASSESSMENT

Following its origins in the 1960s, behavioral assessment enjoyed a honeymoon period in the 1970s. Behavioral assessors basked in conceptual confidence. The assumptions of behavioral assessment began to be stated more explicitly. Various acronyms arose to describe important areas of assessment: Goldfried & Sprafkin's (1976) SORC, which stands for stimulus–organism–response–consequence, and Kanfer and Saslow's (1969) SORKC, which stands for stimulus–organism–response–contingency–consequence. A recognizable list of procedures classified as behavioral assessment techniques emerged (Cone, 1978; Goldfried & Sprafkin, 1976) including direct observation of behavior in naturalistic or analogue situations, self-monitoring, participant observation, self-report in the forms of questionnaires or interviews, physiologic measures, and some standardized tests. A spate of books about behavioral assessment appeared (Barlow, 1981; Ciminero, Calhoun, & Adams, 1977; Cone & Hawkins, 1977; Haynes, 1978; Haynes & Wilson, 1979; Hersen & Bellack, 1976, 1981; Keefe, Kopel, & Gordon, 1978; Mash & Terdal, 1976, 1981) and two behavioral assessment journals were founded, *Behavioral Assessment* and the *Journal of Behavioral Assessment*.

THE DISILLUSIONMENT PERIOD

Following the honeymoon period, there has been a noticeable disillusionment with behavioral assessment. Paradoxically, this disillusionment has often been associated with a misunderstanding of the conceptual foundations of behavioral assessment, or a failure to appreciate their implications. If behavioral assessment is viewed as a content subarea or a subset of techniques, then behavioral assessment may logically be evaluated in terms of the practices and assumptions of traditional assessment. Consequently, it may have been implicitly assumed that certain outcomes, sensible only within a traditional framework, should be achieved by behavioral assessment. In so doing, disillusionment is the inevitable result. If, conversely, behavioral assessment presents a comprehensive alternative to traditional assessment, it must be evaluated against its own set of assumptions and goals.

On the surface, the current disillusionment includes several distinct concerns.

DISILLUSION 1: THE TECHNIQUES ARE IMPERFECT

The first disillusion is the apparent imperfection of current behavioral assessment techniques. Different measures, seemingly of the same behavior, do not always agree with each other. For example, self-report measures of sexual arousal are not always congruent with physiologic measures of sexual arousal (Barlow, 1977). Moreover, similar measures of the same behavior do not agree with each other. For instance, the various questionnaires purporting to measure assertiveness sometimes produce inconsistent responding (Galassi & Galassi, 1980). Even direct observation of behavior in naturalistic settings is not problem-free. For example, high agreement between two or more observers can be obtained and maintained only under very tightly controlled conditions (Kent & Foster, 1977), and often reflect problems such as observer bias or observer drift. In short, few now believe that behavioral assessment techniques will provide ready mirrors of reality.

DISILLUSION 2: THE TECHNIQUES AREN'T STANDARDIZED OR PSYCHOMETRICALLY PURE

The second disillusion is the lack of progress toward standardized psychometrically sound behavioral assessment techniques. It was originally believed by some that through a psychometric distillation process only the most reliable and valid behavioral assessment techniques would be identified and retained (Cone, 1978; Goldfried, 1979; Mash, 1979). Along these lines, Marvin Goldfried has stated:

> Once we have decided on the best procedures for assessing a given variable, we then need to accept the convention of employing only these measures until it can be empirically demonstrated that others may surpass them in validity and discriminability. Until that time occurs, I would even go so far as to suggest that journal editors not consider for publication those studies employing measures having demonstrated inferior validity. (Goldfried, 1979, p. 21)

> The proliferation of nonstandardized behavioral assessment techniques has produced in some a growing sense of frustration. Furthermore, many common behavioral assessment devices do not appear psychometrically sound. For example, split-half reliability of a popular questionnaire may be low, or test-retest reliability of an avoidance test may be inadequate.

DISILLUSION 3: THE TECHNIQUES DO NOT LEAD TO DIFFERENTIAL DIAGNOSIS

A third difficulty is that behavioral assessment packages have not yet emerged to diagnosis clients into discrete groups or disorders. While simply measuring specific target behaviors in a specific client may be worthwhile for treatment purposes, some have hoped that a small set of behavioral assessment devices would eventually reveal what is "really" wrong with a client, or what kind of disorder he or she "really" has. The ad hoc, idiographic nature of behavioral assessment has frustrated the attempt to develop a behavioral diagnostic system.

EVALUATING THE QUALITY OF BEHAVIORAL ASSESSMENT

The difficulties felt by behavioral assessors in the areas of imperfection, standardization, and diagnostic utility, reflect conceptual confusion over the nature and purpose of behavioral assessment. The themes of these conceptual concerns are: How can we evaluate the quality of behavioral assessment? What do we expect it to do? How do we know it is measuring up?

Traditional assessment has sought to achieve quality measurement by developing standardized, psychometrically sound devices that clearly and consistently lead to the identification of distinct diagnostic groups. This psychometric approach is the cornerstone of traditional assessment. So powerful is the theoretical structure of psychometrics that it is difficult at first to see how any assessment approach could be evaluated otherwise. For example, the American Psychological Association (APA) *Standards for educational and psychological testing* (American Psychological Association, 1966) embrace many psychometric principles as necessary requirements of all assessment.

RESOLVING THE ROLE OF PSYCHOMETRICS IN BEHAVIORAL ASSESSMENT

THE USE OF PSYCHOMETRICS IN EVALUATING THE QUALITY OF BEHAVIORAL ASSESSMENT STRATEGIES

The first attempts to evaluate the quality of behavioral assessment strategies outlined a set of familiar concepts and procedures, drawn from classic psychometric theory. While the methods and techniques of behavioral assessment were thought to be distinct from traditional assessment, the means of evaluating them was believed to be the same. To illustrate, Cone (1977, p. 411) wrote: "It is the thesis of the present paper that the concept's of reliability and validity used in traditional assessment are applicable to behavioral assessment as well." Similarily, Curran and Mariotto (1980, p. 33) noted: "A refamiliarization with traditional psychometric theory combined with the utilization of generalizability theory concepts should assist us in improving our assessment procedures." Chapter 3 of the present volume makes a similar, but much more elaborated argument.

Reliability refers to the consistency of scores obtained by the same persons when reexamined with the same assessment device under systematically changing circumstances (e.g., different time, different items, or different examiners), whereas validity refers to what an assessment device measures and how well it does so (Anastasi, 1982). Put another way, reliability deals with relations among scores on the *same* device, while validity deals with relationships among scores on *different* devices (Campbell & Fiske, 1959). The various types of reliability and validity have been categorized more systematically within generalizability theory (Cronbach, Gleser, Nanda, & Rajaratnam, 1972), which relabels the types of reliability and validity into universes of generalization (e.g., across scores, item, time, setting, or method).

These psychometric criteria of reliability and validity have been applied to dozens of behavioral assessment issues and devices. One common type of such research examines the data obtained on one measure of a particular behavior with those of another measure supposedly of the same behavior—a type of concurrent validity. For example, the concurrent validity of role-playing has been examined by comparing data obtained through role-playing with data obtained through contrived situations in the natural environment (e.g., Bellack, Hersen, & Lamparski, 1979). This type of research seems most common in areas where a label for a single type of behavior can encompass many different types or areas of responding, such as anxiety, social skills and the like. For example, studies have compared self-report measures with role-playing measures of heterosocial anxiety and skills (e.g., Heimberg, Harrison, Montgomery, Madsen, & Sherfey, 1980; Nelson, Hayes, Felton, & Jarrett, 1985). Similarly, the concurrent validity and test–retest reliability of several physiologic measures of women's sexual arousal were examined across two measurement sessions (Henson, Rubin, & Henson, 1979).

Research guided by generalizability theory has tended to examine several types of generality in a single study or set of studies. In an exemplar (Jones, Reid, & Patterson, 1975), the following universes of generalization were examined: subjects (13 referred deviant boys and 17 normal control boys), observers (2), and occasions (observations were made on 2 different days during a baseline period). When the observational data for the deviant boys were subjected to an analysis of variance, the subjects factor and the subjects by occasions interaction accounted for most of the variance. For the normal boys, a similar pattern emerged, with more variance accounted for by the subjects by occasion interaction, and less by the subjects main effect. In neither case did the main effect for observer or interactions with the observer factor each significance, permitting generalization across the universe of observers.

PROBLEMS WITH UTILIZING PSYCHOMETRIC PROCEDURES TO EVALUATE BEHAVIORAL ASSESSMENT

It is clear that psychometric and generalizability procedures *can* be applied to behavioral assessment techniques. By so doing, interesting and potentially useful data can be generated. For example, it is interesting and potentially worthwhile to know that self-reports of a given event correlate with other measures of that event. The question remains, however, whether or not these kinds of data by themselves provide an adequate means of evaluating the *quality* of behavioral assessment. In our opinion, the answer is largely "no." In a few instances, psychometrically driven analyses will yield data that do help evaluate behavioral assessment because they happen also to make sense when viewed from the perspective of behavior theory. In some cases, psychometric research will help, once more behaviorally sound methods of evaluation have already established the quality of given methods or techniques. Psychometric and generalizability theory, however, does not provide an adequate theoretical basis for evaluating the quality of behavioral assessment because its assumptions about behavior, its level of analysis, and its model of causality differs fundamentally from a behavioral perspective.

Assumptions about Behavior

In psychometric theory, an observed score is a composite of the true value plus measurement error. The true score is a hypothetical entity, which is typically assumed to be enduring and stable because it reflects an enduring, stable, internal entity. Reliability and validity assess the consistency of measurement. Rather than an event to be explained, consistency is viewed as the hallmark of a good assessment device. If the true score is assumed to be consistent, then consistent measures are thought to be less contaminated by error and more reflective of the true score.

It is an assumption of behavioral assessment, however, that behavior is not necessarily enduring and consistent. Inconsistency in measurement may be produced by actual changes in behavior and not only by an imprecise behavioral assessment technique (Nelson, Hay, & Hay, 1977). When low reliability or validity coefficients are obtained, behavioral assessors ask, "Is it the measure or the behavior?" (Cone, 1981, p. 55). Thus, consistency or inconsistency is an empirical fact to be explained, not an inside route to quality measurement. The behavioral question becomes, What are the variables responsible for the degree of consistency seen? For example, if baseline responding is inconsistent over time, the behavioral assessor begins to look for the factors producing that variability (Barlow, Hayes, & Nelson, 1984; Sidman, 1960). There is no assumption of "measurement error"—although variability in measurement procedures are often one important source of control over variability in responding. For example, the inconsistent sexual responses found by Henson *et al.* (1979) were attributed to changing organismic variables, such as hormone level, and to changing situational variables, such as placement of the measuring device. "Error" has no place in behavioral theory.

In most situations, it does not seem appropriate to expect consistency in responding, given the assumptions of behavioral theory. Since behavior is assumed to be modifiable (often rapidly so), test–retest reliability should not necessarily be expected. Since behavior is assumed to be situation-specific, concurrent validity across assessment situations should not be routinely predicted. Given the assumption that responses are distinguished by the functions they serve, inconsistency across response systems is not surprising. While the results of psychometric investigations of behavioral assessment techniques have been disappointing to some, in fact, the results have simply verified the assumptions underlying behavioral assessment. Thus, when inconsistency across situations, responses, or time is found, it is not necessarily a statement about the quality of behavior assessment. It is, instead, an empirical fact requiring explanation. For example, if behavior is inconsistent across situations, the distinctions between these stimulus situations should be explored. If behavior is inconsistent across time, the reason for a lack of maintenance should be identified.

Level of Analysis

A second reason why psychometric and generalizability theory may not be an appropriate criterion for evaluating behavioral assessment is that their levels of analysis differ. Psychometric research is almost universally based on the analysis of group data, while behavioral assessment emerged from the intensive analysis of individuals. The issue is not one of number (few vs. many) but of the level of analysis (individual vs. group) upon which principles and findings are based.

The history of psychometrics along with its emphasis on variability in group data, has been traced by Johnston and Pennypacker (1980). Central contributors were Legendre who, in 1806, developed a mathematical procedure to derive the one best value from a series of variable values; Adolphe Quetelet who, about 1835, concluded that human characteristics were normally distributed and that variability could be analyzed to determine ideal values of these characteristics; Francis Galton who, in the early 1900s, assumed that among the human characteristics that were normally distributed and assessed through analyses of variability was intelligence or mental ability; and Karl Pearson who, in 1896, developed the product–moment correlation to describe the relationship between two variable distributions.

Psychometrics was built upon an analysis of the variability in scores between individuals in a group—the psychology of "individual differences." For example, in assessing the concurrent validity of two given measures, typically a large group of subjects would be given the two devices at a single point in time. Measures with high concurrent validity would be those in which there is a strong correlation *across* subjects. These data use the group as the level of analysis. For example, from these data we cannot say *for a given individual* if a high score on one measure will be associated with changes in the other measure.

In contrast to this interest in variability across persons, modern behaviorism is built upon an interest in variability in the behavior of an individual across situations and across time. Variability is not seen as "normal variation" or "error" but is the product of variables to be identified (Cone, 1981; Johnston & Pennypacker, 1980; Sidman, 1960). In the psychometric approach, variability creates a kind of rubber ruler against which differences can be measured—what Johnston and Pennypacker (1980) call "vagonometric" assessment. In behavioral assessment, variability is itself the target of interest. It cannot be used to measure something else.

Interindividual variability and intraindividual variability cannot be translated from one to the other. Consider the data shown in Figure 13-1, for example. The top graph shows data with high interindividual variability but low intraindividual variability, while the bottom one shows the reverse. The two types are fundamentally different and no amount of data on variability within a group will yield conclusive data on variability within individuals in the group. For example, suppose two measures of sexual arousal (say, self-report and physiologic measures) are collected in a group of individuals and that the data shown in Table 13-1 are obtained. The correlation between these two measures is very low. We would say, based on psychometric theory, that the measures do not have concurrent validity. Suppose, however, that when we measured these persons repeatedly across time we found

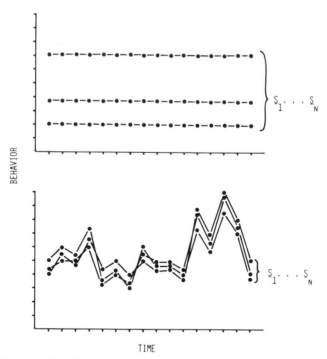

FIG. 13-1. An example of the independence of intrasubject and intersubject variability. In the top graph, intersubject variability is high and intrasubject variability is low. In the bottom graph, the reverse is true. Intrasubject variability, therefore, cannot be estimated by knowledge of intersubject variability.

the patterns show in Figure 13-2. *At the level of the individual,* changes in one measure predict the changes in another across time and situation. Here we would have an example of a psychometrically "poor" set of measures (low concurrent validity, low test–retest reliability)that are nonetheless shown at the level of the individual to respond similarly to situational and temporal variables—that is, to be members of the same response class. A behavioral

TABLE 13-1. Hypothetical Data for Two Measures of Sexual Arousal at the First Assessment Session

Subject	Sexual arousal measure	
	Self-report (1–10)	Physiologic (1–10)
1	8	2
2	10	6
3	3	3
4	6	9
5	3	7

assessor, having such data, could then rely on self-report to measure changes in physiologic arousal over time despite the psychometric results. In fact, a recent study has found just such an effect (Turner & Hayes, 1984) for measures of sexual arousal.

In behavioral assessment, the assessment process must take into account the unique problematic situations and response systems of each client. For each client, target behaviors must be identified, treatment strategies selected, and outcome measures determined. Nomothetic principles must emerge from an understanding of variability in the behavior of individuals. While the same *numbers* of individuals may need to be studied in the two

FIG. 13-2. A hypothetical example of two measures with a high intrasubject correlation, but low intersubject correlation (see Table 13-1).

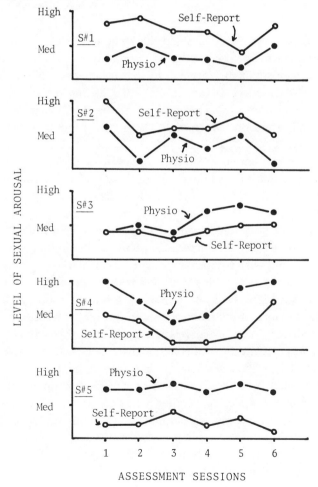

approaches, the level of analysis is different. As the above example shows, group-derived conclusions are not necessarily applicable to the individual.

Models of Causality

The third reason that psychometrics and generalizability theory may not provide adequate criteria for evaluating the quality of behavioral assessment is that the two perspectives differ fundamentally in their view of causality. In psychometrics, events can be explained based on the structure of the organism (e.g., the structure of the mind). That is, structure can assume causal status. In modern behaviorism, the structure of the organism is itself something to be explained by the functional interaction between the organism and the world over both short time frames (e.g., in the lifetime of the individual) and long time frames (e.g., in the lifetime of the species). Structure is not unimportant in this view, but it is not a cause. Instead it is a host for causal agents.

In biology, structuralism examined the structure of an organ or tissue whereas functionalism asked what the function of the organ or tissue was in the life of the organism or the species. As first used in psychology, structuralism examined structures of the mind such as images or sensations, whereas functionalism examined functions of the mind such as memory, imagination, and attention (Murray, 1983). Today, functionalism seeks to define and evaluate psychological concepts by the functions they serve (Skinner, 1974). For example, a behavior is viewed as distinct because of its distinct functions, and the value of a psychological term is itself to be assessed by the functions the term serves. Structuralism seeks to identify the organization of behavior within the individual. Thus, even if traditional assessment agrees that what it seeks to measure is behavior, it seeks to measure it for a structuralistic purpose. Suppose we found that a measure of confidence correlated with performance. In traditional assessment, it would not be uncommon to say that this structure is itself causal. For example, we might be told that high levels of confidence produces good performance. Thus, a stable measure of confidence (e.g., with high test–retest reliability) with good predictive validity (correlation with performance) would be a measure of a causal event. From a functionalistic perspective, these correlations are themselves events to explain. They are caused, not causal. If they have value, it would have to be shown in terms of the functions intended for behavioral assessment: selecting a target behavior, selecting a treatment, or evaluating treatment outcome. To paraphrase a famous sentence of Titchener (1899, p. 291) in order to apply it to assessment: "[Assessment], from a structural standpoint, is observation of an is; [assessment] from the functional standpoint, is observation of an Is-for."

The philosophical source of disagreement in this area is what we take to be a "cause." Modern behaviorism evaluates causes in terms of our ability to predict and to control (and to understand, which relates to the breadth and depth of prediction and control). The difficulty with structural "causes" is that they can sometimes help us predict, but as long as we stay inside the structure we cannot know how to control. Demonstration of control involves manipulation. Manipulation of a structure must be initiated from outside that structure. Thus, structuralistic "causes" (whether they be called behavior, bodily states, traits, or cognitions) cannot serve the functions required of causes in modern behaviorism. As a structural approach, psychometrics can provide data to be evaluated functionally, but cannot functionally evaluate data, including those derived from behavioral assessment.

BEHAVIORAL EVALUATION OF BEHAVIORAL ASSESSMENT

From a behavioral point of view, good measures should help us accomplish meaningful goals, be based on the individual as the appropriate level of analysis, should help us sort out responses that are meaningful from those that are meaningless, and should measure behavior accurately. Each of these goals implies an approach to the evaluation of the quality of behavioral assessment.

TREATMENT UTILITY

One of the main goals of behavioral assessment is to select target behaviors and appropriate treatment. This goal also implies a method of evaluating assessment. If an appropriate target behavior is selected for treatment, presumably clients should improve more than if an inappropriate one has been selected. Similarly, if an appropriate treatment has been selected, clients should get better faster than if an inappropriate treatment had been selected. In other words, in meeting these two goals, behavioral assessment should be able to show that it can contribute to improved treatment outcome—what might be termed "treatment utility."

Treatment utility is a functional approach to evaluating several aspects of behavioral assessment. Among other questions, we can ask if the quality of assessment devices or strategies, if the nature of theoretical distinctions, or if the quantity of assessment contributes to the effectiveness of treatment.

The treatment utility of classifying clients according to particular target behaviors has been shown in several studies. In one example, patients with social skills problems were divided into those with apparent skills deficits and those with apparent suppression of skills due to social anxiety (Trower, Yardley, Bryant, & Shaw, 1978). This had long been a popular distinction in the social skills literature (e.g., Hersen & Bellack, 1977), but its treatment utility had not been examined. The relationship between the identification of skills deficits or social anxiety and the differential selection of treatment had not been studied. Trower *et al.* (1978) showed that socially deficient patients improved more with social skills training than with systematic desensitization but that socially anxious patients improved as well under either treatment. Thus, the distinction has treatment utility. In a similar vein, Ost, Jerremalm, and Johansson (1981) showed that greater effects were achieved when the particular treatment of social phobia matched the subject's pattern of responses (i.e., when subjects with social skills deficits received social skills training, and subjects with anxiety excesses received relaxation training). Recent research in our laboratory has shown treatment utility of distinguishing between cognitive and overt skills deficits in treating depression (McKnight, Nelson, Hayes, & Jarrett, 1984). Depressed women who displayed irrational cognitions improved more when they received cognitive therapy rather than social skills training, whereas depressed women who displayed social skills deficits improved more when they received social skills training. In another illustration of the treatment utility approach, it has been shown that only women suffering from spasmodic dysmenorrhea improved following systematic desensitization; women suffering from congestive dysmenorrhea did not benefit from this treatment (Chesney & Tasto, 1975).

There are a number of other examples, although they are perhaps surprisingly rare in the literature given their importance. Studies have shown the treatment utility of distinctions between types of insomnia (Borkovec, Grayson, O'Brian, & Weerts, 1979), anxiety (Altmaier, Ross, Leary, & Thronbrough, 1982; Elder, Edelstein, & Fremouw, 1981; Shahan & Merbaum, 1981), and depression (Paykel, Prusoff, Klerman, Haskell, & Di Mascio, 1973).

Note that in studies of this type, treatment utility is based upon a nexus of assessment devices, theoretical distinctions, and treatment approaches. It evaluates devices only in the context of what is done with the knowledge obtained from them. Thus, a theoretical distinction can originally have no treatment utility, but may acquire it when treatments that make use of the distinction are later developed. For example, we may suspect that there are two different types of panic disorder, based on two patterns of assessment data, but until we have treatments that use this distinction, it may make no difference in outcome. Similarly, a device may have no treatment utility because the theoretical distinctions to which assessment results are put are incorrect. We may use a new device correctly to identify differences in brain wave patterns in two patient subtypes, but it does not yet have treatment utility because there are no theories to explain the meaning and use of the distinction.

Apparently, no studies have been conducted in behavioral assessment that are designed to measure more directly the treatment utility of given devices. For example, suppose we wished to assess the treatment utility of using self-monitoring, above and beyond that provided by questionnaires. All subjects could complete both questionnaires and self-monitoring, but for only half the subjects would the self-monitoring data be made available to therapists designing their treatment program. If these subjects ultimately improved more than those whose treatment plans were based on question-naires alone, the treatment utility of using self-monitoring data with this disorder would be established. In a similar fashion, the treatment utility of interviews, role-playing, and other devices could be evaluated.

Normally, treatment utility is based on the contribution that an aspect of behavioral assessment makes to treatment effectiveness. For example, relaxation may produce benefits for any anxious client (compared to no treatment) but may produce greater benefits for those suffering from "so-matic" anxiety than for those suffering from "cognitive" anxiety. Sometimes, however, treatment *efficiency* may be the issue, and treatment utility may be established based on resultant lower cost, less therapist time, and so on.

The treatment utility of many other aspects of behavioral assessment remains to be tested. For example, does a functional analysis lead to better treatment than a topographical or static analysis? In other words, is treat-ment improved when the intervention is based on a functional analysis of the individual client's problems, or is it equally effective to use a standard treatment that is generally effective with problems that match the client's in topography? Other questions that need study include: Does the use of multiple assessment methods lead to better treatment than the use of only one method? Does the collection of dependent measures lead to better treatment than not collecting such measures? Does the use of single-subject designs improve treatment more than not using such designs?

The various areas of behavioral assessment that can be evaluated using a treatment utility approach are summarized in Table 13-2. As can be seen, there are multiple methodologies appropriate in each area.

Post Hoc Identification of Dimensions

One approach to treatment validity is to administer the treatments to many persons and to identify post hoc aspects of the assessment devices that help predict therapy responders. This is a well-known strategy with a long tradition in clinical science. For example, a review of research in depression

TABLE 13-2. Types of Treatment Validity Studies and Relevant Methodologies to Answer Particular Treatment Validity Questions

Type of study	Methodology			Treatment utility question
	Typical group comparison	Time-series (single-case)		
		Main Q between subjects	Main Q within subject	
Post hoc	Pre-post correlational	Single-case design correlational	NA	The relationship between patient characteristics and outcome
A priori—single dimension				
Manipulated assessment	Two or more groups randomly assigned. Repeated measures. Treatment varies based on assessment.	Two or more groups randomly assigned. Single-case design (e.g., A-B-A-B) within cell. Treatment varies based on assessment.	Single-case design (e.g., ATD). Treatment varies within subject, based on assessment.	The effect of assessment devices, strategies, and methods on outcome
Manipulated use	Two or more groups randomly assigned. Repeated measures. Treatment varies based on assessment.	Two or more groups randomly assigned. Single-case (e.g., A-B-A-B) within cell. Treatment varies based on assessment.	Single-case design (e.g., ATD). Treatment varies within subject, based on assessment.	The effects of different uses of available assessment data on outcome
Observed differences	Two or more known groups. Repeated measures. Treatment does not vary.	Single-case design. Pure types of patients gathered beforehand. Treatment does not vary.	NA	The relationship between distinct patient types and outcome.
A priori—Multiple dimensions				
Manipulated assessment—manipulated use	Factorial groups randomly assigned. Repeated measures. Treatment varies based on assessment.	Factorial groups randomly assigned. Single-case design (e.g., A-B-A-B) within cell. Treatment	Single-case designs used which allow two or more treatments within subject (e.g., ATD). Assessment	The effect of assessment devices (and so on) on the impact of different uses of assessment data

				on outcome
	varies based on assessment.	& match combinations within subject.		The effect of assessment devices (and so on) on outcome for distinct patient types
Manipulated assessment—observed differences	Factorial groups randomly assigned within known groups. Repeated measures. Treatment varies based on assessment.	Factorial groups randomly assigned within known groups. Single-case design (e.g., A-B-A-B) used within cell. Treatment varies based on assessment	Single-case designs used that allow two or more treatments within subject (e.g., ATD) Treatment varies within subject based on assessment; subjects come from known groups.	
Manipulated use—observed difference	Factorial groups randomly assigned within known groups. Repeated measures. Treatment varies based on assessment.	Factorial groups randomly assigned. Single-case design (e.g., A-B-A-B) used within cell. Treatment varies based on assessment.	Single-case designs used that allow two or more treatments within subject (e.g., ATD). Treatment varies within subject based on assessment; subjects come from known groups.	The effect of the use of assessment data on outcome for distinct patient types
Manipulated assessment—manipulated use—observed differences	Factorial groups randomly assigned within known groups. Repeated measures. Treatment varies based on assessment.	Factorial groups randomly assigned. Single-case design (e.g., A-B-A-B) used within cell. Treatment varies based on assessment.	Single-case designs used that allow two ro more treatments within subject (e.g., ATD). Treatment varies within subject based on assessment; subjects come from known groups.	The effect of assessment devices (and so on) on the impact of different uses of assessment data on outcome for distinct patient types
Observed differences. Two or more treatments.	Factorial. Two or more known groups. Repeated measures. Two or more treatments varying across but not within cells.	Single-case designs. (e.g., A-B-A-B) Pure types of patients gathered beforehand. Each patient gets only one type of treatment.	Single-case design which allow two treatments within subject (e.g., ATD). Pure types of patients gathered beforehand. Each patient gets each treatment.	The effect of different treatments on outcome for distinct patient types

Abbreviations: NA, not applicable; other abbreviations as in text.

by Bielski and Friedel (1976), suggested that higher social class, insidious onset, anorexia, weight loss, middle and late insomnia, and psychomotor disturbance were all positively related to a favorable response to tricyclic medication. In contrast, neurotic, hypochondriacal, and hysterical traits, multiple prior episodes, and delusions predicted a poor response to imipramine and amitriptyline. Similarly, Paykel *et al.* (1973) performed a cluster analysis identifying four subtypes of depressive patients (i.e., psychotic depressives, anxious depressives, hostile depressives, and young depressives with personality disorders) that predicted the degree to which patients would respond to tricyclics.

Unfortunately, research of this sort has often failed to find consistent or strong correlations between assessment measures and outcome. There are several possible sources of this problem: (1) a failure to identify successes and failures at the level of the individual, (2) a failure to identify *differential* treatment effects at the level of the individual, and (3) inconsistencies in target subject populations, subject selection characteristics, therapist characteristics, and treatment implementation.

In a typical post hoc approach to treatment utility, large numbers of subjects have been assessed pretreatment and posttreatment on the target behavior. The degree of pre–post improvement is then correlated with other assessment measures, and certain subject characteristics using these measures are identified that predict treatment outcome. Unfortunately, in this type of study, treatment responsivity is unknown at the level of the individual. Improvement pre–post could be due to extraneous variables (real but uncontrolled sources of changes), or measurement inconsistencies (artificial sources of change) as well as treatment. At the level of the group, we assume that extraneous variables and measurement inconsistency is evenly distributed between groups and is reflected in interindividual variability. Remaining variation is then thought to be treatment-related. At the level of the individual, however, *successes and failures cannot be identified*. Thus, any correlations found between improvement and other variables mixes all three sources of variability in the correlation (treatment, extraneous, measurement). It should be no surprise that such correlations tend to be low and inconsistently obtained.

The same problem of unknown sources of variability plagues this type of study when the treatment utility question requires knowing who responds best to one of two or more treatments. For example, we may want to see if factor A predicts better response on treatment X than treatment Y. Unfortunately typical group-comparison pre–post studies do not allow us to say *specifically who* is improved on treatment X or treatment Y, and cannot even pretend to tell us *specifically who* responds best to X over Y since subjects receive only X or Y.

One solution to these two problems is to identify treatment responsiveness and differential treatment effects at the level of the individual—that is, to use single-case experimental designs. This approach will probably require just as many subjects as the previous approach, but since individual assessment results will now be correlated with individual treatment effects, stronger external validity for these correlations seems likely. Thus, a post hoc approach to treatment utility may be very helpful, once a thorough program of single-case clinical research is established (Barlow, Hayes, & Nelson, 1984). Some types of methodologies for this in a priori treatment utility studies are described below. Even if these problems were solved, the third problem with post hoc studies seems likely to continue. The post hoc approach is very sensitive to any inconsistencies between the original study and subsequent formal cross-validation studies or the clinical environment itself. If a correlation is established between a premeasure and outcome, it may only be obtainable with a specific target population (e.g., persons in a particular part of the country), specific selection criteria (e.g., persons willing to be research subjects), or specific therapist or treatment characteristics. Since these problems are present in virtually all clinical research this is nothing new, but a post hoc approach seems especially vulnerable to them. If a treatment utility relationship is predicted a priori and is successfully demonstrated, then some degree of robustness (external validity) has already been shown.

Especially if built on data meaningful at the level of the individual, the post hoc approach is quite valuable, but it can really only help generate reasonable hypotheses for experimental test. It is also limited because it asks many treatment utility questions in an extremely weak manner. For example, if one were interested in seeing if self-monitoring added to treatment outcome, a post hoc correlation with outcome would be contaminated by (1) subject or therapist variables that lead the therapist to decide to try self-monitoring in the place, and (2) subject variables that lead persons to comply with the use of self-monitoring. Thus, the treatment utility of devices themselves are very difficult to examine post hoc. Similar criticisms apply to the selection of a target behavior or to the quantity of assessment. Only the treatment utility of assessment distinctions based on consistently obtained data (e.g., on patient demographics, scores on universally used measures) can be examined post hoc.

In summary, it has been argued that post hoc methodologies for testing treatment utility questions are most useful when combined within single-case designs. Because the single-case post hoc approach is vulnerable to inconsistencies between the original study and later validation studies, it has been suggested that the post hoc approach be used primarily in generating hypotheses for future study.

A PRIORI GROUP COMPARISON APPROACHES

Single-Dimension Studies

Most experimental treatment utility research that has been done fits into this category. The simplest kinds of studies ask if a single distinction predicts treatment outcome. There are three subtypes: manipulated assessment, manipulated match, and obtained differences.

Manipulated Assessment. In this type (Figure 13-3), it is the nature of available assessment data that is of issue. A single group of subjects is randomly divided into two groups and a single aspect of assessment is varied systematically. For example, information (collected on all subjects) may be made available to therapists in one group but not the other. This might include different quantities of information, information from a given device, diagnostic impressions information from a given device, diagnostic impressions from others, and the like. The therapist then designs and implements treatment according to the assessment data available. Differentail outcomes between groups confirm the treatment utility of the assessment characteristics manipulated.

The essential characteristics is that groups are randomly assigned and treatment is allowed to covary freely with the manipulated assessment differences. Thus, it is the effect of assessment information that is evaluated in this kind of "manipulated assessment" study. It is also possible in this approach to *administer* given assessment procedures to one group and not the other. In this case, what is being evaluated is the direct impact of assessment on the subject, as well as the indirect impact caused by its effect on the therapist. It may be, for example, that taking a Rorschach test is reactive independent of the use to which it is put by the therapist. Typically this is not a question of importance; but, if it is important, the two sources of influence can be distinguished by adding a third group to the arrangement shown in Figure 13-3, which does not even receive the assessment that was withheld from the therapists of one group (i.e., group B in Figure 13-3).

Manipulated Use. These studies are somewhat similar in design to manipulated assessment studies, but they differ fundamentally because all subjects receive the same assessment procedures and this information is available for all subjects. What is manipulated is the *correspondence* between assessment information and treatment. Many assessment questions seem to be of this type. For example, behavior therapists have long claimed that matching treatment to specific client problems will result in improved treatment outcome. Surprisingly, there are few data available on this question. In what appears to have been one of the first studies of this type, Jarrett, Nelson, and Hayes (1981) attempted to compare idiographically based treatment of

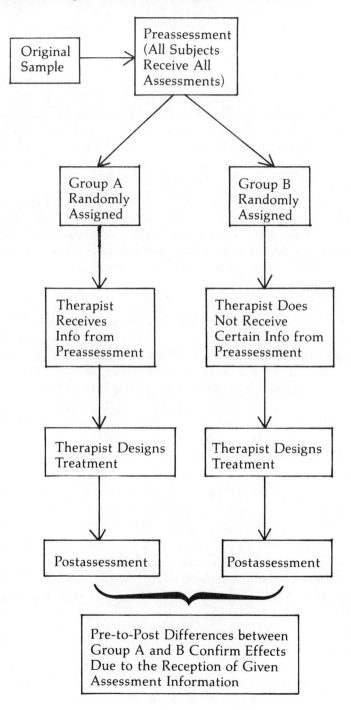

FIG. 13-3. A schematic diagram of a manipulated assessment treatment validity study.

depression with a nomothetic approach. In the idiographic group subjects received treatment modules that matched their specific weaknesses. For example, a subject with frequent irrational thoughts received a cognitive module, subjects with poor social skills received a social skills module, and so on. In the nomothetic group subjects received modules yoked to the idiographic subjects. The results showed no differential effect for treatment matching. An interesting and illuminating methodologist problem was missed, however. Note that this study is virtually identical to a "manipulated assessment" study, because assessment information is used in one group, but ignored in the other. Unfortunately, many in the yoked treatment group *also* (by chance) received needed treatment, as indicated by their pretreatment assessment. A true "manipulated use" study can avoid this by using data to unmatch as well as match assessment and treatment. Two subsequent studies in our laboratory have confirmed the value of idiographically based treatment under these conditions (McKnight *et al.*, 1984; Nelson, Hayes, Jarrett, & McKnight, 1983).

As researchers begin to use treatment utility as an approach for evaluating behavioral assessment, they should consider the possibility that *interactions* exist between behavioral assessment techniques and disorders. The treatment utility of an aspect of behavioral assessment within a certain disorder needs to be demonstrated rather than assumed. For example, if benefits are achieved by matching depressed clients' treatment to their identified problems, this should also then be investigated with other disorders rather than taken as a given. This can be done to some degree within a given study, as will be described below.

Observed Differences. In this third type of a priori group comparison treatment utility study, subjects are divided into groups nonrandomly based on assessment differences. Subjects then receive one type of treatment. Differences between the groups then show the treatment utility of these differences. This is a more common approach than the other two. Essentially, it is the simplest experimental version of post hoc studies that seek to identify treatment responders and nonresponders. For example, socially unskilled sexual deviants without heterosexual arousal and those with heterosexual arousal might all be given a social skills training package. If only those with heterosexual arousal subsequently show changes in sexual deviation, the treatment utility of the distinction between these two groups would be established to some degree.

Note that these three types of studies all examine the interface between assessment and treatment. In manipulated assessment the assessment varies but treatment matching is the same. In manipulated use studies, assessment is the same but methods of matching assessment to treatment varies. In obtained differences studies, assessment outcomes vary, but assessment methods and treatment are constant.

A PRIORI GROUP COMPARISON APPROACHES

Multiple-Dimension Studies

Treatment utility studies can be used to ask more complex questions. These multiple-dimension studies add to or cross the types of questions discussed above. For example, groups developed as in a manipulated assessment study can then be matched with treatment in two or more distinct ways. The factorial design which results asks if assessment information (or the assessment experience per se) has *differential* effects on two or more methods of utilizing assessment information.

A common way "observed differences" studies are elaborated is to cross distinct patient groups with two or more distinct treatment approaches. This kind of research is particularly elegant when the nature of each patient group seems to imply a distinct treatment approach. The factorial design that results tests not only the treatment utility of our patient group distinctions but also the conceptual and theoretical distinctions that gave rise to them and their implied therapies.

For example, suppose we divide patients into cognitive anxiety and somatic anxiety responders. Suppose further that this distinction implies that cognitive therapy should most strongly influence those with cognitive anxiety, while relaxation or other more somatic therapies should work best with persons with somatic anxiety. By crossing the two dimensions, the design shown in Figure 13-4 results.

If our conceptualization is perfectly sound, we should find the results shown. Although only several handfuls of such studies exist, those that do suggest that our conceptualizations are often only partially confirmed (e.g., Trower *et al.*, 1978), or fail to be confirmed at all.

Thus, in addition to enhancing treatment outcome, treatment utility approaches to evaluating aspects of behavioral assessment can improve our understanding of behavior and contribute to an inductive clinical science. To illustrate, the examples of treatment utility studies described above have furthered our understanding of the critical response classes comprising interpersonal difficulties, depression, and dysmenorrhea. If a procedure or experiment contributes to the establishment of general and conceptually consistent principles, it can be said to have "conceptual utility" or theoretical validity (Nelson & Hayes, 1979).

For those interested in assessment as a conceptual area, treatment utility may provide a major avenue for identifying areas of needed conceptual development. Repeated assessment for the purpose of evaluating treatment outcome is one of the hallmarks of behavioral assessment; yet its effect on therapeutic outcome or clinical practice has not been investigated. Presently, it is not known whether the examination of data over time produces

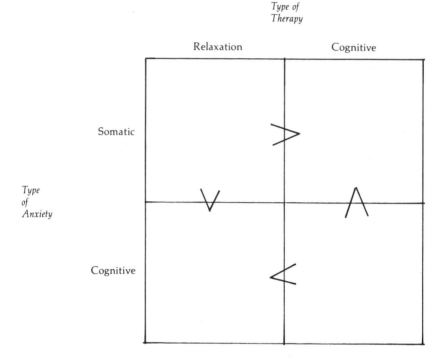

FIG. 13-4. An example of a multiple-dimension, a priori group comparison treatment validity study.

better treatment than collecting data only before and after treatment or than assessment for purely diagnostic purposes.

If repeated assessment can be shown to have treatment utility, in order for it to be conceptually valid one must still identify the variables that control or maximize the contribution that repeated assessment makes to treatment effectiveness. For example, does repeated assessment contribute more to treatment outcome when both the client and the therapist are involved in data collection or when only the therapist is involved (as in observation through a one-way mirror)? Does repeated assessment increase the probability that the clinician will engage in other behaviors (e.g., reinforcing gains) which in turn lead to therapeutic advantages? When clients participate in the assessment process are they more or less compliant with other therapeutic procedures (e.g., homework)? Does a client's self-monitoring of relative improvements serve as a discriminative stimulus for shaping coping behavior that might otherwise have gone unnoticed? Thus, over time, treatment utility is interwoven with conceptual utility because we must not only identify the area within behavioral assessment that contributes to treatment effectiveness, but also the process through which such an effect is produced. An understanding of the variables that control the contribution that assessment makes to treatment produces a field that is, by definition, valid conceptually.

A PRIORI TIME-SERIES APPROACHES

Main Question between Subject

In the various group comparison approaches to treatment utility, the relationship between outcome and assessment is sensible at the level of the group. Unlike post hoc correlations, conclusions are built upon data that allow sources of variability to be separated at the group level. Unfortunately, most group comparison approaches do not allow identification of those who actually improved. By using time-series designs (Barlow *et al.*, 1984), and then collapsing these designs into groups, we can conduct the same types of studies outlined above, but in a more precise manner.

In each of the types of a priori studies described so far, the main question is asked *between* subjects, because the actual manipulations are between subjects. For example, in a "manipulated assessment" study, some subjects would have treatment based on different assessment information than others. By adding time-series designs within subject (e.g., an A-B-A-B) to the usual pre–post measurement, the researcher can: (1) still analyze in a pre–post fashion, if desired, (2) identify at the level of the individual of successes and failures in each group, and (3) begin to correlate observed differences with success and failure, given each assessment approach. Thus, time-series designs can be incorporated within group comparison designs to increase the analytic power of the research. The main questions, however, remain *between* subjects.

A PRIORI TIME-SERIES APPROACHES

Main Question within Subject

It is possible to recast treatment utility questions in a within subject fashion. Generally this requires the use of a design that enables two or more treatments to be compared within subjects. While a B-C-B-C scheme might be used, among others (Barlow *et al.*, 1984; Hayes, 1981), by far the most powerful time-series design for this use in the alternating treatments design (ATD) (Barlow & Hayes, 1979). The ATD consists of the random or semi-random alternation of two or more conditions, where alternations are possible, about once per meaningful unit of measurement. If measures are most meaningful when grouped by the week, for example, conditions should be capable of alternating about once each week (determined randomly or semi-randomly). This allows an individual to be treated in two ways, and differential effectiveness to be determined within an individual.

Each of the main treatment utility questions can be assessed within subject, except for those single dimension studies involving "observed differences," since treatment does not vary and observed differences are not manipulable.

A "manipulated assessment" study can be done by devising treatments based on two sets of assessment data. For example, suppose two groups of expert clinicians are each given a different set of assessment data. One set includes an interview, self-monitoring, and direct behavioral observations. The second includes this same exact information, plus an MMPI, IQ test, Draw-a-Person test, and Rorschach test. Each group of clinicians devises a treatment program. If the two programs are distinct, they could now be delivered within subject, say in an ATD fashion. After a set of subjects have been run, we can determine the impact of assessment on treatment outcome. In addition, the fact that these data are meaningful at the level of the individual allow us to specify (1) the percentage of subjects who will respond best, given treatment based on a particular set of data, and (2) the apparent relationship between observed differences and differential outcome as influenced by assessment.

This same approach is useful in manipulated use, and combined manipulated assessment–manipulated use studies. In each approach, observed differences are implied, because data are meaningful at the level of the individual.

Finally, the approach is useful in "observed differences—two or more treatments" studies. In this study type, subjects may be divided into types of subjects based on assessment data. Unlike a purely post hoc approach, however, relatively "pure types" can be sought and obtained, which allows for a less confounded examination of the relationship between observed differences and outcome. Two or more treatments are then applied within subject, and differential effects are obtained. An example is the study by McKnight *et al.* (1984). Three subjects each were obtained who were depressed and had (1) poor social skills but few irrational cognitions, (2) irrational beliefs but adequate social skills, and (3) problems in both areas. After a short baseline, all subjects received both social skills training and cognitive therapy in an ATD fashion. The outcome data (degree of self-reported depression) are shown in Figure 13-5. As can be seen, the subjects with only social skills problems improved most following social skills training, while the reverse was true for subjects with problems only in the cognitive area. Subjects with problems in both areas improved as rapidly in either condition. Thus, the suspected relationship between these observed differences and two types of therapies was confirmed.

Manipulated Target

There is a final and very important type of study that does not truly evaluate the treatment utility of assessment, but that appears to do so. Often a given syndrome or disorder will contain several possible target behaviors. For example, in depression we could target overt social behavior, cognitive behaviors, and so on. It is then possible to ask if someone is depressed, which target behavior should be selected, cognition or social behavior? If treatments that target cognition are consistently superior to those that target social behavior, we might say that selecting cognition as a target behavior has "treatment utility." Note, however, that this is *not* an evaluation of assessment but instead is an exploration of the nature of a given disorder based on responsiveness to two treatments. We could ask the question with *any* assessment (except that necessary to diagnose depression). In such studies, we may keep track of the targets themselves, but we do nothing with this information other than to evaluate the impact of treatment. Thus, studies of this type do not truly apply treatment utility methodology to behavioral assessment.

Contrast this with similar studies we have already discussed that *do* address assessment quality. In an "observed differences—two or more treatments" study, we might identify categories of clients with distinct combinations of social abilities and cognitive patterns. After identifying categories we might then assign half of each of them to cognitive or social treatments. If there is an interaction between the patient groups and responsivity to treatment, we would say that the observed differences have treatment utility. Note that if there are differences between treatments, but it does *not* interact with patient characteristics, we would say they do not have treatment utility. This is precisely the situation in manipulated target studies, except that the two treatments have distinguishable targets. Thus, this type of study does not evaluate the quality of assessment, though it may evaluate the quality of our theories of disorders that may lead us to target one behavior over another. This could be called a kind of "treatment utility," but it should be made clear that it does not help us evaluate assessment per se.

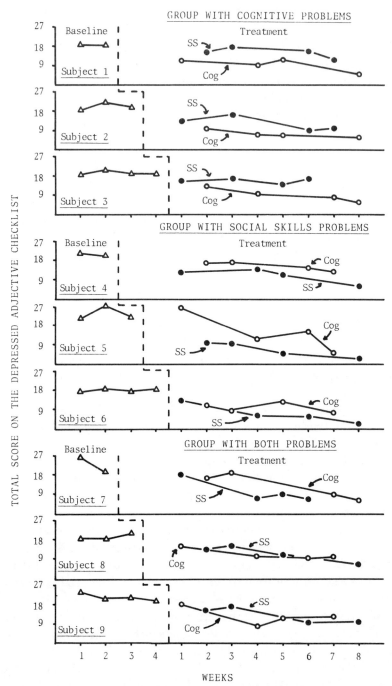

FIG. 13-5. The relationship between depressed subjects individual deficits (cognitive, social skills, or both) and responsivity to cognitive therapy and social skills therapy on a global measure of depression.

SENSITIVITY OF ASSESSMENT DATA TO IDENTIFIED VARIABLES

Generic questions about the accuracy, reliability, or validity of behavioral assessment techniques are probably meaningless. Assessment data vary, depending on the exact circumstances in which the assessment device is used. An alternative way to approach the quality of behavioral assessment is to identify the measurement variables that contribute to the variability in assessment data.

To illustrate, the generic question "Do self-recorders produce accurate data?" cannot be answered. The accuracy of self-recorders' data has been shown to be influenced by a host of variables: training given to the self-recorders, their awareness that their self-monitored data will be compared to some criterion, reinforcement given to self-recorders for accurate data, the number of concurrent response requirements imposed on the self-recorder, the number of behaviors simultaneously self-recorded, and the temporal relationship between the self-recording behavior and the self-recording response (McFall, 1977; Nelson, 1977).

As another illustration, the generic question "Do observers produce accurate data?" cannot be answered. Interobserver agreement has been shown to be influenced by several variables: type of training given to observers, their awareness that their interobserver agreement is being monitored, the complexity of the observational code that is used, and procedures used to calculate interobserver agreement (Kent & Foster, 1977; Wasik & Loven, 1980).

The point is that the same assessment device produces variable data. Instead of considering variability as random error, one approach is to analyze those sources of variability. In behavioral assessment, some variability is due to changes in clients' behavior, but some variability is also due to factors influencing assessment per se.

There are three ways that sensitivity of assessment data to variables can be helpful in evaluating behavioral assessment. First, it can identify techniques that are sensitive to variables that are theoretically troublesome. For example, an observational measure that is extremely sensitive to the motivation of the observer may be ruled out of consideration when we have reason to believe that observer motivation will vary. Similarly, observation of the same event (e.g., on videotape) should not vary much because it shows a sensitivity to variables other than the behavior itself. This issue is implicit in many research areas. For example, negative evaluations of a measure that is sensitive to "demand characteristics," to repeated assessment, and so on, is sensible primarily because we assume that such sensitivity is unwelcome. A measure should not be negatively evaluated based on its sensitivity to known variables, however, unless it can be shown that these variables are problematic and present in uncontrolled ways in the research environment.

Second, this approach can be of use when we can show that the measure *is* sensitive to theoretically expected variables. Often we have very good reason to believe that a given variable will produce *relative* changes in the behavior. If the assessment device is worthwhile, then it too should be sensitive to that variable. For example, we may have good reason to believe that water will get hotter if exposed to flame for a longer period of time. A thermometer that is not sensitive to changes produced by more flame is probably not a good thermometer. In the same way, an assessment device that is not sensitive to changes in behavior produced by situational differences strongly believed to alter the behavior, is probably not desirable. Note that this is almost the opposite of a psychometric approach which often values consistency over variability. This is not the same as accuracy (described below) because we may not be able to give incontrovertible proof that a certain behavior is "really" at a given level. It is only relative changes, not absolute values, that are needed.

Third, a final way that the identified variables approach can be of use is when we already have a criterion against which to evaluate data. Once a criterion is established (e.g., by accuracy or treatment utility), this approach can then allow us to determine how to produce good assessment. To the extent that a measure is sensitive to the same variables in the same way as a measure of known quality, it is also of quality. Note, however, that this sensitivity should be established within subjects, as discussed below. This is similar to concurrent validity, but differs because (1) it is best calculated within subjects; (2) it is thus based on a sensitivity to similar or identical variables, not on a mere correlation when variables are changing in an unknown manner; and (3) it must be built only on measures of known quality, in a behaviorally sensible sense of the term "quality".

In a sense, then, the sensitivity-to-known-variables approach helps us to know what a "meaningful" response is. Presumable "meaningful" responses are those that are sensitive to particular sets of controlling variables. This approach helps establish that.

ASSESSMENT OF INDIVIDUALS

As an alternative to psychometric procedures that focus on *group* data as the unit of analysis, attempts have been made to redirect behavioral assessment to the analysis of individuals as the unit of analysis. An emphasis on the assessment of individuals has been suggested in traditional personality assessment, as well (Harris, 1980; Lamiell, 1981).

What is needed are idiographic approaches in behavioral assessment that are analogous to single-subject experimental designs in behavior therapy. Single-subject designs have proven useful in two ways: first, they are useful in identifying effective treatments for specific clients; and second, they are useful in building an inductive clinical science, that is, one whose general principles are derived from an analysis of many individuals. Similar idiographic approaches are needed in behavioral assessment. Expected benefits would be the discovery of nomothetic principles, as well as the identification of target behaviors, treatment strategies, and outcome measures for individual clients.

Some idiographic approaches to assessment are currently available. The functional analysis is classic as a strategy for determining the controlling variables unique to the responses of an individual (Baer, Wolf, & Risley, 1968; Ferster, 1965; Kanfer & Saslow, 1969). The hypothesis-testing model introduced by Shapiro (1966, 1970) is another strategy to formulate and test hypotheses about individual clients. A third approach to individual assessment is the template-matching approach recently suggested by Cone (1980). In this approach, target behaviors for an individual client are identified by matching the client's current behaviors to a template of individually determined ideal behaviors. In a fourth approach to individual assessment, idiographic correlations among measures, instead of nomothetic correlations, can be computed. Idiographic correlations are produced by correlating the responses of the same individual on different measures across different points in time or across various situations. An idiographic correlation shows the degree of consistency in responding by the same individual on different measures over time and across situations, and thus demonstrates the degree of consistency in the measure's sensitivity since (by definition) all current environmental variables are identical within a given subject at a given time. In a nomothetic correlation, the responses of groups of individuals on different measures are correlated for a single point in time. A nomothetic correlation thus shows the degree of consistency in responding across several individuals on different measures at one point in time. Since situational variables always vary across individuals (if for no other reason than no two people can be at the same place at the same time), nomothetic correlations must confound situational differences with individual differences.

ACCURACY

The use of *accuracy* of measurement as the criterion to evaluate the quality of behavioral assessment has been suggested by Foster and Cone (1980), Cone (1981), and Johnston and Pennypacker (1980). "Accuracy is meant to describe how faithfully a measure represents objective topographic features of a behavior of interest" (Cone, 1981, p. 59). To put it another way: "The goal of my scientific measurement operation or procedure is to arrive at the best possible estimate of the true value of some dimensional quantity of a natural phenomenon. To the extent that this goal is achieved, it is said that the measurement is accurate or valid . . . accuracy may be defined as the extent to which obtained measures approximate values of the 'true' state of mature, perfect accuracy being obtained when equivalence is demonstrated" (Johnston & Pennypacker, 1980, p. 190).

Accuracy, which attempts to evaluate a measurement against "reality," contrasts with psychometrics, which attempts to compare one group or subset of scores against another group or subset of scores. This contrast has been aptly described by Johnston and Pennypacker (1980, p. 75): "Many people who have become accustomed to measuring their own weight in pounds and their consumption of electricity in kilowatt hours have difficulty comprehending a measure of their child's academic achievement given in terms of other children's academic achievement expressed as a unit of time."

The accuracy of an assessment device is established by comparing the measurements that it produces against some standard. In establishing the accuracy of observations made by human observers, for example, the standard might be a mechanical record of the same behavior, records made of a mechanically generated response, or a performance that has been orchestrated according to a redetermined script (Foster & Cone, 1980). Naturally, the same standard could also be applied to the measurement of environmental variables, physiologic states, or other controlling variables. Once the assessment device has been shown to be accurate, data from subsequent applications of the device can then be assessed to have the same levels of accuracy as shown in the original conditions, provided the measure is used in the same way (Foster & Cone, 1980). Thus, "in establishing the accuracy of a behavioral assessment device it is necessary to have: (a) clearly spelled out rules/procedures for using the device, and (b) an incontrovertible index against which data from its use can be compared" (Cone, 1981, p. 57).

This last statement indicates the main problem with using accuracy as a criterion to evaluate behavioral assessment: the difficulty in finding suitable standards against which to evaluate accuracy. Accuracy is, in a sense, a structuralistic view of evaluating the quality of assessment. It is rare when we feel we have "incontrovertible" measures of anything, and in a philosophical sense incontrovertible standards simply do not exist. No matter how fine-grained the measurement, we always only approximate reality. As the uncertainty principle suggests, measurement is always probabilistic. While philosophically questionable due to its inherent structuralism and naive realism, accuracy is still sensible if a good standard exists. However, in many situations, if such a standard exists, the standard itself may actually be the best available assessment device (Foster & Cone, 1980).

Note that treatment utility and accuracy are very different ways of evaluating the quality of assessment. A measure could be accurate and still be useless, or only roughly approximate reality and still be quite valuable. We react to this implicitly in our use of the term "accurate." For example, a ruler is an "accurate" measure of a person's height, but an "inaccurate" measure of the circumference of the globe. A spring scale is an "accurate" measure of a bag of fruit, but an "inaccurate" measure of precious metals. Accuracy, while it appears to refer to "true" values, is always seen relative to the task we have to perform with the measures. This turns accuracy into a variant of the more functional measures of assessment, such as treatment utility or sensitivity to known variables.

COMPARISONS AMONG THE ALTERNATIVES

It may well be true that some questions traditionally asked under the psychometric rubric may be important to behavioral assessment, when considered from these alternative perspectives. For example, on functional grounds, it is probably important that test items have content validity or adequately sample the population of interest, as exemplified in role-playing tests for heterosocial skills (Perri & Richards, 1979) and for employment skills (Mathews, Whang, & Fawcett, 1980). In another example we have already discussed, if the behavior is somehow "captured" so that it cannot change (e.g., through the use of scripts consistently used by actors), then consistent responding across observers or interviewers would be expected. Thus, each area of psychometrics can be relevant, when these analyses fit into a system of evaluation that is philosophically compatible with behavioral assessment. It is not psychometric analyses per se that are objectionable, but rather a psychometric perspective on these analyses.

Four alternative methods of evaluating the quality of behavioral assessment have been proposed: treatment validity, sensitivity to identified variables, idiographic analysis, and accuracy. Each of these four approaches differ significantly from a psychometric approach. For example, accuracy and psychometric properties are not the same thing. Reliable and valid measures need not be accurate (Cone, 1981). Repeated observations of the same behavior may yield consistent, but inaccurate results. Two variables may produce a high degree of concurrent validity, but neither may be an accurate measure of the behavior in question. Accuracy is an excellent criterion for assessment, but its use is often difficult or impossible because it requires an independent knowledge of actual changes in the phenomena. In addition, accuracy is also a structurally based criteria. A measure could be accurate, and still be conceptually or practically useless, for example.

Similarly, while assessment devices with good treatment utility probably have adequate reliability, validity, and/or accuracy, these structural properties are neither necessary nor sufficient for treatment utility. Reliable, valid, and accurate devices are not necessarily useful. Conversely, some useful devices may not be reliable, valid, or accurate. A good example here might be the clinical interview. There is every indication that useful information is obtained through clinical interviews (although much more empirical work is needed here), but chances are that there is little consistency or reliability across interviewers in either conducting interviews or extracting information from them.

Oddly enough, behaviorally based evaluation methods often seem to fit certain traditional assessment devices better than does psychometric theory. Indeed, in some ways a behavioral method of evaluation may be the only way to assess certain beliefs common among traditional clinicians. For instance, a clinician who says that with enough experience giving projective tests helps the clinician in case management, is not making a psychometric claim. The claim is that in experienced hands, giving the tests aids treatment outcome. This could be true, even if the test is not reliable. The process of giving it may somehow put the clinician in better touch with the client, even though the clinician may not be able to *say* what is happening. Thus, even projective tests could have treatment utility. The preceding example suggests that just as psychometrics has heavily influenced behavioral assessment, as behavioral assessment matures the reverse may begin to occur.

IMPLICATIONS

Behaviorally sound methods of evaluation have just begun to have an impact on behavioral assessment. By far the most popular evalulation method to date has been psychometrics. Yet psychometrics may prevent behavioral assessment from moving ahead.

The three sources of disillusionment mentioned earlier provide an example. The search for perfect behavioral assessment devices, and the disillusion in not finding them are both predicated on a nonfunctionalistic, psychometric view of assessment quality. The fact that human behavior (both of the assessor and assessee) is influenced by time and situation should be no source of consternation to a behaviorist. Already we are begining to show that some of our psychometrically impure test devices and distinctions are nevertheless quite useful. Conversely, very few of the "psychometrically pure" devices in traditional assessment have yet shown their treatment utility.

The search for diagnostic groups of pure types of clients (e.g., truly socially unskilled persons) also reflects a psychometric view. Rather than seek the pure group first, perhaps we should let treatment responsiveness or other functional effects select our groups for us. For many purposes we may not need the diagnostic categories we seek. For example, we may find that certain broad categories capture most of the critical differences, and additional distinctions are being made on the basis of topographical, not functional differences. A behavioral view suggests that topographically differences are not the critical ones, yet these are precisely the differences likely to be analyzed psychometrically. Conversely, functional categories may include many dissimilar items (e.g., both shouting and whispering can be attention-getting). Only an assessment technology built on a functional approach is likely to organize behavior functionally. Psychometrics is not such an approach.

The problem of standardization can be viewed two ways. If what is meant is that we should be able to find the one true method (or set of methods) to discover the one true state of affairs, this again amounts to more mixing of behavioral and nonbehavioral assumptions. If what is meant is that we need some practical help in selecting among the range of devices available, then this concern is another form of concern over practicality. Work is needed so that clinicians can utilize behavioral assessment with greater convenience and assurance.

Yet, some difficulty in this area is almost necessary given a behavioral model. For each client, an assessment process must be delineated that takes into account his or her unique problematic situations and response systems. For each client, target behaviors must be identified, treatment strategies selected, and outcome measures determined. Behavioral assessment is *not* a set of techniques, but is rather an approach to assessment. Behavioral assessors need not fear individualization and improvisation. A point of view expressed by Lightner Witmer in 1913 is still applicable here:

I am often asked for a list of the tests which we employ at the Psychological Clinic. I do not furnish such lists, because I am in doubt whether there is a single test which I can recommend to be employed with every case which comes to the Clinic for examination. . . . My very early experience with cases at the Psychological Clinic revealed the necessity for keeping the examination in a fluid state . . . I believe that the clinical psychologist in conducting his examination must proceed directly to the work in hand. I want to know who brings or sends the child to the clinic. Why is he brought? What do his parents or teachers complain of? (p. 103)

CONCLUSION

The view that behavioral assessment consists of a set of techniques to be evaluated by psychometric criterion will lead to pessimism, frustration, and disillusionment. A more constructive view of behavioral assessment is that it is an assessment *approach*, an approach that is individually based, behaviorally sound, and functionally validated. Herein lies the challenges to clinician and researchers alike.

REFERENCES

Altmaier, E. M., Ross, S. L., Leary, N. R., & Thornbrough, M. (1982). Matching stress innoculation's treatment components to clients' anxiety mode. *Journal of Counseling Psychology, 29,* 331–334.

American Psychological Association. (1966). *Standards for educational and psychological tests.* Washington, DC: Author.

American Psychiatric Association. (1980). *Diagnostic and statistical manual of mental disorders* (3rd ed.). Washington, DC: Author.

Anastasi, A. (1982). *Psychological testing.* Fifth edition. New York: Macmillan.

Baer, D. M., Wolf, M. M., & Risley, T. R. (1968). Some current dimensions of applied behavior analysis. *Journal of Applied Behavior Analysis, 1,* 91–97.

Barlow, D. H. (1977). Behavioral assessment in clinical settings: Developing issues. In J. D. Cone & R. P. Hawkins (Eds.), *Behavioral assessment: New directions in clinical psychology* (pp. 283–307). New York: Brunner/Mazel.

Barlow, D. H. (Ed.). (1981). *Behavioral assessment of adult disorders.* New York: Guilford Press.

Barlow, D. H., & Hayes, S. C. (1979). Alternating treatments design: One strategy for comparing the effects of two treatments in a single subject. *Journal of Applied Behavior Analysis, 12,* 199–210.

Barlow, D. H., Hayes, S. C., & Nelson, R. O. (1984). *The scientist–practitioner: Research and accountability in clinical and educational settings.* New York: Pergamon Press.

Bellack, A. S., Hersen, M., & Lamparski, D. (1979). Role-playing tests for assessing social skills: Are they valid? Are they useful? *Journal of Consulting and Clinical Psychology, 47,* 335–342.

Bielski, R., & Friedel, R. O. (1976). Prediction of tricyclic response. *Archives of General Psychiatry, 33,* 1479–1489.

Borkovec, T. D., Grayson, J. B., O'Brien, G. T., & Weerts, T. C. (1979). Relaxation training of pseudoinsomnia and idiopathic insomnia: An electroencephalographic evaluation. *Journal of Applied Behavior Analysis, 12,* 37–54.

Campbell, D. T., & Fiske, D. W. (1959). Convergant and discriminant validation by the multitrait-multimethod matrix. *Psychological Bulletin, 56,* 81–105.

Chesney, M. A., & Tasto, D. L. (1975). The effectiveness of behavior modification with spasmodic and congestive dysmenorrhea. *Behaviour Research and Therapy, 13,* 245–253.

Ciminero, A. R., Calhoun, K. S., & Adams, H. E. (Eds.) (1977). *Handbook of behavioral assessment.* New York: John Wiley & Sons.

Cone, J. D. (1978). The relevance of reliability and validity for behavioral assessment. *Behavior Therapy, 8,* 411–426.

Cone, J. D. (1978). The Behavioral Assessment Grid (BAG): A conceptual framework and a taxonomy. *Behavior Therapy, 9,* 882–888.

Cone, J. D. (1979). Confounded comparisons in triple response mode assessment research. *Behavioral Assessment, 1,* 85–95.

Cone, J. D. (1980, November). *Template matching procedures for idiographic behavioral assessment.* Paper presented at the meeting of the Association for Advancement of Behavior Therapy, New York.

Cone, J. D. (1981). Psychometric considerations. In M. Hersen & A. S. Bellack (Eds.), *Behavioral assessment* (pp. 38–68). New York: Pergamon Press.

Cone, J. D., & Hawkins, R. P. (Eds.). (1977). *Behavioral assessment: New directions in clinical psychology.* New York: Brunner/Mazel.

Cronbach, L. J., Gleser, G. C., Nanda, H., & Rajartnam, N. (1972). *The dependability of behavioral measures.* New York: John Wiley & Sons.

Curran, J. P., & Mariotto, M. J. (1980). A conceptual structure for the assessment of social skills. In M. Hersen, R. M. Eisler, & P. M. Miller (Eds.), *Progress in behavior modification* (Vol. 10, pp. 1–37). New York: Academic Press.

Elder, J. P., Edelstein, B. A., & Fremouw, W. J. (1981). Client by treatment interactions in response acquisition and cognitive restructuring approaches. *Cognitive Therapy and Research, 5,* 203–210.

Ferster, C. B. (1965). Classification of behavioral pathology. In L. Krasner & L. P. Ullmann (Eds.), *Research in behavior modification* (pp. 2–26). New York: Holt, Rinehart & Winston.

Foster, S. L., & Cone, J. D. (1980) Current issues in direct observation. *Behavioral Assessment, 2,* 313–338.

Galassi, M. D., & Galassi, J. P. (1980). Similarities and differences between two assertion measures: Factor analyses of the College Self-Expression Scale and the Rathus Assertiveness Schedule. *Behavioral Assessment, 2,* 43–57.

Goldfried, M. R. (1979). Behavioral assessment: Where do we go from here? *Behavioral Assessment, 1,* 19–22.

Goldfried, M. R., & Kent, R. N. (1972). Traditional versus behavioral assessment: A comparison of methodological and theoretical assumptions. *Psychological Bulletin, 77,* 409–420.

Goldfried, M. R., & Pomeranz, D. M. (1968). Role of assessment in behavior modification. *Psychological Reports, 23,* 75–87.

Goldfried, M. R., & Sprafkin, J. N. (1976). Behavioral personality assessment. In J. T. Spence, R. C. Carson, & J. W. Thibaut (Eds.), *Behavioral approaches to therapy* (pp. 295–321). Morristown, NJ: General Learning Press.

Goodenough, F. L. (1949). *Mental testing.* New York: Rinehart.

Harris, J. G., Jr. (1980). Nomovalidation and idiovalidation: A quest for the true personality profile. *American Psychologist, 35,* 729–744.

Hartmann, D. P., Roper, B. L., & Bradford, D. C. (1979). Some relationships between behavioral and traditional assessment. *Journal of Behavioral Assessment, 1,* 3–21.

Hayes, S. C. (1981). Single-case experimental designs and empirical clinical practice. *Journal of Consulting and Clinical Psychology, 49,* 193–211.

Haynes, S. N. (1978). *Principles of behavioral assessment.* New York: Gardner Press.

Haynes, S. N., & Wilson, C. C. (1979). *Behavioral assessment: Recent advances in methods, concepts, and applications.* San Francisco: Jossey-Bass.

Heimberg, R. G., Harrison, D. F., Montogomery, D., Madsen, C. H., & Sherfey, J. A. (1980). Psychometric and behavioral analysis of a social anxiety questionnaire: The Situation Questionnaire. *Behavioral Assessment, 2,* 403–415.

Henson, D. E., Rubin, H. B., & Hensen, C. (1979). Analysis of the consistency of objective measures of sexual arousal in women. *Journal of Applied Behavioral Analysis, 12,* 701–711.

Hersen, M., & Bellack, A. S. (Eds.) (1976). *Behavioral assessment: A practical handbook.* New York: Pergamon Press.

Hersen, M., & Bellack, A. S. (1977). *Research and Practice in Social Skills Training*. New York: Plenum Press.

Hersen, M., & Bellack, A. S. (Eds.) (1981). *Behavioral assessment: A practical handbook* (2nd ed.). New York: Pergamon Press.

Jarrett, R. B., Nelson, R. O., & Hayes S. C. (1981, November). *An initial investigation of treatment utility: A methodology for evaluating behavioral assessment*. Paper presented at the Association for Advancement of Behavior Therapy, Toronto.

Johnston, J. M., & Pennypacker, H. S. (1980). *Strategies and tactics of human behavioral research*. Hillsdale, NJ: Lawrence Erlbaum.

Jones, R. R., Reid, J. B., & Patterson, G. R. (1975). Naturalistic observation in clinical assessment. In P. McReynolds (Eds.), *Advances in psychological assessment* (Vol. 3, pp. 42–95). San Francisco: Jossey-Bass.

Kanfer, F. H., & Saslow, G. (1969). Behavioral diagnosis. In C. M. Franks (Ed.), *Behavior therapy: Appraisal and status* (pp. 417–444). New York: McGraw-Hill.

Keefe, F. J., Kopel, S. A., & Gordon, S. B. (1978). *A practical guide to behavioral assessment*. New York: Springer.

Kent, R. N., & Foster, S. L. (1977). Direct observation procedures: Methodological issues in naturalistic settings. In A. R. Ciminero, K. S. Calhoun, & H. E. Adams (Eds.), *Handbook of behavioral assessment* (pp. 279–328). New York: John Wiley & Sons.

Lamiell, J. T. (1981). Toward an idiothetic psychology of personality. *American Psychologist, 36*, 276–289.

Mahoney, M. (1974). *Cognition and behavior modification*. Cambridge, MA: Ballinger.

Mash, E. J. (1979). What is behavioral assessment? *Behavioral Assessment, 1*, 23–29.

Mash, E. J., & Terdal, L. G. (Eds.). (1976). *Behavioral therapy assessment*. New York: Springer.

Mash, E. J., & Terdal, L. G. (Eds.). (1981). *Behavioral assessment of childhood disorders*. New York: Guilford Press.

Mathews, R. M., Whang, P. L., & Fawcett, S. B. (1980). Development and validation of an occupational skills assessment instrument. *Behavioral Assessment, 2*, 71–85.

McFall, R. M. (1977). Parameters of self-monitoring. In R. B. Stuart (Ed.), *Behavioral self-management: Strategies, techniques, and outcomes* (pp. 196–214). New York: Brunner/Mazel.

McKnight, D. L., Nelson, R. O., Hayes, S. C., & Jarrett, R. B. (1984). Importance of treating individually-assessed response classes in the amelioration of depression. *Behavior Therapy, 15*, 315–335.

Mischel, W. (1968). *Personality and assessment*. New York: John Wiley & Sons.

Murray, D. J. (1983). *A history of western psychology*. Englewood Cliffs, NJ: Prentice-Hall.

Nelson, R. O. (1977). Assessment and therapeutic functions of self-monitoring. In M. Hersen, R. M. Eisler, & P. M. Miller (Eds.), *Progress in behavior modification* (Vol. 5, pp. 263–308). New York: Academic Press.

Nelson, R. O. (1980). The use of intelligence tests within behavioral assessment. *Behavioral Assessment, 2*, 417–423.

Nelson, R. O. (1983). Behavioral assessment: Past, present, and future. *Behavioral Assessment, 5*, 195–206.

Nelson, R. O., & Barlow, D. H. (1981). Behavioral assessment: Basic strategies and initial procedures. In D. H. Barlow (Ed.), *Behavioral assessment of adult disorders* (pp. 13–43). New York: Guilford Press.

Nelson, R. O., Hay, L. R., & Hay, W. M. (1977). Comments on Cone's "The relevance of reliability and validity for behavioral assessment." *Behavior Therapy, 8*, 427–430.

Nelson, R. O., & Hayes, S. C. (1979). Some current dimensions of behavioral assessment. *Behavioral Assessment, 1*, 1–16.

Nelson, R. O., Hayes, S. C., Felton, J. L., & Jarrett, R. B. (1985). A comparison of data produced by different behavioral assessment techniques with implications for models of social skill inadequacy. *Behaviour Research and Therapy, 23*, 1–12.

Nelson, R. O., Hayes, S. C., Jarrett, R. B., & McKnight, D. L. (1983). *The treatment utility of dimensions of social skills*. Unpublished manuscript.

Ost, L. G., Jerremalm, A., & Johansson, J. (1981). Individual response patterns and the effects of different behavioral methods in the treatment of social phobia. *Behaviour Research and Therapy, 19,* 1–16.

Paykel, E. S., Prusoff, B. A., Klerman, G. L., Haskell, D., & DiMascio, A. (1973). Clinical response to amitriptyline among depressed women. *Journal of Nervous and Mental Disease, 156,* 149–165.

Perri, M. G., & Richards, C. S. (1979). Assessment of heterosocial skills in male college students. *Behavior Modification, 3,* 337–354.

Shahan, A., & Merbaum, M. (1981). The interaction between subject characteristics and self-control procedures in the treatment of interpersonal anxiety. *Cognitive Therapy and Research, 5,* 221–224.

Shapiro, M. B. (1966). The single case in clinical-psychological research. *The Journal of General Psychology, 74,* 3–23.

Shapiro, M. B. (1970). Intensive assessment of the single case: An inductive–deductive approach. In P. Mittler (Ed.), *The psychological assessment of mental and physical handicaps* (pp. 645–666). London: Methuen.

Sidman, M. (1960). *Tactics of scientific research.* New York: Basic Books.

Skinner, B. F. (1945). The operational analysis of psychological terms. *Psychological Review, 52,* 270–277.

Skinner, B. F. (1974). *About behaviorism.* New York: Knopf.

Titchener, E. B. (1899). Structural and functional psychology. *Philosophical Review, 8,* 290–299.

Trower, P., Yardley, K., Bryant, B. M., & Shaw, P. (1978). The treatment of social failure: A comparison of anxiety-reduction and skills-acquisition procedures on two social problems. *Behavior Modification, 2,* 41–50.

Turner, A. E., & Hayes, S. C. (1984). *Idiothetic and nomothetic assessment of response covariation. II. Sexual behavior.* Paper presented at the meeting of the American Psychological Association, Toronto.

Wasik, B. H., & Loven, M. D. (1980). Classroom observational data: Sources of inaccuracy and proposed solutions. *Behavioral Assessment, 2,* 211–227.

Witmer, L. (1913). Clinical records. *The Psychological Clinic, 9,* 1–3.

AUTHOR INDEX

Goldberg, C. R., 58, 59, 118
Goldfried, M. R., 10, 11, 12, 21, 24,
    27, 30, 35, 65, 71, 82, 85, 86, 97,
    157, 158, 194, 236, 332, 333, 335,
    336, 339, 340, 343, 345, 347, 369,
    372, 387, 420, 421, 422, 453, 464,
    465, 466, 467, 468
Goldfried, M. S., 275, 278, 285
Goldiamond, I., 26, 159, 160, 331,
    333, 335, 339, 341, 348, 351, 352,
    353, 354, 356
Goldsmith, J. B., 336, 340, 344, 362,
    369, 372
Goldstein, G., 387
Goldstein, M. K., 160, 187, 191
Goodenough, F. L., 11, 55, 59, 66,
    115, 333, 465
Gordon, S. B., 401, 422, 467
Gottlieb, J., 313
Gottman, J. M., 224, 231, 235, 416
Gough, H. G., 59
Graham, T. A., 217, 224
Grantmyre, J., 149
Grayson, J. B., 478
Green, J. A., 138
Greene, E. B., 157
Greenfield, N. S., 315
Greenspoon, J., 71, 82
Griest, O., 344
Grimm, L. G., 26, 347, 348
Gross, M. C., 255, 256, 257, 260, 262,
    264, 267, 273, 276, 286, 290
Grubb, T. D., 442
Gruenwald, L., 363, 365
Guay, P. F., 257, 262, 264, 267, 276,
    286, 290
Guerra, J. J., 403
Guion, R. M., 99
Guthrie, E. R., 69, 242, 303
Guyton, A. C., 300, 304, 310

Habif, V. L., 387
Hake, D., 159
Hall, D. C., 160, 187, 191
Hall, G. F., 297, 303
Hall, G. S., 58
Hall, R. V., 342
Hammond, O. W., 256, 263
Hamre-Nietupski, S., 363, 365
Hansen, C. L., 344
Harford, R. A., 191
Hargreaves, W. A., 452
Harms, J. Y., 256, 257, 262, 263, 286
Harré, R., 217

Harris, F. R., 32, 276, 342, 343
Harris, J. G., Jr., 12, 118, 121, 495
Harris, S. L., 24
Harrison, D. F., 470
Hart, B. M., 276, 343
Hartley, H. L., 313
Hartley, T. L., 62
Hartmann, D. P., 10, 12, 82, 83, 84,
    86, 87, 88, 89, 90, 91, 92, 104,
    335, 342, 343, 418, 419, 465, 466
Hartshorne, H., 14, 22, 244
Haskell, D., 478, 782
Hatch, J. P., 392, 409
Hathaway, S. R., 58, 452
Haughton, E. C., 195, 375
Hawkins, F. P. 71, 72
Hawkins, K. K., 341, 352
Hawkins, N., 71
Hawkins, R. P., 94, 95, 156, 157, 158,
    166, 190, 276, 331, 332, 335, 336,
    339, 341, 342, 343, 344, 345, 348,
    351, 352, 353, 355, 357, 358, 363,
    370, 371, 373, 374, 386, 451, 467
Hay, L. R., 16, 29, 36, 87, 161, 444,
    452, 472
Hay, W. M., 16, 29, 36, 87, 161, 374,
    444, 452, 472
Hayes, J. E., 355, 374
Hayes, S. C., 4, 7, 12, 21, 23, 26, 28,
    30, 33, 35, 83, 90, 93, 111, 120,
    121, 132, 156, 157, 161, 234, 300,
    349, 352, 360, 366, 367, 369, 374,
    405, 407, 417, 420, 436, 438, 440,
    441, 442, 443, 444, 448, 450, 451,
    453, 454, 456, 464, 470, 472, 475,
    477, 479, 482, 486, 489, 490, 491
Haynes, S. N., 34, 84, 85, 90, 95, 115,
    158, 276, 344, 386, 387, 388, 390,
    391, 392, 393, 395, 398, 399, 400,
    405, 411, 414, 418, 420, 421, 422,
    423, 467
Heard, W. G., 251, 284
Heiby, E. M., 242, 279, 281, 282, 283,
    287, 290, 291
Heider, J. F., 456
Heiman, H. R., 392, 409
Heimberg, R. G., 470
Hefferline, R. F., 191
Hêkmat, H., 268
Helvetius, C. A., 62
Hench, L., 160, 187, 191
Hendee, J. C., 355
Henke, L. B., 343
Henri, V., 55

Moore, J., 366
Moos, R. H., 16, 63, 217
Morgan, B. J., 160
Morgan, C. D., 59
Morris, C. J., 318, 319
Morris, E. K., 360, 366
Morris, L. A., 376
Morris, P., 318, 319
Morris, R. J., 88, 97
Morse, W. H., 375
Moruzzi, G., 306
Moskowitz, D., 137
Mostofsky, D. I., 315
Mowrer, O. H., 17, 69, 156, 242, 250,
    255, 368
Mowrer, W. M., 69
Miller, J., 305
Mullinix, S. D., 404
Munsterberg, H., 58
Murchison, D., 65
Murphy, G., 67
Murphy, L. B., 67
Murray, D. J., 5, 476
Murray, H. A., 222
Murray, H. C., 49, 59, 67
Murray, W. J., 390
Myers, P. E., 313
Myers, R. D., 310
Myerson, W. A., 26, 349, 352, 369

Nagel, E., 162
Nanda, H., 87, 470
Nashby, W., 81
Nathan, P. E., 24, 34, 144, 160, 372,
    373, 377, 392, 399
Nay, W. R., 132
Nedelmann, D. J., 439
Nelson, R. O., 7, 10, 12, 16, 21, 24,
    26, 27, 28, 29, 30, 31, 33, 35, 68,
    83, 87, 88, 90, 91, 93, 111, 115,
    120, 121, 132, 141, 156, 157, 158,
    161, 234, 300, 333, 360, 371, 372,
    374, 402, 405, 420, 421, 436, 438,
    440, 443, 444, 448, 450, 451, 454,
    456, 464, 465, 470, 472, 477, 478,
    483, 486, 488, 489, 490, 491, 493
Neuhaus, O. W., 319, 321
Newcomb, T. M., 66, 67, 244
Newman, J. R., 52
Nietzel, M. T., 5, 191, 409
Nisbett, R. E., 142, 151, 206, 213
Nitko, A. J., 92
Nordheimer, J., 81

Norman, W. T., 118
Norris-Baker, C., 141
Nunnally, J. C., 86, 97, 99, 101, 118,
    121, 122

O'Brian, G. T., 478
O'Brien, F., 191
O'Brien, T., 403
O'Brist, P. A., 146, 147
O'Conner, R. D., 10, 27
Odom, J. V., 115
O'Leary, K. D., 28, 31, 89, 156, 157,
    345, 358, 359, 368, 369, 374
Ollendick, T. H., 389
Olson, W. C., 66
Olweus, D., 222, 223, 245
Olvera, D., 159
Orlando, R., 71
Ornstein, P. A., 226
Orten, J. M., 319, 321
Osgood, C. E., 242, 255, 262
Ossorio, P. G., 338, 340
OSS Assessment Staff, 67
Ost, L. G., 478

Padawer, W., 82
Parker, L., 317
Parley, J. G., 61
Parloff, M. B., 81
Parsonson, B. S., 450
Parten, M. B., 66
Passini, F. T., 118
Paterson, D. G., 61
Patterson, G. R., 14, 71, 91, 392, 396,
    400, 401, 411, 456, 470
Patterson, J. T., 455, 456
Paul, G. I., 443
Paul, G. L., 91, 228, 297, 315, 369
Paunonen, S. V., 245
Pavlov, I. D., 64, 242, 297
Paykel, E. S., 478, 482
Peake, P. K., 15, 88, 89, 208
Pear, J., 332, 344, 345, 350, 354
Pearson, K., 52
Pennypacker, H. S., 6, 9, 21, 115, 125,
    157, 160, 163, 170, 172, 175, 176,
    177, 187, 190, 343, 344, 367, 473,
    496
Pepper, S. C., 7
Perri, M. G., 497
Perry, S., 445
Pervin, L. A., 118, 205, 222, 223
Peterson, D. R., 14, 205, 343
Peterson, G. W., 411

Swartz, J. D., 59
Symonds, P. M., 59

Tailby, W., 377
Takemoto-Chock, N. K., 139
Tasto, D. L., 478
Taylor, C. B., 372, 373
Taylor, T. J., 14
Terdal, L. G., 70, 72, 88, 90, 92, 95,
    101, 157, 158, 341, 342, 344, 387,
    405, 421, 452, 467
Terman, L. M., 57
Tharp, R. G., 28, 374
Thomas, D. R., 17, 122
Thomas, S. S., 66
Thomasius, C., 47
Thompson, W. C., 206
Thoresen, C. E., 315
Thorndike, E. L., 60, 61, 64, 242
Thorpe, J. S., 59
Thorsen, C. E., 420
Thronbrough, M., 478
Thurston, L. L., 59
Tilton, J. R., 70
Timbers, B. J., 27
Timbers, G. D., 27
Titchener, E. B., 7, 476
Tulman, E. C., 242, 250
Topping, D. M., 291
Tredennick, H., 45
Trimble, R. W., 297, 315
Trower, P., 224, 478, 487
Tryon, W. W., 291
Turkat, I. D., 12, 31, 373
Turner, A. E., 23, 442, 475
Tversky, A., 93, 206

Ullman, L. P., 26, 69, 70, 71, 279, 333,
    355, 407
Ulrich, R., 160
Urey, J. R., 455
Usdin, E., 318
Uviller, E. T., 144

Van Houten, R., 26, 195, 337, 371
Van Lehn, R., 313
Van Praag, H. M., 318
Varach, R., 439
Venables, P. H., 315
Verhoeven, W. M., 318
Vernon, P. E., 205, 210, 263, 265, 266
Vincent, J. P., 390, 411, 423
Voeltz, L. M., 23, 25, 101, 118, 131,

    149, 151, 331, 360, 363, 390, 399,
    404, 412, 423, 446
Vogelmann-Sine, S., 144
Vosk, B. N., 387
Vukelich, R., 159

Wachtel, P. L., 205, 214, 277
Wade, T. C., 86, 418, 419
Wagoner, B. L., 146
Wahler, R., 390, 400, 410, 411
Wahler, R. G., 23, 29, 118, 131, 147,
    169, 364, 377
Walder, L. O., 333
Walker, H. M., 195
Wall, S., 140
Wallace, J., 205
Wallace, P. M., 300
Wallace, R. F., 355
Walls, R. T., 161
Walsh, K. W., 307, 312
Walsh, M. J., 307, 312
Walters, R., 256, 260
Wang, M. C., 331, 362
Ward, C. H., 452
Ware, W. B., 417
Warren, D. R., 256, 257, 262, 263,
    286
Warren, S. F., 68
Wasik, B. H., 67, 493
Watchel, P. L., 82
Waters, E., 140
Waters, W. F., 297, 303, 313
Watson, J. B., 62, 63, 64, 81, 156, 242,
    244, 247, 255, 265
Webster's Third New International
    Dictionary, 175
Wechsler, D., 58, 258
Weerts, T. C., 22, 97, 478
Wein, K. S., 115
Weiner, H., 159
Weiss, R. L., 31, 71
Weiss, S. N., 298
Weissman, A. N., 443
Wellman, H., 140
Wells, F. L., 56, 57, 59
Werner, J. S., 369
Werner, T. J., 161
Wetzel, R. J., 28, 374, 421
Whang, P. L., 28, 497
Whatmore, G. B., 148
Whatmore, N. J., 148
Whipple, G. W., 56, 59
White, O. R., 344, 363

SUBJECT INDEX

Abnormal behavior, 249, 279, 280, 282 (*see also* Maladaptive behavior)
Adjustment, 350, 351, 365, 370
Allport-Vernon-Lindzey scale of religiousness, 266
Allport-Vernon-Lindzey study of values, 265
Alternating Treatment Design, 35, 441-442, 490-491
Aristotle, 44
Antecedent events, 406-407
Anthropometry, 48
Anxiety, 347, 348, 352, 367, 368, 369
Ascending reticular activation system (ARAS), 306
Assessment, 56, 61-63, 82, 98-101, 213-216, 234-237, 484 (*see also* Behavioral assessment)
  educational, 60-61
  environmental, 56, 61-63
  history of, 43-46
  models, 53, 73, 92-93, 96-99, 101-102, 105, 231-232
  personality, 58-60
  phases of, 94-105
  preintervention, 387-393, 405-409, 416, 424
Astrology, 43, 44, 46
Autism, 356, 357, 363
Autonomic nervous system, 145-148, 299, 300, 302, 303, 306, 307, 308, 310, 315, 316, 318, (*see also* Sympathetic nervous system)

Behavior analysis, 157, 159-163, 166-170, 248-250, 262, 264, 275, 278, 280, 289-291
Behavior analyst, characteristics of, 413, 414, 423, 424
Behavior dimensions, 177-179
Behavior modification, 248, 259, 269, 270, 273, 275, 276, 278, 279, 288, 291
Behavior movement, 164

Behavior therapy, 65, 69-70
Behavior units, 175-177
Behavior variability, 172, 175, 438-443, 473-474, 493
Behavioral assessment, 3-10, 12, 21, 63-72, 157-159, 165-171, 190, 263, 264, 268, 271, 273, 274-282, 284-291, 331-332, 446-450, 463, 500 (*see also* Assessment)
  cost effectiveness of, 344
  utility of, 93-94, 96
Behavioral consistency, 84-85, 203-217, 244-246, 248, 265, 267-268, 273-274, 283
Behavioral medicine, 298, 317, 313
Behavioral repertoires, 251-264, 269-275, 277-281, 287-289
Behaviorism, 242-243, 247, 253, 255, 283-290 (*see also* Paradigmatic behaviorism)
  radical, 5, 7-8, 297, 311, 322-324
  Watsonian, 64
Behavioristic theory-construction methodology, 251
Between series design (*see* Time-series designs)
Between subject designs, 489
Biofeedback, 304, 311
Binet, A., 55
Biobehavioral model, 298, 300, 303, 307, 308, 310, 311, 312, 313, 314, 317, 322, 323, 324

Card sorts (*see* Self-report measures)
Central nervous system (CNS), 299, 303, 304, 305, 306, 307, 308, 312
Civilian Health and Medical Program of the Uniformed Services (CHAMPUS), 445
Classical conditioning, 297, 302, 303, 311
Classification, 9, 23, 117-118, 230-231 (*see also* Diagnostic classes)
Client goals, 401-402

519

Interactionism, 11, 13, 121, 122, 246, 269, 277–278, 281
Interactionist data, 14–15
Interpersonal attraction, 114, 116, 124
Inter-response structure, 149–151
Intervening variables, 250, 253
Intervention (*see also* Treatment)
  behavioral, 170–171, 400
  decisions, 394–396
  design of, 386–425
  habilitative, 356
  power, 391–392, 412
  selection of, 30–34, 396–397
  systems, 387–388
  termination of, 397

Keystone behavior, 32–33, 119

La Chambre, M. C., 47
Language, 255, 256, 259, 262, 277
Learning, 250, 259, 263, 270–271, 273–274, 277–279, 289
Learning history, 19–21
Legendre, 9, 473

Maladaptive behavior, 336, 349, 350, 351, 355, 366 (*see also* Abnormal behavior)
Measurement, 60, 186–194 (*see also* Assessment, and Behavioral assessment)
  accuracy, 187–188, 493, 496–497
  behavior, 163–166, 171–172, 173–175
  repeated, 34–35, 449–450
Mechanism, 7–9
Medical model, 334
Mind, 3, 4
Minnesota Multiphasic Personality Inventory (MMPI), 59, 419, 463
Modeling, 259, 260, 271, 289
Monism, 4
Motivation, 233, 400–401
Motor responses, 261, 268
Multilevel theory construction, 254–255, 258, 259
Multitest manuals, 56–57

National Center for Health and Technology, 445
Nativism-empiricism, 4 (*see also* Nature-nuture)
Nature-nuture, 237–238
Neurotic paradox, 17

Neurotransmitters, 298, 310, 312, 318, 319, 321, 323
Nomothetic approach, 99, 111–112, 114, 116, 123–125, 214–216, 234–235, 332, 372–373, 466, 486, 495
Norms, 91–92, 93, 96, 97, 98, 102, 104

Observations, 179–181, 183–184
  direct, 48, 65–68, 71, 115, 332, 341–344
  measures, 454–456
  naturalistic, 248
  objective, 276
Operant (radical) behaviorism, 242–243, 247, 249–252, 262, 264, 268, 275–276, 279, 282–286, 288, 290–291
Operant chamber, 288–289
Operant conditioning, 64, 268, 297, 302–303, 311, (*see also* Instrumental conditioning)

Paradigmatic behaviorism, 242–243, 247–262, 264–265, 267–273, 276–283, 285–291
Pearson, K., 9, 473
Person-situation debate, 202–226, 228–230, 237–238, 245, 247
  history, 224–227
  predictive utility, 202, 210–212
  reliability vs validity, 208–212
Personality, 137–138, 243–244, 248, 253–265, 276–279, 283, 289, 290
  abnormal, 280–281
  assessment of, 58–60
  development, 253–273, 277, 282
  traits, 135–140, 143, 149, 152
Personality testing, 248–249, 264, 265, 268, 274, 283, 284, 285, 287, 289
  WPPSI, 259, 261, 269, 272
  geometric design mazes, 260–261, 269, 272
  Strong Vocational Interest Blank, 263, 264, 267
  Allport-Vernon-Lindzey study of values, 263
  Edwards Personal Preference Scale, 263
Personal equation (*see* Person-situation debate)
Personologism, 11, 13, 248 (*see also* Person-situation debate)
Phrenology, 49–51